SOMETHING ABOUT THE AUTHOR®

Something about
the Author *was named
an* **"Outstanding
Reference Source,"**
*the highest honor given
by the American
Library Association
Reference and Adult
Services Division.*

ISSN 0276-816X

something ABOUT THE AUThor®

**Facts and Pictures about Authors
and Illustrators of Books for Young People**

volume 136

GALE®

THOMSON

GALE

Detroit • New York • San Diego • San Francisco • Cleveland • New Haven, Conn. • Waterville, Maine • London • Munich

*LSL
REF
PN
451
.S6
V.136* (handwritten)

Something about the Author, Volume 136

Project Editor
Scot Peacock

Editorial
Katy Balcer, Sara Constantakis, Anna Marie Dahn, Alana Joli Foster, Arlene M. Johnson, Michelle Kazensky, Julie Keppen, Joshua Kondek, Lisa Kumar, Thomas McMahon, Jenai A. Mynatt, Judith L. Pyko, Mary Ruby, Susan Strickland, Anita Sundaresan, Maikue Vang, Tracey Watson, Denay L. Wilding, Thomas Wiloch, Emiene Shija Wright

Research
Michelle Campbell, Sarah Genik, Barbara McNeil, Tamara C. Nott, Gary J. Oudersluys, Tracie A. Richardson, Cheryl L. Warnock

Permissions
Debra Freitas, Margaret Chamberlain

Imaging and Multimedia
Dean Dauphinais, Robert Duncan, Leitha Etheridge-Sims, Mary K. Grimes, Lezlie Light, Michael Logusz, Dan Newell, David G. Oblender, Christine O'Bryan, Kelly A. Quin, Luke Rademacher

Manufacturing
Stacy L. Melson

LIBRARY OF CONGRESS CATALOG CARD NUMBER 72-27107

ISBN 0-7876-5208-3
ISSN 0276-816X

Printed in the United States of America
10 9 8 7 6 5 4 3 2 1

Contents

Authors in Forthcoming Volumes

Below are some of the authors and illustrators that will be featured in upcoming volumes of *SATA*. These include new entries on the swiftly rising stars of the field, as well as completely revised and updated entries (indicated with *) on some of the most notable and best-loved creators of books for children.

*Alma Flor Ada: As an author and translator, Ada has made textbooks and storybooks available to Spanish-speaking children and speakers of English attempting to learn Spanish. Through her many books, Ada also serves as a cultural liaison: she retells traditional Latin American tales, presents stories set in Latin America, offers perspectives on life in Latin American countries, and describes the feelings of children as they confront cultural misunderstanding and learn to take pride in their heritage. *Pio peep!: Traditional Spanish Nursery Rhymes,* her 2003 work cowritten with F. Isabel Campoy, is a bilingual edition.

Shonto Begay: Begay is a respected Native American artist and author whose work reflects both traditional Native and contemporary Euro-American influences. Begay's first self-illustrated children's book was *Ma'ii and Cousin Horned Toad: A Traditional Navajo Story.* In 2002, he illustrated Joseph Bruchac's *Navajo Long Walk: The Tragic Story of a Proud People's Forced March from Their Homeland.*

Becky Citra: Citra, a native of Canada, pens early-reader books, including *My Homework Is in the Mail!,* that are praised for plots filled with suspense and lively action, realistic characters, and child-centered narratives. With *Ellie's New Home,* Citra published her first historical novel. Compared to Laura Ingalls Wilder's "Little House" books for its focus on the pioneer experience, *Ellie's New Home* has a distinctly Canadian flavor.

Quentin Dodd: Dodd combines a day job as a computer network administrator with a night career of creating humorous and outlandish books for young readers. His 2001 title, *Beatnik Rutabagas from Beyond the Stars,* is the tale of two teens who are spirited away in alien space ships to lead competing intergalactic armies. The work was a "Books for the Teen Age" selection by the New York Public Library.

Jon Grupper: Grupper is a prolific writer, producer, and director for television, film, and radio. He has received five Emmy Award nominations, including Outstanding Children's Series, for the TV series *Really Wild Animals.* Grupper is also the author of several books on wildlife for the National Geographic Society. The series' focus on animals, its lush photography, and its conversational yet informative narratives have led reviewers to recommend the titles as introductory texts for units on various regions. *Destination: Rocky Mountains,* one of the National Geographic titles, was published in 2001.

*Ronald Himler: Himler is one of the most visible artists and illustrators in children's literature, for in addition to his own five self-illustrated books and the hundred-plus books he has illustrated for writers such as Eve Bunting, Virginia Driving Hawk Sneve, Byrd Baylor, and Ellen Howard, he has also created the covers of over a hundred young adult titles. Himler published the self-illustrated title *Six is So Much Less Than Seven* in 2002.

*Maira Kalman: Artist Kalman has a cult following; she is known for creating picture books that appeal to both children and parents with an eye for the quirky and contemporary. Noted for her witty, stream-of-consciousness prose, Kalman pairs her texts with energetic illustrations full of visual puns and parodies, strong colors and geometric shapes, and exotic locales. Several of her works focus on the friendly beagle named Max Stravinsky, who first appeared in *Hey Willy, See the Pyramids.* In 2002 Kalman published *Fireboat: The Heroic Adventure of the "John J. Harvey."*

*Mercer Mayer: Popular children's author Mayer is recognized for his versatility, humor, and artistic skill. Noted as one of the first creators of wordless picture books, Mayer also writes and illustrates nonsense fiction, fantasy, and folktales. He is perhaps best known for his "Little Critter" series of picture books, many of which have been created with his wife, Gina. Three books in that series—*The Mixed-up Morning, Play Ball,* and *Just Not Invited*—were published in 2002.

*Donna Jo Napoli: A professor of linguistics at Swarthmore College, Napoli's passion for language can be seen in her novels for young adults and middle-grade readers. Exploring topics ranging from sports to childhood anxieties to fairy tales, Napoli employs both humor and skillful prose to craft award-winning stories of hope and inspiration. *Daughter of Venice,* one of several of the author's works set in Italy, was published in 2002.

*Margaret Shannon Silverwood: Publishing under the name Margaret Shannon, Australian author and illustrator Silverwood has created a small but choice body of humorous books for children, including *Elvira, Gullible's Troubles,* and 2002's *The Red Wolf.* In *The Red Wolf,* Silverwood toys with a classic fairy story—as well as the works of noted American author/illustrator Maurice Sendak—in relating the tale of a seven-year-old princess who receives a gold basket of yarn for her birthday.

Lea Wait: Wait has drawn on her love of New England and its history to author a number of books for young readers. In novels such as *Stopping to Home* and *Seaward Born*, she focuses on self-reliant young people living in the early nineteenth century, who overcome difficult circumstances and gain knowledge and maturity.

Bo Zaunders: On the heels of a long career in advertising that took him from his native Sweden to New York City and many other places in between, Zaunders began a second career as a children's book writer. Working with his wife, illustrator Roxie Munro, he has published nonfiction titles that showcase the daring of men and women from history. In 1998 Zaunders produced *Crocodiles, Camels, and Dugout Canoes: Eight Adventurous Episodes,* and he followed that in 2001 with *Feathers, Flaps, and Flops: Fabulous Early Fliers.*

Introduction

Something about the Author (*SATA*) is an ongoing reference series that examines the lives and works of authors and illustrators of books for children. *SATA* includes not only well-known writers and artists but also less prominent individuals whose works are just coming to be recognized. This series is often the only readily available information source on emerging authors and illustrators. You'll find *SATA* informative and entertaining, whether you are a student, a librarian, an English teacher, a parent, or simply an adult who enjoys children's literature.

What's Inside SATA

SATA provides detailed information about authors and illustrators who span the full time range of children's literature, from early figures like John Newbery and L. Frank Baum to contemporary figures like Judy Blume and Richard Peck. Authors in the series represent primarily English-speaking countries, particularly the United States, Canada, and the United Kingdom. Also included, however, are authors from around the world whose works are available in English translation. The writings represented in *SATA* include those created intentionally for children and young adults as well as those written for a general audience and known to interest younger readers. These writings cover the entire spectrum of children's literature, including picture books, humor, folk and fairy tales, animal stories, mystery and adventure, science fiction and fantasy, historical fiction, poetry and nonsense verse, drama, biography, and nonfiction.

Obituaries are also included in *SATA* and are intended not only as death notices but also as concise overviews of people's lives and work. Additionally, each edition features newly revised and updated entries for a selection of *SATA* listees who remain of interest to today's readers and who have been active enough to require extensive revisions of their earlier biographies.

Autobiography Feature

Beginning with Volume 103, *SATA* features two or more specially commissioned autobiographical essays in each volume. These unique essays, averaging about ten thousand words in length and illustrated with an abundance of personal photos, present an entertaining and informative first-person perspective on the lives and careers of prominent authors and illustrators profiled in *SATA*.

Two Convenient Indexes

In response to suggestions from librarians, *SATA* indexes no longer appear in every volume but are included in alternate (odd-numbered) volumes of the series, beginning with Volume 57.

SATA continues to include two indexes that cumulate with each alternate volume: the Illustrations Index, arranged by the name of the illustrator, gives the number of the volume and page where the illustrator's work appears in the current volume as well as all preceding volumes in the series; the Author Index gives the number of the volume in which a person's biographical sketch, autobiographical essay, or obituary appears in the current volume as well as all preceding volumes in the series.

These indexes also include references to authors and illustrators who appear in Gale's *Yesterday's Authors of Books for Children, Children's Literature Review,* and *Something about the Author Autobiography Series.*

Easy-to-Use Entry Format

Whether you're already familiar with the *SATA* series or just getting acquainted, you will want to be aware of the kind of information that an entry provides. In every *SATA* entry the editors attempt to give as complete a picture of the person's life and work as possible. A typical entry in *SATA* includes the following clearly labeled information sections:

- *PERSONAL:* date and place of birth and death, parents' names and occupations, name of spouse, date of marriage, names of children, educational institutions attended, degrees received, religious and political affiliations, hobbies and other interests.

- *ADDRESSES:* complete home, office, electronic mail, and agent addresses, whenever available.

- *CAREER:* name of employer, position, and dates for each career post; art exhibitions; military service; memberships and offices held in professional and civic organizations.

- *AWARDS, HONORS:* literary and professional awards received.

- *WRITINGS:* title-by-title chronological bibliography of books written and/or illustrated, listed by genre when known; lists of other notable publications, such as plays, screenplays, and periodical contributions.

- *ADAPTATIONS:* a list of films, television programs, plays, CD-ROMs, recordings, and other media presentations that have been adapted from the author's work.

- *WORK IN PROGRESS:* description of projects in progress.

- *SIDELIGHTS:* a biographical portrait of the author or illustrator's development, either directly from the biographee—and often written specifically for the *SATA* entry—or gathered from diaries, letters, interviews, or other published sources.

- *BIOGRAPHICAL AND CRITICAL SOURCES:* cites sources quoted in "Sidelights" along with references for further reading.

- *EXTENSIVE ILLUSTRATIONS:* photographs, movie stills, book illustrations, and other interesting visual materials supplement the text.

How a SATA Entry Is Compiled

A *SATA* entry progresses through a series of steps. If the biographee is living, the *SATA* editors try to secure information directly from him or her through a questionnaire. From the information that the biographee supplies, the editors prepare an entry, filling in any essential missing details with research and/or telephone interviews. If possible, the author or illustrator is sent a copy of the entry to check for accuracy and completeness.

If the biographee is deceased or cannot be reached by questionnaire, the *SATA* editors examine a wide variety of published sources to gather information for an entry. Biographical and bibliographic sources are consulted, as are book reviews, feature articles, published interviews, and material sometimes obtained from the biographee's family, publishers, agent, or other associates.

Entries that have not been verified by the biographees or their representatives are marked with an asterisk (*).

Contact the Editor

We encourage our readers to examine the entire *SATA* series. Please write and tell us if we can make *SATA* even more helpful to you. Give your comments and suggestions to the editor:

BY MAIL: Editor, *Something about the Author,* The Gale Group, 27500 Drake Rd., Farmington Hills, MI 48331-3535.

BY TELEPHONE: (800) 877-GALE

BY FAX: (248) 699-8054

Something about the Author Product Advisory Board

The editors of *Something about the Author* are dedicated to maintaining a high standard of excellence by publishing comprehensive, accurate, and highly readable entries on a wide array of writers for children and young adults. In addition to the quality of the content, the editors take pride in the graphic design of the series, which is intended to be orderly yet inviting, allowing readers to utilize the pages of *SATA* easily and with efficiency. Despite the longevity of the *SATA* print series, and the success of its format, we are mindful that the vitality of a literary reference product is dependent on its ability to serve its users over time. As literature, and attitudes about literature, constantly evolve, so do the reference needs of students, teachers, scholars, journalists, researchers, and book club members. To be certain that we continue to keep pace with the expectations of our customers, the editors of *SATA* listen carefully to their comments regarding the value, utility, and quality of the series. Librarians, who have firsthand knowledge of the needs of library users, are a valuable resource for us. The *Something about the Author* Product Advisory Board, made up of school, public, and academic librarians, is a forum to promote focused feedback about *SATA* on a regular basis. The nine-member advisory board includes the following individuals, whom the editors wish to thank for sharing their expertise:

- **Eva M. Davis,** Teen Services Librarian, Plymouth District Library, Plymouth, Michigan

- **Joan B. Eisenberg,** Lower School Librarian, Milton Academy, Milton, Massachusetts

- **Francisca Goldsmith,** Teen Services Librarian, Berkeley Public Library, Berkeley, California

- **Harriet Hagenbruch,** Curriculum Materials Center/Education Librarian, Axinn Library, Hofstra University, Hempstead, New York

- **Monica F. Irlbacher,** Young Adult Librarian, Middletown Thrall Library, Middletown, New York

- **Robyn Lupa,** Head of Children's Services, Jefferson County Public Library, Lakewood, Colorado

- **Eric Norton,** Head of Children's Services, McMillan Memorial Library, Wisconsin Rapids, Wisconsin

- **Victor L. Schill,** Assistant Branch Librarian/Children's Librarian, Harris County Public Library/Fairbanks Branch, Houston, Texas

- **Caryn Sipos,** Community Librarian, Three Creeks Community Library, Vancouver, Washington

Acknowledgments

Grateful acknowledgment is made to the following publishers, authors, and artists whose works appear in this volume.

ALEXANDER, MARTHA. Alexander, Martha, illustrator. From an illustration in *A You're Adorable,* by Buddy Kaye, Fred Wise, and Sidney Lippman. Candlewick Press, 1994. Illustrations © 1994 by Martha Alexander. Reproduced by permission of the publisher Candlewick Press Inc., Cambridge, MA./ Alexander, Martha, illustrator. From an illustration in her *And My Mean Old Mother Will Be Sorry, Blackboard Bear.* Candlewick Press, 2000. Illustrations © 2000 by Martha Alexander. Reproduced by permission of the publisher Candlewick Press, Inc., Cambridge, MA./ Alexander, Martha, illustrator. From an illustration in her *We're in Big Trouble, Blackboard Bear*. Candlewick Press, 2001. Illustrations © 2001 by Martha Alexander. Reproduced by permission of the publisher Candlewick Press Inc., Cambridge, MA./ Alexander, Martha, photograph. Reproduced by permission.

ALEXANDER, SUE. Gore, Leonid, illustrator. From an illustration in *Behold the Trees,* by Sue Alexander. Arthur A. Levine Books, 2001. Illustrations © 2001 by Leonid Gore. Reproduced by permission./ Alexander, Sue, photograph by Marilyn Sanders. Reproduced by permission.

ANGELOU, MAYA. From a jacket of *I Know Why the Caged Bird Sings,* by Maya Angelou. Random House, 1969. Copyright © 1969 and renewed 1997 by Maya Angelou. Reproduced by permission of Random House, Inc./ From a cover of *Wouldn't Take Nothing for My Journey Now,* by Maya Angelou. Cover Art: "Bow Tie" (quilt) © 1991 by Nancy Crow. Reproduced by permission of Bantam Books, a division of Random House, Inc./ Carter, Dwight, photographer. From a cover of *The Heart of a Woman,* by Maya Angelou. Bantam Books, 1997. Used by permission of Bantam Books, a division of Random House, Inc./ Angelou, Maya, photograph. AP/Wide World Photos. Reproduced by permission.

BARNER, BOB. Barner, Bob, illustrator. From an illustration in *Benny's Pennies,* by Pat Brisson. Bantam Books, 1993. Illustration copyright © 1993 by Bob Barner. Reproduced by permission of Random House Children's Books, a division of Random House, Inc./ Barner, Bob, illustrator. From an illustration in *Dem Bones,* by Bob Barner. Chronicle Books, 1996. Illustrations © 1996 by Bob Barner. Reproduced by permission.

BAYLOR, BYRD. Parnall, Peter, illustrator. From a cover of *This Desert Is Theirs,* by Byrd Baylor. Aladdin Paperbacks, 1975. Illustrations copyright © 1975 by Peter Parnall. Reproduced by permission of Atheneum Books for Young Readers, an imprint of Simon & Schuster Children's Publishing Division./ Baylor, Byrd, illustrator. From a cover of his *Everybody Needs a Rock.* Aladdin Paperbacks, 1985. Illustrations Copyright © 1974 by Peter Parnall. Reproduced by permission of Atheneum Books for Young Readers, an imprint of Simon & Schuster Children's Publishing Division./ Parnall, Peter, illustrator. From an illustration in *I'm in Charge of Celebrations,* by Byrd Baylor. Aladdin Paperbacks, 1995. Illustrations copyright © 1986 Peter Parnall. Reproduced by permission of Atheneum Books for Young Readers, an imprint of Simon & Schuster Children's Publishing Division./ Parnall, Peter, illustrator. From an illustration in *The Table Where Rich People Sit,* by Byrd Baylor. Aladdin Paperbacks, 1998. Illustrations copyright © 1994 by Peter Parnall. Reproduced by permission of Atheneum Books for Young Readers, an imprint of Simon & Schuster Children's Publishing Division.

BLOMGREN, JENNIFER (ALICE). Blomgren, Jennifer, photograph by David Burroughs. Reproduced by permission of Jennifer Blomgren.

BOWEN, FRED. Barrow, Ann G., illustrator. From an illustration in *On the Line,* by Fred Bowen. Peachtree, 1999. Illustrations © 1999 by Ann G. Barrow. Reproduced by permission./ Casale, Paul, illustrator. From an illustration in *Winners Take All,* by Fred Bowen. Peachtree, 2000. Illustrations © 2000 by Paul Casale. Reproduced by permission./ Bowen, Fred, photograph. Reproduced by permission.

BUJOLD, LOIS MCMASTER. Gutierrez, Alan, illustrator. From the cover of *Falling Free,* by Lois McMaster Bujold. Baen, 1988. Copyright © 1988 by Lois McMaster Bujold. All rights reserved. Reproduced by permission./ Gutierrez, Alan, illustrator. From the cover of *Brothers in Arms*, by Lois McMaster Bujold. Baen, 1989. Copyright © 1989 by Lois McMaster Bujold. All rights reserved. Reproduced by permission./ Hickman, Steven, illustrator. From the cover of *Barrayar,* by Lois McMaster Bujold. Baen, 1991. Copyright © 1991 by Lois McMaster Bujold. All rights reserved. Reproduced by permission./ Bujold, Lois McMaster, photograph by David Dyer-Bennet. Reproduced by permission.

BUNKERS, SUZANNE L. Sherer, Stan, photographer. From a cover of *Inscribing the Daily: Critical Essays on Women's Diaries.* Edited by Suzanne L. Bunkers and Cynthia A. Huff. University of Massachusetts Press, 1996. Reproduced by permission./ From a cover of *A Pioneer Farm Girl: The Diary of Sarah Gillespie, 1877-1878.* Edited by Suzanne L. Bunkers with Ann Hodgson. Blue Earth Books, 2000. © 2000 Blue Earth Books. Reproduced by permission of State Historical Society of Iowa-Iowa City./ Bunkers, Suzanne L., photograph. Reproduced by permission.

SOMETHING ABOUT THE AUTHOR

ALEXANDER, Martha 1920-

Personal

Born May 25, 1920, in Augusta, GA; daughter of Guy S. Alexander (an attorney, accountant, and woodworker) and Lillie Mae Camp; married, 1943 (divorced, 1959); children: Kim, Allen. *Nationality:* American. *Education:* Graduated from Cincinnati Academy of Fine Arts, 1939. *Hobbies and other interests:* Gardening of all kinds, pottery, and woodworking.

Addresses

Home—1519 Nuuanu Ave., #1, Honolulu, HI 96817.

Career

Writer and illustrator; Honolulu Academy of Arts, Honolulu, HI, art teacher, 1946-49; children's art teacher; freelance artist; frequent lecturer on the creation of books to children, parents, teachers, and librarians.

Awards, Honors

Outstanding Book citation, *New York Times Book Review,* 1969, for *Blackboard Bear;* Best Books citation, *School Library Journal,* 1970, for *Bobo's Dream;* Children's Spring Book Festival honor book, 1971, for *Sabrina;* Children's Book Showcase title, Children's Book Council, 1972, for *Nobody Asked Me if I Wanted a Baby Sister;* Christopher Award, 1973, for *I'll Protect You from the Jungle Beasts;* Kentucky Bluegrass Award, 1984, for *Move Over, Twerp.*

Writings

SELF-ILLUSTRATED

Out! Out! Out!, Dial (New York, NY), 1968.

Maybe a Monster, Dial (New York, NY), 1968.

Blackboard Bear (also see below), Dial (New York, NY), 1969, Candlewick Press (Cambridge, MA), 1999.

The Story Grandmother Told, Dial (New York, NY), 1969.

We Never Get to Do Anything, Dial (New York, NY), 1970.

Bobo's Dream, Dial (New York, NY), 1970.

Sabrina, Dial (New York, NY), 1970.

Nobody Asked Me if I Wanted a Baby Sister, Dial (New York, NY), 1971.

And My Mean Old Mother Will Be Sorry, Blackboard Bear (also see below), Dial (New York, NY), 1972, Candlewick Press (Cambridge, MA), 2000.

No Ducks in Our Bathtub, Dial (New York, NY), 1973.

I'll Protect You from the Jungle Beasts, Dial (New York, NY), 1973.

(Compiler) *Poems and Prayers for the Very Young,* Random House (New York, NY), 1973, included in *Santa's Take-Along Library: Five Favorite Read-to-Me Books,* Random House (New York, NY), 1985.

I'll Be the Horse If You'll Play with Me (Junior Literary Guild selection), Dial (New York, NY), 1975.

I Sure Am Glad to See You, Blackboard Bear (also see below), Dial (New York, NY), 1976, Candlewick Press (Cambridge, MA), 2001.

Pigs Say Oink: A First Book of Sounds, Random House (New York, NY), 1978.

Martha Alexander

When the New Baby Comes, I'm Moving Out, Dial (New York, NY), 1979, reprinted, Econo-Clad Books (Minneapolis, MN), 1999.

We're in Big Trouble, Blackboard Bear (also see below), Dial (New York, NY), 1980, Candlewick Press (Cambridge, MA), 2001.

Four Bears in a Box (contains *Blackboard Bear; And My Mean Old Mother Will Be Sorry, Blackboard Bear; I Sure Am Glad to See You, Blackboard Bear;* and *We're in Big Trouble, Blackboard Bear*), Dial (New York, NY), 1981.

Marty McGee's Space Lab, No Girls Allowed, Dial (New York, NY), 1981.

Move Over, Twerp, Dial (New York, NY), 1981.

Maggie's Moon, Dial (New York, NY), 1982.

How My Library Grew, by Dinah, H. W. Wilson (New York, NY), 1983.

Three Magic Flip Books (contains *The Magic Hat, The Magic Picture,* and *The Magic Box;* also see below), Dial (New York, NY), 1984.

Even That Moose Won't Listen to Me, Dial (New York, NY), 1988.

My Outrageous Friend Charlie, Dial (New York, NY), 1989.

Where Does the Sky End, Grandpa?, Harcourt (San Diego, CA), 1992.

Lily and Willy, Candlewick Press (Cambridge, MA), 1993.

Where's Willy?, Candlewick Press (Cambridge, MA), 1993.

Willy's Boot, Candlewick Press (Cambridge, MA), 1993.

Good Night, Lily, Candlewick Press (Cambridge, MA), 1993.

The Magic Hat, Puffin Books (New York, NY), 1994.

The Magic Picture, Puffin Books (New York, NY), 1994.

The Magic Box, Puffin Books (New York, NY), 1994.

A You're Adorable, lyrics and music by Buddy Kaye, Fred Wise, and Sidney Lippman, Candlewick Press (Cambridge, MA), 1994.

You're a Genius, Blackboard Bear, Candlewick Press (Cambridge, MA), 1995.

I'll Never Share You, Blackboard Bear, Candlewick Press (Cambridge, MA), 2003.

ILLUSTRATOR

Charlotte Zolotow, *Big Sister and Little Sister,* Harper (New York, NY), 1966.

Janice Udry, *Mary Ann's Mud Day,* Harper (New York, NY), 1967.

Lois Wyse, *Grandmothers Are to Love,* Parents' Magazine Press (New York, NY), 1967.

Lois Wyse, *Grandfathers Are to Love,* Parents' Magazine Press (New York, NY), 1967.

La Verne Johnson, *Night Noises,* Parents' Magazine Press (New York, NY), 1968.

Lois Hobart, *What Is a Whispery Secret?,* Parents' Magazine Press (New York, NY), 1968.

Doris Orgel, *Whose Turtle?,* World (Chicago, IL), 1968.

Lillie D. Chaffin, *I Have a Tree,* D. White (New York, NY), 1969.

Louis Untermeyer, *You,* Golden (New York, NY), 1969.

Liesel Moak Skorpen, *Elizabeth,* Harper (New York, NY), 1970.

Liesel Moak Skorpen, *Charles,* Harper (New York, NY), 1971.

Dorothy Frances Canfield Fisher, *Understood Betsy,* Holt (New York, NY), 1972, new edition with an afterword by Peggy Parish, Dell (New York, NY), 1987.

Joan M. Lexau, *Emily and the Klunky Baby and the Next Door Dog,* Dial (New York, NY), 1972.

Carol K. Scism, *The Wizard of Walnut Street,* Dial (New York, NY), 1973.

Jean Van Leeuwen, *Too Hot for Ice Cream,* Dial (New York, NY), 1974.

Liesel Moak Skorpen, *Mandy's Grandmother* (Junior Literary Guild selection), Dial (New York, NY), 1975.

Amy Ehrlich, *The Everyday Train,* Dial (New York, NY), 1977.

Barbara Williams, *Jeremy Isn't Hungry,* Dutton (New York, NY), 1978.

Judy Malloy, *Bad Thad,* Dutton (New York, NY), 1980.

OTHER

Contributor of reviews to *Atlantic.* Some of Alexander's books have been translated into other languages, including French, Japanese, Spanish, and Dutch.

Adaptations

A set of four filmstrips with cassettes based on the "Blackboard Bear" series, containing *Blackboard Bear, And My Mean Old Mother Will Be Sorry, Blackboard Bear, I Sure Am Glad to See You, Blackboard Bear,* and

We're in Big Trouble, Blackboard Bear, was produced by Spoken Arts, 1984.

Sidelights

Author and illustrator of the ever-popular "Blackboard Bear" series, Martha Alexander is known for her soft pencil and watercolor illustrations and her simple texts, both of which regale young readers with the magic, delights, and frustrations of childhood. Alexander has been an artist since childhood, trying her hand at ceramics, doll-making, fabric and clothing design, portrait painting, children's murals and paintings, decorative collages and mosaics, and teaching art to adults and children. Alexander says she did not find her niche in the art world until, at the age of forty-five, she was given her first children's book to illustrate. She knew then that her long search for the right medium of expression had been more than justified. "I felt for the first time that here it *was,*" Alexander said in *Junior Literary Guild.* "It was as though I had searched all my life to find me—or home." As Alexander went on to produce an impressive selection of picture books, her unique ability to make pictures tell the story and her insightful outlook on children combined to win her popular and critical acclaim.

Alexander was born in Georgia, but her family moved to Ohio when she was nine. Besides being shy and insecure by nature, she was sensitive about her Southern accent and a heritage that included slave-owning. Her books would later reflect her first-hand knowledge of some of childhood's uncertainties. Alexander's interest in art and her teachers' encouragement about her drawing provided her with a solid foundation during her school years.

After graduating from high school, Alexander entered the Cincinnati Academy of Fine Arts. Despite her aspirations to be a portrait painter, she soon found herself drawn into the world of modern art and "art for art's sake" by teachers and fellow-students. Her husband, an artist she met and married while at the academy, also influenced her. "Being married to a serious painter who, I believed, felt a certain disdain for anything other than 'fine arts,'" Alexander once commented, "I found it hard to find my way to a world of my own." The couple moved to Hawaii where, as they raised their two children, Alexander taught art classes and began to sell her paintings, murals, and collages to architects and decorators.

In 1960, after her marriage dissolved, Alexander moved to New York with her two teenaged children and began illustrating for magazines on a freelance basis. She once described this pivotal stage of her career: "After working for about five years freelancing for magazines and a bit in advertising, I felt extremely discouraged and frustrated and I was having a hard time making ends meet. One day I took the day off and did a whole series of drawings of children doing nonsensical things. I had such fun. I put them aside and went back to the grind until several weeks later I came across the drawings and decided 'if I'm going to be poor, I'll be poor doing what I want to do.' I put them together in a little book and went to Harper and Row." At the large publishing company, Alexander was almost immediately given a book to illustrate. With several more books closely following the first, Alexander's career as a children's book illustrator was established.

Alexander's training in the fine arts was invaluable to her in her new medium. While in art school, she was influenced greatly by three artists—modern Swiss painter Paul Klee, fifteenth-century Italian artist Leonardo da Vinci, and twentieth-century French painter Marc Chagall. The beauty of these artists' works impressed her, but she was particularly intrigued by the playfulness of Chagall and Klee and their ability to say so much without words. Alexander remarked in an autobiographical sketch in *Books for Schools and Libraries:* "By viewing their work I discovered how complete stories can be told through images.... It was interesting to see that pictures themselves can enhance a story in ways that words can not. Now I take great pride in telling as much of the story as I can without text, but rather through gestures and expressions."

As she illustrated books for other authors, Alexander came up with ideas for books of her own. She once commented, "As I was working on my first book at Harper, I began to get ideas for books and told them to my editors, although I had no thought of writing them. My editors suggested I write them and my response was 'But I'm not a writer!' She chuckled and said, 'How do you know if you don't try?' My first efforts were very frustrating." Alexander's first publication as author and illustrator, *Out! Out! Out!,* was a wordless picture book, revealing not only Alexander's belief that pictures can tell a story without words but also her initial insecurity as a writer. Alexander once stated that after making many efforts to write her own stories, "it seemed quite hopeless ... they sounded good in my head but not on paper." She resolved her frustrations as a writer by developing a system of creating books that did not

Alexander illustrated children and pets frolicking through the letters of the alphabet in A You're Adorable. *(Words and music by Buddy Kaye, Fred Wise, and Sidney Lippman.)*

Alexander's full-color illustrations grace her work And My Mean Old Mother Will Be Sorry, Blackboard Bear, *in which Anthony and Blackboard Bear run away to the woods when Mother is cross.*

require her to separate the functions of writing and illustrating. Starting with a "dummy"—a book made up of thirty-two bound blank pages—she wrote her story with words and pictures simultaneously. "I found that as I worked on a dummy, words and pictures began to come together as one, and I was hardly aware of the difference between them," she explained.

Alexander's third self-illustrated publication, the popular *Blackboard Bear,* is about a little boy who, rebuffed by the big boys for being too young, goes home and draws a large bear on his blackboard. He then takes his blackboard bear by the leash and parades it in front of the older boys, who long to hold the leash or ride the bear. With his creation of the bear, the little boy has turned the tables: it is his turn to coolly rebuff the big boys. This flight of childhood fantasy is "satisfying poetic justice," Ethel L. Heins observed in *Horn Book,* further summarizing that Alexander "has already shown the ingenuity of her wordless storytelling through pictures in *Out! Out! Out!* Now she proves just as imaginative with the same kind of eloquent drawings accompanied by a minimum of words." A critic in *Books for Keeps,* reviewing a British edition of the book, found that Alexander "builds a variety of needs and coping strategies into a very private, cleverly understated, little book."

The sequels to *Blackboard Bear—And My Mean Old Mother Will Be Sorry, Blackboard Bear, I Sure Am Glad to See You, Blackboard Bear, We're in Big Trouble, Blackboard Bear, You're a Genius, Blackboard Bear,* and the 2003 addition to the series, *I'll Never Share You, Blackboard Bear*—have all been very popular with readers and critics alike. The second title in the series, *And My Mean Old Mother Will Be Sorry, Blackboard Bear,* originally published in 1972, was reprinted in 2000 with full-color illustrations that Alexander adapted from her original three-color artwork. In this installment, the boy manages to get bath water all over the floor and honey all over the kitchen. When he sees his mother's

anger and frustration, he figures it is time to run away with his favorite bear. Together Blackboard Bear and the boy have an evening outing. A reviewer for *Publishers Weekly,* writing about the year 2000 edition, praised Alexander's revamped artwork, commenting on the "twilight colors" of the backgrounds and the bear's "uncanny two-dimensional quality." *Booklist*'s Carolyn Phelan also praised the "memorable" story for its "welcome new look."

In *I Sure Am Glad to See You, Blackboard Bear,* the boy gets a name, Little Anthony, and Bear once again helps him out when other children become cruel and selfish. With *We're in Big Trouble, Blackboard Bear,* Bear learns a hard lesson about leaving the possessions of others alone. Anthony's friends accuse Bear of stealing goldfish from the pond, blueberries from the garden, and honey from a windowsill. Anthony, believing Bear to be innocent, defends him, but then Bear confesses. However, Bear makes up for the thefts, making chalk drawings of the stolen goods and then returning them to their rightful owners. *Booklist*'s Ellen Mandel praised Alexander's "understated yet eloquent pictures" in the 2001 edition of *We're in Big Trouble,* and also pointed out that her "spare text conveys an amazing amount of sentiment."

In 1995, Alexander added a new title to the series with *You're a Genius, Blackboard Bear.* In this outing, Anthony wants to go to the moon. Luckily, Blackboard Bear knows how to build a spaceship. As the two pack their ship with supplies, including sleeping bags, water, and food, Anthony begins to wonder about the monsters that might reside on the moon. Since their ship seems awfully crowded anyway, he sends Bear off on the journey alone. In the end, Bear returns with a star he brought back for Anthony.

Critics found this volume to be just as praiseworthy as the earlier installments. "Alexander's unadorned narrative and her delicate pencil-and-watercolor art complement each other splendidly," wrote a critic for *Publishers Weekly,* "creating a soothing bedtime tale." *Booklist*'s Carolyn Phelan had special acclaim for Alexander's artwork, noting that the "sensitive drawings" lend the book a "beguiling quality that will please both parents and young children." In a review of the British edition, Cliff Moon noted in *School Librarian* that, though the picture book field was inundated with teddy bear books, Alexander's title was "on another plane." "Quite outstanding," he concluded. A critic writing in *Books for Keeps* described *You're a Genius* as a "seemingly simple book which offers countless opportunities for making meanings," and a contributor for *Junior Bookshelf* dubbed the title an "admirable book."

Interaction with the children in her family has been a great source of inspiration for Alexander's books. The idea for *Blackboard Bear* arose on a visit with her four-year-old nephew. "I was utterly fascinated by this child," she explained. "He lived in the country and had never had any children to play with. He had a fantasy world that was unbelievable. I watched him race around playing cops and robbers, cowboys and Indians, elephants, lions, and other games. Whatever he was playing, he became that part. He told me wild tales of how he once fell into a huge pit and how his brave father rescued him. It was endless. Once he handed me a dozen baby kangaroos to keep for him." Alexander believes that the imaginary worlds children create are very real and important aspects of their lives. "Adults should encourage, explore, and be interested in the fantasy world of the child," she stated in a *Publishers Weekly* interview with Jill Korey.

Two picture books, *Nobody Asked Me if I Wanted a Baby Sister* and *When the New Baby Comes, I'm Moving Out,* originated when Alexander's two-year-old grand-daughter indirectly expressed feelings of sibling rivalry about her new baby sister by telling her mother that the baby wanted to live with her grandmother. After thinking about the unvoiced resentment and jealousy that might be behind the two-year-old's statement, Alexander decided to write a story in which an older brother actually gives his baby sister away. She hoped that by reading about the basic, but often unspoken, resentments of sibling rivalry, her young readers will understand they are not alone in these feelings and will find appropriate ways to resolve them.

Childhood frustration and powerlessness are also themes of *Even That Moose Won't Listen to Me,* a book in which a young girl, Rebecca, tries to tell her family that a moose is eating their garden. Her family, assuming that the moose is a figment of Rebecca's imagination, ignores her warnings. The moose, also ignoring Rebecca, continues to munch on the garden until there is

nothing left to munch. When the family finally discovers that their garden has indeed been destroyed and comes to Rebecca for details, she lets them know that she is too busy to discuss it with them. "This book is about small children having power," Alexander stated in *Publishers Weekly.* "I remember what it felt like in my own childhood when no one would listen to me. Children are so often misunderstood, not believed."

Alexander has also created colorful board books for the very young. One quartet of titles has proved particularly popular, the "Lily and Willy" books, which include *Where's Willy?, Willy's Boot, Lily and Willy,* and *Good Night, Lily.* This brother and sister pair star in each of the simple stories, playing hide-and-seek, for example, in *Where's Willy,* with the toddler Willy hiding himself inside a paper bag. With *Willy's Boot,* older sister Lily supervises her brother as he puts away his toys and clothes. In *Good Night, Lily,* the two are in bed with their toys and the sister is reading to Willy. When the siblings fall asleep, the story is continued by Willy's teddy and Lily's doll. A reviewer for *Publishers Weekly* called this quartet of books "understated and alluring." Liza Bliss, writing in *School Library Journal,* praised the "characteristic soft, delicate, and gently realistic style" of Alexander's artwork. Similar positive words came from Sheryl Lee Saunders in *Horn Book Guide,* who called the illustrations "endearing."

Critics have applauded the acute identification with children exhibited in Alexander's expressive drawings and humorously human stories. The author and illustrator says that her understanding of the child's world has been inspired by her children, grandchildren, and great-grandchildren and also by her own memories of child-

In Alexander's self-illustrated **We're in Big Trouble, Blackboard Bear,** *Anthony has to teach Blackboard Bear not to steal.*

hood. But beyond these influences, Alexander is inspired by her readers, as she stated in *Books for Schools and Libraries:* "I want to give something to the child reading my book. The payoff comes when I receive a letter from one of my young readers, and it's evident that I've reached him or her. This affords me the deepest satisfaction of all. You see, I was once the timid, shy, and very insecure child for whom I am writing now."

Alexander more recently told *SATA,* "I owe many people a great deal of thanks along the way, especially Ursula Nordstrom, Charlotte Zolotow, Phyllis Fogelman, [and] Amy Ehrlich."

Biographical and Critical Sources

BOOKS

Kingman, Lee, and others, *Illustrators of Children's Books 1967-1976,* Horn Book (Boston, MA), 1978.

PERIODICALS

Booklist, July, 1994, Annie Ayres, review of *A You're Adorable,* p. 1950; October 1, 1994, Isabel Schon, review of *La bota de Lalo, Lola y Lalo,* and *Buenos noches, Lola,* p. 337; May 1, 1995, Carolyn Phelan, review of *You're a Genius, Blackboard Bear,* p. 1578; November 15, 2000, Carolyn Phelan, review of *And My Mean Old Mother Will Be Sorry, Blackboard Bear,* p. 645; December 15, 2001, Ellen Mandel, review of *We're in Big Trouble, Blackboard Bear,* p. 737.

Books for Keeps, March, 1996, review of *Blackboard Bear,* p. 97; September, 1996, review of *You're a Genius, Blackboard Bear,* p. 96.

Books for Schools and Libraries, Martha Alexander, 1985.

Bulletin of the Center for Children's Books, September, 1969; March, 1977; December, 1979; July-August, 1980; December, 1982; April, 1988.

Horn Book, August, 1969, Ethel L. Heins, review of *Blackboard Bear,* p. 395; February, 1976; December, 1978; February, 1983; September-October, 1995, Elizabeth S. Watson, review of *You're a Genius, Blackboard Bear,* p. 625; January, 2000, review of *Blackboard Bear,* p. 59.

Horn Book Guide, fall, 1993, Sheryl Lee Saunders, review of *Where's Willy?, Willy's Boot, Lily and Willy,* and *Good Night, Lily,* p. 240.

Junior Bookshelf, August, 1995, review of *You're a Genius, Blackboard Bear,* pp. 123-124.

Junior Literary Guild, March, 1975; September, 1975; September, 1978.

Publishers Weekly, February 26, 1988, Jill Korey, biographical sketch of Martha Alexander, p. 117; March 23, 1992, review of *Where Does the Sky End, Grandpa?,* p. 71; April 5, 1993, review of *Where's Willy?, Willy's Boot, Lily and Willy,* and *Good Night, Lily,* p. 74; April 17, 1995, review of *You're a Genius, Blackboard Bear,* p. 57; November 15, 1999, review of *Blackboard Bear,* p. 68; November 6, 2000, "Books with Staying Power," p. 93; December 17, 2001, review of *We're in Big Trouble, Blackboard Bear,* p. 94.

School Librarian, August, 1995, Cliff Moon, review of *You're a Genius, Blackboard Bear,* p. 102.

School Library Journal, July, 1992, Martha Topol, review of *Where Does the Sky End, Grandpa?,* p. 56; October, 1993, Liza Bliss, review of *Where's Willy?, Willy's Boot, Lily and Willy,* and *Goodnight, Lily,* p. 90; June, 1995, Nancy Menaldi-Scanlan, review of *You're a Genius, Blackboard Bear,* p. 76.

* * *

ALEXANDER, Sue 1933-

Personal

Born August 20, 1933, in Tucson, AZ; daughter of Jack M. (an electronic components manufacturer) and Edith (Pollock) Ratner; married second husband, Joel Alexander (a car agency sales manager), November 29, 1959; children: (first marriage) Glenn David; (second marriage) Marc Jeffry, Stacey Joy. *Nationality:* American. *Education:* Attended Drake University, 1950-52, and Northwestern University, 1952-53. *Religion:* Jewish.

Addresses

Home and office—6846 McLaren, Canoga Park, CA 91307; fax: 818-347-2617. *Agent*—Marilyn Marlow, Curtis Brown Ltd., Ten Astor Pl., New York, NY 10003. *E-mail*—suelalexander@earthlink.net.

Career

Writer. Instructor, University of California—Los Angeles.

Member

Society of Children's Book Writers and Illustrators (member of board of directors, 1972—), Southern California Council on Literature for Children and Young People.

Awards, Honors

Children's Choice citations, International Reading Association/Children's Book Council, 1977, for *Witch, Goblin, and Sometimes Ghost,* and 1982, for *Witch, Goblin, and Ghost in the Haunted Woods;* Children's Book of the Year, Child Study Association, 1978, for *Marc the Magnificent;* Dorothy C. McKenzie Award, Southern California Council of Literature for Children and Young People, 1980, for distinguished contribution to the field of children's literature; Golden Kite honor plaque, Society of Children's Book Writers and Illustrators, Notable Children's Book in the Field of Social Studies citation, National Council for the Social Studies/Children's Book Council (NCSS/CBC), both 1980, and High/Low Booklist citation, Young Adult Services Division/American Library Association, 1982, all for *Finding Your First Job;* Teacher's Choice citation, National Council of Teachers of English, *Booklist* Children's Reviewer's Choice, Notable Children's Book in the Field of Social Studies citation, NCSS/CBC, all 1983, Children's Book of the Year, Child Study

Association, and Distinguished Work of Fiction Honor, Southern California Council of Literature for Children and Young People (SCCLCYP), both 1984, all for *Nadia the Willful;* Outstanding Work of Fiction Honor, SCCLCYP, 1987, for *Lila on the Landing;* the Sue Alexander Service and Encouragement Award was created by the Society of Children's Book Writers and Illustrators.

Writings

FOR CHILDREN

Small Plays for You and a Friend, illustrated by Olivia H. H. Cole, Scholastic (New York, NY), 1973.

Nadir of the Streets, Macmillan (New York, NY), 1975.

Peacocks Are Very Special, illustrated by Victoria Chess, Doubleday (New York, NY), 1976.

Witch, Goblin, and Sometimes Ghost, illustrated by Jeanette Winter, Pantheon (New York, NY), 1976.

Small Plays for Special Days, illustrated by Tom Huffman, Clarion (New York, NY), 1977.

Marc the Magnificent, illustrated by Tomie dePaola, Pantheon (New York, NY), 1978.

More Witch, Goblin, and Ghost Stories, illustrated by Jeanette Winter, Pantheon (New York, NY), 1978.

Seymour the Prince, illustrated by Lillian Hoban, Pantheon (New York, NY), 1979.

Finding Your First Job (nonfiction), photographs by George Ancona, Dutton (New York, NY), 1980.

Whatever Happened to Uncle Albert? and Other Puzzling Plays, illustrated by Tom Huffman, Clarion (New York, NY), 1980.

Witch, Goblin, and Ghost in the Haunted Woods, illustrated by Jeanette Winter, Pantheon (New York, NY), 1981.

Witch, Goblin, and Ghost's Book of Things to Do, Pantheon (New York, NY), 1982.

Nadia the Willful, illustrated by Lloyd Bloom, Pantheon (New York, NY), 1983.

Dear Phoebe, illustrated by Eileen Christelow, Little, Brown (Boston, MA), 1984.

World Famous Muriel, illustrated by Chris C. Demarest, Little, Brown (Boston, MA), 1984.

Witch, Goblin, and Ghost Are Back, illustrated by Jeanette Winter, Pantheon (New York, NY), 1985.

World-Famous Muriel and the Scary Dragon, illustrated by Chris C. Demarest, Little, Brown (Boston, MA), 1985.

Lila on the Landing, illustrated by Ellen Eagle, Clarion (New York, NY), 1987.

There's More ... Much More, Said Squirrel, illustrated by Patience Brewster, Harcourt (New York, NY), 1987.

America's Own Holidays (nonfiction), illustrated by Leslie Morrill, F. Watts (New York, NY), 1988.

World-Famous Muriel and the Magic Mystery, illustrated by Marla Frazee, Crowell (New York, NY), 1990.

Who Goes Out on Halloween?, illustrated by G. Brian Karas, Bantam (New York, NY), 1990.

Sara's City, illustrated by Ronald Himler, Clarion (New York, NY), 1995.

What's Wrong Now, Millicent?, illustrated by David Scott Meier, Simon & Schuster (New York, NY), 1996.

One More Time, Mama, illustrated by David Soman, Marshall Cavendish (New York, NY), 1999.

Sue Alexander

Behold the Trees, illustrated by Leonid Gore, Arthur Levine Books (New York, NY), 2001.

Contributor of short stories, poetry, and plays to *Children's Playmate, Weekly Reader, Ladybug, Babybug,* and Walt Disney Studios. Contributor of book reviews to *Los Angeles Times.*

Adaptations

Witch, Goblin, and Sometimes Ghost and *Witch, Goblin, and Ghost Are Back* were adapted for audio cassette by Caedmon in 1987.

Sidelights

Sue Alexander is an award-winning writer of such popular children's picture books as *Witch, Goblin, and Sometimes Ghost, Nadia the Willful,* and *Lila on the Landing.* Her work is characterized by a lively sense of humor, as well as sharp insight into the emotional ups and downs of childhood. "Most of the stories I write are fantasy," Alexander once explained. "That is, they are about goblins and talking peacocks and ghosts instead of real people. But all the stories I write begin the same way: with how I *feel* about something."

Witch, Goblin, and Sometimes Ghost brought Alexander her first large audience, as well as critical notice and awards. In the book, Goblin has difficulty flying his kite, until he figures out he needs wind. Thinking that growing older will make him smarter about such things, he is disappointed when his birthday comes around and he does not automatically become more intelligent. However, Witch's gift of an encyclopedia that he can read and learn from makes him happy again. Set in the form of six read-aloud tales, the book "is useful as additional material for the beginning reader," noted a *Bulletin of the Center for Children's Books* contributor.

The character of Goblin proved so popular with readers that Alexander brought him back in several other books. *Witch, Goblin, and Ghost in the Haunted Woods* is another award-winner in the series, returning to the original scenario of mutually supportive spooky friends in five simple stories, this time focusing on swimming, gardening, and a snow storm. Each tale blends "mystery and the supernatural," according to Virginia Haviland in *Horn Book.* Zena Sutherland commented in *Bulletin of the Center for Children's Books* on the book's "reassuring texts," which deal with, among other things, a treasure hunt and storytelling.

Over thousands of years, the plentiful trees of Israel are destroyed, reducing the land to desert until new inhabitants plant trees to bring the land back to life in **Behold the Trees.** *(Written by Alexander and illustrated by Leonid Gore.)*

"As more of my work was published," Alexander wrote in an essay for *Something about the Author Autobiographical Series (SAAS),* "I began to feel like a professional writer. More importantly, I came to realize that the more of me that went into my writing, the better my stories were. The warm and enthusiastic response of young readers to the first of my books about Goblin, *Witch, Goblin, and Sometimes Ghost,* had given me the insight in a way that was unmistakable. Each of the stories in that book—and in the subsequent books about Goblin and his friends—has, at its core, feelings taken directly from my childhood."

Another book that has its roots in Alexander's childhood is *Lila on the Landing,* which evokes the author's childhood memories of the sense of humiliation and frustration at having to play all by herself on her apartment house landing. Lila succeeds in sharing her landing with Jon and Amy and even manages to win over the scornful Alan. But art does not always reproduce life; in Alexander's case it enhances it. Susan McCord, writing in *School Library Journal,* noted that Alexander "adeptly" deals with childhood loneliness and rejection, and that hers "is a meaningful story for an age for who it's often hard to find something good." A *Bulletin of the Center for Children's Books* contributor commented on Lila's patience and wit in solving her problems, suggesting to readers "the possibility of overcoming rejection," while a *Kirkus Reviews* critic called the book "a winning tale of an old-fashioned, non-high-tech child."

In 1983 Alexander's agent was finally able to find a publisher for a book written eleven years earlier upon the death of Alexander's brother. Devastated by his death, Alexander turned to writing for comfort, dealing with her bereavement in a story. "As I began it, however," she commented in *SAAS,* "I recognized that I couldn't deal emotionally with the subject matter in a here-and-now setting. It would have to take place somewhere far away, preferably in another culture. No sooner had I made that decision than my fifth-grade fascination with Bedouins came to mind." What resulted was *Nadia the Willful,* the story of a young girl who disobeys her disconsolate father's command not to mention the death of his son and her beloved brother, Hamed. However, Nadia must talk to someone: she turns to her mother and then to shepherds who are fearful of the power of her father yet still want to talk about Hamed and thereby keep his memory alive. Ultimately, even Nadia's father learns the simple lesson that no one is truly dead unless they are forgotten. A *Booklist* reviewer found the story "moving" and "universal," and commented upon the desert setting, which is rarely seen in children's books. Maria Salvadore noted in *School Library Journal* that Alexander's language "is soft and fluid" and "affirms universal emotions."

Other popular books by Alexander include the "World-Famous Muriel" series, about a clever little tight-rope walker who loves to solve mysteries. The "Muriel" books once again mine the universal themes Alexander most enjoys: food, magic, mysteries, and friendship.

Bessie Egan, reviewing the third book in the series, *World-Famous Muriel and the Magic Mystery,* concluded in *School Library Journal* that it is "a picture book that will keep children interested and amused."

One More Time, Mama centers on a mother-daughter moment that begins when the daughter, sitting with her mother while watching the evening fireflies, says, "Tell me again about waiting to watch them with me." So begins the mother's story of her wait through three seasons for the birth of her daughter. Tim Arnold, reviewing the book for *Booklist,* wrote: "With simple, poetic prose, Alexander reveals the deep connection of pregnancy and birth and the cyclical passing of the seasons," noting that the author avoids explicit references to the narrator's pregnancy, but instead focuses on the beauty of nature.

GraceAnne A. DeCandido called Alexander's 2001 book *Behold the Trees* "a strong, exquisite, and magical choice." The story begins in 5000 B.C., in the land now known as Israel, when that land was covered with forests. Through centuries of being home to shepherds, farmers, and wars, the trees were cut for land, buildings, and weapons until it became "salt marsh and sand." After World War I, Jews from around the world began sending money to Israel for the planting of trees as memorials to births, deaths, and other events. Once again, the land became filled with trees, "cypress and pine, eucalyptus and acacia, orange and olive." A contributor to *Publishers Weekly* praised Alexander for "delicately but powerfully" implying a parallel between the history of Israel's trees and its people. The result is a story that is "profoundly satisfying," this critic concluded.

In addition to the books she has written, Alexander has been active as a teacher of picture-book writing at the University of California—Los Angeles, and is also a long-time board member with the Society of Children's Book Writers and Illustrators. Taken as a whole, her dynamic involvement in the genre has enriched children's literature. "I love writing stories," she once noted. "It's my work and my joy. It satisfies my sense of fun and my need to share. I wouldn't trade what I do for any profession in the world. I write for young people because they have imaginations that soar, touched off by a word, a phrase, an image . . . a condition I share. To be able to provide the spark for this process gives me the greatest personal joy."

Biographical and Critical Sources

BOOKS

Alexander, Sue, *One More Time, Mama,* Marshall Cavendish (New York, NY), 1999.
Alexander, Sue, *Behold the Trees,* Arthur Levine Books (New York, NY), 2001.
Roginski, James W., *Behind the Covers,* Volume 2: *Interviews with Authors and Illustrators of Books for Children and Young Adults,* Libraries Unlimited, 1989, pp. 1-15.

Something about the Author Autobiography Series, Volume 15, Gale (Detroit, MI), 1993, pp. 51-66.

PERIODICALS

Booklist, September 15, 1976, p. 140; June 1, 1977, pp. 2, 1492; November 1, 1978, p. 473; December 15, 1979, p. 618; October 15, 1980, p. 322; January 15, 1981, p. 695; November 15, 1982, p. 450; April 1, 1983, p. 1022; August, 1983, review of *Nadia the Willful,* p. 1460; September 15, 1984, p. 136; April 15, 1986, p. 1214; September 15, 1987, p. 139; November 15, 1987, p. 557; February 1, 1989, p. 935; March 15, 1990, p. 1440; October 1, 1995, p. 325; November 15, 1999, Tim Arnold, review of *One More Time, Mama,* p. 632; March 1, 2001, GraceAnne A. DeCandido, review of *Behold the Trees,* p. 1276.
Bulletin of the Center for Children's Books, April, 1977, review of *Witch, Goblin, and Sometimes Ghost,* p. 117; September, 1977, p. 1; January, 1980, p. 85; April, 1981, p. 145; October, 1981, Zena Sutherland, review of *Witch, Goblin, and Ghost in the Haunted Woods,* p. 21; September, 1987, review of *Lila on the Landing,* p. 1.
Children's Book Review Service, October, 1999, review of *One More Time, Mama,* p. 181.
Children's Bookwatch, June, 1998, review of *Who Goes Out on Halloween?,* p. 1.
Horn Book, February, 1981, p. 62; June, 1981, Virginia Haviland, review of *Witch, Goblin, and Ghost in the Haunted Woods,* p. 295.
Horn Book Guide, fall, 1998, review of *Who Goes out on Halloween?,* p. 312.
Kirkus Reviews, October 15, 1976, p. 1135; October 1, 1987, review of *Lila on the Landing,* p. 1457.
Publishers Weekly, August 20, 1979, p. 81; March 20, 1981, p. 62; August 20, 1982, p. 72; June 17, 1983, p. 74; February 24, 1984, p. 130; March 2, 1984, p. 93; July 6, 1984, p. 64; September, 25, 1987, p. 108; April 27, 1990, p. 63; October 4, 1999, review of *One More Time, Mama,* p. 73; May 28, 2001, review of *Behold the Trees,* p. 85.
School Library Journal, January, 1975, p. 36; February, 1977, p. 53; September, 1977, p. 99; December, 1978, p. 65; December, 1980, p. 72; March, 1981, p. 153; May, 1981, p. 80; October, 1983, Maria Salvadore, review of *Nadia the Willful,* p. 145; August, 1984, p. 55; January, 1985, p. 62; April, 1986, p. 67; November, 1987, Susan McCord, review of *Lila on the Landing,* p. 102; December, 1987, p. 66; August, 1989, p. 158; July, 1990, Bessie Egan, review of *World Famous Muriel and the Magic Mystery,* p. 55; May, 1991, p. 74; November, 1999, review of *One More Time, Mama,* p. 180; March, 2001, Patricia Lothrop-Green, review of *Behold the Trees,* p. 192.

OTHER

Sue Alexander Web Site, http://www.sue-alexander.com (March 19, 2002).*

ANGELOU, Maya 1928-
(Marguerite Annie Johnson)

Personal

Surname is pronounced "Ahn-ge-low"; born April 4, 1928, in St. Louis, MO; daughter of Bailey (a doorman and naval dietician) and Vivian (a registered nurse, professional gambler, and a rooming house and bar owner; maiden name, Baxter) Johnson; married Tosh Angelos, 1950 (divorced); married Paul Du Feu, December, 1973 (divorced, 1981); children: Guy. *Education:* Attended public schools in Arkansas and California; studied music privately, dance with Martha Graham, Pearl Primus, and Ann Halprin, and drama with Frank Silvera and Gene Frankel; studied cinematography in Sweden.

Addresses

Home—Winston-Salem, NC. *Office*—c/o Dave La Camera, Lordly and Dame, Inc., 51 Church Street, Boston, MA 02116.

Career

Author, poet, scriptwriter, playwright, performer, actress, and composer. *Arab Observer* (English-language newsweekly), Cairo, Egypt, associate editor, 1961-62;

Maya Angelou

University of Ghana, Institute of African Studies, Legon-Accra, Ghana, assistant administrator of School of Music and Drama, 1963-66; freelance writer for *Ghanaian Times* and Ghanaian Broadcasting Corporation, 1963-65; *African Review,* Accra, feature editor, 1964-66. Lecturer at University of California, Los Angeles, 1966; writer-in-residence at University of Kansas, 1970; distinguished visiting professor at Wake Forest University, Wichita State University, and California State University, Sacramento, 1974; Reynolds Professor of American Studies at Wake Forest University, 1981—; visiting professor, universities in the United States; lecturer at various locations in the United States. Southern Christian Leadership Conference, northern coordinator, 1959-60; appointed member of American Revolution Bicentennial Council by President Gerald R. Ford, 1975-76; member of the Presidential Commission for International Women's Year, 1978-79; Board of Governors, University of North Carolina, Maya Angelou Institute for the Improvement of Child & Family Education at Winston-Salem State University, Winston-Salem, NC, 1998.

Appeared in *Porgy and Bess* on twenty-two nation tour sponsored by the U.S. Department of State, 1954-55; appeared in Off-Broadway plays, *Calypso Heatwave,* 1957, and Jean Genet's *The Blacks,* 1961; produced and performed in *Cabaret for Freedom,* Off-Broadway, 1960; appeared in *Mother Courage* at University of Ghana, 1964; appeared in *Medea* in Hollywood, 1966; television narrator, interviewer, and host for African American specials and theater series, 1972—; made Broadway debut in *Look Away,* 1973; directed film, *All Day Long,* 1974; appeared in television miniseries *Roots,* 1977; directed play, *And Still I Rise,* Oakland, CA, 1976; directed play, *Moon on a Rainbow Shawl,* by Errol John, London, 1988; appeared as Aunt June in film, *Poetic Justice,* 1993; appeared as Lelia Mae in television film, *There Are No Children Here,* 1993; appeared in advertising for the United Negro College Fund, 1994; appeared as Anna in film, *How to Make an American Quilt,* 1995; appeared in the film *Down in the Delta,* 1998; appeared in film *The Amen Corner* and television series *Down in the Delta,* both 1999.

Member

American Film Institute (member of board of Trustees, 1975—, Directors Guild of America, Equity, American Federation of Television and Radio Artists, Women's Prison Association (member of advisory board), National Commission on the Observance of International Women's Year, Harlem Writer's Guild, Horatio Alger Association of Distinguished Americans, W. E. B. DuBois Foundation, National Society of Collegiate Scholars, National Society for the Prevention of Cruelty to Children.

Awards, Honors

National Book Award nomination, 1970, for *I Know Why the Caged Bird Sings;* Yale University fellow, 1970; Pulitzer Prize nomination, 1972, for *Just Give Me a Cool Drink of Water 'fore I Diiie;* Tony Award nomination, 1973, for performance in *Look Away;* Rockefeller Foundation scholar in Italy, 1975; named Woman of the Year in Communications, *Ladies' Home Journal,* 1976; Emmy Award nomination, 1977, for performance in *Roots;* appointed first Reynolds Professor of American Studies at Wake Forest University, 1981; Matrix Award in the field of books, Women in Communication, Inc., 1983; North Carolina Award in Literature, 1987; Langston Hughes Award, City College of New York, 1991; Horatio Alger Award, 1992; Inaugural poet for President Bill Clinton, 1993; Grammy, Best Spoken Word Album, 1994, for recording of "On the Pulse of Morning"; etiquette award, National League of Junior Cotillions, 1993; Medal of Distinction, University of Hawaii Board of Regents, 1994; President's Award, Collegiate of Language Association for Outstanding Achievements, 1996; Southern Christian Leadership Conference of Los Angeles and Martin Luther King, Jr., Legacy Association National Award, 1996; named to the New York Black 100 list, Schomburg Center and The Black New Yorkers, 1996; distinguished merit citation, National Conference of Christians and Jews, 1997; Homecoming Award, Oklahoma Center for Poets and Writers, 1997; North Carolina Woman of the Year Award, North Carolina Black Publishers Association, 1997; Presidential & Lecture Series Award, University of North Florida, 1997; Cultural Keeper Awards, Black Caucus of the American Library Association, 1997; Humanitarian Contribution Award, Boston, MA, 1997; Alston/Jones International Civil and Human Rights Award, 1998; Christopher Award, New York, NY, 1998; American Airlines Audience, Gold Plaque Choice Award, Chicago International Film Festival, 1998, for *Down in the Delta;* Sheila Award, Tubman African American Museum, 1999; Lifetime Achievement Award for Literature, 1999; named one of the 100 best writers of the twentieth century, *Writer's Digest,* 1999; Presidential Medal of Arts, 2000; recipient of fifty honorary degrees from institutions including Smith College, 1975, Mills College, 1975, and Lawrence University, 1976.

Writings

AUTOBIOGRAPHY

I Know Why the Caged Bird Sings, Random House (New York, NY), 1970.
Gather Together in My Name, Random House (New York, NY), 1974.
Singin' and Swingin' and Gettin' Merry like Christmas, Random House (New York, NY), 1976.
The Heart of a Woman, Random House (New York, NY), 1981.
All God's Children Need Traveling Shoes, Random House (New York, NY), 1986.
Lessons in Living, Random House (New York, NY), 1993.
Even the Stars Look Lonesome, Random House (New York, NY), 1997.

POETRY

Just Give Me a Cool Drink of Water 'fore I Diiie, Random House (New York, NY), 1971.

Oh Pray My Wings Are Gonna Fit Me Well, Random House (New York, NY), 1975.
And Still I Rise, Random House (New York, NY), 1978.
Shaker, Why Don't You Sing?, Random House (New York, NY), 1983.
Poems, four volumes, Bantam (New York, NY), 1986.
Now Sheba Sings the Song (illustrated poem), illustrations by Tom Feelings, Dutton (New York, NY), 1987.
I Shall Not Be Moved, Random House (New York, NY), 1990.
On the Pulse of Morning, Random House (New York, NY), 1993.
Wouldn't Take Nothing for My Journey Now (short essays), Random House (New York, NY), 1993.
The Complete Collected Poems of Maya Angelou, Random House (New York, NY), 1994.
A Brave & Startling Truth, Random House (New York, NY), 1995.
Phenomenal Woman: Four Poems Celebrating Women, Random House (New York, NY), 1995.

Also author of *The Poetry of Maya Angelou,* 1969. Contributor of poems in *The Language They Speak Is Things to Eat: Poems by Fifteen Contemporary North*

Angelou writes of her traumatic early life in the first of several autobiographical works.

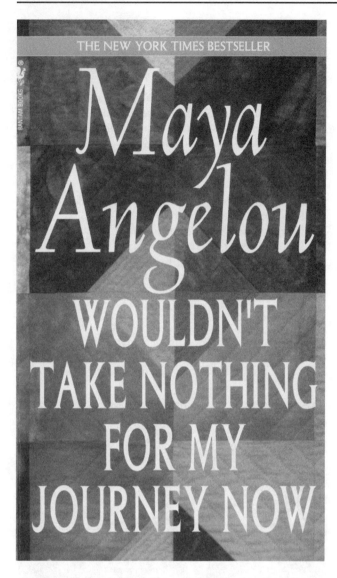

Inspirational reflections on family, spirituality, womanhood, and healing make up Angelou's collection. (Cover photo by J. Kevin Fitzsimons.)

Carolina Poets and to Mary Higgins Clark, *Mother,* Pocket Books (New York, NY), 1996.

CHILDREN'S PICTURE BOOKS

Mrs. Flowers: A Moment of Friendship (selection from *I Know Why the Caged Bird Sings*) illustrations by Etienne Delessert, Redpath Press (Minneapolis, MN), 1986.

Life Doesn't Frighten Me (poem), edited by Sara Jane Boyers, illustrated by Jean-Michel Basquiat, Stewart, Tabori & Chang (New York, NY), 1993.

(With others) *Soul Looks Back in Wonder,* illustrated by Tom Feelings, Dial (New York, NY), 1993.

My Painted House, My Friendly Chicken, and Me, photographs by Margaret Courtney-Clarke, Crown (New York, NY), 1994.

Kofi and His Magic, photographs by Margaret Courtney-Clarke, Crown (New York, NY), 1996.

PLAYS

(With Godfrey Cambridge) *Cabaret for Freedom* (musical revue), produced in New York City at Village Gate Theatre, 1960.

The Least of These (two-act drama), produced in Los Angeles, 1966.

(Adapter) Sophocles, *Ajax* (two-act drama), produced in Los Angeles at Mark Taper Forum, 1974.

(And director) *And Still I Rise* (one-act musical), produced in Oakland, CA, at Ensemble Theatre, 1976.

(Author of poems for screenplay) John Singleton, *Poetic Justice,* screenplay, Columbia Pictures, 1993.

(Author of lyrics with Alistair Beaton) *King,* book by Lonne Elder III, music by Richard Blackford, London, 1990.

Also author of the play *Gettin' up Stayed on My Mind,* 1967, a drama, *The Best of These,* a two-act drama, *The Clawing Within,* 1966, a two-act musical, *Adjoa Amissah,* 1967, and a one-act play, *Theatrical Vignette,* 1983.

FILM AND TELEVISION

Georgia, Georgia (screenplay), Independent-Cinerama, 1972.

(And director) *All Day Long* (screenplay), American Film Institute, 1974.

(Writer of script and musical score) *I Know Why the Caged Bird Sings,* CBS, 1979.

Sister, Sister (television drama), National Broadcasting Co., Inc. (NBC-TV), 1982.

(Writer of poetry) John Singleton, *Poetic Justice* (motion picture), Columbia Pictures, 1993.

Composer of songs, including two songs for movie *For Love of Ivy,* and composer of musical scores for both her screenplays. Author of *Black, Blues, Black,* a series of ten one-hour programs, broadcast by National Educational Television (NET-TV), 1968. Also author of *Assignment America,* a series of six one-half-hour programs, 1975, and of *The Legacy* and *The Inheritors,* two television specials, 1976. Other documentaries include *Trying to Make It Home* (*Byline* series), 1988, and *Maya Angelou's America: A Journey of the Heart* (also host). Public Broadcasting Service Productions include *Who Cares about Kids, Kindred Spirits, Maya Angelou: Rainbow in the Clouds,* and *To the Contrary.* Writer for television series *Brewster Place,* Harpo Productions.

RECORDINGS

Miss Calypso (audio recording of songs), Liberty Records, 1957.

The Poetry of Maya Angelou (audio recording), GWP Records, 1969.

An Evening with Maya Angelou (audio cassette), Pacific Tape Library, 1975.

I Know Why the Caged Bird Sings (audio cassette with filmstrip and teacher's guide), Center for Literary Review, 1978, abridged version, Random House (New York, NY), 1986.

Women in Business (audio cassette), University of Wisconsin, 1981.

Making Magic in the World (audio cassette), New Dimensions, 1988.
On the Pulse of Morning (audio production), Ingram, 1993.
Wouldn't Take Nothing for My Journey Now (audio production), Ingram, 1993.
Phenomenal Woman (audio production), Ingram, 1995.

OTHER

Conversations with Maya Angelou, edited by Jeffrey M. Elliot, Virago Press (London, England), 1989.
(Author of foreword) Margaret Courtney-Clarke, *African Canvas: The Art of African Women,* Rizzoli (New York, NY), 1991.
(Author of foreword) Zora Neale Hurston, *Dust Tracks on the Road: An Autobiography,* HarperCollins (New York, NY), 1991.
(Author of foreword) Rosamund Grant, *Caribbean & African Cooking,* Interlink (Northampton, MA), 1993.
Double Stitch: Black Women Write about Mothers & Daughters, HarperCollins (New York, NY), 1993.
(Author of foreword) Patricia M. Hinds, editor, *Essence: Twenty-five Years Celebrating Black Women,* Harry N. Abrams (New York, NY), 1995.
(Author of introduction) Langston Hughes, *Not without Laughter,* Scribner (New York, NY), 1995.
Maya Angelou (four-volume boxed set), Ingram (London, England), 1995.
(With Mary Ellen Mark) *Mary Ellen Mark: American Odyssey,* Aperture (New York, NY), 1998.

Contributor to volumes such as *Poetic Justice: Filmmaking South Central Style,* Delta, 1993; *Bearing Witness: Contemporary Works by African American Women Artists,* Rizzoli International Publications, 1996; *The Journey Back: A Survivor's Guide to Leukemia,* Rainbow's End Company, 1996. *The Challenge of Creative Leadership,* Shephard-Walwyn, 1998; and *Amistad: "Give Us Free": A Celebration of the Film by Stephen Spielberg,* Newmarket Press, 1998.

Coauthor with Charlie Reilly and Amiri Baraka of *Conversations with Amiri Baraka.* Short stories are included in anthologies, including *Harlem* and *Ten Times Black.* Contributor of articles, short stories, and poems to periodicals, including *Harper's, Ebony, Essence, Mademoiselle, Redbook, Ladies' Home Journal, Black Scholar, Architectural Digest, New Perspectives Quarterly, Savvy Woman,* and *Ms. Magazine.*

Adaptations

I Know Why the Caged Bird Sings was adapted as a television movie by Columbia Broadcasting System, Inc. (CBS-TV), 1979; *And Still I Rise* was adapted as a television special by Public Broadcasting Service (PBS-TV), 1985; *I Know Why the Caged Bird Sings* was produced for audio cassette and compact disk, Ingram, 1996.

Sidelights

Standing before the church congregation, little Marguerite Johnson realized that everyone was looking at her,

and that she wasn't a white girl with long blonde hair. As she remembered that she was a girl with dark skin, a gap between her teeth, and kinky dark hair, she struggled to remember the words of the poem she'd memorized for Easter. It was no use. As Marguerite ran towards the door of the church, "a green persimmon, or it could have been a lemon, caught me between the legs and squeezed. I tasted the sour on my tongue and felt it in the back of my mouth. Then . . . the sting was burning down my legs and into my Sunday socks." Marguerite Johnson—the girl who would grow up to become a performer who flaunted her beauty, power and grace on stages all over the world—the girl who would become a writer whose work would inspire thousands and thousands of readers of all races and genders and ages—had wet herself. Yet that was just the beginning of a traumatic childhood, as the girl would recall in her most famous work, *I Know Why the Caged Bird Sings.*

As a young black woman growing up in the South, and later, in war-time San Francisco, Johnson (who changed her name to Maya Angelou at the beginning of her stage career) faced racism from whites and poor treatment from most men (she was raped when she was seven years old). She found that, in this position, she had few career options, and little chance of leading a fruitful life; she gave birth out of wedlock at seventeen, experimented with drugs, and worked as a madam and prostitute. Instead of letting forces beyond her control overcome her, Angelou began to forge art from her early experiences and change the world as she'd once known it. She became a singer, dancer, actress, composer, and Hollywood's first female black director. She became a writer, editor, essayist, playwright, poet, and screenwriter. She became known, as Annie Gottlieb wrote in the *New York Times Book Review,* as a person who "writes like a song, and like the truth. The wisdom, rue and humor of her storytelling are borne on a lilting rhythm completely her own."

Angelou also became a civil rights activist—she worked at one time for Dr. Martin Luther King and once staged a protest at the United Nations—as well as an educator. By 1975, wrote Carol E. Neubauer in *Southern Women Writers: The New Generation,* "Angelou had become recognized not only as a spokesperson for blacks and women, but also for all people who are committed to raising the moral standards of living in the United States." How had this woman—who had done some things that many would consider immoral—become a leader with a moral agenda? She did so by writing about herself, by fighting for civil and women's rights, and by providing an amazing example of the human potential to rise above defeat. Angelou explained this herself in an interview with George Plimpton in the *Paris Review:* "In all my work, in the movies I write, the lyrics, the poetry, the prose, the essays, I am saying that we may encounter many defeats—maybe it's imperative that we encounter the defeats—but we are much stronger than we appear to be, and maybe much better than we allow ourselves to be."

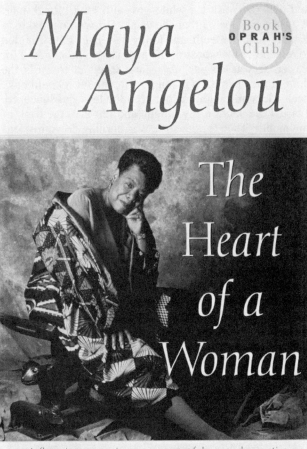

Maya
Angelou

Book
OPRAH'S
Club

The
Heart
of a
Woman

A flowering, a growing son—a powerful personal narrative

Angelou's fourth autobiographical work describes her beginnings as a writer and activist in New York. (Cover photo by Dwight Carter.)

Angelou was born in St. Louis, Missouri, and lived her early years in Long Beach, California. As she related in *I Know Why the Caged Bird Sings,* she was just three years old when her parents divorced. Her father sent Angelou and her four-year-old brother alone by train to the home of his mother in Stamps, Arkansas. In Stamps, a segregated town, "Momma" (as Angelou and her brother Bailey called their grandmother) took care of the children and ran a lunch business and a store. The children were expected to stay clean and sinless, and to do well in school. Although she followed the example of her independent and strong-willed grandmother, and was a healthy child, Angelou felt ugly and unloved. When her mother, who lived in St. Louis, requested a visit from the children, Angelou was shocked by her mother's paler complexion, and by the red lipstick her grandmother would have thought scandalous. Angelou was almost as overwhelmed by her mother's wildness and determination as she was by her beauty.

Life in St. Louis was different from that in Stamps; Angelou was unprepared for the rushing noises of city life and the Saturday night parties. Then, when she was just seven-and-a-half years old, something terrible happened. In one of the most evocative (and controversial)

moments in *I Know Why the Caged Bird Sings,* Angelou described how she was first lovingly cuddled, and later raped by her mother's boyfriend. When the man was murdered by her uncles for his crime, Angelou felt responsible, and she stopped talking. She and her brother were sent back to Stamps. Angelou remained mute for five years, but she developed a love for language and the spoken word. She also read and memorized books. She read the works of black authors and poets, like Langston Hughes, W. E. B. Du Bois, and Paul Lawrence Dunbar. Even though she and Bailey were discouraged from reading the works of white writers at home, Angelou read and fell in love with the works of William Shakespeare, Charles Dickens, and Edgar Allan Poe. When Angelou was twelve and a half, Mrs. Flowers, an educated black woman, finally got her to speak again. Mrs. Flowers, as Angelou recalled in *Mrs. Flowers: A Moment of Friendship,* emphasized the importance of the spoken word, explained the nature of and importance of education, and instilled in her a love of poetry. Maya graduated at the top of her eighth-grade class.

When race relations made Stamps a dangerous place for Angelou and her brother, "Momma" took the children to San Francisco, where Angelou's mother was working as a professional gambler. World War II was raging, and while San Franciscans prepared for air raids that never came, Angelou prepared for the rest of her life by attending George Washington High School and by taking lessons in dance and drama on a scholarship at the California Labor School. When Angelou, just seventeen, graduated from high school and gave birth to a son, she began to work as well. She worked as the first female and black street car conductor in San Francisco. As she explained in *Singin' and Swingin' and Gettin' Merry like Christmas,* she also "worked as a shake dancer in night clubs, fry cook in hamburger joints, dinner cook in a Creole restaurant and once had a job in a mechanic's shop, taking the paint off cars with my hands." For a time, Angelou also managed a couple of prostitutes.

Angelou married a white ex-sailor, Tosh Angelos, in 1950. The pair did not have much in common, and Angelou began to take note of the reaction of people—especially African Americans—to their union. After they separated, Angelou continued her study of dance in New York City. She returned to San Francisco and sang in the Purple Onion cabaret. There, Angelou (who had changed her name to fit Bailey's nickname for her, "My," "Mya," and finally "Maya," combined with her ex-husband's last name) garnered the attention of talent scouts. From 1954 to 1955, she was a member of the cast of *Porgy and Bess;* she visited twenty-two countries before leaving the tour to return to her son. During the late 1950s, Angelou sang in West Coast and Hawaiian nightclubs. After some time living in a houseboat commune in Sausalito, California, she returned to New York.

In New York, Angelou continued her stage career with an appearance in an Off-Broadway show, *Calypso Heatwave.* Then, with the encouragement of writer John

Killens, she joined the Harlem Writers Guild and met James Baldwin and other important writers. It was during this time that Angelou had the opportunity to hear Dr. Martin Luther King speak. Inspired by his message, she determined to become a part of the struggle for civil rights. So, with comedian Godfrey Cambridge, she wrote, produced, directed, and starred in *Cabaret for Freedom* in 1960, a benefit for Dr. King's Southern Christian Leadership Conference (SCLC). Given the organizational abilities she demonstrated as she worked for the benefit, she was offered a position as the northern coordinator for Dr. King's SCLC in 1961. That same year, she appeared in Jean Genet's play, *The Blacks,* which won an Obie Award.

Angelou began to live with Vusumzi Make, a South African freedom fighter; with Angelou's son Guy, they relocated to Cairo, Egypt. There, Angelou found work as an associate editor at the *Arab Observer.* As she recalled in *The Heart of a Woman,* she learned a great deal about writing there, but Vusumzi could not tolerate the fact that she was working. After her relationship with him ended, Angelou went on to Ghana, in West Africa, in 1962. She later worked at the University of Ghana's School of Music and Drama as an assistant administrator. She worked as a freelance writer and was a feature editor at *African Review.* As she related in *All God's Children Need Traveling Shoes,* Angelou also played the title role in *Mother Courage* during this time.

Angelou returned to the United States in the mid-1960s and found a position as a lecturer at the University of California in Los Angeles in 1966. She also played a part in the play *Medea* in Hollywood. In this period, she was encouraged by author James Baldwin and Random House publishers to write an autobiography. Initially, Angelou declined offers, and went to California for the production of a series of ten one-hour programs that she'd written, "Black, Blues, Black," which were broadcast in 1968. Fortunately, however, Angelou changed her mind and wrote *I Know Why the Caged Bird Sings.* The book, which chronicles Angelou's childhood and ends with the birth of her son Guy, bears what Selwyn R. Cudjoe in *Black Women Writers* calls a burden: "to demonstrate the manner in which the Black female is violated ... in her tender years and to demonstrate the 'unnecessary insult' of Southern girlhood in her movement to adolescence." *Caged Bird* won immediate success and a nomination for a National Book Award.

Although Angelou did not write *I Know Why the Caged Bird Sings* with the intention of writing other autobiographies, she eventually wrote four more, which may be read with *Caged Bird* as a series. Most critics have judged the subsequent autobiographies in light of the first, and *Caged Bird* remains the most highly praised. *Gather Together in My Name* begins when Angelou is seventeen and a new mother; it describes a destructive love affair, Angelou's work as a prostitute, her rejection of drug addiction, and the kidnapping of her son. *Gather Together* was not as well received by critics as *Caged Bird.* As Mary Jane Lupton reported in *Black American*

Literature Forum, in this 1974 autobiography, "the tight structure" of *Caged Bird* "appeared to crumble; childhood experiences were replaced by episodes which a number of critics consider disjointed or bizarre." Lupton asserted, however, that there is an important reason why Angelou's later works are not as tight as the first, and why they consist of episodes: these "so-called 'fragments' are reflections of the kind of chaos found in actual living. In altering the narrative structure, Angelou shifts the emphasis from herself as an isolated consciousness to herself as a Black woman participating in diverse experiences among a diverse class of peoples."

Singin' and Swingin' and Gettin' Merry like Christmas is Angelou's account of her tour in Europe and Africa with *Porgy and Bess.* Much of the work concerns Angelou's separation from her son during that time. In *The Heart of a Woman,* Angelou described her acting and writing career in New York and her work for the civil rights movement. She recalled visits with great activists Dr. Martin Luther King and Malcolm X, and the legendary singer Billie Holiday. She also told of her move to Africa, and her experiences when her son was injured in a serious car accident; the book ends with Guy's move into a college dormitory at the University of Ghana. "Angelou's message is one blending chorus: Black people and Black women do not just endure, they triumph with a will of collective consciousness that Western experience cannot extinguish," wrote Sondra O'Neale in *Black Women Writers. All God's Children Need Traveling Shoes* once again explores Guy's accident; it moves on from there to recount Angelou's travels in West Africa and her decision to return, without her son, to America.

Angelou's poetry is often lauded more for its content (praising black beauty and the strength of women, lauding the human spirit, criticizing the Vietnam War, demanding social justice for all) than for its poetic virtue. Yet *Just Give Me a Cool Drink of Water 'fore I Diiie,* which was published in 1971, was nominated for a Pulitzer Prize in 1972. This volume contains thirty-eight poems, some of which were published in *The Poetry of Maya Angelou.* According to Carol Neubauer in *Southern Women Writers,* "the first twenty poems describe the whole gamut of love, from the first moment of passionate discovery to the first suspicion of painful loss." In the other poems, "Angelou turns her attention to the lives of black people in America from the time of slavery to the rebellious 1960s. Her themes deal broadly with the painful anguish suffered by blacks forced into submission, with guilt over accepting too much, and with protest and basic survival." In *Oh Pray My Wings Are Gonna Fit Me Well,* dedicated to her husband at the time, Paul Du Feu, Angelou discussed the plight of the human race, the American potential, and the problems plaguing American Blacks. While Sandra M. Gilbert noted in *Poetry* that Angelou is a "stunningly talented prose writer," she commented that this collection is so "painfully untalented ... that I can't think of any reason, other than the Maya Myth, for it to be in print."

And Still I Rise, which was published in 1978, contains thirty-two poems. Carol Neubauer explained in *Southern Women Writers* that "this series of poems covers a broader range of subjects than the earlier two volumes and shifts smoothly from issues such as springtime and aging to sexual awakening, drug addiction, and Christian salvation. The familiar themes of love and its inevitable loneliness and the oppressive climate of the South are still central concerns. But even more striking than the poet's careful treatment of these subjects is her attention to the nature of woman and the importance of family." The collection *Phenomenal Woman,* wrote Neubauer, displays Angelou's "poetic style, the lines . . . terse and forcefully, albeit irregularly rhymed." *Shaker, Why Don't You Sing?,* dedicated to Angelou's son and grandson, "moves gracefully from the promise of potential strength to the humor of light satire, at all times bearing witness to a spirit that soars and sings in spite of repeated disappointment."

As Angelou wrote her autobiographies and poems, she continued her career in film and television. She was the first black woman to get a screenplay (*Georgia, Georgia*) produced in 1972. She was honored with a nomination for an Emmy award for her performance in *Roots* in 1977. In 1979, Angelou helped adapt her book, *I Know Why the Caged Bird Sings,* for a television movie of the same name.

In the early 1990s, when Angelou was in her sixties, she returned to live in the American South, in what Catherine S. Manegold in the *New York Times* described as a "trim brick house in Winston-Salem." Manegold described Angelou as a woman with broad features, "like chunks of clay collected roughly on a frame," with "dancer's feet," a voice with "a swoop, a lingering vowel, an octave dropped for emphasis," and "the innate and compelling grace of a woman who has constructed a full life, one lived without concession or false excuse." Although Angelou suffers from arthritis, she leads a very busy life. She teaches literature at Wake Forest University in Winston-Salem and is "in great demand on the lecture circuit, making about 80 appearances a year."

Angelou was especially productive in the late 1980s and early 1990s. According to Neubauer, *All God's Children Need Traveling Shoes,* Angelou's fifth autobiography (published in 1986), "swept Angelou to new heights of critical and popular acclaim." Angelou wrote the poetry for the film, *Poetic Justice* (1993) and played the role of Aunt June. She also played Lelia Mae in the 1993 television film, *There Are No Children Here,* and appeared as Anna in the feature film *How to Make an American Quilt* in 1995. Also in 1995, Angelou's poetry helped commemorate the fiftieth anniversary of the United Nations. She had elevated herself to what Richard Grenier in *National Review* called a "dizzying height of achievement." As a title from an article by Freda Garmaise in *Gentleman's Quarterly* proclaimed, "Maya-ness" was "next to godliness."

One of the most important sources of Angelou's fame in the early 1990s was President Bill Clinton's invitation to write and read the first inaugural poem in decades. Americans all across the country watched the six-foot-tall, elegantly dressed woman as she read her poem for the new president on January 20, 1993. "On the Pulse of Morning," which begins "A Rock, a River, a Tree," calls for peace, racial and religious harmony, and social justice for people of different origins, incomes, genders, and sexual orientations. It recalls the civil rights movement, and Dr. Martin Luther King, Jr.'s famous "I have a dream" speech as it urges America to "Give birth again/To the Dream" of equality. Angelou challenged the new administration and all Americans to work together for progress: "Here, on the pulse of this new day,/You may have the grace to look up and out/And into your sister's eyes, and into/Your brother's face, your country/And say simply/Very simply/With hope—Good morning."

While some viewed President Clinton's selection of Angelou as a tribute to the poet and her lifelong contribution to civil rights and the arts, Angelou had her own ideas. She told Catherine S. Manegold in an interview: "In all my work, what I try to say is that as human beings we are more alike than we are unalike." She added, "It may be that Mr. Clinton asked me to write the inaugural poem because he understood that I am the kind of person who really does bring people together."

During the early 1990s, Angelou contributed more poetry and work for children than autobiographical work. *Now Sheba Sings the Song* is just one poem inspired by the work of artist Tom Feelings; the lines or phrases are isolated on each page with eighty-four of Tom Feelings' sepia-toned and black-and-white drawings of black women. *I Shall Not Be Moved* is a collection that takes its title from a line in one of the book's poems. *Phenomenal Woman,* a collection of four poems, takes its title from a poem which originally appeared in *Cosmopolitan* magazine in 1978; the narrator of the poem describes the physical and spiritual characteristics and qualities that make her attractive.

Angelou dedicated *Wouldn't Take Nothing for My Journey Now,* a collection of twenty-four short essays, to Oprah Winfrey, the television talk-show host who celebrated Angelou's sixty-fifth birthday with a grand party. The essays in this book contain declarations, complaints, memories, opinions, and advice on subjects ranging from faith to jealousy. Genevieve Stuttaford, writing in *Publishers Weekly,* described the essays as "quietly inspirational pieces." Anne Whitehouse of the *New York Times Book Review* observed that the book would "appeal to readers in search of clear messages with easily digested meanings." Yet not all critics appreciated this collection. Richard Grenier of the *National Review* concluded that the book "is of a remarkably coherent tone, being from first page to last of a truly awesome emptiness."

Although Angelou's autobiographies are written, in part, for young people, they are beyond the comprehension of most young children. With the publication of *Mrs.*

Flowers: A Moment of Friendship, children can access the world Angelou describes in *Caged Bird.* Like *Now Sheba Sings the Song,* the text of *Life Doesn't Frighten Me* consists of one poem. Each line or phrase is accompanied by the dynamic, abstract and colorful paintings of the late artist Jean-Michel Basquiat.

In *My Painted House, My Friendly Chicken, and Me,* with photographs by Margaret Courtney-Clarke, a young African girl introduces herself and discusses her life. She tells about her friend, a pet chicken to whom she tells all of her best secrets. She displays her beautiful home, and explains how her mother has carefully painted it. The girl also explains how, although she must go to school wearing uniforms her father has purchased in town, she loves to wear her traditional beads and clothing. She expresses a wish that she and the reader can be friends despite the physical and cultural distance that separates them.

Kofi and His Magic is a picture book which allows young readers to get to know an African child, another culture, and another worldview. Through Angelou's text and Courtney-Clarke's colorful photographs, a West African boy named Kofi shows off his beautiful earth-toned home and tells of his life. Kofi's town, Bonwire, is famous for its Kente cloth production. He explains how, even though he is still quite young, he is a trained weaver of Kente cloth. Then, Kofi takes readers on a journey to visit other nearby towns and people, and finally, to see the ocean (which he initially thinks is a big lake). At the end of the book, after Kofi returns to Bonwire, he reveals why he calls himself a magician— Kofi's magic involves allowing the reader to imagine that she or he can visit Kofi and become his friend—the reader must only close her eyes and open her mind for the magic to work.

As Angelou has been busy furthering her career, critics and scholars have attempted to keep up with her, and to interpret her continuing work. While many critics have pointed out that the message in Angelou's prose is universal, Mary Jane Lupton has called attention to the theme of motherhood in Angelou's work. In five volumes of autobiography, Angelou "moves forward: from being a child, to being a mother; to leaving the child; to having the child, in the fifth volume, achieve his independence." In her interview with George Plimpton in the *Paris Review,* Angelou agreed with him that the love of her child was a "prevailing theme" in her autobiographical work.

Some critics have argued that Angelou's poetry is inferior to her prose. Unlike her autobiographical work, Angelou's poetry has not received much of what William Sylvester of *Contemporary Poets* would call "serious critical attention." In Sylvester's opinion, however, Angelou's poetry is "sassy." When "we hear her poetry, we listen to ourselves." In addition, as Lynn Z. Bloom pointed out in *Dictionary of Literary Biography,* "Angelou's poetry becomes far more interesting when she dramatizes it in her characteristically dynamic stage performances." Colorfully dressed, Angelou usually recites her poems before spellbound, if crowded, audiences.

Angelou takes her writing very seriously. She told Plimpton, "Once I got into it I realized I was following a tradition established by Frederick Douglass—the slave narrative—speaking in the first-person singular talking about the first-person plural, always saying I meaning 'we.' And what a responsibility. Trying to work with that form, the autobiographical mode, to change it, to make it bigger, richer, finer, and more inclusive in the twentieth century has been a great challenge for me." A reviewer in *Publishers Weekly* commented that Angelou "casts a keen eye inward and bares her soul in a slim volume of personal essays" titled *Even the Stars Look Lonesome.* Donna Seaman, writing in *Booklist,* described the collection as "20 brief, anecdotal, and spicily provocative essays."

While many critics have described Angelou's ability to write beautiful prose as a natural talent, Angelou has emphasized that she must work very hard to write the way she does. As she has explained to Plimpton and others, very early each morning she goes to a sparse hotel room to concentrate, to lie on the bed and write. She spends the morning on first draft work, and goes home in the afternoon to shower, cook a beautiful meal, and share it with friends. Later that night, she looks at what she's written, and begins to cut words and make revisions. Critics who suggest writing is easy for her, Angelou explained to Plimpton, "are the ones I want to grab by the throat and wrestle to the floor because it takes me forever to get it [a book] to sing. I *work* at the language."

Biographical and Critical Sources

BOOKS

Angelou, Maya, *Gather Together in My Name,* Random House (New York, NY), 1974.

Angelou, Maya, *Singin' and Swingin' and Gettin' Merry like Christmas,* Random House (New York, NY), 1976.

Angelou, Maya, *The Heart of a Woman,* Random House (New York, NY), 1981.

Angelou, Maya, *All God's Children Need Traveling Shoes,* Random House (New York, NY), 1986.

Angelou, Maya, *I Know Why the Caged Bird Sings,* Bantam (New York, NY), 1993.

Angelou, Maya, *Lessons in Living,* Random House (New York, NY), 1993.

Angelou, Maya, *Even the Stars Look Lonesome,* Random House (New York, NY), 1997.

Bloom, Harold, editor, *Maya Angelou's I Know Why the Caged Bird Sings,* Chelsea House Publishers (New York, NY), 1995.

Braxton, Joanne M., editor, *Maya Angelou's I Know Why the Caged Bird Sings: A Casebook,* Oxford University Press (New York, NY), 1999.

Contemporary Poets, St. James Press (Detroit, MI), 1996.

Dictionary of Literary Biography, Volume 38: *Afro-American Writers after 1955: Dramatists and Prose Writers,* Gale (Detroit, MI), 1985.

Evans, Mari, editor, *Black Women Writers (1950-1980): A Critical Evaluation,* Anchor Press-Doubleday (New York, NY), 1984.

Inge, Tonette Bond, editor, *Southern Women Writers: The New Generation,* University of Alabama Press (Tuscaloosa, AL), 1990.

King, Sarah E., *Maya Angelou: Greeting the Morning,* Millbrook Press (Brookfield, CT), 1994.

Lisandrelli, Elaine Slivinski, *Maya Angelou: More than a Poet,* Enslow Publishers (Berkeley Heights, NJ), 1996.

Spain, Valerie, *Meet Maya Angelou,* Random House (New York, NY), 1994.

PERIODICALS

Black American Literature Forum, summer 1990, Mary Jane Lupton, "Singing the Black Mother: Maya Angelou and Autobiographical Continuity," pp. 257-76.

Booklist, August, 1997, Donna Seaman, review of *Even the Stars Look Lonesome,* p. 1842.

Essence, December, 1992, pp. 48-52.

Five Owls, September, 1995, p. 2.

Gentlemen's Quarterly, July, 1995, Freda Garmaise, "Maya-ness Is Next to Godlinesss," p. 33.

Library Journal, October 1, 1995, p. 102.

Mother Jones, May-June, 1995, pp. 22-25.

National Review, November 29, 1993, Richard Grenier, review of *Wouldn't Take Nothing for My Journey Now,* p. 76.

New York Times, January 20, 1993, Catherine S. Manegold, "A Wordsmith at Her Inaugural Anvil," pp. C1, C8; December 19, 1993, Anne Whitehouse, review of *Wouldn't Take Nothing for My Journey Now,* p. 18.

New York Times Book Review, June 16, 1974, Annie Gottlieb, review of *Gather Together in My Name;* June 5, 1994, p. 48.

Paris Review, fall, 1990, Maya Angelou, and George Plimpton, "The Art of Fiction CXIX: Maya Angelou," pp. 145-167.

Poetry, August, 1976, Sandra M. Gilbert, review of *Oh Pray My Wings Are Gonna Fit Me Well.*

Publishers Weekly, September 27, 1993, Genevieve Stuttaford, review of *Wouldn't Take Nothing for My Journey Now,* pp. 53-54; August 4, 1997, review of *Even the Stars Look Lonesome,* pp. 54-55.

School Library Journal, October, 1987, p. 146; May, 1995, p. 57.

B

BARNER, Bob 1947-

Personal

Born November 11, 1947, in Tuckerman, AR; son of Jewel and Jean (McClure) Barner; married; wife's name, Cathie. *Nationality:* American. *Education:* Columbus College of Art and Design, B.F.A., 1970.

Addresses

Home—San Francisco, CA. *Agent*—c/o Author Mail, Chronicle Books, 85 Second St., Sixth Floor, San Francisco, CA 94105.

Career

Riverside Hospital, Columbus, OH, art therapist, 1970-78; Art Institute of Boston, Boston, MA, instructor in art, 1978-79; freelance writer and artist, 1979—. *Exhibitions:* Original art exhibitions with the Society of Illustrators which included artwork from *Benny's Pennies* and *Dem Bones.*

Member

Art Directors Club of Boston.

Awards, Honors

Andy Award for Illustration, Children's International Book Fair, 1975, for *The Elephant's Visit;* Silver Honor Award, Parents' Choice, for *Dem Bones;* Pick of the Lists citation, American Booksellers Association, for *To Everything.*

Writings

SELF-ILLUSTRATED CHILDREN'S BOOKS

The Elephant's Visit, Little, Brown (Boston, MA), 1975.
Elephant Facts, Dutton (New York, NY), 1979.
The Elevator Escalator Book: A Transportation Fact Book, Doubleday (New York, NY), 1990.

Bob Barner illustrated in paper collage how a young boy spends his five pennies on perfect gifts for his mother, brother, sister, dog, and cat. (From Benny's Pennies, *written by Pat Brisson.)*

The Bike Race, Houghton (Boston, MA), 1991.
How to Weigh an Elephant, Bantam (New York, NY), 1995.
Space Race, Bantam (New York, NY), 1995.
Too Many Dinosaurs, Bantam (New York, NY), 1995.
Dem Bones, Chronicle Books (San Francisco, CA), 1996.
Dinosaurs Depart, Bantam (New York, NY), 1996.
To Everything, Chronicle Books (San Francisco, CA), 1998.
Which Way to the Revolution?: A Book about Maps, Holiday House (New York, NY), 1998.
Bugs! Bugs! Bugs!, Chronicle Books (San Francisco, CA), 1999.
Fish Wish, Holiday House (New York, NY), 2000.
Walk the Dog, Chronicle Books (San Francisco, CA), 2000.
Dinosaur Bones, Chronicle Books (San Francisco, CA), 2001.
Stars!, Stars!, Stars!, Chronicle Books (San Francisco, CA), 2002.

A skeleton band offers a rollicking anatomy lesson to the tune of the well-known spiritual **Dem Bones.** *(Written and illustrated by Barner.)*

Parade Day: Marching Through the Calendar, Holiday House (New York, NY), 2003.

ILLUSTRATOR

Eve Bunting, *We Need a Bigger Zoo!,* Ginn (Lexington, MA), 1974.

Van Aarle, *Don't Put Your Cart before the Horse Race,* Houghton (Boston, MA), 1980.

Patty Wolcott, *Double-Decker, Double-Decker, Double-Decker Bus,* Addison-Wesley (Reading, MA), 1980.

Joanne E. Bernstein, *Riddles to Take on Vacation,* A. Whitman (Niles, IL), 1987.

Nat Segaloff, *Fish Tales,* Sterling (New York, NY), 1990.

Patricia Demuth, *Pick Up Your Ears, Henry,* Macmillan (New York, NY), 1992.

Pat Brisson, *Benny's Pennies,* Doubleday (New York, NY), 1993.

Sidelights

Bob Barner is the illustrator of numerous picture books, including many which he wrote himself. His early book *Elephant Facts* came about after work on the purely fanciful *The Elephant's Visit* aroused his interest in real facts about elephants. Similarly, his books on dinosaurs, bugs, dogs, and fish deal with fun yet factual topics in artwork that combines pen and ink, watercolor, and cut- and torn-paper collages. Reviewing his illustrations for the popular *Dem Bones,* a critic for *Publishers Weekly* noted in a starred review that Barner's "cut and torn collages are geared for tickling the funny bones of the early elementary set."

Born in Arkansas, in 1947, Barner grew up in the Midwest, then graduated from the Columbus College of Art and Design in Columbus, Ohio. Thereafter he

worked as an art therapist and an art director in advertising agencies and design studios, even assisting Al Capp for a time with his *Li'l Abner* comic strip. He turned to book production in the 1970s, illustrating a title by Eve Bunting, *We Need a Bigger Zoo!,* before writing and illustrating his own books.

Following his first two titles, *The Elephant's Visit* and *Elephant Facts,* Barner created another nonfiction book with *The Elevator Escalator Book: A Transportation Fact Book,* in which a large brown dog attempts to deliver a package and encounters many different forms of transportation in the process. More facts are served up in a quartet of books in the "Start Smart Math Books," comprised of *Space Race, Too Many Dinosaurs, Dinosaurs Depart,* and *How to Weigh an Elephant.* Each book in the series is designed to get children from four to eight off to a good start in mathematics by blending humorous stories with activities inspired by accepted educational standards. Reviewing *Space Race* and *Too Many Dinosaurs* in *Publishers Weekly,* a contributor called the colorful creatures featured in their pages "painless purveyors of mathematical prowess."

Another playfully educational title by Barner is the award-winning *Dem Bones,* which uses the familiar song to introduce the bones of the human skeleton in a "highly original mixture," as a *Books for Keeps* reviewer described it. "Barner dives gleefully into this clever anatomy lesson," wrote the critic for *Publishers Weekly.* In the pages of this picture book illustrated with torn-paper collages, a jazzy skeleton band blows horns and strums guitars. Each line from the song is given its own spread, with an explanation of form and function of the bones mentioned. For example, with the lyric "Leg bone connected to da knee bone," Barner provides information on how the knee joint functions like a hinge, allowing humans all sorts of movement possibilities. The bone in question is also highlighted on the skeleton. *Booklist*'s Carolyn Phelan found the book overall to be a "snappy introduction to the human skeleton," and Barner's torn- and cut-paper collage artwork "bold in form and vibrant in color."

Barner provides an introduction to map making in his *Which Way to the Revolution?: A Book about Maps.* He employs a well-known historical event, Paul Revere's ride, as an introduction not only to making but also to interpreting maps. Two lights shine in the Old North Church tower, and now Paul must spread the news that the British are coming. But which way should he go? How can he find his way from Boston to Lexington? To his great good fortune, in Barner's take on the story, a clever band of mice are there ready to help him. They have a map and know the route, and they will send one of their band along with Paul so he does not lose the way. But these two must watch out for another enemy besides the British: rats, who will do anything to stop Paul Revere. Barner supplies seven colorful and simple maps for young cartographers to follow the course of Paul Revere's ride in this book that "adds a fantastic— and appealing—element" to the revolutionary tale, according to *Horn Book*'s Mary M. Burns. Writing in

School Library Journal, Lucinda Snyder Whitehurst found *Which Way to the Revolution?* to be "an appealing concept book," and one that "takes a fresh direction that youngsters will enjoy."

Barner turns his attention to the famous verses from Ecclesiastes, "To everything there is a season," with his 1998 title, *To Everything.* A *Publishers Weekly* contributor praised Barner's "snazzy cut- and torn-paper collages" which set the verses "rocking to a jazzy beat." A celebration of the sentiments of the original verse, as well as an exuberant and colorful piece of artwork in its own right, the book is an illustration of the timeless message that everything has its proper time. For the verse, "a time to cry, a time to laugh," for example, Barner created a single monkey on a tree branch while others play together on another bough. A critic for *Kirkus Reviews* called Barner's book a "quite different approach" to the famous verses, and also praised Barner's "vivid collages that are playful, joyous, and happy."

Insects are the inspiration for another colorful title, *Bugs! Bugs! Bugs!,* "an enthusiastic book crawling with splashy bugs," according to a reviewer for *Publishers Weekly.* Barner collects some of children's favorite bugs in this picture book, including the spotted ladybug, butterflies, grasshoppers, bumble bees, and rolypoly bugs, all depicted in brightly colored collage artwork and accompanied by light, whimsical verse. Barner also makes this title an educational experience by including an actual-size bug chart and a "bug-o-meter" which lists the number of legs on each bug, where it lives, how it moves, and if it stings or not. "Budding entomologists will fly to this book like bees to honey," Dawn Amsberry stated in a *School Library Journal* review, concluding that the "bright colors and easy text will be a hit at story time." Lauren Peterson, writing in *Booklist,* likewise praised the "bold colors and rhyming text."

Fish are at the center of things in *Fish Wish,* in which a young boy gazing at a clown fish in an aquarium is taken on an imaginary tour of a coral reef. The boy wonders what it would be like to be such a fish, and then he is hosted by the clown fish on this underwater tour. "A series of eye-popping images accompanies equally vivid language," wrote a reviewer for *Publishers Weekly,* who also found that the characters in the book, from starfish to sea horses, "come together in a visually dynamic and informative grand finale." Barner blends cut and torn paper for the artwork, along with buttons, foil, fabric, and heads for the collages. *Booklist*'s Carolyn Phelan found *Fish Wish* to be a "well-designed picture book, as simple and pleasing as a sea star."

Biographical and Critical Sources

BOOKS

Barner, Bob, *Dem Bones,* Chronicle Books (San Francisco, CA), 1996.
Barner, Bob, *To Everything,* Chronicle Books (San Francisco, CA), 1998.

PERIODICALS

Booklist, December 15, 1993, p. 762; December 1, 1996, Carolyn Phelan, review of *Dem Bones,* pp. 662-663; July, 1999, Lauren Peterson, review of *Bugs! Bugs! Bugs!,* p. 1948; February 1, 2000, Carolyn Phelan, review of *Fish Wish,* p. 1027; November 1, 2001, Carolyn Phelan, review of *Dinosaur Bones,* p. 479.
Books for Keeps, March, 1997, review of *Dem Bones,* p. 19.
Horn Book, November-December, 1990, review of *The Elevator Escalator Book: A Transportation Fact Book,* pp. 774-775; July-August, 1998, Mary M. Burns, review of *Which Way to the Revolution?: A Book about Maps,* p. 506.
Kirkus Reviews, October 1, 1998, review of *To Everything,* p. 1454.
Publishers Weekly, July 19, 1993, p. 251; February 6, 1995, review of *Too Many Dinosaurs* and *Space Race,* p. 86; September 16, 1996, review of *Dem Bones,* p. 81; October 19, 1998, review of *To Everything,* p. 79; May 31, 1999, review of *Bugs! Bugs! Bugs!,* p. 91; February 21, 2000, review of *Fish Wish,* p. 86; June 12, 2000, review of *Walk the Dog,* p. 72; July 9, 2001, review of *Dinosaur Bones,* p. 66; May 6, 2002, review of *Stars!, Stars!, Stars!,* p. 57.
School Library Journal, March, 1980, p. 118; February, 1988, p. 68; September, 1990, pp. 213-214; March, 1993, p. 174; January, 1994, pp. 82-83; November, 1996, Christine A. Moesch, review of *Dem Bones,* pp. 95-96; May, 1998, Lucinda Snyder Whitehurst, review of *Which Way to the Revolution?,* p. 129; November, 1998, Patricia Pearl Dole, review of *To Everything,* p. 102; August, 1999, Dawn Amsberry, review of *Bugs! Bugs! Bugs!,* p. 144; May, 2000, Margaret Rhoades, review of *Fish Wish,* p. 130; July, 2000, Janet M. Blair, review of *Walk the Dog,* p. 91.

OTHER

Bob Barner Web Site, http://www.bobbarner.com (November 13, 2002).*

*   *   *

BAYLOR, Byrd 1924-
(Byrd Baylor Schweitzer)

Personal

Born March 28, 1924, in San Antonio, TX; children: two sons. *Education:* Attended University of Arizona.

Addresses

Home—Arizona. *Office*—c/o Simon & Schuster, Scribner Author Mail, 1230 Avenue of the Americas, New York, NY 01120.

Career

Author of books for children and adults. Worked variously as a reporter for an Arizona newspaper and as

EVERYBODY
NEEDS A
ROCK

by BYRD BAYLOR with pictures by PETER PARNALL

Byrd Baylor presents ten rules for finding the perfect rock to keep forever. *(Cover illustration by Peter Parnall.)*

an executive secretary for the Association for Papago Affairs.

Awards, Honors

Caldecott Honor Book, American Library Association, and Steck-Vaughn Award, Texas Institute of Letters, both 1973, both for *When Clay Sings;* Catlin Peace Pipe Award, 1974, for *They Put on Masks;* Art Books for Children Citation, Brooklyn Public Library, 1976, for *Everybody Needs a Rock;* Steck-Vaughn Award, New York Academy of Sciences Younger Honor, Caldecott Honor Book, and *Boston Globe-Horn Book* Honor Book for Illustration, all 1976, and Art Books for Children Citation, 1977, 1978, and 1979, all for *The Desert Is Theirs;* Caldecott Honor Book, 1977, for *Hawk, I'm Your Brother,* and 1979, for *The Way to Start a Day;* Steck-Vaughn Award, 1978, for *Guess Who My Favorite Person Is;* Outstanding Arizona Author, 1985; *When Clay Sings* and *Everybody Needs a Rock* were named notable books by the American Library Association.

Writings

FOR CHILDREN, EXCEPT AS NOTED; UNDER NAME BYRD BAYLOR, EXCEPT AS NOTED

(Under name Byrd Baylor Schweitzer) *Amigo,* illustrated by Garth Williams, Macmillan (New York, NY), 1963.

(Under name Byrd Baylor Schweitzer) *One Small Blue Bead,* illustrated by Symeon Shimin, Macmillan (New York, NY), 1965.

(Under name Byrd Baylor Schweitzer) *The Chinese Bug,* illustrated by Beatrice Darwin, Houghton Mifflin (Boston, MA), 1968.

(Under name Byrd Baylor Schweitzer) *The Man Who Talked to a Tree,* illustrated by Symeon Shimin, Dutton, 1968.

Before You Came This Way, illustrated by Tom Bahti, Dutton, 1969.

Plink, Plink, Plink, illustrated by James Marshall, Houghton Mifflin (Boston, MA), 1971.

Coyote Cry, illustrated by Symeon Shimin, Lothrop, 1972.

When Clay Sings, illustrated by Tom Bahti, Scribner (New York, NY), 1972.

Sometimes I Dance Mountains, illustrated by Ken Longtemps, photographs by Bill Sears, Scribner (New York, NY), 1973.

Everybody Needs a Rock, illustrated by Peter Parnall, Scribner (New York, NY), 1974.

They Put on Masks, illustrated by Jerry Ingram, Scribner (New York, NY), 1974.

The Desert Is Theirs, illustrated by Peter Parnall, Scribner (New York, NY), 1975.

(Editor) *And It Is Still That Way: Legends Told by Arizona Indian Children,* illustrated by Lucy Jelinek, Scribner (New York, NY), 1976.

We Walk in Sandy Places, photographs by Marilyn Schweitzer, Scribner (New York, NY), 1976.

Hawk, I'm Your Brother, illustrated by Peter Parnall, Scribner (New York, NY), 1976.

Guess Who My Favorite Person Is, illustrated by Robert Andrew Parker, Scribner (New York, NY), 1977.

Yes Is Better than No (for adults), illustrated by Mike Chiago, Scribner (New York, NY), 1977.

The Way to Start a Day, illustrated by Peter Parnall, Scribner (New York, NY), 1978.

The Other Way to Listen, illustrated by Peter Parnall, Scribner (New York, NY), 1978.

Your Own Best Secret Place, illustrated by Peter Parnall, Scribner (New York, NY), 1979.

If You Are a Hunter of Fossils, illustrated by Peter Parnall, Scribner (New York, NY), 1980.

Desert Voices, illustrated by Peter Parnall, Scribner (New York, NY), 1981.

A God on Every Mountain Top: Stories of Southwest Indian Sacred Mountains, illustrated by Carol Brown, Scribner (New York, NY), 1981.

Moon Song, illustrated by Ronald Himler, Scribner (New York, NY), 1982.

The Best Town in the World, illustrated by Ronald Himler, Scribner (New York, NY), 1983.

I'm in Charge of Celebrations, illustrated by Peter Parnall, Scribner (New York, NY), 1986.

The Table Where Rich People Sit, illustrated by Peter Parnall, Scribner (New York, NY), 1994.

Also contributor to *Redbook, McCall's,* and *Arizona Quarterly.*

Adaptations

Hawk, I'm Your Brother, The Way to Start a Day, and *The Other Way to Listen* have been adapted for video in English and Spanish versions by the Cheshire Corporation for its Southwest Series.

Sidelights

Born and raised in the American Southwest, Byrd Baylor has focused many of her writings on the region's landscape, peoples, and values. Her work reflects a familiarity with the area as well as her respect for the

Southwest's unique culture, particularly that of the Native American. Her books of rhythmic prose poetry, written primarily for children, cover a wide range of themes—from exploring the life of prehistoric Indians through their art, to appreciating the environment and its flora and fauna, to realizing one's spiritual connection to nature. Throughout her writings, "Baylor celebrates the beauty of nature and her own feelings of rapport with it," assessed a reviewer in the *Bulletin of the Center for Children's Books.*

As a child, Baylor moved with her family to various locations in the Southwest, including Arizona, Texas, and Mexico, due to her father's work on ranches and in precious metal mines. Spending much of her time outdoors, she learned to value nature and became intrigued with the customs of Native Americans, including their rituals, folklore, and art. When she began her career as an author of children's books, Baylor fused her interests with prose to produce simple stories with important lessons. The alliance has yielded more than twenty-five books and has earned her numerous awards.

Baylor's first published book, *Amigo,* was issued under the name Byrd Baylor Schweitzer. After three more books under the Schweitzer surname, she began using the shortened version of her name. *Before You Came This Way* uses Native American rock carvings, known as petroglyphs, to describe what life may have been like in prehistoric times. Baylor teamed with artist Tom Bahti to explain the significance of the drawings, which depict men, birds, animals, masked figures, and other designs, thereby introducing young readers to an ancient people and lifestyle. The book "treats the drawings for what they are," explained Euple L. Wilson in a review for *School Library Journal,* "the emotional expressions of a non-literate people." Generally well received by both critics and the public alike, *Before You Came This Way* was said to place readers "face to face with the minds and hearts of those people of long ago," according to the *New York Times Book Review*'s Gloria Levitas. Zena Sutherland in *Saturday Review* echoed that the story is "filled with a sense of wonder and quiet reverence, a vivid imagining."

The archaeological study of prehistoric Indian life was again presented by Baylor in works such as *When Clay Sings* and *They Put on Masks.* The former work, a re-teaming with illustrator Bahti, shows how ancient Indians, including the Anasazi, Hohokam, Mimbres, and Mogollon recorded scenes from their everyday lives on their pottery. Revealing the meaning of the motifs painted on the earthenware, Baylor also details how some of the pottery was used and made. *When Clay Sings* received a Caldecott honorable mention and the prestigious Steck-Vaughn Award. *They Put on Masks,* which discusses Indian and Eskimo ceremonial masks, also received the Catlin Peace Pipe Award as well as considerable critical attention.

Among Baylor's other works is *Everybody Needs a Rock,* which tells readers how to choose the rock that is right for them. The book also signified the beginning of

a lengthy and successful collaboration between Baylor and illustrator Peter Parnall, an alliance that produced *The Desert Is Theirs,* one of Baylor's most critically acclaimed works, as well as several Caldecott honor books. *The Desert Is Theirs* investigates the relationship that desert dwellers have with their environment, pointing out the respect these inhabitants have for the land and its animals and resources. Baylor explains in the book that the desert's human inhabitants "say they *like* the land they live on so they treat it well—the way you'd treat an old friend. They sing it songs. They never hurt it. And the land knows." Critical response to the text and art was generally positive, with reviewers calling the work uncompromising, graceful, and striking. The duo, according to Mary M. Burns in *Horn Book,* has "brilliantly integrated myth, folklore, and factual description into a coherent whole."

Baylor continued to delve into humankind's oneness with nature in *Hawk, I'm Your Brother,* which also featured Parnall's artwork. Centering around a young boy's quest to experience the freedom of flying like a bird, the book follows the child as he captures and restrains a baby hawk, thinking that he can bond as its brother and be given the gift of flight. Baylor explains the youth's logic through her rhythmic prose: "And he even thought / that there might be / some special / magic / in a bird / that came from / Santos Mountain. // Somehow / he thought / he'd share / that / magic // and

Baylor describes the land that the Desert People and animals know and love in **The Desert Is Theirs.** *(Illustrated by Peter Parnall.)*

In Baylor's prose poem **I'm in Charge of Celebrations,** *a girl shares her experiences in the desert. (Illustrated by Peter Parnall.)*

he'd *fly.* // They say / it used to / be / that way / when / we / knew how / to / talk / to birds // and how / to call / a bird's / wild spirit / down / into our own. . . . It seemed to him / he'd FLY—// if / a hawk / became / his / brother."

In time the boy realizes that his dream cannot be achieved as long as he denies another being its freedom. As he releases the hawk, a magical experience occurs—he mentally bonds with the creature, witnessing the gift of flight as he watches his "brother" soar through the sky. Elizabeth Martinez explained the story's moral in a review in *Interracial Books for Children Bulletin:* "No one can be truly free if others are not free, and we attain our own freedom by allowing others to be free." The critic also lauded Baylor for keeping the intrinsic identities of both the boy and the hawk intact.

Baylor's subsequent works have continued to be well regarded by both critics and children. Although she has completed more volumes featuring the culture of the American Southwest as a backdrop, she has also explored favorite things, important early morning attitudes, secret hiding places, and small-town life in books like *Guess Who My Favorite Person Is, The Way to Start a Day, Your Own Best Secret Place,* and *The Best Town in the World.* Her writings, particularly those that illuminate the sanctity of the natural wonders of the world, have endeared her to young readers. While many critics laud her evocation of the mystic Native American

spirit, they also praise her lyrical prose, believing that her text demands to be read aloud. "Baylor's sensitivity and eloquence are qualities that indelibly impress [her] readers," observed a *Publishers Weekly* reviewer.

Biographical and Critical Sources

BOOKS

Baylor, Byrd, *Hawk, I'm Your Brother,* illustrated by Peter Parnall, Scribner (New York, NY), 1976.
Children's Literature Review, Volume 3, Gale (Detroit, MI), 1978.

PERIODICALS

Bulletin of the Center for Children's Books, January, 1980, review of *Your Own Best Secret Place,* p. 87; September 15, 1981; November 1, 1986.
Horn Book, April, 1964; June, 1976; February, 1976, Mary M. Burns, review of *The Desert Is Theirs;* February, 1984.
Instructor, August-September, 1972.
Interracial Books for Children Bulletin, Volume 7, number 6, 1976, Elizabeth Martinez, review of *Hawk, I'm Your Brother.*
Junior Bookshelf, August, 1967; August, 1973.
Kirkus Reviews, September 15, 1969; October 15, 1973; April 15, 1974; August 1, 1974; June 15, 1981; July 15, 1981; May 1, 1991.

Mountain Girl's parents assign monetary values to the beauty of nature and family to reveal the true meaning of wealth in Baylor's **The Table Where Rich People Sit.** *(Illustrated by Peter Parnall.)*

New York Times Book Review, December 28, 1969, Gloria Levitas, review of *Before You Came This Way;* November 13, 1977.

Publishers Weekly, November 7, 1977; May 21, 1982, review of *Moon Song,* p. 76.

Saturday Review, November 8, 1969, Zena Sutherland, review of *Before You Came This Way.*

School Library Journal, December, 1969, Euple L. Wilson, review of *Before You Came This Way;* May, 1972; September, 1972; December, 1986.

Scientific American, December, 1969; December, 1972.*

*   *   *

Jennifer Blomgren

BLOMGREN, Jennifer (Alice) 1954-

Personal

Born August 29, 1954, in Forks, WA; daughter of Joseph James (a log truck owner/operator, Air Force Lieutenant, electronics technician, millwright, and mechanic) and Virginia Rosalie Blomgren (secretary, bookkeeper, and musician); married Richard W. Paine, March 18, 1978 (divorced, May, 1989). *Nationality:* American. *Education:* Attended Evergreen State College, 1972-74, University of Washington, 1974, and Peninsula College, 1975-77, 1980-81. *Politics:* Independent. *Religion:* Non-denominational.

Addresses

Home—Washington. *Office*—c/o Author Mail, Sasquatch Books, 119 S. Main St., 4th Fl., Seattle, WA 98104. *E-mail*—applepie@olypen.com.

Career

Children's book author, greeting card designer, illustrator, and formerly a registered nurse.

Awards, Honors

Winner, Pacific Northwest Booksellers Association 2002 Book Awards, for *Where Do I Sleep?: A Pacific Northwest Lullaby.*

Writings

Where Do I Sleep?: A Pacific Northwest Lullaby, illustrated by Andrea Gabriel, Sasquatch Books (Seattle, WA), 2001.

Sidelights

Inspired by the area of Washington State where she was raised and still makes her home, Jennifer Blomgren is the author of *Where Do I Sleep?: A Pacific Northwest Lullaby.* In this verse collection, Pacific Northwest animals are depicted in their natural habitat. Featuring sea otters, bald eagles, moose, gray wolves, and a variety of birds and sea creatures, the book introduces young children to the perhaps unfamiliar nature scape of the northwestern United States, with its forests, rivers, tundra, and coastal regions. Noting that Blomgren's verses "reveal more than sleep preferences," *Booklist* reviewer Lauren Peterson commented that *Where Do I Sleep?* helps young readers "practice map skills, learn about new animals," and adds to their understanding of geography. Praising the pastel illustrations of sleepy animals created by Andrea Gabriel in a review of the picture book for *School Library Journal,* Dona J. Helmer also compared Blomgren's "gentle" text to that of noted twentieth-century children's book author Margaret Wise Brown; she added that "adults will welcome" *Where Do I Sleep?* as "a book designed to produce calm." In *Publishers Weekly,* a reviewer praised the volume as "a tranquil bedtime poem" that "deserves a wide audience."

Blomgren told *SATA:* "I was raised in the temperate rain forest of the Olympic peninsula in Washington State, where nature's beauty abounded, and I became a witness to the epic tragedy of the destruction of a premier wilderness for profit. Even as a child I was saddened and knew that the wholesale, frenzied pace of logging had to end. It did with the [government's] enforced slowdown to save habitat for the spotted owl and other endangered species. This pervasive sense of nature's awesome beauty, fragility, vibrancy, and its delicate balance ... motivates me to write about habitat and its importance.

"I feel it is difficult at best to convince adults of nature's value when left alone unless they are already aware of it. But children are naturally more open, ... [especially] to animals, as though they realize instinctively their place among nature's creatures. Therefore, I feel it important to direct my own concern and love of nature to children.

"Besides, I simply love writing in verse. My grandmother and great grandmother were both published poets, and though I never knew either, they influence me today, as do my parents, who exposed me to books, nature, and an awareness of history and family and the strength we can draw from the past and the people who came before us."

Biographical and Critical Sources

PERIODICALS

Booklist, November 1, 2001, Lauren Peterson, review of *Where Do I Sleep?: A Pacific Northwest Lullaby,* p. 481.

Publishers Weekly, July 16, 2001, review of *Where Do I Sleep?,* p. 179.

School Library Journal, November, 2001, Dona J. Helmer, review of *Where Do I Sleep?,* p. 111.

*   *   *

BOSSE, Malcolm (Joseph, Jr.) 1926-2002

OBITUARY NOTICE—See index for *SATA* sketch: Born May 6, 1926, in Detroit, MI; died of esophageal cancer June 14, 2002, in Manhattan, NY. Educator and author. Bosse was an author of books for both children and adults and was well-known for his stories set in Asia, including *The Warlord* (1983). He got his first exposure to Asia after high school when he worked as a merchant marine, and then later, after earning his bachelor's at Yale and working in New York City for two years as an editorial writer for *Barron's Financial Weekly,* he served in the navy in Vietnam. Vietnam is consequently the setting of his first novel, *Journey of Tao Kim Nam* (1959). Returning home, Bosse earned his master's from the University of Michigan in 1960 and worked as a freelance writer. He continued his studies at New York University, where he received a Ph.D. in 1969. That same year, he began teaching English at the City College of the City University of New York, where he became a professor and eventually retired in 1992. Bosse began writing murder mysteries with his second novel, *The Incident at Naha,* and stories for young adults with 1979's *The Seventy-nine Squares.* Other young adult books by Bosse include *The Barracuda Gang* (1982) and *The Examination* (1994). He also continued to write books for adults, such as the historical novels *The Warlord* (1983) and its sequel, *Fire in Heaven* (1986), and was coeditor of *Foundations of the Novel* (1974) and *The Flowering of the Novel* (1975). During his career, Bosse received considerable praise for both his adult and young adult fiction, including Edgar Allan Poe Award nominations in 1974 and 1975 for *The Incident at Naha* and *The Man Who Loved Zoos* respectively, a Dorothy Canfield Fisher Award in 1981, several honorable and notable book listings from the American Library Association, the Deutscher Jugendliteraturpreis, and the Prix Lecture-Jeunesse.

OBITUARIES AND OTHER SOURCES:

BOOKS

St. James Guide to Young Adult Writers, second edition, St. James Press (Detroit, MI), 1999.

Writers Directory, 16th edition, St. James Press, 2001.

PERIODICALS

New York Times, June 14, 2002, p. C11.

BOWEN, Fred 1953-

Personal

Born August 3, 1953, in Marblehead, MA; married Peggy Jackson (a journalist); children: a son and a daughter. *Nationality:* American. *Education:* University of Pennsylvania, B.A.; George Washington Law School, J.D.

Addresses

Home—Silver Spring, MD. *Agent*—c/o Author Mail, Peachtree Publishers, 1700 Chatahoochee Ave., Atlanta, GA 30318-2112. *E-mail*—sportstory@aol.com.

Career

Lawyer, journalist, and children's author. Lawyer for the federal government; columnist for the *Washington Post,* 2000—.

Awards, Honors

Family Channel Seal of Quality, for *T.J.'s Secret Pitch;* Great Summer Read List citation, *Family Fun* magazine, for *The Kid Coach;* Best Books for the Classroom citation, Virginia Center for Children's Books, 2000,

Fred Bowen

Reading Olympics selection, Bucks Country and Mont-gomery County, PA, 2001-2002, Land of Enchantment Award, New Mexico, Young Hoosier Award, Indiana, Pennsylvania Young Readers Award, and Virginia Young Readers Award, all 2002-2003, and Volunteer State Award masterlist selection, Tennessee, 2003-2004, all for *Winners Take All;* masterlist selection, Maryland Children's Book Award, 2001-2002, for *Full Court Fever.*

Writings

"ALLSTAR SPORTSTORY" SERIES

T.J.'s Secret Pitch, illustrated by Jim Thorpe, Peachtree (Atlanta, GA), 1996.
The Golden Glove, illustrated by Jim Thorpe, Peachtree (Atlanta, GA), 1996.
The Kid Coach, illustrated by Ann Barrow, Peachtree (Atlanta, GA), 1996.
Playoff Dreams, illustrated by Ann Barrow, Peachtree (Atlanta, GA), 1997.
Full Court Fever, illustrated by Ann Barrow, Peachtree (Atlanta, GA), 1998.
Off the Rim, illustrated by Ann Barrow, Peachtree (Atlanta, GA), 1998.
The Final Cut, illustrated by Ann Barrow, Peachtree (Atlanta, GA), 1999.
On the Line, illustrated by Ann Barrow, Peachtree (Atlanta, GA), 1999.
Winners Take All, illustrated by Paul Casale, Peachtree (Atlanta, GA), 2000.

Also author of *The Score,* a weekly sports column for the *Washington Post,* 2000—.

Sidelights

Children's author Fred Bowen "is quickly joining the ranks of today's most popular sports fiction authors," declared Barb Lawler in a *School Library Journal* review of Bowen's *Full Court Fever.* Bowen's winning mixture of sports history and action stories has attracted an ever-increasing fan base since the appearance of his first title, *T.J.'s Secret Pitch,* in 1996. These sports tales, geared for readers between eight and twelve, have managed to reach reluctant readers and sports enthu-siasts alike. Additionally, each book includes a bonus history section at the back, complete with vintage photographs. Commenting on the author's "AllStar SportStory" series, *Newsday* reviewers Nicole Lord and Leeza Menon called Bowen "a natural when it comes to writing sports stories and informing his readers about the past." The two critics found the books "perfect for kids ages eight to twelve."

Born in Marblehead, Massachusetts, in 1953, Bowen is one of seven siblings. "My dad loved sports," Bowen noted on his author's Web site. "One of my earliest memories is watching the 1957 World Series on TV with my dad and my brothers. I was four years old and the TV was black-and-white." His father coached him in Little League, and sports informed much of Bowen's early years. "My best childhood memories are taken

Marcus learns to make free throws with a silly-looking underhand toss but is embarrassed to try the technique during a game in Bowen's **On the Line.** *(Illustrated by Ann Barrow.)*

from playing Little League in the park and basketball on the playground," Bowen recalled on his Web site. "I can remember home runs, bad calls, and great comebacks from games I played more than thirty years ago. My favorite reading back then was sports fiction and the sports section in the newspaper."

Bowen thought he was leaving all this sports craziness behind when he went off to college, first to the University of Pennsylvania, where he majored in history, and then on to George Washington Law School. After graduation, Bowen became a lawyer for the government, but in his free time he still followed sports. He began to get the writing fever when his journalist wife suggested that he try writing movie reviews for the local newspa-per. "The editor liked the idea and I had a lot of fun doing it," Bowen noted on his Web site. "Who wouldn't? I was getting paid to watch the movies. And it was so cool to see my name in the newspaper." Then, when his own son was small and Bowen read sports books to him, he began to see that he could write books like those himself.

In the free time from his busy legal career—during lunch hours, on his commute to work, and on weekend mornings—Bowen began to put down some of his own memories. He soon came up with his first juvenile novel, *T.J.'s Secret Pitch,* the first book in the "AllStar SportStory" series. Young T.J. wants to be a pitcher more than anything, but he is small and he has no speed on his pitches. However, when T.J. discovers the "eephus pitch," a crazy pitching style used by Truett

"Rip" Sewell of the Pittsburgh Pirates in the 1940s, everything changes. Using this pitch, T.J. helps his team to win the championship. This first title from Bowen received critical praise, especially for its blend of play-by-play action and sports history. *School Library Journal*'s Blair Christolson felt that "by interweaving baseball history into the plot, [Bowen] distinguishes this story from typical sports-series fare."

The second book in the series, *The Golden Glove,* deals with Jamie, a shortstop who has lost his lucky glove. He suspects two kids in the neighborhood have stolen it, and his parents refuse to buy him a new one. Finally he is forced to borrow one, but it does not have the same magic as his old mitt. Interwoven into this story is the history of the baseball glove and the fact that early players did not use them. When the first players started to use gloves, they were called sissies. It was not until the Chicago White Stocking pitcher Albert Spalding—the founder of the sporting goods company—wore the glove that it became acceptable.

The Kid Coach, the third title in the series, features the Tigers baseball team, which has lost its coach. The kids end up coaching themselves, and in a big game they

Kyle feels uneasy about faking a catch to win a game in Bowen's Winners Take All. *(Illustrated by Paul Casale.)*

attempt to use the "Williams Shift" to stop a home run hitter. This ploy worked against the great Ted Williams in the 1940s, but the kids are not sure it will work in their game. Bowen blends in the history of the player-coach idea into this tale, particularly the story of Lou Boudreau, who was both shortstop and coach of the Cleveland Indians in the 1940s.

Reviewing the first three titles in the series, sports author Jim Naughton, writing in the *Washington Post Book World,* commended them for not attempting too much. According to Naughton, Bowen's "aims are modest, but he fulfills them almost completely." Naughton also noted that Bowen "weaves female athletes into these 'boy's books' in an admirable way, and he presents a multiracial cast of characters." Naughton further concluded that young readers "who love the game will appreciate that Bowen loves it too and that he makes no attempt to justify this love by enlisting it in the service of grander themes."

In *Playoff Dreams,* the skilled center fielder Brendan is stuck on a team that is not winning. Frustration turns to anger when he sees no way for his team to make it to the playoffs. His parents—a jazz-playing dad and doctor mother—have no clue about athletics, but help comes from a sports-crazy uncle who takes Brendan to a baseball game at Chicago's Wrigley Field. When this uncle tells him the story of the hard-luck Cubs and their Hall-of-Fame player Ernie Banks, Brendan begins to look at the sport differently. Though Banks never went to a playoff or a World Series, he always felt happy to be playing the game at all. Christolson, writing in *School Library Journal,* observed that Bowen's books use "actual sports heroes to reinforce a positive attitude among young athletes." *Booklist*'s Carolyn Phelan also had praise for this title, with its "simple plot and a well-defined problem."

Bowen turns to basketball in the 1998 *Full Court Fever,* in which the Falcons, a team long on skill and spirit but short in stature, try desperately to patch up a losing season. They turn to a tactic devised by the 1964 University of California—Los Angeles Bruins, a team that won championships without any tall players, for help. More basketball action is served up in *Off the Rim.* Here Chris, who spends too much time on the bench, gets some tips from his friend Greta, the star of the girls' team. In this title, Bowen mixes in lore about the history of womens' basketball and how it once differed from men's, being essentially a half-court game.

In *The Final Cut,* four junior high friends will soon be trying out for the eighth-grade basketball team. Though basketball is their life, this quartet is not the best of athletes. They can hold their own in park games, but when it comes time for the big try-outs, will they be able to cut it and keep their friendship intact? Richard Luzer, reviewing this title in *School Library Journal,* noted that Bowen hits a nerve with "the characters' obsessive interest in evaluating the competition and enhancing their own chances of making the team."

On the Line, the eighth title in the "AllStar SportStory" series and the fourth basketball book, deals with a star forward, Marcus, who is tops all over the court, except at the foul line. Unsought help comes from the school custodian, who shows Marcus how to shoot an under-hand foul shot. Bowen again uses a real-life example for this sports story: National Basketball Association star Rick Barry, who played in the 1970s, used the under-hand foul shot to great advantage. "Bowen scores again with a satisfying blend of historical sports commentary and fiction," declared Gerry Larson in *School Library Journal.*

Returning to baseball with the year 2000 title, *Winners Take All,* Bowen tells the story of a good kid who makes a bad decision. Kyle Holt is the Reds center fielder, and they are battling for first place against the Cubs. Kyle wants to win so much that he secretly cheats, pretending to catch a ball he actually drops, and his team wins the game. Everybody is overjoyed, but Kyle feels uneasy about the victory. Then a player from the Cubs discovers the cheating and threatens to tell. Kyle's grandmother gives the young boy a lesson in sports fairness by telling him about Hall-of-Famer Christy Mathewson, a player so honest that umpires would ask his help in making calls. After Kyle confesses to cheating, his team finally beats the Cubs fair and square. Kate Kohlbeck, writing in *School Library Journal,* felt that this was "a story with plenty of play-by-play action, a good plot, a valuable lesson, and some interesting baseball history." Kohlbeck concluded, "Bowen pitches a winner here."

For budding writers, Bowen has this advice on his author's Web site: "Lots of stuff happens in your life. The difference between you and a writer is that a writer writes it down. You can start now. Keep a journal and write your story! You will love reading it when you are older. When you write assignments for school, show them to someone else and listen to their comments and then make changes. My first drafts are never my final books. I make lots of revisions to get it right. One more thing: read a lot. Good readers make better writers."

Biographical and Critical Sources

PERIODICALS

Booklist, November 1, 1997, Carolyn Phelan, review of *Playoff Dreams,* p. 469.
Newsday, March 16, 1998, Nicole Lord and Leeza Menon, "Did You Like It?"
School Library Journal, July, 1996, Blair Christolson, review of *T.J.'s Secret Pitch,* p. 82; March, 1998, Blair Christolson, review of *Playoff Dreams,* pp. 166-167; December, 1998, Barb Lawler, review of *Full Court Fever,* p. 118; July, 1999, Richard Luzer, review of *The Final Cut,* p. 95; April, 2000, Gerry Larson, review of *On the Line,* p. 129; April, 2001, Kate Kohlbeck, review of *Winners Take All,* p. 138.
Washington Post Book World, May 5, 1996, p. 10; May 4, 1997, Jim Naughton, review of *T.J.'s Secret Pitch, The Golden Glove,* and *The Kid Coach,* p. 16.

OTHER

Children's Book Guild, http://www.childrensbookguild.org/ (June 10, 2002), "Fred Bowen."
Fred Bowen Web Site, http://www.fredbowen.com/ (June 10, 2002).

*   *   *

BRANLEY, Franklyn M(ansfield) 1915-2002

OBITUARY NOTICE—See index for *SATA* sketch: Born June 5, 1915, in New Rochelle, NY; died May 5, 2002, in Brunswick, ME. Educator and author. Branley was an innovative educator who became one of the first to teach science to elementary school children, and he was a prolific author of over 140 books explaining scientific concepts to children. He received his teaching license from the New Patlz Normal School (now the State University of New York College at New Paltz), a bachelor's from New York University in 1942, and then his M.A. and Ed.D. from Columbia University in 1948 and 1957 respectively. From 1936 until 1954, Branley was a teacher at various elementary schools in the state of New York. Because science lessons were still new to such young students at the time, Branley worked with other educators to write a pamphlet on how best to teach the subject. This was the first step toward his writing career. He began writing science books for children with Nelson Frederick Beller in the 1940s that taught young students how to perform simple experiments. Branley joined Jersey State Teachers College (now Jersey City State College), where he was a science professor from 1954 to 1956, but it was his work as director of educational services at the American Museum of Natural History's Hayden Planetarium that sparked his interest in astronomy and space exploration. What followed was a series of books on astronomy, including the "Exploring Our Universe," "Mysteries of the Universe," and "Voyage into Space" series. Branley remained at the planetarium, becoming its astronomer in 1963, and chairman of the planetarium in 1968, before he retired in 1972. In addition to his series on astronomy, Branley authored many other science books explaining a wide variety of concepts to young readers; he also wrote and edited college textbooks. Many of Branley's books received awards as outstanding science books, and in 1970 he was named New Jersey's Children's Book Writer of the Year.

OBITUARIES AND OTHER SOURCES:

BOOKS

Something about the Author Autobiography Series, Volume 16, Gale (Detroit, MI), 1993.

PERIODICALS

New York Times, May 9, 2002, p. A29.

BUJOLD, Lois McMaster 1949-

Personal

Surname is pronounced "*boo*-jhold"; born November 2, 1949, in Columbus, OH; daughter of Robert Charles (an engineering professor) and Laura Elizabeth (a home-maker; maiden name, Gerould) McMaster; married John Fredric Bujold, October 9, 1971 (divorced, December, 1992); children: Anne Elizabeth, Paul Andre. *Nationality:* American. *Education:* Attended Ohio State University, 1968-72.

Addresses

Agent—Eleanor Wood, Spectrum Literary Agency, 320 Central Park W., Suite 1-D, New York, NY 10025.

Career

Ohio State University Hospitals, pharmacy technician, 1972-78; homemaker, 1979—; writer, 1982—. Writing workshop instructor at Thurber House, spring, 1988, and Ohio State University, summers, 1990-92.

Member

Science Fiction Writers of America, Novelists, Inc.

Awards, Honors

Nebula Award for Best Novel, Science Fiction Writers of America, 1988, for *Falling Free,* and 1995, for

Lois McMaster Bujold

Mirror Dance; Nebula Award for Best Novella, Science Fiction Writers of America, 1989, for *The Mountains of Mourning;* Hugo Award for Best Novella, World Science Fiction Society, 1989, for *The Mountains of Mourning;* Hugo Award for Best Novel, World Science Fiction Society, 1990, for *The Vor Game,* 1991, for *Barrayar,* and 1995, for *Mirror Dance;* first place Locus Award, *Locus* (magazine), 1991, for *Barrayar,* and 1995, for *Mirror Dance;* Mythopoeic Award, 2002, for *Curse of Chalion.*

Writings

SCIENCE FICTION

Shards of Honor, Baen Books (Riverdale, NY), 1986.
Ethan of Athos, Baen Books (Riverdale, NY), 1986.
The Warrior's Apprentice, Baen Books (Riverdale, NY), 1986.
Falling Free (first published serially in *Analog Science Fiction/Science Fact,* December, 1987-February, 1988), Baen Books (Riverdale, NY), 1988.
Brothers in Arms, Baen Books (Riverdale, NY), 1989.
Borders of Infinity, Baen Books (Riverdale, NY), 1989.
The Vor Game, Baen Books (Riverdale, NY), 1990.
Vorkosigan's Game (contains *Borders of Infinity* and *The Vor Game*), Science Fiction Book Club (New York, NY), 1990.
Barrayar (first published serially in *Analog Science Fiction/Science Fact,* July-October, 1991), Baen Books (Riverdale, NY), 1991.
Mirror Dance (sequel to *Brothers in Arms*), Baen Books (Riverdale, NY), 1994.
Cetaganda: A Vorkosigan Adventure, Baen Books (Riverdale, NY), 1996.
Memory, Baen Books (Riverdale, NY), 1996.
Young Miles, Baen Books (Riverdale, NY), 1997.
Komarr: A Miles Vorkosigan Adventure, Baen Books (Riverdale, NY), 1998.
A Civil Campaign: A Comedy of Biology and Manners, Baen Books (Riverdale, NY), 1999.
Miles, Mystery, and Mayhem, Baen Books (Riverdale, NY), 2001.
Diplomatic Immunity, Baen Books (Riverdale, NY), 2002.

Also author of novella *The Mountains of Mourning,* published in *Analog,* May, 1989. Contributor to periodicals, including *American Fantasy, Analog Science Fiction/Science Fact, Columbus Dispatch, Far Frontiers, New Destinies,* and *Twilight Zone.*

OTHER

The Spirit Ring (fantasy novel), Baen Books (Riverdale, NY), 1992.
Dreamweaver's Dilemma: Short Stories and Essays, edited by Suford Lewis, New England Science Fiction Association Press (Framingham, MA), 1995.
(Editor, with Roland J. Green) *Women at War,* Tor (New York, NY), 1995.
The Curse of Chalion (fantasy novel), Eos (New York, NY), 2001.

Bujold's novels have been translated into Spanish, Italian, German, French, Polish, Romanian, Japanese,

Hebrew, Lithuanian, Croatian, Korean, Bulgarian, Greek, Czech, and Russian.

Adaptations

Bujold's short story "Barter" was adapted for the syndicated television program *Tales from the Darkside,* 1986. The Reader's Chair publishes Bujold's work on audiocassette and MP3-CD.

Sidelights

Lois McMaster Bujold is widely known in the science-fiction field for her witty, believable tales of Miles Vorkosigan, the protagonist of a series that is over a dozen books and growing. Bujold is considered a master at character development and the nuances of human interaction—qualities not always found in modern science fiction. Although best known as the creator of Vorkosigan, the disabled military genius and mercenary, Bujold has written many other critically acclaimed science fiction novels, as well as two well-received fantasy books.

Born in Columbus, Ohio, in 1949, Bujold has been a self-confessed voracious reader all her life. Beginning with horse stories as a young reader, she graduated to adult science fiction at the age of nine. She acquired this taste from her father, who was an engineer, a professor at Ohio State, and a graduate of Cal Tech. The novels and science fiction magazines he would buy to read while flying to various consulting jobs would invariably end up with his daughter. Bujold also began writing at an early age, already crafting look-alike snippets of prose that emulated her favorite writers. A friend and Bujold would collaborate on extended story lines as after school entertainment.

After graduating from high school, Bujold attended Ohio State University from 1968 to 1972, but she did not graduate. "I dabbled with English as a major in college," the author noted on her Web site, "but quickly fell away from it—my heart was in the creative, not the critical end of things." As a student of photography and biology, she traveled to East Africa collecting slides of insects while still in college. Bujold noted on her author Web site that her real education came not from her classes in college, but from "reading five books a week for ten years from the Ohio State University stacks [and] reading enormous amounts of SF as a teenager." After leaving college, Bujold worked as a pharmacy technician by day while continuing to experiment with various writing forms, including a Sherlock Holmes pastiche. When her old school chum, Lillian Stewart Carl, began writing again and publishing, Bujold was inspired to do the same. Married, with two children, no day job, and in need of money, she decided to give writing a try.

"I quickly discovered that writing was far too demanding and draining to justify as a hobby," Bujold wrote on her Web site, "and that only serious professional recognition would satisfy me. Whatever had to be done, in terms of writing, re-writing, cutting, editorial analysis,

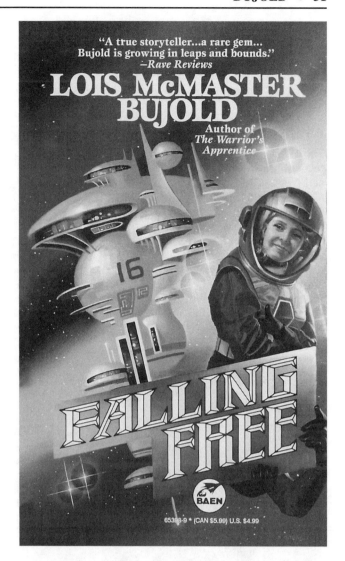

Engineer Leo Graf leads the genetically created quaddies, who have four hands but no legs, to freedom. (Cover illustration by Alan Gutierrez.)

and trying again, I was determined to do. This was an immensely fruitful period in my growth as a writer, all of it invisible to the outside observer."

Her hard work paid off. By 1982 she had settled on science fiction as her field, and in quick succession she wrote *Shards of Honor, The Warrior's Apprentice,* and *Ethan of Athos.* As these novels made the rounds of New York publishers, she broke into print in *Twilight Zone* magazine with a short story. Then, in 1985, Bujold accomplished the feat of receiving publishing contracts for all three of her novels.

Bujold's first book, *Shards of Honor,* is a science-fiction romance that describes events prior to Miles's birth. In this novel, Cordelia Naismith is the leader of a scientific survey group; Aral Vorkosigan is the commander of a military force which destroys the survey camp. Though enemies, the two must work together to survive, and by the time they return to their opposing societies they have fallen in love. "Bujold has a nice hand with the complications" of the story, asserted Tom Easton in *Analog Science Fiction/Science Fact.* Granting the plot's predictability, he commended Bujold for delving into dilemmas of personal and cultural honor, exploitation of science by government, and love that crosses political boundaries.

Miles Vorkosigan is the son of Cordelia and Aral, and in *The Warrior's Apprentice* Bujold begins his story, recounting his efforts to follow in his father's footsteps and, failing, to find his own path in life. Born into the warrior class, Miles tries unsuccessfully to enter the military academy despite having been deformed before birth and afflicted with extremely fragile bones. After this failure he begins traveling to complete his education in other ways. Comparing *The Warrior's Apprentice* to *Shards of Honor,* which had been hailed as a highly promising first novel, Martha A. Bartter, writing in *Fantasy Review,* found Miles's story "better: more unified, faster-paced, funnier." Recommending the book highly, the critic observed, "Bujold may be a new voice

On the run from the Cetagandans, Miles Vorkosigan arrives on Earth where he faces assassins and a clone of himself. (Cover illustration by Alan Gutierrez.)

among science fiction writers, but she knows how to make a story work."

In 1988 Bujold won her first Nebula Award, for *Falling Free,* which depicts a human engineer's efforts to liberate an exploited race. Genetically created with four hands and no legs, the "quaddies" live and work in a low-gravity environment under the control of a huge corporation. Leo Graf, with all the individuality and integrity of a good engineer, leads them to freedom by his own example. Reviewing the book for *Washington Post Book World,* Kathryn Cramer criticized Bujold's conception of the quaddies' revolution as simplistic, but she praised the book for its "portrayal of the emotional experience of being an engineer." Remarked Cramer, "The ability to portray scientists and engineers at work has long been one of the strengths of science fiction, now sadly lacking in much contemporary sf."

Bujold continued the story of Miles Vorkosigan in the subsequent novels *Brothers in Arms, Borders of Infinity, The Vor Game, Barrayar, Mirror Dance, Cetaganda, Memory,* and *Komarr.* Hugely popular with fans of the series, the Miles Vorkosigan books were also lauded by critics; *Barrayar* earned Bujold her third Hugo Award, while *Mirror Dance* won both the Locus and Hugo Awards for best novel in 1995. One novel in the series, *Barrayar,* looks back at the events that happened during Cordelia Naismith's pregnancy with Miles. Shortly after Cordelia and Aral Vorkosigan are married, the Emperor of Barrayar dies and the highly-ranked Aral Vorkosigan is appointed regent of the planet. Mary K. Chelton commented in *Voice of Youth Advocates* that "Bujold has a genius for blending technological speculation, the conventions of classic military science fiction, and cultural anthropology" to create "wonderfully plotted stories." Bartter, writing in *Twentieth-Century Science Fiction Writers,* observed that "Bujold doesn't preach; her characters must make hard choices, and pay the price for them." And Faren Miller declared in *Locus* that "in many respects her new book, *Barrayar,* is the best yet," adding, "This is sf fully equipped with brains, humor, and heart."

Bujold's 1994 title, *Mirror Dance,* also won a Hugo Award for science fiction. In this novel, Miles has more in-depth encounters with his clone, Mark. Despite the fact that they are made from the same basic genetic materials, the two are very different. Unbeknownst to Miles, Mark has taken his place as Admiral Naismith, head of a fleet of mercenaries, in order to stage a raid on a cloning facility whose products are scheduled to become brain-transplant hosts. Unfortunately, his lack of experience and his tendencies for introspection are hampering him. When Miles finds out about his plan, the more impulsive "brother" rushes to get in on the action. However, Miles is killed by a stray bullet, put into cryogenic freeze, and then dropped in an anonymous mail chute with little hope of his friends finding his correct shipping address. Mark then is taken to visit Miles's parents to tell them of the news, and finds that they are willing to accept and love him as if he had been born to them. In this book, Mark finally gets a chance to find out who he really is. A critic in *Publishers Weekly* claimed the book is "peopled with introspective but genuine heroes who seize the reader's imagination and intellect." Calling the plot "as good a story as ever was offered as science fiction," *Booklist* reviewer Roland Green asserted that the book "deserves the highest recommendation and a hoard of eager readers." Miller, reviewing the work in *Locus,* observed that *Mirror Dance* is "often darker than anything Bujold has achieved before," but the critic concluded by encouraging readers to "go discover this impressive book for yourself: you're in for some surprises, but I don't think you'll be disappointed."

The 1995 release *Cetaganda* returns once again to the world of Miles Vorkosigan, prior to his death in the last series novel. In this adventure, he calls upon his diplomatic skills in a trip to the planet Cetaganda, where he is to attend the funeral of the empress. In the follow-up to *Mirror Dance,* the 1996 *Memory,* Miles is resurrected and explores all the ramifications, both physical and spiritual, of his near death experience. Though he is not fully recovered, he takes on a mission for the Barrayan secret service, only to be dismissed for covering up an incident. There is no time to sulk, however; he is soon called back from civilian life to help save the empire. A contributor for *Publishers Weekly* noted that the Vorkosigan books "started out as fairly lightweight space opera," but in the process of writing the series Bujold "has matured as a writer."

In *Komarr,* Miles Vorkosigan, forced to give up his military career and become an Imperial Auditor, investigates a space accident at the planet Komarr, which is occupied by the Barrayar and is the front line of defense against the enemy Cetagandians. Miles soon uncovers plots within plots in the process of his investigations, as he finds the band of terrorists who are responsible for the accident. Miles also discovers a possible love interest in Ekaterin. *Booklist*'s Green called this novel another "fine effort from one of sf's outstanding talents." Paula Lewis, writing in *Voice of Youth Advocates,* similarly wrote that "Bujold retains the wit, intelligence, action, and great character development that have made the Miles Vorkosigan series so superior."

Bujold's sequel to *Komarr* was the 1999 novel *A Civil Campaign: A Comedy of Biology and Manners.* In this outing, Miles pursues his love for Ekaterin. One big stumbling block, however, is the fact that he is partially responsible for the death of her husband. Critics continued to respond positively to the series. A *Publishers Weekly* reviewer concluded: "Bujold successfully mixes quirky humor with just enough action, a dab of feminist social commentary and her usual superb character development." And Carolyn Cushman, writing in *Locus,* called this tale "a romantic romp" in which "Miles learns that the only way to win at love is to surrender." The series continues with the 2002 publication of *Diplomatic Immunity.*

In addition to her highly successful series about Miles Vorkosigan, Bujold has also penned two well-received

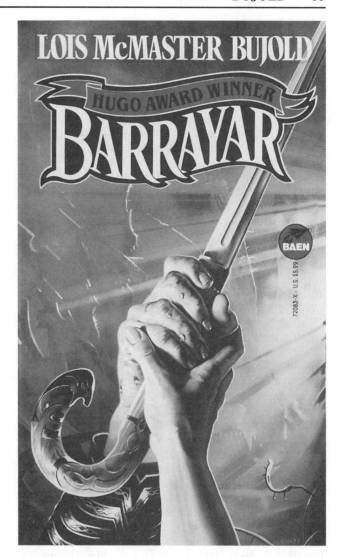

Lady Vorkosigan, pregnant with her son, takes action when a palace coup threatens the life of her family in this work, part of the "Miles Vorkosigan" series. (Cover illustration by Stephen Hickman.)

fantasy novels, *The Spirit Ring* and *The Curse of Chalion.* In the first fantasy, Bujold travels to Renaissance Italy, which in this novel is changed into a fantasy world. The novel focuses on Fiametta Beneforte, the teenage daughter of the powerful magician Prospero. Fiametta begs her father to teach her his magical talents, but he refuses because of her gender. Then their duchy is invaded and the Duke killed, and as Fiametta and her father flee, he drops dead from cardiac arrest. His body is taken back to the occupied castle to be used in an act of unspeakable black magic that will bind his soul. With the help of Thur Ochs, a man who fits Fiametta's true-love ring perfectly, they overtake the castle's invaders and free her father's spirit. Although peopled with ghosts and demons, *The Spirit Ring* "is solidly grounded in human psychology and the ways of the real world," Miller claimed in *Locus.* Susan Rice wrote in *Voice of Youth Advocates* that Bujold had made the transfer from science fiction to fantasy quite readily, claiming that "with this new setting and characters, Bujold is the best yet," and concluding to the reader: "Don't miss this one, it's a keeper."

The Curse of Chalion presents a political fantasy in which the former soldier Cazaril is betrayed and sold into slavery. Managing to escape years later, he returns to Chalion, the homeland which he once served so faithfully. Once back, he takes the menial job of secretary to a young noblewoman, sister to the heir to the throne. Things begin to heat up for Cazaril when he is caught in a web of political intrigue as well as black magic and forced to fight a curse that threatens the royal house. "Science fiction's loss is fantasy's gain," wrote Don D'Ammassa in *Science Fiction Chronicle*. Noting that Bujold always delivers at least a good story, D'Ammassa concluded, "This is one of the great ones." Paul Brink, writing in *School Library Journal*, also commended this fantasy novel, calling it a "finely balanced mixture of adventure, swordplay, court intrigue, romance, magic, and religion." *The Curse of Chalion* went on to win the 2002 Mythopoeic Award for Adult Literature.

Bujold has long been cited for her exceptional character development. Mary K. Chelton observed in *Voice of Youth Advocates* that Bujold's "characters are so vivid and easily beloved that they master the plot and the reader simultaneously. It is an honor to have read her work, and a debt of honor repaid to encourage others to introduce her to kids." Bujold remarked in *Twentieth-Century Science Fiction Writers* that character development is one of her main considerations: "I try to write the kind of book I most like to read: character-centered adventure." Chelton concluded that Bujold's "people wear their civilization on the inside. And can she write about it! But then, science fiction has always been about that. Bujold just does it better than almost anybody else."

Biographical and Critical Sources

BOOKS

Authors and Artists for Young Adults, Volume 19, Gale (Detroit, MI), 1997.

Bishop, Michael, editor, *Nebula Awards 24: SFWA'S Choices for the Best Science Fiction and Fantasy,* Harcourt (New York, NY), 1990.

Encyclopedia of Science Fiction, edited by John Clute and Peter Nicholls, St. Martin's Press (New York, NY), 1993.

St. James Guide to Science Fiction Writers, 4th edition, St. James Press (Detroit, MI), 1996.

Twentieth-Century Science Fiction Writers, 3rd edition, St. James Press (Detroit, MI), 1991.

PERIODICALS

Analog Science Fiction/Science Fact, January, 1987, Tom Easton, review of *Shards of Honor,* pp. 179-180.

Booklist, February 1, 1987, Roland Green, review of *Ethan of Athos,* p. 822; March 1, 1988, Roland Green, review of *Falling Free,* p. 1098; December 1, 1988, Roland Green, review of *Brothers in Arms,* p. 618; September 1, 1992, Roland Green, review of *The Spirit Ring,* pp. 37-38; January 1, 1994, Roland Green, review of *Mirror Dance,* p. 811; November 15, 1995, Roland Green, review of *Cetaganda,* pp. 538, 541; September 1, 1996, Roland Green, review of *Memory,* p. 69; May 15, 1998, Roland Green, review of *Komarr,* p. 1600; May 15, 1999, Ray Olson, "Top 10 SF/Fantasy," p. 1678; September 1, 1999, Roland Green, review of *A Civil Campaign,* p. 75; May 1, 2001, Roland Green, review of *The Curse of Chalion,* p. 1672.

Book Watch, April, 1996, p. 2.

Chicago Sun-Times, October, 1991; November, 1992.

Extrapolation, fall, 1996, Anne L. Haehl, "Miles Vorkosigan and the Power of Words: A Study of Lois McMaster Bujold's Unlikely Hero," pp. 224-233; winter, 1996, Donald M. Hassler, review of *Dreamweaver's Dilemma,* pp. 370-371.

Fantasy Review, October, 1986, Martha A. Bartter, review of *The Warrior's Apprentice,* p. 20.

Kirkus Reviews, January 1, 1994, p. 23; October 1, 1995, p. 138; August 1, 1999, review of *A Civil Campaign,* p. 1182.

Kliatt, January, 1994, p. 14; November, 1996, p. 40; July, 1997, p. 51; January, 1998, p. 40; September, 1999, review of the audio version of *Vor Game,* p. 61.

Library Journal, December, 1995, Jackie Cassada, review of *Cetaganda,* pp. 163-164; September 15, 1996, p. 114; April 15, 1997, p. 138; December, 1997, Kristen L. Smith, review of the audio version of *Barrayar,* p. 173; September 15, 1999, Jackie Cassada, review of *A Civil Campaign,* p. 115; April 1, 2000, Dean James, review of *A Civil Campaign,* p. 160; July, 2001, Jackie Cassada, review of *The Curse of Chalion,* p. 131.

Locus, September, 1991, Faren Miller, review of *Barrayar,* pp. 15, 17; August, 1992, Faren Miller, review of *The Spirit Ring,* pp. 17, 55-56; January, 1994, Faren Miller, review of *Mirror Dance,* p. 15; October, 1999, Carolyn Cushman, review of *A Civil Campaign,* p. 27.

Publishers Weekly, August 31, 1992, review of *The Spirit Ring,* pp. 67-68; January 3, 1994, review of *Mirror Dance,* p. 76; October 30, 1995, p. 48; December 11, 1995, review of *Cetaganda,* p. 61; September 23, 1996, review of *Memory,* p. 60; April 27, 1998, review of *Komarr,* p. 49; August 23, 1999, review of *A Civil Campaign,* p. 52; December 3, 2001, review of *Miles, Mystery and Mayhem,* p. 46.

School Library Journal, October, 2001, Paul Brink, review of *The Curse of Chalion,* p. 194.

Science Fiction Chronicle, February, 1996, p. 44; May, 1996, p. 61; October, 1996; May, 2001, Dan D'Ammassa, review of *The Curse of Chalion,* p. 40.

Sol Rising, May, 1991.

Starlog, May, 1990.

Voice of Youth Advocates, December, 1986, Margrett J. McFadden, review of *Shards of Honor,* p. 233; February, 1987, Eleanor Klopp, review of *The Warrior's Apprentice,* p. 290; February, 1991, Judy Kowalski, review of *The Vor Game,* p. 361; December, 1991, Mary K. Chelton, "A Debt of Honor Repaid: The Science Fiction Novels of Lois McMaster Bujold—'My Word On It'," pp. 295-297; February, 1992, Mary K. Chelton, review of *Barrayar,* pp. 378-379; April, 1993, Susan Rice, review of *Spirit Ring,* p. 36; June,

1996, Kim Carter, review of *Cetaganda,* pp. 106-107; June, 1996, Vicky Burkholder, review of *Women at War,* p. 112; October, 1998, Paula Lewis, review of *Komarr,* p. 282.

Washington Post Book World, July 30, 1989, Kathryn Cramer, review of *Falling Free.*

Writer's Digest, July, 1994, Bart Kemper, "Dancing on the Edge," pp. 6-7.

OTHER

The Bujold Nexus, http://www.dendarii.com (November 3, 2002).

*   *   *

BUNKERS, Suzanne L. 1950-

Personal

Born April 20, 1950, in Le Mars, IA; daughter of Jerome A. (a rural letter carrier) and Verna (a homemaker; maiden name, Klein) Bunkers; children: Rachel Susanna. *Nationality:* American. *Education:* Iowa State University, B.S., 1972, M.A., 1974; University of Wisconsin-Madison, Ph.D., 1980. *Politics:* Democrat. *Hobbies and other interests:* Travel, Luxembourg history, genealogy, immigration history, Holocaust studies.

Addresses

Home—317 Carroll St., Mankato, MN 56001. *Office*—Department of English, Minnesota State University, Mankato, MN 56001. *E-mail*—suzanne.bunkers@ mnsuedu.

Career

Minnesota State University, Mankato, MN, assistant professor, 1980-84, associate professor, 1984-89, professor of English, 1989—. Manuscript reviewer for mass market and university presses, 1982—; host of "The Weekly Reader" program on KMSU-Radio, 1990—; consultant for the Capstone Press series "Diaries, Letters, and Memoirs," 1996-2001. Girl Scouts, troop leader, 1994-97.

Member

American Council of Learned Society Fellows, Fulbright Commission Fellows, Modern Language Association of America, Midwest Modern Language Association, Women's Caucus for the Modern Languages, Minnesota Historical Society, Phi Kappa Phi Honor Society, Luxembourg Society of America, Midwest Center for Holocaust Education.

Awards, Honors

National Endowment for the Humanities fellowship, 1986-87; Fulbright senior research fellowship, 1987-88; Bush Foundation fellowship, 1995; Jerome Foundation fellowship, 1996; Minnesota Historical Society research fellowship, 1997-98; Norcroft Writing Retreat fellow-

Suzanne L. Bunkers

ship, 2002; Minnesota State University teaching fellow, 2002.

Writings

(With Frank W. Klein) *Good Earth, Black Soil,* St. Mary's College Press (Winona, MN), 1981.

(Editor) *The Diary of Caroline Seabury, 1854-1863,* University of Wisconsin Press (Madison, WI), 1991.

(Editor) *"All Will Yet Be Well": The Diary of Sarah Gillespie Huftalen,* University of Iowa Press (Iowa City, IA), 1993.

(Editor, with Cynthia A. Huff) *Inscribing the Daily: Critical Essays on Women's Diaries,* University of Massachusetts Press (Amherst, MA), 1996.

In Search of Susanna (autobiography), University of Iowa Press (Iowa City, IA), 1996.

(Editor and author of foreword, with Ann Hodgson) *A Pioneer Farm Girl: The Diary of Sarah Gillespie, 1877-1878,* Blue Earth Books (Mankato, MN), 2000.

(Editor) *Diaries of Girls and Women: A Midwestern American Sampler,* University of Wisconsin Press (Madison, WI), 2001.

Contributor to anthologies, including *The Intimate Critique: Autobiographical Literary Criticism,* edited by Olivia Frey, Frances Zauhar, and Diane Freedman, Duke University Press, 1993; *Communication and Women's Friendships: Parallels and Intersections in Literature and Life,* edited by JoAnna S. Mink and Janet D. Ward, Bowling Green State University Popular Press, 1993; *American Women Humorists: Critical Essays,* edited by Linda A. Morris, Garland, 1994; and *Nineteenth-Century American Women and Literacy,* edited by Catherine Hobbs, University Press of Virginia, 1995. Contributor to periodicals, including *a/b: Autobiography Studies, Legacy, Minnesota English Journal, The Lion and the Unicorn, Plainswoman,* and *Iowa Woman.*

Work in Progress

"Researching immigration history, Midwestern American women's diaries, and the theory of autobiography. At present I'm also working on a sequel to *In Search of Susanna*. This memoir will take readers (and myself) further back into the past as well as bring readers up into the present."

Sidelights

Suzanne L. Bunkers is a professor of English and the author and editor of several books of memory—both personal history as well as diary reminiscences of women and young girls. Working primarily in the field of autobiography, memoir, and diaries, she blends an interest in women's studies, Midwestern-American history, and immigration history with her literary pursuits. As an editor, Bunker prepared the late-nineteenth-century diary of a young farm girl for publication as *A Pioneer Farm Girl: The Diary of Sarah Gillespie, 1877-1878,* a book for middle-grade readers. Several years before this publication, Bunkers also edited Gillespie's

Bunkers and Cynthia A. Huff examine women's diaries written in America and Europe during the past two centuries. (Cover photo by Stan Sherer.)

entire diary, *"All Will Yet Be Well": The Diary of Sarah Gillespie Huftalen,* kept until a few years before that woman's death at age eighty-nine. Adult readers might also be interested in Bunker's memoir, *In Search of Susanna,* about several generations of women in her own family, and in particular her great-great-grandmother. Also, her *Diaries of Girls and Women: A Midwestern American Sampler* provides extensive samplings from several dozen diaries of girls and women from 1837 to 1999. And in her *Diary of Caroline Seabury, 1854-1863,* Bunkers presents the story of a young woman making her way in the world during the Civil War.

A native Midwesterner, Bunkers was born in Le Mars, Iowa, in 1950, and attended Iowa State University and the University of Wisconsin—Madison, where she earned her doctorate in 1980. Since that time, she has taught at Minnesota State University, acting as director of the honors program from 1999-2002, teaching creative writing and literature in the English department, and hosting a weekly radio program on the university's public radio station.

Her first major publication was the 1991 *The Diary of Caroline Seabury, 1854-1863,* which she edited from the original diary kept by this woman from ages twenty-seven to thirty-six. Hired as a teacher of French, Seabury left her home in New York to go to her new posting in Mississippi; she remained in the South until after the Civil War began. Joined by her sister in Mississippi, Seabury wanted her journal to become the joint record of two teachers in what was for them a new and sometimes foreign land. In the diary the reader finds an initial naivete about the institution of slavery, but her writing became more and more informed and condemning the longer Seabury was in the South. Her sister died of tuberculosis not long after joining her, and then in 1862 Seabury lost her teaching job and had to make her way North again to New York through enemy lines. A reviewer for *Publishers Weekly* called the diary an "illuminating memoir" and "an eloquent historical record."

"Because I write scholarly and popular works, there is not one over-arching motivation for my work nor one expression of my work," Bunkers once commented to *SATA*. "As a teacher and scholar, I have been inspired by the works of authors whom I've read and taught in classes over the past twenty-five years. As a writer, I have been especially interested in the interaction of memory and imagination as it manifests itself in such forms as memoir, essay, diary, and historical fiction."

Bunker further added: "As a writer of creative nonfiction, I believe that I have a responsibility to work in good faith as I strive to bring past events and individuals into the present through the interaction of my memory and imagination. Doing so means waiting to write until I have talked with others and, even more importantly, listened to their stories and examined how their memories are interwoven with my own. As I fashion creative nonfiction, I interweave diary entries, excerpts from letters, newspaper clippings, photographs, oral histories, and family stories to lay out patterns of dailiness. My hope is that, by doing so, I can make more visible the lives of women and men within the context of families, generations, and cultures."

In *"All Will Yet Be Well,"* Bunkers presents about a fifth of the total diaries of Sarah Gillespie Huftalen, who lived from 1865 to 1955. Early entries record life on her Iowa farm when Sarah was a child along with the usual problems of childhood, and some unusual ones, as well. Her father, prone to depression, was abusive to her and cruel to the rest of the family. Later on, Sarah taught in rural schools, but she was torn between her work and her need to care for her ailing mother. An early suffragist, Sarah went on to serve as superintendent of schools, earn a master's degree, teach at Upper Iowa University, and have a happy marriage for twenty-two years. However, late in life, her duty drew her back to the Iowa farm to care for her unmarried brother, a man as verbally abusive as her father had been.

Bunkers reworked part of this material for her year 2000 editing of *A Pioneer Farm Girl: The Diary of Sarah Gillespie, 1877-1878.* Focusing on just two years in the life of young Sarah, the book includes excerpts from the diaries, sidebars, activities, and a time line of the era, along with full-color photographs. Part of the Capstone Press series of "Diaries, Letters, and Memoirs," the book is geared for young readers. *School Library Journal*'s Carolyn Janssen noted that the book provides "personal glimpses into our history" and introduces "young readers to primary sources in historical context."

"I like to call my creative process 'making a word quilt,'" Bunkers explained to *SATA.* "As I plan and write, I gather and select stories, cut and shape them, lay them out in various ways to create the narrative's pattern, then stitch them into the finished quilt. Stories from my life as a daughter and mother as well as from my work as a teacher and writer make up some of the pieces stitched into this word quilt. So do excerpts from the diaries I have kept since I was ten, as well as information gleaned from the study of religious and cultural artifacts and records. My creative nonfiction is not the result of objective, scientific study. It is intensely personal. It reflects my thoughts and feelings about myself and others. While my stories include imaginative detail, they are as true as I can make them, given that my interpretations of people and events bear the unmistakable marks of my own experience and personality." This working process can best be seen in Bunkers's 1996 book, *In Search of Susanna,* in which she draws on family records, memories, and her own research in the United States and in Europe to tell the story of her great-great-grandmother, Susanna. In doing so, Bunkers sheds new light on her own life and her relationship with her daughter, Rachel Susanna, whom she is raising as a single mother.

In *Diaries of Girls and Women,* Bunkers returns to her role as editor, providing extensive excerpts from forty-six girls' and women's previously unpublished diaries, spanning almost two centuries of Midwest history. A

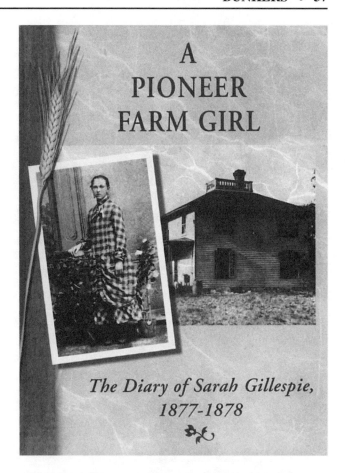

In this work, Bunkers and Ann Hodgson include diary excerpts, sidebars, activities, and a timeline of a girl's life in nineteenth-century Iowa. (Cover photos from the State Historical Society of Iowa.)

fascinating index and guide to the times, this "remarkable collection" offers "compelling and interesting voices," according to Karen L. Kilcup, writing in *Biography.*

Bunkers concluded to *SATA,* "In her essay '"Noon Wine": The Sources,' Katherine Anne Porter explains that a writer's imagination 'works and reworks its recollections in a constant search for meanings' and that it is the 'endless remembering which surely must be the main occupation of the writer' as he or she works to blend memory with imagination to craft stories. This is what I hope to do in the creative nonfiction that I write."

Biographical and Critical Sources

PERIODICALS

Belles Lettres, winter, 1992, Virginia Walcott, review of *The Diary of Caroline Seabury,* pp. 13-14.
Biography, fall, 2001, Karen L. Kilcup, review of *Diaries of Girls and Women: A Midwestern American Sampler,* pp. 959-964.
Georgia Review, spring, 1997, Jeanne Braham, review of *In Search of Susanna,* pp. 155-160.

Journal of Southern History, November, 1993, Cynthia A. Kierner, review of *The Diary of Caroline Seabury,* pp. 761-762.

Journal of Women's History, winter, 1999, Sarah M. Liros, review of *Inscribing the Daily: Critical Essays on Women's Diaries,* p. 220.

Library Journal, January, 1995, Patricia A. Beaber, review of *"All Will Yet Be Well": The Diary of Sarah Gillespie Huftalen,* p. 130.

Mississippi Quarterly, winter, 1991, Bridget Smith Pieschel, review of *The Diary of Caroline Seabury,* pp. 97-104.

Publishers Weekly, March 29, 1991, review of *The Diary of Caroline Seabury,* p. 86.

School Library Journal, September, 2000, Carolyn Janssen, review of *A Pioneer Farm Girl: The Diary of Sarah Gillespie, 1877-1878,* p. 246.

Signs, spring, 2001, Elaine Neil Orr, review of *Inscribing the Daily,* p. 892.

Western Historical Quarterly, summer, 1995, Susan Sessions Rugh, review of *"All Will Yet Be Well,"* pp. 231-232.

Women's Review of Books, July, 1996, Rebecca Steinitz, review of *Inscribing the Daily,* pp. 41-42.

OTHER

Suzanne L. Bunkers Web Site, http://krypton.mnsu.edu/ ~susanna (April 8, 2002).

C

CASANOVA, Mary 1957-

Personal

Born February 2, 1957, in Duluth, MN; daughter of Eugene (a business manager) and Joyce (a homemaker; maiden name, Anderson) Gazelka; married Charles Casanova (an insurance agent), July 1, 1978; children: Katie, Eric. *Nationality:* American. *Education:* University of Minnesota, B.A., 1981. *Religion:* "Judeo-Christian/ Lutheran." *Hobbies and other interests:* Reading, writing, cross-country and downhill skiing, camping, canoeing, hiking, running, horseback riding, and playing the piano.

Addresses

Home—P.O. Box 141, Ranier, MN 56668. *Agent*—Andrea Cascardi, Transatlantic Literary Agency, Inc., P.O. Box 349, Rockville Centre, NY 11571. *E-mail*—Mary@MaryCasanova.com.

Career

Author, speaker, visiting author, writing workshop instructor. Keynote speaker at state reading associations, young author conferences, and literary festivals; visiting author to elementary and middle schools; speaker at writing conferences, including Society of Children's Book Writers and Illustrators, Paris, France, 2002; presenter at American Library Association, International Reading Association, National Council of Teachers of English, and National Council of Teachers of Social Studies.

Member

Society of Children's Book Writers and Illustrators, Children's Literature Network, Loft Literary Center, International Reading Association.

Mary Casanova

Awards, Honors

Emily Johnson Award, Children's Literature Conference, 1990, for "Father's Boots"; Career Development Grant, Minnesota State Arts Board, 1992; Career Opportunity Grants, Arrowhead Regional Arts Council, 1992-94; Fellowship in Literature, Arrowhead Regional Arts Council/McKnight Foundation, 1995; Children's Book of the Month, 1995, Flicker Tale Children's Book Award, North Dakota Library Association, 1997, Iowa Readers' Choice Book Award, 1998, and Indian Paintbrush Book Award, 1998, all for *Moose Tracks;* Quick Picks for Reluctant YA Readers citation, American

Marius must save the life of his brother, believed to be marked with the curse of the werewolf, from villagers intent upon destroying enemies of the Church in sixteenth-century France. (Cover illustration by Cliff Nielsen.)

Library Association (ALA), Oklahoma Children's Crown Award list, Junior Library Guild selection, and Sequoyah Book Award list, all for *Riot;* Wyoming Indian Paintbrush Book Award list, 1999-2000, Indiana Best-Read Alouds Booklist, 1999-2000, Iowa Children's Choice Award list, 2000-2001, Lamplighter Award list, 2000-2001, and Missouri Mark Twain Book Award list, all for *Wolf Shadows;* Top 100 Books for 2000 citation, New York Public Library, Notable Children's Book citation, ALA, Minnesota Book Award, 2001, Gold Award, Parent's Choice, Editor's Choice, *Booklist,* Pick of the List, American Bookseller's Association, Aesop Accolade, American Folktale Society, and Blue Ribbon List, *Bulletin of the Center for Children's Books,* all for *The Hunter;* Minnesota Book Award, 2001, for *Curse of a Winter Moon;* Iowa Children's Choice Award, 2002-2003, for *Stealing Thunder.*

Writings

The Golden Retriever (nonfiction), Crestwood House/Macmillan (New York, NY), 1990.

Moose Tracks (middle-grade novel), Hyperion (New York, NY), 1995.

Riot (middle-grade novel), Hyperion (New York, NY), 1996.

Wolf Shadows (middle-grade novel; sequel to *Moose Tracks*), Hyperion (New York, NY), 1997.

Stealing Thunder (middle-grade novel), Hyperion (New York, NY), 1999.

Curse of a Winter Moon (middle-grade novel), Hyperion (New York, NY), 2000.

(Reteller) *The Hunter: A Chinese Folktale* (picture book), illustrated by Ed Young, Atheneum (New York, NY), 2000.

When Eagles Fall (middle-grade novel), Hyperion (New York, NY), 2002.

Cécile: Gates of Gold, illustrated by Jean-Paul Tibbles, Pleasant (Middleton, WI), 2002.

One Dog Canoe (picture book), illustrated by Ard Hoyt, Farrar, Straus & Giroux (New York, NY), 2003.

Sidelights

Author of a number of award-winning titles for middle grade readers, Mary Casanova blends a love for the outdoors with insightful and dramatic coming-of-age stories that pull no punches. Her *Moose Tracks* and its sequel, *Wolf Shadows,* deal with issues of wildlife preservation, while *Stealing Thunder* is a heroic story about animal cruelty and saving a horse. With *Curse of a Winter Moon,* the versatile Casanova takes readers back to seventeenth-century France, and in her 2002 novel *When Eagles Fall* the author returns to the wilderness of northern Minnesota, where she makes her home, to tell a tale of family break up and one girl's ability to cope. Casanova has also written two picture books, *The Hunter* and *One Dog Canoe.*

Mary Casanova told *SATA:* "When I set out to write for children, I had two main goals: to write books that kids couldn't put down and to write books that matter. Coming from a family of ten children—seven boys and three girls—I was always active: riding horses, playing tag off the pontoon boat in the summer and ice-hockey with our own 'team' in the winter. I was also a reluctant reader. I loved being outside, and if a book was going to hold my attention it had to be a fast-paced story. *Moose Tracks,* my first novel, hooks the kind of reader I was."

The protagonist of *Moose Tracks* is twelve-year-old Seth, who tries to save a wounded moose calf from poachers. The book opens with Seth out hunting with his stepfather's shotgun but without his permission. He shoots a rabbit and takes its foot as a good luck charm. However, the boy is soon tormented by his action, partly because his stepfather is the local game warden, and partly because he feels guilty himself. When he later sees a couple of poachers killing a cow moose, he is warned by them not to tell his stepfather, but Seth fixates on the poachers and determines to save the injured moose calf that they have orphaned. With his friend Matt, Seth is soon in deep danger, trapped in an abandoned mine by the poachers, but finally he is able both to save the calf and to catch the poachers.

Critical reception for this first novel was generally positive. Marilyn Courtot, writing in *Meet Authors and Illustrators,* noted that the book "moves at a good pace and it should keep middle readers turning the pages." Similarly, a contributor for *Kirkus Reviews* wrote that "the attention-grabbing action and emotional struggles of the hero will hook reluctant readers." *School Library Journal* reviewer Todd Morning said that "Casanova's precise and evocative descriptions" add depth to the adventure story that culminates when Seth orchestrates the capture of poachers and confesses to his own misdeed. Reviewing this debut novel in *Publishers Weekly,* a critic noted that Casanova "earnestly conveys the ugliness of killing animals for financial gain."

Casanova continued to *SATA:* "I love to throw my character in the midst of issues, issues I can't quite get my arms around. *Riot* is that kind of story. After living through a two-year labor dispute that erupted into violence in my small northern town in 1989, I knew I'd have to write about it and somehow make sense of it. The result is the fictionalized account of a riot through twelve-year-old Bryan Grant's eyes; his father is increasingly involved in the fervor, protesting the work he doesn't get at the paper mill. Bryan's mother, on the other hand, is a union member and teacher who desires a peaceable solution to the dispute." Critical response to this book was also positive. "Casanova has created an exciting, realistic novel," Cheryl Cufari commented in a *School Library Journal* review of *Riot.* Although Elizabeth Bush complained in a review in *Bulletin of the Center for Children's Books* that "good guy/bad guy treatment of the labor action grossly oversimplifies the issues," Lauren Peterson concluded in a review in *Booklist* that "this fast-paced story poses challenging questions that have no easy answers."

With her third novel, *Wolf Shadows,* Casanova created a sequel to *Moose Tracks.* Set just a week after the end of that first novel, the second installment finds Seth's life still complicated by the impending birth of a first child to his mother and stepfather. Added to this, his friend Matt turns against a wolf protection program in light of the fact that it appears wolves have been killing his family's livestock. Further complications come from the orphaned moose calf; Seth knows he should release the animal soon, but he is fearful of doing so as the first day of deer hunting season approaches. That day, Seth's mother goes into labor with the new baby, and Seth joins Matt for the opening of the season. But when Matt illegally shoots a wolf, this causes a nearly insurmountable rift in his longtime friendship with Seth, who vehemently opposes poaching. *Booklist*'s Chris Sherman once again had praise for Casanova, noting that she "offers a well reasoned argument for wolf protection in this tense, fast-paced story."

In her fourth novel, Casanova presents a female protagonist in this tale of a girl who desperately wants to save an Appaloosa horse from danger. A novel inspired by the author's own love of horses, *Stealing Thunder* features young Libby, who has always longed for her own horse. Her neighbor, Jolene Porter, has let Libby take care of her horse, Thunder. Though the animal was skittish at first around Lilly, the two have become close. Suddenly, Jolene Porter leaves her husband, and Libby is cut off from her favorite horse. Her family cannot afford to buy the horse from Mr. Porter, but when Libby discovers that he is mistreating Thunder, perhaps in hopes of cashing in on the insurance on him, she determines to save the horse. Libby and her friend Griff, whom she has enlisted into the cause, soon find themselves over their heads in trouble in this "fast-paced adventure," filled with "precise and evocative" descriptions, as Janet Gillen described the novel in *School Library Journal.* Gillen further commented that both Libby and Griff are "personable characters" in this "compelling story of intrigue and heroism."

Casanova's next work, *The Hunter,* was a change of pace. In this picture book retelling of a Chinese folktale, Hai Li Bu learns to understand the language of animals and becomes a more effective hunter. However, in a time of scarce game, he must sacrifice himself in order to save the lives of his villagers. "The tale of his sacrifice is well told in measured, poetic prose, unified by repeating word patterns," wrote *School Library Journal*'s Margaret A. Chang, who concluded that this is a "handsome addition to any folktale collection." David Russell, writing in *Five Owls,* commented that the "union of a moving and simply told tale and subtly evocative illustrations make this an especially beautiful picture book—one that deserves to be treasured."

With *Curse of a Winter Moon,* Casanova returns to the novel length story, but departs from her usual nature terrain to tell a tale of sixteenth-century France. Young Marius must put off his own apprenticeship in order to take care of his six-year-old brother, Jean-Pierre. The birth of this younger brother on Christmas Eve took their mother's life and has convinced superstitious villagers that the younger boy is a werewolf. Their misguided belief is reinforced by the Church, which overtaxes the peasants and burns heretics. Soon Marius finds his world turned upside down when his father is arrested as a heretic and his brother is taken into custody. While a *Publishers Weekly* reviewer felt that *Curse of a Winter Moon* had "flat characters," other critics had praise for it. Barbara Scotto, writing in *School Library Journal,* called the book a "solid look at a period not often written about in novels for this age group," while *Booklist*'s Ilene Cooper noted that Marius "comes across as a real boy in extraordinary circumstances."

In her next middle-grade novel, *When Eagles Fall,* Casanova brings thirteen-year-old Alex Castille-Reid, who has gotten into trouble in San Jose, to the wilderness of northern Minnesota. There she joins her father, an eagle researcher, while he conducts field work. Trying to prove herself, she steals off to remove a lure from an eagle's nest and ends up stranded in bad weather with an injured eaglet. "Casanova has written an eco-adventure story that also provides valuable information about eagle research," claimed *School Library Journal* contributor Doris Losey. Describing the book as "a good choice for reluctant readers, *Booklist*'s Jean

Franklin found *When Eagles Fall* "an obviously well-researched survival novel with lots of local color and a teenage heroine who turns out to have plenty of grit."

As part of the debut series "Girls of Many Lands," Casanova returned to France to research a second novel, *Cécile: Gates of Gold.* The story follows the life of twelve-year-old Cécile Revel, a servant at the court of King Louis XIV in 1711, who finds following royal protocol a challenging task. Writing in *School Library Journal,* reviewer Kristen Oravec claimed the book's "action builds steadily and will sustain readers' interest."

"If it's true that writers should 'write to express, not to impress,' then nowhere is this more important than in writing for children," Casanova noted on her Web site. "They are the toughest critics, demanding first and foremost a good story. It's the writer's responsibility to write honestly, from the heart, and to give something of lasting value to the reader. Every writer offers a unique gift; if expressed clearly enough, true enough, it is a gift of story that a young reader will remember for a long time."

Biographical and Critical Sources

PERIODICALS

Booklist, July, 1995, Chris Sherman, review of *Moose Tracks,* p. 1878; November 1, 1996, Lauren Peterson, review of *Riot,* p. 497; October 1, 1997, Chris Sherman, review of *Wolf Shadows,* p. 328; October 15, 2000, Ilene Cooper, review of *Curse of a Winter Moon,* p. 437; June 1, 2002, Jean Franklin, review of *When Eagles Fall,* p. 1704.
Bulletin of the Center for Children's Books, January, 1997, Elizabeth Bush, review of *Riot,* p. 165.
Five Owls, March-April, 2001, David Russell, review of *The Hunter,* p. 90.
Horn Book Guide, spring, 1998, Peter D. Sieruta, review of *Wolf Shadows,* p. 69; fall, 1999, Carolyn Shute, review of *Stealing Thunder,* p. 289; spring, 2001, Peter D. Sieruta, review of *Curse of a Winter Moon,* p. 70.
Kirkus Reviews, May 15, 1995, review of *Moose Tracks,* p. 708.
Los Angeles Times, November 24, 1996.
Pioneer (Bemidji, MN), May 14, 1997, p. 6.
Publishers Weekly, June 19, 1995, review of *Moose Tracks,* p. 60; August 21, 2000, review of *Curse of a Winter Moon,* p. 74.
School Library Journal, June, 1995, Todd Morning, review of *Moose Tracks,* p. 108; October, 1996, Cheryl Cufari, review of *Riot,* p. 120; October, 1997, Claudia Morrow, review of *Wolf Shadows,* p. 131; October, 1999, Janet Gillen, review of *Stealing Thunder,* p. 148; August, 2000, Margaret A. Chang, review of *The Hunter,* p. 168; October, 2000, Barbara Scotto, review of *Curse of a Winter Moon,* p. 156; July, 2002, Doris Losey, review of *When Eagles Fall,* p. 114; September, 2002, Kristen Oravec, review of *Cécile: Gates of Gold,* p. 220.
Star Tribune (Minneapolis, MN), October 22, 1995, p. F13.

OTHER

Mary Casanova, Children's Book Author, http://www.marycasanova.com (April 9, 2002).
Meet Authors and Illustrators, http://www.childrenslit.com/ (April 9, 2002), Marilyn Courtot, review of *Moose Tracks.*

* * *

CLINTON, Cathryn
See HOELLWARTH, Cathryn Clinton

* * *

COBB, Vicki 1938-

Personal

Born August 19, 1938, in Brooklyn, NY; daughter of Benjamin Harold (a labor arbitrator) and Paula (Davis) Wolf; married Edward Scribner Cobb (a psychology professor), January 31, 1960 (divorced 1975); married Richard Trachtenberg (a financial executive), 1996; children: (first marriage) Theodore Davis, Joshua Monroe. *Education:* Attended University of Wisconsin, 1954-57; Barnard College, B.A. (zoology), 1958; Columbia University Teachers College, M.A. (secondary school science education), 1960.

Addresses

Agent—Susan Schulman, A Literary Agency, 2 Bryan Plaza, Washington Depot, CT 06794.

Career

Writer and lecturer. Sloan-Kettering Institute and Pfizer & Company, Rye, NY, scientific researcher, 1953-61; high school science teacher, Rye, NY, 1962-64; Tele-prompter Corp., New York, NY, hostess and principal writer of television series *The Science Game,* beginning 1972; American Broadcasting Company, New York, NY, writer for *Good Morning America,* 1976; Scott Publishing Company, public relations director, 1978-83; Pinwheel Publishers, vice president.

Member

Authors Guild, Authors League of America, Society of Children's Book Writers, PEN, American Society of Journalists and Authors.

Awards, Honors

Cable television award for best educational series, 1973, for *The Science Game;* Outstanding Science Trade Books for Children Award, Children's Book Council-NSTA, 1975, for *Supersuits,* 1980, for *Bet You Can't!: Science Impossibilities to Fool You,* 1981, for *Lots of Rot,* and 1982, for *The Secret Life of Hardware;* Book of the Year Award, Child Study Children's Book Committee, 1979, for *Truth on Trial: The Story of Galileo Galilei;* Children's Book Selections, Library of Congress, 1979, for *More Science Experiments You Can Eat,* 1981, for *How to Really Fool Yourself: Illusions for All Your Senses,* and 1983, for *The Monsters Who Died: A Mystery About Dinosaurs;* Children's Choice Selection, International Reading Association-Children's Book Council, 1980, for *More Science Experiments You Can Eat;* Children's Science Book Award, New York Academy of Sciences, 1981, for *Bet You Can't!;* Notable Book Citation, American Library Association, 1982, for *How to Really Fool Yourself;* Washington Irving Children's Book Choice Award for nonfiction, Westchester Library Association, 1984, for *The Secret Life of School Supplies;* Eva L. Gordon Award, American Nature Study Society, 1985; Parents' Choice Award; American Book Association "pick of the list" citation; SLMSSE-NY Award for Outstanding Contributions to Children's Literature.

Writings

FOR CHILDREN; NONFICTION

Science Experiments You Can Eat, illustrated by Peter Lippman, Lippincott (Philadelphia, PA), 1972, revised and updated edition, illustrated by David Cain, HarperCollins (New York, NY), 1994.

How the Doctor Knows You're Fine, illustrated by Anthony Ravielli, Lippincott (Philadelphia, PA), 1973.

Arts and Crafts You Can Eat, illustrated by Peter Lippman, Lippincott (Philadelphia, PA), 1974.

Supersuits, illustrated by Peter Lippman, Lippincott (Philadelphia, PA), 1975.

More Science Experiments You Can Eat, illustrated by Giulio Maestro, Lippincott (Philadelphia, PA), 1979.

Magic . . . Naturally!: Science Entertainments and Amusements, illustrated by Lance R. Miyamoto, Lippincott (Philadelphia, PA), 1979, revised edition, illustrated by Lionel Kalish, HarperCollins (New York, NY), 1993.

Truth on Trial: The Story of Galileo Galilei, illustrated by George Ulrich, Coward (New York, NY), 1979.

(With Kathy Darling) *Bet You Can't!: Science Impossibilities to Fool You,* illustrated by Martha Weston, Lothrop (New York, NY), 1980.

How to Really Fool Yourself: Illusions for All Your Senses, illustrated by Leslie Morrill, Lippincott (New York, NY), 1981, revised edition, illustrated by Jessica Wolk-Stanley, Wiley (New York, NY), 1999.

Lots of Rot, illustrated by Brian Schatell, Lippincott (New York, NY), 1981.

The Secret Life of School Supplies, illustrated by Bill Morrison, Lippincott (New York, NY), 1981.

The Secret Life of Hardware: A Science Experiment Book, illustrated by Bill Morrison, Lippincott (New York, NY), 1982.

Fuzz Does It!, illustrated by Brian Schatell, Lippincott (New York, NY), 1982.

(With Kathy Darling) *Bet You Can!: Science Possibilities to Fool You,* illustrated by Stella Ormai, Avon (New York, NY), 1983, hardcover edition, Lothrop (New York, NY), 1990.

Gobs of Goo, illustrated by Brian Schatell, Lippincott (New York, NY), 1983.

The Monsters Who Died: A Mystery About Dinosaurs, illustrated by Greg Wenzel, Coward (New York, NY), 1983.

Chemically Active!: Experiments You Can Do at Home, illustrated by Theo Cobb, Lippincott (New York, NY), 1983.

The Secret Life of Cosmetics: A Science Experiment Book, illustrated by Theo Cobb, Lippincott (New York, NY), 1985.

Inspector Bodyguard Patrols the Land of U, illustrated by John Sanford, Simon & Schuster (New York, NY), 1986.

Skyscraper Going Up!: A Pop-Up Book, design and paper engineering by John Strejan, Crowell (New York, NY), 1987.

Why Doesn't the Earth Fall Up?: And Other Not Such Dumb Questions About Motion, illustrated by Ted Enik, Lodestar Books (New York, NY), 1988.

Scraps of Wraps, illustrated by Doffy Weir, A&C Black (London, England), 1988.

Getting Dressed, illustrated by Marylin Hafner, Lippincott (New York, NY), 1989.

Keeping Clean, illustrated by Marylin Hafner, Lippincott (New York, NY), 1989.

Writing It Down, illustrated by Marylin Hafner, Lippincott (New York, NY), 1989.

Feeding Yourself, illustrated by Marylin Hafner, Lippincott (New York, NY), 1989.

For Your Own Protection: Stories Science Photos Tell, Lothrop (New York, NY), 1989.

Natural Wonders: Stories Science Photos Tell, Lothrop (New York, NY), 1990.

Why Doesn't the Sun Burn Out?: And Other Not Such Dumb Questions About Energy, illustrated by Ted Enik, Lodestar Books (New York, NY), 1990.

Why Can't You Unscramble an Egg?: And Other Not Such Dumb Questions About Matter, illustrated by Ted Enik, Lodestar Books (New York, NY), 1990.

Fun and Games: Stories Science Photos Tell, Lothrop (New York, NY), 1991.

(With Josh Cobb) *Light Action!: Amazing Experiments with Optics,* illustrated by Theo Cobb, HarperCollins (New York, NY), 1993.

(With Kathy Darling) *Wanna Bet?: Science Challenges to Fool You,* illustrated by Meredith Johnson, Lothrop (New York, NY), 1993.

Vicki Cobb's Papermaking Book and Kit, HarperFestival, 1993.

Why Can't I Live Forever?: And Other Not Such Dumb Questions About Life, illustrated by Mena Dolobowsky, Lodestar Books (New York, NY), 1997.

Blood and Gore Like You've Never Seen, Scholastic (New York, NY), 1997.

Dirt and Grime Like You've Never Seen, Scholastic (New York, NY), 1998.

(With Kathy Darling) *Don't Try This at Home!: Science Fun for Kids on the Go,* illustrated by True Kelley, Morrow (New York, NY), 1998.

You Gotta Try This!: Absolutely Irresistible Science, illustrated by True Kelley, Morrow (New York, NY), 1999.

Bangs and Twangs: Science Fun with Sound, illustrated by Steve Haefele, Millbrook Press (Brookfield, CT), 2000.

Squirts and Spurts: Science Fun with Water, illustrated by Steve Haefele, Millbrook Press (Brookfield, CT), 2000.

Whirlers and Twirlers: Science Fun with Spinning, illustrated by Steve Haefele, Millbrook Press (Brookfield, CT), 2001.

See for Yourself: More Than 100 Experiments for Science Fairs and Projects, illustrated by Dave Klug, Scholastic (New York, NY), 2001.

I Get Wet, illustrated by Julia Gorton, HarperCollins (New York, NY), 2001.

I See Myself, illustrated by Julia Gorton, HarperCollins (New York, NY), 2002.

Sources of Forces: Science Fun with Force Fields, illustrated by Steve Haefele, Millbrook Press (Brookfield, CT), 2002.

I Fall Down, illustrated by Julia Gorton, HarperCollins (New York, NY), 2003.

I Face the Wind, illustrated by Julia Gorton, HarperCollins (New York, NY), in press.

Fireworks: Where's the Science Here?, Millbrook Press (Brookfield, CT), in press.

"FIRST BOOK" SERIES

The First Book of Logic, illustrated by Ellie Haines, Franklin Watts (New York, NY), 1969.

The First Book of Cells: The Basic Structure of Life, illustrated by Leonard Dank, Franklin Watts (New York, NY), 1970.

The First Book of Gases, illustrated by Ellie Haines, Franklin Watts (New York, NY), 1970.

The First Book of Heat, illustrated by Robert Byrd, Franklin Watts (New York, NY), 1973.

"STEPPING-STONE" SERIES

Making Sense of Money, illustrated by Olivia H. H. Cole, Parents' Magazine Press (New York, NY), 1971.

Sense of Direction: Up, Down, and All Around, illustrated by Carol Nicklaus, Parents' Magazine Press (New York, NY), 1972.

The Long and Short of Measurements, illustrated by Carol Nicklaus, Parents' Magazine Press (New York, NY), 1973.

"HOW THE WORLD WORKS" SERIES

The Scoop on Ice Cream, illustrated by G. Brian Karas, Little, Brown (Boston, MA), 1985.

Sneakers Meet Your Feet, illustrated by Theo Cobb, Little, Brown (Boston, MA), 1985.

More Power to You!, illustrated by Bill Ogden, Little, Brown (Boston, MA), 1986.

The Trip of a Drip, illustrated by Eliot Kreloff, Little, Brown (Boston, MA), 1986.

"IMAGINE LIVING HERE" SERIES; ILLUSTRATED BY BARBARA LAVALLEE

This Place Is Cold: Alaska, Walker (New York, NY), 1989.

This Place Is Dry: Sonoran Desert, Walker (New York, NY), 1989.

This Place Is Wet: Amazon Basin, Walker (New York, NY), 1989.

This Place Is High: Andes Mountains, Walker (New York, NY), 1989.

This Place Is Lonely: Australia, Walker (New York, NY), 1991.

This Place Is Crowded: Japan, Walker (New York, NY), 1992.

This Place Is Wild: East Africa, Walker (New York, NY), 1998.

"THE FIVE SENSES" SERIES; ILLUSTRATED BY CYNTHIA C. LEWIS

Follow Your Nose: Discover Your Sense of Smell, Millbrook Press (Brookfield, CT), 2000.

Your Tongue Can Tell: Discover Your Sense of Taste, Millbrook Press (Brookfield, CT), 2000.

Feeling Your Way: Discover Your Sense of Touch, Millbrook Press (Brookfield, CT), 2001.

Perk Up Your Ears: Discover Your Sense of Hearing, Millbrook Press (Brookfield, CT), 2001.

Open Your Eyes: Discover Your Sense of Sight, Millbrook Press (Brookfield, CT), 2002.

OTHER

Brave in the Attempt: The Special Olympics Experience (adult nonfiction), photographs by Rosemarie Hausherr, Pinwheel, 1983.

Also editor of *Biology Study Prints,* 1970. The author's papers and manuscripts are held in the de Grummond Collection at the University of Southern Mississippi.

Sidelights

Vicki Cobb, author of science books for children, once commented: "When you think about the great teachers who influenced you, who they were as human beings was at least as important as what they taught you. The passion and energy they brought to their teaching—their humanity—somehow touched their students. I believe that revealed humanity is the bridge to authentic and powerful communication, both oral and written. Students and readers learn best when they are moved—when feelings are associated with concepts. The feelings and personalities of top fiction writers are part of their 'voice' as storytellers. Personal voices are beginning to be heard in children's nonfiction, but such writing is a break with tradition. There is an underlying assumption that nonfiction gains authority by being dispassionate and straightforward, although the result may be dry and perhaps boring. But does the word from 'on high' have any more validity than the word communicated with wit or enthusiasm? Why can't the real world be presented in lively prose as fictional worlds are? I consider myself to be a storyteller of the real world. It is my job to present that world in a manner that is engaging to my readers."

Cobb has credited her childhood experiences for her hands-on approach to science and her interest in books. She began reading at an early age and at The Little Red School House in Greenwich Village, she learned to grind corn to make cornmeal, as well as learned to make candles and soap. At sixteen, under an early enrollment program for promising high school students, Cobb entered the University of Wisconsin. While at Wisconsin, Cobb found that she liked to study the sciences. After transferring to Barnard College in Manhattan and graduating, she worked for several years as a researcher testing anti-cancer drugs on mice. During that time she married Edward Cobb.

Two years after her marriage, Cobb became a junior high school teacher and discovered that she liked explaining basic concepts to her students. While pregnant with her first child, Cobb left her job and turned her attention to writing science texts. In the early and mid-1970s, Cobb worked as a writer for television programs. In 1972 Cobb wrote and hosted *The Science Game,* which featured experiments that could be reproduced at home, for a cable television company in New York. In 1976 Cobb became a writer for *Good Morning America,* the ABC-TV talk show, but she lost her job when a new executive producer brought in his own staff. The author then resumed her career as a writer of science books for children, and has published nearly seventy books for young readers. In addition to writing, Cobb conducts science demonstrations based on her writings, and she also holds science workshops for teachers.

Cobb has cited *Science Experiments You Can Eat,* published in 1972, as the first book in which she could be creative. Commenting on her research for the book, the author stated: "In the morning I got the boys off to day camp and then went prowling through the supermarket aisles looking for ideas. I tried out all kinds of experiments, which often failed. Nevertheless, my family was game about eating them." A *Scientific American* review called *Science Experiments You Can Eat* "a first-rate introduction to the sciences of matter for boys and girls old enough to work by themselves."

Cobb's writings have won several awards, including the Children's Science Book Award in 1981 for *Bet You Can't!: Science Impossibilities to Fool You* and the Eva L. Gordon Award for children's literature in science in 1985. Her titles, such as *Lots of Rot, See for Yourself: More Than 100 Experiments for Science Fairs and Projects, I See Myself,* and *I Get Wet,* have received praise from reviewers. *Lots of Rot* was judged by an *Appraisal* reviewer to be "a wonderful introduction to the subject of decay and the agents and condition that cause it." According to Eunice Weech of *School Library Journal, See For Yourself* contains "a wealth of fun and exploration." A reviewer for *Horn Book Magazine* noted that the "simple yet well-conceived activities ... help young kids draw conclusions from their observations."

Among Cobb's most recent titles are several books in a series that explores the five senses with her hallmark combination of fun and learning: *Follow Your Nose, Your Tongue Can Tell, Feeling Your Way, Perk Up Your Ears,* and *Open Your Eyes.* Reviewer Lauren P. Gattilia, on the *Education World* Web site, commended Cobb's collection of experiments, demonstrations, and craft projects in *Follow Your Nose* and *Your Tongue Can Tell*

for a "kid-friendly, casual style that never talks down to readers" as well as for "solid explanations of the way the senses work." Gillian Engberg, in a *Booklist* review, pointed out the "hip collage and lively text" in the "Five Senses" volumes. Engberg noted that "the text weaves basic concepts into anecdotes and suggestions for easy experiments, which are illustrated with kitchy, irreverent collages contributed by Cynthia Lewis."

Cobb introduces young readers to some of the basics of physics in a recent series that includes *Bangs and Twangs: Science Fun with Sound, Squirts and Spurts: Science Fun with Water, Whirlers and Twirlers: Science Fun with Spinning,* and *Sources of Forces: Science Fun with Force Fields. Booklist* reviewer Gillian Engberg, commenting on the "lively cartoon format" and "rowdy fun" of *Bangs and Twangs* and *Squirts and Spurts,* found that "both titles hook the reader from the start." Noting that the books "will encourage enthusiastic learning," Engberg felt that the books successfully "[convey] sophisticated concepts" and credited Cobb's "accessible language" and "Steve Haefele's drawings of an exuberant, grinning narrator and her robot sidekick."

Commenting on her departure from the traditional approach to writing about science, Cobb once noted that "traditional written treatment of information often requires that the reader have an agenda, such as a school assignment, before coming to the material. Thus, the reasons a reader wants access to information may have nothing to do with the intrinsic nature of the material or the reader's basic curiosity. When something is required reading, dry, impersonal writing is likely to stifle further inquiry, rather than nurture and support it. My books are a departure from the traditional. I've used a slightly irreverent tone—'science is not the mysterious process for eggheads it's cracked up to be.'"

Biographical and Critical Sources

BOOKS

Children's Literature Review, Volume 2, Gale (Detroit, MI), 1976.

McElroy, Lisa Tucker, *Meet My Grandmother: She's a Children's Book Author,* photographs by Joel Benjamin, Millbrook Press (Brookfield, CT), 2001.

Silvey, Anita, editor, *Children's Books and Their Creators,* Houghton Mifflin (Boston, MA), 1995.

Wyatt, Flora R., and others, *Popular Nonfiction Authors for Children,* Libraries Unlimited (Englewood, CO), 1998.

PERIODICALS

Appraisal, fall, 1974, review of *Heat;* winter, 1982, review of *Lots of Rot,* p. 22.

Booklist, December 1, 1995, Carolyn Phelan, reviews of *Light Action: Amazing Experiments with Optics* and *Why Doesn't the Sun Burn Out?: And Other Not Such Dumb Questions About Energy,* p. 632; April, 1998, Carolyn Phelan, *Don't Try This at Home!: Science Fun for Kids on the Go,* p. 1316, and Shelley Townsend-Hudson, review of *This Place Is Wild: East Africa,* p. 1316; August, 1999, Carolyn Phelan, review of *You Gotta Try This!: Absolutely Irresistible Science,*

p. 2048; October 15, 2000, Gillian Engberg, reviews of *Squirts and Spurts: Science Fun with Water* and *Bangs and Twangs: Science Fun with Sound,* p. 432; November 15, 2000, Gillian Engberg, reviews of *Your Tongue Can Tell: Discover Your Sense of Taste* and *Follow Your Nose: Discover Your Sense of Smell,* p. 636.

Horn Book, April, 1977, p. 197.

Horn Book Magazine, November/December, 2002, review of *I Get Wet* and *I See Myself,* pp. 774-775.

School Library Journal, May, 1997, Carolyn Angus, review of *Why Can't I Live Forever?: And Other Not Such Dumb Questions About Life,* p. 118; May, 1998, Anne Chapman, review of *This Place Is Wild: East Africa,* p. 130; July, 1998, Kathryn Kosiorek, *Don't Try This at Home!,* p. 104; August, 1999, Marion F. Gallivan, review of *You Gotta Try This!,* p. 167; March, 2001, Eunice Weech, review of *Bangs and Twangs,* p. 232; May, 2001, Wendy S. Carroll, review of *Feeling Your Way: Discover Your Sense of Touch,* p. 140; March, 2002, Eunice Weech, review of *See for Yourself: More Than 100 Experiments for Science Fairs and Projects.*

Scientific American, December, 1972, review of *Science Experiments You Can Eat,* p. 119.

OTHER

AuthorsDen, http://www.authorsden.com/ (December 10, 2002).

Education World, http://education-world.com/ (May 26, 2000), Lauren P. Gattilia, reviews of *Follow Your Nose, Your Tongue Can Tell,* and *How to Really Fool Yourself.*

Vicki Cobb's Kid's Science Page, http://www.vickicobb. com/ (December 10, 2002), author's Web site.

*   *   *

Autobiography Feature

Vicki Cobb

When you are a child, you learn things about yourself that never change for your lifetime. By the time I was eight years old, I had learned two things about myself that shaped the way I've lived my life. The lessons were hard ones because in each case I lost something important. And both losses had to do with noses.

I went to a private elementary school in Greenwich Village called "The Little Red School House." Private schools in New York are not usually neighborhood schools. My school friends lived all over the city and we had to make plans to spend time together. So on most days, after school, I spent time alone. My sister, Elly, who is four years younger than I, was not a suitable playmate when I was eight. My dolls became my friends. I created a powerful fantasy world around my dolls. I loved making all kinds of clothes for them and dressing them up for adventure. One of my favorite books was called *Story of the Live Dolls.* It was about some dolls who came to life and became best friends to the girl who owned them. I loved imagining that the same thing happened to me.

One day, I was given a new doll. She was the most beautiful doll I had ever seen, with golden hair and blue eyes that opened and closed. I named her Priscilla, after my best friend. I made her an elegant cape out of gray wool lined with grape-colored satin. I daydreamed about her at school. I could hardly wait to get home and act out my fantasies. Then, one day, a terrible accident happened. Priscilla rolled off my bed and landed on her face on the floor. In those days, dolls were not made of plastic. Their faces were molded out of some kind of sawdust and adhesive. Priscilla's face did not survive the fall. Her nose was smashed. All that was left was a hole. We rushed Priscilla to a doll hospital. But she could not be repaired. My mother reminded me that she was only a doll and she could be replaced. But I was inconsolable. I didn't want to replace Priscilla. I decided then and there that I would never again care that much about some *thing.* Things must be just things to me, not love objects. This was the first important thing I learned about myself.

At "Little Red" it was strongly believed that children learned by doing things. When we studied the Indians, we built a tepee in the classroom and we ground corn to make cornmeal the way the Indians did. When we studied the early American colonists, we made candles and soap. We wrote stories and did arts-and-crafts projects. We wrote plays and performed them for each other.

That same year, I made my first puppet. First I sculpted the head out of plasticine clay. Then I covered the clay with strips of newspaper soaked in paste. I put several layers of paper strips over the clay so that the paper had the same shape as the clay. Several days later, after the paste had dried, I cut the head in half and took out the clay. The paper was now quite stiff and it was easy to put the rigid halves of the head together with more strips of paper and paste. Finally I painted the head. He had a turned-up nose and glasses. I made his hair by pasting short lengths of yarn all around the back of his head. I made him bald, just like my father. He was going to be a hand puppet, with his hollow head and a suit like a glove for my fingers. I could make his head and his hands move.

My puppet was going to be the star of our show. Everyone in my class admired him. Then, something terrible happened over the weekend. A mouse ate off his nose and left a giant hole, right in the center of his adorable face! There was no way to repair the damage. My teacher made the discovery first thing Monday morning. She worried how she would tell me. She shouldn't have. I was amazed how little it mattered. I remember thinking that the finished puppet wasn't important. What was important was my ability to make such a puppet and no mouse could take *that* away from me. From that point on, I was aware that *doing* things was what was important. That I was happiest when I was involved in creating something. And when I was finished, I really didn't care if my product continued to exist. I had already had my fun making it. This was the second important thing I learned about myself.

I was the first of two daughters of Ben and Paula Wolf. My mother was a beautiful woman with a radiant personality. People were attracted to her light. My father was a man of many accomplishments. He had worked his way through college and law school as a jazz pianist. He later developed his music by studying classical piano music and composing songs for our summer community's annual Labor Day show. He was a serious chess player and studied the games of the masters, playing them by himself. He also was a gifted artist. He would take his sketchbook on trips and later transform his sketches into watercolor paintings. The one thing my father did not do well was earn money. He graduated law school at the end of the depression and was unsuccessful in his attempt to launch a private law practice. Just before I was born, he became a civil service worker. Later he went into labor mediation for the state. My parents felt it was important for my mother to stay home for us children. So my father supplemented his income by taking all kinds of jobs that used his talents. He directed choruses and sold his paintings and taught labor law. We always had enough. It never occurred to me that we weren't rich.

The importance of being a doer obviously came from my home. I painted and did woodwork with my father. I cooked and sewed and knitted with my mother. I had four years as an only child, four years as the sole apple of my parents' eyes before my sister Elly was born. All that exclusive adult attention helped me become a reader at age four. Reading became my most important form of entertainment. One of my favorite books was *The Secret Garden* by Frances Hodgson Burnett. My father started reading it to me when I was quite young. It is the story of a lonely girl who discovers an abandoned and locked garden on the estate where she lives. She begins to cultivate the garden. I made my father stop reading the book to me because I was terrified of what would happen to her when she was discovered. Years later, I decided my fears were silly. I confronted them and finished reading the book myself. And yes, it did have a happy ending.

The best year of my childhood was the year I was eleven. I had a talented teacher named Louis Sarlin. In my

Vicki Cobb, 2002

school, we called our teachers by their first names. Louis taught me so much about my capabilities. He would give us paper and say, "Write a story." And I discovered I could write a story. He would say, "Write a poem." And I could. Here's one of the poems I wrote that year. It's called "A Boring Day."

On a dreary, gray, cloudy day
There's nothing for me to do or play.
"Why don't you dance," my mother says,
"Or cook a meal, or make the beds,
"Or read a book, or play with Elly,
"And if you're hungry, make bread and jelly,
"Play the piano or fuss with your hair,
"Don't just sit around and stare.
"I can name hundreds of things you can do."
"I know that," I say, "But I don't want to."

The next year we moved out of the city to Tarrytown, New York where I went to the public junior high school. For the first time in my life I didn't fit in with the other kids in my school. I was different. I was Jewish in a town that did not have a large Jewish population. And I found out that being smart did not win one any popularity contests. For the first time in my life I got grades on my schoolwork. Little Red had prepared me well. I received quite high grades without really working very hard. My best friend was Ilana Rahmani, also an outsider. Ilana had been born in Israel and she was interested in music. We were not included in the social life of our schoolmates. We would never be chosen as cheerleaders or class officers. We were not invited to the parties and activities of the others. So we spent almost all of our spare time together.

*

When I was in tenth grade, the guidance counselor of the school approached my parents and said that there was a new, experimental program for bright kids that selected candidates for various colleges. The Ford Foundation Early Admissions Scholarships program was interested in placing tenth and eleventh graders in college, letting them skip the last one or two years of high school. The guidance counselor suggested that I should, at least, take the tests. They would be a good experience for me.

What a surprise when I won admission to several colleges and universities! Suddenly I had to make a decision. And with great credit to my parents, they allowed it to be my decision. I discussed my options with them, with a respected family friend, and, of course, with Ilana. It was Ilana's advice that was the clincher. We both felt that there was nothing for us in Tarrytown. When I looked forward to the next two years, finishing high school in Tarrytown paled in comparison with the possibilities of college. Ilana's vote to go for it was the mark of a truly unselfish friend. After all, she had to face her senior year (she was a year older than I) without me. So I accepted the Ford Scholarship to enter the University of Wisconsin, a thousand miles from home, in the fall of 1954, a few weeks after my sixteenth birthday.

The summer before I entered college, I was a counselor-in-training at Buck's Rock Work Camp in New Milford, Connecticut. Buck's Rock was a teenage camp where campers and CITs, like me, had the opportunity to choose some kind of work for which we would be paid. Buck's Rock had many craft shops that produced products that were sold to the public. Creative campers could design products for production. Campers who were not as talented in design could work in the production of these products if they wished. Everyone was paid for their work in shop hours. At the end of the summer, the income from our sales gave us a rate for each shop hour, and we were paid according to the number of shop hours we had accumulated. In those days I was interested in being an artist. I created all kinds of designs for production, such as silk-screened stationary, a tiled tea tray, and fabric silk screened with a farm design. Each design had to be approved by the Shop Planning Committee in order to be put into production. No other camper or CIT had as many items in production as I. I loved thinking up products that the public might enjoy having and then creating them. My success this last summer, before entering college, played an important part in my becoming what I am today.

I entered the University of Wisconsin in the fall of 1954 and was thrust into the spirit of the times: namely, that girls went to college to find husbands. Dating was the most important thing in a female college student's life. This way of thinking was clearly stated and acted upon by my first roommate, an eighteen-year-old freshman from a small Wisconsin town. Mary Lou promptly found "Roger-Poger," an engineering student due to graduate that next January. It took her only one semester to find her man, land him, quit school, and marry in February.

When I entered college at the tender age of barely sixteen, I had never really dated. Marriage seemed far off, something for grown-ups. My first semester I did focus on my studies and discovered my love for science in a course called "Physical Universe," or PU for short. My grades were good. But by second semester, the social atmosphere had eroded my good intentions and I put my considerable creative energies into the dating game. I became engaged the summer I was eighteen to a boy from New York, which prompted my transfer to Barnard College in Manhattan in the middle of my junior year.

The engagement broke up shortly after I returned to New York, but Barnard was very good for me. At Wisconsin I was smart enough to get reasonably good grades without working very hard. But there was no way I could "wing it" at Barnard. I had three semesters to cram in all of the courses in my major, which was zoology, plus fulfill two language requirements and write a senior thesis. I had to work very hard to get unremarkable grades and graduate on schedule in May of 1958. But even at Barnard, the mark of distinction at graduation time was not personal grades or achievements but the size of the diamond on the ring finger of one's left hand.

*

Upon graduation, having failed to find a husband (I was by then nineteen), I took a job in cancer research, the only job open to many of us educated females not going on to graduate school. The pharmaceutical house that hired us also assumed that we would soon be lost to them because of marriage, so the job was far from being on a career track.

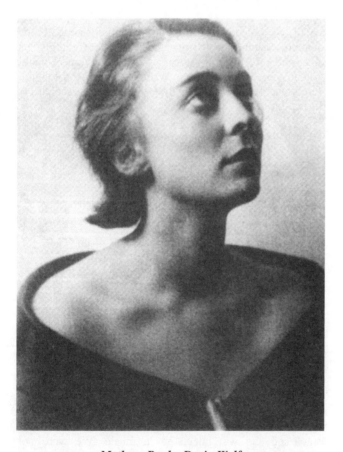

Mother, Paula Davis Wolf

It was like factory work, injecting hundreds of mice twice a day to test the effect of various drugs on the size of tumors. It was a dead end job and deadly to boot. So that fall I enrolled at Teachers College, Columbia University, for a graduate degree in high school science education.

A year and a half later, right after I received my master's from Columbia, I married Edward Scribner Cobb, a graduate student in experimental psychology at Columbia. Now I needed a job to support the two of us. Getting a teaching job proved to be impossible. There were no openings for young married women because it was assumed they would soon be leaving to start a family. My assurance that I could at least promise several years of service because my husband was a student and we depended on my income fell on deaf ears. So I took another job doing the same boring kind of cancer research, hoping that it would be temporary, that a teaching job would soon materialize.

My teaching career finally began in the fall of 1962. But I was not able to get an assignment as a high school science teacher. A novice, like me, was assigned to the much less desirable junior high classroom. I loved teaching and I especially loved teaching junior high. My students were old enough to understand the basic science concepts that interested me most and we did not have to dwell on difficult details. I didn't have to teach to any particular standardized exam and the curriculum topics were broad enough for me to teach each unit as I wished. I quickly learned that the texts were boring. I discovered that there were wonderful books in the library that could give me the background to bring science alive. My biggest frustration with teaching was not enough time for lesson preparation. I had three preparations and five classes to teach every day. My gut feeling was that I could really bring science to life if only I had enough time to think about it.

In the middle of my third year of teaching, I did what had been expected: I left to have a child. I stopped teaching in January and had three months to go before my first son, Theo, would arrive. I quickly discovered that staying home and keeping house was not something I was particularly well suited to. Besides, we needed money. Ed had finished his course work for his Ph.D. and was a teaching assistant at Barnard, not a well-paying job to say the least. So I looked in the *New York Times* and found an ad for teachers to write on specific subject areas. I figured if I could talk about science, I could write about it. So I drove to Brooklyn for a meeting with the publisher.

University-College Tutors, Inc. was a storefront on Avenue J in Brooklyn. The front room, visible from the street, had four workers busily marching around a rack, collating the pages that would become a book. The books produced by UCT were paperback outline student guides. The UCT slogan was "Simplicity Is Worth Millions." Wishful thinking, no doubt, on the part of the UCT publisher, Mr. Baker. I was ushered into the room behind the front room where Mr. Baker indulged in his hobby of roasting coffee beans from different parts of the world. He didn't grind his roasted beans, however, but brewed coffee by soaking the intact beans in water which took on the color of very weak tea. Each time I went there I was offered a different variety of this strangely prepared brew he called "coffee." They all tasted terrible.

Father, Benjamin Harold Wolf

Mr. Baker invited me into his office, a room directly to the right and behind the coffee-bean roasting room. He showed me a manuscript in progress and asked me what I thought. While I looked it over he returned to his typing, which he did machine-gun style. Not only could he type quickly, but he could talk on the telephone while he was typing! Of course, my opinion of the manuscript was that I could do better. I told him how. At the end of the interview he said, "You sound intelligent even if you are pregnant." (That remark stuck in my mind although this was 1964, long before the women's movement took off.) He asked me if I could write a high school chemistry text. After I said, "Yes," he said, "Write a chapter. But it must sound simple." I left saying that I would.

It took me about ten days to write that first chapter. I returned to UCT and Mr. Baker looked over my efforts while he talked on the phone and typed. "It's not simple enough," he said, handing the pages to me. I went home and rewrote it and returned to Avenue J a week later. "It's still not simple enough," he said, returning the script to me. Discouraged but not daunted I returned to my typewriter. On the fourth attempt he kept the script, saying he wanted to read it. Two days later he called offering me a contract. I've had many contracts since, but I still remember the feeling of elation that came from that call. I was offered a flat fee for my work, my name would not go on the book, but I had a chance to earn money at home doing something interesting, using my brains and education.

My son, Theo, was born when I was in the middle of the chemistry book. I finished it when he was three months

"My sister, Elly (left) and me, with Priscilla"

old, staring up at me from his infant seat while I worked. Mr. Baker paid me most of what he owed me, but he never published the book and went out of business not long afterwards. I was disappointed, of course, but I had learned something. I had learned that I could write something book length and that I could earn money at home. So I proceeded to look for other jobs I could do.

The lack of money for our little household was an ongoing problem. And, while I could find work as a freelance science writer, we needed a more regular income from me. In the spring of 1966, when I was six months pregnant with my second child, I took a part-time teaching job in New York City three afternoons a week. My son, Josh, was conveniently born in July of that year so that I could continue teaching in the fall.

Again, I was teaching junior high science. I had to teach a unit on chemistry, so I brought my chemistry book to my class. My students liked it and understood it. I felt encouraged and kept on looking for work as a writer. Through a family friend I found another small publisher and won a contract to write two high school texts titled "Molecular Biology" and "Biological Measurement." But again, I was fated not to be published, for this publisher declared bankruptcy shortly after I submitted the finished works.

Although I was teaching and running a household with two small children, I kept "beating the bushes" looking for work as a writer. Part of "beating the bushes" was telling everyone I met or knew that I was looking for work. I had an old friend at Grolier, an educational publishing house, who put me in touch with an editor at Franklin Watts. The editor took me to lunch, my first heady experience of the "publishing lunch." Back at his office he asked, "What have you written?" I promptly pulled out my three unpublished books, an impressive pile of pages. He gave a quick look to the top sheet of the first manuscript. "Vicki," he said, "you simply must write a book for us. How about *The First Book of Logic?*" I had taken a one-semester course in logic in my freshman year of college so I wasn't totally uninformed on the subject. I took a deep breath and

said, "Yes." The editor smiled and said, "You give me an outline and I'll give you a contract. When can you have the outline?" "Six weeks," I unhesitatingly replied. I figured that I could learn enough logic in six weeks to write an outline. After I got the contract I'd worry about writing the book.

The First Book of Logic was published in 1969 when Theo was five years old. In the process of producing a book, publishers send the typeset manuscript, called "galley proofs," to authors for final corrections before the book goes to press. The day I remember best was the day the galleys arrived and I first saw "by Vicki Cobb" in type. I must have spent hours gazing at those three words. Suddenly, it was real. After five years, three unpublished books, and countless small writing jobs, I would finally be an author.

It would be nice to say that I was now off and running. But that's not how it works. I still had to "beat the bushes." No contract came easily and we constantly needed money. In 1969 I landed some work with McGraw-Hill writing the material that went on the back of a series of large photographs. This contract paid enough for me to stop teaching. So I made the decision to risk living without my small but steady teaching salary and take my chances making the same amount of money as a writer, job by job.

The children's nonfiction books that I wrote during this time were parts of series. I wrote books on navigation, economics, cells, gases, heat, and other topics. When you write for a series, your job as author is to sound like all the other authors in the series. My editors made sure of it. When I look back on these early books now, I cringe. The writing is so flat and dull! I'm glad these books are out of print.

One day Ellie Haines, a good friend who was also an artist, called up and said, "Let's do a cookbook for kids together, Vicki. We both like to cook and I'll do the illustrations." I said, "Let me think about it." I remember hanging up the phone and walking to the living room window overlooking the Hudson River. I thought to myself, "I don't want to write a cookbook for kids. I want to write science for kids." Then, as I gazed into the sky, the title *Science Experiments You Can Eat* popped into my head. I instantly knew it was a good idea. But good ideas mean nothing unless you can make them happen. So I ran to my desk and sat down and wrote an outline that was practically identical to the table of contents of the book.

We presented the idea to an editor who appeared interested but hesitant. I later found out why. She called me and said that she wanted to do the book but that she didn't want Ellie's art. I said, without a moment's pause, "If you don't want the art, I must withdraw the book." It was hard to be loyal to Ellie because I really needed money, but I had made my deal with her first and there were other publishing companies where we could submit the idea. I called Ellie and told her what I had done. I also told her the reason the publisher had passed on the project. We hung up the phone on the note that we would submit it elsewhere. Half an hour later Ellie called back. "It's really your project, Vicki, and I know how much you need the money. So I'll withdraw." A true friend! But I had been a good friend to her as well.

I wrote *Science Experiments You Can Eat* during the summer of 1970. It was a very happy time for me. We rented a house in South Hadley, Massachusetts. In the morning I got the boys off to day camp and then went prowling through the supermarket aisles looking for ideas. I tried out all kinds of experiments, which often failed. Nevertheless, my family was game about eating them. I was absorbed in my work until the early afternoons. Then I spent the afternoons playing tennis with my husband and enjoying my children. I didn't realize that Ed was becoming increasingly involved with the sickness that would ultimately end our marriage five years later. Ed rode off on his bicycle daily to a local bar to drink enough to kill the pain of his lack of productivity. He became skilled at keeping his drinking from me. It was years later that I realized that that summer had been shrouded in the illusion of security.

When I was a child, I became a reader because it was the best form of entertainment. We didn't get a television until I was twelve. But my children were brought up on television. I was fascinated and sometimes appalled at the impact it had on them. At first, I tried to control what they watched. But Theo discovered cartoons at a friend's house and after that I gave up. Television was the common ground for children of their generation, and I made a conscious decision to let them watch what they wanted as long as they did other things as well.

But as a writer for children, the medium fascinated me. I thought it could be used to teach all kinds of things because there was no question that children learned from it. So I began looking for opportunities to write for television.

One day I went to a convention called "Concerned Citizens for Broadcasting" in a New York hotel. The afternoon session was about cable television, which was well established in New York. At that time, cable television was more promise than actuality, and it promised television in abundance. Instead of perhaps ten channels, it offered forty or more. The presidents of several competing cable TV stations were on the panel. They were all intent on "wiring the nation," much as the phone company had been fifty years earlier. These companies were competing with each other, wooing different towns and villages for the right to bring them clear reception and the promise of programming. One president was even developing his own programming to give his company a competitive edge. "What kind of programming are you going to make?" asked a man in the audience. The executive shrugged his shoulders, "I'm open to suggestion," he said. "If anyone has any ideas, tell me about them."

I was sitting in the front row in anticipation of any opportunity. When the session was over I ran to the dais before the speaker could make his exit. "I have an idea for you," I said. "Who are you?" he asked. I gave him my name. "I'm just a writer," I said, "but I have an idea that would be easy for you to do." He told me to call his secretary for an appointment.

It took several weeks of constant calling to finally nail down an appointment. But finally the day of the meeting arrived. "What's your idea?" the executive asked. I reached into my briefcase and pulled out a neatly typed proposal in a blue folder and put it on his desk. He looked at the title and said, "I'll read this later, tell me about it." I spoke for about ten minutes. The president was sufficiently interested

in me to want to extend our meeting past the originally scheduled twenty minutes. He then began telling me about the history of his company and the role of cable television in the future of America. He told me his life story, how he built the company up from nothing. He told me what he thought of me, that I just might be smart. Then he leaned back in his chair, folded his hands behind his head, and said, "Now you know what I think of you. What do you think of me?" I looked him straight in the eye and said, "I'm sorry, but you'll just have to guess." He laughed and said that he wanted me to speak to his programming director. The meeting had lasted an hour and a half.

Needless to say, the meeting with the programming director was easy to arrange. "Irving is very high on you," were his first words to me. "What's your idea?" I spent a few minutes outlining my idea to him. "That's a good idea," he said. "Do you have any others?" Off the top of my head I said, "How about a science show for kids?" "That's a very good idea," he said. "Who would do it?" "I could do it," I answered. "Okay," he said. "Let's do a pilot next week." That's how I got my own television show, one of the first three shows ever syndicated nationally on cable television. The meeting had taken all of five minutes.

Cable television in the early seventies must have been like network television twenty years earlier. Production was on a shoestring and a staff of three had to do everything. The work was intense but fun. My show was called "The Science Game." It was hands-on science in the studio with two kids as my guests. All of the experiments were things my viewers could easily do at home. My assistant and I made sure the experiments worked, we found the guests, I

"An artist at Buck's Rock," 1954

wrote the show, and we filmed two shows back to back on the days we were in the studio. In a year and a half we produced twenty-three shows that were aired all over the country.

You might think that having your own television show would make you rich and famous. Neither happened to me. A science show for kids has a small audience at best. Not many people had cable television at that time. I had almost no indication that anyone watched the show. We got my show in my house and it was on the cable station three times a day. My kids would see me on TV, say "Oh, Mom's on again," and instantly switch to some other channel. Aside from the fun I had creating the show, and the award the show won in the cable television industry, there was no lasting effect of it on my life or on the world.

At this time, I was struck with a brainstorm for children's television. It was clear that my children loved the good guys vs. bad guys conflicts of cartoons. Why not take a conflict found in the real world and present it as a fantasy? My idea was "Inspector Bodyguard," an imaginary superhero who lived in the human body and acted as a quarterback to the body's team of natural defenses against germs and other threats to life. Through a friend, I presented my idea to a major pharmaceutical producer of children's vitamins. They were interested enough to give

"Getting my MRS. degree," 1960

me money to go to Hollywood and work with some animators. It was my first trip to California.

I created a "storyboard" of two Inspector Bodyguard adventures with "story-sketch" man, Bob Ogle. A storyboard is something like a comic strip. It tells the action in words as it shows what is going on on the screen. Bob and I sat in an office for three days and laughed and imagined things and brought the Inspector to life. I returned to New York and presented the work to the pharmaceutical company. They loved it and said to take it to the next step, to sell it to a network. However, the Inspector didn't make it. Just at that time, the networks decided not to permit advertising for children's vitamins. After all, a vitamin is a pill that can make you feel good and they didn't want this message to be misinterpreted. So Inspector Bodyguard went into a drawer in my house where he remained for many years. Recently he has been published as the book *Inspector Bodyguard Patrols the Land of U.*

In 1974, my husband's alcoholism began to disrupt our lives. He did not receive tenure at the college where he was teaching and it was clear that he would be out of a job. His response was to increase his drinking. The boys and I lived without knowing if he would show up for dinner, when he would come home, indeed, if he was even dead or alive. Now I had to make even more money, enough to support the three of us, if not four. In January of 1975 I signed a contract to write a college physics textbook with two professors from the University of Wisconsin. The sum of money I was to receive made me independent of my husband's salary, which he would be drawing until May. So I ended the marriage in February of that year.

I have always thought of myself as extremely competent. But the emotional strain of ending my marriage and assuming full responsibility for myself and the children made me vulnerable and less effective than I had always been. Several months into the physics text, the whole project fell apart and was cancelled. I was numb. I had no idea what to do next. I knew children's books could not pay me enough to live. I needed a full-time job. A friend put me in touch with the executive producer of a brand-new morning talk show for ABC. It was going to be called "Good Morning America."

Like a sleepwalker, I went to the interview. GMA needed four writers. My television experience had consisted of doing my own show, although I had other experience writing for visual media. I had written several filmstrips. At the end of the interview I said, "I'm not sure I want this job. I don't think I want to be a newswriter." When I left, the secretary pulled me over to show me how many resumes were in the "keep file." There was one other beside mine. I was called back for a second interview with the head writer, a playwright. He said to bring some recent samples of my writing. I brought the first few chapters of the physics text.

The head writer read my material and kept shaking his head. "This is clean writing," he said. Unbelievably, I got the job! Becoming a network television newswriter for a major morning talk show was a job many others would have given their right arm for. But for me, it was not a career step. It was simply a job that enabled me to hire a housekeeper and support myself and my kids. It was not a job for a working mother. The three other writers were ambitious, while I needed to leave at the end of the day. It didn't matter to them that I had finished my assignments. They stayed late, getting points with the management. The pressure was on us to have a hit show. We were all expected to give it everything it needed, no matter how much time it took. Did I work overtime? You bet! Hours and hours, weekends, late nights. I came home at night exhausted. My housekeeper left dinner for me which was usually cold. I was too tired to give my kids much attention. I needed weekends to recover.

The work itself at GMA started off as an interesting challenge. Each writer was responsible for a half-hour script each day. We wrote "continuity," the chitchat between segments. We did something called a "pre-interview" which was talking to a guest over the phone so that we could write the questions for David Hartman or the female host. We did "produced spots" which were scripted segments filmed on location. We made decisions about editing film and we wrote "voice overs," the words you hear spoken over film. Although a talk show looks as if there is no script, there is *always* a script because the networks have a contract with a writers' union. At the end of my script I wrote David Hartman's sign off. "Make it a good day" were the words. They were words I used when I said good-bye to my friends. The first time I wrote them, I watched the show. "Have a good day," said David. The next script I wrote my sign off again and again David changed it. I caught David in the halls. "Listen," I said, "I wrote '*make* it a good day' because it implies that you have control over your life. If you want a good day the choice is up to you to make it so." "That's very good, Vicki. I'll use it." And those words, actually the words "make it," became David Hartman's signature, and they were the only words I wrote that I could be certain would be actually spoken on the air.

"Good Morning America" was an expensive new show and ABC was very nervous about it. Typical of start-up operations, there were a lot of changes the first year of its existence. Whenever the network brass got panicky that the show wasn't going to make it, they fired the executive producer. The next executive producer typically brought in his own people. To make room, staff was fired. I lasted ten months on the job. The third executive producer fired me. I was notified that I had no job in a phone call from the office manager on a Friday night as I was leaving on vacation. There was no real cause to fire me, so the executive producer had had someone else do it in a cowardly way. I decided that he would not get away with it. I called my writers' union. I demanded that the union officials set up a meeting with my boss where I could be told face to face why I was fired.

The day of the meeting, the head of the union showed up with two lawyers. I marched into the meeting with my head high, my fellow writers silently cheering me on. I knew that the meeting would not restore my job. My replacement was already on staff. But at least I would have the opportunity of showing everyone that the producer had no real cause to fire me. I ultimately had the satisfaction of knowing I was the last person to be fired in such a capricious manner.

With husband Edward Scribner Cobb, and sons, Josh and Theo, 1969

At this time, there was a new man in my life who was proving to be a worse alcoholic than my husband. I decided that I had to get rid of him and start my life over again. I needed to live out of the city because I wanted good schools for my children. At the moment I had nothing except my unemployment insurance. I was at the lowest point of my life. I began preparing myself to restructure my life. I thought about my work. It was clear that I was talented and competent enough to get a well-paying job in public relations. At one point during this period, I actually took such a job. I found I could do public relations as well as anyone. But the business was very undependable. I lost that job after three weeks because the firm failed to land the account they had initially hired me for. I could also be a journalist. I worked briefly as a writer for *Us* magazine doing several stories, including an interview with Senator Ted Kennedy. I could be a teacher again.

Then I thought, "What do I really want to do? I want to write science books for children. That's what the world has rewarded me for the most. That is where I can be distinctive."

My family and friends said, "But you can't earn a living writing children's science books." "That may be true," I thought to myself, "but if I take a PR job, I'll only be trying to earn enough money to free myself to write for kids. I don't want to look back on my life twenty years from now and think, 'If only I had tried.' I'll try now. If I fail I can always take that public relations job."

The first thing I did was to sign up two book contracts. One was for *More Science Experiments You Can Eat* and the other was *Truth On Trial: The Story of Galileo Galilei*. I hadn't written a book in three years. I wasn't sure I still could. Next I began looking for an apartment. By luck I found one in Mamaroneck, New York. It had two large bedrooms. Mine would also be my office and the other was large enough for my boys to share. It was located within walking distance to everything they would be doing so that I didn't have to worry about interrupting my work to chauffeur them about. The apartment was more than I thought I could afford but it met so many of my other requirements that I took it on the spot. Besides, it had the added attraction of a working fireplace and a small balcony.

Shortly after moving to Mamaroneck I took a part-time job as public relations director for Scott Publishing Company, the publisher of an annual stamp catalogue listing the prices of stamps for collectors. The Scott job paid the rent and got me out of the house to midtown Manhattan one day a week. The rest of my time I spent doing as many books as I could, constantly beating the bushes. I was growing as a writer. It's easy to see how if you compare the opening paragraphs of *Science Experiments You Can Eat* with those of *More Science Experiments You Can Eat,* published eight years later. The later book speaks with an informal and witty tone while the earlier book is more traditional. Nonfiction writing in general is bound by the conventions of journalism where the writer is never a presence in the work but simply serves as a conduit from the real world to the reader. Most newspapers have style sheets with rules for their staff so that the material submitted by a variety of reporters all sounds pretty much the same. But literature depends on a writer developing a distinctive "voice," bringing her own vision and personality to the work. The author's voice is crucial to high quality fiction. This is a recognized and established standard for judging fiction, for an effective author's voice can greatly enhance a story. But this standard has not been applied to very much nonfiction, particularly "informational books" such as the ones I wanted to write. Most editors are bound by tradition, making authors tell it straight and tell it simply, usually in a boring manner.

With her father, as the recipient of the Eva L. Gordon Award from the American Nature Society, 1985

Without quite knowing what I was doing, I made a break with tradition. I signed a contract to write a book for second-grade readers on the microorganisms that make things rot. I knew that the first job of any writer is to engage the attention of the reader. Here is my opening paragraph for *Lots of Rot:*

Want to smell something rotten? Take a deep breath by the garbage can. If it's rotten your nose knows. All it takes is one sniff. Yukk!

The manuscript came back from my editor covered with blue marks. Here's how she rewrote the first two sentences:

Have you ever smelled something rotten? You probably have if you've ever taken a deep breath by a garbage can.

She went through the rest of the book taking out all the spark and life and playfulness and, of course, the "Yukk!" All the active verbs were changed to passive ones; the personal, intimate tone was changed to make the subject more distant from the reader. I felt sick when I read it. I called my editor and asked to come in and speak to her about the book. When I did, and she could see how upset I was, she asked me to return when her boss was available. I prepared well for this all-important meeting. I wrote out a defense of my book chapter by chapter, telling why I was doing what I was doing. My book looked deceptively simple, it read easily. But it was packed with information that built one idea upon another. The day of the meeting I wore a new suit. I was going to make my case and then leave the fate of the book in their hands.

When I left the meeting, I felt satisfied that I had done everything I could think of to defend my work. They said they would let me know. Three days later the chief editor called my agent. "If Vicki won't write the book the way we want it, we won't publish it," she said. And, although I needed the money, I withdrew the book and promptly sold it to Harper & Row. The book was published in my voice, the way I wrote it. The day I first saw a finished copy, I was sitting at the Harper & Row booth at a convention. A number of my books were on display. A child walked by. She picked up *Lots of Rot* and opened it. "Will she turn the page?" I wondered hopefully. My hands were so tightly clasped, my knuckles were white. The girl turned the page and I wondered, "Will she turn the next page?" The suspense was killing. Yes, she kept reading. She settled her chin on her hand as she stood and read. Her mother said, "It's time to go." "I want to finish this," said my reader. And she did! A young person picked up my book out of all the books in the convention, and without knowing that the author was watching, stood and read my book, a science book, cover to cover! I have had many awards and good reviews and recognition for my work over the years. But that moment was the one I needed to absolutely validate my approach to my work. I vowed that I would never ever give in to some editor's opinion if I strongly disagree.

Over the years, like many other authors, I have been invited to speak to children at schools. Often I am the first nonfiction author to be invited. Instead of talking about

Demonstrating the fun of science to schoolchildren

writing, I like to talk about science. I do a program that demonstrates some of the fun and magic based on science. In many ways, I still consider myself a teacher except, instead of talking directly to a class, I use my craft of writing to communicate a love for science. Science is a subject that many people find difficult, including elementary-school teachers. Science textbooks are not well written so it's no surprise that flat, boring reading turns students off the subject.

A few years ago, a science curriculum specialist in a school district in Washington State called me and asked if I did science programs for teachers based on my books. I hadn't put anything together yet, but I said that I could. That started me doing in-service programs for educators. The response from teachers was amazing. Many of them said that they were afraid to teach science but that they felt confident that they could teach from my books. Appearing before teachers has been yet another challenge. At the end of a six-hour day of hands-on science under my direction, teachers write evaluations. They do not have to put their names on them so they say exactly what they think of me. It is always a shock to discover that although most give me very high marks, I can't win them all. Despite doing my

very best there will always be some who will not understand. Tough lesson!

Doing in-service programs for teachers all over the country has made me think hard, again, about education. I am more firmly convinced than ever that the Little Red educational philosophy was right. I look back over my life and see that my fulfillment in my work comes from repeating the same kinds of activities I enjoyed as a child. I recall sixth grade as a magic year of self-discovery and discovery of the world around me. In many ways, I now recreate sixth grade for myself through my work. When I think of new ideas for books, I am recreating that summer at Buck's Rock when I was dreaming up products to sell to the public.

My life has been a surprise to me. I never expected to have a big career where people would pay me for my words and opinions. I thought that my life would be based on my marriage and on the achievements of my husband and children. I do not minimize the effect of financial need on my productivity. The road to achievement is simply to turn stuff out. Would I have been as productive if I had married a good provider? I doubt it.

I like where I am today and I know that getting here wasn't easy. Recently, I met a pretty young teacher, a new bride excited by her first teaching job. The school I was visiting was making a big fuss over me. She was curious about the path I had traveled to this point. How does one get to be a celebrated author? I thought to myself, "If I told her about my life—my husband's illness, the constant worry about money, the many harsh rejections from editors, the criticism from the public, the loneliness of my profession, and the reality that leadership and speaking out is often isolating—would she choose to walk in my shoes? Not likely." I probably wouldn't have chosen it either. But now, if you asked me if I could have lived my life any differently, would I? Emphatically not! There are no short cuts; every life is defined as much by the choices that we make as by events. My choices seem to always put me at risk and set up challenges. Sometimes I find myself in hot water. But all along the way, there's been joy in the struggle. As my life continues to unfold I expect to keep creating, to collect unusual experiences, not things, and to find myself continually surprised.

POSTSCRIPT

Vicki Cobb contributed the following update to *SATA* in 2002:

I am often asked what I wanted to be when I grew up. I know exactly what the answer is because I wrote an essay about it when I was eleven, which I still have. "In college, I will major in art and minor in dramatics. After college I want to act. When I marry, I want my husband to be a producer. I want three children, three dogs, and a horse. After I have my children I will stay home because I think a mother should raise her children herself. Then I will design clothes and illustrate books. I want to travel a lot, too."

Now that I'm a senior citizen I can start to see how my life is turning out. I didn't do a lot of things I said I wanted to do when I was eleven. I didn't become an actress and marry a producer. I had only two children and can barely keep my plants alive, let alone take care of pets. Instead of being an artist at home, I became a writer. But the main

In Uganda with co-author Barbara Lavallee (right), researching **This Place Is Wild***, 1994*

message I get from my early desires is that I wanted to live life fully; I wanted to accomplish a lot. And to that end I have certainly fulfilled my dreams.

Travel seemed to me to be the ultimate learning experience. But travel takes money, and when I was young, we didn't have any. If I were going to travel, I'd have to find a way not to pay for it myself. In 1982, I had my first chance to go to Europe. I was hired by a chain of retail florists in Sweden to develop an herb-growing kit for kids. I had to go to Malmo, in southern Sweden, to meet with their experts. The trip, of course, was at their expense. On the way home, I stopped in London. A second trip was required six months later. This time I flew to Amsterdam and took a train north to Copenhagen. By now, I was bitten by the travel bug big time. I began traveling around the U.S. speaking at schools. I was invited to Alaska two years in a row. I went to Ketchikan in southeast Alaska, to Nome, to an Eskimo village on the Bering Sea, to Valdez, and down the Kenai Peninsula. I fell in love with the people and their pioneer spirit and the scenery, with its black beaches and mountains rising from the sea. Alaska is truly heart-stoppingly beautiful.

On my second trip I was introduced to Barbara Lavallee, a wonderful Alaskan artist. Barbara had never illustrated a children's book but I thought she'd be good at it. Plus, I thought it would be fun to work with her. Despite the four thousand miles between our homes, our lives were remarkably similar. She, too, was divorced with two sons and had decided to make her living freelance from her art. My agent suggested that I write a book about Alaska and have Barbara illustrate it. It wouldn't be a science book but I thought I could do it. Since I would make more money from writing a series rather than a single title about Alaska, I created the "Imagine Living Here" series. The idea was that there were places on earth that had some over-riding characteristic that affected the lives of plants and animals, people, life-style, art, and culture. We would present our view, Barbara's and mine, of these places—not a dry and factual one. We had a hard time selling the series because many people felt that Barbara's art was too stylized for nonfiction. But I didn't agree, nor did a very visionary editor, Amy Shields, at Walker Books.

Alaska became the subject of *This Place Is Cold,* the first book of the "Imagine Living Here" series. I didn't need to make another trip to Alaska to write it, since I had already been all over the state and Barbara was Alaskan. But Barbara and I met in Arizona to research *This Place Is Dry.* What fun we had! We took a jeep trip through the desert, we visited the Sonoran Desert Museum outside of Tucson, we went to archeological digs and museums. When we were finished collecting information for the book, we took a mule trip down the Grand Canyon. In the process of making arrangements for the trip, I discovered an interesting way to help pay for it. I had called the Arizona tourist board and told them I had a book contract to write about their desert. Could they help? Aside from sending me lots of information and printed material, they got us a reduced rate at a hotel.

Aha! I now knew how to do it. In order to write *This Place Is Wet* we needed to see a rain forest. Our dream, of course, was the Amazon River Basin, but a trip to South America was way out of our price range. As a fallback, I thought we could afford a trip to a Puerto Rican rain forest but it would not be the same. Not to worry; the Brazilian Tourism Foundation generously came to our assistance, as did the Bolivians and Peruvians for our book on the Andes Mountains, *This Place Is High.* We were off to see the world, and oh, what a time we had. We celebrated Mother's Day in Rio, without our kids. We took a cruise up the Amazon, we took a train ride through the Sacred Valley of the Incas on our way to Machu Picchu, we ate exotic seafood, heard haunting music, met all kinds of interesting people and, of course, we shopped—something Barbara and I especially love doing together. The next year we went to Japan for *This Place Is Crowded* and to Australia for *This Place Is Lonely.* Finally, we went on the ultimate trip to Kenya and Uganda to research *This Place Is Wild.* Barbara always said that these trips were like "eating dessert first." The hard work began when we got home and had to produce the book. The eighth book was to be titled *This Place is Ancient.* We made a trip to Turkey to research it, but for some unclear reasons, my publisher decided not to publish it, so the series stands at seven books.

By 1991 I had lost both my parents. Aside from missing them terribly, it is strange to be the oldest member of a family. I had to finish growing myself up and take a hard look at the direction of my own life. I was alone. Theo was married and living in Wisconsin. Josh was working as an optical engineer in upstate New York. With my small inheritance I could afford to buy a place to live in. So I purchased a brand-new, three-bedroom townhouse with a pond in the backyard. The downstairs had a walk-out basement and a fireplace. It was the largest room in the house and I designed it as my dream office. Heaven! Upstairs, there is plenty of room for my sons and their growing families to come and visit. It didn't seem too big for just one person. But that was about to change.

My school-visit business was thriving. I had been to almost all of the fifty states doing programs for kids and teachers. In December of 1993 I was invited to the Eagle Valley School District in Vail, Colorado. Since I ski, I was thrilled. I managed to put in eight days of skiing around six days of work. Toward the end of my work-vacation, I was skiing all alone one morning when a gentleman invited me to share the chairlift with him and his buddy. By the time we reached the top of the mountain I knew that he, too, came from New York and he skied the same part of Vermont I skied, although it was a different mountain. He invited me to spend the day skiing with them and I accepted. His name was Richard Trachtenberg and we were married in 1996. Richard made my life complete. There was plenty of room for him in my new home.

It's fair to say that our marriage would never have happened if I didn't ski. I first learned how on my honeymoon back in January of 1960. We had wooden skis and leather boots with straps that connected the boot to the ski so that if you fell and came out of your binding, the ski wouldn't sail independently down the mountain—a frightening danger to other skiers. I skied every winter for twelve years. Then, as my marriage to Ed Cobb ended, I couldn't afford it any longer. But in 1982, I was out in Park City, Utah, promoting a book I had written on the Special Olympics. Park City generously offered equipment and lift tickets to anyone associated with the Special Olympics and I took them up on the offer. The equipment had changed so much in ten years and it was so much fun, that I vowed to

Dancing with her husband Richard Trachtenberg, in his silver skiing top hat, at their wedding, May 1996

put skiing back into my life. When I came home, I joined a ski house in Vermont and spent many wonderful winter weekends trying to break out of the intermediate skier level. When I met Richard, I was still far from expert and could only dream of mastering a black diamond trail. Richard, however, was an excellent skier. His style is perfectly linked, carved turns with his legs together so you can't see daylight between them. He is extremely graceful and his technique allows him to ski everything from ice to powder to moguls to extremely steep slopes while making it look easy. He taught himself to ski by reading ski magazines and practicing mentally in his office all week until he could get on a slope over the weekend. He also skis a lot! Since we met, we ski over sixty days a winter. We bought a small condo in Manchester, Vermont, and every Friday night we have a picnic in the car as we make the three-hour drive north. (Richard is famous at our local mountain for skiing in a sparkling silver party top hat. I call him my "Fred Astaire on skis.") With that much skiing, one can't help improving. I'm happy to say that this old dog has learned some new tricks and become an excellent skier although I'll never have the young legs needed for the truly challenging stuff.

Richard also brought boating into my life. He owns a thirty-seven foot sport fisherman called "Summer Snow." It sleeps four, has a full galley (kitchen) and a head (bathroom) with a tiny bathtub in it. I have learned how to tie lines (not ropes), keep from getting seasick, and navigate with a Global Positioning System (GPS). We have gone on cruises from New York to Montauk Point to Martha's Vineyard. I've learned how to deal with getting stuck on a sandbar, losing an anchor in New York Harbor during Op-Sail 2000, and riding my (folding) bicycle around Fire Island. I have been a tennis player since I first met Ed Cobb. So between tennis, boating, and skiing, this female, who was not brought up with athletics, is pretty active.

These days, life is very sweet. And the bonus is my wonderful grandchildren. Theo has two daughters: Abby and Lexie. Abby, born in 1990 is always into some creative project. There is a book about us called *Meet My Grandmother: She's a Children's Book Author,* by Lisa McElroy. Lexie, born in 1994, is very athletic and has already spent time skiing with us. Richard's son, Eric, is father of Benjamin (the same name as my father), born on Josh's birthday in 1997. Ben is going to my elementary school, The Little Red School House, where they call him "Mister Idea Man." Josh's son, Jonathan, also born in 1997, is a fearless athlete and hilariously funny. Jillian, born in 2000, is a tough and determined little girl, no matter what she tries. My job as a grandmother is to keep them all supplied with books. They each have a collection of signed books from other authors I meet in my travels. They have books from my many publishers, which I shamelessly ask for when I meet with my editors. And, of course, they have the books I write.

A very famous philosopher once said that life must be lived forward. So I have a list of unfinished business: There are still many places in the world I have yet to see. Richard and I still have many trails yet to ski and many ports to visit. And, of course, many more books to write. Recently I have put together a book of short funny poems that my son Theo will illustrate. I am a young enough grandmother to see my grandchildren grow up. Richard and I are putting our hard-won knowledge of life to good use. We know it doesn't get any better than this, and for that we are grateful.

COCCA-LEFFLER, Maryann 1958-

Personal

Born July 25, 1958, in Everett, MA; daughter of Theodore F. (an engineer) and Rose (a homemaker; maiden name, Vivilecchia) Cocca; married Eric M. Leffler (in finance), April 5, 1981; children: Janine, Kristin. *Nationality:* American. *Education:* Massachusetts College of Art, B.F.A., 1980.

Addresses

Home and office—14 Holt Rd., Amherst, NH 03031. *E-mail*—MCLeffler@aol.com.

Career

Freelance children's book illustrator and author.

Member

Society of Children's Book Writers and Illustrators.

Awards, Honors

Pick of the Lists citation, American Booksellers Association, for *Missing: One Stuffed Rabbit, Wanda's Roses, Mr. Tanen's Ties,* and *Bus Route To Boston;* Parents' Choice Approved Book, for *Bus Route to Boston;* Children's Book Award, Florida Reading Association, 2001, for *Mr. Tanen's Ties.*

Writings

SELF-ILLUSTRATED

Wednesday Is Spaghetti Day, Scholastic (New York, NY), 1990.

Grandma & Me (board book), Random House (New York, NY), 1990.
Ice Cold Birthday (easy reader), Grosset & Dunlap (New York, NY), 1992.
Count the Days till Christmas, Scholastic (New York, NY), 1993.
What a Pest! (easy reader), Grosset & Dunlap (New York, NY), 1994.
Clams All Year, Boyds Mills Press (Honesdale, PA), 1996.
Lots of Hearts, Grosset & Dunlap (New York, NY), 1996.
Silly Willy, Grosset & Dunlap (New York, NY), 1996.
Mommy Hugs, Little Simon (New York, NY), 1997.
Daddy Hugs, Little Simon (New York, NY), 1997.
Missing: One Stuffed Rabbit, A. Whitman (Morton Grove, IL), 1998.
Princess for a Day, Grosset & Dunlap (New York, NY), 1998.
Mr. Tanen's Ties, A. Whitman (Morton Grove, IL), 1999.
Jungle Halloween, A. Whitman (Morton Grove, IL), 2000.
Bus Route to Boston, Boyds Mills Press (Honesdale, PA), 2000.
Edgar Degas: Paintings That Dance, Grosset & Dunlap (New York, NY), 2001.
Bravery Soup, A. Whitman (Morton Grove, IL), 2002.
Mr. Tanen's Tie Trouble, A. Whitman (Morton Grove, IL), 2003.

ILLUSTRATOR

Eileen Spinelli, *Thanksgiving at the Tappletons,* Addison Wesley (Reading, MA), 1982, re-illustrated edition, HarperCollins (New York, NY), 1992.
Susan Alton Schmeltz, *Oh So Silly!,* Parents Magazine Press (New York, NY), 1983.
Rita Goldan Gelman and Susan Kovacs Buxbaum, *Splash! All about Baths,* Little, Brown (Boston, MA), 1987.
Stephen Krensky, *Big Time Bears,* Little, Brown (Boston, MA), 1989.
Ruth Young, *A Trip to Mars,* Orchard Books (New York, NY), 1990.

Wendy Cheyette Lewison, *MUD,* Random House (New York, NY), 1990.

Marcia Leonard, *Alphabet Bandits,* Troll (Mahwah, NJ), 1990.

My ABC's at Home (board book), Grosset & Dunlap (New York, NY), 1990.

Marcia Leonard, *The Kitten Twins,* Troll (Mahwah, NJ), 1990.

These Are Baby's Things, Random House (New York, NY), 1990.

Hey Diddle Diddle (nursery rhymes), Grosset & Dunlap (New York, NY), 1991.

John Schindel, *Something's Fishy,* Simon & Schuster (New York, NY), 1993.

The Elves and the Shoemaker, Grosset & Dunlap (New York, NY), 1993.

Pat Brisson, *Wanda's Roses,* Boyd's Mills Press (Honesdale, PA), 1994.

Wendy Cheyette Lewison, *Hello Snow!,* Grosset & Dunlap (New York, NY), 1994.

Eve Bunting, *I Don't Want to Go to Camp,* Boyds Mills Press (Honesdale, PA), 1996.

Eve Bunting, *My Backpack,* Boyds Mills Press (Honesdale, PA), 1997.

Michelle Poploff, *Tea Party for Two,* Delacorte Press (New York, NY), 1997.

Diane Cocca-Spofford, *The Good-Bye Game,* Infinity Plus One (Ridgewood, NJ), 1998.

Barbara Juster Esbensen, *Jumping Day,* Boyds Mills Press (Honesdale, PA), 1999.

Wendy Cheyette Lewison, *The Big Snowball,* Grosset & Dunlap (New York, NY), 2000.

Diane Cocca-Spofford, *Do You Love Me?,* Infinity Plus One (Ridgewood, NJ), 2001.

Judy Donnelly, *The Pilgrims & Me,* Grosset & Dunlap (New York, NY), 2002.

Sidelights

Author/illustrator Maryann Cocca-Leffler is the creator of many self-illustrated titles and the illustrator of dozens more. Known for the bright colors and cheerful presentation of her artwork and her simple, clear texts which are appropriate for beginning readers, Cocca-Leffler once told *SATA:* "As long as I can remember, I've always wanted to be an artist. I used to draw and paint on anything; paper bags, rocks, sea-shells, and even a mural on my parent's garage door (my parents still regret the day I painted over it!)."

Born in 1958, in Everett, Massachusetts, the author grew up in an Italian family where, as she noted on her Web site, "dinnertime was always a major feast. Many days you could find my mother, Rose, in the kitchen, rolling meatballs or my father, Ted, in his garden picking tomatoes." The second oldest of five children, Cocca-Leffler liked to play school, listen to the music of the Beatles, and draw and paint as a child. She determined early on that she wanted to be an artist when she grew up. "I remember back in fourth grade, my teacher, Sister Isabel Thomas, saw promise in me as an artist and gave me my very first set of pastels," the author told *SATA.* "I still have them! In high school, my Uncle Dan and I took

Maryann Cocca-Leffler

sculpting classes at night. He and my entire family were always encouraging. I always did well in school, but art class was my favorite. When it came time to decide on a college, I submitted my portfolio to Massachusetts College of Art. My parents were a bit worried; they couldn't believe anyone could make a living as an artist. I remember them saying, 'You need something to fall back on.' They suggested I try a liberal arts college. I wanted and needed intense art training, therefore I went on to study at Massachusetts College, majoring in illustration. During my junior year, my style began to take shape. It did not fit into the editorial role. While other illustration majors found it easy to depict 'the Iran-hostage-crisis,' I found it difficult. I remember a classmate saying, 'Maryann, you can never draw anything that looks MEAN!' Children book illustration, on the other hand, seemed to be a perfect fit for my style."

Cleaning out a corner of her parents' cellar, she turned it into a space for her first studio. She painted a bright mural on the oil tank in the process, one of several she created as a young painter. For four years she used this dark cellar studio, all the while dreaming of becoming a children's book illustrator. "After graduation, I lined up several freelance elementary textbook jobs, one on an elementary math book for Houghton Mifflin," Cocca-Leffler further explained to *SATA.* "I drew a million little objects, but it was a start. Fearing that I would never make any real money as an illustrator, my father, with good intentions, got me a job, three days a week, drawing aircraft and missiles for a defense contractor. I lasted three months."

Finally Cocca-Leffler decided to freelance full-time. "I took many jobs just for the money, including drawing toilet plumbing supplies. But at the same time I continued to illustrate children's textbooks. I was determined to find work using my own style of illustration instead of styling my illustration to fit a job. I made the rounds with my portfolio to Boston-area publishers. In 1981 I got an offer to illustrate my first children's book, *Thanksgiving at the Tappletons.*" Written by Eileen Spinelli, this picture book deals with calamity in the preparation of Thanksgiving dinner at the Tappleton house. However, despite their difficulties, the family realizes that they do indeed have something to be thankful for. Reviewing the revised 1992 edition of *Thanksgiving at the Tappletons* in *Booklist,* Ilene Cooper found that the "art captures the slapstick fun" of Spinelli's text. Cocca-Leffler's artwork for this book set her off on her new career, but at first progress was slow.

"1981 was also the year I got married," Cocca-Leffler recalled for *SATA.* "When we returned from our honeymoon, my husband, Eric, played our phone number in the state lottery. We won $3,500.00! With the money we printed eight full-color greeting cards which I

Janine loses her classroom's stuffed rabbit at the mall and sets the whole class on the search in Cocca-Leffler's self-illustrated **Missing: One Stuffed Rabbit.**

designed and started our own greeting card company, Marcel & Co. I worked in the greeting card business for the next five years, accumulating one hundred of my own designs and selling them through sales representatives around the country. It was tough competing with the big guys, so we sold our line to a company in Arizona. My years illustrating greeting cards helped me establish my style and aided in the development of my characters. With these skills and the use of my greeting cards as a promotional tool, I was able to re-enter the children's book field. I have been illustrating and writing children's book ever since."

Further illustration jobs came her way, but during this time Cocca-Leffler also turned her hand to her own self-illustrated title. "*Wednesday Is Spaghetti Day* was the first book I both wrote and illustrated. I got the idea when I was cat-sitting my cousin Laura's two cats. One day, after coming home to a mess, I said, 'I wonder what these cats do when you leave them home alone?' That's when the idea was born. Six years and seven publishers later, *Wednesday Is Spaghetti Day* was finally published." Cocca-Leffler's debut picture book tells of Catrina the cat who can not wait until the Termonte family leaves, for she has invited all her feline friends over for an Italian feast. When the guests arrive, Catrina tosses her cat food out and proceeds to put together a real Italian banquet. "I grew up in a close Italian family where there was always plenty of love, togetherness, and FOOD!" the author told *SATA.* "The recipe the cats use in *Wednesday Is Spaghetti Day* is my Mom's. In *Thanksgiving at the Tappletons* some of the characters look suspiciously like my relatives (my Dad, Uncle Dan, and my Mom and Aunt Hilda who really did work at a bakery)."

For her next work, *Grandma & Me,* Cocca-Leffler took inspiration not from her own childhood, but from that of her children. "My best creations, by far, are my two daughters, Janine and Kristin," Cocca-Leffler told *SATA.* "Though at times it is very difficult to work with small children, they are truly an inspiration. *Grandma & Me* is based on my daughter Janine, who spent every Tuesday with her Nana Rose, so I could spend time in my studio. Ever since they were babies, I have enjoyed sharing books with my daughters."

Cocca-Leffler's daughters as well as events from her own childhood have inspired other books by the author/illustrator. "The two sisters in *Ice Cold Birthday* and its sequel *What a Pest!* are sometimes my two daughters and sometimes my sister and I. The idea for the ice cream-cookie cake in *Ice Cold Birthday* came from a hastily made cake we made for my sister when we forgot her birthday. And like in *What a Pest!,* I actually did get the chicken pox right before I was to perform on stage."

With *Clams All Year,* Cocca-Leffler returned to her own childhood for inspiration, the story being based on one summer her family spent in Hull, Massachusetts. One night a big storm brought in lots of clams: so many, in fact, that the family was eating clams all year. Sheila M. Geraty, writing in *Horn Book Guide,* praised Cocca-

Leffler's "sprightly gouache and colored-pencil illustrations," while Kathy Piehl, writing in *School Library Journal,* also commended the artwork, which, she said, captures "the love and exuberance of an extended family." A contributor for *Publishers Weekly* similarly concluded that "this simply told tale of a close-knit family has a timeless, understated warmth."

As her children grew, they provided inspiration for more self-illustrated titles, including *Missing: One Stuffed Rabbit, Mr. Tanen's Ties, Princess for a Day,* and *Jungle Halloween.* An experience her daughter Janine had in the first grade brought about *Missing: One Stuffed Rabbit.* In her class, one of the students got to take the prized Coco home each night and write about the events in a diary. In the fictional Janine's case, this visit is cut short when the rabbit is lost in a mall, and when she later learns that the toy has been given as part of a toy distribution to a hospital, the students agree that the wheelchair-bound girl who gets Coco should keep the stuffed animal. "There is plenty to look at here—and sharp eyes will spot where and when Coco gets lost," wrote *Booklist*'s Cooper. DeAnn Tabuchi also lauded the "bold, colorful" artwork in a *School Library Journal* review, calling it "appealing, as is the totally satisfying conclusion."

Mr. Tanen's Ties "is based on the REAL Mr. Tanen, who is the principal of my daughters' former elementary school," Cocca-Leffler noted on her Web site. In the book, this principal is very well known for his brightly colored and unusual ties that announce various events, and the students love both his ties and the man. However, Mr. Tanen's boss, Mr. Apple, is not so approving. He orders Tanen to get rid of this neckwear and don a more sensible plain blue tie. When Mr. Tanen takes some time off, Mr. Apple substitutes for him, and the students manage to give the dour man some zany neckwear of his own, with miraculous results. This award-winning title was praised by a critic for *Kirkus Reviews* for making the world of adults "a lot less formidable, and a lot more eccentric." *Booklist*'s Cooper lauded this "fresh and upbeat" book, and its artwork, which is "just as bright as Mr. Tanen's ties."

Daughter Kristin's fourth birthday party provided inspiration for *Princess for a Day,* while a jungle mural the author painted on her bedroom wall prompted *Jungle Halloween.* In the latter picture book, rhyming verses relate the tale of jungle animals who get all dressed up for a Halloween party. *School Library Journal*'s Linda M. Kenton commented that Cocca-Leffler's book stays away from traditional Halloween motifs which "can easily frighten preschoolers," and went on to call *Jungle Halloween* a "surefire showstopper for storytimes."

A girl named Kristin is also the fictional author of a school report on a French Impressionist painter in *Edgar Degas: Paintings That Dance,* part of the "Smart about Art" series. The book, like others in the series, uses the school report format to tell the events of the artist's life, and it also employs reproductions as well as child-like cartoons to illustrate the "report." *Booklist*'s Gillian

Engberg, in a starred review of *Edgar Degas,* felt the book was a "successful blend of fact and humor that makes sophisticated concepts completely accessible and even entertaining." A reviewer for *Publishers Weekly* also praised the "clear, accessible format" of the series and Cocca-Leffler's contribution to it.

Cocca-Leffler reverts once again to her early childhood experiences for the year 2000 title *Bus Route to Boston.* "I grew up on a bus route," Cocca-Leffler noted on her Web site. "As a young girl, I remember frequent Saturday bus trips, which traveled down our street, through crowded neighborhoods, over the bridge, then all the way to Boston. My mother, sister, and I went bargain hunting in Filene's Basement, enjoyed ice cream at Bailey's, shopped for vegetables at Haymarket, and ventured into the North End for pizza and cannoli. Through my story and paintings I have shared these warm childhood memories of Boston." In the book, a day on the bus is presented, from the first meeting with Bill the driver to stops at all of the special places from Cocca-Leffler's memory, ending with a homecoming in the late afternoon. *Booklist*'s Cooper praised the title as a "warm, loving memoir [that] will have plenty of resonance for today's children," and further commented that the "oversize, nicely crowded acrylic artwork ... is lots of fun." Marianne Saccardi, reviewing the title in *School Library Journal,* similarly called attention to the "simple and unadorned" language and the artwork which contains "touches of humor." Saccardi concluded that *Bus Route to Boston* is a "charming slice of life in a time past."

For her 2002 title, *Bravery Soup,* Cocca-Leffler, as usual, delved into personal experience for a story line. "I got the idea ... when I had to do something that I didn't look forward to doing," Cocca-Leffler recounted on her Web site. "(I think we have all been there.) I had to dig deep to find the bravery I needed." Similarly, the young raccoon Carlin, who is frightened by everything, even his own shadow, wants to sip some of Big Bear's Bravery Soup and become like this fearless animal. But first Carlin must make a dangerous journey through the Forbidden Forest and up Skulk Mountain to the lair of a terrible monster in order to bring back a vital ingredient for the soup. Along the way, Carlin discovers that he already possesses bravery inside of himself. Calling the work "a satisfying example of how facing fears helps to conquer them," *Booklist*'s Connie Fletcher noted that Cocca-Leffler's use of "bright acrylics and humorous details" keep children from being too frightened by scary elements in the story. A reviewer for *Publishers Weekly* also felt that the illustrations "convey suspense as well as the warm friendship between the animal friends."

"I haven't changed much since I was a kid ... except I got older!" Cocca-Leffler noted on her Web site. "I still think like an eight-year-old, which really helps when you write for kids." The author/illustrator concluded to *SATA,* "To be able to express these ideas and images through my books and at the same time experience the shared joy of illustrating is the best job in the world."

Biographical and Critical Sources

PERIODICALS

Booklist, October 1, 1992, Ilene Cooper, review of *Thanksgiving at the Tappletons,* p. 338; January 1, 1996, p. 842; June 1, 1996, Susan Dove Lempke, review of *Clams All Year,* p. 1730; March 15, 1998, Ilene Cooper, review of *Missing: One Stuffed Rabbit,* p. 1246; May 15, 1999, Ilene Cooper, review of *Mr. Tanen's Ties,* p. 1702; February 1, 2000, Ilene Cooper, review of *Bus Route to Boston,* p. 1028; September 1, 2000, Hazel Rochman, review of *Jungle Halloween,* p. 131; November 15, 2001, Gillian Engberg, review of *Edgar Degas,* p. 572; April 15, 2002, Connie Fletcher, review of *Bravery Soup.*

Horn Book Guide, fall, 1996, Sheila M. Geraty, review of *Clams All Year,* p. 251; fall, 1998, Christine Heppermann, review of *Missing,* p. 288; fall, 1999, Susan Halperin, review of *Mr. Tanen's Ties,* p. 248; spring, 2001, Martha Sibert, review of *Jungle Halloween,* p. 13.

Kirkus Reviews, March 15, 1999, review of *Mr. Tanen's Ties,* p. 449; February 15, 2002, review of *Bravery Soup,* p. 252.

Publishers Weekly, November 5, 1982, review of *Thanksgiving at the Tappletons;* December 11, 1987, p. 63; July 13, 1990, p. 52; April 12, 1993, p. 61; May 16, 1994, p. 64; May 27, 1996, review of *Clams All Year,* p. 78; May 12, 1997, review of *My Backpack,* p. 76; February 21, 2000, review of *Bus Route to Boston,* p. 87; September 25, 2000, review of *Jungle Halloween,* p. 62; November 19, 2001, review of *Edgar Degas,* p. 70; March 1, 2002, review of *Bravery Soup,* p. 70.

School Library Journal, March, 1983, p. 167; December, 1984, pp. 76-77; December, 1989, p. 84; March, 1990, Laura Culberg, review of *Wednesday Is Spaghetti Day,* p. 189; May, 1990, p. 88; October, 1990, pp. 105-106; September, 1992, p. 201; September, 1993, p. 218; December, 1994, p. 71; March, 1996, p. 166; July, 1996, Kathy Piehl, review of *Clams All Year,* pp. 57-58; February, 1998, Jan Shepherd Ross, review of *Tea Party for Two,* p. 90; May, 1998, DeAnn Tabuchi, review of *Missing,* p. 113; March, 1999, Shelley Woods, review of *Mr. Tanen's Ties,* pp. 171-172; April, 1999, Linda Ludke, review of *Jumping Day,* pp. 92-93; April, 2000, Marianne Saccardi, review of *Bus Route to Boston,* p. 94; September, 2000, Linda M. Kenton, review of *Jungle Halloween,* p. 186; November, 2001, Susan Lissim, review of *Edgar Degas,* p. 143.

OTHER

Boyds Mills Press, http://www.boydsmillspress.com/ (April 9, 2002), "Authors and Illustrators: Maryann Cocca-Leffler."

Maryann Cocca-Leffler Web Site, http://www.maryanncoccaleffler.com/ (June 30, 2002).*

COLE, Brock 1938-

Personal

Born May 29, 1938, in Pittsburgh, PA; married Susan Cole (a classical studies professor); children: two sons. *Education:* Kenyon College, B.A.; University of Minnesota, Ph.D.

Addresses

Home—158 Lombard Ave., Oak Park, IL 60302.

Career

University of Minnesota, instructor in English composition; University of Wisconsin, instructor in philosophy, until 1975; writer and illustrator, 1975—.

Awards, Honors

Juvenile Award, Friends of American Writers, 1980, for *The King at the Door;* California Young Reader Medal, California Reading Association, 1985, and Young Reader's Choice Award, Pacific Northwest Library Association, both for *The Indian in the Cupboard,* which was also named a *New York Times* outstanding book, 1981; Smarties "Grand Prix" for children's books, Book Trust, 1985; Parent's Choice Award, 1986, for *The Giant's Toe;* Carl Sandburg Award, Friends of Chicago Public Library, 1988, for *The Goats,* which was also named a *New York Times* notable book, an American Library Association (ALA) best book for young adults, and an ALA notable book, all 1987; *Booklist* Editors' Choice citation, and Notable Children's Book of the Year citation from *Publishers Weekly,* both for *Celine; School Library Journal*'s Best Books of 1997 list, and National Book Award nominee, 1997, both for *The Facts Speak for Themselves.*

Writings

FOR CHILDREN; SELF-ILLUSTRATED

The King at the Door, Doubleday (New York, NY), 1979.
No More Baths, Doubleday (New York, NY), 1980.
Nothing but a Pig, Doubleday (New York, NY), 1981.
The Winter Wren, Farrar, Straus (New York, NY), 1984.
The Giant's Toe, Farrar, Straus (New York, NY), 1986.
Alpha and the Dirty Baby, Farrar, Straus (New York, NY), 1991.
Buttons, Farrar, Straus (New York, NY), 2000.
Larky Mavis, Farrar, Straus (New York, NY), 2001.

OTHER

(Illustrator) Lynne Reid Banks, *The Indian in the Cupboard,* Avon (New York, NY), 1980.
(Illustrator) Jill Paton Walsh, *Gaffer Samson's Luck,* Farrar, Straus (New York, NY), 1984.
The Goats (young adult novel), Farrar, Straus (New York, NY), 1987.
Celine (young adult novel), Farrar, Straus (New York, NY), 1989.

The Facts Speak for Themselves (young adult novel), Front
Street (Arden, NC), 1997.
(Illustrator) Deborah Chandra and Madeleine Comora,
George Washington's Teeth, Farrar, Straus (New York,
NY), 2003.

Work in Progress

Lost above the Timberline, for Farrar, Straus.

Sidelights

A philosophy professor turned painter, illustrator, and
writer, Brock Cole has created picture books critically
acclaimed for their expressiveness as well as depth of
detail, and three young adult novels which have won
numerous awards for their realistic portrayal of contemporary issues. While his picture books range in theme
and content from broad humor to allegory and drama,
Cole's novels "set out to ... uplift, comfort, amuse or
expand the horizons of those readers known, perhaps
condescendingly as 'young adults,'" according to Lynn
Freed writing in the *New York Times Book Review.*
"They manage to accomplish all this and much more,
simply by telling fine stories about unforgettable characters." "I want children to read like adults," Cole told Kit
Alderdice in a *Publishers Weekly* interview. "I don't
know whether that's their interest or not. But that's the
kind of book I write ... where things are not clear.
Where there's ambiguity. Where there's uncertainty.
And where something is really well written and is a joy
to read just because you get things right."

Cole grew up in the small town of Charlotte, Michigan,
and small-town life influenced him greatly. In *Junior
Literary Guild,* he recalled that Charlotte was "a place
where a six year old could wander into the feed mill or
the auto body shop and watch men work without being
chased out." His family moved to different places in the
Midwest several times during his childhood, and he
ended up graduating from high school in Royal Oak,
Michigan. After graduation he attended Kenyon College
in Ohio. He briefly considered writing as a career, but
instead decided that he wanted to be a teacher. He taught
English at the University of Minnesota, where he was
also studying for a graduate degree. After completing his
Ph.D., Cole began teaching philosophy at the University
of Wisconsin.

In 1975, Cole's wife, Susan, got a job at the University
of Illinois, and the family moved to the Chicago area
with their two sons. By that time, Cole realized that
teaching was not really his interest. He was mainly
interested in writing books for children. Realizing that
the books would need to be illustrated, Cole also decided
to learn how to illustrate. He had no previous art
training, and he did not take classes to learn. Instead, he
studied the work of other illustrators whom he admired.
It seemed like a monumental task for the author to
undertake, but he had a very simple, yet effective, plan
of action. "I looked at illustrators I liked and tried to
draw like they did," Cole told Christine McDonnell in an
interview in *Horn Book* magazine. In particular, Cole

*Sixteen-year-old artist Celine must demonstrate
maturity while living with her young stepmother,
finishing high school, and helping her seven-year-old
neighbor through his parents' divorce. (Cover
illustration by Elaine Norman.)*

studied the work of Maurice Sendak, Ernest Shepard,
Margot Zemach, and Edward Ardizzone. This technique
worked well for him and his first picture book, *The King
at the Door,* was published in 1979, just a few years
after he decided to write and illustrate full-time.

The King at the Door is a moral fable set in a time long
ago. It is the story of a king who, while dressed in
beggar's rags, asks at an inn for food and drink. While
the innkeeper looks at the poorly dressed man and offers
only pitiful scraps, the young chore-boy, Little Baggit is
able to look deeper than the clothing to see the real
identity of the king. The boy shares his own humble
dinner with the king and is later richly rewarded when
the royal coach arrives for him. Critical praise welcomed
this debut book. "Cole proves that familiar plots can be
fashioned into new, refreshing and mighty diverting
tales by a gifted craftsman," a *Publishers Weekly* critic

wrote. A *Kirkus Reviews* contributor commented that the book was "crisply told, energetically pictured, and unmistakably amusing." In 1980 Cole won a Juvenile Award from the Friends of American Writers for the book.

Several more picture books followed. *No More Baths* features a rebellious young girl named Jessie McWhistle. After a particularly dirty day, her parents have the audacity to try to bathe her in the middle of the day. She decides to leave home so she will never have to take baths again. "The author-artist tells a fresh, funny story with a clear text," McDonnell related in a review in *Horn Book.* Moving onto another social satire with *Nothing but a Pig,* Cole once again scored a hit. This tale focuses on a pig who is a social climber. A few critics thought the tale was too fantastical, but Karla Kuskin, writing in the *New York Times Book Review,* praised the illustrations highly, indicating that the village where the story is set is "filled with color and clutter and always on the verge of coming apart at the picturesque seams." *The Winter Wren,* published in 1984, is an allegorical tale of Simon and his sister Meg who take a journey to wake Spring at Winter's farm. But cold Winter has overheard their plan, and he drenches the children with an ice storm which turns Meg into a wren. Barbara Elleman praised the artistry of the book in *Booklist,* commenting that "strikingly composed double-page spreads flow gracefully across the pages." A few critics found the text confusing, but Elleman wrote that "others will use the ambiguity as a springboard to discuss the tale's transformation and renewal theme." Cole showed a quirkier sense of humor with the 1986 book, *The Giant's Toe.* In a variation on the "Jack and the Beanstalk" stories, this tale follows an elderly, dull-

In Brock Cole's self-illustrated, original tale Buttons, *three daughters come up with far-fetched plans to get buttons to replace the ones their father popped off his britches after eating too much.*

witted giant who cuts off his toe by mistake while hoeing cabbages. The toe transforms into an elf-like creature who eludes the giant's attempts at capturing him. Luann Toth, writing in the *School Library Journal,* called *The Giant's Toe* "Cole's best effort to date."

Having carved out a successful career in illustration—creating the artwork for Lynne Reid Banks's *The Indian in the Cupboard* and for Jill Paton Walsh's *Gaffer Samson's Luck*—and his own picture books, Cole wanted to attempt something that had been tempting him for many years: writing a novel. Showing the beginnings of such a project to Stephen Roxburgh, then an editor at Farrar, Straus, he received hopeful words. "There's no encouragement like an editor's encouragement," Cole told Alderdice. He went on to write the first draft of this debut novel in a bare six weeks.

Most of Cole's books have been parables. Cole's first young adult novel, *The Goats,* was a parable of another kind. In this book, two thirteen year olds—a boy and a girl—are stripped and marooned on Goat Island by their fellow campers. The cruel ritual at Camp Tall Pine is to find two socially backward campers to be "Goats," and leave them overnight to spark their interest in the opposite sex. The prank backfires because Howie and Laura decide to escape when they see someone returning to the island. It turns out to be the counselors, attempting to save them. But the two teens decide to ride to the mainland on a floating log and barely make it to land alive. They break into a boarded-up cottage where they sleep and borrow clothes for their journey.

"It's an old story," Cole told McDonnell, reminiscent of Adam and Eve in the Garden of Eden. "The twist is that the kids are searching for Paradise, rather than being driven from it." Realizing that they have been cruelly treated by their campers, the children decide to strike out on their own, battling their way through what Cole has called "a fallen world." They steal clothing and money from people on the beach, yet somehow keep a sense of morality because they realize they have to pay it back. "Without clothing or housing or food, the preteen-age couple feel compelled to lie and steal and trespass over and over again, but there is a rightness and authenticity to that, and they make a rigorous accounting of 'things they would have to come back and pay for' and 'things they had borrowed without asking,'" Ron Hansen wrote in the *New York Times Book Review.* They skillfully find their way around in a world that has completely rejected them. In the end, the pranksters have their way, because the boy and the girl do come closer, but in a caring, affectionate way rather than sexually.

In contrast to the competence of the lost children, the adults in the story appear crass, irresponsible, and incompetent. "I decided not to sweeten it up," Cole commented to McDonnell. "It's a fair view, not a complete view. It's fragmentary, but it's an honest view." "Critics of the book," wrote Anita Silvey in *Horn Book,* "are concerned with the absence of positive adult characters ... and the change in the young protagonists from innocents to thieves." Cole believes that children have a natural sense of morality. "I have much more faith in children's ability and judgment than a lot of people. They turn away if they find something too scary or too burdensome. I would like to think they can put the book down," he told McDonnell.

Cole's 1989 novel, *Celine* is a wryly-funny tale about a teenager who practically has to grow up by herself. The sixteen-year-old artist is living in a loft in Chicago with her twenty-two-year-old stepmother, Catherine. Celine's mother happens to live on a beautiful yacht off of the island of Antigua. Her father has gone off on a lecture tour of Europe, leaving the teen and her barely-adult stepmother in the hope that they will grow closer together. He leaves with an admonition that his daughter "show a little maturity." "Really," Celine remarks, "it's hard not to be offended. If I was any more mature, I'd have Alzheimer's disease." In fact it is Celine's voice that formed the heart of the novel for Cole. "It's a kind of sustained, arch, ironic, self-aware, humorous voice," Cole told Alderdice. "And I can hear her voice in my head so clearly. Sometimes when I was working on [the novel] it was just as if I was writing down what she told me."

Celine virtually takes possession of her neighbor Jake Barker, whose parents are going through a divorce. Jake's mother claims that she loves spending time with him, but Celine ends up being his foster mother most of the time. At the same time, she is attempting to finish high school a year early, partly because she feels like a misfit there. Celine finds herself having a crush on Jake's father, Mr. Barker, while she tries to deal with the cute but stupid Dermot, who has a crush on her. She rushes home from school with an idea for a painting that is so compelling, she is afraid she will die before she finishes it, only to be coaxed into polishing Catherine's toenails instead.

"Start to finish, this book is a delight," wrote Freed in *The New York Times Book Review.* "It is funny, witty and poignant.... At the end of the novel, the reader emerges curious to know what becomes of Celine as an adult. What becomes of such sharp vision, such wry insight, such wise innocence?" A critic writing in *Publishers Weekly* felt that one of the strengths of the novel is Celine's "wry comments on everything from modern art to divorce." Karen Berlin observed in *Voice of Youth Advocates* that "events and people just seem to swirl about Celine, filtering through her artist's eyes into the meaningful patterns of an adolescent's life." An *Entertainment Weekly* critic observed "since (Celine's) mind shoots off in daring flights of speculation at the slightest provocation, we're in for a wild, funny ride."

Readers would have to wait until 1997 for a third novel; meanwhile Cole published a further picture book, *Alpha and the Dirty Baby,* in which a heroine must "contend with a pesky, lazy family of imps," according to a critic for *St. James Guide to Young Adult Writers.* The writing for Cole's third novel turned out to be more difficult than he had anticipated. Writing from the point of view of a thirteen-year-old girl, Cole had trouble finding his

Larky Mavis cherishes the odd creature she finds in a peanut and is rewarded when Heart's Delight turns out to be an angel who carries her away into the sky. (From Larky Mavis, *written and illustrated by Cole.)*

protagonist's voice, less worldly wise and humorous than Celine's. With young Linda in *The Facts Speak for Themselves,* there is none of the perspective or wit of his other young narrators. However, once her flat, matter-of-fact speech was established, Cole moved on with this gritty and sometimes painful look at youthful sexuality.

The opening of *The Facts Speak for Themselves* finds Linda being questioned about a murder she has witnessed. As her social worker begins to document her case, Linda finds errors in such a transcription of events and wants to set the record straight with her own version. One of three children of a single mother, Linda takes over motherly duties for the younger children—none by the same father—when her mother abrogates this responsibility. At one point her mother marries an older man, and when he is struck down by a stroke, Linda's mother simply leaves, and her daughter once again steps into the breech and becomes a caregiver to this stepfather. Finally reunited with her mother, Linda meets her mother's newest boyfriend, Frank, and tries to be pleasant to him. Jack, her mother's realtor boss, takes a fancy to Linda and arranges liaisons between them in houses he is showing. When Frank learns of this, he shoots the realtor as much out of jealousy as out of disgust.

"These are the facts," wrote *Booklist*'s Ilene Cooper in a starred review of *The Facts Speak for Themselves.* "As Cole sets them forth in Linda's unemotional voice, they are more than compelling. Readers can hardly tear their eyes from the pages." Cooper went on to note, "It is Cole's skill in maintaining Linda's straightforward narrative, the juxtaposition between the shocking and the everyday details, that makes the recounting of Linda's story such a triumph." Reviewing the novel in *Horn*

Book, Patty Campbell praised "the flat, matter-of-fact, but hypnotic voice" which Cole created, calling it an "impressive literary creation" and "Cole's triumph, and also a risk." With Linda, "Cole goes beyond adolescent sexual attraction," noted Wendy J. Glenn in an *ALAN Review* overview of the author's novels, "to examine weightier issues, those of motive and power, manipulation and victimization." And despite the bleakness of this novel—a National Book Award nominee—Glenn still saw "glimmers of Cole's typical humor and insight."

More straightforward humor and brightness is served up in two picture books from Cole published at the turn of the new millennium. With *Buttons,* he presents a "delectable tall tale with events akin to those in the familiar English folktale, 'The Three Sillies,'" according to a *Horn Book* reviewer, who further commented, "Cole's narrative has a humorous lilt that's as much fun as his rollicking illustrations" which exhibit "the panache of Caldecott himself." "Cole's comical illustrations add flair to the zany adventures of the three silly girls," noted Shirley Lewis in *Teacher Librarian,* while *School Library Journal*'s Carol Ann Wilson dubbed the picture book a "charming combination of romance, adventure, and mirth." And a reviewer for *Publishers Weekly* concluded, "Cole treats the ridiculous characters with affection, not mockery, inviting readers into the story to laugh right along with them."

With the 2001 title, *Larky Mavis,* "Cole delivers a lyrical and ever-relevant picture book," according to a critic for *Publishers Weekly.* A fable about a simple woman whose treasure—scoffed at by the other villagers—turns out to be an angel, *Larky Mavis* is more than a "simple moral tale," thought the *Publishers Weekly* reviewer: "Brock draws materials from fables, fairy tales and mythic archetypes to create a story that will resonate deeply with readers." *Booklist*'s Cooper felt that the story was "laced with magic."

Brock Cole explained his approach to writing children's books in his interview with McDonnell: "Don't falsify. Be honest. Be responsible to the characters you're writing about." Furthermore, he commented that "It's not right to create a book with messages or to look for messages in books. Books with messages are confidence tricks. This is fiction. To persuade people by means of fiction seems dishonest." Instead, he wants his readers to come up with their own insights, their own answers. "I think that the duties of a writer are ... to create experiences which are meaningful to people, that people can draw on for enriching their own lives, and in dealing with their own lives," he told Alderdice. "I want [readers] to know—well, what it's like to be bullied. [And] the satisfactions of being a bully. All of this stuff. I want access to the world. And in a queer way, I think fiction can give you that."

Biographical and Critical Sources

BOOKS

Cole, Brock, *Celine,* Farrar, Straus (New York, NY), 1989.

St. James Guide to Young Adult Writers, 2nd edition, St. James Press (Detroit, MI), 1999.

PERIODICALS

ALAN Review, winter, 1999, Wendy J. Glenn, "Brock Cole: The Good, the Bad, and Humorously Ironic."

Booklist, November 1, 1984, Barbara Elleman, review of *The Winter Wren,* p. 366; October 15, 1989, pp. 440, 441; June 1, 1992, p. 1768; October 1, 1997, Ilene Cooper, review of *The Facts Speak for Themselves,* p. 318; June 1, 1998, p. 1793; July, 1998, p. 1899; February 15, 2000, p. 1104; July, 2001, Ilene Cooper, review of *Larky Mavis,* p. 2016.

Bulletin of the Center for Children's Books, December, 1989, pp. 75-76.

English Journal, December, 1990, pp. 77-78.

Entertainment Weekly, May 4, 1990, review of *Celine,* p. 114.

Horn Book, August, 1980, Christine McDonnell, review of *No More Baths,* pp. 393-394; January-February, 1988, Anita Silvey, review of *The Goats,* p. 23; September-October, 1989, Christine McDonnell, "New Voices, New Visions: Brock Cole," pp. 602-605; March-April, 1990, pp. 205-206; November-December, 1997, Patty Campbell, review of *The Facts Speak for Themselves,* pp. 678-679; March-April, 2000, review of *Buttons,* p. 182.

Junior Literary Guild, September, 1979, Brock Cole, autobiographical sketch.

Kirkus Reviews, September 15, 1979, review of *The King at the Door,* p. 1063.

New York Times Book Review, November 15, 1981, Karla Kuskin, "The Art of Picture Books," pp. 57, 60; November 8, 1987, Ron Hansen, "Discovering the Opposite Sex," p. 31; April 15, 1990, Lynn Freed, review of *Celine,* p. 23; April 15, 1991, Lynn Freed, "Children's Books," p. 23.

Publishers Weekly, October 29, 1979, review of *The King at the Door,* p. 82; October 27, 1989, review of *Celine,* p. 70; August 2, 1991, pp. 71-72; February 17, 1997, Kit Alderdice, "Brock Cole: Children Braving an Adult World," pp. 197-198; September 1, 1997, pp. 105-106; January 3, 2000, review of *Buttons,* p. 75; July 16, 2001, review of *Larky Mavis,* p. 180.

School Library Journal, October, 1986, Luann Toth, review of *The Giant's Toe,* p. 158; November, 1989, p. 125; November, 1991, p. 91; October, 1997, p. 131; April, 2000, Carol Ann Wilson, review of *Buttons,* p. 96; August, 2001, Lee Bock, review of *Larky Mavis,* p. 144.

Teacher Librarian, June, 2000, Shirley Lewis, review of *Buttons,* p. 49.

Voice of Youth Advocates, February, 1990, Karen Berlin, review of *Celine,* p. 341.*

*   *   *

CORREY, Lee
See STINE, G(eorge) Harry

D

DADEY, Debbie 1959-

Personal

Last name is pronounced "Day-dee"; full name, Debra Sue Gibson Dadey; born May 18, 1959, in Morganfield, KY; daughter of Voline (a model maker) and Rebecca (a teacher; maiden name, Bailey) Gibson; married Eric Dadey (a chemist), June 11, 1981; children: Nathan, Becky, Alex. *Nationality:* American. *Education:* Western Kentucky University, B.S., M.S.L.S. *Politics:* Democrat. *Religion:* Catholic. *Hobbies and other interests:* Hiking, biking, making crafts, scrapbooking, and playing with her children.

Addresses

Home—Fort Collins, CO. *Agent*—Susan Cohen, Writer's House, 21 West 26th St., New York, NY 10010.

Career

St. Romuald Elementary School, Hardinsburg, KY, teacher, 1981-83; St. Leo Elementary School, Versailles, KY, teacher, 1983-84; Sayre School, Lexington, KY, began as teacher, became librarian, 1986-1990; Tates Creek Elementary School, Lexington, KY, librarian, 1990-92. Freelance writer, Argus Communications, 1989; instructor, University of Kentucky, 1990-92, and Southern Methodist University, 1995-97; writing consultant, Scott County Schools, 1991-92; contributing editor, *Writer's Digest,* 1998-2002.

Member

International Reading Association (Bluegrass Chapter vice president), Society of Children's Book Writers and Illustrators, National Education Association, Kentucky Education Association, Fayette County Education Association.

Awards, Honors

Best Children's Books of the Year citation, Bank Street College, 2000, and master list, Kentucky Bluegrass Award, 2001-2002, both for *Cherokee Sister;* Elba Award, for *Wizards Don't Need Computers;* Children's Choice Award, for *Vampires Don't Wear Polka Dots;* Milner Award, 2002, for body of work.

Writings

Buffalo Bill and the Pony Express: A Historical Novel, illustrated by Mike Gordon, cover illustrated by Daniel O'Leary, Disney Press (New York, NY), 1994.

My Mom the Frog, Scholastic (New York, NY), 1996.

Shooting Star: Annie Oakley, the Legend, illustrated by Scott Goto, Walker (New York, NY), 1997.

Bobby and the Great, Green Booger ("Bobby" series), illustrated by Mike Gordon, Willowisp Press (St. Petersburg, FL), 1997.

Bobby and the Big Blue Bulldog ("Bobby" series), illustrated by Mike Gordon, Willowisp Press (St. Petersburg, FL), 1998.

Will Rogers: Larger Than Life, illustrated by Scott Goto, Walker (New York, NY), 1999.

(With Marcia Thornton Jones) *Story Sparkers: A Creativity Guide for Children's Writers,* Writer's Digest Books (Cincinnati, OH), 2000.

Cherokee Sister, Delacorte (New York, NY), 2000.

King of the Kooties, illustrated by Kevin O'Malley, Walker (New York, NY), 2001.

Whistler's Hollow, Bloomsbury (New York, NY), 2002.

Swamp Monster in Third Grade, Scholastic (New York, NY), 2002.

(With son, Nathan) *Slime Wars,* Scholastic (New York, NY), 2002.

Contributing editor of *Kidstuff* magazine. Contributor to *Kicks* magazine.

"MARTY" SERIES

Marty the Maniac, illustrated by Mel Crawford, Willowisp Press (St. Petersburg, FL), 1996.

Debbie Dadey

Marty the Mud Wrestler, illustrated by Mel Crawford, Willowisp Press (St. Petersburg, FL), 1997.

Marty the Millionaire, illustrated by Mel Crawford, Willowisp Press (St. Petersburg, FL), 1997.

"ADVENTURES OF THE BAILEY SCHOOL KIDS" SERIES; WITH MARCIA THORNTON JONES

Vampires Don't Wear Polka Dots, illustrated by John Steven Gurney, Scholastic (New York, NY), 1990.

Werewolves Don't Go to Summer Camp, illustrated by John Steven Gurney, Scholastic (New York, NY), 1991.

Santa Claus Doesn't Mop Floors, illustrated by John Steven Gurney, Scholastic (New York, NY), 1991.

Leprechauns Don't Play Basketball, illustrated by John Steven Gurney, Scholastic (New York, NY), 1992.

Ghosts Don't Eat Potato Chips, illustrated by John Steven Gurney, Scholastic (New York, NY), 1992.

Aliens Don't Wear Braces, illustrated by John Steven Gurney, Scholastic (New York, NY), 1993.

Frankenstein Doesn't Plant Petunias, illustrated by John Steven Gurney, Scholastic (New York, NY), 1993.

Genies Don't Ride Bicycles, illustrated by John Steven Gurney, Scholastic (New York, NY), 1993.

Pirates Don't Wear Pink Sunglasses, illustrated by John Steven Gurney, Scholastic (New York, NY), 1993.

Witches Don't Do Back Flips, illustrated by John Steven Gurney, Scholastic (New York, NY), 1994.

Skeletons Don't Play Tubas, illustrated by John Steven Gurney, Scholastic (New York, NY), 1994.

Cupids Don't Flip Hamburgers, illustrated by John Steven Gurney, Scholastic (New York, NY), 1995.

Gremlins Don't Chew Bubble Gum, illustrated by John Steven Gurney, Scholastic (New York, NY), 1995.

Monsters Don't Scuba Dive, illustrated by John Steven Gurney, Scholastic (New York, NY), 1995.

Zombies Don't Play Soccer, illustrated by John Steven Gurney, Scholastic (New York, NY), 1995.

Dracula Doesn't Drink Lemonade, illustrated by John Steven Gurney, Scholastic (New York, NY), 1995.

Elves Don't Wear Hard Hats, illustrated by John Steven Gurney, Scholastic (New York, NY), 1995.

Martians Don't Take Temperatures, illustrated by John Steven Gurney, Scholastic (New York, NY), 1995.

Gargoyles Don't Drive Buses, illustrated by John Steven Gurney, Scholastic (New York, NY), 1996.

Wizards Don't Need Computers, illustrated by John Steven Gurney, Scholastic (New York, NY), 1996.

Mummies Don't Coach Softball, illustrated by John Steven Gurney, Scholastic (New York, NY), 1996.

Cyclops Doesn't Roller Skate, illustrated by John Steven Gurney, Scholastic (New York, NY), 1996.

Angels Don't Know Karate, illustrated by John Steven Gurney, Scholastic (New York, NY), 1996.

Dragons Don't Cook Pizza, illustrated by John Steven Gurney, Scholastic (New York, NY), 1997.

Bigfoot Doesn't Square Dance, illustrated by John Steven Gurney, Scholastic (New York, NY), 1997.

Mermaids Don't Run Track, illustrated by John Steven Gurney, Scholastic (New York, NY), 1997.

Bogeymen Don't Play Football, illustrated by John Steven Gurney, Scholastic (New York, NY), 1997.

Unicorns Don't Give Sleigh Rides, illustrated by John Steven Gurney, Scholastic (New York, NY), 1997.

Knights Don't Teach Piano, illustrated by John Steven Gurney, Scholastic (New York, NY), 1998.

Hercules Doesn't Pull Teeth, illustrated by John Steven Gurney, Scholastic (New York, NY), 1998.

Ghouls Don't Scoop Ice Cream, illustrated by John Steven Gurney, Scholastic (New York, NY), 1998.

Phantoms Don't Drive Sports Cars, illustrated by John Steven Gurney, Scholastic (New York, NY), 1998.

Giants Don't Go Snowboarding, illustrated by John Steven Gurney, Scholastic (New York, NY), 1998.

Frankenstein Doesn't Slam Hockey Pucks, illustrated by John Steven Gurney, Scholastic (New York, NY), 1998.

Trolls Don't Ride Roller Coasters, illustrated by John Steven Gurney, Scholastic (New York, NY), 1999.

Wolfmen Don't Hula Dance, illustrated by John Steven Gurney, Scholastic (New York, NY), 1999.

Goblins Don't Play Video Games, illustrated by John Steven Gurney, Scholastic (New York, NY), 1999.

Dracula Doesn't Rock and Roll, illustrated by John Steven Gurney, Scholastic (New York, NY), 1999.

Ninjas Don't Bake Pumpkin Pies, illustrated by John Steven Gurney, Scholastic (New York, NY), 1999.

Sea Monsters Don't Ride Motorcycles, illustrated by John Steven Gurney, Scholastic (New York, NY), 1999.

The Bride of Frankenstein Doesn't Bake Cookies, illustrated by John Steven Gurney, Scholastic (New York, NY), 2000.

Robots Don't Catch Chicken Pox, illustrated by John Steven Gurney, Scholastic (New York, NY), 2000.

Vikings Don't Wear Wrestling Belts, illustrated by John Steven Gurney, Scholastic (New York, NY), 2000.

Ghosts Don't Ride Wild Horses, illustrated by John Steven Gurney, Scholastic (New York, NY), 2000.

Wizards Don't Wear Graduation Gowns, illustrated by John Steven Gurney, Scholastic (New York, NY), 2000.

Sea Serpents Don't Juggle Water Balloons, illustrated by John Steven Gurney, Scholastic (New York, NY), 2000.

Swamp Monsters Don't Chase Wild Turkeys, illustrated by John Steven Gurney, Scholastic (New York, NY), 2001.

Aliens Don't Carve Jack-O-Lanterns, illustrated by John Steven Gurney, Scholastic (New York, NY), 2001.

Mrs. Claus Doesn't Climb Telephone Poles, illustrated by John Steven Gurney, Scholastic (New York, NY), 2001.

Leprechauns Don't Play Fetch, illustrated by John Steven Gurney, Scholastic (New York, NY), 2002.

Ogres Don't Hunt Easter Eggs, illustrated by John Steven Gurney, Scholastic (New York, NY), 2002.

"BAILEY SCHOOL KIDS SUPER SPECIALS"; WITH MARCIA THORNTON JONES

Mrs. Jeepers Is Missing, illustrated by John Steven Gurney, Scholastic (New York, NY), 1996.

Mrs. Jeepers' Batty Vacation, illustrated by John Steven Gurney, Scholastic (New York, NY), 1997.

Mrs. Jeepers' Secret Cave, illustrated by John Steven Gurney, Scholastic (New York, NY), 1998.

Mrs. Jeepers in Outer Space, illustrated by John Steven Gurney, Scholastic (New York, NY), 1999.

Mrs. Jeepers' Monster Class Trip, illustrated by John Steven Gurney, Scholastic (New York, NY), 2001.

Mrs. Jeepers on Vampire Island, illustrated by John Steven Gurney, Scholastic (New York, NY), 2001.

"BAILEY CITY MONSTERS" SERIES; WITH MARCIA THORNTON JONES

The Monsters Next Door, illustrated by John Steven Gurney, Scholastic (New York, NY), 1998.

Howling at the Hauntlys', illustrated by John Steven Gurney, Scholastic (New York, NY), 1998.

Vampire Trouble, illustrated by John Steven Gurney, Scholastic (New York, NY), 1998.

Kilmer's Pet Monster, illustrated by John Steven Gurney, Scholastic (New York, NY), 1999.

Double Trouble Monsters, illustrated by John Steven Gurney, Scholastic (New York, NY), 1999.

Spooky Spells, illustrated by John Steven Gurney, Scholastic (New York, NY), 1999.

Vampire Baby, illustrated by John Steven Gurney, Scholastic (New York, NY), 1999.

Snow Monster Mystery, illustrated by John Steven Gurney, Scholastic (New York, NY), 1999.

The Hauntlys' Hairy Surprise, illustrated by John Steven Gurney, Scholastic (New York, NY), 1999.

Happy Boo Day, illustrated by John Steven Gurney, Scholastic (New York, NY), 2000.

"TRIPLET TROUBLE" SERIES; WITH MARCIA THORNTON JONES

Triplet Trouble and the Talent Show Mess, illustrated by John Speirs, Scholastic (New York, NY), 1995.

Triplet Trouble and the Runaway Reindeer, illustrated by John Speirs, Scholastic (New York, NY), 1995.

Triplet Trouble and the Red Heart Race, illustrated by John Speirs, Scholastic (New York, NY), 1996.

Triplet Trouble and the Field Day Disaster, illustrated by John Speirs, Scholastic (New York, NY), 1996.

Triplet Trouble and the Cookie Contest, illustrated by John Speirs, Scholastic (New York, NY), 1996.

Triplet Trouble and the Pizza Party, illustrated by John Speirs, Scholastic (New York, NY), 1996.

Triplet Trouble and the Class Trip, illustrated by John Speirs, Scholastic (New York, NY), 1997.

Triplet Trouble and the Bicycle Race, illustrated by John Speirs, Scholastic (New York, NY), 1997.

"BARKLEY'S SCHOOL FOR DOGS" SERIES; WITH MARCIA THORNTON JONES

Playground Bully, illustrated by Amy Wummer, Volo (New York, NY), 2001.

Puppy Trouble, illustrated by Amy Wummer, Volo (New York, NY), 2001.

Top Dog, illustrated by Amy Wummer, Volo (New York, NY), 2001.

Dadey writes a tongue-in-cheek tale of the famous Annie Oakley in* Shooting Star: Annie Oakley, the Legend. *(Illustrated by Scott Goto.)

Nate teaches his friend Donald how to use his wits against Louisa, the fourth-grade bully, in Dadey's chapter book **King of the Kooties**. *(Illustrated by Kevin O'Malley.)*

Ghost Dog, illustrated by Amy Wummer, Volo (New York, NY), 2001.

Snow Day, illustrated by Amy Wummer, Volo (New York, NY), 2001.

Sticks and Stones and Doggie Bones, illustrated by Amy Wummer, Volo (New York, NY), 2002.

Buried Treasure, illustrated by Amy Wummer, Volo (New York, NY), 2002.

Blue Ribbon Blues, illustrated by Amy Wummer, Volo (New York, NY), 2002.

Santa Dog, illustrated by Amy Wummer, Volo (New York, NY), 2002.

Tattle Tails, illustrated by Amy Wummer, Volo (New York, NY), 2002.

Puppy Love, illustrated by Amy Wummer, Volo (New York, NY), 2002.

Prize-Winning Parade, illustrated by Amy Wummer, Volo (New York, NY), 2003.

Sidelights

Debbie Dadey has written scores of popular and compelling easy-reader novels for primary grade and middle grade readers which blend tongue-in-cheek horror with fast-paced storytelling skills. Working with Marcia Thornton Jones on such popular series as the "Adventures of the Bailey School Kids," the "Bailey City Monsters," "Triplet Trouble," and "Barkley's School for Dogs," Dadey has attracted legions of young readers to a jaunty world of gremlins, wizards, pirates, and aliens. Dadey's solo efforts have also produced the "Marty" series and the "Bobby" series for younger readers, as well as humorous stand-alone titles such as *King of the Kooties* and *My Mom the Frog.* Other of Dadey's solo books, such as *Cherokee Sister* and *Whistler's Hollow,* are for somewhat older readers and of a more serious nature.

"I have always been a daydreamer, sometimes to my teachers' chagrin," Debbie Dadey told *SATA.* "I think anyone who can dream can write. All it takes is the desire and the dream." Dadey began achieving her dream, with the help of Marcia Thornton Jones, when Dadey was working as a librarian at an elementary school where Jones was a teacher. "It was one of those days when the kids didn't seem to be paying attention to anything we had to say," Dadey recalled for *SATA.* "We decided if we grew horns, sprouted fangs, had steam rolling out of our ears, and were fifteen feet tall the kids in our school would really pay attention to us. That's the reason we wrote *Vampires Don't Wear Polka Dots.* It's a story about a tough group of third graders who get an even tougher teacher [Mrs. Jeepers] ... she might even be a monster or vampire!"

The success of their first book encouraged Dadey and Jones to continue collaborating, work which was done largely during lunch in their school cafeteria. Memories of summer camp inspired the pair's next book, *Were-wolves Don't Go to Summer Camp.* "We had been to short little camps as kids," Dadey told *SATA,* but the book expanded on their rather ordinary experiences to focus on a week-long camp where the counselor is rumored to be a real werewolf. Despite the fun of writing books with werewolves and vampires as characters, Dadey and Jones told *SATA* that their favorite book so far is *Santa Claus Doesn't Mop Floors* because of its insight into the character of Eddie, whom they describe as a "stinker." The book shows how Eddie discovers "that miracles really can happen," Dadey said.

Leprechauns Don't Play Basketball is a story which pits a vampire and a leprechaun against one another right in the middle of an elementary school. "It was interesting because of the research we did into leprechauns and vampires," the authors told *SATA.* "If we write about a certain creature, we always read as much as we can about it. We come up with some interesting tid-bits and try to include them in our stories." While writing *Ghosts Don't Eat Potato Chips,* the pair "read so many ghost books we had to check under our beds before we went to sleep at night!"

In the forty-fourth book in the series, *Ghosts Don't Ride Wild Horses,* the kids from Bailey School are on a trip to a ghost town. This school outing turns dangerous when the ghost of a cowboy picks on redheaded Eddie, whom the ghost sees as the incarnation of Blackheart Eddie who stole his gold. Can the school kids, including Liza, Melody, and Howie, save their friend? In the 2001 title *Swamp Monsters Don't Chase Wild Turkeys,* Melody,

Liza, Eddie, and Howie once again find something strange going on at their school. The ecology project coordinator, claiming to be from Australia, actually turns out to be a swamp monster, and the kids at Bailey School are the only ones who that can save the town from his evil intentions.

So popular was the "Adventures of the Bailey School Kids" that Dadey and Jones branched out into companion series. The "Bailey City Monsters" series features Ben and his sister, who are sure that their new neighbors, the Hauntlys, are actually as creepy as their name implies. They strive through the volumes in this series to prove that the Hauntlys are in fact monsters and that their hotel, the Hauntly Manor Inn, is a hotel for monsters. "Triplet Trouble" is a series geared for slightly younger readers, featuring the mischief that the Tucker triplets make in the classroom. These adventures do not include monsters as in the "Bailey School Kids." Dadey and Jones have also teamed up on "Barkley's School for Dogs," twelve titles strong and growing.

Dadey, who eventually left teaching to write full time, no longer collaborates with Jones over the lunch table, but by e-mail and fax, as they live in different states now. They take turns writing chapters of their fast-selling books, employing what they refer to as the "hot potato" method of writing. Beginning with research on various topics, they then move on to an outline, and then one collaborator begins writing a chapter, forwarding this portion to the other, who then takes the "hot potato" and continues the tale.

In addition to these collaborative efforts, Dadey has also carved out a successful writing career on her own, penning several novels and picture books. Dadey's first solo effort, *Buffalo Bill and the Pony Express,* is a short fictional account of that legend of the Wild West and of the opening of travel and communication routes. Dadey continued to write about Western themes with her picture book *Shooting Star: Annie Oakley, the Legend,* a tall tale about the famous sharp-shooter. In this "spirited yarn," as a contributor for *Publishers Weekly* described the book, Oakley not only outshoots the Grand Duke of Russia and shoots candles out with her bullets, but she also manages to shoot craters in the moon and to take the points of celestial stars. Ilene Cooper noted in a *Booklist* review of *Shooting Star* that Dadey mixes fact and fantasy in this book with a "sassy" tone. Shirley Wilton, writing in *School Library Journal,* felt that this is a "great book for reading aloud or for introducing children to a colorful historical figure."

For *Will Rogers: Larger Than Life,* Dadey again teamed up with the same artist who illustrated *Shooting Star,* Scott Goto, to present an account of the laconic lasso artist who became one of the most beloved humorists of his day. Dadey once more blends fact and tall tale in this recounting of Rogers's life, spinning "historical straw into tall-tale gold for a memorable introduction to an American humorist," according to *Booklist*'s John Peters. Dadey's account has Rogers roping a horse at five years of age and proceeding to plow three hundred acres

with his feet, and when he lassos the Earth, the backlash sends him sailing to Mars.

Dadey has also crafted primary and middle grade novels that are full of the same sort of fun and irreverent humor that she serves up in her series work with Jones. Her books about Marty, *Marty the Maniac, Marty the Mud Wrestler,* and *Marty the Millionaire,* as well as her "Bobby" books, *Bobby and the Great, Green Booger* and *Bobby and the Big Blue Bulldog,* are easy readers for primary grades, as is *My Mom the Frog.* In that book, young Jason discovers a wart on his hand. His mother, being supportive, promises to buy some medicine for it, and meanwhile gives it a kiss to make it better. The next day, Jason discovers that his mom is missing. When his sister tells him about the old wives' tale that you will turn into a frog if you touch a wart, Jason is soon convinced that his mother has been turned into the frog that he finds on the kitchen floor next to his mother's purse.

King of the Kooties is a humorous tale about bullying, which is "a topic of concern to elementary school children," as Carolyn Phelan noted in *Booklist.* Nate has a new friend, Donald, who has just become his neighbor and will be in his fourth grade class this year. However, they will have to share their class with Louisa, a bully who loves to tease and ridicule. Her newest target, it seems, is Donald, whom she calls the Kootie King. The two friends try a number of defenses to ward off her attacks, including a bribe of cookies, but they finally decide that their best tactic would be to create a good offense. They decide to set up the Kingdom of the Kooties and to establish Louisa as its first princess. A contributor for *Kirkus Reviews* noted that this exploration of "one approach to the age-old problem of bullies" is "never didactic."

More serious in tone and geared for middle grade readers are *Cherokee Sister* and *Whistler's Hollow.* The former title, set in 1838, is full of "vivid descriptions. . . [which] transport readers back to the 1830s," Sarah O'Neal wrote in *School Library Journal.* Twelve-year-old Allie's best friend is Leaf, a young Cherokee girl. One Sunday, Allie slips away from church and goes to visit Leaf, where, with her tanned skin and Leaf's buckskin dress, she blends in very well—so well, in fact, that the soldiers who have been sent to remove the Cherokee from their land mistake Allie for one and send her off to a relocation camp for the Trail of Tears. "*Cherokee Sister* took me eight years to write," Dadey told Julia Durango in *By the Book.* "It was an education for me because I did a lot of research and rewrote the story so many times. Of course, in that same time period I also did five series."

Adapting a tale from her own grandmother, Dadey follows the trials of a young girl who becomes orphaned after World War I in *Whistler's Hollow.* When her mother dies, eleven-year-old Lillie Mae is sent to the Kentucky farm of a great uncle and aunt by another greedy aunt. These nurturing older relatives raised Lillie Mae's father, now missing in the First World War. The young girl hopes against hope that her father will return to claim her, but meanwhile she finds that something is terribly wrong at the farm. There is a terrible smell emanating from the attic, and mysterious sounds come at night. Although her neighbor, Paul, knows the source of the smells and sounds—her great-uncle has a still set up in the attic—Paul convinces her that the house is haunted. To further make Lillie Mae's life miserable, Paul turns the other children at school against her. While a reviewer for *Publishers Weekly* complained that Dadey's "heavy-handed revelations and forced dialogue exacerbate the feel of melodrama" in this novel, a contributor for *Kirkus Reviews* praised Dadey's ability to paint her characters in a "few short strokes." The same critic further noted that readers will have "no problem identifying with [Lillie Mae's] most universal desire ... to be connected to people she can love and be loved in return."

Responding to a question from Durango as to whether she had run out of ideas after so many books, Dadey replied, "I have lots of ideas, after all they are all around me." Dadey further noted, "My problem is having enough time to write all the ideas that come to me."

Biographical and Critical Sources

BOOKS

Reginald, Robert, *Science Fiction and Fantasy Literature, 1975-1991*, Gale (Detroit, MI), 1992.

PERIODICALS

Booklist, September 15, 1992, Sheilamae O'Hara, review of *Leprechauns Don't Play Basketball*, p. 148; March 15, 1997, Ilene Cooper, review of *Shooting Star: Annie Oakley, the Legend*, p. 1245; April 1, 1999, John Peters, review of *Will Rogers: Larger Than Life*, p. 1419; September 15, 1999, Carolyn Phelan, review of *King of the Kooties*, p. 256; April 1, 2000, Susan Dove Lempke, review of *Cherokee Sister*, p. 1476.

Bulletin of the Center for Children's Books, June, 1997, Elizabeth Bush, review of *Shooting Star*, pp. 353-354.

Horn Book Guide, fall, 1999, Jackie C. Haine, review of *Will Rogers*, p. 249; spring, 2001, Carolyn Shute, review of *Cherokee Sister*, p. 71.

Kirkus Reviews, April 1, 1997, review of *Shooting Star*, p. 552; July 15, 1999, review of *King of the Kooties*, p. 1131; June 1, 2002, review of *Whistler's Hollow*, p. 803.

Publishers Weekly, March 24, 1997, review of *Shooting Star*, p. 83; October 4, 1999, review of *King of the Kooties*, p. 75; June 10, 2002, review of *Whistler's Hollow*, p. 61.

School Library Journal, April, 1997, Shirley Wilton, review of *Shooting Star*, p. 122; September, 1999, Ruth Semrau, review of *Will Rogers*, p. 180; November, 1999, Anne Knickerbocker, review of *King of the Kooties*, p. 112; April, 2000, Sarah O'Neal, review of *Cherokee Sister*, p. 134.

OTHER

By the Book, http://www.geocities.com/juliadurango/ (March 13, 2001), Julia Durango, "Debbie Dadey Does It All."

Debbie Dadey and Marcia Thornton Jones Web Site, http://www.baileykids.com/ (April 9, 2002).

Scholastic Book Clubs, http://www.scholastic.com/ (April 9, 2002), "Debbie Dadey and Marcia Thornton Jones."

*   *   *

DEANS, Sis Boulos 1955-

Personal

Born November 4, 1955, in Portland, ME; daughter of James (an electrician) and Velma (a nurse; maiden name, Pellitier) Boulos; married John Deans (a farrier), October 7, 1978; children: Jessica Emily, Rachel Marie, Emma Lee. *Nationality:* American. *Education:* University of Maine—Orono, A.S., 1976; graduated from the Maine Medical Center School of Surgical Technology, 1985. *Politics:* Democrat. *Religion:* Roman Catholic. *Hobbies and other interests:* Camping, photography, sports.

Addresses

Home—260 Gray Rd., Gorham, ME 04038.

Career

Mercy Hospital, Portland, ME, surgical technician, 1985—. Worked for nine years as an animal medical technician for veterinarians; also worked variously as a lifeguard, a waitress, and a writing instructor.

Member

Association of Surgical Technologists, Maine Writers and Publishers Alliance, Pejepscot Historical Society.

Awards, Honors

Maine Chapbook Award, 1995, for *Decisions and Other Stories;* Lupine Honor Book, Maine State Library Association, 2001, for *Racing the Past.*

Writings

FOR CHILDREN

Chick-a-dee-dee-dee: A Very Special Bird, illustrated by Nantz Comyns, Gannett Books (Portland, ME), 1987.

Emily Bee and the Kingdom of Flowers, illustrated by Nantz Comyns, Gannett Books (Portland, ME), 1988.

The Legend of Blazing Bear, illustrated by Nantz Comyns, Windswept House Publishers (Mount Desert, ME), 1992.

Brick Walls, Windswept House Publishers (Mount Desert, ME), 1996.

Racing the Past, Henry Holt (New York, NY), 2001.

FOR ADULTS

Decisions and Other Stories, Maine Writers and Publishers Alliance (Brunswick, ME), 1995.

His Proper Post: A Biography of Gen. Joshua Lawrence Chamberlain, Belle Grove (Kearny, NJ), 1996.

Also author of adult short fiction, poetry, and plays, published in periodicals including *Tableau, Maine Scholar,* and *Portland Review of the Arts.*

Work in Progress

Every Day and All the Time, a young adult novel, for Henry Holt (New York, NY), 2003.

Sidelights

The author of several picture books and middle-grade novels, Sis Boulos Deans is a busy woman. "I'm hyper, work well under pressure, and require little sleep," she told *SATA.* Her home is always a center of activity. She shares a farm in Maine with her husband, their three daughters, two horses, two dogs, a cat, a rabbit, and three chickens. "My husband and children share my love for camping, and vacations for us usually involve sleeping in a tent," Deans says. "My girls swim competitively and are also active in other sports, church, and school activities, so I'm usually en route to a pool or a ball field.

"Besides being a wife, mother, and writer, I work three days and a night of call in the operating room as a surgical technician. My specialty is orthopedics; my favorite cases are total knee and hip replacements. People usually ask how I manage to balance such a hectic life and still write. My answer: 'I write when normal people are sleeping.' Which is true—it's the only time our house is quiet."

"For me, writing is like breathing—something that comes naturally and is a necessity of life," Deans told *SATA.* "Since childhood, I've been motivated by a creative desire to capture with words the world around me. Dialogue is one of my favorite vehicles, and humor is usually in the driver's seat." In addition to children's books, Deans has written plays, stories, and biographies for adults, including *Decisions and Other Stories* and *His Proper Post: A Biography of Gen. Joshua Lawrence Chamberlain.*

"I didn't start writing children's books until my eldest daughter was four," she told *SATA.* "After seeing one of my short stories published in a magazine that she was too young to read, she said, 'Momma, you write for everyone but me.' My guilt kicked in, and I immediately called Nantz Comyns, a good friend and an artist I'd known since college. 'Nantz,' I said, 'I'm going to write a kid's book and you're going to illustrate it.'"

Since then, Deans and Comyns have worked on several books together. Their third book, *The Legend of Blazing Bear,* was the Maine Writers and Publishers Alliance best-selling children's book for 1992. In the book, an Abenaki father gently teaches his son through storytelling, with an emphasis on his nation's culture and customs. However, Jeanette K. Cakouros, writing in the *Maine Sunday Telegram,* declared that *Blazing Bear* is "more than a storybook," citing the book's added glossary of American Indian words and terms, a chart of Maine's Kennebec and Abenaki Indians, a map showing the locations and place names of the tribes, a bibliography for further reading, and, of course, colorful artwork. "Nantz and I have an excellent working relationship," Deans explained, "and our successful collaborations have been, and continue to be, rewarding and fun."

In 1996, Deans published her first children's novel, *Brick Walls.* In this story, Leona, also known as Leo, and her sister are sent to a Catholic boarding school by their mother, who wants to get the children away from their alcoholic father. The brick walls of the school are nothing, however, compared to the walls Leo puts up around her emotions in this coming-of-age story.

"The lonely stoicism of the long-distance runner is physical fact as well as metaphor in" *Racing the Past,* a "powerful" novel, declared *Booklist*'s Hazel Rochman. Eleven-year-old Ricky is confused and disoriented after the death not only of his father, but also of a neighbor who was something of a stand-in grandmother to him. Bugsie, the school bully, makes Ricky's trips to school on the bus miserable. At first Ricky stops taking the bus and starts walking the three and a half miles to school simply to avoid the jeers of "white trash" thrown at him, and the fights that sometimes follow. In a way he agrees with Bugsie: the best thing his dad has done in his life is die in the drunk-driving accident. Ricky is worried that he will turn out like his father, or like his uncles, who are in prison. Even after the death of his father, the memories of his physical abuse remain. But then Ricky discovers long-distance running. Soon Ricky avoids taking the bus to improve his running speed, and eventually he can beat the bus home. By the time the story ends, Ricky has learned to stand up to Bugsie, brought the attention of the track coach to his running skills, and even found a degree of self-understanding.

Reviewing this novel in *School Library Journal,* Todd Morning felt that though "not all of the disparate threads" of the story "come together," still Deans did a "good job of capturing the often rough, cruel, and foul-mouthed world of early adolescents." A *Publishers Weekly* reviewer similarly called *Racing the Past* a "hard-hitting novel" about one youth's attempts "to find self-respect and a sense of purpose." The same critic concluded that "Deans's persuasive and informed sympathy encourages readers to cheer Ricky for his perseverance and his triumphs." A *Horn Book* contributor also added praise, noting that "the reader will be cheering for [Ricky's] determined and admirable character."

Biographical and Critical Sources

PERIODICALS

Booklist, June 1, 2001, Hazel Rochman, review of *Racing the Past,* p. 1880.

Horn Book, July-August, 2001, review of *Racing the Past,* p. 449.

Maine Sunday Telegram, September 20, 1992, Jeanette K. Cakouros, review of *The Legend of Blazing Bear.*

Publishers Weekly, June 11, 2001, review of *Racing the Past,* p. 86.

School Library Journal, February, 1993, Lisa Mitten, review of *The Legend of Blazing Bear,* p. 92; June, 2001, Todd Morning, review of *Racing the Past,* p. 148.*

*   *   *

DENNARD, Deborah 1953-

Personal

Born October 8, 1953, in Houston, TX; daughter of Margaret (Kelly) Ward; married Robert Marion Dennard (an engineer), December 22, 1973. *Nationality:* American. *Education:* Texas A & M University, B.A., 1976; University of Texas—Arlington, B.M., 2000, M.M. (music education), 2002. *Religion:* Methodist. *Hobbies and other interests:* Community theater, dogs, music, bird watching, tap dancing, travel.

Addresses

Agent—c/o Author Mail, Northword Press, 18705 Lake Drive E., Chanhassen, MN 55317.

A young coyote hunts for food in a backyard before returning to the pinon forest in **Coyote at Pinon Place,** *written by Deborah Dennard and illustrated by John Paul Genzo.*

Career

Writer. Fort Worth Zoo, Fort Worth, TX, zoo educator, 1976-92.

Member

Society of Children's Book Writers and Illustrators.

Writings

How Wise Is an Owl?, illustrated by Michelle Neavill, Carolrhoda (Minneapolis, MN), 1993.

Do Cats Have Nine Lives?, illustrated by Jackie Ubanovic, Carolrhoda (Minneapolis, MN), 1993.

Can Elephants Drink through Their Noses?, illustrated by Terry Boles, Carolrhoda (Minneapolis, MN), 1993.

Travis and the Better Mousetrap (fiction), Cobblehill Books (New York, NY), 1996.

Coyote at Pinon Place, illustrated by Jon Paul Genzo, Soundprints (Norwalk, CT), 1999.

Koala Country: A Story of an Australian Eucalyptus Forest, illustrated by James McKinnon, Soundprints (Norwalk, CT), 2000.

Lemur Landing: A Story of a Madagascan Tropical Dry Forest, Soundprints (Norwalk, CT), 2001.

Hedgehog Haven: The Story of an English Hedgerow Community, Soundprints (Norwalk, CT), 2001.

Bullfrog at Magnolia Circle, Soundprints (Norwalk, CT), 2002.

Gorillas, Northword Press (Chanhassen, MN), 2002.

Chimpanzees, Northword Press (Chanhassen, MN), 2002.

Orangutans, Northword Press (Chanhassen, MN), 2002.

Monkeys, Northword Press (Chanhassen, MN), 2002.

Snakes, Northword Press (Chanhassen, MN), 2003.

Lizards, Northword Press (Chanhassen, MN), 2003.

Turtles, Northword Press (Chanhassen, MN), 2003.

Crocodiles and Alligators, Northword Press (Chanhassen, MN), 2003.

Work in Progress

"I am always doing research for at least ten projects at once. All (or most) of my projects are animal or nature oriented. Some are serious, some are frivolous, all are fun."

Sidelights

Deborah Dennard has written several well-received fiction and nonfiction titles for young readers which explore facets of wildlife. Born in Houston, Texas, Dennard attended Texas A & M University and worked as a zoo educator before she began writing for children. After her initial publications, Dennard told *SATA:* "As an author with a track record of seventeen books, I feel that the greatest motivation behind my writing is a desire to excite children and hopefully to inspire in them a lifelong interest in reading, animals, and nature. I am available as a visiting author, an activity which I greatly enjoy, and hope to continue publishing both my nonfiction and fiction works in the future. What could be more exciting than to see your name on the cover of a book?"

Readers experience life in the Australian eucalyptus forest through the eyes of a koala in **Koala Country,** *written by Dennard and illustrated by James McKinnon.*

Dennard has continued to enjoy seeing her name in print on picture books for young readers. *Travis and the Better Mousetrap* is the story of a young boy named Travis whose aunt sees a mouse in their house. The little boy decides to create a better mousetrap, but he is even more successful in his endeavors than he planned. Not only does he capture a mouse as big as he is, but also the Easter Bunny, the Groundhog, the Thanksgiving Turkey, and then one of Santa's reindeer. Meanwhile, the mouse for which this trap was intended remains free to race about his room. When Travis calls for his aunt to come and help, all of the animals disappear back into the machine before she can see them.

Coyote at Pinon Place follows a young coyote as it wanders into a backyard and drinks from a small plastic wading pool while searching for food. Bothered by a blue jay and then a rattlesnake, the coyote finally catches a wood rat for its meal. *School Library Journal*'s Emily Herman felt that "Dennard's fictionalized account of coyote's adventure is rich in nature detail." Reviewing the same title in *Childhood Education,* Jeanie Burnett similarly praised Dennard's "well-chosen descriptions [that] paint vivid pictures."

With *Koala Country: A Story of an Australian Eucalyptus Forest* and *Lemur Landing: A Story of a Madagas-*

can *Tropical Dry Forest,* Dennard uses fictional techniques to impart real information by telling the stories of individual animals in relation to their environment, focusing on their adaptation and search for food and water. In *Koala Country,* Dennard follows the endangered koala, explaining "marsupial eating, sleeping, mating, and parenting habits," according to *Booklist*'s Gillian Engberg. The book follows a mother and her infant, called a joey, through forays in the forest. *School Library Journal* contributor Louise L. Sherman felt that Dennard's narrative was "enjoyable as well as informative." The lemur gets a similar treatment in *Lemur Landing,* which follows a troop of ring-tailed lemurs on their daily routine. Well-illustrated, with an accompanying glossary and map, this title may have "more appeal for youngsters than the typical nonfiction treatment," *Booklist*'s Lauren Peterson commented.

Biographical and Critical Sources

PERIODICALS

Booklist, June 1, 1993, Janice Del Negro, review of *How Wise Is an Owl?, Do Cats Have Nine Lives?,* and *Can Elephants Drink through Their Noses?,* p. 1843; June 1, 2001, Gillian Engberg, review of *Koala Country: A Story of an Australian Eucalyptus Forest,* p. 1879; March 1, 2002, Lauren Peterson, review of *Lemur Landing: A Story of a Madagascan Tropical Dry Forest,* p. 1136.
Childhood Education, fall, 2000, Jeanie Burnett, review of *Coyote at Pinon Place,* p. 45.
Horn Book Guide, fall, 1996, Peter D. Sieruta, review of *Travis and the Better Mousetrap,* p. 53.
School Library Journal, February, 1996, Judith Constantinides, review of *Travis and the Better Mousetrap,* p. 82; May, 2000, Emily Herman, review of *Coyote at Pinon Place,* p. 76; November, 2001, Louise L. Sherman, review of *Koala Country,* p. 119; March, 2002, Lisa Radmer, review of *Lemur Landing,* p. 90.

* * *

DEVLIN, Harry 1918-

Personal

Born March 22, 1918, in Jersey City, NJ; son of Harry George (general manager of Savarin Co.) and Amelia (Crawford) Devlin; married Dorothy Wende (an artist and writer), August 30, 1941; children: Harry Noel, Wende Elizabeth (Mrs. Geoffrey Gates), Jeffrey Anthony, Alexandra Gail (Mrs. James Eldridge), Brion Phillip, Nicholas Kirk, David Matthew. *Education:* Syracuse University, B.F.A., 1939. *Religion:* Congregationalist.

Addresses

Home and office—443 Hillside Ave., Mountainside, NJ 07092.

Career

Artist, 1939—. Freelance cartoonist for periodicals, c. 1940s; *Collier's,* New York, NY, editorial cartoonist, 1945-54; Union College, Cranford, NJ, lecturer in history of fine arts and history of American domestic architecture, 1962-64. Painter of stamps for U.S. Postal Service. President, Mountainside Public Library, 1968-69; served as grants chairman and vice chairman, New Jersey State Council on the Arts, 1970-79; chairman, Union County, NJ, Advisory Board on the Arts, 1972-75; trustee, Morris Museum, Morristown, NJ, 1980—; member, New Jersey Committee for the Humanities, 1984—; founding member, Rutgers University Advisory Council on Children's Literature. *Exhibitions:* One-person art exhibitions at Morris Museum, 1979, General Electric World Headquarters, Fairfield, CT, 1980, Union League Club, New York City, 1981, A. T. & T. World Headquarters, 1986, Schering Plough, 1986, Jane Voorhees Zimmerli Art Museum, Rutgers State University, New Brunswick, NJ, 1990-91, and International Museum of Cartoon Art, Boca Raton, FL. Works represented in permanent collections, including Midlantic Bank, Crum & Foster, First Atlantic Bank, and City Federal Savings Corporate Headquarters. *Military service:* U.S. Naval Reserve, 1942-46; served as artist; became lieutenant, Office of Naval Intelligence.

Member

Society of Illustrators (life member), National Cartoonists Society (president, 1956-57), Associated Artists of New Jersey (president, 1984-85), Artists Equity Association (New Jersey), Graphic Artists Guild, Dutch Treat Club.

Awards, Honors

Best in Advertising Cartoon awards, National Cartoonists Society, 1956, 1962, 1963, 1977, 1978, and 1991; Special Citation for Husband-Wife Writers of Children's Books, New Jersey Institute of Technology, 1969; New Jersey Teachers of English Award, 1970, for *How Fletcher Was Hatched!;* Award of Excellence, Chicago Book Fair, 1974, for *Old Witch Rescues Halloween;* New Jersey Institute of Technology Award, 1976, for *Tales of Thunder and Lightning;* Arents Award for Art and Literature, Syracuse University, 1977; elected to Hall of Fame in Literature, New Jersey Institute of Technology, 1980; Chairman's Award for painting "House on High Street," Society of Illustrators, 1981; elected to New Jersey Advertising Hall of Fame, 1983; D.H.L., Kean College, 1985; inducted into New Jersey Literary Hall of Fame, 1987.

Writings

SELF-ILLUSTRATED; JUVENILE

The Walloping Window Blind, Van Nostrand (New York, NY), 1968.

What Kind of House Is That?, Parents' Magazine Press (New York, NY), 1969.

Tales of Thunder and Lightning, Parents' Magazine Press (New York, NY), 1975.

WITH WIFE, WENDE DEVLIN; JUVENILE; SELF-ILLUSTRATED

Old Black Witch!, Parents' Magazine Press (New York, NY), 1963.

The Knobby Boys to the Rescue, Parents' Magazine Press (New York, NY), 1965.

Aunt Agatha, There's a Lion under the Couch, Van Nostrand (New York, NY), 1968.

How Fletcher Was Hatched!, Parents' Magazine Press (New York, NY), 1969, thirtieth-anniversary edition, Town Book Press (Westfield, NJ), 1999.

A Kiss for a Warthog, Van Nostrand (New York, NY), 1970, thirtieth-anniversary edition, Town Book Press (Westfield, NJ), 2000.

Old Witch and the Polka Dot Ribbon, Parents' Magazine Press (New York, NY), 1970.

Cranberry Thanksgiving, Parents' Magazine Press (New York, NY), 1971.

Old Witch Rescues Halloween, Parents' Magazine Press (New York, NY), 1973.

Cranberry Christmas, Parents' Magazine Press (New York, NY), 1976, reprinted, Aladdin (New York, NY), 1991.

Cranberry Mystery, Four Winds Press (New York, NY), 1978.

Hang on Hester, Lothrop (New York, NY), 1980.

Cranberry Halloween, Four Winds Press (New York, NY), 1982.

Cranberry Valentine, Macmillan (New York, NY), 1986.

Cranberry Birthday, Macmillan (New York, NY), 1988.

Cranberry Easter, Macmillan (New York, NY), 1990.

Harry Devlin

A dog thinks hatching from an egg and learning to say "peep" will regain the favor of his chick-loving mistress in How Fletcher Was Hatched!, *written by Wende Devlin and illustrated by Harry Devlin.*

Cranberry Summer, Four Winds Press (New York, NY), 1992.

Cranberry Autumn, Four Winds Press (New York, NY), 1993.

Cranberry Moving Day, Aladdin (New York, NY), 1994.

Cranberry First Day of School, Aladdin (New York, NY), 1995.

Cranberry Lost at the Fair, Aladdin (New York, NY), 1995.

The Trouble with Henriette!, Simon & Schuster (New York, NY), 1995.

OTHER

(Illustrator) Harold Longman, *The Wonderful Tree House,* Parents' Magazine Press, 1962.

To Grandfather's House We Go: A Roadside Tour of American Homes, Parents' Magazine Press, 1967.

Portraits of American Architecture (adult nonfiction), East View Editions, 1982, published as *Portraits of American Architecture: Monuments to a Romantic Mood, 1830-1900,* David Godine (New York, NY), 1989, published as *Portraits of American Architecture: A Gallery of Victorian Homes,* Gramercy (New York, NY), 1996.

Also author and host of four-film series *Fare You Well, Old House,* 1976-81, and of films *Houses of the Hackensack,* 1976, and *To Grandfather's House We Go,* 1981, all for New Jersey Public Broadcasting Corp.

Adaptations

Old Black Witch! was filmed by Gerald Herman as *The Winter of the Witch,* starring Hermione Gingold, Parents' Magazine Films, 1972; *How Fletcher Was Hatched!, A Kiss for a Warthog, The Knobby Boys to the Rescue,* and *Aunt Agatha, There's a Lion under the Couch* were adapted as film strips by Spoken Arts, Inc., in 1985; *Cranberry Halloween, Cranberry Thanksgiving, Cranberry Christmas,* and *Cranberry Mystery* were adapted as film strips by Spoken Arts, Inc., in 1986.

Sidelights

An accomplished master of the arts of cartooning, painting, and advertising, as well as an expert on historic American architecture, artist Harry Devlin collaborates on children's books with his wife, author Wende Devlin. "Our first book," he once explained, referring to their 1963 picture book *Old Black Witch!,* "sold over a million copies, which beguiled us into the belief that we could write." The team has since proved that they can indeed write—and illustrate—books for children, their efforts earning them numerous fans, heaps of critical praise, and a special citation from the New Jersey Institute of Technology for their collaboration work in children's literature. Many of their books, including their

The citizens of two feuding cities are brought together by a warthog from Africa in A Kiss for a Warthog, *written by Wende Devlin and illustrated by Harry Devlin.*

popular, long-running "Cranberryport" series about life in a small New England town, have been best sellers.

Born in Jersey City, New Jersey, in 1918, Devlin received his art training at the University of Syracuse, graduating in 1939. Although he began working as an artist immediately after graduation, Devlin's career didn't really kick into high gear until after World War II when he left the U.S. Naval Reserve and became an editorial cartoonist for *Collier's* magazine, a position he held for nine years. His cartoons won him acclaim as a shrewd and clear-headed commentator on the political and social scene of the 1950s. During that time he also created art for two short-lived comic strips, "Fullhouse" and "Raggmopp," the latter strip described by Jerry Robinson in *The Comics* as "stylishly drawn with a tasteful use of white space." The strips were written by Devlin's wife, Wende Devlin, a fellow Syracuse student who he married in 1941, and recounted humorous incidences involving the rearing of their seven children. Ever since making a splash in the world of children's book publishing, Devlin has continued to do artwork for magazine and newspaper advertising, and has won six awards for his advertising work from the National Cartoonists Society.

Devlin credits the diversity of his work—he has done everything from magazine illustrations to portrait and mural painting to editorial cartoons—for his ability to sustain a successful artistic career for over seven decades. "As I have survived as an artist and writer, I can say that diversity is the key to survival," he explained in *Contemporary Graphic Artists.* Another reason for his success in the children's book field is his collaborator. "Wende writes more and better than I can," Devlin readily admitted; "I write only about those things that I think may fascinate and pay no heed to trends or styles." Their sense of fun permeates each of their books, which include *How Fletcher Was Hatched!, A Kiss for a Warthog,* and *The Trouble with Henriette!* and often feature unique animal characters. Each book is enlivened by Devlin's highly detailed pen-and-ink renderings, finished with watercolor, which "abound with minute, often amusing details," as a *Publishers Weekly* contributor noted of *The Trouble with Henriette!*

Books by the Devlins often focus on seemingly normal situations ... until something unusual happens that makes things quickly become topsy turvy. In *Old Black Witch!,* young Nicky and his mother decide to buy a colonial-era house in a small New England town, with the idea of opening a small, cozy tea room for little old ladies, called the Jug and Muffin. However, their plans

Trapped by ghosts in an old house, Maggie and Mr. Whiskers must find a way out and deliver the money for a new dock to the townspeople of Cranberryport. (From Cranberry Halloween, *written by Wende Devlin and illustrated by Harry Devlin.)*

become thwarted when they realize that their house is already occupied by a not-so-nice old lady—the crotchety, black-garbed witch of the title. Fortunately for all involved, the witch has a knack for making blueberry pancakes in addition to casting spells, and with her help the tearoom becomes a success.

Another Devlin collaboration finds the towns of Quimby and Oldwick engaged in an ongoing battle to see which will be most successful: both towns fight to see who will have the best football team, the nicest parade, the prettiest downtown. But the town of Quimby has a secret weapon that always makes it come out on top: a cantankerous, crusty old warthog skulking around in its town zoo. In the Devlin's whimsical *A Kiss for a Warthog,* the mayor of Oldwick decides that he's had enough and puts in an order for his own warthog, straight from Africa. Allegra, the cute little creature that soon arrives in Oldwick, looks exactly like what the mayor had in mind, but when she refuses to get off the boat until she gets a welcoming smooch on her hairy, betusked snout, she brings the feuding towns together.

Dogs have a major role in several of Devlin's books, including *The Trouble with Henriette!,* about a truffle—a type of mushroom—sniffing pup whose sensitive sniffer suddenly fails to work. And in *How Fletcher Was Hatched!,* Devlin humorously brings to life the story of a hound dog whose young mistress becomes distracted by some baby chicks she is raising in science class. Suddenly Fletcher finds himself ignored, and the advice from his four-legged friends Otter and Beaver is simple: If Alexandra likes chicks, then do like a chick and hatch! The giant pink egg Beaver puts together around Fletcher causes Alexandra's science-teacher's eyeballs to pop, but when it hatches, Fletcher gets all the attention he has missed.

Because of his stature as an artist and illustrator, Devlin was asked to become a member of the New Jersey State Council on the Arts in 1970. Membership in that organization enabled him to gather sufficient funds to found the Rutgers University Collection of Children's Art and Literature at the Jane Voorhees Zimmerli Museum of Rutgers University. In 1998 a video recording of Devlin's career was produced. Titled *Harry Devlin: An Artist's Odyssey,* the film includes interviews with Devlin regarding his life, artistic techniques, and the competing demands on commercial art versus creative expression, as well as discussions with family members and an exhibition of his works.

Biographical and Critical Sources

BOOKS

Contemporary Graphic Artists, Volume 1, Gale (Detroit, MI), 1986.
Gauley, Sherrie, *Harry Devlin: Illustrations for Children's Literature: Essay and Annotated Catalogue,* Jane Voorhees Zimmerli Art Museum (Rutgers, NJ), 1990.
Robinson, Jerry, *The Comics: An Illustrated History of Comic Strip Art,* Putnam, 1974.

PERIODICALS

Booklist, May 15, 1992, Carolyn Phelan, review of *Cranberry Summer,* p. 1686; December 15, 1992, Emily Melton, review of *Old Black Witch,* p. 744; August, 1993, Ilene Cooper, review of *Cranberry Autumn,* p. 2069; May 15, 1995, Leone McDermott, review of *The Trouble with Henriette!,* p. 1651.
Library Journal, May 15, 1969; May 15, 1970; April, 1998, Jeff Dick, review of *Harry Devlin: An Artist's Odyssey,* p. 1335.
New York Times Book Review, May 9, 1965; January 4, 1970.
Publishers Weekly, October 8, 1982, review of *Cranberry Halloween,* p. 62; May 29, 1995, review of *The Trouble with Henriette!,* p. 84.
School Library Journal, May, 1980, review of *Hang on Hester!,* p. 81; January, 1987, Peggy Forehand, review of *Cranberry Valentine,* p. 62; November, 1988, Joanna G. Jones, review of *Cranberry Birthday,* p. 84; March, 1990, Marcia Hupp, review of *Cranberry Easter,* p. 190; June, 1992, Virginia Opocensky, review of *Cranberry Summer,* p. 91; September, 1993, Jody McCoy, review of *Cranberry Autumn,* p. 206; September, 1995, review of *The Trouble with Henriette!,* p. 168.

OTHER

Harry Devlin: An Artist's Odyssey (video recording), 1998.
Town Book Press Web site, http://www.townbookpress. com/ (August 29, 2001), "Harry Devlin."*

*   *   *

DUDEN, Jane 1947-

Personal

Born August 27, 1947, in Red Wing, MN; daughter of Robert (a restaurant owner and quality control inspector) and Mary Lee (a school principal's assistant) Goodwin; married Larry Duden (a teacher), March 29, 1969 (divorced, 1990); children: Margaret. *Nationality:* American. *Education:* University of Minnesota, A.L.A. (magna cum laude), 1967; Mankato State University, B.S. (magna cum laude), 1969. *Hobbies and other interests:* Competing in triathlete contests, cooking, traveling, hiking, pets.

Addresses

Home—4508 47th Ave. S., Minneapolis, MN 55406. *E-mail*—duden001@gold.tc.umn.edu.

Career

Elementary-school teacher in Norwood and Waconia, MN, 1969-70, Frankfurt, Germany, 1971, and Augsburg, Germany, 1972-73; Carlson Marketing, Minneapolis, MN, incentive travel planner, 1974-77, 1988-89. Freelance writer and education specialist, 1977—. Volunteer writing helper in elementary schools.

Member

International Reading Association, various environmental groups.

Awards, Honors

Best Books of 1989, Children's Reading Roundtable of Chicago, for *Nineteen Seventies, Nineteen Sixties, Nineteen Fifties,* and *Nineteen Forties;* Best Children's Science Books, *Science Books & Films,* 1990, for *The Ferret; Skipping Stones* Honor Award, 2001, for *Oil Spills: The Perils of Petroleum.*

Writings

Shirley Muldowney, Crestwood House (New York, NY), 1988.

Animal Handlers and Trainers, Crestwood House (New York, NY), 1989.

Nineteen Seventies ("Timelines" series), Crestwood House (New York, NY), 1989.

Nineteen Sixties ("Timelines" series), Crestwood House (New York, NY), 1989.

Nineteen Fifties ("Timelines" series), Crestwood House (New York, NY), 1989.

Nineteen Forties ("Timelines" series), Crestwood House (New York, NY), 1989.

Christmas, Crestwood House (New York, NY), 1990.

The Ferret, Crestwood House (New York, NY), 1990.

The Harp Seal, edited by Julie Bach, Crestwood House (New York, NY), 1990.

The Ozone Layer, Crestwood House (New York, NY), 1990.

Thanksgiving, Crestwood House (New York, NY), 1990.

(With Gail B. Stewart) *Nineteen Eighties* ("Timelines" series), Crestwood House (New York, NY), 1991.

The Olympics ("Sportslines" series), Crestwood House (New York, NY), 1991.

Baseball ("Sportslines" series), Crestwood House (New York, NY), 1991.

(With Susan Osberg) *Basketball* ("Sportslines" series), Crestwood House (New York, NY), 1991.

(With Susan Osberg) *Football* ("Sportslines" series), Crestwood House (New York, NY), 1991.

Nineteen Ninety-one ("Timelines" series), Crestwood House (New York, NY), 1992.

Nineteen Ninety ("Timelines" series), Crestwood House (New York, NY), 1992.

Great Moments in Sports ("Sportslines" series), Crestwood House (New York, NY), 1992.

Men's & Women's Gymnastics ("Sportslines" series), Crestwood House (New York, NY), 1992.

The Super Bowl ("Sportslines" series), Crestwood House (New York, NY), 1992.

The World Series ("Sportslines" series), Crestwood House (New York, NY), 1992.

Earthquake! On Shaky Ground, Perfection Learning (Logan, IA), 1997.

Helping Paws: Service Dogs, Perfection Learning (Logan, IA), 1998.

Jane Duden

The Sea Otters of California, Capstone Press (Mankato, MN), 1998.

The Giant Pandas of China, Hilltop Books (Mankato, MN), 1998.

The Florida Panther, Capstone Press (Mankato, MN), 1998.

(With Susan Walker) *Oil Spills!: The Perils of Petroleum,* Perfection Learning (Logan, IA), 1999.

Floods!: Rising, Raging Waters, illustrated by Kay Ewald, Perfection Learning (Logan, IA), 1999.

Avalanche: The Deadly Slide, Perfection Learning (Logan, IA), 2000.

Vegetarianism for Teens ("Nutrition and Fitness" series), Capstone Press (Mankato, MN), 2001.

Betsy Ross: Let Freedom Ring, Bridgestone Books (Mankato, MN), 2002.

Jefferson Davis, Capstone Press (Mankato, MN), 2002.

Also author of *Humpback Whale,* Capstone Press (Mankato, MN). Author of several student and teacher editions to accompany elementary and middle-school textbooks, educational films, and CD-ROMs.

Work in Progress

Whoop Dreams: The Historic Migration, "A book on the first human-assisted migration of an endangered species—the whooping cranes led by ultra-lite aircraft in the fall of 2001."

Sidelights

Jane Duden told *SATA:* "I wrote my first book, *Inky the Cricket,* at age eight—to help me get over my fear of the crickets in our basement! Inky went on to adventures like ice fishing, which I did as a child with my father. Years later, I wrote books for different reasons. I believe humans need the inspiration and solace that comes from nature and animals, so I believe passionately in our responsibility to preserve natural areas and wildlife. That passion fuels many of my books. My books on endangered species, *The Ozone Layer* and *Oil Spills!,* came about through those convictions. Another reason I write is to share fun trivia and important facts that can enrich our imaginations and spark new interests, such as the 'Timelines' and 'Sportslines' series. I also write to tell about heroes who uplift and inspire, such as the people and dogs in *Helping Paws.* And I write to explain complex things in simpler ways, as in my books on natural disasters. I hope my readers find wonderment, respect, and understanding from what they read.

"After teaching in Minnesota and in U.S. Army schools in Frankfurt and Augsburg, Germany, I joined the corporate world at Carlson Marketing Group and traveled widely in that position. Although I'm now a freelance writer working at home, I still enjoy frequent classroom visits as a guest author to write with children. I feel the best part about writing is meeting fascinating people to interview and traveling far and wide. My topics have taken me on travels from Alaska to Antarctica, and from the gray whale nurseries of Baja Mexico, to the Olympics in Seoul, and to puppy training classes at home. Believe it or not, I think the second best part about writing is rewriting—reworking the words over and over again until they please me. That's why my advice to young writers is: be curious, meet people, go places, ask questions, and never forget that writing is about rewriting. I'd also like to caution writers to carefully select their sources, and to try for primary sources whenever possible.

"Writing children's nonfiction is a joyful blend of all my favorite things: discovering, teaching, learning, and sharing. I have also written teacher and student editions for textbook publishers, lessons for PBS's *Newton's Apple,* program booklets for *Sesame Street Live,* and a student magazine to teach agriculture in the classroom. Each spring, writing wildlife migration updates for *Journey North,* an online science education program, lets me share the dependable miracles taking place in the natural world."

A former elementary-school teacher, Duden is the author of several nonfiction books, covering topics as diverse as animals, the environment, and nutrition. In her books about animals, Duden has penned titles such as *The Sea Otters of California, The Giant Pandas of China,* and *Helping Paws.* The award-winning *The Ferret* explains

to readers the rediscovery of the black-footed ferret, once thought to be extinct. Complete with photographs, *The Ferret* shows readers how the creature exists in the wild as well as scientists' attempts at restoring a plentiful, healthy supply of ferrets for reintroduction to the wild. Describing the book as "clearly written," *Science Books & Films* critic Karen J. Goldsmith found *The Ferret* a "very well-written and entertaining book for the young nature student."

Two of Duden's titles about the environment, *Oil Spills!: The Perils of Petroleum* and *The Ozone Layer,* introduce young readers to the potential benefits and dangers of important natural resources. Discussing with children many of the products resulting from the petrochemical industry, including everyday objects like ball-point pens, the author also explains the damage oil causes when inadvertently spilled. Disasters such as the Exxon *Valdez* oil spill in Alaska are featured, as well as one of the largest oil-accidents in history, the *Castillo de Bellver* spill, which contaminated miles of South African coast land with over seventy-nine million gallons of oil. Reviewing the book for *Skipping Stones,* contributor Amanda Marusich found *Oil Spills!* "clear, informative, and shocking," going on to call the volume "a gripping read." Similarly, *The Ozone Layer* also garnered high marks from *Science Books & Films* reviewer Nathan S. Washton, who appreciated the way Duden informs

Duden discusses vegetarianism and how to build a healthy diet in this fact-filled book. (Cover photo by Paul Barton.)

young readers about the role of the ozone in the Earth's environment. Recommending *The Ozone Layer* for fourth through eighth-grade students, Washton decided that children "will benefit greatly from reading this concise book, emerging with an understanding of the benefits and dangers of ozone."

How to follow a vegetarian diet is the focus of Duden's *Vegetarianism for Teens*. Here she explores the option of eating a meatless diet, including the variations within a vegetarian diet such as avoiding dairy and egg products in addition to animal flesh. Duden presents her teen readers with information about nutritional requirements, thus allowing them to make their own decisions about how to create a healthy diet suitable for them. In addition, *Vegetarianism for Teens* offers advice for adolescents who might face family resistance to their new diet and tips for sticking to a vegetarian diet while eating outside of the home. Reviewing *Vegetarianism for Teens* as well as another book in the "Nutrition and Fitness" series, *School Library Journal* critic Joyce Adams Burner thought that both books provide "good overviews of aspects of nutrition." Noting that *Vegetarianism for Teens* touches on an issue popular with teens, *Booklist* contributor Lauren Peterson said that the book has "a user-friendly format."

Biographical and Critical Sources

PERIODICALS

Booklist, August, 1988, Ilene Cooper, review of *Shirley Muldowney,* p. 1917; July, 2001, Lauren Peterson, review of *Vegetarianism for Teens,* p. 2001.

School Library Journal, September, 1988, Susan Schuller, review of *Shirley Muldowney,* p. 189; April, 1990, Sylvia S. Marantz, review of *Nineteen Seventies, Nineteen Sixties, Nineteen Fifties,* and *Nineteen Forties,* p. 131; January, 1991, Janie Schomberg, review of *Thanksgiving,* p. 100; April, 1991, Meryl Silverstein, review of *The Ozone Layer,* p. 144; February, 1992, Janice C. Hayes, review of *Football* and *The Olympics,* p. 94; July, 2001, Joyce Adams Burner, review of *Vegetarianism for Teens,* p. 122; July, 2002, Karen Land, review of *Betsy Ross: Let Freedom Ring,* p. 133.

Science Books & Films, November-December, 1990, Karen J. Goldsmith, review of *The Ferret,* p. 130; April, 1991, Nathan S. Washton, review of *The Ozone Layer,* p. 78.

Skipping Stones, May-August, 2001, Amanda Marusich, review of *Oil Spills!: The Perils of Petroleum,* p. 6.

Voice of Youth Advocates, February, 1992, Susan Rice, review of *Baseball, Basketball, Football,* and *The Olympics,* p. 392.

E–F

ERICKSON, John R. 1943-

Personal

Born October 20, 1943, in Midland, TX; son of Joseph and Anna Beth Erickson; married Kris Dykema, August 26, 1967; children: Scot, Ashley, Mark. *Nationality:* American. *Education:* University of Texas, B.A., 1966; attended Harvard Divinity School, 1966-68. *Hobbies and other interests:* Ranching, playing five-string banjo, church choir, fathering.

Addresses

Home—2010 Southwest 22nd Ave., Perryton, TX 79070. *Office*—Gulf Publishing Company, 3301 Allen Pkwy., Houston, TX 77019.

Career

Cowboy and ranch manager in Texas and Oklahoma, 1972-82; full-time author, 1982—. Maverick Books, Houston, TX, founder, 1982; affiliated with Gulf Publishing Company, Houston, TX, 1989—. Performs at schools and libraries across the United States.

Awards, Honors

Teddy Book Award, Austin Writers' League, 1998, for *The Mopwater Files.*

Writings

"HANK THE COWDOG" SERIES

The Original Adventures of Hank the Cowdog, illustrated by Gerald L. Holmes, Maverick Books (Houston, TX), 1983.
The Further Adventures of Hank the Cowdog, illustrated by Gerald L. Holmes, Maverick Books (Houston, TX), 1983.
It's a Dog's Life, illustrated by Gerald L. Holmes, Maverick Books (Houston, TX), 1984.
Murder in the Middle Pasture, illustrated by Gerald L. Holmes, Maverick Books (Houston, TX), 1984.

Cowboy John R. Erickson writes about the art of ranch roping and its part in life on the range. (Cover photo by John A. Stryker, courtesy of Texas and Southwestern Cattle Raisers Foundation.)

Faded Love, illustrated by Gerald L. Holmes, Maverick Books (Houston, TX), 1985.
Let Sleeping Dogs Lie, illustrated by Gerald L. Holmes, Maverick Books (Houston, TX), 1986.

The Curse of the Incredible Priceless Corncob, illustrated by Gerald L. Holmes, Texas Monthly Press (Austin, TX), 1989.

The Case of the One-Eyed Killer Stud Horse, illustrated by Gerald L. Holmes, Texas Monthly Press (Austin, TX), 1989.

The Case of the Halloween Ghost, illustrated by Gerald L. Holmes, Texas Monthly Press (Austin, TX), 1989.

Every Dog Has His Day, illustrated by Gerald L. Holmes, Texas Monthly Press (Austin, TX), 1989.

Lost in the Dark Uncharted Forest, illustrated by Gerald L. Holmes, Texas Monthly Press (Austin, TX), 1989.

The Fiddle-Playing Fox, illustrated by Gerald L. Holmes, Texas Monthly Press (Austin, TX), 1989.

The Wounded Buzzard on Christmas Eve, illustrated by Gerald L. Holmes, Texas Monthly Press (Austin, TX), 1989.

Monkey Business, illustrated by Gerald L. Holmes, Texas Monthly Press (Austin, TX), 1990.

The Case of the Missing Cat, illustrated by Gerald L. Holmes, Gulf Publishing (Houston, TX), 1990.

Lost in the Blinded Blizzard, illustrated by Gerald L. Holmes, Gulf Publishing (Houston, TX), 1991.

The Case of the Car-Barkaholic Dog, illustrated by Gerald L. Holmes, Gulf Publishing (Houston, TX), 1991.

The Case of the Hooking Bull, illustrated by Gerald L. Holmes, Gulf Publishing (Houston, TX), 1992.

The Case of the Midnight Rustler, illustrated by Gerald L. Holmes, Gulf Publishing (Houston, TX), 1992.

The Case of the Double Bumblebee Sting, illustrated by Gerald L. Holmes, Gulf Publishing (Houston, TX), 1994.

Moonlight Madness, illustrated by Gerald L. Holmes, Puffin Books (New York, NY), 1994.

The Case of the Black-Hooded Hangmans, illustrated by Gerald L. Holmes, Gulf Publishing (Houston, TX), 1995.

The Case of the Swirling Killer Tornado, illustrated by Gerald L. Holmes, Gulf Publishing (Houston, TX), 1995.

The Case of the Kidnapped Collie, illustrated by Gerald L. Holmes, Puffin Books (New York, NY), 1996.

The Case of the Night-Stalking Bone Monster, illustrated by Gerald L. Holmes, Maverick Books (Houston, TX), 1996.

The Case of the Vampire Vacuum Sweeper, illustrated by Gerald L. Holmes, Puffin Books (New York, NY), 1997.

The Mopwater Files, illustrated by Gerald L. Holmes, Gulf Publishing (Houston, TX), 1997.

The Case of the Haystack Kitties, illustrated by Gerald L. Holmes, Puffin Books (New York, NY), 1998.

The Case of the Vanishing Fishhook, illustrated by Gerald L. Holmes, Viking (New York, NY), 1998.

The Case of the Measled Cowboy, illustrated by Gerald L. Holmes, Viking (New York, NY), 1999.

The Case of the Vampire Cat, illustrated by Gerald L. Holmes, Puffin Books (New York, NY), 1999.

The Phantom in the Mirror, illustrated by Gerald L. Holmes, Puffin Books (New York, NY), 1999.

Slim's Goodbye, illustrated by Gerald L. Holmes, Puffin Books (New York, NY), 2000.

The Case of the Raging Rottweiler, illustrated by Gerald L. Holmes, Puffin Books (New York, NY), 2000.

The Case of the Saddle House Robbery, illustrated by Gerald L. Holmes, Viking (New York, NY), 2000.

The Case of the Deadly Ha-Ha Game, illustrated by Gerald L. Holmes, Puffin Books (New York, NY), 2001.

The Fling, illustrated by Gerald L. Holmes, Puffin Books (New York, NY), 2001.

The Case of the Missing Bird Dog, illustrated by Gerald L. Holmes, Puffin Books (New York, NY), 2002.

The Secret Laundry Monster Files, illustrated by Gerald L. Holmes, Puffin Books (New York, NY), 2002.

The Case of the Shipwrecked Tree, illustrated by Gerald L. Holmes, Puffin Books (New York, NY), 2003.

Also author of *Hank the Cowdog's Greatest Hits,* three volumes, 1985-91. Creator of audio versions of "Hank the Cowdog" books for Maverick Books.

OTHER

Through Time and the Valley, illustrated by Bill Ellzey, 1978, Maverick Books (Houston, TX), 1983.

Panhandle Cowboy, photographs by Bill Ellzey, foreword by Larry McMurtry, University of Nebraska Press (Lincoln, NE), 1980.

The Modern Cowboy, University of Nebraska Press (Lincoln, NE), 1981.

The Devil in Texas and Other Cowboy Tales, illustrated by Gerald L. Holmes, Maverick Books (Houston, TX), 1982.

Cowboys Are Partly Human, illustrated by Gerald L. Holmes, Maverick Books (Houston, TX), 1983.

The Hunter, Doubleday (New York, NY), 1984.

Alkali County Tales, illustrated by Gerald L. Holmes, Maverick Books (Houston, TX), 1984.

Ace Reid: Cowpoke, illustrated by Ace Reid, Maverick Books (Houston, TX), 1984.

Essays on Writing and Publishing, Maverick Books (Houston, TX), 1985.

Cowboy Country, illustrated by Kris Erickson, Maverick Books (Houston, TX), 1986.

Cowboys Are a Separate Species, illustrated by Gerald L. Holmes, Maverick Books (Houston, TX), 1986.

Cowboys Are Old Enough to Know Better, illustrated by Gerald L. Holmes, Gulf Publishing (Houston, TX), 1988.

(With Frankie McWhorter) *Cowboy Fiddler,* Texas Tech Press (Lubbock, TX), 1992.

Catch Rope: The Long Arm of the Cowboy, University of North Texas Press (Denton, TX), 1994.

Some Babies Grow Up to Be Cowboys: A Collection of Articles and Essays, University of North Texas Press (Denton, TX), 1999.

Moonshiner's Gold, Viking (New York, NY), 2001.

Friends: Cowboys, Cattle, Horses, Dogs, Cats, and 'Coons, University of North Texas Press (Denton, TX), 2002.

Contributor to periodicals, including *Cattleman, Livestock Weekly,* and *Texas Highways.*

Work in Progress

More books in the "Hank the Cowdog" series.

Sidelights

"When I started out, the dog was working for me," author John R. Erickson told Annette Drowlette in the *American-Statesman.* "Now I'm working for the dog." The canine in question is the fictional Hank, protagonist and first-person narrator of dozens of books in the enormously popular "Hank the Cowdog" series of books for young people. With several million copies of print books and audio books sold, the canine detective Hank, self-proclaimed Head of Ranch Security at an establishment somewhere in the Texas panhandle, is one of the best known dogs in modern literature. Ranch hand turned author, Erickson now lives on his own 6,000-acre spread in the Texas panhandle, where he gets up each morning at 5:30 a.m. to spend his morning working on the current "Hank" story for four to five hours. Then it is on to ranch chores for the rest of the day. "The truth is," wrote Drowlette, "the man behind the dog is a bright determined entrepreneur who is one of Texas' best-known children's authors. His books capture the flavor of ranch life in the Lone Star State in a way matched by few others."

Born in 1943, Erickson grew up with first-hand knowledge of ranch life. The grandson of a rancher, he began working on them himself when he was a fifth grader. "I thought it was fun," Erickson told Jodi Duckett in the *Morning Call.* "I'd go out in the country with a friend and help his dad. At some point, he thought I was worthy paying money to." Erickson graduated from the University of Texas, having passed through its prestigious honors program. "It was a great education," Erickson told Drowlette, "but it was very nonspecific and it didn't prepare me to get a job anywhere." Married, Erickson went on to divinity school at Harvard. He thought for a time that he wanted to become a minister, but a bout of homesickness prompted him to drop out and return to Texas just three credits shy of a master's degree.

It was at university that Erickson first became interested in writing, penning plays, essays, and fiction. He never thought that he could make a living from writing, though, so he worked as a cowboy to support his growing family. "I didn't know you could be a writer in a place like Perryton," Erickson told Duckett. Writing became a free-time activity for Erickson, though he did begin publishing stories and articles in trade journals such as *Cattleman, Livestock Weekly,* and *Western Horseman.* Some of these articles were nonfiction and fact-filled; others were humorous. "I really didn't know what I should be writing about," Erickson admitted to Duckett. "It is obvious I should have been writing about Texas and country subjects and humor, but it was a very humorless time. It was during the Vietnam War and everybody was mad about everything."

Erickson sent out dozens of manuscripts to New York publishers, but these were all rejected. Slowly, however, he was beginning to find his own voice, as he realized that he appreciated the oral storytelling traditions of cowboys and their great sense of humor. He never thought of himself as humorous, though. "I'm kind of a boring person most of the time," he told Duckett. "I don't like to do much of anything but work. I love work. I hate fun." Still, at one point, he decided to write a humorous piece about a couple of dogs he had once observed on a ranch where he was working. When people responded well to his readings of this story, he thought he might be on to something.

Meanwhile, he continued to work as a cowboy. In 1982, things came to a head, as the author noted on his Web site. "I was working out in the cold; there was eight inches of snow on the ground. I had just gotten a couple of rejection slips from New York publishers; and I had a wife with two kids and another one on the way." Erickson decided to stop waiting for breaks, and to make his own instead. Borrowing $2,000, he started up his own publishing company, Maverick Books. His first publishing effort was a full-length book featuring the cowdog he had already successfully written about in magazine pieces. He sold copies of *The Original Adventures of Hank the Cowdog* from the back of his pickup truck at cattle auctions, rodeos, and any other event that drew numbers of people. This title was not necessarily aimed at children, as Erickson told Drowlette. "The common denominator in my audience was agriculture." Because he was writing for an audience of any age, his "Hank" book did not talk down to young readers. As a result, that original book and its sequels in the ongoing series appeal to both children and parents.

When Erickson managed to sell two thousand copies of the book in six weeks, he was encouraged to develop an audio version of the book, read by him and accompanied with original songs for the banjo. He began to take his show on the road and perform his books as well as sell them. "My kids grew up on stage doing 'Hank' programs and going to the back of the hall and selling books," Erickson told Duckett. Soon schools began using his books, a mainstream Texas publisher picked up the series, and "Hank" was on the way to stardom.

Each title in the "Hank" series is narrated by the cowdog Hank in a laconic Texas drawl, not unlike that of Erickson's. The Head of Ranch Security, Hank tries to boss around a cast of others, including his mutt sidekick, Drover, a barn cat with an acid tongue named Pete, Slim, who is a somewhat insecure cowboy, and the owners of the ranch, High Loper and Sally Mae. The books are heavily loaded with dialogue and are also thick with detail about ranch life. Each tells the story of some adventure, or more likely misadventure, with Hank pursuing various monsters or solving mysteries. Modeled after an Australian shepherd that Erickson once knew on a ranch, Hank is representative of the comical aspects of such dogs, who are not always well trained and end up "getting in trouble," as Erickson told Duckett. Erickson himself is the model for Slim the cowboy, while Sally Mae is drawn from Erickson's wife, Kris. Loper also comes from life, modeled after a cowboy Erickson once knew.

The series has been praised for its humorous plots, witty characters, and lively dialogue. Hank's "dogservations are so doggone right on that they are little jewels of chuckle, chortle, or guffaw," asserted George Gleason in *School Library Journal.* In addition to amusing children, "Hank the Cowdog" books attempt to make reading easy for them. Erickson's "writing style is geared toward slow readers and those with short spans of attention," pointed out Janet Schnol in *Publishers Weekly.* Schnol quoted the author: "I write my stories to be like an amusement park water slide—once you're on, you can't get off and before you know it, it's over." "Hank the Cowdog" books can be heard on audio cassette, and their canine hero has inspired a fan club, "Hank's Security Squad," as well as a newsletter, *Hank Times.*

In addition to the books about Hank, Erickson has also written several nonfiction titles, including *Some Babies Grow Up to Be Cowboys,* and a mystery/adventure novel for middle grade readers titled *Moonshiner's Gold.* In the former title, Erickson collects two dozen articles and essays on cowboy life in a "finely crafted collection," according to Si Dunn of the *Dallas Morning News.* A reviewer for *Publishers Weekly* also praised that work, noting that Erickson should be a "campfire-storyteller-for-hire," as he proves in these essays about the myth and reality of life in the Texas panhandle. With *Moonshiner's Gold,* Erickson breaks new ground, telling the tale of a young teen in the 1920s who has to act beyond his years to save the family ranch when his father dies, moonshiners set up a still on their property, and the family gets an eviction notice. Janet Hilburn, reviewing the novel in *School Library Journal,* commended the "well developed and exciting" story, its "historical basis and accuracy," and "strong" characters, elements which add up to make a "portrayal of an exciting era in a setting that is usually ignored."

Erickson once commented: "My wife and I are trying to raise three kids in an age that seems determined to steal their innocence. I write stories that are worthy of my own children, which stimulate their imaginations and give them some spiritual nourishment, but which are also full of innocent fun. The award I value the most is a mother who writes me and says, 'Thank you for giving us something worth reading.'" Writing on his Web site, Erickson gives advice to young writers: "Write about something you know. Try to leave your readers better off than they were before."

Biographical and Critical Sources

PERIODICALS

American-Statesman (Austin, TX), January 18, 1997, Annette Drowlette, "The Man behind 'Hank the Cowdog,'" p. D1; May 2, 1998, Anne Morris, "Cowdog Rounds Up 1st Place in Children's Book Awards," p. C4.

Booklist, March 15, 1994, p. 1319.

Dallas Morning News, August 10, 2000, Si Dunn, review of *Some Babies Grow Up to be Cowboys,* p. 2C.

Library Journal, October 15, 1980, p. 2196.

Morning Call (Allentown, PA), February 9, 1998, Jodi Duckett, "Author Has Doggone Good Time with Children's Series," p. D1.

Publishers Weekly, September 25, 1981, p. 80; April 19, 1991, Janet Schnol, p. 42; July 24, 2000, review of

Some Babies Grow Up to Be Cowboys, p. 82; August 5, 2002, "Back at the Ranch," p. 25.

School Library Journal, September, 1988, George Gleason, review of *The Original Adventures of Hank the Cowdog, It's a Dog's Life,* and *The Further Adventures of Hank the Cowdog,* p. 198; October, 1994, p. 79; March, 1996, p. 194; November 1, 1998, Kathleen Nester, review of *The Case of the Haystack Kitties,* p. 84; April, 1999, Julie Shatterly, review of *The Case of the Vanishing Fishhook,* p. 92; August, 2001, Janet Hilburn, review of *Moonshiner's Gold,* p. 178.

Texas Monthly, October, 1983, pp. 192-193; January, 1990, Anne Dingus, review of *The Original Adventures of Hank the Cowdog,* p. 132.

OTHER

John R. Erickson Web Site, http://www.hankthecowdog.com/ (April 10, 2002).*

*   *   *

FLEISCHER, Jane
See OPPENHEIM, Joanne

*   *   *

FLOWERS, Pam 1946-

Personal

Born September 19, 1946, in Sault Ste. Marie, MI; daughter of Earl (a machinist) and Shirley (a dental assistant; maiden name, Piehl) Flowers. *Nationality:* American. *Education:* Houston Community College, Houston, TX, A.A., 1975. *Hobbies and other interests:* "Reading adventure books and books by explorers, walking with my dogs every day."

Addresses

Home—P.O. Box 874924, Wasilla, AK 99687. *E-mail*—pamflowers@pocketmail.com.

Career

Public speaker, writer, dog musher. Respiratory therapist in Texas, 1975-81.

Member

International Reading Association.

Awards, Honors

Outsider of the Year, *Outside* magazine, 1991; Gold Medal, Society of Woman Geographers, 1996.

Writings

Hug a Husky, Three-Dog Night Press (Wasilla, AK), 1996.

Pam Flowers

(With Ann Dixon) *Alone across the Arctic: One Woman's Epic Journey by Dog Team,* Alaska Northwest Books (Portland, OR), 2001.

Contributor of short stories to magazines, including *Dog World, Alaska, Fur-Fish-Game,* and *Up Here.*

Work in Progress

Scarhead, a novel about an Inuit boy in the Arctic, to be completed in 2004.

Sidelights

In 1993, Pam Flowers followed a dream of Arctic adventure few would think of tackling. Traveling alone with an eight-dog team, she mushed 2,500 miles from Barrow, Alaska, to Repulse Bay, Canada, retracing the steps of the Danish explorer Knud Rasmussen during his 1923-24 expedition along the length of the North American coast. Though Flowers recorded bits and pieces of that momentous journey in various magazines, it was not until 2001 that she, in collaboration with Ann Dixon, published a book-length account of her travels: *Alone across the Arctic: One Woman's Epic Journey by Dog Team.*

"For over twenty years I have been traveling alone by dog team around Alaska and through the Canadian Arctic," Flowers told *SATA.* "I often wrote short stories

about these adventures for magazines. People seem endlessly fascinated with dog sledding and the far north, so after writing more short stories and presenting a narrated slide show about a trans-Arctic expedition, I finally decided to make the time to write this story in the form of a book."

Born in Sault Ste. Marie, Michigan, in 1946, Flowers was entranced by books about exploration as a kid. "During most of my life I have read books about polar explorers," Flowers explained. "These books inspired me, but only a few were really helpful to aspiring polar types. When the author included specifics such as lists of gear, type of dog, mileage, weather, dates, maps, what they did right and confessed mistakes, I learned a lot."

Attending Houston Community College, Flowers earned an associate degree in respiratory therapy and for the next six years worked as a respiratory therapist in Texas. However, the pull of the North always drew her, and finally, in 1981, she moved to Alaska. Two years later she already had enough experience in mushing to run the grueling, 1,200-mile Iditarod race. Her ultimate goal, however, was to re-trace the Rasmussen expedition.

Finally, in 1993, she was prepared. With a team of eight young dogs and no sponsor, she set out in the dark of winter from Alaska. She survived Arctic storms, animal predators, and even the disappearance of her sole lead dog, Douggie, for twelve days. At one point she considered giving up because of unsafe summer ice, but in the end, she made it to Repulse Bay in Canada's Northwest Territory. Her diary records some of the more harrowing times during the journey: "My eyelashes freeze together and I can't open my eyes, I have to crawl back to the tent on my knees . . . and frantically claw the snow away from my eyes." He sole companions on this journey were the sled dogs, each of whom she came to know very closely. One dog, for example, Roald, was "intelligent" but "lacked confidence, which sometimes caused him to clown around rather than try his hardest."

When it came time to write the book, Flowers decided that she needed a collaborator. "Writing with a collaborator is like writing the book, it is always a work in progress and egos have to go into hiding until the book is finished," Flowers told *SATA.* "The most important tool in the writing of this book was my expedition journal, for without it I would have forgotten many details. I gave a transcription to Ann Dixon who would write a chapter and give it to me to read. I learned right away to be sitting at my computer when reading the chapter so I could quickly put down my thoughts. Sometimes I would make only a few changes, often I wrote insert paragraphs to add crucial information, once I re-wrote an entire chapter. Ann would add, change, and delete as necessary to keep the story flowing. What made the partnership between Ann and me successful was our willingness to read what the other wrote and consider what was best to tell the story."

Published by Alaska Northwest Books, *Alone across the Arctic* included color photographs by Flowers, as well as much of that extra material that Flowers herself appreciates in other books: lists of gear packed and tips on Arctic travel. The book met with warm critical response. John Kenny, writing in *Library Journal,* called it a "delightful and well-written story of perseverance," while *Booklist*'s David Pitt similarly found the book to be "an inspiring story, well told." *School Library Journal*'s Lee Bock, who found the message of self-respect through achievement conveyed in this "exciting book" to be very important, concluded that *Alone across the Arctic* "is an engaging survival story with broad appeal."

"I still spend considerable time presenting narrated slide shows to schools, environmental groups, dog clubs, museums, and corporations," Flowers told *SATA,* "and I greatly enjoy the immediacy of direct audience interaction. But the book has allowed me to tell more anecdotes and include many facts that are not in the slide show. Best of all, it has allowed me to leave something tangible behind that the reader can enjoy many times over."

Biographical and Critical Sources

BOOKS

Flowers, Pam, and Ann Dixon, *Alone across the Arctic: One Woman's Epic Journey by Dog Team,* Alaska Northwest Books (Portland, OR), 2001.

PERIODICALS

Booklist, September 15, 2001, David Pitt, review of *Alone across the Arctic,* p. 188.
Library Journal, March 1, 2002, John Kenny, review of *Alone across the Arctic,* p. 128.
School Library Journal, November, 2001, Lee Bock, review of *Alone across the Arctic,* p. 175.
Woman's Sports and Fitness, March, 1987, Naomi Klouda, "Dog-Sledder Goes It Alone," p. 20.

*   *   *

FRIEDMAN, Ina R(osen) 1926-

Personal

Born January 6, 1926, in Chester, PA; daughter of Jacob Sidney (a paper jobber) and Libby (a homemaker; maiden name, Leibowitz) Rosen; married Sol Friedman, August 11, 1946 (died November 15, 1973); married Sam D. Starobin, March 12, 1977; children: (first marriage) Ronne, Wendy, Lynn, Loren. *Nationality:* American. *Education:* Pennsylvania State University, B.A., 1946; Lesley College, M.A. *Politics:* Democratic. *Religion:* Jewish. *Hobbies and other interests:* Theater, gardening, cooking, traveling, swimming, collecting oral histories.

Ina R. Friedman

Addresses

Home—311 Dean Rd., Brookline, MA 02445-4142. *E-mail*—info@inafriedman.com.

Career

Writer, lecturer, filmmaker, and storyteller. Producer of slide tape "It Wasn't Just the Nazis," and video *Escape or Die.*

Member

Authors Guild, Authors League of America, Society of Children's Book Writers and Illustrators, National Writer's Union, New England Storytelling Center, National Association for Storytelling, PEN, Hadassah, League of Women Voters.

Awards, Honors

Christopher Award, 1985, *Reading Rainbow* selection, Public Broadcasting System (PBS), and Notable Book selection, American Library Association (ALA), all for *How My Parents Learned to Eat;* Best Book selection, ALA, 1990, for *The Other Victims;* Notable Book selection, ALA, Pick of the List selection, American Booksellers Association, and Sugarman Family Award runner-up, all 1995, all for *Flying against the Wind.*

Writings

(With Ethel Dalmat) *Poetry in Prayer* (religious service), Temple Sinai (Washington, DC), 1965.
A Collection of Temple Sinai Religious School Poetry, Temple Sinai (Washington, DC), 1969.
Black Cop: A Biography of Tilman O'Bryant, Westminister Press (Philadelphia, PA), 1974.
Escape or Die: True Stories of Young People Who Survived the Holocaust, Addison Wesley (Reading, MA), 1982.
How My Parents Learned to Eat, illustrated by Allen Say, Houghton (Boston, MA), 1984.
The Other Victims: First-Person Stories of Non-Jews Persecuted by the Nazis, Houghton (Boston, MA), 1990.
Flying against the Wind: The Story of a Young Woman Who Defied the Nazis, Lodgepole Press (Brookline, MA), 1995.

Adaptations

How My Parents Learned to Eat has been released on audio tape; *Escape or Die* has been adapted into a video produced by the author and released by Hodgepole Publications (Brookline, MA), 2002.

Sidelights

Ina R. Friedman once told *SATA:* "For the past several years I have been a storyteller and lecturer in addition to being a writer. I tell stories from my books on the Holocaust, including *Escape or Die: True Stories of Young People Who Survived the Holocaust, The Other Victims: First-Person Stories of Non-Jews Persecuted by*

Facing overwhelming evil with courage and moral conviction, real-life heroine Cato Bjontes van Beek worked against the Nazis in World War II Germany. (Cover illustration by Michael Lenn.)

the Nazis, and *Flying against the Wind: The Story of a Young Woman Who Defied the Nazis,* and Native American, Japanese, New England, Jewish, and other types of stories. I also tell the story of Isabella Stewart Gardner, the founder of the Gardner Museum in Boston. I got into storytelling through lecturing on my book *Escape or Die.* Several people heard me tell stories and suggested I work up a program solely of storytelling, which I did. I joined the National Association for the Preservation and Perpetuation of Storytelling [now National Association for Storytelling], and also the New England Storytelling Center. I also give workshops to students on writing, publishing, and publicizing books. In 2002, I produced a storytelling video of three stories from *Escape or Die.*

"I have always been interested in writing, but as an adolescent I became afraid to show anyone my work after one aunt who had a master's degree in social work declared, 'She has no talent.' Her judgment was based solely on one story I had written. My advice to would-be writers: Keep writing, take writing courses to help you improve, show your work to people who can give you constructive criticism, and have faith in yourself.

"My first published book, *Black Cop,* was written about a friend on the police force. My children enjoyed listening to his detective stories so I thought other students would, too. His life mirrored the civil rights movement of the 60s and 70s, and I thought this would be a good area to explore.

"To obtain material for *Escape or Die,* I traveled over 60,000 miles to five continents. I wanted to show the effect of the Nazis on individual lives, and I wanted the stories of young people to whom students could relate. *How My Parents Learned to Eat* grew out of my friendship with a Japanese woman who married an American. I thought how fortunate their children were to be brought up in two cultures. It was very exciting to receive the Christopher Award for this book."

Friedman's next work about individuals who suffered under the Nazi regime came in 1990. *The Other Victims: First-Person Stories of Non-Jews Persecuted by the Nazis* shares with readers the wide range of non-Jewish people whom the Nazis targeted for mistreatment and death, including homosexuals, Gypsies, blacks, people with physical and mental handicaps, and Jehovah's Witnesses. While many people know that over six million Jews perished in Adolph Hitler's death camps, Friedman takes care to share with readers some of the stories of the nearly five million non-Jews who also suffered the same fate. In *The Other Victims,* the author presents the stories of men and women she interviewed about their experiences in German-occupied Europe and the means they took to live another day. Personal accounts of being forced to undergo sterilization because of physical handicaps are detailed as well as stories about Gypsy boys who were sent to labor camps to be worked to death and individuals targeted for concentration camps just because they followed the Jehovah's Witnesses religion. A *Publishers Weekly* reviewer wrote, "Suspenseful vignettes are enlivened by historical background, dialogue and a not-always happy yet satisfying afterword, telling what happened to each individual." Other critics found Friedman's words a strong warning to youngsters about the dangers of totalitarianism. *School Library Journal* contributor Jack Forman, for example, commented favorably on the author's reminder "about the responsibility we all have not to let this happen again." Describing the book as "dramatic, ghastly, and all too real," *Voice of Youth Advocates* contributor Luvada Kuhn believed that *The Other Victims* "fills a need for first-hand information about this blot on the human race."

Friedman's next work, *Flying against the Wind: The Story of a Young Woman Who Defied the Nazis,* came about through the individuals she contacted for interviews for *The Other Victims.* Initially wanting to include the story of Cato Bontjes van Beek, a young German woman, in the previous book, the author decided to devote a whole book to Cato's short but inspirational life. While searching for information about Cato, Friedman came into contact with her family, who gave her the names of other people who knew Cato as well as access to her diary and letters. Using this firsthand research, the author constructs the story of Cato Bontjes van Beek, a Christian born into a family of independent thinkers in 1920. Recognized as a leader in her childhood and unafraid to voice her opinions, Cato refused to join the Hitler Youth organization and began to question the ideas of the Nazi movement. As a teenager, she moved to Berlin to be with her divorced father and became involved with the resistance movement there, helping Jews and others flee the tyranny of the Nazis. Eventually, though, this secret life caught up with Cato, as she was arrested for being a member of a group that, unknown to her, had Communist affiliations.

Charged with treason, Cato was sentenced to death and spent her remaining days in Berlin's infamous Alexanderplatz Prison. While offered a chance to escape by a sympathetic German officer who thought her punishment too harsh for such a young woman, Cato refused, preferring to be put to death with the rest of her friends who were also imprisoned for treason. Hoping her death sentence would be commuted to life in jail, Cato learned her fate on August 5, 1943, as she was executed in her twenty-second year. According to *Booklist*'s Hazel Rochman, "young people will be greatly moved by her story of courage and compelling moral choice." Noting that *Flying against the Wind* offers a good look at growing up in Nazi Germany, *Voice of Youth Advocates* reviewer Susan Levine found that Friedman's "writing helps the reader feel Cato's suffering and her great courage."

Biographical and Critical Sources

BOOKS

Beacham's Guide to Young Adult Literature, Volume 15, Gale (Detroit, MI), 2002.

PERIODICALS

Booklist, July, 1995, Hazel Rochman, review of *Flying against the Wind: The Story of a Young Woman Who Defied the Nazis,* p. 1870.
Publishers Weekly, January 19, 1990, review of *The Other Victims: First-Person Stories of Non-Jews Persecuted by the Nazis,* p. 111.
School Library Journal, April, 1990, Jack Forman, review of *The Other Victims,* p. 132.
Voice of Youth Advocates, June, 1990, Luvada Kuhn, review of *The Other Victims,* p. 124; April, 1996, Susan Levine, review of *Flying against the Wind,* p. 53.

OTHER

Remember.org, http://remember.org/ (August 10, 2002), "Ina R. Friedman."

G

GERSON, Mary-Joan

Personal

Female. *Nationality:* American. *Education:* Cornell University, B.A., 1961; New York University, Ph.D., 1978; New York University Postdoctoral Program in Psychoanalysis and Psychotherapy, certificate, 1986. *Hobbies and other interests:* Tennis, painting, photography, collecting folk art.

Addresses

Office—80 Central Park West, New York, NY 10023. *E-mail*—mjg5@nyu.edu.

Career

Professor, lecturer, teacher, and author. New York University Postdoctoral Program in Psychotherapy and Psychoanalysis, New York, NY, supervising analyst and clinical professor, 1989—, and codirector of the "Project in Family Theory and Therapy."

Awards, Honors

Aesop Prize, American Folklore Society (Children's Folklore Section), 2001, for *Fiesta Femenina: Celebrating Women in Mexican Folktales.*

Writings

Omoteji's Baby Brother, illustrated by Elzia Moon, H. Z. Walck (New York, NY), 1974.
Why the Sky Is Far Away: A Folktale from Nigeria, illustrated by Hope Meryman, Harcourt (New York, NY), 1974, revised edition edited by Ann Rider, illustrated by Carla Golembe, Joy Street Books (Boston, MA), 1992.
How Night Came from the Sea: A Story from Brazil, edited by Ann Rider, illustrated by Carla Golembe, Little, Brown (Boston, MA), 1994.

Mary-Joan Gerson retells a Nigerian folktale about humankind's waste and greed in Why the Sky Is Far Away. *(Illustrated by Carla Golembe.)*

(Reteller) *People of Corn: A Mayan Story,* illustrated by Carla Golembe, Little, Brown (Boston, MA), 1995.
The Embedded Self: A Psychoanalytic Guide to Family Therapy, Analytic Press (Hillsdale, NJ), 1996.
(Reteller) *Fiesta Femenina: Celebrating Women in Mexican Folktales,* illustrated by Maya Christina Gonzalez, Barefoot Books (New York, NY), 2001.

Author of scholarly articles to professional journals and periodicals, including *Psychology of Women Quarterly, Contemporary Psychoanalysis, Women and Therapy,* and *American Journal of Family Therapy.*

Sidelights

Mary-Joan Gerson is a psychotherapist, psychoanalyst, and professor of clinical psychology who has lived and worked in such diverse places as Nigeria and Peru. In addition to her scholarly and academic publications,

Gerson is known for her children's stories, which are based on ancient folktales, mythology, and cultural traditions. *Omoteji's Baby Brother,* her debut work, tells the story of a young African boy's special gift to his newborn brother during his ceremonial naming ritual. Omoteji creates a poem of praise for the baby and arranges for drummers to accompany his presentation. A critic for the *Bulletin of the Center for Children's Books* praised the book for its "engaging" story, complete "with the authenticity of cultural details." A *Publishers Weekly* reviewer also predicted that the work will "delight the young reader."

Gerson's next story, *Why the Sky Is Far Away: A Folktale from Nigeria,* is a retelling of an ancient myth originating from the Bini tribe in Nigeria. According to the narrative, the sky once provided food to the people—stew, corn, and pineapple—but grew angry when the people began to waste its gifts. As a punishment, the sky moved so far out of reach that, forever afterward, humans could no longer just take what they wanted, but instead had to work and grow their own crops. The tale, passed down orally for over five hundred years, has been described as comparable to the Biblical story of manna from heaven and the Zuni tribe's mythological Corn Maidens who often chastised people for wasting food. Ellen Fader noted in a *Horn Book* review that the book is "a splendid contribution to the already existing body of African folk tales and a timely reminder to those who would squander the earth's riches." Sam Swope wrote in the *New York Times Book Review* that Gerson's narrative "gives the story a contemporary environmental message."

Gerson's third book for children features a legend from Brazil. In *How Night Came from the Sea: A Story from Brazil,* Gerson tells how an African sea goddess brings the gift of nighttime to Brazil. The daughter of Iemanjá, the goddess of the sea, leaves her mother's quiet, dark, and tranquil underwater kingdom to marry a mortal who lives on the newly created Earth, where there is no break from the light. Though she loves her husband and new life outside of the sea, the young bride misses the darkness of her mother's world and feels compassion for the men and women who work twenty-four hours a day, having no nighttime to interrupt their labor. Sensing his new wife's sadness, the husband dispatches three men to ask Iemanjá for help, and the goddess gives the men a bag with the warning that they are to deliver it to her daughter without opening it. Tempted by the mysterious bag's contents, the men open the package, letting loose all of the wild night spirits, including the moon, stars, and other inhabitants of the dark. Fortunately, Iemanjá's daughter is able to tame the night elements so all of the people on Earth can enjoy an interruption from the harsh daylight. Describing *How Night Came from the Sea* as "a beautiful book that will find many uses," a *Kirkus Reviews* critic believed that "the lyrically retold story makes a rich contrast to other creation myths." *Booklist*'s Hazel Rochman lauded the work as well, calling it "a beautiful story, lyrically told, in some ways reminiscent of the myth of Persephone and the seasons."

Gerson retells eight folktales celebrating women from various Mexican cultures in **Fiesta Femenina.** *(Illustrated by Maya Christina Gonzalez.)*

For her next two children's works, Gerson turns to the land of Mexico in both *People of Corn: A Mayan Story* and *Fiesta Femenina: Celebrating Women in Mexican Folktales.* In "graceful, flowing prose," according to *Horn Book*'s Ellen Fader in a review of *People of Corn,* the author retells the ancient Mayan legend of creation where two gods make various attempts at developing creatures who will worship them. The duo's first efforts result in mute animals and puppet-like humans lacking true affection for their creators. After discovering corn, however, the Plumed Serpent and Heart of Sky find a proper medium from which to make the Mayans, the first people of Earth. Though the Mayans give their creators exactly the worship and praise the gods expected, Plumed Serpent and Heart of Sky realize that humans are much wiser than anticipated and may one day tire of praising them. To avoid this from ever taking place, the two gods decide to partially obscure human intelligence by limiting it to the "near and real." Only in their dreams, according to the Mayan legend, is the veil lifted, exposing humans to a wide-ranging variety of experiences, some of which can be seen in the famous weavings of Mayan women. Writing in *Booklist,* Annie Ayres found *People of Corn* "mysterious and complex," going on to claim that "ancient Mayan mythology has rarely been made so accessible and appealing."

In *Fiesta Femenina* Gerson offers young readers a collection of eight tales from a variety of Mexican peoples, including the Mayans, Aztecs, Mixtec, Yaqui, and descendants of the Spanish colonists. Each featuring a strong female protagonist, the stories range from the religious, in a story about the Virgin of Guadalupe, to the ancient, in an Aztec tale about a goddess becoming Mother Earth, and the humorous, in a retelling of how the moon avoids the sun's romantic overtures. *Booklist* critic Ayres argued that "this collection will be a sparking treasure in any folktale collection," while *School Library Journal* reviewer Ann Welton found "these selections soundly composed, diverse, and celebratory of both the women and the land from which they come."

Gerson once told *SATA:* "At a time when children live in an electronic world, in which images and words—and in a sense relationships—can be produced and erased at a finger's touch, the power and mystery of folklore becomes more compelling and more enriching. Whatever our technological development, the mystery and dilemmas of human life remain, and demand attention and imagination."

Biographical and Critical Sources

BOOKS

Gerson, Mary-Joan, reteller, *People of Corn: A Mayan Story,* illustrated by Carla Golembe, Little, Brown (Boston, MA), 1995.

PERIODICALS

Booklist, August, 1992, Hazel Rochman, review of *Why the Sky Is Far Away: A Nigerian Folktale,* p. 2017; September 1, 1994, Hazel Rochman, review of *How Night Came from the Sea: A Story from Brazil,* p. 51; January 1, 1996, Annie Ayres, review of *People of Corn: A Mayan Story,* p. 839; September 15, 2001, Annie Ayres, review of *Fiesta Femenina: Celebrating Women in Mexican Folktales,* p. 226.

Bulletin of the Center for Children's Books, November, 1974, review of *Omoteji's Baby Brother,* p. 42; October, 1992, Betsy Hearne, review of *Why the Sky Is Far Away,* pp. 42-43; October, 1994, Elizabeth Bush, review of *How Night Came from the Sea,* p. 46.

Horn Book, September, 1992, Ellen Fader, review of *Why the Sky Is Far Away,* pp. 591-592; March-April, 1995, Mary M. Burns, review of *How Night Came from the Sea,* p. 205; November-December, 1995, Ellen Fader, review of *People of Corn,* p. 751; January-February, 2002, Anita Burkham, "Awards," p. 125.

Kirkus Reviews, March 1, 1974, p. 24; July 15, 1992, review of *Why the Sky Is Far Away,* p. 920; August 15, 1994, review of *How Night Came from the Sea,* 1128.

New York Times Book Review, November 8, 1992, Sam Swope, review of *Why the Sky Is Far Away,* p. 36.

Publishers Weekly, July 8, 1974, review of *Omoteji's Baby Brother,* p. 74; August 24, 1992, review of *Why the Sky Is Far Away,* p. 79; July 18, 1994, review of *How Night Came from the Sea,* p. 245.

School Library Journal, September, 1992, Linda Boyles, review of *Why the Sky Is Far Away,* p. 216; November, 1994, Harriett Fargnoli, review of *How Night*

Came from the Sea, p. 75; December, 1995, Wendy Lukehart, review of *People of Corn,* p. 96; October, 2001, Ann Welton, review of *Fiesta Femenina: Celebrating Women in Mexican Folktales,* p. 183.

OTHER

Mary-Joan Gerson Web Site, http://www.mjgerson.com/ (August 3, 2002).

*   *   *

GREGORY, Kristiana 1951-

Personal

Born June 12, 1951, in Los Angeles, CA; daughter of Harold (an inventor) and Jeanne (a recreation supervisor; maiden name, Kern) Gregory; married, 1982; children: two. *Nationality:* American. *Religion:* Christian. *Hobbies and other interests:* Reading, swimming, camping, studying French, "hanging out with girlfriends," yard sales, Bible study, long walks.

Addresses

Home and office—Boise, ID. *Agent*—c/o Author Mail, Scholastic, 555 Broadway, New York, NY 10012. *E-mail*—kgregorybooks@yahoo.com.

Career

Gardena Valley News, Gardena, CA, freelance feature writer, 1977-79, freelance reporter, 1978; *Southern California Business,* Los Angeles, CA, associate editor, 1978; *Los Angeles Times,* Los Angeles, CA, book reviewer and columnist, 1978-91; *San Luis Obispo County Telegram-Tribune,* San Luis Obispo, CA, reporter, 1980-81; homemaker and writer, 1982—.

Member

Society of Children's Book Writers and Illustrators, Authors Guild.

Awards, Honors

Golden Kite Award for Fiction, Society of Children's Book Writers and Illustrators, Notable Children's Trade Book in Social Studies citation, National Council for the Social Studies/Children's Book Council (NCSS-CBC), and Book for the Teen Age citation, New York Public Library, all 1989, all for *Jenny of the Tetons;* Best Book for Young Adults citation, American Library Association, and citation from NCSS-CBC, both 1992, both for *Earthquake at Dawn.*

Writings

HISTORICAL FICTION

Jenny of the Tetons, Harcourt (San Diego, CA), 1989.
The Legend of Jimmy Spoon, Harcourt (San Diego, CA), 1990.
Earthquake at Dawn, Harcourt (San Diego, CA), 1992.

Jimmy Spoon and the Pony Express, Scholastic (New York, NY), 1994.

The Stowaway: A Tale of California Pirates, Scholastic (New York, NY), 1995.

The Winter of Red Snow: The Revolutionary War Diary of Abigail Jane Stewart, Scholastic (New York, NY), 1996.

Across the Wide and Lonesome Prairie: The Oregon Trail Diary of Hattie Campbell, Scholastic (New York, NY), 1997.

Orphan Runaways, Scholastic (New York, NY), 1998.

Cleopatra VII: Daughter of the Nile, Scholastic (New York, NY), 1999.

The Great Railroad Race: The Diary of Libby West, Scholastic (New York, NY), 1999.

Seeds of Hope: The Gold Rush Diary of Susanna Fairchild, Scholastic (New York, NY), 2001.

Five Smooth Stones: Hope's Diary, Philadelphia, Pennsylvania, 1776, Scholastic (New York, NY), 2001.

We Are Patriots: Hope's Revolutionary War Diary, Scholastic (New York, NY), 2002.

Eleanor of Aquitaine, Scholastic (New York, NY), 2002.

Contributor of a short story, "The Gift," to *Moody Monthly.*

Sidelights

Kristiana Gregory is the author of over a dozen historical fiction works for children and young adults. In novels such as *Jenny of the Tetons, The Legend of Jimmy Spoon* and its sequel, *Jimmy Spoon and the Pony Express,* and *Orphan Runaways,* Gregory transforms historical documents into full-fledged stories of eighteenth, nineteenth, and early-twentieth-century American life. Central to her works are the adventures of young people who, like their modern counterparts, face emotional crises and hard choices. Careful research distinguishes her books, which have received a number of commendations.

Books were always an important part of Gregory's life. As she once told *SATA:* "We had books everywhere, and my parents read to me a lot. If we had questions, my father would say, 'Let's look it up in the encyclopedia.' Then we'd get in this long, involved, fun adventure going through an encyclopedia, and I think that's where I got my love for research. All the historical things I write remind me of my childhood and the excitement of exploring something and finding out about it."

Gregory's love of books served her well in school. In her *SATA* interview, she commented: "I was a very good student when I was in elementary school. I loved writing and English and history. I remember I loved doing reports. I would go home and read an encyclopedia—not a whole encyclopedia, but if I was researching apples, I would pick up the *A,* and I would rarely get around to writing my report on apples. I would get so enthralled in the volume *A* that I would end up finding something else I wanted to write about."

One subject Gregory chose to write about as an adult, Native American history and culture, was also part of

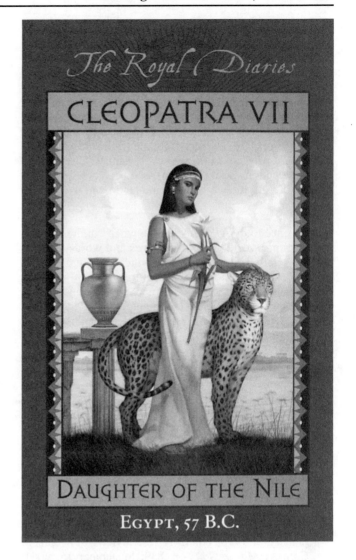

In Kristiana Gregory's work, twelve-year-old Cleopatra records her fears for her life and her hope to become queen of Egypt. (Cover illustration by Tim O'Brien.)

her upbringing. "When we moved to New Mexico we were very close to the Mescalero Apache Indian reservation," she commented. "My parents were interested in the Native Americans, and they would take us around to the different powwows and pueblos. They had almost a reverent respect for them, and they passed that on to us. Anything that had to do with Native Americans they were interested in. We would go to museums, and we had Navajo rugs in our home and trinkets and that sort of thing."

Gregory's first taste of professional writing came during the 1970s when she became a freelance writer for newspapers. "I went to the editor of the *Gardena Valley News* and said, 'I don't have any writing experience but I love to write—will you hire me?' I can't believe I did this, because I had no experience. He hired me to write feature stories for ten dollars each, plus they would give me a byline. Eventually that editor became editor of the Los Angeles Chamber of Commerce's weekly tabloid, *Southern California Business,* and asked me to come along. Later I met a *Los Angeles Times* editor through a college course on writing who offered me a job there."

Children's books became an increasingly important part of Gregory's life after she married and started a family in Pocatello, Idaho. "I was invited to write a children's book column for the *Los Angeles Times Book Review,*" she explained. "I was in the middle of nowhere, in very cold weather—it was below zero for weeks at a time, which was difficult for a native Californian, plus I had a toddler and an infant—and the United Parcel Service would deliver these huge boxes of books, brand-new children's books. It was quite a thrill, because the editor said, 'Just write a column, pick eight or so books per column.' The column appeared every other week and I had all these wonderful books to choose from.

"When my children were a little older I started tutoring at the Pocatello High School. I got to know a lot of the Native Americans from Fort Hall, which was seven miles north of Pocatello. That was the real spark of the desire to write, when I saw how hungry these teenagers were to know about their culture. We would try to find books to interest them in reading, and very little is written about their ancestors. That was my main motivation for writing *Jenny of the Tetons.* I found a real

Young Hope records the confusion of her life as the American Revolution begins in Philadelphia in 1776.

Shoshone woman with nothing written about her, and I wanted to honor her and honor the culture."

In *Jenny of the Tetons,* Gregory tells of Jenny and Beaver Dick's lives from the point of view of a fictional immigrant orphan, Carrie Hill, adopted by the Leighs. Grieving for her parents, who were killed in an Indian raid, fifteen-year-old Carrie agrees to help Beaver Dick's wife tend their many children, unaware that this woman is herself an Indian. Once Carrie arrives at the Leighs' rustic home, she struggles to reconcile her hatred and Jenny's kindness. Gradually the family's love eases her grief. When tragedy strikes the Leighs, she fully shares the emotional pain. According to Richard Peck, assessing the book in the *Los Angeles Times Book Review,* "The strength of the writing lies in its research and the underplayed description of unqualified sorrow."

Gregory stayed with Native themes for her next book, *The Legend of Jimmy Spoon,* the tale of a young white boy who goes to live among the Shoshone. It was based on the memoirs of a nineteenth-century pony express rider. Twelve-year-old Jimmy is frustrated with both his father's refusal to give him a horse and the boredom of working at the family store. After meeting two Indian youths outside of town, he decides to accept their gift of a horse in return for a visit to their camp. The tribe wants him to stay permanently, however, and for the next three years Jimmy works to learn and understand Shoshone ways as the adopted son of the chief's mother. Eventually Jimmy's father discovers his whereabouts and threatens war if he does not return; to preserve the peace, Jimmy leaves the tribe. *Los Angeles Times Book Review* writer Eileen Heyes found the book "skimpy in the basics of story," but she judged it "rich in its portrait of Indian philosophy and daily life." Paula J. Lacey, reviewing *The Legend of Jimmy Spoon* in *Voice of Youth Advocates,* described it as "well researched" and "exciting."

The idea for Gregory's third book came only after some setbacks. "After another book I had been trying to sell was again rejected, I was so depressed I said I was never going to write again," she told *SATA.* "I had kind of an angry conversation with God and said, 'If you want me to write again, you're going to have to show me a character, an event, and an original source document,' which is basically what I've done with the other two books. So I was in my orthodontist's office, and normally I don't get to read the magazines; this time he kept me waiting for forty-five minutes, and I had a chance to go through all the magazines on my lap. The last magazine was a *National Geographic* from 1990, and it was about the 1989 San Francisco earthquake with a sidebar about the 1906 earthquake. There were some never-before-published photographs taken by a young woman, and there was a little photo of her. It told this very tiny story, and there was an excerpt from a letter never before published describing what one woman had seen in the 1906 earthquake. There were incredible details—things that I had never heard or thought about—like looters being shot and babies being born in the parks. A set of triplets had been born after the earthquake. My heart started beating rapidly, and I said, 'Oh, this is a character, it's a young woman, there is a major event—the earthquake—and here's a document.'

"So I went home and called *National Geographic* to see if I could contact these people. They put me in touch with the owner of the letter and told me about Brigham Young University, which had the photos, and the photographer's nephew James Irvine, of the Irvine family of southern California. It was a big California story, not only because of where it happened, but because the Irvine family was one of the first white landowners in California."

In *Earthquake at Dawn,* Gregory chronicles the experiences of photographer Edith Irvine and her traveling companion, the fictional Daisy Valentine, in San Francisco at the time of the great earthquake of April 18, 1906. The two young women come to the city early on the morning of the quake to board a ship to Australia and, ultimately, Paris, where Edith has been invited to show her photographs. The earthquake shatters their plans. They spend the next several days trying to find Edith's father, from whom they have been separated, and sharing the trials of several residents who become like family to them. One of their new friends is Mary Exa, whose 1906 letter about the earthquake provided revealing quotes for the beginning of each chapter. Despite thirst, hunger, exhaustion, fires, rats, and additional earth tremors, Edith makes time to photograph the devastation. This itself endangers them, for authorities trying to conceal the extent of the catastrophe have been destroying cameras and photographic plates. Mary Hedge, assessing the book for *Voice of Youth Advocates,* wrote, "The emotional impact ... blends well with the adventure plot, making it an excellent choice for the rare teenage historical fiction lover."

"The theme that I tried to pull through in *Earthquake at Dawn,*" Gregory explained to *SATA,* "was that you can survive. No matter how terrible something is that you might dread, often when you actually experience it, it is not as bad as you had feared. You do get through it, and there are ways to get water. In the book they got water from the dew that gathered during the night and from melted ice and a lake, and eventually they brought river water over. They were eating frogs, they were making dandelion tea, and most of all, they were banding together. Strangers became friends, and within a matter of hours they became family members because of how much they depended on each other. I'm hoping that whatever events kids go through, they see that there is hope in anything."

Gregory's readers soon prompted her to write again, returning to an earlier subject. "I got so many letters from children all over the country asking for a sequel to *The Legend of Jimmy Spoon* that I said okay. It was called *Jimmy Spoon and the Pony Express.* I spent months researching the pony express. Because I couldn't get to Nevada, I called bookstores and museums all along the pony express trail and asked them to tell me what titles they had. I had bookstores send me things

about Nevada flowers and the terrain and immigrant diaries from that era. One man sent me a videotape of the pony express trail that he had done all the way from Missouri to California so I could see what the terrain was like in Nevada. I would have loved to travel myself, but when you have children in school, you just don't have the time."

In *Jimmy Spoon and the Pony Express,* seventeen-year-old Jimmy is itching for adventure after working in his father's store. He liked his time with the Shoshone far better than his staid life in Salt Lake City. When he comes across an ad for riders for the Pony Express, he sees it as a way out of his boring life and as an opportunity to travel once again through Shoshone territory. However, Jimmy soon learns that delivering the mail, despite some small adventures, is not quite as exciting as he hoped it would be. Reviewing the novel in *Booklist,* Chris Sherman noted that "Gregory packs her short chapters with enough action, drama, and humor to please even hard-core reluctant readers." Similarly, Sarah Guille Kuilhaug, writing in *Horn Book Guide,* called the novel a "sure-fire good read."

In her next novel, *The Stowaway: A Tale of California Pirates,* Gregory takes middle grade readers from the prairie to the sea with eleven-year-old Carlito, who stows away on a pirate ship to seek revenge for the killing of his father. Partially set in Monterey, California, in the nineteenth century, the book is based on the adventures of a real pirate, Hipolyte de Bouchard. Barbara Chatton praised *The Stowaway* in a *School Library Journal* review, calling it "exciting," and further noting that Gregory "brings to life events and perspectives not often found in the standard history texts."

Gregory has also penned many titles in the "Dear America" series, in which aspects of American history are illuminated by the fictional diaries of young people of the time. She has taken a look at America's Revolutionary War experience in three such titles, *The Winter of the Red Snow: The Revolutionary War Diary of Abigail Jane Stewart, Five Smooth Stones: Hope's Diary, Philadelphia, Pennsylvania, 1776,* and *We Are Patriots: Hope's Revolutionary War Diary.* In *The Winter of the Red Snow,* Gregory relates the hardships of the Revolutionary Army during the bitter winter of 1777-78 at Valley Forge through the eyes of eleven-year-old Abby, whose family lives nearby. "Although Gregory's overall tone is positive," noted Ann W. Moore in *School Library Journal,* "she doesn't neglect ... the horrors of war."

Gregory returns to the topic of the Revolution in two companion volumes. With *Five Smooth Stones,* she looks at the events of 1776 through the eyes of nine-year-old Hope Potter—"one brave, young girl," according to Mary Laub of *Childhood Education*—who records daily life and her brushes with famous patriots in and around Philadelphia at the beginning of the war. Denise Wilms had positive words for the novel in *Booklist,* remarking that Gregory does "an effective job of evoking the times." Elizabeth Bush reached a similar conclusion in her review for *Bulletin of the Center for Children's Books.* "Kid-pleasing, authentic details of everyday life abound," Bush wrote, citing details from the humorous "to the severe discomforts of life without electricity and central heating."

Hope's story is continued in *We Are Patriots.* The Potter family has fled the city for the country, but they still find no peace. Hope's brother, gone off to fight with the British, has been arrested as a spy, and her father is fighting for the Americans. Meanwhile, there is a new baby to care for, and concern for the safety of the family forces Hope's mother to bring them back to Philadelphia, where they must deal with the invading British troops. Trying to regain normalcy, they reopen their bakery, but when her father returns from the front, he has fearful stories to relate. A contributor for *Kirkus Reviews* noted, "Strong imagery and well-researched details make this an engrossing as well as educational selection."

A journey west on the Oregon Trail is the subject for another diary-novel, *Across the Wide and Lonesome Prairie: The Oregon Trail Diary of Hattie Campbell.* Set in 1847, this journal-novel chronicles the hardships of a thirteen-year-old girl, Hattie, and her family as they travel from Missouri west along the Oregon Trail. Although disaster strikes the group on more than one occasion, once when Hattie herself makes a fatal mistake, the youngster also makes friends and has her horizons broadened in this tale "rich with details of pioneer life," as *Booklist*'s Carolyn Phelan described it. Phelan further observed that though it is a fictional diary, Gregory's book "has a good deal of truth in it." These "details of life on the trail will be fascinating to young readers," thought *School Library Journal*'s Connie Parker.

A further trek west is at the heart of *The Great Railroad Race: The Diary of Libby West,* which chronicles the construction of the transcontinental railroad in 1868 as seen through the eyes of the fourteen-year-old daughter of a newspaper reporter in Utah Territory who is covering the story. The building of the railway connected the West with the East, reducing the arduous six-month stagecoach or wagon train journey to a mere week by rail. A contributor for *Kirkus Reviews* commented that "history is brought to life through Libby's candid narration."

Gregory deals with the California Gold Rush of 1849 in *Seeds of Hope: The Gold Rush Diary of Susanna Fairchild* and in *Orphan Runaways.* The former title focuses on the journals of another fourteen-year-old-girl, Susanna, who has traveled with her parents from New York to the West by ship. The family intended to head for Oregon Territory, but Susanna's mother is lost at sea on the journey. Once they land in San Francisco on New Year's Day of 1849, her father is struck with gold fever and takes his children off into the wilds of California in search of the elusive yellow metal. Life in the mining camps is "richly detailed in Susanna's vivid entries," wrote Ellen Mandel in a *Booklist* review. Mandel went

on to call this book a "gripping, realistic fictional glimpse of history."

Orphan Runaways provides a look at the Gold Rush through the eyes of twelve-year-old Danny and his younger brother, Judd, who run away from a San Francisco orphanage in search of an uncle residing in one of the California boom towns. Upon finding Uncle Hank, Danny decides to stay with a kindly hotel operator because he is prejudiced against his uncle's new wife, a Chinese woman. Finally, however, the young boy comes around, learning to accept his new aunt. Critical views of this novel were mixed. *School Library Journal*'s Faith Brautigam complained that the "characters don't come to life." However, *Booklist*'s Kay Weisman felt this novel supplied a good "exploration of racial prejudice of the time," while Kristi Steele, writing in *Children's Book Review Service,* praised the "many memorable characters" in *Orphan Runaways.*

Cleopatra VII: Daughter of the Nile takes the reader far from Gregory's usual fictional and historical territory. Part of the "Royal Diaries" series, *Cleopatra VII* transports readers to ancient Egypt and Rome, following Cleopatra as a twelve-year-old as she meets such luminaries as the soldier and statesman Mark Antony (who, many years later, will become her lover), the famous Roman orator Cicero, and Octavian, who will later become Augustus Caesar and defeat Cleopatra and Mark Antony for control of the Roman Empire. "The attention to detail draws readers headlong into Egypt," wrote a contributor for *Kirkus Reviews.* Susan Dove Lempke, reviewing the novel in *Booklist,* praised Gregory's narrative style, noting that she "writes evocatively," and also commenting that the author "has clearly done her research." Cynthia M. Sturgis, writing in *School Library Journal,* called the book an "enjoyable story," and further remarked that characters "are well drawn ... and historical background is well integrated into the text." Deborah Stevenson, writing in *Bulletin of the Center for Children's Books,* further lauded the book, noting that Gregory "paints an exciting picture of riches, heritage, and conspiracy," as the youthful Cleopatra tries to navigate treacherous diplomatic waters in Rome in an attempt to shore up her father's Egyptian reign.

In all her writing, Gregory tries to convey the need for love and hope. "What I'm gradually learning—I wish I'd learned it younger—is that your family is those you love, and you can have a family anywhere. Our society is very disrupted, full of broken families, and there are a lot of kids ... who have lost a parent to murder. The gang population is very high, and the violence is pretty bad, and it's astounding to me the grief that some of these kids must feel. What do you do? Does that mean you have no family anymore? Part of my motivation is I'm hoping that kids, as I said, see that there is hope, there is always hope, and there is always somebody to love, and there is always someone who will love you." Love is paramount in her books, Gregory asserted: "Love for your fellow human being regardless of color or circumstances, taking time to try to understand another person and not make snap judgments."

Biographical and Critical Sources

BOOKS

Something about the Author, Volume 74, Gale (Detroit, MI), 1993.

PERIODICALS

Booklist, April 15, 1992, p. 1527; November 15, 1994, Chris Sherman, review of *Jimmy Spoon and the Pony Express,* p. 590; September 15, 1995, Linda Perkins, review of *The Stowaway: A Tale of California Pirates,* pp. 162-163; April 15, 1997, Carolyn Phelan, review of *Across the Wide and Lonesome Prairie: The Oregon Trail Diary of Hattie Campbell,* p. 1428; February 15, 1998, Kay Weisman, review of *Orphan Runaways,* p. 1011; April 1, 1999, GraceAnne A. DeCandido, review of *The Great Railroad Race: The Diary of Libby West,* p. 1426; January 1, 2000, Susan Dove Lempke, review of *Cleopatra VII: Daughter of the Nile,* p. 922; March 1, 2000, Sally Estes, review of *Orphan Runaways,* p. 1212; January 1, 2001, Denise Wilms, review of *Five Smooth Stones: Hope's Diary, Philadelphia, Pennsylvania, 1776,* p. 960; September 1, 2001, Ellen Mandel, review of *Seeds of Hope: The Gold Rush Diary of Susanna Fairchild,* p. 104.

Book Report, May-June, 1997, Jo Clarke, review of *Orphan Runaways,* p. 34.

Bulletin of the Center for Children's Books, October, 1995, Elizabeth Bush, review of *The Stowaway,* p. 55; October, 1996, Elizabeth Bush, review of *The Winter of Red Snow: The Revolutionary War Diary of Abigail Jane Stewart,* pp. 55-56; December, 1999, Deborah Stevenson, review of *Cleopatra VII,* p. 130; April, 2001, Elizabeth Bush, review of *Five Smooth Stones,* p. 303.

Childhood Education, winter, 2001, Mary Laub, review of *Five Smooth Stones,* p. 110.

Children's Book Review Service, June, 1998, Kristi Steele, review of *Orphan Runaways,* p. 130.

English Journal, December, 1992, p. 77.

Horn Book Guide, spring, 1995, Sarah Guille Kuilhaug, review of *Jimmy Spoon and the Pony Express,* p. 77; fall, 1998, Christine Hinsdale, review of *Orphan Runaways,* p. 330; fall, 1999, Anne St. John, review of *The Great Railroad Race,* p. 292.

Kirkus Reviews, April 1, 1999, review of *The Great Railroad Race,* p. 534; July 15, 1999, review of *Cleopatra VII,* p. 1133; May 1, 2002, review of *We Are Patriots: Hope's Revolutionary War Diary,* p. 654.

Los Angeles Times Book Review, May 28, 1989, Richard Peck, "A Blending of Two Cultures," p. 8; October 28, 1990, Eileen Heyes, review of *The Legend of Jimmy Spoon,* p. 12.

Publishers Weekly, April 28, 1989, p. 81; September 2, 1996, review of *The Winter of Red Snow,* p. 131.

School Library Journal, June, 1989, p. 105; August, 1992, p. 154; November, 1994, Sally Bates Goodroe, review of *Jimmy Spoon and the Pony Express,* p. 102; September, 1995, Barbara Chatton, review of *The Stowaway,* p. 200; September, 1996, Ann W. Moore, review of *The Winter of Red Snow,* p. 202; March, 1997, Connie Parker, review of *Across the Wide and Lonesome Prairie,* p. 187; March, 1998, Faith Brautigam, review of *Orphan Runaways,* p. 212; August, 1999, Cathy Coffman, review of *The Great Railroad Race,* p. 158; October, 1999, Cynthia M. Sturgis, review of *Cleopatra VII,* p. 150; July, 2001, Janet Gillen, review of *Seeds of Hope,* p. 108.

Tribune Books (Chicago, IL), May 4, 1997, Katherine Seigenthaler, "Dear Diarists," pp. 1, 9.

Voice of Youth Advocates, December, 1990, Paula J. Lacey, review of *The Legend of Jimmy Spoon,* p. 281; June, 1992, Mary Hedge, review of *Earthquake at Dawn,* p. 94; April, 1995, Darlene Kelm, review of *Jimmy Spoon and the Pony Express,* p. 23.

OTHER

KidsReads, http://www.kidsreads.com/ (July 2, 2002), Shannon Maughan, "Kristiana Gregory Interview."

Kristiana Gregory Web Site, http://www.kgregorybooks.com/ (November 16, 2002).

* * *

GRIMES, Nikki 1950-
(Naomi McMillan)

Personal

Born October 20, 1950, in Harlem, NY; daughter of James (a violinist) and Bernice (a keypunch operator; maiden name, McMillan) Grimes; children: Tawfiqa (daughter; deceased). *Education:* Rutgers University, B.A., 1974. *Religion:* Christian. *Hobbies and other interests:* Knitting, reading, long walks, talking with friends, cooking, playing word games.

Addresses

Home—903 North 71st St., Seattle, WA 98103.

Career

Writer. Blackafrica Promotions, Inc., New York, NY, talent coordinator, 1970-71; Rutgers University, Livingston College, New Brunswick, NJ, instructor in writing and applied sociolinguistics, 1972-74; Harlem Teams for Self-Help, New York, NY, documentary photographer, 1975-76; WBAI-FM Radio, New York, NY, scriptwriter and producer of *The Kid Show,* 1977-78; Riksradio, Sweden, scriptwriter and producer, 1979-80; AB Exportsprak Translators, Sweden, proofreader and translator, 1980-84; freelance writer and editor, 1984-89; Walt Disney Co., Burbank, CA, writer and editor, 1989-91; freelance writer, 1991—. University of California, Los Angeles, CA, library assistant, 1986-88; Swedish/English translator of computer systems manuals. Lecturer at colleges, universities, and workshops, including Pratt Institute, City University of New York, Studio Museum of Harlem, University of Massachusetts, and New York University; consultant to Swedish Educational Radio and New York's Cultural Council Foundation.

Nikki Grimes

Member

Society of Children's Book Writers and Illustrators, Pen Center U.S.A. West, Authors Guild, Academy of American Poets.

Awards, Honors

Ford Foundation grant for research in Tanzania, 1974-75; Best Books of the Year selection, Child Study Association, and Children's Book of the Year Award, Bank Street College, both for *Growin';* Books for Free Children citation, *Ms.,* Children's Book citation, Library of Congress, Best Books of the Year, *Philadelphia Inquirer,* Best Books of the Season, *Saturday Review,* all 1978, and Notable Books citation, American Library Association (ALA), 1978-79, all for *Something on My Mind;* Benjamin Franklin Picture Book Award, for *From a Child's Heart;* Coretta Scott King Honor Book Award, ALA, and Notable Books citation, ALA, both for *Meet Danitra Brown;* 100 Titles for Reading and Sharing, New York Public Library, for both *Meet Danitra Brown* and *C Is for City;* Notable Books citation, ALA, 1997, for *Come Sunday;* Coretta Scott King Honor Book Award, ALA, 1998, for *Jazmin's Notebook;* Books for Youth Editors' Choice, *Booklist,* 1999, for *My Man Blue.*

Writings

FOR YOUNG PEOPLE

Growin' (novel for children), illustrated by Charles Lilly, Dial (New York, NY), 1977.

Something on My Mind (poems), illustrated by Tom Feelings, Dial (New York, NY), 1978.

Oh, Bother! Someone's Baby-Sitting! illustrated by Sue DiCicco, Western Publishing (Racine, WI), 1991.

Oh, Bother! Someone's Fighting, illustrated by Darrell Baker, Western Publishing (Racine, WI), 1991.

Malcolm X: A Force for Change, Fawcett Columbine (New York, NY), 1992.

Minnie's New Friend, illustrated by Peter Emslie and Darren Hunt, Western Publishing (Racine, WI), 1992.

(Adapter) *Walt Disney's Pinocchio,* illustrated by Phil Ortiz and Diana Wakeman, Western Publishing (Racine, WI), 1992.

From a Child's Heart (poems), illustrated by Brenda Joysmith, Just Us Books (East Orange, NJ), 1993.

(Reteller) *Cinderella,* illustrated by Don Williams and Jim Story, Western Publishing (Racine, WI), 1993.

Meet Danitra Brown (poems), illustrated by Floyd Cooper, Lothrop, Lee & Shepard Books (New York, NY), 1994.

C Is for City, illustrated by Pat Cummings, Lothrop, Lee & Shepard Books (New York, NY), 1995.

Come Sunday, illustrated by Michael Bryant, Eerdmans (Grand Rapids, MI), 1996.

Wild, Wild Hair, illustrated by George Ford, Scholastic (New York, NY), 1996.

At the Break of Day, illustrated by Jan Spivey Gilchrist, Eerdmans (Grand Rapids, MI), 1997.

It's Raining Laughter (poems), photographs by Myles Pinkney, Dial (New York, NY), 1997.

Someone's Fighting, Golden Books (New York, NY), 1997.

Jazmin's Notebook, Dial (New York, NY), 1998.

Talkin' 'bout Bess: The Story of Aviator Bessie Coleman, Orchard Books (New York, NY), 1998.

A Dime a Dozen, Dial (New York, NY), 1998.

Hopscotch Love: A Family Treasury of Love Poems, Lothrop, Lee & Shepard Books (New York, NY), 1999.

At Break of Day, Eerdmans (Grand Rapids, MI), 1999.

My Man Blue (poems), illustrated by Jerome Lagarrigue, Dial (New York, NY), 1999.

Aneesa Lee and the Weaver's Gift, illustrated by Ashley Bryan, Lothrop, Lee & Shepard (New York, NY), 1999.

When Daddy Prays, Eerdmans (Grand Rapids, MI), 2000.

Stepping Out with Grandma Mac, Simon & Schuster (New York, NY), 2000.

Shoe Magic, illustrated by Terry Widener, Orchard Books (New York, NY), 2001.

A Pocketful of Poems, illustrated by Javaka Steptoe, Clarion Books (New York, NY), 2000.

Is It Far to Zanzibar? (poems), illustrated by Betsy Lewin, Lothrop, Lee & Shepard Books (New York, NY), 2000.

Bronx Masquerade, Dial (New York, NY), 2001.

Danitra Brown Leaves Town (poems), illustrated by Floyd Cooper, HarperCollins (New York, NY), 2002.

Under the Tree: Poems of Christmas, illustrated by Kadir Nelson, HarperCollins (New York, NY), 2002.

UNDER PSEUDONYM NAOMI McMILLAN

Wish You Were Here, illustrated by Vaccaro Associates, Disney Press (New York, NY), 1991.
(Reteller) *Cinderella,* McClanahan (New York, NY), 1995.
(Reteller) *Jack and the Beanstalk,* McClanahan (New York, NY), 1995.

"GOLDEN BOOKS" BOARD BOOKS; UNDER PSEUDONYM NAOMI McMILLAN

Baby's Colors, illustrated by Keaf Holliday, Western Publishing (Racine, WI), 1995.
Baby's Bedtime, illustrated by Sylvia Walker, Western Publishing (Racine, WI), 1995.
Busy Baby, illustrated by Anna Rich, Western Publishing (Racine, WI), 1996.

OTHER

Also author of several books based on Walt Disney characters, including *Mickey Mouse Tales* and *The Little Mermaid,* published by Running Press (Philadelphia, PA); *Disney Babies Bedtime Stories; The Viking's Eye* and *Sky Island,* both in the "Mickey Mouse Adventures" series; *My Favorite Book* and *The Great Castle Contest,* in the "Minnie 'n' Me" series; *Fast Friends, Eeyore's Tail Tale,* and *Rabbit Marks the Spot,* in the "Winnie the Pooh Twin" series; *Her Chance to Dream,* in the "Tale Spin" series; and *Fake Me to Your Leader* and *Catteries Not Included,* in the "Rescue Rangers" series.

FOR ADULTS

Poems By, CB Broadside Publications, 1970.
Portrait of Mary (historical novel), Harcourt (San Diego, CA), 1994.

Work represented in anthologies, including *Night Comes Softly,* edited by Nikki Giovanni. Theater and arts critic, *New York Amsterdam News,* 1975-76. Contributor to magazines and newspapers, including *Essence, Today's Christian Woman, Vision, Black World, Time Capsule,* and *Sunday Woman.* Contributing editor, *Unique NY,* 1977-78.

Work in Progress

A collection of inner-city haiku and a collection of young adult poetry.

Sidelights

Poet, novelist, and author of picture books, Nikki Grimes manages to reach many audiences with her works—from very young children, to middle readers and young adults, and also adults. Two-time Coretta Scott King Honor Book winner, Grimes once told *SATA:* "The word, both written and spoken, has always held a special fascination for me. It seemed uncanny that words, spread across a page just so, had the power to transport me to another time or place. But they could. I spent many hours ensconced in the local library, reading—nay, devouring—book after book after book. Books were my

soul's delight. Even so, in one sense, the stories I read betrayed me. Too few gave me back my mirror image. Fewer still spoke to, or acknowledged, the existence of the problems I faced as a black foster child from a dysfunctional and badly broken home. I couldn't articulate it then, but I sensed a need for validation which the books I read did not supply. 'When I grow up,' I thought, 'I'll write books about children who look and feel like me.'"

Whether writing poetry or fiction, Grimes has succeeded in creating works featuring young African-American characters with whom children and young adults can identify. Drawing upon scenes from her own childhood in New York City, Grimes is noted for successfully conveying the black experience and universal themes such as friendship, tolerance, family and community relationships, and children surviving adolescence. Despite a difficult childhood, her stories are characterized by optimism and warmth.

Tisa tries to hide to avoid having her thick, unruly hair combed and braided but ends up happy with her twenty beautiful braids in Grimes's **Wild, Wild Hair.**
(Illustrated by George Ford.)

"I was moved around a lot as a child," Grimes explained to *SATA,* "always having to adjust to new neighborhoods, new schools, new faces. The most difficult aspect of my constant uprooting was struggling to make new friends, leaving them behind, moving to a new neighborhood, and starting the whole process over again. Yet I had no choice, but I both needed and wanted friends. The fact that each friendship was bound to be short-lived only made it the more precious to me. It is little wonder that friendship is a theme to which I return again and again. *Growin',* my first book for children, had friendship as its primary focus."

Featuring a poetry-writing African-American fifth grader named Yolanda, and nicknamed Pump for Pumpkin, *Growin'* recounts the child's troubles as she tries to adjust to her father's death, the resultant move to a strange neighborhood, and ongoing friction with her mother. Pump, however, makes friends with the bully at her new school as they discover mutual artistic interests and find themselves aligned against their peers and school authorities. A *Kirkus Reviews* critic commended "the black ghetto setting and conspicuously non-sexist relationship," while Zena Sutherland in *Bulletin of the Center for Children's Books* praised the author for her competent writing style and warm story. Although reviewers concurred that Grimes needed to develop her characters more fully, they complimented her for a heartening tale, ample adventure, and a believable resolution to conflict.

Grimes went on to tell *SATA* that the subject of friendship recurs in the poems of *Something on My Mind* and *From a Child's Heart.* About the first book, Jeanne McLain Harms and Lucille J. Lettow, writing in *School Library Journal,* described Tom Feelings' black-and-white sketches and Grimes' free-verse responses to black children's urban experiences as "simple, eloquent, and in tune." A *Publishers Weekly* reviewer observed that "the artist and lyricist couldn't reveal the thoughts of the boys and girls portrayed here more acutely if they were inside their subjects' skins." *School Library Journal* contributor Ruth M. McConnell further noted that reflections are not only of the African-American experience but "the universal marking-time, growing pains, and perplexities of youth in poignant, funny, and sad ways." *From a Child's Heart,* described by a *Kirkus Reviews* contributor as "thirteen subtly cadenced, accessible poems in an authentically childlike voice," contains "a modicum of rhyme, a conscious if informal sense of innocence, and more than a little sentimentality," according to Betsy Hearne of *Bulletin of the Center for Children's Books.*

"The subject [of friendship] is most squarely dealt with in *Meet Danitra Brown,* an ode to friendship if ever there was one!" Grimes continued. In a collection of thirteen poems, narrator Zuri talks about herself and her admiration for her good friend Danitra Brown. Cyrisse Jaffee, writing in *Women's Review of Books,* summarized it as an "affectionate portrait of friendship and individuality" and lauded the language "filled with energy and rhythm" which lent itself to reading aloud. In

School Library Journal, Barbara Osborne Williams concluded that the book provides a glimpse of "touching moments of friendship with universal appeal." Although Betsy Hearne, writing in *Bulletin of the Center for Children's Books,* was concerned that some readers might be put off by such an effusive display of admiration, she pointed out that for those uncomfortable with more formal poetry, "this book will prove a satisfying introduction and sturdy friend." In addition, a reviewer for *Publishers Weekly* noted that "issues of race, feminism and family structure are delicately incorporated."

Grimes comes by her urban insights quite naturally. "Born in Harlem, I have since lived in every borough of New York City save Staten Island. Consequently, cityscapes form the backdrop of most of my writing." This is most evident in her *C Is for City,* where the delights of city life are described in alliteration, rhythm, and rhyme from A to Z. *Booklist* reviewer Julie Yates Walton called the book a "hustling, bustling, urban ABC book" that city children will surely "identify with."

Grimes's *Come Sunday* is a collection of fourteen poems about LaTasha, a vivacious little girl who loves to attend the community church: Paradise Baptist. As Elizabeth Bush pointed out in *Bulletin of the Center for Children's Books,* here are "just the details children find fascinating about Sunday rituals," as well as a "sensitive look at a child's spirituality." A *Kirkus Reviews* critic lauded the "suite of pitch-perfect poems" and concluded: "Whatever their religious background, readers will smile at the jubilation." Similarly, a *Publishers Weekly* commentator summarized *Come Sunday* as "reverent, funny and wildly energetic all at the same time."

Although Grimes has always maintained that she writes for children *first,* she has not limited herself to juvenile literature. As she told *SATA:* "In addition to children's books, I write books and magazine articles for adults." Critics responded favorably to her biography for young adults entitled *Malcolm X: A Force for Change,* in which she examined the contributions and dreams of the renowned Black Muslim leader. In *Portrait of Mary,* Grimes wrote a fictionalized version of the life of the mother of Jesus. "Passages from the Gospels punctuate the text and serve to give it a homogenized storyline," stated a critic from *Kirkus Reviews.* Susan Salter Reynolds, writing in the *Los Angeles Times Book Review,* referred to the details Grimes interjected of lentil stew and wet hay, commenting that "it breathes life into the story to be able to picture Mary's daily life and her hopes and fears for her son." "Grimes' Mary is a fully realized character," observed Ilene Cooper in *Booklist,* calling her novel "A compelling narrative."

Grimes presents a middle grade novel in *Jazmin's Notebook,* the story of an African-American teenager living with her sister in a small Harlem apartment. Set during the late 1960s, the novel describes the difficult life of young Jazmin and the way in which she is able to find strength and meaning by writing poetry and keeping a journal of her life. *Booklist*'s Hazel Rochman felt that

In fourteen poems, an African-American boy tells how a man named Blue has taught him to survive in a rough world.
(From My Man Blue, *written by Grimes and illustrated by Jerome Lagarrigue.)*

Jazmin's journal entries and occasional poems "are funny, tender, angry, and tough." Through the course of these writings, the reader comes to know a teen who has spunk and is resourceful. Bounced around from one foster home and relative to the next, she finally has found her place with her older sister. Picked on at school for her thick glasses, she is an A student and will not take the bad advice of her counselor who tries to talk her out of pursuing academics. "Many teens will relate to Jazmin, whether she is talking about the power of religion, friendship, or laughter, or about her attraction to a luscious guy," Rochman wrote. "Readers will be drawn into Jazmin's neighborhood," observed a reviewer for *Publishers Weekly,* who went on to call Jazmin an "articulate, admirable heroine ... [who] leaps over life's hurdles with agility and integrity."

However, it is in poetry that Grimes most often expresses herself, telling autobiographical verse stories as well as tales of the city, the family, and of relationships. Grimes mines her own past in the verse

collection *A Dime a Dozen,* presenting scenes from her childhood playing hopscotch with her big-footed father or detailing the prickly relations between her father and mother which ultimately ended in divorce. "Free-flowing and very accessible, the poetry may inspire readers to distill their own life experiences into precise, imaginative words and phrases," thought Susan Dove Lempke in a *Booklist* review of *A Dime a Dozen.* The twenty-two poems of *Hopscotch Love* are short and "upbeat," according to *Booklist*'s Rochman, sometimes bordering on "greeting-card sentimental," while the 1999 collection, *My Man Blue,* tells a more poignant story in fourteen "knowing, heartfelt poems," as a contributor for *Publishers Weekly* described the verse. Here the reader learns of the friendship between an African-American boy, Damon, who is fatherless, and Blue, a rough-looking character who lost his own son to the streets. Together the two shoot hoops and make outings to the park, and slowly learn to trust one another. Rochman, reviewing *My Man Blue* in *Booklist,* felt it is a "great picture book for older readers."

More poetry is served up in *Aneesa Lee and the Weaver's Gift*, a collection of thirteen short, interlocking poems which "skillfully uses the metaphor of weaving to explore the world of a talented girl," according to a contributor for *Publishers Weekly*. These poems describe the art of weaving from gathering the materials to making dyes, to spinning yarn, preparing the loom, and finally weaving the tapestry. Aneesa Lee, the weaver, is herself a warp and woof of black, white, and Japanese heritages, and her weaving is a form of connecting with a larger community. "For adult weavers, the book will be a treasure," wrote the reviewer for *Publishers Weekly*, "and for children, it serves as a glimpse into the intricacies not only of weaving, but the patterns of daily life." Moving far afield from her usual realistic verse about kids in American cities, Grimes ventures from this familiar urban stage to the more exotic world of Tanzania in *Is It Far to Zanzibar?*, a collection of "rhyming, sing-song verse" at once both "light and playful," as Rochman commented in *Booklist*. Here Grimes tells of children picking coffee or being chased by a lion. The verse collection is, as Rochman further noted, "an outsider's view of a Tanzania where everyone's having fun." Writing in the *New York Times Book Review*, Julie Yates Walton commented that Grimes, during her long career in prose and poetry, has demonstrated a "breathtaking range in tone and style," and in this introduction to Tanzania "offers a lively peek at the great big world." With *Shoe Magic*, Grimes again employs metaphor to look at lives, this time using children's shoes as a window to their lives. "This collection clearly celebrates its child readers," wrote Kathleen Whalin in a *School Library Journal* review, while *Booklist*'s Gillian Engberg felt that young poets "will find inspiration" in this verse collection. And with her 2001 collection, *A Pocketful of Poems*, "Grimes boils poetry down to its essence in this picture book homage to words," according to a reviewer for *Publishers Weekly*. "A must read for aspiring poets and writers." "There is so much vibrant energy and freshness in this collaboration," wrote *Booklist*'s GraceAnne A. DeCandido, "the book will dance into the hearts of children right away." Lauralyn Persson, reviewing the same title in *School Library Journal*, found it to be a "playful and thoroughly successful pairing of words and pictures."

"I inherited my father's passion for travel," Grimes once told *SATA*, "and have been to such places as China, Russia, Austria, Trinidad, and Tanzania, where I spent one year. My longest sojourn was in Sweden, where I lived for six years. In fact, I have Sweden to thank for my favorite hobby: knitting. I like to read, of course, go on long walks, talk with friends, cook, and play word games. But most of all, I love to write!" And write Grimes does. In over fifty collections of poetry, prose novels, and children's picture books she has celebrated the world of children—both the hard-edged realities of inter-urban youth, as well as the gentler and softer worlds of young children. Her writings speak of friendships, families, and the power of words to unite and inspire.

Biographical and Critical Sources

BOOKS

Children's Literature Review, Volume 42, Gale (Detroit, MI), 1997, pp. 88-95.
St. James Guide to Children's Writers, 5th edition, St. James Press (Detroit, MI), 1999.

PERIODICALS

Booklist, July 15, 1978, pp. 1732-1733; February 15, 1994, p. 1085; September 15, 1994, Ilene Cooper, review of *Portrait of Mary*, p. 114; October 1, 1995, Julie Yates Walton, review of *C Is for City*, p. 322; October 1, 1997, p. 334; September 15, 1998, Hazel Rochman, review of *Jazmin's Notebook*, p. 228; December 1, 1998, Susan Dove Lempke, review of *A Dime a Dozen*, p. 664; January 1, 1999, p. 782; February 15, 1999, Hazel Rochman, review of *Hopscotch Love*, p. 1064; October 1, 1999, p. 374; October 15, 1999, Hazel Rochman, review of *My Man Blue*, p. 42; January 1, 2000, p. 821; March 15, 2000, Hazel Rochman, review of *Is It Far to Zanzibar?*, p. 1381; September 15, 2000, Gillian Engberg, review of *Shoe Magic*, p. 234; February 15, 2001, GraceAnne A. DeCandido, review of *A Pocketful of Poems*, p. 1154; April 1, 2001, p. 1473; May 15, 2001, p. 1750; February 15, 2002, Gillian Engberg, review of *Bronx Masquerade*, p. 1024; February 15, 2002, Hazel Rochman, review of *Danitra Brown Leaves Town*, p. 1033.
Bulletin of the Center for Children's Books, April, 1978, Zena Sutherland, review of *Growin'*, p. 127; October, 1978, p. 30; February, 1994, Betsy Hearne, review of *Something on My Mind*, p. 188; July-August, 1994, Betsy Hearne, review of *Meet Danitra Brown*, p. 357; March, 1997, Elizabeth Bush, review of *Come Sunday*, pp. 248-249; January, 1998, p. 161.
Five Owls, September-October, 1994, p. 14.
Horn Book, July-August, 1994, p. 467.
Kirkus Reviews, December, 1977, review of *Growin'*, p. 1266; July 15, 1978, p. 747; October 15, 1993, review of *From a Child's Heart*, p. 1329; July 15, 1994, review of *Portrait of Mary*, p. 935; July 1, 1996, review of *Come Sunday*, p. 822; October 15, 1998, p. 1532; October 1, 1999, p. 1580; November 15, 1999, p. 1809.
Los Angeles Times Book Review, September 11, 1994, Susan Salter Reynolds, review of *Portrait of Mary*, p. 6; April 8, 2001, p. 6.
New York Times Book Review, June 4, 2000, Julie Yates Walton, review of *Is It Far to Zanzibar?*, p. 449; November 19, 2000, p. 32.
Publishers Weekly, November 14, 1977, p. 67; May 29, 1978, review of *Something on My Mind*, p. 51; January 4, 1993, p. 74; October 18, 1993, p. 73; April 11, 1994, review of *Meet Danitra Brown*, p. 65; April 8, 1996, review of *Come Sunday*, p. 63; June 29, 1998, review of *Jazmin's Notebook*, p. 60; May 17, 1999, review of *My Man Blue*, p. 79; November 8, 1999, review of *Aneesa Lee and the Weaver's Gift*, p. 67; November 29, 1999, p. 69; January 17, 2000, p. 58; January 15, 2001, review of *A Pocketful of Poems*, p. 76; May 21, 2001, p. 109; December 17, 2001, review of *Bronx Masquerade*, p. 92.

School Library Journal, December, 1977, p. 49; September, 1978, Ruth M. McConnell, review of *Something on My Mind,* p. 137; January, 1987, Jeanne McLain Harms and Lucille J. Lettow, "The Cupboard Is Bare: The Need to Expand Poetry Collections"; August, 1993, p. 196; December, 1993, p. 104; May, 1994, Barbara Osborne Williams, review of *Meet Danitra Brown,* p. 322; November, 1995, p. 71; June, 1997, p. 107; December, 1997, p. 90; July, 1998, p. 95; January, 1999, p. 142; May, 1999, p. 107; December, 1999, p. 119; January, 2000, p. 121; May, 2000, p. 161; October, 2000, Kathleen Whalin, review of *Shoe Magic,* p. 148; May, 2001, Lauralyn Persson, review of *A Pocketful of Poems,* p. 141; July, 2001, p. 124; January, 2002, Lynn Evarts, review of *Bronx Masquerade,* p. 132; February, 2002, Catherine Threadgill, review of *Danitra Brown Leaves Town,* p. 101.

Teacher Librarian, November, 1998, p. 45.

Voice of Youth Advocates, October, 1998, p. 274.

Women's Review of Books, November, 1994, Cyrisse Jaffee, "A World of Words," pp. 31-32.*

H

HALEY, Gail E(inhart) 1939-

Personal

Born November 4, 1939, in Charlotte, NC; daughter of George C. (an advertising manager and artist) and P. Louise Bell (an artist) Einhart; married Joseph A. Haley (a mathematician), August 15, 1959; married husband, Arnold F. Arnold (an artist, writer, and designer), February 14, 1966; married husband, David Considine (a professor of mass media), September 3, 1983; children: Marguerite Madeline, Geoffrey David. *Education:* Attended Richmond Professional Institute, 1957-59, and University of Virginia, 1960-64.

Addresses

Home—P.O. Box 1023, Blowing Rock, NC 28605. *Office*—Department of Curriculum and Instruction, Edwin Duncan Hall, Appalachian State University, Boone, NC 28608. *Agent*—Sheldon Fogelman, 10 East 40th Street, New York, NY 10016. *E-mail*—Haley_Gail@ hotmail.com.

Career

Manuscript Press, New York, NY, vice-president, beginning 1965; Appalachian State University, Boone, NC, currently writer-in-residence and curator of Gail Haley Collection of the Culture of Childhood. Artist, author, and illustrator of children's books and educational material, and designer of toys and fashion items. Graphics and illustrations exhibited at libraries and museums in southern states and New York. Work included in permanent collections at the University of Minnesota, Jacksonville (FL) Children's Museum, University of Southern Mississippi, and Appalachian State University. Toured Great Britain in one-woman multimedia show "Get into a Book." Actively involved in the design and utilization of puppetry in education.

Gail E. Haley

Member

Puppeteers of America and its UNESCO affiliate, UNIMA.

Awards, Honors

Boston Globe-Horn Book honor award for illustration, 1970, and Caldecott Medal, American Library Association, 1971, both for *A Story, a Story;* Czechoslovak Children's Film Festival Award for best animated children's film of the year, 1974; Kate Greenaway Medal for illustration, British Library Association, 1976, and Kadai Tosho award (Japan), both for *The Post Office Cat;* Parents Choice Award for illustration, 1980, for *The Green Man;* Children's Book Council children's choice selection for *Birdsong,* 1984; Kerlan Award from the University of Minnesota Kerlan Collection, 1989, for lifetime achievement and contribution to children's literature; National Council for the Social Studies Notable Children's Book award, 1986, for *Jack and the Bean Tree.*

Writings

FOR CHILDREN; SELF-ILLUSTRATED

My Kingdom for a Dragon, Cozet Print Shop, 1962.
The Wonderful Magical World of Marguerite: With the Entire Cast of Characters Including Rocks, Roses, Mushrooms, Daisies, Violets, Snails, Butterflies, Breezes, and Above All—the Sun, McGraw (New York, NY), 1964.
Round Stories about Our World, Follett (Chicago, IL), 1966.
Round Stories about Things That Grow, Follett (Chicago, IL), 1966.
Round Stories about Things That Live in Water, Follett (Chicago, IL), 1966.
Round Stories about Things that Live on Land, Follett (Chicago, IL), 1966.
(Reteller) *A Story, a Story: An African Tale,* Atheneum (New York, NY), 1970.
Noah's Ark, Atheneum (New York, NY), 1971.
Jack Jouett's Ride, Viking (New York, NY), 1973.
The Abominable Swampman, Viking (New York, NY), 1975.
The Post Office Cat, Scribner (New York, NY), 1976.
Go Away, Stay Away!, Scribner (New York, NY), 1977.
Costumes for Plays and Playing, Methuen (London, England), 1978.
The Green Man, Scribner (New York, NY), 1979.
A Story, a Day, Methuen (London, England), 1979.
Gail Haley's Costume Book, Volume I: *Dress Up and Have Fun,* Magnet Books (New York, NY), 1979.
Gail Haley's Costume Book, Volume II: *Dress Up and Play,* Magnet Books (New York, NY), 1980.
Birdsong, Crown (New York, NY), 1984.
Jack and the Bean Tree, Crown (New York, NY), 1986.
Jack and the Fire Dragon, Crown (New York, NY), 1988.
Marguerite, Lion Books (New York, NY), 1988.
Sea Tale, Dutton (New York, NY), 1990.
Puss in Boots, Dutton (New York, NY), 1991.
Mountain Jack Tales, Dutton (New York, NY), 1992, new edition, Parkway Publishers (Boone, NC), 2001.
Dream Peddler, Penguin Putnam (New York, NY), 1993.
Two Bad Boys: A Very Old Cherokee Tale, Dutton (New York, NY), 1996.

ILLUSTRATOR

Francelia Butler, editor, *The Skip Rope Book,* Dial (New York, NY), 1962.

Haley retells an African myth about Ananse the spider man in her self-illustrated **A Story, a Story.**

Jane Yolen, editor, *One, Two, Buckle My Shoe: A Book of Counting Rhymes,* Doubleday (New York, NY), 1964.
James Holding, *The Three Wishes of Hu,* Putnam (New York, NY), 1964.
Bernice Kohn, *Koalas,* Prentice-Hall (Englewood Cliffs, NJ), 1965.
Lois Wyse, *P.S., Happy Anniversary,* World Publishing (New York, NY), 1966.
Hannah Rush, *The Peek-A-Boo Book of Puppies and Kittens,* T. Nelson (London, England), 1966.
Solveig Russell, *Which Is Which?,* Prentice-Hall (Englewood Cliffs, NJ), 1966.
(With other illustrators) E. L. Konigsburg, *All Together, One at a Time,* Atheneum (New York, NY), 1971, reprinted, Aladdin Paperbacks (New York, NY), 1998.

FOR ADULTS; NONFICTION

Play People: Puppetry in Education, Appalachian State University (Boone, NC), 1988.
(With David Considine) *Visual Messages: Integrating Imagery into Instruction, K-12 Resource,* Libraries Unlimited (Englewood, CO), 1992, new edition, 1999.
(With David Considine and Lyn Ellen Lacy) *Imagine That: Developing Critical Thinking and Critical Viewing through Children's Literature,* Teacher Idea Press, 1994.

OTHER

Contributor of articles to periodicals, including *New Advocate, Children's Literature Association Quarterly,* and *Puppetry Journal.* Illustrator of syndicated column, "Parents and Children," written by Arnold F. Arnold. Author and narrator of "Wood and Linoleum Illustration," Weston Woods, 1978.

Adaptations

A Story, a Story was made into a filmstrip, 1972, and an animated film, 1973, both produced by Weston Woods; *Jack Jouett's Ride* was made into a filmstrip and an animated film, both produced by Weston Woods, 1975; *Taleb and His Lamb,* based on *A Story, a Story,* was produced by Arthur Barr Productions, 1975; *Go Away, Stay Away!* was made into a filmstrip produced by Weston Woods, 1978; *Tracing a Legend: The Story of the Green Man,* based on *The Green Man,* was produced as a filmstrip by Weston Woods, 1980; *Tradition and Technique: Creating Jack and the Bean Tree* was made into a filmstrip produced by Weston Woods, 1987.

Sidelights

For the past four decades, American author and illustrator Gail E. Haley has produced books with strong, socially relevant themes that entertain and educate children about the world in which they live. Her works include messages about the environment, racism, and illiteracy. Haley is also a noted reteller of stories based on myth and folklore. She was the first illustrator to receive the two most prestigious awards for illustration in children's literature: the Caldecott Medal for *A Story, a Story* in 1971, and its British equivalent, the Kate

Trickster Jack meets kings, giants, and talking animals during his adventures in Mountain Jack Tales, *written and illustrated by Haley.*

Greenaway Medal, for *The Post Office Cat* in 1976. Haley is widely acclaimed as an artist who skillfully utilizes a variety of media and styles to visually convey the essence of her ideas.

Haley was born in Charlotte, North Carolina, and raised in nearby Shuffletown, a rural community complete with sprawling farms and open woods, which she avidly explored. She received much attention as the first child of George and Louise Einhart, and her precociousness was encouraged from a very young age. When she was four years old her father was drafted into the U.S. infantry during World War II; the entire family made an unplanned, weeklong trip aboard a military train to his California base. This was the beginning of Haley's lifelong love of travel and adventure.

Following her father's departure for Japan, Haley and her mother returned to Charlotte to live with Haley's grandparents. "My grandmother, who had grown up in Kings Mountain, North Carolina, was my mentor and earliest fan," Haley wrote in her essay for *Something about the Author Autobiography Series* (SAAS). "She worked in an engraving house, and she brought me endless supplies of paper, pencils, empty books, silk cords, and anything else I might need to be creative.... My grandparents and aunt spoiled me rotten. Whatever I drew was beautiful. My stories were brilliant."

When the war ended, Haley's family was reunited, and they returned to their home in Shuffletown. By this time Haley was in the second grade but had not yet learned to read; her father taught her in a matter of days, beginning an enduring love of books. As a child, "My temple was the Charlotte Public Library—a stately old building with a whole wing for children's literature," Haley recalled in an essay published in *Five Owls.* "It had stained-glass windows depicting fairy tales mounted above the bookcases." Haley devoured as much literature as she could during the long bus rides (ten miles each way) to and from school, including some material that was not allowed at home. She acquired her first typewriter at age ten and immediately began writing her first "book," about a crusader from a Middle-Eastern country. Her stories became more advanced as she grew older.

"When I emerged from the world of books," Haley recalled in *Five Owls,* "I didn't like what I saw. I grew up in the South of the '40s and '50s. There was still rabid segregation evident at water fountains, motels, and the Woolworth's lunch counter. Schools and even churches were segregated. The *real* world made no sense to me.... I fled from a world in which I did not fit and went looking for one in which I did. I found that world in the magic of books."

Haley became a big sister when she was eight years old, and again when she was twelve. Rather than feeling deprived of the spotlight, she was delighted by her younger sisters and enjoyed telling them stories, making dolls and tiny accessories and even wooden puppets like the one her father had made for her. Haley reveled in the Saturday mornings she spent in town with her father in his office at the *Charlotte Observer* and was significantly influenced by her experiences there. "The art department was like an alchemist's laboratory," Haley told *SAAS*. "There were jars of rubber cement, airbrushes, kneaded erasers, french curves, T squares, and machines to create almost any kind of line imaginable to mankind. I would hang around the artists for hours, watching the magic they did. Then I'd wander around the building talking to the writers.... The act of communicating through the printed word was something I knew I wanted to be a part of."

After graduating from high school, Haley attended art school for two years in Richmond, Virginia, a compromise she and her parents reached following their refusal to allow her to attend the school of her choice in New York City. Haley undertook a double major and studied graphics and painting as well as fashion illustration. She met her first husband while in school and, following graduation, was married at age nineteen. A job as a technical illustrator left her unfulfilled, and when she had accumulated enough money she returned to school. It was there that she received encouragement from a professor, Charles Smith, to pursue her interest in writing and illustrating children's books seriously. Later, when she had written a half dozen books, Haley traveled to New York to call on publishers but was unable to sell her work. She waited for several months before taking matters into her own hands.

"I borrowed five hundred dollars from the bank, bought a stack of woodblocks, some ink and paper," said Haley in *SAAS*. "I wrote an allegory about my need to write and illustrate books. It was called *My Kingdom for a Dragon* and told the story of a knight who made friends with a dragon, even though he realized it would cost him his knighthood and the princess whom he loved." Haley produced the book with the help of a local printer, traveled to Washington to secure the copyright, then made her first sale of 250 copies to Brentano's bookstore. She besieged the publishing industry with the remaining copies and sent copies to writers and illustrators she admired, asking their advice about how to get started.

Several years after her first marriage ended, Haley remarried and spent a year in the Caribbean with her new husband. Her experiences there led her to research Caribbean folklore and eventually write and illustrate *A Story, a Story,* the Caldecott-award-winning retelling of the Ashanti myth of the Sky God, Nyame, and the Spider-man, Ananse. Haley is credited as the first children's author to introduce the concept of a black god. Several years later the film version of *A Story, a Story* won the Czechoslovak Children's Film Festival Award. Following the book's success, Haley's retelling of *Noah's Ark* was published. The book, inspired in part by the two children she now had, focused on the conservation of natural resources and the importance of educating children about ecology.

Haley has always drawn story ideas from her surroundings, as was the case when the family moved from New York to Virginia, where she wrote *Jack Jouett's Ride.* Haley examined library archives and traveled to England in order to research the history of the local Revolutionary War hero before writing her book. It met with great success and was made into an animated film.

Within a year the family moved to England and Haley's work went in a new direction. Inspired by the British custom of "employing" cats in post offices to catch mice, she wrote and illustrated the award-winning *The Post Office Cat.* This book went on to win an important Japanese book award. Also while in London, Haley researched the origins of the country's mythical "Green Man" and produced another popular book based on this figure; in 1990 she served as advisor for the BBC television production of *Return of the Green Man.*

By 1983, Haley had returned to the United States and married for a third time. She and her husband, David Considine, both joined the faculty at Appalachian State University in North Carolina, where Haley taught courses in writing and illustrating for children as well as a course in puppetry. The rich Blue Ridge Mountain folklore became a new source of story ideas for Haley, and her subsequent books with mountain themes include *Jack and the Bean Tree* and *Jack and the Fire Dragon.* In 1992 Haley produced *Mountain Jack Tales,* a book that "in a lucid, vibrant voice" recounts traditional stories of the region, according to a *Publishers Weekly* reviewer.

In 1984, Haley's love of puppetry and children's theater culminated in a presentation of her work at the Smithsonian Institution. A permanent marionette collection was established at Appalachian State that is enriched by puppets acquired during Haley's world travels to Bali, Thailand, and Australia. "Puppets are an extension of my work with picture books," she told *SAAS*. "They allow me to use the skills I've gained over the years, plus the added dimensions of form, music, and movement." Haley is also the author of a nonfiction work for adults, *Play People: Puppetry in Education,* published in 1988.

In 1996 Haley published *Two Bad Boys: A Very Old Cherokee Tale,* a "retelling" in the tradition of *A Story, a Story.* In this collection of Native American folklore, the beginning of Cherokee culture is described via a boy whose reflection in the water comes to life, albeit as a mischief-making "Wild Boy" who tempts his twin into trouble. Eventually, their pranks cause the end of ready food, and the boys' progeny must forever after hunt and grow food to survive. The author's prose style, "essentially realistic but lightly infused with mysticism, subtly evokes a paradise lost," said a *Publishers Weekly* reviewer.

Commenting in *Contemporary Authors,* Haley said that her work, "more than a personal catharsis, ... is an effort designed to stimulate verbal and visual responses and a preparation for literacy." She acknowledged the challenge to reading posed by other media, such as television: "A child brings his own understanding and experience to the book and is enriched by what the book gives him back. He must supply movement, image, sound, and sequence of time. This is a far greater challenge to his brain than sitting passively before a TV set and having these things fed to him without any effort on his part."

Biographical and Critical Sources

BOOKS

Children's Literature Review, Volume 21, Gale (Detroit, MI), 1990.
Contemporary Authors New Revision Series, Volume 14, Gale (Detroit, MI), 1985.
De Montreville, Doris, and Donna Hill, editors, *Third Book of Junior Authors,* Wilson (New York, NY), 1972.
Kingman, Lee, editor, *Newbery and Caldecott Medal Books: 1966-1975,* Horn Book (Boston, MA), 1975.
Kingman, Lee, and others, compilers, *Illustrators of Children's Books: 1967-1976,* Horn Book (Boston, MA), 1978.
Kirkpatrick, D. L., *Twentieth-Century Children's Writers,* St. Martin's Press (New York, NY), 1978.
Something about the Author Autobiography Series, Volume 13, Gale (Detroit, MI), 1991.

PERIODICALS

Charlotte Observer, July, 1973.
Children's Literature Association Quarterly, fall, 1986.
Five Owls, May-June, 2000, Gail E. Haley, "Pages and Ages: Reflections of an Author-Illustrator," pp. 112-113.
Journal of Children's Literature, spring, 1996, pp. 20-21.
Language Arts, November, 1984.
Library Talk, November-December, 1989.
New Advocate, winter, 1990.
New York Times Book Review, April 12, 1970; November 8, 1979; January 6, 1985.
Publishers Weekly, February 22, 1971; September 6, 1971.
School Library Journal, April, 1986.
Top of the News, April, 1971; summer, 1985.

OTHER

Gail E. Haley's Home Page, http://www.gailehaley.com (April 13, 2002).*

*   *   *

HALL, Patricia 1948-

Personal

Born October 2, 1948; daughter of Verl (an architect) and Frances Rodgers (a teacher) Hall; married William Ivey (divorced); married Barry Cohen (a management consultant), April 21, 1984; children: David S. H. *Nationality:* American. *Education:* University of California—Santa Cruz, B.S. (psychology; with honors), 1970; University of California—Los Angeles, M.A. (folklore and mythology), 1975.

Patricia Hall

Addresses

Home and office—13089 Candela Pl., San Diego, CA 92130. *E-mail*—pattyhall2@yahoo.com.

Career

Country Music Foundation, Nashville, TN, intern, 1975-76; American Association for State and Local History, Nashville, TN, director of education, 1977-84. Johnny Gruelle & Raggedy Ann Museum, Arcola, IL, historical consultant. Museum consultant; freelance folklorist. Secretary, Tennessee Association of Museums, 1980s-1990s; chair, Folklife Panel, Tennessee Arts Commission, 1990s.

Awards, Honors

National Endowment for the Humanities grant, 1998, for research on Johnny Gruelle.

Writings

Johnny Gruelle, Creator of Raggedy Ann and Andy, Pelican (Gretna, LA), 1993.
Raggedy Ann and Andy: Johnny Gruelle's Dolls with Heart (video documentary), Sirocco Productions (Norfolk, VA), 1995.
Raggedy Ann and Andy Postcard Book, Pelican (Gretna, LA), 1999.

Raggedy Ann and More: Johnny Gruelle's Doll's and Merchandise, Pelican (Gretna, LA), 2000.

Raggedy Ann and Johnny Gruelle: A Bibliography of Published Works, Pelican (Gretna, LA), 2001.

Raggedy Ann and Andy: A Retrospective Celebrating Eighty-five Years of Storybook Friends, illustrated by Johnny Gruelle, Simon & Schuster (New York, NY), 2001.

The Real-for-Sure Story of Raggedy Ann, illustrated by Joni Gruelle Wannamaker, Pelican (Gretna, LA), 2001.

Hooray for Reading! (based on the characters by Johnny Gruelle), Simon & Schuster (New York, NY), 2002.

Old Friends, New Friends (based on the characters by Johnny Gruelle), Little Simon (New York, NY), 2002.

Message for Santa (based on the characters by Johnny Gruelle), Little Simon (New York, NY), 2002.

Also contributor of articles to *Traces of Indiana and Midwestern History, Table Rock Sentinel, Toybox, Connecticut, Blue Ridge Country, Doll World, The Encyclopedia of Indianapolis,* and *Cloth Doll.* Contributor to *Rags* and *For the Heart's Sake,* two national newsletters for Raggedy Ann and Andy fans.

"CLASSIC RAGGEDY ANN AND ANDY" SERIES; BASED ON THE CHARACTERS BY JOHNNY GRUELLE

Day at the Fair, illustrated by Kathryn Mitter, Little Simon (New York, NY), 2000.

School Day Adventure, illustrated by Kathryn Mitter, Little Simon (New York, NY), 2000.

Easter Treats!: A Book of Colors, illustrated by Kathryn Mitter, Little Simon (New York, NY), 2001.

Fridays Are Fun!: Days of the Week, illustrated by Alison Winfield, Little Simon (New York, NY), 2001.

Going to Grandma's, illustrated by Kathryn Mitter, Little Simon (New York, NY), 2001.

I Spy!, illustrated by Kathryn Mitter, Little Simon (New York, NY), 2001.

All That We Love, illustrated by Alison Winfield, Little Simon (New York, NY), 2001.

Hooray for Reading!, illustrated by Kathryn Mitter, Little Simon (New York, NY), 2002.

Old Friends, New Friends, illustrated by Alison Winfield, Little Simon (New York, NY), 2002.

Message for Santa, illustrated by Alison Winfield, Little Simon (New York, NY), 2002.

Work in Progress

Additional Raggedy Ann books.

Sidelights

Patricia Hall is author of a number of historical books about Johnny Gruelle and his beloved children's storybook characters Raggedy Ann and Andy. Since 1967, Hall has collected and researched Gruelle's books, dolls, artwork, and periodical appearances. The author related that since that time, her collection has won awards at college-sponsored competitions, has been featured in national magazines, and has been exhibited nationally by Toy Town Museum in 1997 and the Target Corporation in 1998. Gruelle has also been the subject of a biography

by Hall, *Johnny Gruelle, Creator of Raggedy Ann and Andy,* a documentary video, *Raggedy Ann and Andy: Johnny Gruelle's Dolls with Heart,* and a volume celebrating the literary and artistic legacy of Raggedy Ann and Andy since their creation by Gruelle in 1915, *Raggedy Ann and Andy: A Retrospective Celebrating Eighty-five Years of Storybook Friends.* Additionally, the author is known for her articles about Gruelle, which have appeared in magazines across the United States. Devoting much of her professional career to the life of Gruelle and his characters, Hall serves as Historical Consultant for the Johnny Gruelle & Raggedy Ann Museum in Arcola, Illinois, and presents programs about Gruelle and his Raggedys to audiences nationwide.

Beginning in 2000, the author began to pen the "Classic Raggedy Ann and Andy" series of children's books based on Gruelle's original Raggedy Ann and Andy characters. Intended for young readers, the board books and Ready-to-Read primers share with children concepts such as love in *All That We Love,* colors in *Easter Treats!: A Book of Colors,* and shapes in *I Spy!.* Other books in the series include *Day at the Fair, School Day Adventure, Fridays Are Fun!: Days of the Week, Going to Grandma's,* and *Hooray for Reading!.*

Biographical and Critical Sources

PERIODICALS

Americana, November, 1990, Patricia L. Hudson, "Still Smiling at Seventy-Five," pp. 52-55.

Booklist, October 15, 1995, Nancy McCray, review of *Raggedy Ann and Andy: Johnny Gruelle's Dolls with Heart,* p. 419.

Indianapolis Star, July 10, 1993, Rich Gotshall, review of *Johnny Grulle: Creator of Raggedy Ann and Andy,* p. E-1.

Nashville Banner, September 24, 1993, Larry D. Woods, review of *Johnny Grulle: Creator of Raggedy Ann and Andy,* p. C-8.

Publishers Weekly, January 14, 2002, "The Real Raggedy Ann," p. 62.

School Library Journal, November, 2001, Jane Marino, review of *The Real-for-Sure Story of Raggedy Ann,* p. 146.

*   *   *

HINES, Gary (Roger) 1944-

Personal

Born August 12, 1944, in Oakland, CA; son of W. Roger (a contractor and realtor) and Helen (a secretary; maiden name, Lassen) Hines; married Anna Grossnickle (a children's author and illustrator), June 19, 1976; children: Beth Carlson, Sarah Stephens, Lassen. *Nationality:* American. *Education:* Attended University of California—Davis, 1962-63, and College of Siskiyous, 1963-64; California State University—Chico, B.S., 1967. *Politics:* "Liberal." *Hobbies and other interests:* Reading, theater, skiing, history.

Addresses

Home—P.O. Box 1456, Gualala, CA 95445. *Office*—U.S. Forest Service, Box 188, Milford, PA 18337. *Agent*—Ginger Knowlton, Curtis Brown Ltd., Ten Astor Place, New York, NY 10003.

Career

Writer. Worked variously in construction and as a firefighter, 1959-67; U.S. Forest Service, budget analyst in San Francisco, CA, 1968-73, administrative assistant in Pinecrest, CA, 1973-75, public affairs director in Pinecrest, CA, 1976-90; children's author, 1991—. Composer and musician, San Francisco, CA, 1968-73; Card, Pinkerton, and Hines (acoustic folk group), San Francisco, CA, member, 1969-72; affiliated with Hines Sight and Sound (freelance audio/visual business), Twain Harte, CA, 1980-90; Sierra Repertory Theatre, Sonora, CA, sound designer, 1980-90; actor, appearing in productions including *Something's Afoot, The Secret Affairs of Mildred Wild, The Fantasticks,* and *Gifford Pinchot: From the Other Side* (also see below), 1981—. Grey Towers National Historic Landmark, outreach coordinator, 1991-98; Grey Towers National Historic Landmark, deputy director, 1998-2001.

Member

Society of Children's Book Writers and Illustrators.

Awards, Honors

Distinguished Service Award, U.S. Department of Agriculture, 1990, for theatrical production on conservationist Gifford Pinchot; recipient of numerous awards for educational programs for the U.S. Forest Service, including a national merit award in 1999.

Writings

(And creator) *Gifford Pinchot: From the Other Side* (play), first produced in Sonora, CA, 1988.
A Ride in the Crummy (picture book), illustrated by wife, Anna Grossnickle Hines, Greenwillow (New York, NY), 1991.
Flying Firefighters (picture book), illustrated by Anna Grossnickle Hines, Clarion Books (New York, NY), 1993.
The Day of the High Climber (picture book), illustrated by Anna Grossnickle Hines, Greenwillow (New York, NY), 1994.
A Christmas Tree in the White House, illustrated by Alexandra Wallner, Holt (New York, NY), 1998.
Thanksgiving in the White House, illustrated by Alexandra Wallner, Holt (New York, NY), 2003.

Work represented in anthologies, including *The Haunted House,* edited by Jane Yolen, HarperCollins (New York, NY), 1993; contributor to *Writers in the Kitchen,* compiled by Tricia Gardella. Composer of music for the 1974 Spokane, WA, World's Fair promotional film; also composer of jingles for radio advertisements.

Work in Progress

Several picture books; coauthoring a science fiction series; a novel; a nonfiction book; several short stories for an anthology.

Sidelights

Gary Hines once told *SATA:* "I grew up in a small community in the Cascade mountains of northern California. Surrounded by beautiful peaks and forests, my hometown was a terrific place for my imagination to run wild. The one part of myself I have always tried to nurture is the ability to see life through the eyes of wonder. Sometimes I do this well, sometimes not. But I continually try to remind myself that life is an incredible (though often difficult) journey and that everything one needs to experience it is magically tucked away inside us already. We are all born with the essentials. The trick is not forgetting where they are and to have the courage to search for them when they've been elusive.

"Of course, throughout my growing up years, and especially in my adult years, there have been and still are numerous barriers to wonder and imagination. We've all bumped up against them from time to time. But if you believe in yourself, the barriers eventually fall away and let you pass.

"At one time or another, I have been an outhouse builder, a firefighter, a construction worker, a bricklayer's assistant, a musician, a songwriter, a recording engineer, a forest ranger, an actor, and a writer. All of these experiences have shaped who I am today.

"Much of my professional career has dealt with the field of conservation. I know firsthand how precious, limited, and often abused the world's natural resources are. I cannot, however, think of a natural resource more valuable and special than children. This is why I choose to write for young people. They are the future and deserve the very best we can give."

Hines has written several well-received picture books, three of which have been illustrated by his wife, Anna. Publishing his first work for young readers in 1991 about a young boy's train ride, Hines noted on the Web site he shares with his wife that he entered the world of children's literature "because Anna suggested it. After all, some of my work with the Forest Service involved working with kids and developing slide presentations—putting words with pictures, like a picture book but different."

Tactics firefighters use to combat forest fires are featured in *Flying Firefighters.* Here Hines introduces to children many of the tactics used to battle fires in "an exciting, action-packed portrayal of helicopter and sky-diving firefighters," according to *School Library Journal* critic Susannah Price. Beginning with the dispatching of crews, *Flying Firefighters* covers many aspects of firefighting, including the types of equipment used, strategies employed in extinguishing the flames, and how fires originate in nature. Told through dialogue, *Flying Firefighters* earned the praise of *Booklist*'s Hazel Rochman, who believed "the present-tense drama of the picture book will hold children with its fast-paced action and exciting facts."

Hines's *The Day of the High Climber* is a companion volume to his picture book about a young boy's experience on a train, *A Ride in the Crummy*. Planning to spend the summer with his family at his father's logging camp, a young boy waits for the arrival of Puss Tompkins, a high climber whose job it is to chop off the tops of trees before they are felled. Wishing to witness the dangerous task, the boy looks forward to seeing Tompkins, whom his father calls the best around, in action. Finally, the high climber reaches the logging camp, and the young narrator can see the brave Tompkins in action. Calling the story "simply and quietly told," *School Library Journal* contributor Donna L. Scanlon described the narrative as "laced with logging terminology that is enhanced by carefully executed and detailed watercolor paintings."

Trees are again the focus of Hines' *A Christmas Tree in the White House,* a story loosely based on a true event. Set during the administration of President Teddy Roosevelt, the noted conservationist leader decrees that no tree shall be cut merely for Christmas decoration in the White House. However, his sons Archie and Quentin decide their holiday will not be complete without a tree, and so the two conspire to hide a small evergreen in their shared bedroom. The sons fear the worst when their father learns of their actions, but rather than reprimanding the children, Roosevelt takes them to his chief forester. Expecting the forester to lecture the children on the value of every tree, Roosevelt is surprised when he instead explains how careful thinning of a forest can be beneficial to smaller trees. Lesson learned, the President allows a small tree to be put up for decoration during the subsequent Christmas seasons. Writing in *Booklist*, Helen Rosenberg found *A Christmas Tree in the White House* "an interesting historical piece as well as a book for any Christmas collection," while a *Publishers Weekly* reviewer predicted that "kids will be charmed by the irreverent behavior of the Roosevelt children."

Biographical and Critical Sources

PERIODICALS

Booklist, October 15, 1993, Hazel Rochman, review of *Flying Firefighters,* p. 447; May 15, 1994, Julie Cosaro, review of *The Day of the High Climber,* p. 1683; October 1, 1998, Helen Rosenberg, review of *A Christmas Tree in the White House,* p. 335.
New York Times Book Review, December 20, 1998, Margaret Moorman, review of *A Christmas Tree in the White House.*
Publishers Weekly, March 29, 1991, review of *A Ride in the Crummy,* p. 92; September 28, 1998, review of *A Christmas Tree in the White House,* p. 57.
School Library Journal, June, 1991, Louise L. Sherman, review of *A Ride in the Crummy,* p. 79; January, 1994, Susannah Price, review of *Flying Firefighters,* p. 108; June, 1994, Donna L. Scanlon, review of *The Day of the High Climber,* p. 101; October, 1998, Mary M. Hopf, review of *A Christmas Tree in the White House,* p. 41.

OTHER

Anna Grossnickle and Gary Hines Web Site, http://www.aghines.com/ (July 30, 2002).

*   *   *

HITE, Sid 1954-

Personal

Born April 12, 1954, in Richmond, VA. *Nationality:* American. *Education:* Attended a community college for one year.

Addresses

Home—Sag Harbor, NY. *Agent*—c/o Author Mail, Scholastic, Inc., 557 Broadway, New York, NY 10012.

Career

Novelist. Has also worked in various odd jobs.

Writings

YOUNG ADULT NOVELS

Dither Farm, Holt (New York, NY), 1992.
It's Nothing to a Mountain, Holt (New York, NY), 1994.
Answer My Prayer, Holt (New York, NY), 1995.
An Even Break, Holt (New York, NY), 1995.
Those Darn Dithers, Holt (New York, NY), 1996.
The Distance of Hope, Holt (New York, NY), 1998.
Cecil in Space, Holt (New York, NY), 1999.
Stick and Whittle, Scholastic (New York, NY), 2000.
A Hole in the World, Scholastic (New York, NY), 2001.
The King of France, Scholastic (New York, NY), 2003.

Work in Progress

The King of France, due 2003.

Sidelights

Sid Hite is the author of a number of young adult novels that feature complex teen characters, interesting settings, and compelling plots. Imbuing his novels with the quiet pace of small-town life, Hite often layers everyday occurrences with fantasy elements and relates his stories in a style that critics have characterized as quiet and laid-back. "To read a Sid Hite novel is to travel to a timeless place where miracles lie around every corner," maintained a *Publishers Weekly* contributor upon reviewing Hite's *Answer My Prayer.* While some miracles are fantastic in origin, others are more spiritual, as in *A Hole in the World* and *An Even Break,* which affirm basic human goodness while dealing with the molding of basic values and a young teen's coming of age.

Born in 1954, Hite was raised in the same atmosphere that permeates his fiction. "I grew up outside of the small, country town of Bowling Green, Virginia," he once told *SATA.* "A stoplight went up at the main intersection when I was sixteen. Most of my childhood was spent outdoors—either playing baseball, basketball, and football, or exploring the vast stretches of woods that still exist in Caroline County.

"Instead of pursuing a formal education, I traveled extensively after leaving high school, managing to step foot in twenty countries by the time I was twenty-one. I fell in love with novels in my late teens and decided then I wanted to write one myself." Although it took several years and a series of jobs to make Hite's aspiration a reality, he published his first novel, *Dither Farm,* in 1992.

Dither Farm, along with its sequel, *Those Darn Dithers,* introduces readers to an unusual family living in Willow County, Virginia. Henry and Clementine Dither have four children—Holly, Emmet, Matilda, and Archibald— all of whom are energetic, curious, and able to get into trouble at least once during the course of Hite's story. In *Dither Farm* a visit from a distant aunt results in mayhem when the carpet she brings with her is found to

Sid Hite

be magical—and sought after by a gang of ne'er-do-wells. Critical reaction to the novel was mixed. "Hite has a charming way with language and a feeling for rural life that makes this a pleasure to read," commented Paula Rohrlick in a review for *Kliatt,* while in *Publishers Weekly* a contributor found the author's fiction debut to be full of "subplots and digressions" that "will deter all but the most patient reader." *Those Darn Dithers* won over many critics, however, with its story of a summer filled with Wild West shows, secret inventions, and a ghostly presence. Noting that Hite manages to juggle "main plots and characters ... with aplomb," *School Library Journal* contributor Marilyn Payne Phillips praised the author as "a master at wordplay."

Romance enters the energetic mix of plot and character in Hite's *It's Nothing to a Mountain.* Taking place in 1969, the novel finds fourteen-year-old Lisette and her younger brother, Riley, orphaned when their parents are killed in a car accident. Moving to their grandparents' home in the Blue Ridge mountains, the children begin to learn the ways of the country with the help of Thorpe, a runaway teen who lives in a nearby cave and who saves Riley's life. As Thorpe becomes more of a presence in Lisette and Riley's lives, he also learns to trust his new friends and becomes infatuated with Lisette. Noting the presence of Hite's characteristic otherworldly atmosphere, a *Publishers Weekly* contributor praised *It's Nothing to a Mountain* for its "boldly defined characters" and action-filled plot, "including a death-defying underground journey."

Teen romance is at the core of *Cecil in Space,* which, despite its sci-fi title, is grounded squarely in a small town that seventeen-year-old narrator Cecil assures readers is anything but adventure-filled and exciting. Cecil is found to be well read in everything from Freud to astronomy, leaving a *Publishers Weekly* critic with the observation that *Cecil in Space* "wouldn't be a Hite novel if there wasn't a little philosophical musing." But in Bricksburg, Virginia, baseballs are the only things that ever leave the ground, and Cecil admits to being as captivated by the local baseball teams as anyone in town, until he begins to notice girls. Cecil relates the day-to-day events of his summer trapped in Bricksburg "in a funny, irreverent manner that moves the story along well and keeps the reader smiling," explained *Voice of Youth Advocates* contributor Sue Krumbein. A *Kirkus Reviews* critic praised "Hite's keen sense of the absurd" as contributing to Cecil's "witty observations and ... morose pronouncements about life on Earth."

Hite draws readers into the past in *Stick and Whittle,* which finds two men named Melvin on the plains of northern Texas in the years just after the U.S. Civil War. Melvin "Stick" Fitchett fought in the war on the side of the Confederacy and hopes to rebuild his life as a cattleman, while Melvin "Whittle" Smyte is a teen determined to make something of his life after realizing that through his carelessness he may have caused Chicago's great fire. The two pair up and go in search of Stick's sweetheart, who has been abducted by bandits. Their journey is hampered by everything from tornados

A surly dog, a beautiful girl, and a ghost keep things interesting during fifteen-year-old Paul's summer on a Virginia farm. (Cover illustration by Limbert Fabian.)

to unfriendly Indians. Noting that both unbelievable coincidences and "stock characters ... are here in abundance," a *Horn Book* critic nevertheless claimed that the author's "tongue-in-cheek telling defines the adventure as a diversionary romp." "Hite's offbeat Western is sure to draw new fans as they relish the book's dry humor, colorful language, and passel of surprises," maintained a *Publishers Weekly* reviewer, while in *School Library Journal* Vicki Reutter praised the book as a "lighthearted Western" that is "peppered with challenging vocabulary."

Biographical and Critical Sources

PERIODICALS

Booklist, May 15, 1992, Deborah Abbott, review of *Dither Farm,* p. 1676; May 15, 1994, Deborah Abbott, review of *It's Nothing to a Mountain,* p. 1674; May 1, 1995, Ilene Cooper, review of *Answer My Prayer,* p. 1567; November 1, 1995, Stephanie Zvirin, review of *An Even Break,* p. 473; December 15, 1996, Randy Meyer, review of *Those Darn Dithers,* p. 721; March 15, 1998, Ilene Cooper, review of *The Distance of Hope,* p. 1236; April 15, 1999, Hazel Rochman,

review of *Cecil in Space,* p. 1523; November 1, 2000, Debbie Carton, review of *Stick and Whittle,* p. 539.

Bulletin of the Center for Children's Books, September, 1995, Roger Sutton, review of *Answer My Prayer,* p. 16.

Horn Book, September-October, 1995, Ann A. Flowers, review of *Answer My Prayer,* p. 609; January, 2001, review of *Stick and Whittle,* p. 92.

Kirkus Reviews, October 15, 1995, review of *An Even Break,* p. 1493; April 15, 1998, review of *The Distance of Hope,* p. 581; February 15, 1999, review of *Cecil in Space,* p. 300; September 1, 2001, review of *A Hole in the World,* p. 1291.

Kliatt, May, 1996, Paula Rohrlick, review of *Dither Farm,* p. 16.

Publishers Weekly, May 18, 1992, review of *Dither Farm,* p. 71; April 25, 1994, review of *It's Nothing to a Mountain,* p. 80; May 8, 1995, review of *Answer My Prayer,* p. 296; October 8, 1995, review of *An Even Break,* p. 86; November 26, 1996, review of *Those Darn Dithers,* p. 76; May 10, 1999, review of *Cecil in Space,* p. 69; August 21, 2000, review of *Stick and Whittle,* p. 74; November 12, 2001, review of *A Hole in the World,* p. 60.

School Library Journal, May, 1992, Cindy Darling Codell, review of *Dither Farm,* p. 133; June, 1995, Alice Casey, review of *It's Nothing to a Mountain,* p. 148; December, 1995, Tom S. Hurlburt, review of *An Even Break,* p. 104; December, 1996, Marilyn Payne Phillips, review of *Those Darn Dithers,* p. 122; May, 1998, Patricia A. Dollisch, review of *The Distance of Hope,* p. 142; May, 1999, Connie Tyrrell Burns, review of *Cecil in Space,* p. 125; September, 2000, Vicki Reutter, review of *Stick and Whittle,* p. 231; October, 2001, Sylvia V. Meisner, review of *A Hole in the World,* p. 162.

Voice of Youth Advocates, August, 1994, Ruth Cline, review of *It's Nothing to a Mountain,* p. 146; February, 1996, Jacqueline Rose, review of *An Even Break,* p. 372; June, 1999, Sue Krumbein, review of *Cecil in Space,* p. 113.

*   *   *

HOBAN, Russell (Conwell) 1925-

Personal

Born February 4, 1925, in Lansdale, PA; son of Abram T. (an advertising manager for the *Jewish Daily Forward*) and Jeanette (Dimmerman) Hoban; married Lillian Aberman (an illustrator), January 31, 1944 (divorced, 1975); married Gundula Ahl (a bookseller), 1975; children: (first marriage) Phoebe, Abrom, Esme, Julia; (second marriage) Jachin Boaz, Wieland, Benjamin. *Education:* Attended Philadelphia Museum School of Industrial Art, 1941-43. *Hobbies and other interests:* Stones, short-wave listening.

Russell Hoban

Addresses

Home and office—Fulham, London, England. *Agent*—David Higham Associates Ltd., 5-8 Lower John St., Golden Sq., London WlR 4HA, England.

Career

Artist and illustrator for magazine and advertising studios, New York, NY, 1945-51; Fletcher Smith Film Studio, New York, NY, story board artist and character designer, 1951; Batten, Barton, Durstine & Osborn, Inc., New York, NY, television art director, 1952-57; J. Walter Thompson Co., New York, NY, television art director, 1956; freelance illustrator for advertising agencies and magazines, including *Time, Life, Fortune, Saturday Evening Post,* and *True,* 1957-65; Doyle, Dane, Bembach, New York, NY, copywriter, 1965-67; novelist and author of children's books, beginning 1967. Art instructor at the Famous Artists Schools, Westport, CT, and School of Visual Arts, New York, NY. *Military service:* U.S. Army, Infantry, 1943-45; served in Italian campaign; earned the Bronze Star.

Member

Authors Guild, Authors League of America, Society of Authors, PEN.

Awards, Honors

The Sorely Trying Day, The Mouse and His Child, How Tom Beat Captain Najork and His Hired Sportsmen, and *Dinner at Alberta's* have all been named notable books by the American Library Association; *Bread and Jam for Frances* was selected as a Library of Congress Children's book, 1964; Boys' Club Junior Book Award, 1968, for *Charlie the Tramp; Emmet Otter's Jug-Band Christmas* was selected as one of *School Library Journal's* Best Books, 1971, and received the Lewis Carroll Shelf Award and the Christopher Award, both 1972; Whitbread Literary Award, 1974, and International Board on Books for Young People Honor List, 1976, both for *How Tom Beat Captain Najork and His Hired Sportsmen; A Near Thing for Captain Najork* was selected as one of the best illustrated children's books of the year by the *New York Times,* 1976; *Riddley Walker* received John W. Campbell Memorial Award for the best science fiction novel of the year from Science Fiction Research Association, 1981, and was nominated as the most distinguished book of fiction by National Book Critics Circle and for the Nebula Award by Science Fiction Writers of America, both 1982, and the Australian Science Fiction Achievement Award, 1983; Recognition of Merit, George G. Stone Center for Children's Books, 1982, for his contributions to books for younger children.

Writings

CHILDREN'S NONFICTION

(Self-illustrated) *What Does It Do and How Does It Work?: Power Shovel, Dump Truck, and Other Heavy Machines,* Harper (New York, NY), 1959.

(Self-illustrated) *The Atomic Submarine: A Practice Combat Patrol under the Sea,* Harper (New York, NY), 1960.

CHILDREN'S FICTION

Bedtime for Frances, illustrated by Garth Williams, Harper (New York, NY), 1960, new edition, HarperTrophy (New York, NY), 1995.

Herman the Loser, illustrated by Lillian Hoban, Harper (New York, NY), 1961.

The Song in My Drum, illustrated by Lillian Hoban, Harper (New York, NY), 1961.

London Men and English Men, illustrated by Lillian Hoban, Harper (New York, NY), 1962.

(With Lillian Hoban) *Some Snow Said Hello,* Harper (New York, NY), 1963.

The Sorely Trying Day, illustrated by Lillian Hoban, Harper (New York, NY), 1964.

A Baby Sister for Frances, illustrated by Lillian Hoban, Harper (New York, NY), 1964, new edition, HarperTrophy (New York, NY), 1993.

Nothing to Do, illustrated by Lillian Hoban, Harper (New York, NY), 1964.

Bread and Jam for Frances, illustrated by Lillian Hoban, Harper (New York, NY), 1964, revised edition, HarperCollins (New York, NY), 1993.

Tom and the Two Handles, illustrated by Lillian Hoban, Harper (New York, NY), 1965.

The Story of Hester Mouse Who Became a Writer and Saved Most of Her Sisters and Brothers and Some of Her Aunts and Uncles from the Owl, illustrated by Lillian Hoban, Norton (New York, NY), 1965.

What Happened When Jack and Daisy Tried to Fool the Tooth Fairies, illustrated by Lillian Hoban, Scholastic (New York, NY), 1965.

Henry and the Monstrous Din, illustrated by Lillian Hoban, Harper (New York, NY), 1966.

The Little Brute Family, illustrated by Lillian Hoban, Macmillan (New York, NY), 1966.

(With Lillian Hoban) *Save My Place*, Norton (New York, NY), 1967.

Charlie the Tramp, illustrated by Lillian Hoban, Four Winds (New York, NY), 1967, book and record, Scholastic (New York, NY), 1970.

The Mouse and His Child, illustrated by Lillian Hoban, Harper (New York, NY), 1967, new edition illustrated by David Small, Arthur A. Levine (New York, NY), 2001.

A Birthday for Frances, illustrated by Lillian Hoban, Harper (New York, NY), 1968, reprinted, HarperTrophy (New York, NY), 1994.

The Stone Doll of Sister Brute, illustrated by Lillian Hoban, Macmillan (New York, NY), 1968.

Harvey's Hideout, illustrated by Lillian Hoban, Parents' Magazine Press (New York, NY), 1969.

Best Friends for Frances, illustrated by Lillian Hoban, Harper (New York, NY), 1969, new illustrated edition, HarperCollins (New York, NY), 1994.

Ugly Bird, illustrated by Lillian Hoban, Macmillan (New York, NY), 1969.

The Mole Family's Christmas, illustrated by Lillian Hoban, Parents' Magazine Press (New York, NY), 1969.

A Bargain for Frances, illustrated by Lillian Hoban, Harper (New York, NY), 1970, reprinted, HarperFestival (New York, NY), 1999.

Emmet Otter's Jug-Band Christmas, illustrated by Lillian Hoban, Parents' Magazine Press (New York, NY), 1971.

The Sea-Thing Child, illustrated by son Abrom Hoban, Harper (New York, NY), 1972, new edition illustrated by Patrick Benson, Candlewick Press (Cambridge, MA), 1999.

Letitia Rabbit's String Song (Junior Literary Guild selection), illustrated by Mary Chalmers, Coward (New York, NY), 1973.

How Tom Beat Captain Najork and His Hired Sportsmen, illustrated by Quentin Blake, Atheneum (New York, NY), 1974.

Ten What?: A Mystery Counting Book, illustrated by Sylvie Selig, J. Cape (London, England), 1974, Scribner (New York, NY), 1975.

La Corona and the Tin Frog (originally published in *Puffin Annual*, 1974), illustrated by Nicola Bayley, J. Cape (London, England), 1978.

Crocodile and Pierrot: A See the Story Book, illustrated by Sylvie Selig, J. Cape (London, England), 1975, Scribner (New York, NY), 1977.

Dinner at Alberta's, illustrated by James Marshall, Crowell (New York, NY), 1975.

A Near Thing for Captain Najork, illustrated by Quentin Blake, J. Cape (London, England), 1975, Atheneum (New York, NY), 1976.

Arthur's New Power, illustrated by Byron Barton, Crowell (New York, NY), 1978.

The Twenty-Elephant Restaurant, illustrated by Emily Arnold McCully, Atheneum (New York, NY), 1978, illustrated by Quentin Blake, J. Cape (London, England), 1980.

The Dancing Tigers, illustrated by David Gentlemen, J. Cape (London, England), 1979.

Flat Cat, illustrated by Clive Scruton, Philomel (New York, NY), 1980.

Ace Dragon Ltd., illustrated by Quentin Blake, J. Cape (London, England), 1980.

They Came from Aargh!, illustrated by Colin McNaughton, Philomel (New York, NY), 1981.

The Serpent Tower, illustrated by David Scott, Methuen/Walker (London, England), 1981.

The Great Fruit Gum Robbery, illustrated by Colin McNaughton, Methuen (London, England), 1981, published as *The Great Gum Drop Robbery*, Philomel (New York, NY), 1982.

The Battle of Zormla, illustrated by Colin McNaughton, Philomel (New York, NY), 1982.

The Flight of Bembel Rudzuk, illustrated by Colin McNaughton, Philomel (New York, NY), 1982.

Big John Turkle, illustrated by Martin Baynton, Walker (London, England), 1983, Holt (New York, NY), 1984.

Jim Frog, illustrated by Martin Baynton, Walker (London, England), 1983, Holt (New York, NY), 1984.

Lavinia Bat, illustrated by Martin Baynton, Holt (New York, NY), 1984.

Charlie Meadows, illustrated by Martin Baynton, Holt (New York, NY), 1984.

The Rain Door, illustrated by Quentin Blake, J. Cape (London, England), 1986, HarperCollins (New York, NY), 1987.

The Marzipan Pig, illustrated by Quentin Blake, J. Cape (London, England), 1986.

Ponders, illustrated by Martin Baynton, Walker (London, England), 1988.

Monsters, illustrated by Quentin Blake, Scholastic (New York, NY), 1989.

Jim Hedgehog and the Lonesome Tower, illustrated by Betsy Lewin, Clarion Books (New York, NY), 1990.

Jim Hedgehog's Supernatural Christmas, illustrated by Betsy Lewin, Clarion Books (New York, NY), 1992.

M.O.L.E.: Much Overworked Little Earthmover, J. Cape (London, England), 1993.

The Court of the Winged Serpent, illustrated by Patrick Benson, Trafalgar Square (New York, NY), 1995.

Trokeville Way, Knopf (New York, NY), 1996.

Trouble on Thunder Mountain, illustrated by Quentin Blake, Orchard Books (New York, NY), 2000.

Jim's Lion, illustrated by Ian Andrew, Candlewick Press (Cambridge, MA), 2001.

CHILDREN'S VERSE

Goodnight, illustrated by Lillian Hoban, Norton (New York, NY), 1966.

The Pedaling Man, and Other Poems, illustrated by Lillian Hoban, Norton (New York, NY), 1968.

Egg Thoughts, and Other Frances Songs, illustrated by Lillian Hoban, Harper (New York, NY), 1972.

NOVELS

The Lion of Boaz-Jachin and Jachin-Boaz, Stein & Day (New York, NY), 1973.

Kleinzeit, J. Cape (London, England), 1974.

Turtle Diary, J. Cape (London, England), 1975, Random House (New York, NY), 1976.

Riddley Walker, J. Cape (London, England), 1980, Summit Books (New York, NY), 1981, expanded edition with new foreword, Indiana University Press (Bloomington, IN), 1998.

Pilgermann, Summit Books (New York, NY), 1983.

The Medusa Frequency, edited by Gary Fisketjohn, Atlantic Monthly (New York, NY), 1987.

Fremder, J. Cape (London, England), 1996.

Mr Rinyo-Clacton's Offer, J. Cape (London, England), 1998.

Angelica's Grotto, Carroll & Graf (New York, NY), 2001.

Also author of *Amaryllis Night and Day.*

OTHER

(Illustrator) W. R. Burnett, *The Roar of the Crowd: Conversations with an Ex-Big-Leaguer,* C. N. Potter (New York, NY), 1964.

The Carrier Frequency (play), first produced in London, England, 1984.

Frances tries everything to keep from going to sleep in Hoban's classic **Bedtime for Frances.** *(Illustrated by Garth Williams.)*

Riddley Walker (stage adaptation of his novel), first produced in Manchester, England, 1986.

(Author of introduction) Wilhelm K. Grimm, *Household Tales,* illustrated by Mervyn Peake, Schocken (New York, NY), 1987.

A Russell Hoban Omnibus, Indiana University Press (Bloomington, IN), 1999.

Contributor of articles to *Granta, Fiction,* and *Holiday.* Author of *Come and Find Me* (television play), 1980. Hoban's papers are included in the Kerlan Collection at the University of Minnesota.

Adaptations

The Mouse and His Child was made into a feature-length animated film by Fario-Lockhart-Sanrio Productions in 1977 and featured the voices of Cloris Leachman, Andy Devine, and Peter Ustinov (who also read an abridged version of the novel for a Caedmon recording in 1977); Glynnis Johns recorded selections from *Bedtime for Frances, A Baby Sister for Frances, Bread and Jam for Frances,* and *A Birthday for Frances* in a sound recording titled *Frances,* as well as selections from *A Bargain for Frances, Best Friends for Frances,* and *Egg Thoughts, and Other Frances Songs* in a sound recording titled *A Bargain for Frances and Other Stories,* both released by Caedmon in 1977; *Turtle Diary* was adapted for the screen by United British Artists/Brittanic in 1986, featuring a screenplay by Harold Pinter and starring Glenda Jackson and Ben Kingsley; *Riddley Walker* was staged by the Manchester Royal Exchange Theatre Company, also in 1986.

Sidelights

"Russell Hoban is a writer whose genius is expressed with equal brilliance in books both for children and for adults," wrote Alida Allison in *Dictionary of Literary Biography.* Largely self-educated, Hoban has moved masterfully from being an artist and illustrator to writing children's fables and adult allegorical fiction. Praising his "unerring ear for dialogue," his "memorable depiction of scenes," and his "wise and warm stories notable for delightful plots and originality of language," Allison considered Hoban to be "much more than just a clever and observant writer. His works are permeated with an honest, often painful, and always uncompromising urge toward self-identity." Noting that "this theme of identity becomes more apparent, more complex as Hoban's works have become longer and more penetrating," Allison stated, "Indeed, Hoban's writing has leaped and bounded—paralleling upheavals in his own life."

In an interview with Rhonda M. Bunbury in *Children's Literature in Education,* Hoban indicated that as a child he was "good with words and good with drawing. It just happened my parents more or less seized on the drawing and thought that I'd probably end up being a great painter. I did become an illustrator, but I think that the drawing formula was always a little bit poisoned by the expectations that were laid on me, while the writing was allowed to be my own thing." He wrote poetry and short stories in school, and won several prizes. Having attended the Philadelphia Museum School of Industrial Art, Hoban worked as a freelance illustrator before he began writing children's stories. He would drive throughout Connecticut, occasionally stopping at construction sites and sketching the machinery being used. A friend saw his work and suggested that it might make a good children's book; Hoban's first published work was about construction equipment—*What Does It Do and How Does It Work?: Power Shovel, Dump Truck, and Other Heavy Machines.*

Although Hoban has since originated several well-known characters in children's literature, including Charlie the Tramp, Emmet Otter, and Manny Rat, he is especially recognized for a series of books about an anthropomorphic badger named Frances. Reviewers generally concurred that these stories depict ordinary family life with much humor, wit, and style. Benjamin DeMott suggested in the *Atlantic Monthly* that "these books are unique, first, because the adults in their pages are usually humorous, precise of speech, and understandingly conversant with general life, and second, because the author confronts—not unfancifully but without kinky secret garden stuff—problems with which ordinary parents and children have to cope." *Bedtime for Frances,* for instance, concerns nighttime fears and is regarded by many as a classic in children's literature. According to a *Saturday Review* contributor, "The exasperated humor of this book could only derive from actual parental experience, and no doubt parents will enjoy it."

"Hoban has established himself as a writer with a rare understanding of childhood (and parental) psychology, sensitively and humorously portrayed in familiar family situations," noted Allison. He and his first wife, Lillian, also an illustrator and author of books for children, collaborated on many successful works, including several in the "Frances" series. Allison added that although their work together was usually well-received, "there were pans as well as paeans." While some books have been faulted for "excessive coziness, for sentimentality, and for stereotyped male-female roles," Allison said that a more general criticism of their work together is that "it tends toward repetition." However, commenting in *Children and Books,* May Hill Arbuthnot and Zena Sutherland found that all of Hoban's stories about Frances show "affection for and understanding of children" as well as "contribute to a small child's understanding of himself, his relationships with other people, and the fulfillment of his emotional needs." Further, they said, "These characters are indeed ourselves in fur." Yet as a *Times Literary Supplement* contributor observed, "Excellent as [the "Frances" books] are, they give no hint that the author had in him such a blockbuster of a book as *The Mouse and His Child.*"

Revered in England as a modern children's classic, *The Mouse and His Child* was described in the *New York Times Book Review* by Barbara Wersba as a story about two wind-up toy mice who are discarded from a toyshop

Emmet and his mother try to get together enough money to buy a Christmas gift for each other and learn the true meaning of wealth in Emmet Otter's Jug-Band Christmas, *illustrated by Lillian Hoban.*

and are then "buffeted from place to place as they seek the lost paradise of their first home—a doll house—and their first 'family,' a toy elephant and seal." Ill-equipped for the baffling, threatening world into which they are tossed, the mouse and his child innocently confront the unknown and its inherent treachery and violence, as well as their own fears. The book explores not only the transience and inconstancy of life but also the struggle to persevere. "Helpless when they are not wound up, unable to stop when they *are,* [the mice] are fated like all mechanical things to breakage, rust and disintegration as humans are to death," writes Margaret Blount in her *Animal Land: The Creatures of Children's Fiction.* "As an adult," said Blount, "it is impossible to read [the book] unmoved." Distressed, however, by the "continuing images of cruelty and decay," Penelope Farmer remarked in *Children's Literature in Education* that *The Mouse and His Child* is "like Beckett for children." But assessing whatever cruelty and decay there is in the novel as the "artful rendering of the facts of life," Allison affirmed, "If there is betrayal, there is also self-sacrifice. If there is loss, there is also love. If there is homelessness, there is also destination. The mouse child gets his family in the end; children's literature gets a masterpiece."

"Like the best of books, [*The Mouse and His Child*] is a book from which one can peel layer after layer of meaning," said a *Times Literary Supplement* contributor. Some critics, however, questioned the book's suitability for children. Hoban responded to these critics in an essay for *Books for Your Children:* "When I wrote [*The Mouse and His Child*] I didn't think it was [a children's book]. I was writing as much book as I was capable of at the time. No concessions were made in style or content. It was my first novel and ... it was the fullest response I could make to being alive and in the world." Hoban indicated to Bunbury that the book has become his favorite book for children, the one that has given him the most satisfaction, "Though it may not be the best of my novels, it is the closest to my heart because of that." Believing the book reveals "an absolute respect for its subject—which means its readers as well," Isabel Quigley added in the *Spectator*, "I'm still not sure just who is going to read it but that hardly seems to matter.... It will last." Hoban felt that within its limitations, the book is suitable for children, though. "Its heroes and heroines found out what they were and it wasn't enough, so they found out how to be more," he says in his essay. "That's not a bad thought to be going with."

A pair of tin wind-up mice persevere through numerous trials on their quest for happiness and security in Hoban's The Mouse and His Child. *(Illustrated by David Small.)*

Nominated as the most distinguished book of fiction by the National Book Critics Circle, and for the Nebula Award by the Science Fiction Writers of America, *Riddley Walker* received the John W. Campbell Memorial Award from the Science Fiction Research Association as the year's best science fiction novel and the Australian Science Fiction Achievement Award. *Riddley Walker* imagines a world and civilization decades after a nuclear holocaust; the story of what remains is narrated in a fragmented, phonetical English by a twelve-year-old boy struggling to comprehend the past so that its magnificence might be recaptured. "Set in a remote future and composed in an English nobody ever spoke or wrote," wrote DeMott in the *New York Times,* "this short, swiftly paced tale juxtaposes preliterate fable and Beckettian wit, Boschian monstrosities and a hero with Huck Finn's heart and charm, lighting by El Greco and jokes by Punch and Judy. It is a wrenchingly vivid report on the texture of life after Doomsday."

Detecting similarities in *Riddley Walker* to other contemporary works such as Anthony Burgess's *A Clockwork Orange,* John Gardner's *Grendel,* and the complete works of William Golding, DeMott believed that "in vision and execution, this is an exceptionally original work, and Russell Hoban is actually his own best source." *Riddley Walker* "is not 'like' anything," suggested Victoria Glendinning in the *Listener.* As A. Alverez expressed in the *New York Review of Books,* Hoban has "transformed what might have been just another fantasy of the future into a novel of exceptional depth and originality."

Critically lauded and especially popular in England, *Riddley Walker* has been particularly commended for its inventive language, which Alverez thought "reflects with extraordinary precision both the narrator's understanding and the desolate landscape he moves through." Reviewing the book in the *Washington Post Book World,* Michael Dirda believed that "what is marvelous in all this is the way Hoban makes us experience the uncanny familiarity of this world, while also making it a strange and animistic place, where words almost have a life of their own." "What Hoban has done," suggested Barbara A. Bannon in a *Publishers Weekly* interview with Hoban, "is to invent a world and a language to go with it, and in doing both he remains a storyteller, which is the most significant achievement of *Riddley Walker.*"

Alverez called *Riddley Walker* an "artistic tour de force in every possible way," but Natalie Maynor and Richard F. Patteson suggested in *Critique* that even more than that, it is "perhaps the most sophisticated work of fiction ever to speculate about man's future on earth and the implications for a potentially destructive technology." Eliot Fremont-Smith maintained in the *Village Voice* that "the reality of the human situation now is so horrendous and bizarre that to get a hold on it requires all our faculties, including the imaginative. We can't do it through plain fact and arms controllers' reasoning alone.... Read *Riddley,* too." Although Kelly Cherry referred to the novel in the *Chicago Tribune Book World* as a "philosophical essay in fictional drag," DeMott thought that Hoban's focus on what has been lost in civilization "summons the reader to dwell anew on that within civilization which is separate from, opposite to, power and its appurtenances, ravages, triumphs." *Riddley Walker,* said DeMott, is "haunting and fiercely imagined and—this matters most—intensely ponderable."

An American by birth but an Englishman at heart, Hoban has made his home in London for much of his adult life. In a 1998 *Pure Fiction Reviews* interview with the author, John Forsyth declared that Hoban's enthusiasm for his adopted city "remains undiminished, decades after moving here . . . and that this affection places him in a whole tradition of English writing." As Hoban told Forsyth, "I came here because I was a great admirer of British ghost stories and supernatural stories. . . . I've been at great pains to have [my narrators] speak in an English manner, and to make their background a credible English background."

During the same interview Hoban revealed one more attraction of London—its subway system, the Underground. "I hate buses, you know; they never turn up, people rush ahead of you and all that," he elaborated. "At most Tube stations it tells you how long it's going to be till the next Wimbledon train or whatever. And then there's the perpetual nocturnal mood of the Underground; it never seems like daytime down there, it always seems like night. I'm a nocturnal kind of person, and I like to work at night."

The Underground plays a role in Hoban's 1998 adult novel, *Mr Rinyo-Clacton's Offer.* The story follows one Jonathan Fitch as he is approached in the Piccadilly Circus subway station by the title character, an eccentric aristocrat. The offer of the title is of the Faustian variety: Rinyo-Clacton offers Fitch a million pounds in exchange for his life in one year. "What kind of weirdo are you?," asks Fitch. "The kind with lots of money," is the reply. The book then goes on to examine the tragic circumstances that impel Fitch to consider the fateful deal.

For all their suspense, though, "in my books there aren't characters who are simply bad or simply good," Hoban told Fred Hauptfuhrer in *People.* "Nothing in life is that simple." Writing for adults has added both breadth and depth to Hoban's work; and as his work has grown in complexity, he has commented upon the process by which an idea evolves into a book. As he explained to Bannon: "There always seems to be something in my mind waiting to put something together with some primary thought I will encounter. It's like looking out of the window and listening to the radio at the same time. I am committed to what comes to me, however it links up."

Biographical and Critical Sources

BOOKS

Allison, Alida, editor, *Russell Hoban/Forty Years: Essays on His Writings for Children,* Garland Publishing (New York, NY), 2000.

Arbuthnot, May Hill, and Zena Sutherland, *Children and Books,* 4th edition, Scott, Foresman (Glenview, IL), 1972.

Blount, Margaret, *Animal Land: The Creatures of Children's Fiction,* Morrow (New York, NY), 1974.

Children's Literature Review, Volume 3, Gale (Detroit, MI), 1978.

Contemporary Literary Criticism, Gale (Detroit, MI), Volume 7, 1977, Volume 25, 1983.

Dictionary of Literary Biography, Volume 52: *American Writers for Children since 1960: Fiction,* Gale (Detroit, MI), 1986, pp. 192-202.

Hoban, Russell, *The Thorny Paradise: Writers on Writing for Children,* edited by Edward Blishen, Kestrel (Harmondsworth, England), 1975.

Hoban, Russell, *Mr Rinyo-Clacton's Offer,* J. Cape (London, England), 1998.

Twentieth-Century Children's Writers, 3rd edition, St. James Press (Chicago, IL), 1989.

Wilkie, Christine, *Through the Narrow Gate: The Mythological Consciousness of Russell Hoban,* Fairleigh Dickinson University Press (Rutherford, NJ), 1989.

PERIODICALS

American Artist, October, 1961.

Antioch Review, summer, 1982.

Atlantic Monthly, August, 1976, Benjamin DeMott, "The Way You Slide," pp. 83-84; December, 1983.

Booklist, January 1, 2002, Cynthia Turnquest, review of *Jim's Lion,* p. 865.

Books for Your Children, winter, 1976, Russell Hoban, "'The Mouse and His Child': Yes, It's a Children's Book," p. 3.

Chicago Tribune Book World, July 12, 1981, Kelly Cherry, review of *Riddley Walker.*

Children's Literature in Education, March, 1972, Penelope Farmer, review of *The Mouse and His Child;* spring, 1976; fall, 1986, Rhonda M. Bunbury, interview with Russell Hoban, pp. 139-149.

Critique, fall, 1984, Natalie Maynor and Richard F. Patteson, review of *Riddley Walker.*

Economist, January 27, 2001, p. 4.

Educational Foundation for Nuclear Science, June, 1982.

Encounter, June, 1981.

Globe and Mail (Toronto, Canada), March 29, 1986.

Harper's, April, 1983.

Junior Bookshelf, July, 1963.

Listener, October 30, 1980, Victoria Glendinning, "The 1 Big 1," p. 589.

Los Angeles Times, February 14, 1986.

New Statesman, May 25, 1973; April 11, 1975.

Newsweek, March 1, 1976; June 29, 1981; December 7, 1981; May 30, 1983; February 17, 1986.

New Yorker, March 22, 1976; July 20, 1981; August 8, 1983.

New York Review of Books, November 19, 1981, A. Alvarez, "Past, Present, & Future," pp. 16-18.

New York Times, June 28, 1981, Benjamin DeMott, "2,000 Years after the Berstyn Fyr," pp. 1, 25; November 1, 1981; June 20, 1983; February 14, 1986.

New York Times Book Review, February 4, 1968, Barbara Wersba, review of *The Mouse and His Child;* March

21, 1976; June 6, 1982; May 29, 1983; November 27, 1983.

Observer (London, England), March 13, 1983.

People, August 10, 1981, Fred Hauptfuhrer, interview with Russell Hoban.

Publishers Weekly, May 15, 1981, Barbara A. Bannon, interview with Russell Hoban; June 4, 2001, p. 57.

Saturday Review, May 7, 1960, review of *Bedtime for Frances;* May 1, 1976; December, 1981.

School Library Journal, January, 2002, Faith Brautigam, review of *Jim's Lion,* p. 101.

Spectator, May 16, 1969, Isabel Quigley, "Nice Mice," pp. 654-655; April 5, 1975; March 12, 1983.

Time, February 16, 1976; June 22, 1981; May 16, 1983.

Times (London, England), January 7, 1982; March 24, 1983.

Times Literary Supplement, April 3, 1969, review of *The Mouse and His Child,* p. 357; March 16, 1973; March 29, 1974; October 31, 1980; March 7, 1986; April 3, 1987; September 4, 1987.

Village Voice, June 15, 1982, Eliot Fremont-Smith, review of *Riddley Walker.*

Washington Post, February 28, 1986.

Washington Post Book World, June 7, 1981, Michael Dirda, "Riding Out a Canterbury Tale," pp. 1, 14; June 27, 1982; May 29, 1983; July 12, 1987; October 14, 1990.

Wilton Bulletin, September 26, 1962.

OTHER

Pure Fiction Reviews, http://www.purefiction.com (October 2, 2001), interview with Russell Hoban.*

*   *   *

HOELLWARTH, Cathryn Clinton 1957-
(Cathryn Clinton)

Personal

Born December 12, 1957, in Bridgeton, NJ; daughter of J. Robert (a seminary professor) and Marilyn (a seminary administrator; maiden name, Dodge) Clinton; married Dan Hoellwarth (a minister), January 1, 1978; children: Jena, Marshall. *Nationality:* American. *Education:* University of Iowa, B.A. (English), 1989; Vermont College (of Norwich University), M.F.A., 2000. *Religion:* Christian. *Hobbies and other interests:* Gardening, exercising, reading.

Addresses

Home—Lancaster, PA. *Agent*—c/o Author's Mail, Candlewick Press, 2067 Massachusetts Ave., 5th Fl., Cambridge, MA 02140. *E-mail*—CathrynC@Juno.com.

Career

Picture book author and poet. Minister and speaker in Lancaster, PA, 1987—; Eastern Mennonite Missions, Salunga, PA, program director, 1992-95; ordained minister, Teaching the Word Ministries, 2001.

Awards, Honors

Parents' Choice Gold Award, 2001, for *The Calling.*

Writings

The Underbed (picture book), Good Books (Intercourse, PA), 1990, revised edition, 2001.

(As Cathryn Clinton) *The Calling* (middle-grade novel), Candlewick Press (Cambridge, MA), 2001.

(As Cathryn Clinton) *A Stone in My Hand* (middle-grade novel), Candlewick Press (Cambridge, MA), 2002.

Contributor of poetry to periodicals, including *MCC Women's Concerns Report* and *Gospel Herald.*

Work in Progress

Dogday and the Insect Orchestra, a picture book; *By the Light of Van Gogh,* a novel about a girl who attempts suicide and lives, expected 2003.

Twelve-year-old Esta Lea is called to the Lord and begins a journey of healing throughout South Carolina in Cathryn Clinton's book. (Cover illustration by Wendell Minor.)

Sidelights

Inspiration for Cathryn Clinton Hoellwarth's first book for young readers came from a common source: the needs of her own child. However, she has since continued to work in the field, expanding her talents from picture books to novels for middle-grade readers. Hoellwarth's first teen novel, *The Calling,* received enough praise to encourage her to continue working in the genre. While her first book was published under her full name, *The Calling* and her other books for older readers have been published under the name Cathryn Clinton.

The Calling takes place in the early 1960s in a small town in South Carolina. It follows the dramatic changes that occur in the life of twelve-year-old Esta Leah Ridley after she has a vision of Jesus and discovers she has healing powers. After Esta Leah's touch helps her deaf grandmother regain her hearing, the young girl is catapulted into regional renown by her smooth-talking and recently "saved" uncle, her crusade wholeheartedly supported by her devoutly religious parents. Traveling the area as a minister newly ordained in the Beulah Land Healing and Holiness Church, she performs a number of healings, but she begins to question whether she is being used by her uncle for less-than-charitable purposes. "As Esta's faith and her worries escalate, she struggles with how best to share her gift," explained *Booklist* contributor Gillian Engberg, adding that "even readers who aren't religious will be moved" by Esta Lea's growing faith in her own judgment. Praising *The Calling* as a "humorous, sincere account of faith healing," Joel Shoemaker described the work as a "fun, quick-reading, gently provocative narrative" in his review for *School Library Journal.*

The Calling focuses on a subject close to Hoellwarth's heart: like her protagonist, she is descended from several generations of ministers and has herself been ordained to preach the Christian faith. As the author noted in a *Publishers Weekly* interview with Elizabeth Devereaux, "God and faith tend to be taboo subjects for YA fiction." In *The Calling* she addresses both subjects, couching them in a humorous setting to make them less threatening to teen readers. "I want to be able to say it's okay to question, and as readers are asking those serious questions, I want them to be able to laugh too," she explained to Devereaux.

Hoellwarth told *SATA:* "I began writing poetry while attending the University of Iowa as an undergraduate English major. I decided to write a picture book because I couldn't find one to help my son with his fears. We'd already gone through all the ones at the library." That picture book, *The Underbed,* was published in 1990, the year after Hoellwarth earned her B.A. degree from the University of Iowa. Inspired by her publishing success, as well as the strong creative community she witnessed at the school's noted Iowa Writer's Workshop each year, Hoellwarth determined to continue her own studies in creative writing.

"I decided to try writing fiction because of the encouragement of teachers in the Master of Fine Arts Writing program at Vermont College of Norwich University," Hoellwarth continued. "Norma Fox Mazer and Amy Ehrlich, who later became my editor at Candlewick Press, influenced me as a writer. Each in their own way taught me how to ask myself the necessary questions to reveal character motivation, plot, and the other good stuff. Life taught me how to be an observer and memory keeper, two qualitites that are essential in writing for children."

Hoellwarth's second middle-grade novel, *A Stone in My Hand,* focuses on the plight of an eleven-year-old Palestinian girl named Malaak whose father is killed in a terrorist act near their home on the Gaza strip. Malaak's family is further torn apart when her older brother, seeking revenge for his father's death, decides to join a group of Islamic extremists. *Booklist*'s Hazel Rochman offered warm words for the novel, finding that "the young girl's narrative captures the experience of the occupation and the never-ending cycle of anger and retaliation."

"What continues to guide me in writing is my belief that 'art' is a calling," concluded the author. "Through it we can reveal reality and truth so that we can laugh and cry for ourselves and others."

Biographical and Critical Sources

PERIODICALS

Booklist, October 1, 2001, Gillian Engberg, review of *The Calling,* p. 331; September 15, 2002, Hazel Rochman, review of *A Stone in My Hand,* p. 232.
Publishers Weekly, December 24, 2001, Elizabeth Devereaux, "Flying Starts: Six First-Time Authors and Illustrators Talk about Their Fall Debuts," p. 30.
School Library Journal, August, 2001, Joel Shoemaker, review of *The Calling,* p. 177.*

*   *   *

HOEYE, Michael 1947-

Personal

Born April 12, 1947; married Martha Banyas. *Nationality:* American. *Education:* Washington University at St. Louis, B.A. (English literature); graduate work in psychology and religion at Union Theological Seminary.

Addresses

Home—1825 Southeast 7th Ave., Portland, OR 97214-3530.

Career

Terfle House, Portland, OR, founder. Marylhurst University, Marylhurst, OR, instructor in M.B.A. program. Has also worked as a textile designer, stagehand at

Studio 54, agent, therapist, and fashion photographer in New York, NY.

Writings

NOVELS

Time Stops for No Mouse: A Hermux Tantamoq Adventure, Terfle Books (Portland, OR), 2000, Putnam (New York, NY), 2002.

The Sands of Time: A Hermux Tantamoq Adventure, Terfle Books (Portland, OR), 2001, Putnam (New York, NY), 2002.

Work in Progress

A third Hermux Tantamoq novel, for Putnam.

Sidelights

A former college instructor, author Michael Hoeye entered the world of children's literature with his highly successful *Time Stops for No Mouse: A Hermux Tantamoq Adventure.* Discussing his inspiration for the book on the Web site *BookBrowse,* Hoeye claimed the name for the hero of the book came to him while playing a word game with his wife, Martha Banyas. After picking a number of random letters, players each had one minute to arrange their selection of letters into a character's name and create a fictional story about the character. "I drew the letters that formed the name Hermux Tantamoq," recalled Hoeye. "And immediately saw him as an ordinary, but likable, city mouse who was a watchmaker."

While the game was short-lived, the character of Hermux Tantamoq endured in the author's mind, with Hoeye gradually fleshing out the small creature in his head. For many months, the story of Tantamoq remained a series of stories Hoeye had written both on paper and in his imagination. It was not until his wife went on a two-month long journey to Southeast Asia that the author finally began to develop Tantamoq's adventures into a coherent tale. While keeping in contact with Banyas through e-mails, Hoeye decided to deviate from the standard rote letter detailing the weather back home and events of his usual existence. Instead, he began writing the first chapter of *Time Stops for No Mouse,* a mystery featuring the watchmaking rodent. Subsequent chapters followed via e-mail until Valentine's Day arrived, and looking for a thoughtful present, the author bound his now thirty-page book and gave it to his wife. Other copies of the book he sent to friends, some of whom implored Hoeye to finish the story, a challenge he took up, eventually finishing the mystery.

However, as the author attempted to find a publishing house for his manuscript, Hoeye became disappointed at the lack of interest he received. Undeterred, Hoeye decided to publish the work himself, setting up a company called Terfle House. Little did he realize that "being a self-publisher is like being a washing machine on permanent spin cycle," as he commented on the *Penguin Putnam* Web site. "There are always twelve

Michael Hoeye

things that should have been done yesterday. And a hundred more things before you go home for the day." The author persevered, though, and in the summer of 2000 *Time Stops for No Mouse* made its debut through Terfle.

Selling the book posed another challenge, one Hoeye undertook by taking his work directly to the individuals who sold it—booksellers. Using eye-catching mailings and displays at trade shows, Hoeye convinced booksellers to stock his title, eventually selling over ten thousand books. "While sales figures may seem modest compared with those from larger houses, this mouse's success has been won without benefit of any national publicity," claimed *Publishers Weekly* contributor Barbara Roether. But, seeing the popularity of the work, big publishing companies did not stay away for long, with Penguin Putnam eventually buying the rights to republish the three books in the series, *Time Stops for No Mouse, The Sands of Time: A Hermux Tantamoq Adventure,* and a yet unnamed third book.

In the first of *Hermux Tantamoq*'s adventures, *Time Stops for No Mouse,* the mouse in question receives a request from the beautiful Linka Perflinger to repair a watch as quickly as possible. After the noted aviatrix does not return for the watch, Tantamoq decides to investigate, not only out of concern for the mouse's safety but also out of curiosity about the attractive female. Doing some sleuthing, Tantamoq unwittingly

Mouse watchmaker Hermux Tantamoq investigates the disappearance of a beautiful aviatrix and discovers that the entire city of mice, rats, minks, and moles is in danger from a cosmetics tycoon. (Cover illustration by Dale Champlin.)

discovers the ugly truth about the desire for youthfulness pervading the cosmetics industry. The more information the watchmaker finds, the more convinced he is that Perflinger is not the only one in trouble, but rather the whole metropolis of Pinchester. "In this first novel, Hoeye has created a hilarious community of city-dwelling animals and an appealing hero, Hermux Tantamoq," claimed *Commonweal* critic Darla Donnelly. *School Library Journal* contributor Saleena L. Davidson also offered kind words for *Time Stops for No Mouse*, writing that "Hoeye mixes an interesting cast of characters with a multi-leveled story that will keep readers' attention from beginning to end."

Tantamoq tackles a new mystery in *The Sands of Time*. Here the watchmaker must rescue his artist-friend Mirrin Stentrill after his paintings of cats causes a riot. Considered to be mythical creatures, cats are a taboo topic among the rodents of Pinchester. But when a mysterious chipmunk, chased away years earlier after deciphering a map leading to the secret land of the cats, reappears in the city and claims to have new information about cats, he unwittingly sets off a race among Tantamoq and other villains to discover the ancient resting place of Ka-Narsh-Pah and the secrets of the long-lost cat kingdom. "Hoeye's galloping plot," according to a *Publishers Weekly* critic, is filled with "evocative descriptions" and "exuberantly sophisticated wit" that will "keep the pages rapidly turning."

When asked by a *Publishers Weekly* writer about his first book, the author claimed "that he hoped the book would invite adults back into a more childlike world, while children would be taken to a world with more adult themes." Receiving wide-spread appeal from a broad readership, Hoeye's first entries in the "Hermux Tantamoq Adventures" appear to have done just that.

Biographical and Critical Sources

PERIODICALS

Bookseller, September 14, 2001, "Little Creature Helps Land Author with a Giant Deal," p. 40.

Carousel, summer, 2002, Chris Stephenson, "A Funny Thing Happened to Michael Hoeye on His Way to Hermux Tantamoq," p. 29.

Commonweal, April 8, 2001, Darla Donnelly, review of *Time Stops for No Mouse,* p. 22.

Kirkus Reviews, August 15, 2001, review of *The Sands of Time,* p. 1214.

Publishers Weekly, July 9, 2001, Barbara Roether, "Northwest Mouse Sneaks into National Market," p. 19; August 20, 2001, "Big Money for Kids's Mouse Book," p. 17; September 10, 2001, review of *The Sands of Time,* p. 93; March 4, 2002, Shannon Maughan, "Moving on Up: A Look Behind Some Current Children's Bestsellers," p. 36.

School Library Journal, May, 2002, Saleena L. Davidson, review of *Time Stops for No Mouse,* p. 154.

OTHER

BookBrowse, http://www.bookbrowse.com/ (March 6, 2002), "Michael Hoeye."

Hermux Tantamoq Web Site, http://www.hermux.com/ (August 15, 2001).

Penguin Putnam, http://www.penguinputnam.com/ (March 6, 2002), "Michael Hoeye on *Time Stops for No Mouse*" and "Michael Hoeye on Michael Hoeye."

*   *   *

HOLEMAN, Linda 1949-

Personal

Born December 24, 1949, in Winnipeg, Manitoba, Canada; daughter of Leon and Donna Freeman; married Jon Holeman; children: Zalie, Brenna, Kitt. *Education:* University of Winnipeg, B.A., 1972; University of Manitoba, B.Ed., 1976, M.Ed., 1982. *Avocational interests:* Reading, traveling, gardening, cycling.

Addresses

Home—728 South Dr., Winnipeg, Manitoba, Canada R3T 0C3. *E-mail*—lholeman@shaw.ca.

Career

Writer, 1991—. Frontier School Division, South Indian Lake, Manitoba, Canada, classroom and resource teacher, 1974-76; Ryerson School, Fort Garry School Division, Winnipeg, Canada, classroom and resource teacher, 1977-84; University of Winnipeg, Continuing Education Division, creative writing instructor, 1996—; Winnipeg Public Library, writer-in-residence, 1999-2000. Conducts courses, workshops, and seminars on writing.

Member

International Board on Books for Young People (Canada), Canadian Children's Book Centre, Canadian Society of Children's Authors, Illustrators, and Performers (CANSCAIP), Writers' Union of Canada, Manitoba Writers' Guild.

Awards, Honors

Winner, *Canadian Living* Annual Writing Competition, 1991, for "Sweet Bird of Youth"; runner-up, Thistledown Press National Young Adult Short Story Competition, 1992, for "Saying Good-bye"; winner, *Winnipeg Free Press*/Canadian Authors Association Annual Non-Fiction Contest, 1993, for "On the Road Again"; third place, Canadian Authors Association Annual Poetry Competition, 1993; finalist, *Zygote* magazine's poetry contest, 1995, for "Two Hands, Ten Fingers"; winner, Thistledown Press Second National Young Adult Short Story Competition, 1995, for "How to Tell Renata"; nominee, John Hirsch Award for Most Promising Manitoba Writer, 1996; Journey Prize finalist, 1996; Canadian Library Association Young Adult Book Award finalist, and McNally Robinson Book for Young People Award finalist, both 1996, and Our Choice selection, Canadian Children's Book Centre, all for *Saying Good-bye;* McNally Robinson Book of the Year finalist, 1997, for *Flying to Yellow;* Best Fiction, *Quill & Quire,* and Geoffrey Bilson Award for Historical Fiction shortlist, both 1997, Books for the Teen Age, New York City Public Library, Our Choice selection, Canadian Children's Book Centre, Young Adult Canadian Book Award honor book, Canadian Library Association, 1998, Blue Heron Book Award shortlist, Red Maple Award finalist, and McNally Robinson Book for Young People finalist, all 1998, CNIB Tiny TORGI Award shortlist, 1999, finalist, National Christian Library Association Lamplighter Award, 1999-2000, and Manitoba Young Readers Choice Award shortlist, 2000, all for *Promise Song;* CBC Literary Award finalist, 1998 and 1999; Vicky Metcalf Short Story Editor Award, 1999; Best Books for the Teen Age, New York City Public Library, finalist, Mr. Christie's Book Award, finalist, Canadian Library Association Young Adult Book Award, finalist, McNally Robinson Book for Young People, and Red Maple Award shortlist, all 1999, all for *Mercy's Birds;* McNally Robinson Book of the Year Award finalist, 2000, for *Devil's Darning Needle;* Our Choice Award, Canadian Children's Book Centre, 2001-2001, McNally Robinson Book for Young People Award, Red Maple Award shortlist, and Young Adult Canadian Book Award nominee, Canadian Library Association, all 2001, Manitoba Young Readers Choice Award Honour Book and Books for the Teen Age, New York Public Library, both 2002, and Saskatchewan Young Readers Choice Award shortlist, 2002-2003, all for *Raspberry House Blues;* Larry Turner Award for Nonfiction, 2001; Poetry in Motion, Manitoba Writers Guild, 2002; nominee, American Library Association's Best Books for Young Adults, 2002-2003.

Writings

Saying Good-bye (young adult short stories), Lester (Toronto, Ontario, Canada), 1995, published as *Toxic Love,* Tundra (Toronto, Ontario, Canada), 2003.
Frankie on the Run (chapter book), illustrated by Heather Collins, Boardwalk Books (Toronto, Ontario, Canada), 1995.

YOUNG ADULT NOVELS

Promise Song, Tundra (Toronto, Ontario, Canada), 1997.
Mercy's Birds, Tundra (Toronto, Ontario, Canada), 1998.
Raspberry House Blues, Tundra (Toronto, Ontario, Canada), 2000.
Search of the Moon King's Daughter, Tundra (Toronto, Ontario, Canada), 2002.

OTHER

Flying to Yellow (short stories; for adults), Turnstone, 1996.
Devil's Darning Needle (short stories; for adults), The Porcupine's Quill, 1999.

Contributor of short stories for adults and young adults to anthologies, including *The Blue Jean Collection,* edited by Peter Carver, Thistledown Press, 1992; *Success Stories for the 90's,* edited by Dorothy Snowman, Institute of Children's Literature, 1994; *Due West,* edited by Wayne Tefs, Turnstone Press, 1996; *Winds Through Time,* edited by Ann Walsh, Beach Holme Press, 1998; *Sight Lines 9,* Prentice Hall, 1999; *Close Ups,* edited by Peter Carver, Red Deer College Press, 2000; and *Girls' Own,* edited by Sarah Ellis, Penguin Books, 2001. Poems and articles have appeared in newspapers, magazines, and journals and anthologies, including *Room of One's Own, Contemporary Verse 2, Canadian Living, NeWest Review, Prarie Fire, Other Voices,* and *Prairie Books Now.* Contributor to *CM: A Reviewing Journal of Canadian Materials for Young People,* 1989-1994. Guest editor for the special young adult issue of *Prairie Fire Magazine,* fall, 1998.

Work in Progress

YA and adult novels.

Sidelights

When she was growing up in Winnipeg, Manitoba, reading and books were an important part of Linda Holeman's life. She kept a diary and scribbled stories and story ideas in journals and scrapbooks. A story she wrote in grade five was selected for broadcast on Canadian Broadcasting Corporation (CBC) Radio's *Story Broadcast Journal.* Although she thought about becoming a writer, Holeman never really believed she could actually do it.

"As a young reader, I dreamed of being a writer in England," she told Dave Jenkinson of *Resource Links,* "because I didn't really think there were any Canadian writers, let alone writers in Winnipeg." As a result, Holeman pushed her dream to the back of her mind and became a teacher.

When her second daughter was born in 1984, she left teaching to stay home with her children—and her thoughts turned to writing again. But five years passed before she woke up one morning and declared that today was the day she would start writing. Keeping her word to herself, she turned out her first manuscript, a seven-hundred-page historical novel for adults that involved a great deal of research. Though Holeman has never tried to have this book published, she believes that writing it was an important exercise. It introduced her to the craft of writing and helped her realize that she needed to learn more.

In 1990, Holeman enrolled in a weekend workshop in writing for children at the University of Manitoba. The piece she took with her to the workshop eventually became "Starlight, Star Bright," the first story in *Saying Good-bye,* her collection for young adults. Although Holeman often started her short stories with adults in mind, they seemed to be taken over by young adult voices. "This young adult voice seems to come to me, not with ease, but ... more readily in many cases than other voices do," she told Jenkinson in *Resource Links.*

When she had completed several stories, Holeman selected three and sent them to publishers, to see if there was any interest. There was, and eventually, ten of Holeman's stories were published in a book entitled *Saying Good-bye,* which was later published under the title *Toxic Love.* In this collection, ordinary teens struggle through the awkward period between dependence on parents and the freedom of adulthood, learning lessons about family, friends, and society along the way. Each story allows the narrator an opportunity to become educated about such life experiences as befriending people unlike oneself, handling an abusive relative, or discovering that affairs of the heart are more complicated than they seem. Reviewing the collection in Toronto *Globe and Mail,* Elizabeth MacCallum said, "At her best, [Holeman] creates characters so familiar that it's almost impossible not to place yourself right in the story. This is a writer who can weave such a spell that a dilemma can become your dilemma and your gut tightens with the stress."

Buoyed by her early success and the praise garnered by her first collection, Holeman gained the confidence to start thinking of herself as a writer. Her next book, *Frankie on the Run,* was a chapter book for young readers. Based on a true story about a hog named Francis who had escaped from a slaughterhouse and was living wild in Red Deer, Alberta, the book started as a story for Holeman's younger daughter, Brenna. Eager to find out what happened to Frankie, Brenna encouraged her mom to finish the story. When it was published, *Quill & Quire* critic Fred Boer called it a "straightforward and entertaining story ... with a comfortably happy ending."

At about the same time, Holeman enrolled in the mentor program sponsored by the Manitoba Writers' Guild and found a way to express her adult voice. The result was *Flying to Yellow,* a collection of fourteen short stories for adults. Though intended for an older audience than the stories in *Saying Good-bye, Flying to Yellow* explores many of the same themes—family, relationships, love, loss, and change—and received similar critical praise.

After focusing on short stories, Holeman was inspired to write her first novel for young adults when she came across a reference to "home boys" in Annie Proulx's prize-winning novel *The Shipping News.* Intrigued, she started digging into the story and discovered that from 1868 to 1925, orphanages in Britain sent abandoned children to Canada to provide farmers with cheap labor. Though the idea behind the scheme was to improve the lot of these orphans, many of them were shamefully mistreated in their new homes. The research sparked Holeman's imagination, and the result was *Promise Song,* the story of fourteen-year-old Rosetta Westley, who is separated from her six-year-old sister and sent to work for a mean-spirited farmer. Despite the harsh situation in which she finds herself, Rosetta is determined to reunite with her sister and to become a teacher. *School Library Journal* contributor Carol A. Edwards said that "Rosetta's pluck and determination make her an admirable heroine, and the story is exciting."

Despite Holeman's successful short stories, she began to feel that she was moving away from the genre. "My short stories are getting longer and longer," she said in *Resource Links.* "They're running away, and I'm finding it harder and harder to rein them in.... It [is] much more freeing to work on one plot, one set of characters, one era, than to work for several weeks in a row, or maybe two weeks here and another two weeks six months later, on one story that's only ten pages long."

Holeman completed another collection of short stories for adults, *Devil's Darning Needle,* and followed up *Promise Song* with three more novels for young adults. In *Mercy's Birds,* Holeman delves into the troubled life of fifteen-year-old Mercy, whose family circumstances have been deteriorating. Mercy must care for her alcoholic aunt and her mother, who is clinically depressed, while dealing with her own fears and insecurities. "The characters are well-developed and realistic; Holeman addresses poverty, abuse, and depression with compassion and a perceptive eye," wrote Shelle Rosenfeld in *Booklist*. "Eloquent and impacting, Mercy's story is an engrossing one." In *Raspberry House Blues,* the reader learns the story of Poppy, whose adoptive mother leaves with her boyfriend, leading to Poppy's decision to live with her adoptive father and his new family. Poppy's odyssey to find her birth mother and a family is one of self-discovery. Janet Hilbun, writing in the *School Library Journal,* called *Raspberry House Blues* "an appealing book with a host of unusual characters that will worm their way into readers' hearts."

Set in England in the 1830s, during the Industrial Revolution, *Search of the Moon King's Daughter* deals with child exploitation. This work of historical fiction follows fifteen-year-old Emmaline from her peaceful life in Lancashire into the dark heart of the cotton mill area surrounding Manchester. When her mother succumbs to the lure of laudanum and sells Emmaline's beloved younger brother into the chimney sweep business, Emmaline journeys into London to find him. "Issues involving the use of children through the epochs—their exploitation and the treatment they have received at unscrupulous hands—have always held a grim fascination for me," Holman told *SATA*. "And of course it still exists, which is even more difficult for me to come to terms with. Perhaps writing about it is my way of dealing with it. When we write, I believe there is a certain element of us coming face-to-face with our own fears."

"[Writing] never gets easier," Holeman once commented, "but, underneath all the pain, there is deep, abiding love for this thing I do, this thing that 'belongs' to me, which I am responsible for and can never abandon. This blessing—this love of taking words and creating stories."

Biographical and Critical Sources

BOOKS

Pendergast, Tom, and Sara Pendergast, editors, *St. James Guide to Young Adult Writers,* 2nd edition, St. James Press (Detroit, MI), 1999.

PERIODICALS

Booklist, December 15, 1998, Shelle Rosenfeld, review of *Mercy's Birds,* p. 748.
Children's Book News, spring, 1996, pp. 18-19.
Globe and Mail (Toronto, Canada), April 15, 1995, Elizabeth MacCallum, "Writer's Skill Puts Reader Right into the Story."
Publishers Weekly, December 18, 2000, review of *Raspberry House Blues,* p. 79.
Quill & Quire, April, 1995, p. 38; April, 1996, p. 30; February, 1997, pp. 55-56; December, 1995, Fred Boer, review of *Frankie on the Run,* p. 39; February, 1998, Susan Lawrence, "The Best in 1997 Children's Books," p. 42.
Resource Links, October, 1996, Dave Jenkinson, "Profiles: Linda Holeman," pp. 8-11.
School Library Journal, October, 1997, Carol A. Edwards, review of *Promise Song,* pp. 132-133; March, 1999, Lucinda Lockwood, review of *Mercy's Birds,* p. 748; December, 2000, Janet Hilbun, review of *Raspberry House Blues,* p. 145.
Voice of Youth Advocates, December, 1998, Joyce Sparrow, review of *Mercy's Birds,* p. 356.

OTHER

Achuka, http://achuka.com/can/holeman.htm/ (January 16, 2001), "Linda Holeman Special Feature."
Linda Holeman's Home Page, http://www.lindaholeman.com/ (November, 19, 2001).

* * *

Autobiography Feature

Linda Holeman

My earliest memories are of noise and colour. I spent my first ten years living in a tall, narrow house on Aikens Street, in Winnipeg's ethnic and much written about "North End." In the province of Manitoba, the North End has always been a haven for new citizens to Canada, and sings with a cacophony of different languages and music.

The North End was also home to my father. He was born to Russian immigrants—his father Tonia had arrived in the States via Paris, born in St. Petersburg, his mother Luba came alone to Ellis Island, a fifteen-year-old girl from a village near Odessa. It was prior to World War I. Tonia and Luba met in Hartford, Connecticut, had a whirlwind courtship, and married within a few months. They were unlike as any two people ever thrown together.

My grandfather Tonia was from a family of dreamers and armchair philosophers with a love of travel. They worked hard and money was often a problem, but they still found time for reading, study, and heated discussions on politics, literature, and history. Grandma Luba was from a peasant family; her mother gave birth to twelve children, but only four survived childhood.

With the lure of free land that was offered to immigrants in the second decade of the twentieth century, Tonia and Luba, along with Tonia's parents, some of his ten siblings and their families, chose to come to Canada. They had also been offered land in Texas. With only a map to help them make their decision, they chose Manitoba, in central Canada, more familiar geographically to their home of Russia.

They were given and settled on a plot of land around Camper, about 130 miles north of Winnipeg. My father, Leon, the first of four children, was born shortly after they moved to "the farm" in Camper. Although they had no experience as farmers, the extended family managed to eke out a simple livelihood. Speaking only Russian, they lived in close, fairly primitive quarters in the scrub landscape of Manitoba's Interlake region. It must have been terribly difficult for my grandmother, a young girl thrown into the midst of a large family that quite possibly looked down on her for her inexperience and youth. At sixteen, she was thirteen years younger than her husband, and had nowhere near his level of education or worldly understanding. I think she was a bit wild—pictures of her as a newlywed show a big, robust girl with thick black wavy hair and long green eyes. I imagine her as possessing an enchanting gypsy persona, for somehow she had charmed my quiet-spoken, philosophical, and gentlemanly grandfather.

When it was time for my father to start school, my grandparents left the farm and moved into the North End of Winnipeg, where their own voices mixed comfortably with the blend of Polish, Yiddish, and Ukrainian.

It's important to know that Manitoba has always been a cultural melting pot. Situated squarely in the centre of Canada, the "keystone" province, so named for its shape, it's bordered on the south by North Dakota; if you go far enough north you will hit Hudson Bay. It's prairie land, but there are over one hundred thousand lakes in Manitoba, so basically we're about water and wheat. In winter the temperature can drop below minus thirty, while in the summer the high nineties can be expected. There is a lot of wind, and yearly summer plagues of mosquitoes. If there is too much snow in the winter the Red River, which runs through Winnipeg, may flood its banks. The ground can alternately be described as stony or "gumbo." This is not a place for the fainthearted. But we have the sky—the huge, open sky, and out beyond the city limits you really can see forever. Nothing stops the vision. Our sunsets are worth painting; our vast stretches of land inspire poetry.

Tonia got a job with General Steelwares, and his feet had to stay planted on the ground to feed his family of three sons and a daughter. Later he worked for the Canadian National Railroad, and my father told me that Grandpa Tonia loved the sound of the trains coming and going—it gave him a bittersweet feel of journeys so close, although because of his family responsibilities he could no longer travel. Even though he died before I could know him, I'm sure it is from this man that I inherited a restlessness, a shuffling unease at staying in one spot, a desire to see and know the world, and a curiosity about the human condition.

When my father started school he could only speak Russian, but he was a quick learner. Education was stressed, but even though he graduated from high school with top marks, and sometimes poignantly spoke of a boyish dream of medical school, further education was out of the question. Instead, he entered the blue-collar work-force alongside his father at General Steelwares, and later at Manitoba Hydro, in order to help out at home.

My mother's family was, in contrast, steeped in Anglo-Saxon heritage. No obvious dreamers, they were thrifty and lived by the strict Protestant work ethic—work before pleasure, nose to the grindstone, stiff upper lip. My mother's father, Robert, of Scottish descent, grew up on a farm near the town of Miami, in the fertile rolling fields of southern Manitoba. My maternal grandmother, Lily, was born to Irish parents in Iowa, but the family, in search of greener pastures, moved to Canada when Lily was a young adult. Tiny, opinionated, and strong-willed, she met Bob in Winnipeg as he recovered from a severe leg wound suffered in World War I (he eventually lost his leg, and I always knew him with a wooden leg, which fascinated and distressed me when I was a child). When they married, Lily, a practising Catholic, gave up her religion for Robert. She loved him enough to relinquish her creed and raise their seven children in her husband's Anglican faith—even though he never again set foot inside a church once they were married.

My mother, Donna, was the second oldest of the six daughters and one son born to Bob and Lily. She had the striking Irish combination of blue-black hair and brilliant blue eyes, and a ready, generous smile. A rebellious spirit, she was as strong-willed as her own mother—and for that reason the two were always at loggerheads. She didn't like school, but struggled through, eventually going into nurses' training.

She and my father met at a dance in Winnipeg in the 1940s while my mother was completing her nursing degree. During the war years my father trained armed forces in communications, including Morse code. He had a knack for electronics which would eventually lead him into his own lifelong business. My father was quite handsome—dapper is the word that comes to mind when I look at pictures of him while he was in his twenties—very suave and polished. He also had great physical skill and endurance, and, for a number of years belonged to the Winnipeg Athletics Association. With this troupe of young men and women he travelled around the province, putting on impressive shows including gymnastic routines, building human pyramids, tossing wooden clubs, and other acts of physical prowess. He impressed my mother with his manners and quiet sense of humour. They were married when the war ended.

So there they were, these two people with completely dissimilar backgrounds. My father—the child of Russian emigrants, whose past lives carried a kind of hushed intrigue with their tales of tzars and a younger brother stolen by Tatars and the terror of the Russian Revolution and hurried exchanges of suitcases of money in a Paris hotel room. My mother—the offspring of farmers who mainly knew the land, who studied the sky and rubbed soil between their fingers.

They found their own home in the North End, and my father started a radio (and later television) repair business in the basement of the house. My mother quit nursing; my

Linda Holeman, 2001

brother Gregory was born in 1947; I was born Christmas Eve, 1949. Next came my brothers Randall, in 1953, and Tim, in 1955, and finally a sister, Shannon, in 1958. We all lived in the old and rather cramped house on Aikens Street, its backyard the size of a handkerchief and no front yard at all. The street was lined with other narrow houses set within an arm's reach of each other, most filled with three generations. The cracked sidewalks were always teeming with bicycles and baby carriages and dogs. My school—Champlain Elementary—was just around the corner. St. John's United Church, where I attended Sunday school, was a five-minute walk away. Going east for two blocks I hit Main Street, with its delicatessens and ethnic restaurants and shops and both the College and the Deluxe, movie theatres that played a double bill and cartoons every Saturday for fifteen cents. If I went one block west I was at the St. John's Public Library. And best of all was

Rosenblatt's Grocery, right next door to our house, on the corner of Aikens and Machray. The store was in the front of the building, and Mr. and Mrs. Rosenblatt and their three children lived at the back. The Rosenblatts were good neighbours and kind people. I was in and out of that store a dozen times a day—running errands for my mother or grandmother, or simply to press my nose against the glass window of the candy counter.

Adelman's was on the corner of Anderson and Salter, and I had to run in and out of the store at least four times a day for things Baba Lu needed for her cooking and baking.

Mr. and Mrs. Adelman never closed their store. They lived in the back and only locked the front door when they went to bed at night. Sometimes Mrs. Adelman would motion for me to come in to the tiny, crowded kitchen behind the linoleum-covered counter. She always wanted me to have a bite to eat. "So skinny, Natalie," she'd say, wringing her hands and pinching my cheeks. Then she'd offer me matzo spread thinly with sharp horseradish, or a spoonful of steaming chicken broth swimming with eyes of fat, or a nut-powdered cookie shaped like a slice of the moon.

"Baba Lu," from *Saying Good-bye*

It was a microcosm—my own little world, with everything I thought was needed to make life complete. My now-widowed grandma Luba lived in a series of small apartments, always within a few blocks of our home. She would stop by our house every day, and often I would walk to visit her. She was a huge part of my life, and I loved her deeply. I never saw her read, but on Saturday nights she'd listen to opera on the radio, her fingers always moving over the cutwork or cross-stitch in her lap. She created beautiful handiwork—tablecloths and runners and pillowcases—some of which I still own and treasure today.

Like Grandma, my parents were not readers. I never remember seeing either read a book; in essence, they found life too busy for any form of recreation. My father worked night and day to establish his business. My mother had five children within eleven years. Money was always tight, and she worked hard to make ends meet. She also helped my father with his growing business the entire time, answering phones and dealing with customers during the day and doing the paperwork at night. She also kindly and patiently gave Grandma, who was often depressed through the early years after Grandpa's death, daily attention. My oldest brother Gregory was diagnosed with brain cancer when he was five. I was three. Greg survived, after treatments of cobalt bomb—the only course open to cancer patients at the time. My mother had a full plate.

I learned the wonder of the printed word when I started school. How well I remember the absolute pleasure of realizing that I could read. It was grade one, and I was in Miss Anderson's class. We had the very typical and unimaginative Dick and Jane books of the fifties: Dick. Here is Dick. Look, Dick. Here is Jane, and so on. It seemed that from the time I picked up that first book, I understood the black marks. Miss Anderson saw me reading through the book, turning the pages quickly, and gently scolded me. I must only read with the class, one or two pages a day, and then spend endless time printing out the word of the day. I could barely stand it. The worst part was that the whole class, probably thirty children or more, all had to move at the same pace. And Miss Anderson, bless her well-meaning soul—she was a very sweet, older lady—devised a ridiculous method of making sure none of us who finished our work before the others got into mischief (like reading ahead in the book). She would assign our rows of printing or workbook page, and when we were done, we had to lay down our pencils and stand beside our desks. Think of the logistics of this. I was always done first. One by one, the rest of the class would finish and stand up. It must have played havoc on the psyche of those children who were always last. All I know is that I spent much of grade one standing beside my desk, impatient and frustrated.

The pattern for my success in the classroom continued through grade four. I loved reading, and was always at the library. I suppose my mother must have taken me the first time, to get a library card, but I only have memories of going by myself. I loved the library, its broad stone steps leading to thick double doors, the hushed atmosphere and comforting bookish smell. There were warm hardwood floors, gleaming deep wooden shelves, and even a working fireplace. Story Time was on Saturday mornings, and although I was capable of reading the book chosen by the "story lady," I liked the feeling of being read to.

Mine was a very typical North American working-class family of the fifties. My father was soft-spoken, kind, yet distracted by his work. My mother disciplined us and oversaw our lives. We had no money for extras—although my mother somehow found enough to pay for my piano lessons—but we didn't lack for anything. All my friends were in the same situation; we wore hand-me-downs and played with whatever was available. During good weather we roved in small bands of children dragging toddler sisters and brothers, dogs at our heels, to the schoolyard. There we played scattered rounds of baseball, or threw balls against the school in games of Seven-Up, or skipped rope. In the winter we skated on the outside rink in nearby Peanut Park; we built snow forts. We stayed outside until it was dark or we were hungry. Every night, in bed, I read: a habit I have never lost.

The Christmas I was eight I was given a small white Bible. I made a pact with myself to read the whole Bible

The Freeman family, 1957: (back, left) Greg, Linda, parents Donna and Leon, (front) Randy, Tim, and Bimbo

that year. I did read all of Genesis and made it partway through Exodus, and then gave it up, guiltlessly, for the pleasures of Enid Blyton and her Adventure Series. I also read all the sad dog stories I could find. I wept as I read *Lassie Come Home* and *Greyfriar's Bobby,* enjoying the melancholy that these tales of loyalty and blind devotion brought out in me. I read the requisite Nancy Drew and Trixie Belden and Cherry Ames and Hardy Boy books, and then all that Louisa May Alcott and Laura Ingalls Wilder had written. And, strangely enough, I devoured, with great interest, a collection of books about scientists. I can see them today on that library shelf labeled Nonfiction: the plain, dull covers with only the scientist's name printed on the front. George Washington Carver. Thomas Alva Edison. All the scientists had three names.

Life was incredibly simple. I wasn't aware of my brother's illness, or my parents' struggle with money, or my grandmother's depression. We had dogs and cats that I adored, I had a best friend—Vera—as well as lots of others, I loved school.

I had only one fear—that my mother would die.

I was haunted by that image a lot—my mother dying. I loved my mother with a fierce neediness that she was never aware of. When she wasn't home I grew restless and uneasy. And I learned, early, the weight of separation and longing.

My first experience with these emotions came when I was five. My mother sent me to her sister in the country for a visit with my cousin, who was my age. This pattern kept up for a number of years, being sent to Manitoba farms and small towns to stay with one or another of my mother's sisters and their families (I had twenty-three cousins on my mother's side). I suffered so badly from homesickness that I thought it might kill me. I missed my mother with unbearable longing—but never told her. So she continued sending me (often by Greyhound Bus, alone, which was also frightening to me as a child) for what she imagined was an enjoyable holiday.

Every night on those imposed "holidays," as soon as I got into whatever bed I was sleeping in with whatever cousin or cousins, I would cry, always trying to stifle my sobbing. All I could envision in the darkness was the last image I had seen from the bus window—my mother's smiling face, her hand lifted in a wave as the bus pulled away from the depot. I knew, with a grim certainty, that while I was away she would be killed in some terrible mishap. The mishaps varied, but the deadly outcome was inevitable. I couldn't stop the stories and pictures unfolding in my head. I even played out her funeral over and over, creating scenes from the books I had read. I was always standing near the open plot as her coffin was being lowered. I wept with unbelievable fervour. Most certainly my cousins heard me; surely my eyes were puffy and red each morning, but nothing was ever said. I didn't tell my mother this fear until I was an adult. She's still alive today, over eighty, funny and spirited and loving. What brought out that dark side of me, those obsessive fears? My mother attributes it to an overly active imagination, to being oversensitive. All my life I've been told by a long succession of family and friends that I'm too sensitive. But how lucky to feel too much, rather than too little. After all, aren't imagination and sensitivity to the world a necessary facet of a writer's makeup?

I didn't want to spend my July here, at my aunt and uncle's farm. But I wasn't given a choice; I had been left there for four long weeks while my parents had 'time to themselves.'... And so I took a Greyhound to the town nearest my aunt and uncle's farm and was picked up by my Auntie Tess, my mother's only sister, who acted as if my visit was a wonderful event that she and Uncle Mike and my cousins, Marsha and Loreen, were thrilled about. But Auntie Tess was the only one who could carry out this charade of joy at my arrival.

"The Summer Goldie Died," from *Devil's Darning Needle*

In spite of the unspoken fear, mine was a good childhood: although unenhanced by an excess of material goods, mind-broadening travel, or cultural inspiration, it was secure.

I knew every street and alley of my neighbourhood, and roamed freely. The routines of my home rarely varied; my parents were even-tempered and openly supported each other. I felt loved, although the word was never spoken and rarely physically demonstrated. I was simply one of five children, not particularly singled out, not particularly ignored. I was asked for little, and asked little in return. I was oblivious to even the possibility of anything ever changing.

The changes began when we left the North End. My mother had wanted to move away for some time; the area had a certain roughness to it, the recklessness that occurs when people come and go, when houses are rented out, when a lifestyle is temporary. She was tired of the crowded house with its steep narrow stairs, the lack of yard for us to play. She was concerned for our safety, weary of barking dogs and neighbours' arguments keeping her awake at night. My mother had dreams of a bungalow—no stairs—of green spaces for us to play, of safe, wide streets. Of a garden. My father's business was doing well: he had recently moved from our basement into a building on Main Street.

My mother found a "ranch house"—the darling architecture of the late fifties and early sixties—on Rowandale Crescent, on the new edge of the suburb of East Kildonan. Most houses didn't have lawns yet, just mud. There were no mature trees, but shrubs and twiggy saplings held in place by poles and twine. We had a large, pie-shaped back yard. A two-car garage. There were four bedrooms on the main floor; the basement had a panelled rec room, a big playroom, and another bathroom. Luxury! My mother was in her glory.

But I was thrown into a panic. I was a stranger in a strange land, an alien set down on a treeless planet. The quiet street outside our sealed living room picture window seemed uninhabited. There were no endless shouts and laughter from neighbours, no ringing of bicycle bells, no honks from the delivery trucks at Rosenblatt's Grocery. The main street, Henderson Highway, had big, new, and impersonal stores. There were no theatres, no tantalizing odors of home-cooked food, no daily visits with my beloved grandmother. And no library.

I spent a miserable summer, sulkily playing with my brothers or looking after my sweet two-year-old sister—

whom I adored—while my mother happily planted her dreamed-of garden, complete with rows and rows of raspberry canes. In the fall I started grade five at a small school, Angus McKay. It was about three-quarters of a mile away; I had to walk there, then home for lunch and back, then finally home at four o'clock. Winter in Winnipeg is bitterly cold. I suffered painful frostbite on my cheeks and nose. The white, empty streets made my home appear even more barren, and I learned the term pathetic fallacy. My emotions were reflected in what I saw as a cold, barren environment.

School was a wholly different experience now. At Champlain School the teachers had held up my work as an example to the other students. I received awards for being first in class. I confidently spoke out, often recounting stories that related to class topics. I was relied on to run notes to the office. Of course I was a teacher's pet. But in spite of what must have been a gagging Pollyanna persona, I had been popular. Not so here, at Angus McKay. Many other kids excelled at their work, and I was simply one of a number of good students. And something else happened. I stopped telling stories.

It was because of a boy named Bruce. As I eagerly raised my hand, yet another time, to add something to what the teacher was saying, Bruce turned and stared at me. Then he said, to no one in particular and yet to everyone, "There she goes again. Linda thinks she has a story about everything. She never shuts up." I clearly remember the look on his face, the tone of his voice.

I put down my hand, deeply shamed. Bruce was making fun of me. It was a terrifying moment of self-consciousness, the awakening of the realization that I was—at least in Bruce's opinion—a fool. Did everyone else feel the same? A painful hot flush ran through my body. The teacher, Mrs. Bean, strict but fair, reprimanded him, and asked what it was I had to say, but I just shook my head. And that was the end of my storytelling, at least in class.

I was—to use the phrase of that era—crushed. Why? Bruce was just one kid, one loud-mouth. But what happened was to set the tone for me from then on. I can no more explain my sudden painful consciousness of self than I can explain the sound of my laugh or the thickness of my hair. Maybe my mother was right—I was just oversensitive. But all I know is that I stopped talking in class. I did my work, and I answered when called upon, but I didn't want to be noticed. I tried to make myself small, which was difficult, seeing as I grew to my adult height of five feet six inches that year. And I realized I was a bit of a loner.

But all was not lost that first year at Angus McKay. As well as making a new best friend, Anita (she continues to be my "best friend" to this day), I discovered the joy of writing.

As a treat, for one hour each week for a month—it was November, grey skies and scattering of hard snow against the classroom windows—we listened to an hour-long radio show on CBC called "Let's Write a Story Broadcast." During this hour, a disembodied voice would read stories, talk about the writing of these tales, and then give out a writing assignment. One week the assignment was "Three Magic Words." With the three words given, I wrote "An African Adventure." Apparently teachers were encouraged to send their students' work in to the show. Mine was one

sent, and one chosen to be published in a booklet that highlighted what the program considered the "best" writing of the entries submitted. Mrs. Bean told me about my success in front of the class, and gave me the booklet. I still have it—my first publication. As well, my story was read over the radio later that week, and I sat in class, cheeks burning and head down, listening to my own words read in a sonorous male voice. It was a moment of quiet triumph, a realization that for me, it was much better to write my stories than to tell them.

I still continued to read with wild passion—and what made my friendship with Anita so wonderful was that like me, she had loner tendencies, and she loved to read every bit as much as I did. In contrast to our serious sides, we were giggly and totally spontaneous and uninhibited when it was just the two of us.

Later that year, a small library was built in the basement of a strip mall near my house. Henderson Library had no deep wooden shelves of books, no hardwood floors, no fireplace. No windows. It was a rectangular box filled with row after row of metal bookshelves, its floors cold linoleum. And, in a convoluted twist of planning, directly across the hall from the library was a bowling alley. The drop and rumbling roll of heavy balls, the crash of spares and strikes and the ensuing cheers and whistles of happy bowlers echoed through the glass doors into the library.

But there were books. Not many at first; the shelves were quite empty when the library first opened. But there were enough for Anita and me to go to that library every day, on our way home from school. We'd make our choices, then go to either her house or mine. We'd lay across our beds, or on the floor, or, weather permitting, in the backyard, and read. The next day, on our way to the library again, we'd talk about what we'd read. We were our own literary circle of two. We were thinking about how stories worked, and how they made us feel.

We decided to become writers when we grew up. We would move to England and write our books in the tower of an old castle. We would, naturally, be quite famous. That fantasy floated in my head for a long time.

Then junior high brought me back to earth with a resounding thud.

I realized this "loner" aspect of my personality more and more as I entered my teens. I'd never wanted to participate in any childhood organizations—no sports teams, no summer camps, no Girl Guides. I was happiest on my own, or in the company of a few good friends. It was obvious, even then, that I was a very private person, and I suppose I created a kind of invisible barrier around myself.

Those three years at John Henderson Junior High passed in a kind of slinking anonymity. Anita went to a private school, so I lost my ally in this unforgiving no-man's land. A number of the girls I knew were already into heavy makeup and parties where they mastered the Twist, the Pony, and the Mashed Potato, as well as the fine art of making out with boys. I was reading, riding my bike through the twisting monkey trails near the river, collecting leaves and ironing them between wax paper, keeping copious journals and recording what I'd dreamed each night, and writing carefully rhymed poetry and attempts at stories.

I didn't really feel left out; the activities of so many other girls weren't appealing to me. But I was mesmerized by finding out the details of their lives. I became a voyeur in the girls' washroom at school, watching the application of makeup, the torture of the lash curler, the "tsking" over runs in nylon stockings. I watched, and listened. It was the beginning of my training to be a writer—any writer will tell you that observing and listening are ways to "find" stories.

Six months after her mother's accident, Lila started junior high. She had no real friends in the noisy school with the battered lockers and dingy narrow halls. She knew she had nothing to attract the other girls—no older sister with a wardrobe and diary to plunder, no older brother who might attract a friend or two, no TV, no record player and pile of 45s to dance to, nothing. She hadn't had a best friend since Betty Ann.

Lila was overcome with a desire to be more acceptable, to be like the girls she admired, the girls with high back combed hair, thick pancake make-up, and puzzling trails of small bruises on their heavily perfumed necks. Betty Ann was now one of these girls, a girl with sideways glances from under half-lowered lids, a swaying walk.

"Sighs for Lila," from *Flying to Yellow*

But no one ever teased or bullied me; actually I was treated with a kind of respectful distance. I was simply there, on the fringes of the school population. My marks were decent. I loved singing in the school choir. I was competent in sports, but was completely noncompetitive. I never drew attention to myself.

I liked it this way. I didn't want to be noticed. If people were watching me, then I couldn't watch them. I liked being on the outside of the main circle, where I could study the often mysterious behaviour of my peers and teachers.

Large events took place outside my little world of junior high. President Kennedy was assassinated, men were being sent into space, bomb shelters were being built in case of nuclear attack. What were my thoughts about these things? I recorded them all, in great detail, on those evenings I spent with my journals.

I was never, ever, without a number of books on the go. The one that had the greatest impact on me, during my thirteenth year, was *The Diary of Anne Frank.*

I was babysitting for a neighbour. After I put the kids to bed I read the book from cover to cover. As I finished the last page, I finally looked up, unaware of where I was or how long I'd been reading. I was sitting in a comfortable easy chair, the only illumination in the house the bright circle from the floor lamp behind my chair. I sat in that enclosed ring of light, something stirring deep inside me. This was a girl, my age, who had lived an extraordinary life, although at the time she of course couldn't see the larger picture, or how this registering of her life would affect generations to come. She had simply recorded her life, and now it was a book. And it was a book that had a huge impact on me, as I realized that while the lives of presidents and astronauts were large, small lives also had an impact. They could make people *feel.* And I was feeling so much, in that darkened living room, in the late hours of that night, that I had to fight to control my breathing.

Linda at age eight, with her beloved Grandma Luba

One girl had done this to me—and to how many other thousands? That a piece of writing could do this was overwhelming. Imagine. *This is what I want to do.* But in the same instant I dismissed it. After all, who was I to dare think this way? Who did I think I was?

It appeared to me, around this time, that I was destined to live a life where nothing real happened. I was sure I would live without knowing real love, or real grief, and exist only on the details of the lives I read about. But just before the final days of school, in June of 1963, something real did happen.

My brother Greg died, a month short of his sixteenth birthday, finally a victim of the cancer that had been waiting to reemerge from the time he was five.

This was perhaps the most troubling and confusing time I have had in my life. Of course there was grief, but more than that was suppressed anger and confusion. The days leading up to Greg's death, and that long and dreadful summer afterward, had a surreal feeling, as if I were trapped inside a foggy bubble, unable to hear or see properly. I was just waiting it out, waiting for the bubble to pop, so that I could understand. But there was no pop. The bubble simply evaporated over time, eking away with infuriating slowness.

I think this—the silence and confusion and my ensuing anger—affected me more than the actual death of my brother. I was angry at Greg and at my parents, and also somehow ashamed, as if our family had committed an unspeakable crime, something that had to be covered up and never spoken of again.

But I believe that summer—the silent, sad summer I was slowly marching toward my fourteenth birthday—had an impact on me, as did my ungrounded terror over losing my mother, that was to shape much of what I wrote about decades later. I know that those fears—loss and separation, a desperate attempt to make sense of what was hurting, to find the way to connect again—was to become my theme.

I was terribly unworldly. There was no art in my home, no classical music, few books, no excursions to galleries or museums. But I did have one tiny thread to the world outside of Rowandale Crescent and Winnipeg, through Alex, my father's cousin.

Alex lived in New York, travelled widely with his job, and sent us postcards from all over the globe. And, as a present to my parents one year, he gave them a subscription to the *New Yorker,* which he renewed every Christmas for over a decade.

I was fascinated by the cosmopolitan essence of the *New Yorker.* I memorized, without understanding, the magazine's poetry. I whispered the free verse to myself in the bathtub, or while I ironed my father's shirts, or roamed the monkey trails. I loved the rhythm and cadence of the words in my mouth. I read short stories by John Cheever and Eudora Welty and John Updike. While I struggled to make sense of them I savoured the flow and shape of the work, the strange edge to these stories that were unlike any I had ever read.

Alex's postcards and the *New Yorker* helped to open my eyes to what I considered the real world. By the time I was ready for high school, that world felt tantalizing, agonizing, just beyond my fingertips.

When I started River East Collegiate, I tentatively opened the barrier I had kept around me for the last five years. My circle of good friends grew, although Anita remained a constant. I had boyfriends, went to parties, and grew as concerned about my appearance as those girls in the washroom in junior high. I still wasn't big on group activities, but I did join the Travelogue Club, and I signed on to the staff of the school newspaper, the *Scope.* Both of these had an impact on my future.

I loved Travelogue—sitting in the darkened classroom after school on Wednesdays while blurry reels of Malta or Iceland droned on the projector. I watched, each week, with growing excitement, sometimes even researching the country later. I pored over the ever-growing collection of postcards from Alex. I couldn't believe that I had never left Winnipeg—never been further than a hundred miles outside of the city. It infuriated me—that the whole world was out there, and I was stuck in this windy city in the middle of the Canadian prairies. It was during those Travelogue classes that I vowed I would see the world. I didn't know how, but I knew I couldn't wait too long. I still have a quote by Marcel Proust that I copied back then: "The voyage of discovery lies not in finding new land-scapes, but in having new eyes." But I wanted my eyes made new *through* new landscapes.

As to the *Scope*—I'm ashamed to say now that I did not make strong political statements or explore current events. No. My contribution to each issue was the Fashion Column. Fashion! I cringe as I write this, but I was suddenly into fashion in a big way. I studied the latest magazines with fervour, writing that column with true passion. If nothing else, I did learn to write a tight column, and realized how natural writing about anything felt to me. I realized it was something I could do well.

My interest in clothes had hit as I was finishing junior high. There was no money at home for anything but a few very serviceable and conservative outfits; if I wanted new and stylish clothes it was up to me to get them. So that summer before I started high school I got my first "real" job, other than babysitting. I was an A&W car hop. I made sixty cents an hour.

With my carefully saved earnings, I bought material and patterns. We had an ancient, unpredictable portable Singer sewing machine in the basement. I eventually mastered the stubborn old thing, and using some of the scant knowledge I had gleaned in junior high home ec classes, taught myself how to sew—how to put in zippers and use a buttonholer and even to devise my own patterns.

For my sixteenth birthday my parents gave me a new sewing machine. It was green, a Brother cabinet, and an amazing improvement over the Singer. I was thrilled, and there were many nights when my mother had to come to my bedroom door and tell me to get to sleep—it was after two in the morning and there I was, hunched over the sewing machine as it whirred along, the material pliant and willing under my fingertips—and I had to be up for school in five hours. I made all my clothes through high school. I do think now that part of this obsession with designing and making clothes was a form of my need to create things. It had been a pattern through my life to that point, whether building structures with my brothers' Meccano sets, doing jigsaw or crossword puzzles, or making dollhouse furniture out of cardboard and toothpicks. The pattern was a desire to create a whole from single pieces that must fit together smoothly. Exactly what goes into writing a story or novel.

I always had a job. When A&W lost its charm I worked at the snack bar at the local Safeway, and after that made pizza at a hole-in-the-wall called Pizza To Go Go. For one summer I worked as a file clerk in a huge old building downtown. I was cloistered in a long windowless room made up of tall wood cabinets. I had to file manila folders containing uninteresting purchase and shipping orders from a massive wire basket. When my basket was empty I took it back to a main office and was handed another full one. In a strange way the job suited me; I could do the work effortlessly, and was free to dream and make up stories to my heart's content. I could even talk out loud, in the voices of my characters. There was no one there but me. I realize I was in the very situation that I now urge my creative writing students to search out as time to think through the stories they are working on—a time involving silence, monotony, and rhythm. This is a pattern where my best productive thoughts come—in the repetition of mindless tasks, such as raking leaves, painting a wall, or, terrible thought—washing dishes. So those times in the file room were peaceful, creative times for me.

But all of this: the jobs, the sewing late into the night, and my active social life were taking a toll on my interest in school, and on my marks.

Things were changing at home. My parents were recovering from Greg's death. My father's business was doing well. My mother now had a bit of her own time, and began reading, finding special interest in metaphysics. She also worked as a private nurse.

I awoke to the fact that my mother and father were truly interesting. They were fun-loving and each had a wonderful and different sense of humour, and had no problem laughing at themselves. My mother was a consummate storyteller. She always saw the funny side of a situation. When Randy and Tim and I were teenagers, and Shannon on the cusp of adolescence, she regaled all of us—and any friends we had over for supper—with hilarious tales. Many were of her own childhood, and a great many more were of her days in nursing. She didn't mince words, and had a delicious sense of timing. There was a great deal of laughter around our dinner table in those years. We were also encouraged to tell our stories. My forte was imitating teachers—emphasizing small behaviours or idiosyncrasies, and making everyone laugh. I was filled with reckless joy at capturing my family's attention. I told stories of what transpired at school or at my part-time job or with my friends. Usually these stories were huge exaggerations, strictly for humour or shock effect. It was here, safe and comfortable with my parents and siblings and good friends, that I honed my storytelling skills.

I never stopped reading, or recording my life, although I was still too shy in school to speak out much. The only class I really loved was English, because an assignment to read a novel was a treat. My favourites of those assigned novels were Hardy's *Tess of the D'Urbervilles* and *Ethan Frome,* by Edith Wharton. English was the one bright light in an otherwise long and, sadly, boring day. I can't blame anybody for my failure to be engaged or even vaguely interested in what I was learning. My reticence to ask for help or voice an opinion added to the situation. I also didn't think of asking my parents to help with my homework when I was stuck. I simply did the work with as little effort as possible, and my marks were an indication of that attitude. My parents were very casual about school; my mother's mantra was "do your best." Actually my mother and father didn't impose many heavy-handed rules. They expected us to go on to university, but other than that were rarely critical and didn't appear disappointed in our choices. They were confident in our abilities; they trusted us to make our own way in the world. In many ways this was incredibly freeing.

My first escapes from Winnipeg were in 1967, when I was seventeen—hitchhiking from place to place with friends—down into the States and east into Ontario. I didn't tell my parents about my method of travel, because I knew they'd forbid it. But hitchhiking saved money, and the experiences—very fortunately—were always positive. There were lots of young people on the road in the late sixties—in vans and beat-up old cars, the beginning of the Love and Peace, flowers-in-your-hair era. The ease of that time lulled us all into the belief that it was one big old road, and anyone with a thumb out deserved a ride by a friendly stranger.

I loved being a young person in the late sixties, even though the U.S. involvement in Vietnam was devastating for families across the border. Occasionally I met boys who had slipped up to Winnipeg from the States, but it all felt far-away and unreal. To me, life was new and shiny and exciting. School took a back burner. I was having a great time—so great that I didn't do well enough to graduate with my grade-twelve class. I was short one subject, having failed math repeatedly, which meant I couldn't start university until I made up that credit. It only bothered me a little, this glitch in my future. There is no excuse for my lax attitude, although perhaps I can attribute it to the spirit of the times, part of the flower-child generation's axiom—to "go with the flow" and hang loose.

At my father's insistence that I have some training that would get me a "decent" job for the year before I went to university, I sullenly signed up for a short-term secretarial course. Although I refused to admit it, I actually derived great pleasure in the typing classes—in a room full of clacking old manual Underwoods—and learning shorthand. I loved the idea of transcribing words into this secret language of tiny chicken scratches. For a number of months I even wrote in my nightly journal in shorthand.

As soon as I'd completed the course I hopped on a series of trains and made my way to Indiana to stay with Anita in her dorm at Goshen College. I hung out all day, sometimes going to classes with Anita, and partied at night for over a month. My time there made me anxious to start university—and not just for the parties. I suddenly felt that I was wasting time, and was annoyed at myself for not working harder at high school.

Eventually I came back to Winnipeg and got a job at Household Finance, a money-lending firm. I hated every-

At age sixteen, with sister, Shannon

World travels in an old van, Spain, 1973

thing about the conservative office job, but needing the money, I stuck it out until the beginning of September, when I started university.

My dream, initially, was for a degree in journalism. I imagined I could make a career out of the one thing I loved—writing. But the only university in Canada offering journalism then was Carleton, in Ottawa, twelve hundred miles east. The expenses involved in going to an out-of-province university were prohibitive for my family. I suppose if my will had been strong enough, I would have saved and borrowed enough money and gone, but the idea of venturing there alone, with no real support system, was too huge for me to get my head around at that time. So I opted for a basic bachelor of arts program at the University of Winnipeg, a small and friendly down-town campus.

I assumed I'd major in English. But my Intro English class didn't excite me the way I thought it would. I did read, outside of classes, widely and wildly, with no real direction. I'd spend hours in bookstores at the remainder bins, looking for books that I could afford. Now I wanted to own them rather than borrow them from the library. There was something about the weight of a book in my hand, the smell of ink, that was intoxicating. My bookshelves filled with writers disparate as Ayn Rand, F. Scott Fitzgerald, Alice Munro, Dostoyevsky, Agatha Christie, and Franz Kafka.

And then, during that first year at the University of Winnipeg, I met Jon.

He wore small, round John Lennon glasses and had fabulous long hair. He was a bit of a bad boy, and I'd always had a thing for bad boys. He had big dreams and ideas, and, like me, he couldn't wait to get out into the world. He wrote me poetry. The next year we got married, very simply, at the tiny university chapel. I wove garden flowers into my hair; Jon wore a suede tie made by a friend. I was twenty-one. We drove down to Minneapolis—five hundred miles south of Winnipeg, for a four-day honeymoon, all the time we could afford.

Instead of English I ended up majoring in sociology and psychology, entranced with relationships and how the human thought process—especially children's—developed. Once I found my rhythm at university, the excitement of learning that I had lost somewhere in my teens returned. My first year of marriage I took all of my classes in the morning, then walked ten blocks down Portage Avenue, eating my lunch on the way, to my job as receptionist at an engineering firm, working from one until six. Jon had a full-time night job in the office of an abattoir, Canada Packers. Between our salaries we paid our tuition fees, bought our books, and covered the rent on our tiny apartment—a little gem with lots of tall windows looking out onto gracious old trees—on the second floor of an old house in Osborne Village, the "hippie" centre of Winnipeg. When we both graduated with our B.A.s, we had managed to save enough money to quit our jobs. We set out for western Canada in our beat-up VW van. It was 1972. We took cans of baked beans and jars of peanut butter and jam, and bought bread and fruit and cheap red wine along the way. We slept in the back of our van, through the hot, mosquito-filled nights of flat Saskatchewan, into the chilly heights of Lake Louise and Banff in Alberta, and finally through the Rockies of British Columbia, all the way to Vancouver. The radio was always blasting—the Stones and the Doors and Bob Dylan. We shared our first sight of mountains and the ocean. It was idyllic.

I felt good about my future; I had applied for a new program—it had only run one year—offered in the Education Department at the University of Manitoba. It was called Early Childhood, and it was geared toward obtaining a teaching certificate for working with the tiniest of "students"—preschoolers two and a half to five years old. I loved kids, and had loved studying about them in my psychology classes. The new program was popular and innovative, and there was a lengthy and stringent application process. Only twenty-eight students were selected, and I was one of them.

Jon had decided to go into elementary education; by the end of 1973 we held teaching certificates which, along with our undergraduate degrees, qualified us as teachers. And then we sold our car, gave up the lease on our bright little apartment, stored our bits and pieces in my parents' basement, and took off to see the world.

We bought student tickets from Toronto to Amsterdam—touted as a "champagne flight"—for ninety nine dollars each. We flew through the night with a planeload of noisy students—and yes, the crew actually did serve champagne and orange juice before we circled over the Amsterdam airport in the early hours of the morning. We stumbled off the plane, bleary-eyed, collected our luggage and bikes, and bought a map of the world. The world. That's how unsophisticated we were.

Driving an old van we bought off the street in Amsterdam, our bikes strapped to its roof, and using that one ragged map, we saw as much of the world as we could. To keep extending the trip we tried to earn money at every chance—picking apples in Switzerland, giving blood in Greece, working on a collective dairy farm in Israel.

I kept a number of detailed journals, and wrote a flurry of letters home. My mother was wonderful, replying with her own endless letters sent to the "Poste Restante" of the major city of each country I informed her we'd next be travelling through. More than once she encouraged me to write a series of travel articles on our experiences when we got home. I thought about it, but the old "who do you think you are?" reared its head, and I didn't really believe a newspaper or magazine would care what I had to say about the camel market in Israel's Beersheba, or the palace of Knossos on Crete, or the Grand Bazaar in Istanbul.

After a year we came back to Canada completely broke—no jobs and no place to live, and my parents opened their home to us. I did a terrible thing that summer. Rooting through some old boxes I'd left in my parents' basement when I moved out, I discovered huge stacks of scribblers—all my adolescent journals and stories and poetry and dream books. I started reading them, and, at the

ripe old age of twenty three, found them shallow and embarrassing. Inconsequential. In one swift and thoughtless move, I threw them out. How often I've thought about that huge box of my secret thoughts and my first attempts at writing. They would have been useful to me as a writer for young adults—not only to remember the girl *I* was, but certainly as a tool in helping me remember what it felt like to be a teenager. But at the time I was annoyed by what I saw as my silly youthful self, and I didn't want to be reminded of my self-pity and the pain I wrote about.

Six weeks later Jon and I were on the move again. We'd secured our first teaching jobs, in an isolated northern Manitoba community.

South Indian Lake, population seven hundred Cree and Métis, was over seven hundred miles north of Winnipeg. The community spread out over several islands, and was accessible only by small plane. There was a Hudson Bay store, a nursing station, and the school. It was a wonderful and eye-opening two-year experience. I taught six and seven year olds, many of whom could only speak Cree when they first came to school. We lived in a trailer on the edge of the lake, cross-country skied through the endless winters, and I took correspondence courses from the University of Manitoba, attaining a bachelor of education with special education qualifications by 1976. I learned to bake bread and make quilts, and Jon and I took basic lessons in Cree from one of the locals. We were given fish and fresh slabs of moose and venison and beautiful beaded moccasins by the friendly community, and learned more about our own Canadian First Nations culture than I would have over a lifetime had we not come to live at South Indian Lake. I had a lot of time there, to read and think, and my childhood dream of writing a book awakened.

When we returned to Winnipeg, we had saved enough money to buy a tiny old farmhouse on a long, two-acre strip of land on the Red River, about ten miles outside of the city. Busy with making the ramshackle house liveable, and financially stable for once, we decided not to teach that year. I found an interesting job in the physiology department of a medical facility, and Jon worked in a funky furniture store.

I also took my first writing course. It was the winter of 1977, and the ten-week course in creative writing was on Saturday mornings. I decided that it really was time to stop dreaming about being a writer and do something about it.

I went to the first class, eagerly listened to the instructor, went home and jumped into the assignment, honing the pages over the week, loving the look of my own words on the page. I felt my "natural talent" for writing would automatically shine. I envisioned my words and sentences and paragraphs sparkling on those clean pages like uncut diamonds. I pictured how the instructor would pull me aside after that first assignment and tell me that, yes, I was truly meant to be a writer, and he could tell from this one ten-page writing assignment that my future was assured, that I had remarkable talent. I was so full of myself, and so incredibly naive.

I quickly realized that I was disappointed in the actual course. The middle-aged instructor appeared tired and not completely enthusiastic about his Saturday morning job.

His teaching was less than inspired, and he seemed to prefer talking about his own writing (he had had two books published locally) to what I saw as helping us to learn about writing. As he handed back that first assignment, I tried to meet his eye, sure he would give me a sign, something to indicate that he knew I was special, but he didn't look up from the stack of stapled assignments as he called our names.

I stared at the red-penned mark on the first page. Six out of ten. SIX. Even though I was twenty-seven years old, I felt as though I were back in school, and had just bombed on a test. I surreptitiously tried to see the marks on the papers of those around me. There was an eight. A seven and a half. A nine—NINE. And I had a six. I was devastated, and determined I would do better with the future assignments. I tried. How I tried. I wrote and rewrote, I took out library books on writing and poured over them, and I even read *both* of the instructor's books. I took my assignments with me to my job and typed them up cleanly on the electric typewriter there, thinking that perhaps my ancient manual Remington with its faint ribbon and *p* with the missing tail was bringing down my mark. But it was not to be. I never got beyond a seven. The instructor sometimes scribbled *this is working,* or put an exclamation mark behind a sentence, writing *yes,* but that was about all. I never knew what I was doing wrong, or why I couldn't bring my marks higher than that dismal seven. I didn't bother going to the tenth and final class. I

was discouraged and felt I had wasted my time and money, convinced it was my lack of talent that resulted in the despairing results and my feeling of bad karma.

I should have simply chalked up that class as a bad experience. But instead I decided that I'd made a mistake, all these years, thinking that I might be able to write. I'd made a *colossal* mistake. I really didn't have what it would take.

Now I shake my head in frustration at the thought of that narrow-visioned young woman being so easily discouraged, so unsure of her ability and desire that she would allow a few Saturday mornings and one person to shatter her dream. Then again, maybe this was all just part of the major plan, that I really wasn't *ready* to begin my writing career. If I had been, I might have thumbed my nose at that instructor (only figuratively, for if nothing else, I was polite) and worked at my writing on my own, or investigated other writing classes.

The next year, Jon and I got back into teaching, and I decided to go ahead with my master's degree, as a part-time student. I narrowed my focus to educational psychology. I had never stopped being interested in the intellectual and emotional makeup of children and young people. I loved kids and was completely comfortable with them. My favourite period each teaching day was, naturally, story time, when I'd hunker down on the floor with my seven- and eight-year-old students around me, and read aloud to them—even though most of them could read for them-

The author's children, 2002: (from left) son, Kitt, with daughters Brenna and Zalie

selves. My favourite book was *Charlotte's Web*. I cried over that book for five straight years.

As much as I loved being with and teaching the kids, though, I felt restricted by the administrative side of school life: the bells, committees, the strict adherence to curriculum, and the endless paperwork. The "free spirit" side of me inwardly rebelled at all the rules. But those years were good times for Jon and me. We were making decent salaries, we were renovating and adding on to our house, creating vegetable and flower gardens and planting trees on our country property, and, of course, we had the summers off, and kept travelling. We went across Canada and into the States, visited the Hawaiian islands and took other forays to Europe—Scandinavia, Germany, Monaco, Portugal—wherever the mood took us.

We had been married for almost ten years when our first daughter, Zalie, was born in early 1981. I took the basic four-month maternity leave, and that same month Jon left teaching and went into the investment business. When Zalie was three months old I had to go back to work. I wanted to be home with my baby, but financially, with Jon's new career just getting started, it was impossible. I suffered terrible guilt. I cried a lot, but got Zalie to and from the babysitter every day, taught full-time and completed my master's degree in 1982. This enabled me to leave the classroom and work as a resource teacher, concentrating on one-to-one or very small group work with kids who were having trouble with the regular classroom curriculum. I continued as a resource teacher until our second daughter, Brenna, was born in 1984. By then I was able to stay home with my little girls.

That year of 1984-85, as I turned thirty-five, was a first for me. It was the only time, apart from our year of living in Europe, that I hadn't been working or going to university or both at the same time. I was almost giddy, playing with the girls and endlessly reading to them. I know I read hundreds—no, thousands—of children's books over the next few years. I took a correspondence course from the Institute of Children's Literature in Connecticut, which I found very helpful in learning to shape a story for children. I did complete some short stories and sent them out to publishers that I found in market guides, but received only rejections. Again, the dream of being a writer started to slip away. I was so easily discouraged.

We continued to travel, with the girls now, and we moved into the city, buying a big old house that needed a complete renovation. By the time Zalie was in grade two, and Brenna ready for kindergarten, I was growing restless. I had been an "at home" mom for almost five years; I loved my time with my children, and was grateful that I had had that choice. But I had too much energy, and knew I would need something more once they were both in school. I didn't want to return to what I saw as the confines of teaching, so decided that once Brenna started kindergarten that fall of 1989 I would enter a Ph.D. program, specializing in child behaviour. But my heart wasn't in it. It wasn't my *dream*. My dream was to be a writer. I was thirty-nine, and I hadn't made that dream into a reality. I tried not to feel disappointed in myself, tried to tell myself that my life was full, and good—which it was—but that niggling thought that I'd let myself down wouldn't leave.

I was working on my Ph.D. proposal and complaining to Jon about how I didn't know if this was the right thing to

do after all. And it was Jon who said, "Linda, all these years I've heard you say that the one thing that you really wanted to do—to be—was a writer. And now you're going to spend all this time and energy, for the next three or four years, writing research, when you want to write fiction. What's stopping you?"

He had a good point, but I still hadn't completely made up my mind whether to drop my plans for university when I discovered, to my great delight, that I was expecting our third child. It seemed to be the excuse I needed to give up or at least delay my plans to go back to university.

Again, was this part of the master plan? I didn't want to start the long years of study needed for a Ph.D. with a newborn. In December 1989, three weeks before my fortieth birthday, our son Kitt was born.

And I started to write.

It had sounded like a good idea: write for all those hours the baby naps. Unfortunately, Kitt wasn't a napper. And he didn't sleep through the night as his sisters had. But I was determined to write. Jon brought home an old computer from work, and I struggled to master it. Often Kitt sat on my lap, happy with his soother and some small toy, as I typed with an almost alarming frenetic energy around his chubby body. I'm not sure exactly what awakened that passion, what winds blew away all my self-doubts, but it was obviously the "right time." That first year it was as if a magic button had been pushed in me; I wrote every minute I could. I wrote short stories for children and for adults, I wrote poetry, I wrote articles, and I started a novel. There was a certain liberty, brought on by my ignorance. I didn't know what I was doing, but I had nothing to lose. I told myself I would give it a few years. If nothing "big" had happened by then, well . . . I didn't want to think that far. So I wrote, and sent out my work with crossed fingers. The mail held too many rejections to count, but somehow, instead of discouraging me, they fuelled my determination. And I did get a few short stories and poems published in small magazines and journals in both Canada and the U.S. that first year. Although I was only paid in copies, and they were very small publications, it was enough to keep me going. But I certainly didn't feel I could actually say the words "I'm a writer" to anyone. It was a bit of a secret. Only Jon knew how hard I was working at the makeshift desk in our bedroom.

In the spring of 1991 I entered a short story into a national writing competition sponsored by one of Canada's largest circulation magazines, *Canadian Living*. As with all my submitted work, I tried to forget about it, not really believing I had a chance. And then the phone rang, just after noon one cool fall day. The girls were home from school for lunch, Kitt was banging on his high chair tray with a spoon, and our cockatiel, Basil, was shrieking in the background as he always did when the phone rang. A bubbly voice told me I'd won the *Canadian Living* contest; my story had been selected over eight hundred entries. The prize was a word processor, to be delivered within a few weeks. If it was convenient, could a photographer come to my house the next day? My picture and a profile, as well as my story, would be in the next issue of the magazine, read by thousands and thousands across Canada.

With husband, Jon Holeman, 1996

I hung up the phone and stood in the noisy kitchen, watching the soup on the stove come to a boil. I remember thinking, "This is it. I'm a writer." It was the most intense high, apart from the birth of my children, that I had ever had.

The publication of that story really did start my career—not only because it boosted my publication credits, but, more importantly, because of what it did for my confidence. The next year, 1992, I put together a collection of ten of my short stories for young adults, and then attempted to find a publisher for the collection. It was a nerve-wracking and unsettling time, checking the mailbox constantly, wondering if anyone would be interested enough in my writing to actually publish a book. Eventually someone did.

That first book was titled *Saying Good-bye,* and it was published by Lester Publishing in Toronto in March of 1995.

In the time between the acceptance and the publication of *Saying Good-bye* (two long years), I continued to write, and to learn about writing as I went along. Writing *Saying Good-bye* had been my apprenticeship, I realized. I had to write a book to learn how to write a book, if that makes sense.

Other books quickly followed that first young adult book—a first chapter book that same year, then a collection of stories for adults. Young adult novels and another story collection for adults followed, and my writing career was in full swing within a few years. As I gradually became known through my published books, I was offered jobs teaching creative writing—both in workshops and in continuing education university courses. I was hired to critique manuscripts, as a mentor for emerging writers, and as a writer-in-residence.

Here I was teaching writing and mentoring other writers. It amazed me. I had never taken a university English class except for that one in first year, had read

voraciously but never studied any particular form of literature. Anything concrete I knew about story structure I'd basically learned on my own, studying books on writing and the work of writers I admired. I often felt like a sham, that any minute it would be discovered that I didn't know a thing about writing—that I was an imposter, just waiting to be caught and cast in disgrace from the writing world.

But I accepted everything I was offered, afraid that if I said no to anything it might mean I'd never be asked again. In retrospect, I almost burned myself out—trying to be the best writer I could be, studying writing in great detail so that I could be a helpful instructor or mentor to emerging writers, eventually writing speeches and presentations that I would give to students in classrooms, or to teachers or librarians, or to writing groups or fledgling writers across Canada and eventually into the U.S. and the U.K. At times I was completely overwhelmed. But I bit the bullet and just got on with it—something I'd learned from my mother's disciplined and stoic side of the family.

My life continues to open. When I was twenty-one and just married, I started a new journal by writing this first line: "Every year of my life I must do one new thing that scares or challenges me."

I've tried to live by that.

I've been on safari in the plains of South Africa, white-water rafted down the Snake River in Colorado, stroked the backs of ancient sea turtles while snorkelling off the coast of Maui, sat in a tiny Zodiac among thousands of beluga whales in the icy waters of Hudson Bay, cycled through the wilds of West Ireland, flown over the Grand Canyon in a six-seater Cessna. And I've written books. You can find out about my books by visiting my website at www.lindaholeman.com. My sense of searching, a driven need for adventure, for movement, for discovery, for testing myself, hasn't flagged, much as the stories in my head never stop spinning.

I've learned to pace myself. My life today revolves around my family, my writing life, and—still—travelling. Through the many ups and downs and successes and failures of this life I've tried to carve out, Jon has been behind me, totally supportive in all ways. I owe much of my accomplishment to his generosity and understanding of my "wild writer's mind" (to quote writer Natalie Goldberg).

As I write this, in the spring of 2002, my daughters are spreading their wings—Zalie is at the University of Manitoba and Brenna will be attending university in Nova Scotia in the fall. Both girls—genetically disposed to wanderlust—have already travelled extensively on their own, undergoing remarkable experiences which have opened their eyes and matured them. Kitt, at twelve, is in middle school, into skateboarding and playing his electric guitar. All three kids have been an endless source of interest to me. They're bright, confident, and strong-willed yet softhearted. I love watching them experience the world around them, and am always fascinated by their cognitive and emotional processes.

My children have also been a great resource for me as I write for young people. I've never stopped watching and listening to them. I run story ideas by them, and sometimes they read drafts of various work. I take their opinions seriously.

Although my father passed away in 1999, my mother, and Randy, Tim, and Shannon and their partners and families are closely connected by thought, even though often the physical distance is great. Whenever possible, we try to get together around the table on Rowandale Crescent. Our laughter is just as loud, our stories just as wild as all those decades ago. That creative thread—the imagination and need to watch and listen has surfaced in all of us. My mother began writing in her sixties, and has a long list of publications. She regularly visits elementary schools to tell her stories of life as a child in the 1920s. Shannon writes a weekly column for a newspaper, and has published books of both fiction and nonfiction. Randy produces videos, Tim is a counsellor. We are all avid readers.

I hope that you will stop for a moment and be thankful that you, too, have this sense of wonder, for that's what life is for readers. Whether you need, like I do, to actually travel to far off places, or whether you never leave the comfort of your home, when you read, you go on a journey of understanding and self-discovery. Over my desk is a quote by an unnamed author: "Travel is fatal to prejudice, bigotry and narrow-mindedness."

The same might be said for one who reads literature with an inquisitive mind and open heart.

Thanks for taking the time to find out about my journey to being a writer. And never stop reading and dreaming. Both will take you farther than you can ever imagine.

HOROWITZ, Ruth 1957-

Personal

Born May 28, 1957, in Newark, NJ; daughter of Irvin (a newspaper editor) and Marjorie (a school librarian; maiden name, Brailove) Horowitz; married David Christensen (a professor of philosophy), July 26, 1981; children: Sophie, Samuel. *Education:* Hampshire College, B.A., 1979; University of Pittsburgh, M.L.S., 1980. *Politics:* Democrat. *Religion:* Jewish. *Hobbies and other interests:* Photography, reading.

Addresses

Home—35 Brookes Ave., Burlington, VT 05401. *E-mail*—horowitz@sover.net.

Career

Inglewood Public Library, Inglewood, CA, librarian; Notre Dame Academy, Los Angeles, CA, librarian, until 1987; freelance writer, 1987—. Presenter of writing workshops, 1998—; teacher at local Hebrew school, 2000—. Burlington Library Commission, member, 1991-96, chair, 1993-95. Worked as press secretary for a statewide political campaign, 1996.

Awards, Honors

Crab Moon was cited among "outstanding science trade books for children" by National Science Teachers Association and included in a "choice list" for children's literature, both 2001.

Writings

Bat Time, illustrated by Susan Avishai, Four Winds Press (New York, NY), 1991.

Mommy's Lap, illustrated by Henri Sorensen, Lothrop, Lee & Shepard (New York, NY), 1993.

Crab Moon, illustrated by Kate Kiesler, Candlewick Press (Cambridge, MA), 2000.

Ruth Horowitz

Breakout at the Bug Lab, illustrated by Joan Holub, Dial (New York, NY), 2001.

Contributor of short stories, articles, essays, and reviews to periodicals, including *Seven Days.*

Work in Progress

Other children's books; a novel for adults.

Sidelights

Ruth Horowitz told *SATA:* "I've always loved telling myself stories. When I was little, I acted out stories with my toys, wrote poems, and felt frustrated because I wanted to write long, serious adult novels—books I wasn't yet able to read, yet alone write. The fact that I was a horrendous speller didn't help matters, either.

"Over the years, I've done lots of different kinds of writing, sometimes in my own name, sometimes on behalf of other people. I've written press releases for non-profits, political pieces for candidates and elected officials, classified ads for a house painter, and sermons that I've delivered from the pulpit at my synagogue. For several years, the mainstay of my work has been newspaper stories for *Seven Days,* an alternative weekly that covers northern Vermont. My newspaper stories have included news features about community-based policing and lake water quality, profiles of composers and medical examiners, humor pieces about lawn ornaments and Ken dolls, book reviews, personal essays, and even a love advice column.

"No matter what sort of writing I'm doing, I love the process of learning something new: imagining what it's like to be a tattoo artist, or a refugee from Kosovo, or a scientist who tracks down rare birds on Vermont's highest peak; explaining the advantages of restoring old buildings downtown, or the dangers of lead paint; or discovering a lesson about grief in the way Abraham mourns his wife Sarah in the Bible. I love the challenge of finding the appropriate voice for the particular type of writing I'm doing, and of making my material easy to understand and interesting to read. I try to find words that are both accurate and beautiful, and details that will make my readers laugh or let them see something familiar in an unexpected new way.

"Writing on behalf of someone else is a lot like creating a fictional character. You have to climb inside the person's head and figure out what he or she has to say. There's nothing more wonderful than coming up with the words that make someone say, 'That's exactly how I feel!' Even more satisfying than putting the right words into someone else's mouth, though, is evoking in a reader that same 'Aha!' of recognition about something I've written on my own behalf, in a voice that's entirely my own. I'm learning that readers tend to recognize themselves most clearly when I've written most honestly about myself.

"I began writing for children when my first child was just old enough to sit in my lap and hear a story. I was working as a children's librarian at the time, so the pace of picture books had worked itself into my brain. The first picture book I wrote, *Mommy's Lap,* seemed to arise spontaneously one day when I was taking my

Daniel witnesses the annual coming ashore and spawning of thousands of horseshoe crabs in **Crab Moon.** *(Illustrated by Kate Kiesler.)*

daughter for a walk in her stroller and thinking about what might happen when her baby brother or sister was born. I made the words up as I walked, and by the time I got home, I had the whole book pretty much written.

"Getting that first book accepted for publication was almost as easy as writing it: the second editor who considered it offered me a contract. The whole experience was so ridiculously easy, in fact, that I assumed I must be exempt from the toil and frustrations less privileged people suffer to become children's authors. But I learned my lesson soon enough. Not only did it take seven years for *Mommy's Lap* actually to make it into print, but writing—and finding publishers for—the books that followed was a long and difficult process. My files are filled with unpublished manuscripts and letters of rejection.

"Looking at the children's books I've published since I wrote *Mommy's Lap,* I see that each one celebrates a species of animal that people have unfairly maligned. An underlying goal of my work, it seems, has been to open children's eyes to the value and beauty of creatures that defy traditional standards of beauty.

"*Bat Time,* which depicts Leila and her father's summertime bedtime ritual of going outside and watching for bats, describes a favorite pastime of my husband and daughter the first few summers after we moved to Vermont. I wanted to draw a connection between the familiar evening routine inside the house and the natural events taking place outside.

"*Crab Moon,* in which Daniel discovers the annual miracle of horseshoe crabs coming ashore by the thousands to spawn, was inspired by a series of e-mail messages from my Aunt Susan, who rescues stranded horseshoe crabs on Long Island. I didn't actually witness the phenomenon in person until after the book came out. I was thrilled—not to mention relieved—when the horseshoe crabs actually did just what I'd described in the book.

"Max, the hero of *Breakout at the Bug Lab,* is an entomologist's pet giant hissing Madagascar cockroach who escapes from his tank on the day of a gala celebration. The story grew out of a profile I wrote about an entomologist who keeps a tank full of pet cockroaches in her lab. The scientist, Trish, turns out to be a wonderful storyteller, and the tale of Max's escape is based on some of the true adventures she described. After I wrote *Bug Lab,* Trish convinced me to adopt some roaches of my own, and kids have—mostly—enjoyed meeting them when I've brought them to schools and libraries."

Biographical and Critical Sources

PERIODICALS

Dallas Morning News, June 11, 2000, review of *Crab Moon.*
Honolulu Advertiser, March 3, 2001, Jolie Jean Cotton, review of *Crab Moon.*

Horn Book, July-August, 2001, review of *Breakout at the Bug Lab,* p. 453.
Kirkus Reviews, July 1, 1991, review of *Bat Time;* April 15, 2001, review of *Breakout at the Bug Lab.*
New York Times, November 30, 2000, Christopher Lehmann-Haupt, "For a Child, a Safe Haven Can Be a Picture Book."
Reading Teacher, March, 1994, review of *Mommy's Lap.*
Reading Time, August, 2000, review of *Crab Moon.*
School Library Journal, November, 1991, Marilyn Iarusso, review of *Bat Time;* May, 1993, Mary Lou Budd, review of *Mommy's Lap;* May, 2000, Patricia Manning, review of *Crab Moon;* April, 2001, Leslie S. Hilverding, review of *Breakout at the Bug Lab,* p. 112.
Smithsonian, November, 1991, review of *Bat Time.**

*   *   *

HUCK, Charlotte S. 1922-

Personal

Born October 6, 1922, in Evanston, IL; daughter of Carl M. (a wholesale jeweler) and Mildred (a homemaker; maiden name, Bridges) Huck. *Nationality:* American. *Education:* Attended Wellesley College, 1940-41; Northwestern University, B.S., 1944, M.A., 1951, Ph.D., 1955. *Religion:* Episcopalian. *Hobbies and other interests:* Genealogy, "reading aloud in schools and the library."

Addresses

Home—706 West Fern Ave., Redlands, CA 92373.

Career

Price School, LaDue City, MO, middle grade teacher, 1944-45; Halsey School, Lake Forest, IL, middle grade teacher, 1945-46; Joseph Sears School, Kenilworth, IL, primary teacher, 1946-51; Northwestern University, Evanston, IL, instructor, 1951-55; Ohio State University, Columbus, OH, assistant professor, 1955-59, associate professor, 1959-62, professor, 1962-86, professor emeritus, 1986—. University of Denver, Denver, CO, visiting professor, summer, 1964; University of Hawaii, visiting professor, summer, 1965; Senior Warden, St. Stephen's Episcopal Church, 1986-87; member, Redlands YWCA's board of directors, 1993-94; member, Redlands Day Nursery's board of directors, 1994—. Founder of *The WEB* (Wonderfully Exciting Books), an Ohio State University quarterly which focuses on the use of children's literature in the classroom.

Member

National Council of Teachers of English (chair, elementary section, 1967-69; president, 1975-76), American Library Association (chair, May Hill Arbuthnot Lecture Committee, 1973-74), Caldecott Committee (chair, 1980-81), Friends of Smiley Library.

Awards, Honors

Distinguished Teaching Award, Ohio State University, 1972; Landau Award, 1979; Distinguished Service Award, National Council of Teachers of English (NCTE), 1987; Reading Hall of Fame, 1988; Arbuthnot Award, International Reading Association, 1988; inducted into Hall of Fame, Ohio State University College of Education, 1990; Arbuthnot Honor Lecture, American Library Association (ALA), 1992; NCTE Award for Outstanding Educator in the Language Arts, 1997; Best Books of 2001 selection, Chicago Public Library, Notable Children's Book selection, ALA, 2002, Notable Social Studies Trade Book for Young People, Children's Book Council/National Council for the Social Studies, and Notable Children's Books of the Year selection, NCTE, all for *The Black Bull of Norroway;* Dorothy C. McKenzie Award for Distinguished Contributions to the Field of Children's Literature, Children's Literature Council of Southern California, 2002. The annual Charlotte Huck Children's Literature Festival at the University of Redlands is named in Huck's honor.

Writings

(With Doris A. Young) *Children's Literature in the Elementary School* (textbook), Holt (New York, NY), 1961, 7th edition (with others), McGraw-Hill (Dubuque, IA), 2001.

(Reteller) *Princess Furball* (folktale), illustrated by Anita Lobel, Greenwillow (New York, NY), 1989.

(Editor) *Secret Places* (poetry), illustrated by Lindsay Barrett George, Greenwillow (New York, NY), 1993.

(Reteller) *Toads and Diamonds,* illustrated by Anita Lobel, Greenwillow (New York, NY), 1996.

A Creepy Countdown, illustrated by Joseph A. Smith, Greenwillow (New York, NY), 1998.

(Reteller) *The Black Bull of Norroway: A Scottish Tale,* illustrated by Anita Lobel, Greenwillow (New York, NY), 2001.

Princess Furball has been published in Japan and France.

Sidelights

A long-time educator in language arts, Charlotte S. Huck has blended an academic approach to children's literature with an appreciation for the conventions of the picture book to write a much-used text as well as several children's books of her own. In the words of Ilene Cooper and Denise Wilms in *Booklist,* Huck's *Children's Literature in the Elementary School,* in print for over forty years, is a "trustworthy standby." This textbook was in its fourth printing before Huck, the respected expert on children's literature, began to make her mark as a children's book writer with the picture book titles *Princess Furball, A Creepy Countdown, Toads and Diamonds,* and *The Black Bull of Norroway: A Scottish Tale,* as well as the poetry collection she edited, *Secret Places.*

Charlotte S. Huck

Huck explained to *SATA* how she wrote both *Children's Literature in the Elementary School* and *Princess Furball,* her first children's book. "After completing my Ph.D. at Northwestern University, I began teaching at Ohio State. I stayed through one very hot August in order to teach my first class in children's literature. From that single course, we developed a program that offered specialization in children's literature at both the M.A. and Ph.D. levels. I wrote a textbook with Doris A. Young called *Children's Literature in the Elementary School.* With graduate students and teachers, we started a review quarterly titled *The WEB* (Wonderfully Exciting Books) which focused on the classroom uses of children's literature, and we began a yearly conference on children's literature which currently attracts over two thousand participants."

Huck, busy with academic life, finally found the opportunity to write *Princess Furball.* She related to *SATA:* "When I retired from Ohio State, I moved to Redlands, California, where my twin sister's children lived. Now I had the time to fulfill one of my secret desires; to retell my favorite fairy tale. I had wondered why no one had made a picture book of this gutsy variant of 'Cinderella.' In researching the story, I found my answer. The Grimm version had incest in it, but others did not. So I retold *Princess Furball* and Anita Lobel created stunning pictures for it."

Princess Furball tells the story of a princess whose father has betrothed her to an ogre in exchange for fifty wagons of silver. The Princess refuses to marry until she receives one dress of gold, one of silver, and one made of starlight. Finally, she demands a coat made of one thousand furs. When she receives these gifts from her father, she runs away instead of marrying the ogre. Princess Furball is found in the forest by men of another kingdom, and she goes to work in the king's kitchen. Like Cinderella, however, she gets attention from the prince at a ball when she wears her gown of gold. Wearing her two other dresses, she attends two more balls. The prince places a ring on her finger before she disappears at the third ball, and thus he is able to identify her even when he sees her in her rags. According to Linda Boyles in *School Library Journal,* this retelling is "smooth and graceful." Boyles describes Furball as "a strong female character ... she is resourceful and charming throughout" and relies "on her own abilities."

Huck told *SATA* how *Secret Places,* a collection of poems, developed. "All children have secret places that are special to them. At our summer cabin in Northern Wisconsin I had two—one down by the lake where I went when I had been scolded or I was angry, and one that was almost a little room in the pines where my twin and I played house. I decided to gather together a collection of poems about the various secret places of children."

The nineteen poems in *Secret Places* are, in the opinion of Kathleen Whalin, a reviewer in *School Library Journal,* "strong and sure." They include the writings of Byrd Baylor, Gwendolyn Brooks, Rose Burgunder, Elizabeth Coatsworth, Rachel Field, Aileen Fisher, Karla Kuskin, Myra Cohn Livingston, David McCord, A. A. Milne, and Nancy Dingman Watson. Whalin concluded that this anthology "should be welcomed universally." A reviewer for *Publishers Weekly* also praised this collection, calling it a "reflective anthology."

Readers count scary things from one to ten and ten to one in Huck's **A Creepy Countdown.** *(Illustrated by Joseph A. Smith.)*

Huck's next project was a "snappy retelling" of *Toads and Diamonds,* a fairy tale from Charles Perrault, as a critic noted in *Publishers Weekly.* Once again teaming up with Lobel, Huck retells the story of the sweet maiden Renee, who comes from a stepfamily not known for its kindness. Helping an old woman at a well get water, young Renee receives a magical gift. Whenever she talks, both jewels and flowers will flow from her mouth. Seeing this miraculous gift, Renee's lazy and cruel stepsister, Francine, prompted by the evil stepmother, goes in search of the same blessing. But Francine, who is continually cruel to animals, receives a curse instead: snakes and toads come from her mouth in place of jewels. Meanwhile, the well-deserving Renee wins a prince charming because of her innate kindness and honesty and not because of her newfound wealth. Writing in *Bulletin of the Center for Children's Books,* Betsy Hearne lauded this "elaborate production" with its "detailed narrative, an exemplary source note, and operatically dramatic art." *Booklist's* Carolyn Phelan also felt Huck's retelling had merit, noting that it "reads aloud well."

From classic fairy tales, Huck turned to the world of numbers with a counting book in *A Creepy Countdown,* a "bit of fun keyed to Halloween," according to Stephanie Zvirin writing in *Booklist.* Employing simple rhymes, Huck takes little ones through the numbers from one to ten and then back down. Beginning with "one tall scarecrow standing on a hill," Huck leads the reader on to "ten tiny mice, feeling very brave, [who] squeaked BOO TO YOU TOO!" Barbara Elleman, writing in *School Library Journal,* called this book a "surefire Halloween treat."

Huck once again teamed up with Lobel for another retelling of a traditional story, this time a Scottish tale in *The Black Bull of Norroway.* The three daughters of a widow all seek husbands. In the case of the two oldest, they seek wealthy, powerful husbands, but the youngest, Peggy Ann, declares that she is not necessarily after wealth or title in a husband: she would rather have a man who is kind and good and gives her his love. The girl also says that if this were the case, she would even be satisfied with the Black Bull of Norroway, an infamous local creature. The bull appears at her door when Peggy Ann decides to go off on her own to seek her fortune. On three successive nights the bull takes the girl to different castles, each owned by one of his human brothers. In the process, Peggy Ann removes a thorn from the bull's hoof, and this breaks a spell, transforming him back to the handsome duke that he is. But all does not end happily right away; the couple becomes separated for years before they are finally reunited once again.

This tale was widely commended by reviewers. A contributor for *Publishers Weekly* found that the long-delayed reunion was "roundly satisfying." *Horn Book's* Mary M. Burns also had praise for the title, noting that "Huck's talents are impressively demonstrated in a blithesome retelling" whose text is "fluid and precise," with "just enough repetition to suggest the authentic voice of the storyteller." Similarly, a critic for *Kirkus*

Huck retells the Scottish tale of three sisters and what they want in a husband in **The Black Bull of Norroway.** *(Illustrated by Anita Lobel.)*

she also stays connected to her academic roots. Leaving Ohio for the sunnier climes of California, she has built ties with the University of Redlands in her new hometown. Starting in 1996, the Charlotte Huck Children's Literature Festival has been hosted annually at that school, gathering artists and illustrators from around the United States for a celebration of children's books.

Biographical and Critical Sources

BOOKS

Huck, Charlotte, *A Creepy Countdown,* illustrated by Joseph A. Smith, Greenwillow (New York, NY), 1998.

Huck, Charlotte, reteller, *The Black Bull of Norroway: A Scottish Tale,* illustrated by Anita Lobel, Greenwillow (New York, NY), 2001.

PERIODICALS

Booklist, April 1, 1987, p. 1212; May 15, 1990, Ilene Cooper and Denise Wilms, review of *Children's Literature in the Elementary School,* p. 1811; October 1, 1993, p. 348; November 1, 1996, Carolyn Phelan, review of *Toads and Diamonds,* p. 496; September 1, 1998, Stephanie Zvirin, review of *A Creepy Countdown,* p. 133; September 15, 2001, Shelle Rosenfeld, review of *The Black Bull of Norroway,* p. 228.

Bulletin of the Center for Children's Books, October, 1989, p. 35; January, 1997, Betsy Hearne, review of *Toads and Diamonds,* pp. 173-174; October, 1998, Janice M. Del Negro, review of *A Creepy Countdown,* p. 62; May, 2001, Janice M. Del Negro, review of *The Black Bull of Norroway,* p. 339.

Childhood Education, spring, 1990, p. 177.

Horn Book, November-December, 1996, Maria B. Salvadore, review of *Toads and Diamonds,* pp. 750-751; May, 2001, Mary M. Burns, review of *The Black Bull of Norroway,* p. 339.

Kirkus Reviews, March 15, 2001, review of *The Black Bull of Norroway,* pp. 410-411.

Language Arts, November, 1997, p. 546.

Publishers Weekly, October 11, 1993, review of *Secret Places,* p. 88; March 7, 1994, p. 73; July 29, 1996, review of *Toads and Diamonds,* p. 88; September 28, 1998, review of *A Creepy Countdown,* p. 48; March 19, 2001, review of *The Black Bull of Norroway,* p. 99.

School Library Journal, September, 1989, Linda Boyles, review of *Princess Furball,* p. 240; August, 1993, Kathleen Whalin, review of *Secret Places,* p. 175; September, 1996, Donna L. Scanlon, review of *Toads and Diamonds,* p. 197; September, 1998, Barbara Elleman, review of *A Creepy Countdown,* p. 174.

Teacher Librarian, September, 1998, Shirley Lewis, review of *A Creepy Countdown,* p. 47.

Reviews remarked that "Huck's text is powerful and sweet," and that her effort "to find 'traditional tales that show plucky girls' pays off here." Reviewing the same title in *Bulletin of the Center for Children's Books,* Del Negro concluded that this "is a solid addition to comparative folktale and storytelling collections."

Huck believes that it is important to read books aloud to children. "I still have wonderful memories of both my mother and father reading aloud to my twin sister and me," she recalled to *SATA.* "It was only natural that when I became a teacher I read aloud not once but several times a day to my students. I also gave them time each day to read books of their own choosing. For only as children hear stories lovingly read aloud and have time to read themselves, do they develop a love of reading."

Pleased with her new writing career, Huck told *SATA,* "the transition from writing about children's literature to creating books for children has been exciting, indeed. I feel fortunate that my life's work has been involved with a field that brings so much joy and satisfaction to all." Now in her eighties, Huck continues to be a force for children's literature. Not only does she write books, but

*   *   *

HUME, Stephen Eaton 1947-

Personal

Born May 13, 1947, in Dallas, TX; children: Georgia, Natalie. *Nationality:* American; Canadian. *Education:*

Trinity College, B.A., 1969; University of Toronto, M.A., 1971.

Addresses

Home—12-1240 Newport Ave., Victoria, British Columbia V8S 5E7, Canada. *Office*—c/o University of Victoria, P.O. Box 1700, Victoria, British Columbia V8W 2YZ, Canada. *E-mail*—midnight@islandnet.com.

Career

Author, journalist, and educator. *Daily Colonist* and *Times-Colonist,* Victoria, Canada, reporter, 1976-89; Camosun College, instructor, 1998-99; University of Victoria, Victoria, Canada, sessional instructor in children's literature, 1999—.

Member

Writers' Union of Canada.

Awards, Honors

Second prize, MacMillan Bloedel Journalism Award, second prize, 1978; Our Choice selection, Canadian Children's Book Centre, 1973, for *Midnight on the Farm, Rainbow Bay,* 1998, *A Miracle for Maggie,* 2001, *Red Moon Follows Truck,* 2002; Best Environmental

Stephen Eaton Hume

Children's Books, *Amicus Journal,* 1999, for *Rainbow Bay;* Canadian Library Association Book of the Year Award for Young-Adult Fiction nomination, 2000, for *A Miracle for Maggie.*

Writings

Midnight on the Farm, illustrated by Regolo Ricci, Oxford University Press (Toronto, Canada), 1992.

Rainbow Bay, illustrated by Pascal Milelli, Raincoast Books (Vancouver, Canada), 1997.

A Miracle for Maggie, Beach Holme Publishing (Vancouver, Canada), 2000.

Frederick Banting: Hero, Healer, Artist, XYZ Publishing (Montreal, Canada), 2001.

Red Moon Follows Truck, illustrated by Leslie Elizabeth Watts, Orca Book Publishers (Victoria, Canada), 2001.

Contributor to periodicals, including the Toronto *Globe and Mail, Journal of the American Medical Association, Vancouver Sun, Toronto Star, Georgia Straight,* and *Medical Post.*

Work in Progress

Ben Franklin's War, a historical novel with elements of fantasy.

Sidelights

Stephen Eaton Hume is an American-born Canadian who worked as a journalist in British Columbia for over a dozen years before beginning a new career as a children's book author. His published picture books include *Midnight on the Farm, Red Moon Follows Truck,* and *Rainbow Bay,* the last an award-winning story about a young boy and his life on an island.

Hume was born in Dallas, Texas, in 1947, and lived in a small town near the border until his family moved to rural Maryland. He spent much of his childhood on a farm, the memories of which inspired his first book for children. As he told *SATA,* "My first child, Georgia, was only a few weeks old when I began writing *Midnight on the Farm.* It was four in the morning. My wife and I were living in a small apartment near the water. It was dark outside, and I could hear foghorns blowing. I started thinking about the farm where I grew up in southern Maryland. I could see it in every detail. As a child, I used to look out my bedroom window at midnight and wonder what all the creatures were doing at that late hour. That is what the book is about. A big thrill for me was seeing Regolo Ricci's illustrations. They were perfect. It was just as I had imagined the scene."

Midnight on the Farm attracted the favorable attention of critics in Canada. *Books in Canada* reviewer Phil Hall, for one, described it as "a moody, dreamy, quiet sort of book" that recalls stories of generations past. The *London Free Press* called *Midnight on the Farm* "a small masterpiece," adding "This one is destined to become a classic." Hume's 2001 offering *Red Moon*

Follows Truck also gained praise. Ellen Mandel, in her *Booklist review* of the story about a boy moving to a new home, described it as a "warm boy-and-dog story [that] will have special appeal for children ... uprooted to a new home." *Quill and Quire* reviewer Lian Goodall commented on Red Moon's "gentle humor," and "plain, strong, understated text."

"I wrote *A Miracle for Maggie* because I imagined what would happen to a diabetic child in the 1920s just before the discovery of insulin," Hume explained to *SATA*. "My mother was diagnosed with diabetes when she was a child, just a few years after Dr. Frederick Banting discovered insulin (Banting appears as a character in the book). Before his discovery, children with diabetes did not live very long, and young diabetic women were not able to have children. Banting was a decorated war hero, but he was untrained as a researcher. No one thought he would discover a treatment for diabetes, but he did." *A Miracle for Maggie* is set in Nova Scotia and features a young teen protagonist. Dr. Banting makes a second appearance in Hume's biography, *Frederick Banting: Hero, Healer, Artist. Canadian Book Review Annual* contributor, Christina Pike said of *A Miracle for Maggie,* "This moving account of human endurance in the face of incredible odds is impossible to put down until the last page is read."

"I hope my picture books and novels for young readers are fun to read," Hume added, "and take you to a world where time stands still and magic is alive." Dedicating most of his books to his daughters, Georgia and Natalie, Hume continues to write in between teaching and working as a journalist. "I don't have regular hours," he explained. "My advice for beginning writers is to read as often as you can. And, of course, write. You have to practice writing. Writing is a bit like driving in the dark. You don't know what spectacular scenery is just around the next bend in the road. Don't worry about trends. Write and revise until you have done the best you can do."

Biographical and Critical Sources

PERIODICALS

Booklist, January 1, 2002, Ellen Mandel, review of *Red Moon Follows Truck,* p. 865.

Books in Canada, October, 1992, Phil Hall, review of *Midnight on the Farm,* pp. 50-53.

Canadian Book Review Annual, 2000, Christina Pike, review of *A Miracle for Maggie,* p. 6195.

London Free Press, September 26, 1992, review of *Midnight on the Farm.*

Quill and Quire, August, 1992, Janet McNaughton, review of *Midnight on the Farm,* p. 24; October 2001, Lian Goodall, review of *Red Moon Follows Truck,* p. 41.

School Library Journal, February, 2002, Kathleen Simonetta, review of *Red Moon Follows Truck,* p. 107.

OTHER

Stephen Eaton Hume Web Site, http://www.finearts.uvic.ca/~sehume/home.html/ (August 20, 2002).

J

JASSEM, Kate
See OPPENHEIM, Joanne

*   *   *

JENNINGS, Richard (W.) 1945-

Personal

Born October 25, 1945, in Memphis, TN; married Linda Siggins (a nurse), 1987; children: five. *Nationality:* American. *Education:* Rhodes College, B.A. (English). *Religion:* Methodist.

Addresses

Home—Leawood, KS. *Agent*—George Nicholson, Sterling Lord Literistic, 65 Bleecker St., New York, NY 10012. *E-mail*—rjennings@kcrr.com.

Career

Rainy Day Books, Kansas City, KS, cofounder, 1975—; *Kansas City Magazine,* editor, 1987-88; Bernstein-Rein Advertising, vice president and creative director, 1988-98. Cochairman, Kansas City Book Fair, 1984.

Member

Authors Guild.

Awards, Honors

First place award, Southern Literary Festival, South-western-at-Memphis, 1967; *Booklist* Editor's Choice, 2000, for *Orwell's Luck.*

Writings

The Tragic Tale of the Dog Who Killed Himself, Bantam (New York, NY), 1980.
Orwell's Luck, Houghton Mifflin (Boston, MA), 2000.

Richard Jennings

The Great Whale of Kansas, Houghton Mifflin (Boston, MA), 2001.
La Chance de ma vie, Pere Castor (Paris, France), 2001.
My Life of Crime, Houghton Mifflin (Boston, MA), 2002.

Feature columnist for *Kansas City Magazine,* 1990-2000.

Sidelights

Richard Jennings has added several unusual volumes to the array of novels available to middle-grade readers. *Orwell's Luck,* for example, finds a young girl attempting to heal an injured wild rabbit, only to have the tables quickly turn after the rabbit, Orwell, gains back his strength and starts communicating with her through coded messages published in the newspaper. "Quirky details and a warm, precocious twelve-year-old narrator add up to an engaging and imaginative novel," said a *Publishers Weekly* contributor, adding that *Orwell's Luck* delves into both the philosophical and the practical. Noting that the book's "Christian symbolism is sometimes obvious," a *Horn Book* contributor praised Jennings' protagonist, "whose always-searching mind poses lots of good questions." "Thoughtful readers will enjoy looking for the answers," the reviewer added, "in this quirky story that hints at mysteries just out of reach." In *School Library Journal,* critic Judith Everitt also had praise for the book, calling the novel "a challenging and thought-provoking" read and commenting that "Jennings writes with natural grace and has a clear understanding" of the way a preteen views the world.

Jennings continues in the same unique vein in his second novel, *The Great Whale of Kansas,* in which the author's "refreshing style and distinctive voice are once again in evidence," according to *Horn Book* contributor Jonathan Hunt. In this 2001 work, an imaginative and curious eleven-year-old boy living in Melville, Kansas, makes an incredible find while digging holes in his yard: He finds a set of mysterious bones that draws him into the field of paleontology, as well as fame, as he attempts to make sense of his find.

Hunt praised Jennings' approach to writing for children, comparing the author to Daniel Pinkwater and noting that "his novels are laced with droll tongue-in-cheek observations, philosophical musings, and slight hints of absurdity" designed to challenge and entertain middle-grade readers. In reflecting on his work as a writer, Jennings quoted twentieth-century French playwright Eugene Ionesco: "I still feel surprised, sometimes, that I am no longer twelve years old."

Biographical and Critical Sources

PERIODICALS

Horn Book, September, 2000, review of *Orwell's Luck,* p. 571; September, 2001, Jonathan Hunt, review of *The Great Whale of Kansas,* p. 588.
Publishers Weekly, September 11, 2000, review of *Orwell's Luck,* p. 91.
School Library Journal, October, 2000, Judith Everitt, review of *Orwell's Luck,* p. 161.

OTHER

Richard Jennings Web Site, http://www.richardwjennings. com/ (August 25, 2002).*

JOHNSON, Marguerite Annie
See ANGELOU, Maya

*   *   *

JONES, Patrick 1961-

Personal

Born August 6, 1961, in Flint, MI; son of Vaughn Paul (an auto worker) and Betty Lou (a homemaker) Jones. *Nationality:* American. *Education:* University of Michigan—Flint, B.A. (English and political science; with honors), 1983, A.M.L.S., 1984.

Addresses

Home—6914 Pillsbury Ave. S., Richfield, MN 55423. *E-mail*—patrick@connectingya.com.

Career

Chatham-Effingham-Liberty Library, Savannah, GA, reference librarian, 1985-86; Springfield City Library, Springfield, MA, young-adult specialist, 1986-88; Cuyahoga County Public Library, Cleveland, OH, young-adult manager of Mayfield Regional Library, 1988-91; Allen County Public Library, Fort Wayne, IN, manager of Tecumseh Branch, 1991-96; St. Agnes Academy Library, Houston, TX, assistant librarian, 1996-98; Houston Public Library, Houston, TX, youth services coordinator, program manager, and developer of the "Power Card Challenge" program, 1998-2000; library consultant and lecturer, 2000—; Hennepin County Library, Minnetonka, MN, outreach services manager, 2002—.

Member

Young Adult Library Service Association (YALSA), Minnesota Library Association, Public Library Association, National Writers Union.

Awards, Honors

Project of the Year, Texas Library Association, John Cotton Dana Award, American Library Association, all 1999, all for "Power Card Challenge" program; Frances Henne Research Award, YALSA, 2000.

Writings

Connecting Young Adults and Libraries: A How-to-Do-It Manual, Neal-Schuman (New York, NY), 1992, second edition, 1998.
What's So Scary about R. L. Stine?, Scarecrow Press (Lanham, MD), 1998.
(With Joel Shoemaker) *Do It Right!: Best Practices in Customer Service to Young Adults in Schools and Public Libraries,* Neal-Schuman (New York, NY), 2001.

Patrick Jones

(Editor, with Linda Waddle) *New Directions for Library Services to Young Adults,* American Library Association (Chicago, IL), 2002.

Running a Successful Library Card Campaign Program: A How-to-Do-It Manual, Neal-Schuman (New York, NY), 2002.

Contributor to books, including *Children's Books and Their Creators,* Houghton-Mifflin (Boston, MA), 1995; *Libraries and Problem Patrons,* American Library Association (Chicago, IL), 1995; *Twentieth-Century Young Adult Authors,* Gale (Detroit, MI), 1996; *Young Adults and Public Libraries,* Greenwood Press (Westport, CT), 1998; *St. James Encyclopedia of Popular Culture,* St. James Press (Detroit, MI), 1999; and *Beacham's Guide to Literature for Young Adults.* Contributor to periodicals, including *ALAN Review, American Libraries, Booklist, Emergency Librarian, Grassroots, Horn Book, Journal of Youth Services in Libraries, Kliatt, RQ, School Library Journal, Today's Librarian, Voice of Youth Advocates,* and *Voices from the Middle.*

Work in Progress

Things Change, a young-adult novel.

Sidelights

Patrick Jones is a library consultant whose specialization in the needs of young-adult readers has made him an expert in the field. In addition to lecturing and publishing articles in a number of journals devoted to the concerns of librarians, Jones has authored several books designed to aid his colleagues in developing young adults' interest in reading. His first published book, *Connecting Young Adults and Libraries: A How-to-Do-It Manual,* presents practical advice and useful resources for public libraries wishing to serve not only college-bound teens but also latchkey students, homeless teens, and those whose circumstances have forced them to leave school early and enter the working world. "Jones not only understands both libraries and teenagers ... ," commented Cathi Dunn MacRae in *Wilson Library Bulletin,* "but he also has a flair for boiling issues down to essentials, listing ideas in absorbable small doses" that can be easily adopted by libraries of many sizes and budgets. Dubbing the book "the definitive soup-to-nuts manual for young adult librarians," *School Library Journal* contributor Bette D. Ammon praised in particular Jones's inclusion of "a plethora of strategies for enticing readers," among them developing book talk and volunteerism programs, creating advisory boards, and addressing confidentiality and censorship issues.

"The first article I wrote for publication was when I was twelve years old," Jones commented to *SATA.* "It was a profile of Bobo Brazil for a professional wrestling magazine called *In This Corner.* A little over twelve years later I published one of my first professional articles, called 'Wrestling with Magazines for Teenagers,' for the *Voice of Youth Advocates.* In both cases, the reason for writing the article was simple: It was something I wanted to read. Much of my professional writing stems from wanting to find the answer to a question: What was the best young-adult book? What are the best series books for young adults? How do libraries connect young adults with their services? Unable to find the answers already existing, I did the research and wrote the article.

"While most of my writing has been in the field of young adult librarianship, working in this field has allowed me to branch out. For example, I published several essays for the *St. James Encyclopedia of Popular Culture,* several, of course, on professional wrestling. After years of reviewing young adult literature, I started publishing longer essays for reference books, such as *Beacham's Guide to Literature for Young Adults,* as well as the book *What's So Scary about R. L. Stine? Things Change,* a young-adult novel I wrote one caffeine-filled weekend in the late 1980s in reaction to reading so many boring novels for teens, I finally reworked during 2001 and [it] is being considered for publication."

In his *What's So Scary about R. L. Stine?* Jones addresses the concern of many in the field that the proliferation of easy-reading "series" books such as those by Stine—as well as the "Babysitters's Club" books popular during the 1980s and 1990s—have diminished the skills of teen readers. Jones "believes that if kids love Stine's books there has to be a legitimate reason," explained Annette Curtis Klause in her review for *Voice of Youth Advocates*. In making his case in support of Stine's work as a prolific author of such series as the "Goosebumps" and "Fear Street" books, Jones "debunks assumptions about what is 'good' reading and emphasizes the importance of books that answer the emotional needs of YA readers," Klause explained. Noting that the book would be worthwhile reading for budding writers considering work in the YA horror genre as well as older Stine afficionados, the critic called Jones's analysis of Stine's successful formula "fascinating and informative" and his own writing "lively and enthusiastic." Jones's "respect for young people and their reading tastes shines through," concluded Klause of *What's So Scary about R. L. Stine?* In a *School Library Journal* assessment of Jones's book, Molly S. Kinney also voiced approval, noting that the author presents "a powerful argument for appreciating and evaluating Stine's style, popularity, and contribution to young adult literature."

"A professor in college once told me that 'writing is a way of knowing,'" Jones explained to *SATA*, "and I realize that what she meant is when we write, we learn. When we teach, we discover how much we know. All writers, no matter if they write the great American novel or an article for *School Library Journal*, write because they are curious. I suppose as long as I remain curious and ask questions, I'll continue writing and trying to know more."

Biographical and Critical Sources

PERIODICALS

Booklist, August, 1998, Susan Rosenzweig, review of *Connecting Young Adults and Libraries: A How-to-Do-It Manual*, p. 2019.

Book Report, March-April, 1993, Kathleen Morrissey McBroom, review of *Connecting Young Adults and Libraries*, p. 51.

Bulletin of the Center for Children's Books, March, 1999, Deborah Stevenson, review of *What's So Scary about R. L. Stine?*, pp. 261-262.

Journal of Adolescent and Adult Literacy, March, 2000, Shirley A. Proctor, review of *What's So Scary about R. L. Stine?*, p. 583.

Library Journal, October 1, 2001, Rachel Quenk, review of *Do It Right!: Best Practices for Serving Young Adults in School and Public Libraries*, p. 150; May 15, 2002, Shari Goldsmith, "Hennepin County Library," p. 34.

School Library Journal, September, 1992, Bette D. Ammon, review of *Connecting Young Adults and Libraries*, p. 152; July, 1999, Molly S. Kinney, review of *What's So Scary about R. L. Stine?*, pp. 117-118; August, 2001, Miranda Doyle, review of *Do It Right!*, p. 214.

Voice of Youth Advocates, October, 1997, Susan Rosenzweig, review of *Connecting Young Adults and Libraries*, p. 226; June, 1999, Annette Curtis Klause, review of *What's So Scary about R. L. Stine?*, p. 145.

Wilson Library Bulletin, January, 1993, Cathi Dunn MacRae, review of *Connecting Young Adults and Libraries*, pp. 85-86.

*   *   *

JORDAN, June (Meyer) 1936-2002 (June Meyer)

OBITUARY NOTICE—See index for *SATA* sketch: Born July 9, 1936, in New York, NY; died of breast cancer, June 14, 2002, in Berkeley, CA. Educator, poet, playwright, librettist, and author. Jordan has been described as a writer for every person who ever felt like an outsider. The prolific, award-winning author wrote from a perspective distinctly African-American, in a voice resoundingly female, but her themes and her message of hope were directed at everyone willing to listen and learn. Jordan was born in Harlem and grew up in Brooklyn. She began her teaching career in the 1960s. At the State University of New York at Stony Brook in the 1980s, she directed the Poetry Center. At the University of California at Berkeley in the 1990s, Jordan taught African-American studies and women's studies. She also founded the Poetry for the People program, where undergraduate students learned how to teach poetry and reach out to the community, at schools or prisons, among the poor and homeless, wherever they found people in need of a voice. Jordan championed the cause of women, children, and the African-American community above all. She often employed the dialect of "Black English," and her poetry in particular has been described as alternately blunt and exquisitely tender. Jordan was nominated for the National Book Award in 1971 for the children's book *His Own Where—*, and she won the Herald Angel Award from the Edinburgh Arts Festival in 1995 for the opera libretto *I Was Looking at the Ceiling and Then I Saw the Sky*. She was also a playwright. Critics have been especially drawn to Jordan's essay collections, in which she discussed her views on many subjects, often controversial and always rooted in her experience as an African-American woman. These collections include *Technical Difficulties: African-American Notes on the State of the Union* and *Affirmative Acts: New Political Essays*. In all, Jordan penned nearly thirty books, including *The Haruko: Love Poetry of June Jordan* and *Kissing God Goodbye: New Poems*. Prior to 1969 she wrote under the name June Meyer.

OBITUARIES AND OTHER SOURCES:

BOOKS

Contemporary Poets, 7th edition, St. James Press (Detroit, MI), 2001.

Jordan, June, *Civil Wars: Selected Essays, 1963-1980*, Beacon Press, 1981, revised edition, Scribner (New York, NY), 1996.

Jordan, June, *Soldier: A Poet's Childhood*, Basic Civitas Books, 1999.

PERIODICALS

Los Angeles Times, June 15, 2002, obituary by Jon Thurber, p. B19.

New York Times, June 18, 2002, obituary by Dinitia Smith, p. A23.

Washington Post, June 16, 2002, obituary by Jon Thurber, p. C8.

K

KOONTZ, Robin Michal 1954-

Personal

Born July 29, 1954, in Wheaton, MD; daughter of Warren Steele (in government) and Virginia (an art teacher; maiden name, Mullins) Koontz; married Marvin Denmark (a carpenter), April 1, 1977. *Nationality:* American. *Education:* Attended Maryland Institute of Art, 1973-74. *Hobbies and other interests:* "Walking; trail maintenance; nature-gazing; flower, vegetable, and junk gardening; playing with puppies; bicycling short distances; going to garage sales."

Addresses

Home—Walton, OR. *Office*—P.O. Box 336, Noti, OR 97461.

Career

Production artist, illustrator, and writer. Worked as a veterinarian's assistant and nursing home activities director, 1974-76; Monterey Bay Publishing Co., Monterey, CA, typesetter, 1976-77; Express Press Printing, Eugene, OR, typesetter/camera, 1978-84; freelance advertising production artist in Eugene, OR, 1984-85; freelance illustrator/computer graphic artist/writer, 1985—. Robin's Light-Arted Design Co., Noti, OR, owner; designer of gift tags, enclosures, and greeting cards, 1981-88. Conductor of writing, illustrating, and HTML workshops for various organizations, including the Society of Children's Book Writers and Illustrators.

Member

Society of Children's Book Writers and Illustrators (member of board for Northwest chapter, 1990—; member of steering committee for Oregon chapter, 1990—; Oregon regional advisor, 1996—).

Robin Michal Koontz

Awards, Honors

Notable Trade Book for Language Arts citation, Children's Literature Assembly, 1988, for *This Old Man;* Children's Choice selection, International Reading Association, 1992, for *In a Cabin in a Wood;* winner of Gold Award (with others), AIM International Convention, 1996, for excellence in graphic concept, graphics, and interactive design.

Writings

SELF-ILLUSTRATED

Pussycat Ate the Dumplings, Dodd, Mead (New York, NY), 1987.
Dinosaur Dream, Putnam (New York, NY), 1988.

This Old Man, Putnam (New York, NY), 1988.
I See Something You Don't See: A Riddle-Me Picture Book, Cobblehill Books (New York, NY), 1992.
Chicago and the Cat: A Little Chapter Book, Cobblehill Books (New York, NY), 1993.
Chicago and the Cat: The Camping Trip, Cobblehill Books (New York, NY), 1994.
Chicago and the Cat: The Halloween Party, Cobblehill Books (New York, NY), 1994.
Chicago and the Cat: The Family Reunion, Cobblehill Books (New York, NY), 1996.
The Complete Backyard Nature Activity Book: Fun Projects for Kids to Learn about the Wonders of Wildlife and Nature, Learning Triangle Press (New York, NY), 1998.
Why a Dog?: By A. Cat, Scholastic (New York, NY), 2000.
Chicago and the Cat: The County Fair, iPicturebooks, 2001.
How Is a Moose Like a Goose?, Millbrook Press (Brookfield, CT), 2002.

ILLUSTRATOR

Becky Ayres, *Victoria Flies High,* Cobblehill Books (New York, NY), 1990.
Darcie McNally, *In a Cabin in a Wood,* Cobblehill Books (New York, NY), 1991.
Sarah Tattler, *Whoops!,* Scott, Foresman (Glenview, IL), 1992.
Joan Hoffman, *I Don't Like Peas,* School Zone Publishing (Grand Haven, MI), 1993.
Etta Wilson, *Music in the Night,* Cobblehill Books (New York, NY), 1993.
Linda Hayward, *It Takes Three,* Millbrook Press (Brookfield, CT), 2003.

Also illustrator for the book series "Think Big Books," 1987-88, "Lift Off Books," 1990, and "I Know It Books," 1993, and for the flashcard sets "Pictures and Words," 1992, and "Phonics Made Easy," 1992, all for School Zone Publishing; contributing illustrator for the book series "Fast Forward Books," School Zone Publishing, 1986. Contributor to "Is It Alive?" and "Who's Hiding?," Creative Teaching Press, 1994. Illustrator and designer for *Alphabet Express,* an interactive CD-ROM, for School Zone Publishing, 1995.

OTHER

Editor of *NewsWorthy,* the newsletter for the Oregon chapter of the Society of Children's Book Writers and Illustrators. Contributor of short story "The Story Quilt" to the anthology *On Her Way: Stories and Poems That Celebrate Growing Up in America,* compiled by Sandy Asher, Dutton (New York, NY), 2004.

Adaptations

Several of the "Chicago and the Cat" books are available in electronic book format from iPicturebooks.

Sidelights

Robin Michal Koontz is best known for her self-illustrated "Chicago and the Cat" books that follow the

Chicago the rabbit and his feline friend are the main attractions in the "Chicago and the Cat" series, written and illustrated by Koontz.

adventures of a large white bunny named Chicago and her buddy, the Cat. Koontz has also written nonfiction, including *The Complete Backyard Nature Activity Book: Fun Projects for Kids to Learn about the Wonders of Wildlife and Nature,* and her year 2000 title, *Why a Dog?: By A. Cat,* is an irreverent look at feline-canine relations, from the viewpoint of a cat.

"I have been illustrating and writing books for children since 1987," Koontz noted on her illustrator/author Web site. After attending the Maryland Institute of Art in 1974, she set out on a variety of jobs before she began doing art full time in 1984. In 1985 she decided to visit publishers in New York, portfolio in hand, and managed to land a book contract with Dodd, Mead for *Pussycat Ate the Dumplings,* her first picture book and one that employs cat rhymes from Mother Goose. "My editors there moved to Putnam, and then to Cobblehill Books," Koontz explained on her Web site. She moved with them, publishing *Dinosaur Dream* and *This Old Man* at Putnam. The latter, a counting song book, was a Junior Literary Guild selection. Her first illustrating work was for Becky Ayres's *Victoria Flies High,* published by Cobblehill Books. Also working as an illustrator, she provided artwork for *In a Cabin in a Wood,* by Darcie McNally, which employs the traditional song in a story about a little man who offers a rabbit a safe hiding place from a hunter. However, other forest creatures also seek the safety of this small cabin, and soon it is overflowing with animals. A reviewer for *Publishers Weekly* praised Koontz's "large-scale watercolors [that] are loaded with humor."

Her first self-illustrated title for Cobblehill Books was *I See Something You Don't See,* a "fresh book of riddles delivered in a rhyming, narrative format," according to a contributor for *Publishers Weekly*. A brother and sister wake up, have breakfast, and as they work, play, and end the day at grandmother's house, a riddle comes out of each activity. There are thirteen such teasers in all. Visual clues are supplied in each case, as with the following: "Round like a plate, / flat as a chip, / holes like eyes, / but can't see a bit." On the facing page, Koontz illustrates the little girl buttoning her brother's shirt; there are also a needle and thread pictured to supply further clues to the correct answer to this puzzler.

"I spend a few days a year presenting to elementary schools," Koontz told *SATA*. "It is exhausting, although rewarding work. School visits have helped me to keep in touch with my audience. I show them slides of my house and all the animals that inspire me. We create a one-page illustrated story, acting first as the author, then as the illustrator. We are careful to honor the authors' words while going beyond them to enhance the story. I try out new ideas on them. I let them look through early sketches and the final pieces from my books so they can see the whole process. I let them read the letters and comments from my editor, which they delight in. They discuss her opinions of my drawings. We have a great time together and everyone learns something. At a recent visit, I read a story that had the kids absolutely howling with laughter, but the teachers were frowning. I think it important to know your audience if you think you want to write and/or illustrate for children, but you have to remember that it is an adult who publishes the book! We wound up having a great discussion about why the kids loved it and the teachers did not, and I came away with some ideas for revising the story."

The rabbit and cat of *Chicago and the Cat* make numerous appearances in early chapter book titles from Koontz. In the first title in the series, the rather loud cat charges into Chicago's house one snowy night. At first the shy rabbit gives the cat some food and a place to stay but insists that the visitor be on her way in the morning. The boisterous cat proves helpful, however, by showing that she can cook—carrot pancakes, in this case—and the two slowly become best friends. Koontz divides the action into four brief chapters, further detailing the relationship between the two, which survives Cat's reckless disregard for Chicago's garden. A reviewer for *Publishers Weekly* noted that the "upbeat text" of this book features "terse, humorous dialogue" between two "endearing but decidedly different characters."

Koontz continues the adventures of this unlikely pair in *Chicago and the Cat: The Camping Trip,* in which the two head off for the woods on a camping expedition. Chicago proves to be more of an outdoors animal than Cat, enjoying cooking, hiking, sleeping in a tent, and even river rafting. Cat, on the other hand, would rather take a bus than hike, and she likes her tuna canned. *Booklist*'s Deborah Abbott noted that the "gentle humor-spiced" interaction between Chicago and Cat is "enhanced by the droll watercolor paintings." Abbott also felt that this five-chapter easy reader was an "ideal choice." Writing in *School Library Journal*, Gale W.

Sherman similarly thought that this book from Koontz was "another fine selection for young readers."

More adventures are served up in *Chicago and the Cat: The Halloween Party,* in which the duo prepares for a masquerade party. Chicago thinks that a horse costume will be just the thing, but Cat is not so sure once she finds out that there will be a contest for best costume. Nonetheless, the two set off for the party as a horse and decide to trick-or-treat along the way. This bit of holiday merry-making gets them to the party late, however, after the best costume has been selected. *Booklist*'s Kay Weisman lauded Koontz's illustrations, which "add humor and bring out the many childlike qualities of the characters." Weisman further commented that the book was "sure to please beginning readers."

The fourth title in the series, *Chicago and the Cat: The Family Reunion,* tells of the arrival of a busload of the rabbit's relatives, laden with all sorts of delicacies, including dandelion casserole and zucchini popsicles. To Cat such food is completely inedible, and the relatives further alienate the feline when they take over her bedroom and proceed to play baseball by whatever rules they want. Finally, at the end, Cat is ready for another reunion, this time with her own cat relatives.

Koontz's first nonfiction title, *The Complete Backyard Nature Activity Book,* was four years in the research and writing, and was a "great learning experience," according to Koontz on her Web site. The book details many science-based activities for youngsters age nine to twelve. These include construction of a hummingbird feeder, a bat house, and a window box nest for swallows, among others. Subtitled *Fun Projects for Kids to Learn about the Wonders of Wildlife and Nature,* the book combines facts, anecdotes, and insights about wildlife with easy-to-make projects for naturescaping in virtually any available environment. These projects include construction of feeders, houses, and habitats to attract insects, birds, frogs, and other small creatures, along with ideas for planting live habitat. Many of the projects use recycled materials, such as a trash-can-lid bird bath.

Koontz finds inspiration for her nature-based books in her own life. "My husband Marvin and I live on a hill in western Oregon," Koontz noted on her Web site. "We also have a farm across the road from us which we call 'The Funny Farm.' There we have fourteen bat houses and about forty nesting boxes for cavity-dwelling birds, most of which are seasonally occupied. . . . We also have shelves and other inviting structural enhancements on our outbuildings which host barn swallows and cliff swallows by the dozens. At summer's end, we'll see hundreds of birds swooping over the pasture, snapping up insects." Koontz's "Funny Farm" also hosts an array of domesticated animals, including two Icelandic horses, two dogs—Buddy the Borderline Collie and Miss Mollie (who was her mother's miniature schnauzer), and three cats—FuzzButt, Koodie, and Moo.

"Now that I've been illustrating and writing for children for several years," Koontz told *SATA*, "I don't know what else I would do if I was forced to make a change. It's something I pretty much stumbled into, with the support and encouragement of friends and family, but now I wouldn't trade it for anything, even though I have to come up with other means to pay the bills part of the time. The constant challenge of the creative process itself along with the marketing/business aspect of getting and staying published is sometimes frustrating, but always exciting. I've learned a lot and like to share what I've learned with others. My volunteer work for SCBWI [Society of Children's Book Writers and Illustrators] Oregon is very satisfying—I love to be with people who share the same passion. But what is most exhilarating and satisfying of all is seeing kids react positively to my work. I can't think of anything more rewarding than that."

Biographical and Critical Sources

BOOKS

Koontz, Robin Michal, *I See Something You Don't See: A Riddle-Me Picture Book,* Cobblehill Books (New York, NY), 1992.

PERIODICALS

Booklist, February 15, 1992, Sheilamae O'Hara, review of *I See Something You Don't See,* pp. 1108-1109; February 15, 1993, Deborah Abbott, review of *Chicago and the Cat,* p. 1060; February 1, 1994, Deborah Abbott, review of *Chicago and the Cat: The Camping Trip,* p. 1012; September 15, 1994, Kay Weisman, review of *Chicago and the Cat: The Halloween Party,* p. 147.
Junior Literary Guild, April-September, 1988, p. 7.
Publishers Weekly, February 13, 1987, review of *Pussycat Ate the Dumplings,* p. 92; October 28, 1988, review of *This Old Man,* p. 77; November 25, 1988, review of *Dinosaur Dream,* p. 65; November 30, 1990, review of *In a Cabin in a Wood,* p. 69; November 29, 1991, review of *I See Something You Don't See,* p. 51; January 4, 1993, review of *Chicago and the Cat,* p. 73.
School Library Journal, May, 1987, pp. 87-88; February, 1989, pp. 72, 76; June, 1990, p. 96; March, 1991, pp. 188-189; March, 1992, Nancy Menaldi-Scanlan, review of *I See Something You Don't See,* p. 231; March, 1994, Gale W. Sherman, review of *Chicago and the Cat: The Camping Trip,* p. 200; September, 1994, Judy Constantinides, review of *Chicago and the Cat: The Halloween Party,* p. 187; September, 1996, Elisabeth Palmer, review of *Chicago and the Cat: The Family Reunion,* p. 182.
Wilson Library Bulletin, November, 1987, p. 63.

OTHER

Robin Michal Koontz Web Site, http://users.rio.com/robink/ (July 4, 2002).

KRENSKY, Stephen (Alan) 1953-

Personal

Born November 25, 1953, in Boston, MA; son of Paul David (a business executive) and Roselyn (Gurewitz) Krensky; married Joan Frongello (a textbook editor), April 7, 1984; children: Andrew, Peter. *Nationality:* American. *Education:* Hamilton College, B.A., 1975.

Addresses

Home and office—12 Eaton Rd., Lexington, MA 02420.

Career

Freelance writer and critic, 1975—.

Awards, Honors

Notable Book, American Library Association (ALA), 1982, for *Dinosaurs, Beware!;* Children's Books of the Year citation, Child Study Association of America, 1985, for *Maiden Voyage: The Story of the Statue of Liberty;* Children's Books of the Year citation, Child Study Children's Book Committee, 1987, for *Lionel in the Fall,* 1993, for both *Lionel and Louise* and *Christopher Columbus,* and 1995, for *Lionel in the Winter;* Pick of the Lists citation, American Booksellers Association, 1992, for *Lionel in the Spring,* 1994, for *Lionel in the Winter,* and 1996, for *Breaking into Print: Before and after the Invention of the Printing Press;* Children's Choice selection, International Reading Association, 1992, for *George Washington: The Man Who Would Not Be King;* Reading Magic award, *Parenting* magazine, 1996, for *Lionel and His Friends;* Notable Children's Trade Book in the Field of Social Studies, National Council for the Social Studies/Children's Book Council (NCSS/CBC), 1996, for *Breaking into Print;* Notable Book, ALA, 1998, for *How Santa Got His Job.*

Writings

FOR YOUNG PEOPLE

A Big Day for Scepters, illustrated by Bruce Degen, Atheneum (New York, NY), 1977.
The Dragon Circle, illustrated by A. Delaney, Atheneum (New York, NY), 1977.
Woodland Crossing, illustrated by Jan Brett Bowler, Atheneum (New York, NY), 1978.
The Perils of Putney, illustrated by Jeurg Obrist, Atheneum (New York, NY), 1978.
Castles in the Air and Other Tales, illustrated by Warren Lieberman, Atheneum (New York, NY), 1979.
A Troll in Passing, Atheneum (New York, NY), 1980.
My First Dictionary, Houghton (Boston, MA), 1980, reprinted as *The American Heritage First Dictionary* and *Houghton Mifflin Primary Dictionary,* illustrated by George Ulrich, Houghton (Boston, MA), 1986.
The Witching Hour, illustrated by A. Delaney, Atheneum (New York, NY), 1981.

Stephen Krensky

Conqueror and Hero: The Search for Alexander, illustrated by Alexander Farquharson, Little, Brown (Boston, MA), 1981.

(With Marc Brown) *Dinosaurs, Beware!: A Safety Guide,* illustrated by Marc Brown, Atlantic-Little, Brown (Boston, MA), 1982.

The Wilder Plot, Atheneum (New York, NY), 1982.

The Lion Upstairs, illustrated by Leigh Grant, Atheneum (New York, NY), 1983.

The Wilder Summer, Atheneum (New York, NY), 1983.

(With Marc Brown) *Perfect Pigs: An Introduction to Manners,* illustrated by Marc Brown, Little, Brown (Boston, MA), 1984.

A Ghostly Business, Atheneum (New York, NY), 1984.

Maiden Voyage: The Story of the Statue of Liberty, illustrated by Richard Rosenblum, Atheneum (New York, NY), 1985.

Scoop after Scoop: A History of Ice Cream, illustrated by Richard Rosenblum, Atheneum (New York, NY), 1986.

Who Really Discovered America?, illustrated by Steve Sullivan, Hastings House, 1987.

Snow and Ice, Scholastic (New York, NY), 1989.

Witch Hunt: It Happened in Salem Village, illustrated by James Watling, Random House (New York, NY), 1989.

Big Time Bears, illustrated by Maryann Cocca-Leffler, Little, Brown (Boston, MA), 1989.

Christopher Columbus, illustrated by Norman Green, Random House (New York, NY), 1991.

The Missing Mother Goose, illustrated by Chris Demarest, Doubleday (New York, NY), 1991.

Children of the Earth and Sky, illustrated by J. Watling, Scholastic (New York, NY), 1991.

George Washington: The Man Who Would Not Be King, Scholastic (New York, NY), 1991.

Four against the Odds: The Struggle to Save Our Environment, Scholastic (New York, NY), 1992.

The Pizza Book: Fun, Facts, a Recipe—the Works!, illustrated by R. W. Alley, Scholastic (New York, NY), 1992.

All about Magnets, Scholastic (New York, NY), 1993.

Fraidy Cats, illustrated by Betsy Lewin, Scholastic (New York, NY), 1993.

The Iron Dragon Never Sleeps, illustrated by John Fulweiler, Delacorte (New York, NY), 1994.

Children of the Wind and Water: Five Stories about Native American Children, illustrated by J. Watling, Scholastic (New York, NY), 1994.

The Three Blind Mice Mystery, illustrated by Lynn Munsinger, Yearling (New York, NY), 1995.

The Printer's Apprentice, illustrated by Madeline Sorel, Delacorte (New York, NY), 1995.

Breaking into Print: Before and after the Invention of the Printing Press, illustrated by Bonnie Christensen, Little, Brown (Boston, MA), 1996.

My Teacher's Secret Life, illustrated by JoAnn Adinolfi, Simon & Schuster (New York, NY), 1996.

Striking It Rich: The Story of the California Gold Rush, illustrated by Ann DiVito, Simon & Schuster (New York, NY), 1996.

Pocahontas Official Game Book, Brady Computer Books, 1996.

A Good Knight's Sleep, illustrated by Renee Williams-Andriani, Shaw's Candlewick Press (Cambridge, MA), 1996.

Sharks Never Sleep, Candlewick Press (Cambridge, MA), 1997.

We Just Moved!, illustrated by Larry Difiori, Scholastic (New York, NY), 1998.

Write Away!: One Author's Favorite Activities That Help Ordinary Writers become Extraordinary Writers, Scholastic Professional Books (New York, NY), 1998.

How Santa Got His Job, illustrated by S. D. Schindler, Simon & Schuster Books for Young Readers (New York, NY), 1998.

My Loose Tooth, illustrated by Hideko Takahashi, Random House (New York, NY), 1999.

Bones (nonfiction), illustrated by Davy Jones, Random House (New York, NY), 1999.

The Youngest Fairy Godmother Ever, illustrated by Diana Cain Bluthenthal, Simon & Schuster Books for Young Readers (New York, NY), 1999.

Taking Flight: The Story of the Wright Brothers, illustrated by Larry Day, Simon & Schuster Books for Young Readers (New York, NY), 2000.

What a Mess!, illustrated by Joe Mathieu, Random House (New York, NY), 2001.

The Moon Robber, illustrated by Dean Morrissey, HarperCollins (New York, NY), 2001.

Pearl Harbor, illustrated by Larry Day, Aladdin Paperbacks (New York, NY), 2001.

Egypt, Scholastic Reference (New York, NY), 2001.

(Adapter) Charles Dickens, *A Christmas Carol,* pictures by Dean Morrissey, HarperCollins (New York, NY), 2001.

Shooting for the Moon: The Amazing Life and Times of Annie Oakley, Melanie Kroupa Books/Farrar, Straus and Giroux (New York, NY), 2001.

(Adapter) A. A. Milne, *Eeyore Has a Birthday,* with decorations by Ernest H. Shepard, Dutton Children's Books (New York, NY), 2001.

(Adapter) A. A. Milne, *Winnie-the-Pooh and Some Bees,* with decorations by Ernest H. Shepard, Dutton Children's Books (New York, NY), 2001.

How Santa Lost His Job, illustrated by S. D. Schindler, Simon & Schuster Books for Young Readers (New York, NY), 2001.

The Winter King, pictures by Dean Morrissey, HarperCollins (New York, NY), 2002.

Paul Revere's Midnight Ride, illustrated by Greg Harlin, HarperCollins (New York, NY), 2002.

Abe Lincoln and the Muddy Pig, illustrated by Greshom Griffith, Aladdin Paperbacks (New York, NY), 2002.

Ben Franklin and His First Kite, illustrated by Bert Dodson, Aladdin Paperbacks (New York, NY), 2002.

Sacagawea and the Bravest Deed, illustrated by Diana Magnuson, Aladdin Paperbacks (New York, NY), 2002.

(Adapter) A. A. Milne, *Pooh Goes Visiting,* decorations by Ernest H. Shepard, Dutton Children's Books (New York, NY), 2002.

(Adapter) A. A. Milne, *Tigger Comes to the Forest,* decorations by Ernest H. Shepard, Dutton Children's Books (New York, NY), 2002.

Contributor of short stories to *Cricket* and reviews to magazines and newspapers, including *New York Times Book Review, New Republic,* and *Boston Globe.*

"ARTHUR" CHAPTER BOOK SERIES; BASED ON THE CHARACTERS BY MARC BROWN; ADAPTED FROM THE "ARTHUR" TELEVISION SERIES

Arthur's Mystery Envelope, illustrated by Marc Brown, Little, Brown (Boston, MA), 1998.

Arthur and the Scare-Your-Pants-Off Club, illustrated by Marc Brown, Little, Brown (Boston, MA), 1998.

Arthur Makes the Team, illustrated by Marc Brown, Little, Brown (Boston, MA), 1998.

Arthur and the Crunch Cereal Contest, illustrated by Marc Brown, Little, Brown (Boston, MA), 1998.

Santa tries life as a postal worker and chimney sweep before meeting a group of elves and finding his true calling in Krensky's **How Santa Got His Job.** *(Illustrated by S. D. Schindler.)*

A young boy tells about his loose tooth in rhyme in Krensky's **My Loose Tooth.** *(Illustrated by Hideko Takahashi.)*

Arthur Accused, illustrated by Marc Brown, Little, Brown (Boston, MA), 1998.

Locked in the Library, illustrated by Marc Brown, Little, Brown (Boston, MA), 1998.

Buster's Dino Dilemma, illustrated by Marc Brown, Little, Brown (Boston, MA), 1998.

The Mystery of the Stolen Bike, illustrated by Marc Brown, Little, Brown (Boston, MA), 1998.

Arthur and the Popularity Contest (based on a teleplay by Sandra Willard), illustrated by Marc Brown, Little, Brown (Boston, MA), 1998.

Arthur Rocks with Binky (based on a teleplay by Sandra Willard), illustrated by Marc Brown, Little, Brown (Boston, MA), 1998.

Arthur and the Lost Diary, illustrated by Marc Brown, Little, Brown (Boston, MA), 1998.

Who's in Love with Arthur? (based on a teleplay by Peter Hirsch), illustrated by Marc Brown, Little, Brown (Boston, MA), 1998.

Arthur and the Cootie-Catcher, illustrated by Marc Brown, Little, Brown (Boston, MA), 1999.

Buster Makes the Grade (based on a teleplay by Peter Hirsch), illustrated by Marc Brown, Little, Brown (Boston, MA), 1999.

King Arthur (based on a teleplay by Peter Hirsch), illustrated by Marc Brown, Little, Brown (Boston, MA), 1999.

Francine, Believe It or Not, illustrated by Marc Brown, Little, Brown (Boston, MA), 1999.

Muffy's Secret Admirer (based on a teleplay by Sandra Willard), illustrated by Marc Brown, Little, Brown (Boston, MA), 1999.

Arthur and the Poetry Contest (based on a teleplay by Joe Fallon), illustrated by Marc Brown, Little, Brown (Boston, MA), 1999.

Buster Baxter, Cat Saver (based on a teleplay by Joe Fallon), illustrated by Marc Brown, Little, Brown (Boston, MA), 2000.

Buster's New Friend (based on a teleplay by Matt Steinglass), illustrated by Marc Brown, Little, Brown (Boston, MA), 2000.

Arthur and the Big Blow-Up (based on a teleplay by Joe Fallon), illustrated by Marc Brown, Little, Brown (Boston, MA), 2000.

Francine the Superstar, illustrated by Marc Brown, Little, Brown (Boston, MA), 2000.

Arthur and the Perfect Brother (based on a teleplay by Joe Fallon), illustrated by Marc Brown, Little, Brown (Boston, MA), 2000.

Binky Rules (based on a teleplay by Sandra Willard), illustrated by Marc Brown, Little, Brown (Boston, MA), 2000.

Arthur and the Double Dare, illustrated by Marc Brown, Little, Brown (Boston, MA), 2002.

Also adapter of ten traditional bedtime tales for *Arthur's Really Helpful Bedtime Stories* (based on the characters by Marc Brown), illustrated by Marc Brown, Random House (New York, NY).

"ARTHUR GOOD SPORTS" SERIES; WITH MARC BROWN

Arthur and the Race to Read, illustrated by Marc Brown, Little, Brown (Boston, MA), 2001.

Arthur and the Best Coach Ever, illustrated by Marc Brown, Little, Brown (Boston, MA), 2001.

Arthur and the Goalie Ghost, illustrated by Marc Brown, Little, Brown (Boston, MA), 2001.

Arthur and the Pen-Pal Playoff, illustrated by Marc Brown, Little, Brown (Boston, MA), 2001.

Arthur and the Recess Rookie, illustrated by Marc Brown, Little, Brown (Boston, MA), 2001.

Arthur and the Seventh-Inning Stretcher, illustrated by Marc Brown, Little, Brown (Boston, MA), 2001.

"LIONEL" SERIES

Lionel at Large, illustrated by Susanna Natti, Dial (New York, NY), 1986.

Lionel in the Fall, illustrated by Susanna Natti, Dial (New York, NY), 1987.

Lionel in the Spring, illustrated by Susanna Natti, Dial (New York, NY), 1990.

Lionel and Louise, illustrated by Susanna Natti, Dial (New York, NY), 1992.

Lionel in the Winter, illustrated by Susanna Natti, Dial (New York, NY), 1994.

Lionel and His Friends, illustrated by Susanna Natti, Dial (New York, NY), 1996.

Lionel in the Summer, illustrated by Susanna Natti, Dial (New York, NY), 1998.

Lionel at School, illustrated by Susanna Natti, Dial (New York, NY), 2000.

Lionel's Birthday, illustrated by Susanna Natti, Dial (New York, NY), 2003.

"LOUISE" SERIES

Louise Takes Charge, illustrated by Susanna Natti, Dial (New York, NY), 1998.

Louise Goes Wild, illustrated by Susanna Natti, Dial (New York, NY), 1999.

Louise, Soccer Star?, illustrated by Susanna Natti, Dial (New York, NY), 2000.

Adaptations

Krensky adapted his novel *The Wilder Summer* into a special for Home Box Office (HBO) Family Playhouse; the film was produced by Learning Corporation of America, 1984. *Dinosaurs, Beware!* was adapted into a filmstrip with cassette, Random House/Miller-Brody, 1985.

Sidelights

Stephen Krensky is the prolific and popular author of over sixty books for children. His picture books, easy readers, fiction, and nonfiction reflect his eclectic interests as well as those of the primary and middle graders for whom he usually writes. Krensky has written about dinosaurs, summer camp, Alexander the Great, Native American children, the private lives of teachers, the invention of the printing press, the discovery of America, and the further adventures of familiar Mother Goose characters, among other subjects, and he has even written a dictionary for primary graders and a social history of ice cream. Noted for investing all of his books with his appealing sense of humor and clear, fluid literary style, Krensky is perhaps best known as the creator of the "Lionel" series of beginning readers, stories that describe the experiences and feelings of a young boy at home and at school. Krensky is acknowledged for treating Lionel's concerns with sensitivity and respect, and the series is praised for providing early readers with an appropriate, enjoyable link between picture books and chapter books.

Born in Boston, in 1953, Krensky never thought of becoming a writer when he was young, though he did develop an early interest in both fiction and illustrating. His earliest stories were not written; rather, they were bedtime games of making up stories, attempting to visualize characters such as Robin Hood and Gandalf, the wizard from *The Lord of the Rings,* in his dreams. "I started writing stories for children while in college, something I backed into after becoming interested in illustrating children's books," Krensky wrote in an autobiographical sketch for *Sixth Book of Junior Authors and Illustrators.* More comfortable with writing than drawing, he stuck with the former. "For me writing is as much a craft as an art," Krensky noted in his sketch. Early on he developed a businesslike approach to

writing, not waiting to be visited by muses or struck by inspiration, but working at it every day and revising until he is satisfied with the end result. Unlike some authors, Krensky never viewed children's books as a stepping stone to writing for adults. "I think of it simply as writing the kind of stories I like best," he reported in *Sixth Book of Junior Authors and Illustrators.*

Krensky's first book for young readers appeared in 1977, just two years after he left college. *A Big Day for Scepters* tells the story of Calendar, a young sorcerer and collector of magic who searches for and finds a mysterious scepter with his thirteen-year-old companion. Krensky's second novel, *The Dragon Circle,* also deals with fantasy and magic; in this book, the Wynd family gets involved with dragons who need help recovering a long-lost treasure. Notable in these early books is Krensky's tongue-in-cheek humor, a mischievous glint in the eye of the narrator. A *Kirkus Reviews* contributor noted that the action in *A Big Day for Scepters* was "trippingly related," and Craighton Hippenhammer, writing in *School Library Journal,* commented that Krensky's first book was a "light, fast-moving, and humorous fantasy." Hippenhammer, also reviewing *The Dragon Circle* for *School Library Journal,* concluded that it was "simply but nicely plotted" and that it would carry young readers along "on wave after wave of action-packed spells until the last fiery dragon breath is quenched forever."

Krensky also wrote about the Wynd family from *The Dragon Circle* in two other books, *The Witching Hour* and *A Ghostly Business.* The latter describes how the five Wynd children, visiting their Aunt Celia in Boston, discover a ghost in her house—a sad and sensitive creature suffering from a curse. Fine practitioners of magic, the children help both aunt and ghost in a blend, according to a reviewer for *Bulletin of the Center for Children's Books,* of "humor . . . magic, and . . . triumph of good over evil" that provides "an entertaining reading experience."

Krensky's early books set the tone for much of his children's fiction. His combination of humor and magic earned the author the title of "talented fabulist" from one *Publishers Weekly* critic for another of his books involving magic and fantasy, *A Troll in Passing.* In this work, the young troll Morgan has no love for the nocturnal pursuits of his brethren. Instead of spending his time mining, he would rather roam the countryside gathering mistletoe—a useless occupation, it would seem, until the day that the fearsome trolls of the Simon clan plan to attack Morgan's people and his mistletoe becomes their one defense. A *Bulletin of the Center for Children's Books* contributor concluded that Krensky's "fluent and sophisticated" writing style was "well worth pursuing in a nicely crafted story that has pace, humor, and momentum."

Two books featuring ninth grader Charlie Wilder, *The Wilder Plot* and *The Wilder Summer,* provide a bit of a change for Krensky: both stories leave magic for the realistic world of junior high. In *The Wilder Plot,*

Charlie unwillingly gets the lead role in the student production of *A Midsummer Night's Dream* and spends much of the rest of the book attempting to get out of this uncomfortable situation before being saved just before showtime. Amy L. Cohn noted in *School Library Journal* that Krensky captured the intensity of school in "a novel of high-spirited good humor."

Set at summer camp, *The Wilder Summer* describes Charlie's attempts to get to know Lydia, with whom he falls in love at first sight, despite the endeavors of Lydia's jealous friend Willoughby. "Charlie's shy reluctance to approach Lydia leads to a string of humorous situations," commented a reviewer for *Voice of Youth Advocates,* and creates a book that "should appeal to the youngest YAs." The reviewers proved to be right about the book's popularity: *The Wilder Summer* was appealing enough to be adapted for a television movie.

Krensky continued in this more realistic yet still humorous vein with the "Lionel" series of easy-to-read books. The first in the series, *Lionel at Large,* introduces the youthful protagonist and his family in five "warm, down-to-earth stories" which are by turns "humorous and touching," according to a *School Library Journal* critic. In this book, Lionel visits the doctor, refuses to eat his vegetables, and stays overnight with a friend. "There's quiet humor in the writing," noted a reviewer for *Bulletin of the Center for Children's Books.*

This same humor has continued in several subsequent installments, each presented in short vignettes featuring Lionel and his family and friends. With *Lionel in the Spring,* the reader follows Lionel in such seasonal activities as planting a garden and spring housecleaning. Carolyn K. Jenks, reviewing the book for *Horn Book,* felt that Lionel's "cheerful attitude" and the "amusing, believable situations" all enhanced this "well-written ... series of stories for beginning readers." Another addition to the series, *Lionel in the Winter,* takes a look at cold weather activities in four easy-to-read stories "that will invite warm smiles on any day, cold or not," according to Carol Fox in *Bulletin of the Center for Children's Books.* Lionel explores his backyard Arctic, learns about New Year's resolutions, and keeps company with a snowman in these "gently funny stories."

In the fourth book of the series, *Lionel and Louise,* Lionel experiences some new adventures with his sister. He rescues Louise from a dragon(fly), builds a sand castle on the beach, cleans up a mess at home, and goes on a camping expedition in the backyard. Reviewing *Lionel and Louise* in *Booklist,* Julie Corsaro felt that these stories introducing imaginative play were "warm and funny," while Sharron McElmeel concluded in *School Library Journal* that the book was an "entertaining addition to beginning-reader collections."

Krensky has also written a number of nonfiction books for both older and younger readers. Included in the latter are *Dinosaurs, Beware!: A Safety Guide* and *Perfect Pigs: An Introduction to Manners,* both cowritten with popular author/illustrator Marc Brown. An ALA Notable Book in 1982, *Dinosaurs, Beware!* presents sixty safety tips for youngsters through the use of dinosaurs, while *Perfect Pigs* is an introduction to good manners.

Krensky's nonfiction for older readers is noted for providing accurate and thoroughly researched introductions to their subjects. For example, *Conqueror and Hero: The Search for Alexander* "offers a clear, concise account of the brilliant and enigmatic Macedonian leader," according to Ethel R. Twichell in *Horn Book.* A reviewer for *Bulletin of the Center for Children's Books* noted that the conciseness of that text "may appeal to reluctant readers," and *School Library Journal* critic Elizabeth Holtze commented that when "readers put down this good book, they will want to learn more about its fascinating subject." Although *Maiden Voyage: The Story of the Statue of Liberty* was one of the many books on its subject to appear in the statue's centennial year, it is often thought to stand out from the rest, according to Elizabeth S. Watson in *Horn Book,* because of its "brevity and humor." *Maiden Voyage* appeared on the Child Study Association of America's Book of the Year list in 1985.

Two of Krensky's books that deal with the discovery of America are *Who Really Discovered America?* and *Christopher Columbus.* The former title details the voyages that preceded that of Columbus, including those of Asian nomads, Polynesians, Phoenicians, and Scandinavians. The familiar Krensky mix was noticeable in this nonfiction. "Though Krensky treats his subject with respect and precision, his text is leavened with humor," noted a *Kirkus Reviews* contributor. Krensky's easy-reading biography of Columbus takes a "middle ground in the hero-antihero controversy," according to Carolyn Phelan in *Booklist,* who concluded that the "straightforward account is [a] good choice at this reading level."

Lighter in tone are *The Pizza Book* and *Scoop after Scoop: A History of Ice Cream.* In both, Krensky gives an overview of the history of the subject along with various recipes. Carolyn Jenks commented in *School Library Journal* that *The Pizza Book* takes a "lighthearted look at the evolution of this crowd pleaser." In *Booklist,* Ilene Cooper concluded that Krensky's *Scoop after Scoop* was a book "written with verve and humor," which "could be used for curriculum support or as an interesting commentary in its own right." Betsy Hearne, reviewing *Scoop after Scoop* in *Bulletin of the Center for Children's Books,* summed the matter up thusly: "Since many of [the consumers of ice cream] are children, they might as well get a taste of interesting history along with their cavities."

Other Krensky nonfiction titles include a history of the California gold rush, *Striking It Rich: The Story of the California Gold Rush;* a collective biography of four environmentalists, *Four against the Odds: The Struggle to Save Our Environment;* and a history of the written word and printing, *Breaking into Print: Before and after the Invention of the Printing Press.* Catherine M. Clancy, writing in *Voice of Youth Advocates,* thought that *Four against the Odds,* featuring profiles of John

Muir, Rachel Carson, Chico Mendes, and Lois Gibbs, "offers an excellent introduction to the 'environmental issue,'" while Chris Sherman, reviewing the same book in *Booklist,* noted that "Krensky's style is very readable." Assessing Krensky's overview of the printed word, *Breaking into Print,* a critic for *Kirkus Reviews* concluded that Krensky's text and Bonnie Christensen's illustrations worked in tandem to create "a gorgeous format that does complete justice to the subject."

Krensky has also used his fiction to deal with history, as with his *Printer's Apprentice,* in which a young apprentice in 1735 learns of the importance of freedom of speech the hard way, and with *The Iron Dragon Never Sleeps,* which addresses the plight of the Chinese workers constructing the transcontinental railroad. A *Kirkus Reviews* contributor noted that Krensky "makes good use of historical fact" in *The Printer's Apprentice* and that "his plot moves along smoothly, and the ideas and ideals are worth reading about." Reviewing the same novel in *Horn Book,* Margaret A. Bush commented that Krensky "creates a lively adventure story." Another *Kirkus Reviews* contributor found *The Iron Dragon Never Sleeps* to be an "interesting adjunct to the study of Westward expansion," while a *Publishers Weekly* critic concluded that Krensky avoided "a pat, happy ending" to this story of the friendship of a white girl and a Chinese boy and that he devised "a bittersweet conclusion that renders his historically accurate story even more powerful."

Krensky continued to write for newly independent readers with such tales as 1998's *We Just Moved!.* In it, a little boy voices his anticipation and anxiety about his family's impending move to a new home—while Larry Difiori's illustrations slyly show the family home to be a medieval castle. One line of text, "We packed all our clothing," is accompanied by an illustration showing a cart laden with suits of armor. In other humorous touches that chronicle his adjustment, the boy is excited about the "modern kitchen" in the new, improved castle, which turns out to be a fireplace in the kitchen. However, "the occasional comedy in the well-drawn, colorful illustrations is balanced by the emotional truth of the words," noted *Booklist*'s Carolyn Phelan.

Krensky gave the indomitable sister of Lionel her own series in 1998 with *Louise Takes Charge.* Again, the works were illustrated by Susanna Natti, who collaborated with Krensky on the previous Lionel titles. In the debut story, Louise's first few days of the new school year are blighted by the sudden change in personality in her friend Jasper. After a summertime growth spurt, Jasper returns to become the class bully. One day Lionel tells Louise a story about a knight and his apprentice, which gives Louise an idea: she offers to serve as Jasper's apprentice, and soon others in her class follow suit. "The setup isn't entirely plausible, but the dialogue is snappy," wrote *Booklist*'s Susan Dove Lempke. The series continued with *Louise Goes Wild,* in which the little girl laments that she is too boring and predictable, and *Louise, Soccer Star?,* where the heroine dreams of greatness on the soccer pitch, but she is irate when a new

schoolmate from England usurps her center forward spot on the team. Trelawney even takes Louise's lucky number—but Louise, after working hard to best her nemesis, in the end befriends her. "Krensky creates believable characters," noted *Booklist* writer Lempke in a review of *Louise, Soccer Star?,* "nicely depicting realistic, not-always-pretty feelings with empathy."

A comic prequel to the Santa story was the basis for Krensky's *How Santa Got His Job.* The story depicts a very young Santa applying for jobs in his suit and tie. He works as a chimney sweeper—but remains clean. He finds a job at the post office—but prefers to deliver in the middle of the night. At the zoo, he befriends the reindeer, and then runs away to join the circus with them. All are rescued by elves and find a new home and new calling at the North Pole. Across the pages, Krensky's protagonist ages into an older, avuncular Santa in S. D. Schindler's images. "The story is smart and funny, and Schindler knows exactly how to make his artwork play off the humor," noted *Booklist* critic Ilene Cooper.

The Youngest Fairy Godmother Ever gives Krensky fans another indomitable heroine facing a challenge: Mavis wants desperately to be a fairy godmother, as in the Cinderella story. She tells her parents that she wants to make the wishes of others come true, to which they respond by saying they wish she would take out the garbage. Mavis studies hard to perform magic and tries to make her own magic wand, but she is seemingly stymied in the realization of her career goal. At school, she tries to turn a pet classroom mouse into a coachman, which leads to some minor chaos and suddenly causes her to notice a new classmate. Shabbily dressed Cindy lives with her two mean stepsisters, who order her about. Mavis learns that Cindy does not have a Halloween costume, so she decides to sew one for her—making her indeed someone's fairy godmother. "As sympathetic as it is witty, this prince-less 'Cinderella' should charm its readers," noted a *Publishers Weekly* contributor.

Krensky has also penned a number of juvenile biographies. These include *Taking Flight: The Story of the Wright Brothers,* which recounts the achievements of brothers Orville and Wilbur Wright in their attempt to make and send aloft a "flying machine" in North Carolina in 1903. Krensky has also written about a nineteenth-century Ohioan and famed sharpshooter Annie Oakley in *Shooting for the Moon: The Amazing Life and Times of Annie Oakley.*

Krensky teamed with Schindler again for a sequel to his first Santa story. In 2001's *How Santa Lost His Job,* the Christmas stalwart suddenly realizes that Muckle the Elf is planning to make him obsolete with the help of a new machine called the Deliverator. Predictably, it fails at the worst possible time, and Santa is saved from compulsory early retirement. In this book, noted a *Kirkus Reviews* contributor, its author "has crafted a tale with an obvious lesson, but somehow this does not detract. Rather, it highlights the importance of personal attention and the 'little things' in the celebration of Christmas."

Krensky once told *SATA* where his books and ideas come from: "People often ask me how I can write something that twelve-year-olds or nine-year-olds will want to read. I'm not sure, but I do know that the part of me that was once twelve and nine and six is not neatly boxed and tucked away in some dusty corner of my mind. It's spread throughout the place like crepe paper or bunting. So far I think it's given the place a festive air. If I'm lucky, it always will."

Biographical and Critical Sources

BOOKS

Krensky, Stephen, *We Just Moved!*, illustrated by Larry Difiori, Scholastic (New York, NY), 1998.

Sixth Book of Junior Authors and Illustrators, edited by Sally Holmes Holtze, H. W. Wilson (New York, NY), 1989.

PERIODICALS

Booklist, November 15, 1986, Ilene Cooper, review of *Scoop after Scoop: A History of Ice Cream*, p. 513; December 1, 1991, Julie Corsaro, review of *Lionel and Louise*, p. 709, and Carolyn Phelan, review of *Christopher Columbus*, p. 111; June 1, 1992, Chris Sherman, review of *Four against the Odds: The Struggle to Save Our Environment*, p. 1759; July, 1998, Carolyn Phelan, review of *We Just Moved!*, and *Lionel in the Summer*, p. 1890; September 1, 1998, Ilene Cooper, review of *How Santa Got His Job*, p. 112; October 1, 1998, Susan Dove Lempke, review of *Louise Takes Charge*, p. 330; March 15, 1999, review of *How Santa Got His Job*, p. 1302, and Ilene Cooper, review of *My Loose Tooth*, p. 1337; July, 1999, Lauren Peterson, review of *Louise Goes Wild*, p. 1946; May 15, 2000, Carolyn Phelan, review of *Taking Flight: The Story of the Wright Brothers*, p. 1740; June 1, 2000, Carolyn Phelan, review of *Arthur and the Big Blow-Up*, p. 1894; July, 2000, Ilene Cooper, review of *The Youngest Fairy Godmother Ever*, p. 2040; October 1, 2000, Hazel Rochman, review of *Lionel at School*, p. 352; March 1, 2001, Susan Dove Lempke, review of *Louise, Soccer Star?*, p. 1278; April 15, 2001, Roger Leslie, review of *The Moon Robber*, p. 1559; May 15, 2001, Connie Fletcher, review of *Arthur and the Seventh-Inning Stretcher*, p. 1753; September 15, 2001, Stephanie Zvirin, review of *How Santa Lost His Job*, p. 235, and Carolyn Phelan, review of *Shooting for the Moon: The Amazing Life and Times of Annie Oakley*, p. 228.

Bulletin of the Center for Children's Books, May, 1980, review of *A Troll in Passing*, p. 175; January, 1982, review of *Conqueror and Hero: The Search for Alexander*, p. 88; November, 1984, review of *A Ghostly Business*, p. 49; April, 1986, review of *Lionel at Large*, p. 113; February, 1987, Betsy Hearne, review of *Scoop after Scoop: A History of Ice Cream*, p. 111; February, 1994, Carol Fox, review of *Lionel in Winter*, pp. 190-191.

Children's Book Review Service, February, 1979, p. 68; July, 1980, p. 127; January, 1982, p. 48; February,

1983, p. 71; spring, 1983, p. 119; March, 1986, p. 89; December, 1989, p. 40; December, 1991, p. 40.

Five Owls, September, 1991, p. 20.

Horn Book, December, 1981, Ethel R. Twichell, review of *Conqueror and Hero*, pp. 677-678; January-February, 1986, Elizabeth S. Watson, review of *Maiden Voyage: The Story of the Statue of Liberty*, pp. 76-77; July-August, 1990, Carolyn K. Jenks, review of *Lionel in the Spring*, p. 477; March, 1992, p. 219; March, 1994, p. 195; September-October, 1995, Margaret A. Bush, review of *The Printer's Apprentice*, pp. 600-601.

Kirkus Reviews, April 1, 1977, review of *A Big Day for Scepters*, p. 352; January 1, 1988, review of *Who Really Discovered America?*, p. 56; June 1, 1994, review of *The Iron Dragon Never Sleeps*, p. 776; June 15, 1995, review of *The Printer's Apprentice*, p. 858; July 15, 1996, review of *Breaking into Print: Before and after the Invention of the Printing Press*, p. 1051; September 15, 2001, review of *How Santa Lost His Job*, p. 1360;

New York Times Book Review, June 19, 1977, p. 28; April 30, 1978, p. 46; November 9, 1980, p. 56; January 5, 1997, p. 22.

Publishers Weekly, June 13, 1980, review of *A Troll in Passing*, p. 72; May 27, 1983, p. 67; January 6, 1984, p. 84; June 27, 1986, p. 88; October 9, 1987, p. 86; October 18, 1991, p. 61; May 2, 1994, review of *The Iron Dragon Never Sleeps*, p. 309; December 18, 1995, p. 55; June 5, 2000, review of *The Youngest Fairy Godmother Ever*, p. 93; June 11, 2001, review of *The Moon Robber*, p. 86; October 8, 2001, review of *Shooting for the Moon: The Amazing Life and Times of Annie Oakley*, p. 64.

School Arts, April, 1997, Kent Anderson and Ken Marantz, review of *Breaking into Print: Before and after the Invention of the Printing Press*, p. 63.

School Library Journal, April, 1977, Craighton Hippenhammer, review of *A Big Day for Scepters*, p. 68; October, 1977, Craighton Hippenhammer, review of *The Dragon Circle*, p. 115; November, 1981, Elizabeth Holtze, review of *Conqueror and Hero*, pp. 106-107; January, 1983, Amy L. Cohn, review of *The Wilder Plot*, p. 77; May, 1986, review of *Lionel at Large*, p. 113; April, 1992, Sharron McElmeel, review of *Lionel and Louise*, p. 95; February, 1993, Carolyn Jenks, review of *The Pizza Book*, p. 100; June, 2000, Gay Lynn Van Vleck, review of *The Youngest Fairy Godmother Ever*, p. 118; August, 2000, Susan Knell, review of *Taking Flight*, p. 171; September, 2000, Helen Foster James, review of *Lionel at School*, p. 202; January, 2001, Blair Christolon, review of *Louise, Soccer Star?*, p. 102; July, 2001, Susan Lissim, review of *Pearl Harbor*, p. 95; September, 2001, Devon Gallagher, review of *The Moon Robber*, p. 200; October, 2001, review of *How Santa Lost His Job*, p. 67.

Times Educational Supplement, September 24, 1982, p. 35.

Voice of Youth Advocates, February, 1984, review of *The Wilder Summer*, p. 339; October, 1992, Catherine M. Clancy, review of *Four against the Odds: The Struggle to Save Our Environment*, p. 254.

Wilson Library Bulletin, fall, 1992, p. 82.*

L–M

LEWIS, Kim 1951-

Personal

Born May 26, 1951, in Montreal, Quebec, Canada; married Flea (a farm manager); children: Sara, James. *Nationality:* Canadian; British. *Education:* Sir George Williams University, B.F.A. (with distinction), 1972; Hornsey College of Art, certificate, 1973.

Addresses

Home—The Riding, Bellingham, Hexham, Northumberland, NE48 2DU, England.

Career

Camden Arts Centre, London, England, assistant to the gallery administrator, 1973-75; Middlesex Polytechnic Fine Art Department, London, England, fine art printmaking technician, 1975-78; Charlotte Press Printmaking Workshop, Newcastle upon Tyne, England, resident lithographer, 1978-80; self-employed artist and printmaker, 1980—; author and illustrator of children's books, 1988—. *Exhibitions:* Group exhibitions include National Exhibition of Modern British Prints, London, England, 1975; Royal Academy Summer Show, London, England, 1976; Charlotte Press Printmaking Shows at Bondgate Gallery, Alnwick, England, Callerton Gallery, Ponteland, England, and Sallyport Gallery, Berwick upon Tweed, England, all 1978; Marsil Museum, Montreal, Canada, 1978; Old School Arts Workshop, Middleham, England, 1979; and Northern Print Workshops, Laing Art Gallery, Newcastle, England, 1979. Solo exhibitions include Spectro Arts Workshop, Newcastle, England, 1978; Wallington Hall, Cambo, England, 1979; Stamfordham Galley, Stamfordham, England, 1984; Gossipgate Gaslight Gallery, Alston, England, 1985; Queen's Hall Arts Centre, Hexham, England, 1987; and Gossipgate Garden Gallery, Carlisle, England, 1989.

Two children have to decide which of Floss's puppies they should keep in Kim Lewis's self-illustrated **Just Like Floss.**

Awards, Honors

Board of Governors Medal for Creative Expression, 1971; A. E. Pinsky Medal, 1972; Birks Medal, 1972; Kate Greenaway Medal shortlist, British Library Association, 1990, for *The Shepherd Boy;* Sheffield Children's Book Award shortlist, 1996, for *My Friend Harry;* Parents' Choice Silver Honour, 1998, for *Emma's Lamb;* Children's Book Award shortlist, 1999, for *Just Like Floss.*

Writings

SELF-ILLUSTRATED

The Shepherd Boy, Walker Books (London, England), 1990.
Emma's Lamb, Walker Books (London, England), 1991.
Floss, Walker Books (London, England), 1992.
First Snow, Walker Books (London, England), 1993.

The Last Train, Walker Books (London, England), 1994.

My Friend Harry, Walker Books (London, England), 1995.

One Summer Day, Walker Books (London, England), Candlewick Press (Cambridge, MA), 1996.

Friends, Walker Books (London, England), Candlewick Press (Cambridge, MA), 1997.

Just Like Floss, Walker Books (London, England), Candlewick Press (Cambridge, MA), 1998.

Little Calf, Walker Books (London, England), Candlewick Press (Cambridge, MA), 2000.

Little Lamb, Walker Books (London, England), Candlewick Press (Cambridge, MA), 2000.

Little Puppy, Walker Books (London, England), Candlewick Press (Cambridge, MA), 2000.

Little Baa, Walker Books (London, England), Candlewick Press (Cambridge, MA), 2001.

A Quilt for Baby, Walker Books (London, England), Candlewick Press (Cambridge, MA), 2003.

ILLUSTRATOR

Berlie Doherty, *Willa and Old Miss Annie,* Walker Books (London, England), 1994.

Sam McBratney, *I'm Not Your Friend,* HarperCollins (London, England), 2001, published as *I'll Always Be Your Friend,* HarperCollins (New York, NY), 2001.

Also illustrator of several book covers for Bloodaxe Books.

Sidelights

Kim Lewis told *SATA:* "When I first came to Northumberland, it struck me as the part of England most like the countryside where I come from in Canada, so in that sense, I felt I had travelled a long way to 'come home.'

"Landscape dominates Northumberland with its high moors and huge skies—one becomes very aware of changes in land due to changes in the weather. Also, because we live and work on a farm, land and weather daily affect what my husband has to do in his job. Trying to create the atmosphere and feeling of living and working in a Northern landscape has thus formed the main theme in both my fine art and children's work.

"Northern landscape, as well as hill farming life, can seem bleak to some, but it prevents sentimentality. The ideas in my books are influenced by this. A border collie is used for work, not play; a winsome lamb belongs to a ewe, however much a child would like to keep it for herself; a shepherd's son has to learn to watch and wait before he can take his wished for place in the scheme of things; snow isn't just lovely and fluffy—it can blot out a familiar landscape, a favourite toy, and even the way home.

"I write about what I know and like to draw realistically from what I see, never trusting my imagination to come up with any material more amazing than what is around. I like to include those quiet corners of a farm where machinery and tools rest, after work, in dark barns where rugged wool sacks are stacked and the wood is weathered to a hundred years' sort of soft grey. The

cycle of farm work which follows the seasons, from lambing time to hay making and clipping, from calving to winter feeding, provides so much visual material that I never seem to tire of it. I have made lithographs and watercolours of these things, and now children's books. Each pencil drawing takes two weeks to complete. Each book takes a year.

"When I did a series of book covers for the Newcastle-based Bloodaxe Books, it was the first time I'd used coloured pencil illustrations instead of printmaking, and the start of producing pictures to go with words. Encouraged by a writer/illustrator friend and inspired by watching my husband's work on the sheep farm, I decided to tell the story of the farming year in a simple way for young children, such as my son who was three at the time.

"I wanted other farm children to recognise their own lives in the stories and city children to be able to 'walk into' the books as if visiting a hill farm for themselves. As a result, *The Shepherd Boy* was sent to Walker Books, London, who loved the artwork but sent me away to rewrite the story as I wanted to, instead of how I thought a children's book should be written. Such freedom was the start of a happy publishing relationship which has been in place ever since, book by book."

Author/illustrator Lewis is strongly influenced by the locale of her adopted country, England. Born in Canada, Lewis moved to rural Northumberland after finishing her bachelor's degree. Enchanted by the landscape that was so similar to the area outside her native Montreal, she quickly fell in love with life in the English countryside. Her two children also became involved with the daily routines of working on a farm, and so it was a natural progression for Lewis to base the characters in her stories on her own children and their adventures, sometimes even naming her characters after them.

Lewis was inspired to write her first children's book, *The Shepherd Boy,* when her husband landed a job as manager at a sheep farm in the North Tyne Valley. *The Shepherd Boy* tells of James's longing to be just like his father, who is a shepherd. By the end of the story, James receives a shepherd's crook and a sheepdog to raise as his own. A sheepdog is also featured in *Floss,* in which the title character, a border collie, has to learn the difference between work and play. Floss was reprised in the 1998 title, *Just Like Floss,* in which two children have to decide which of the pups from Floss's litter they will keep. When the smallest pup, Sam, stands fast eyeball-to-eyeball with a big ewe, the children know immediately he is the one—a born sheepdog like his mother.

Two children are at the heart of *One Summer Day,* as well. Little Max loves tractors, and he always wants to follow when one goes by the window. When his friend Sara takes him for a walk, Max sees the tractor go by again, and now he feels both excited and satisfied. Hanna B. Zeiger, writing in *Horn Book,* praised the "gentle, sun-dappled illustrations" which "capture the unhurried pace of a small child's happy adventures," while a contributor for *Kirkus Reviews* called *One Summer Day* a "book with a drop of humor and a spoonful of wistfulness."

Another little boy, James, has a special relationship with a toy elephant in *My Friend Harry,* a picture book that shows "great finesse in portraying the relationship between a young child and his silent companion," according to *Booklist*'s Carolyn Phelan. A real-life friendship is at the center of *Friends,* in which toddlers Sam and Alice get together on Sam's farm for a day of play. Hearing the clucking of a chicken as it lays an egg, they go to retrieve the egg, but on the way back to the house have a quarrel and break it. Everything works out fine, however, for when they hear the tell-tale clucking again, they get another egg and bring this one safely home. "You can almost smell the hay," wrote Miriam Lang Budin in *School Library Journal.* "Masterful."

Lewis sticks with rural themes in *Little Puppy, Little Calf,* and *Little Lamb.* These books all feature Katie's first gentle and magical moments with the newborn animals on her farm. She touches the newborn calf's nose, for example, and is licked on the face by the puppy. "What saves these books from sentimentality," noted *Booklist*'s Hazel Rochman, "are the facts about each animal" that Lewis integrates into her stories. Piper L. Nyman, reviewing the same three books in *School Library Journal,* commented on the "lush, rural landscapes" on the endpapers and the "gentle nature" of these tales.

In *Little Baa,* Lewis presents a lamb dancing through the fields while its Ma nibbles grass nearby. Suddenly, when she looks up, Baa is gone. While the other baby lambs return to their mothers, Baa stays missing, and Ma wanders through the countryside in search of her baby. Floss, the border collie, helps out, finding the baby lamb and reuniting him with his mother, a reunion which *Booklist*'s Ilene Cooper found "quite touching." Cooper further felt that the book was "tender and lovely, a nice mix of animal behavior and human emotion." Rachel Fox, writing in *School Library Journal,* concluded that young readers "will find its happy ending quite satisfying."

Lewis continued to *SATA:* "Now that my children have grown up, I am finding that areas of my own childhood are surfacing. Subject matter is blurring into overlays of remembrance, still with a strong feeling of the countryside—where I have always wanted to be.

"It is a great pleasure to write and draw about the small corners of country life for children, where the world is up close and new. Drawing is my favourite thing, so I've always done it, regardless."

Biographical and Critical Sources

PERIODICALS

Booklist, February 15, 1992, p. 1110; September 15, 1992, p. 158; October 15, 1995, Carolyn Phelan, review of

My Friend Harry, p. 412; April 15, 1998, Hazel Rochman, review of *Friends,* p. 1450; January 1, 1999, Kathleen Squires, review of *Just Like Floss,* p. 888; March 15, 2000, Hazel Rochman, review of *Little Puppy, Little Calf,* and *Little Lamb,* p. 1387; May 1, 2001, Ilene Cooper, review of *Little Baa,* p. 1691.
Books for Keeps, January, 1996, review of *First Snow,* p. 6; November, 1996, review of *The Last Train,* p. 8.
Horn Book, September-October, 1994, p. 586; July-August, 1996, Hanna B. Zeiger, review of *One Summer Day,* pp. 450-451; November-December, 1998, Marilyn Bousquin, review of *Just Like Floss,* pp. 715-716.
Horn Book Guide, July, 1990, p. 39; fall, 1991, p. 236; fall, 1992, p. 238; spring, 1994, p. 42; spring, 1999, p. 14.
Kirkus Reviews, January 15, 1992, p. 122; July 15, 1994, p. 989; June 15, 1996, review of *One Summer Day,* p. 901; November 1, 1998, review of *Just Like Floss,* p. 1601.
Publishers Weekly, March 9, 1992, review of *Floss,* p. 55.
School Librarian, spring, 1998, Beverly Mathias, review of *Friend,* p. 19.
School Library Journal, December, 1990, p. 82; July, 1991, Barbara Chatton, review of *Emma's Lamb,* p. 60; April, 1992, p. 96; November, 1993, p. 86; October, 1994, p. 92; September, 1995, p. 181; July, 1996, Christine A. Moesch, review of *One Summer Day,* p. 67; July, 1998, Miriam Lang Budin, review of *Friends,* p. 78; January, 1999, Kathy M. Newby, review of *Just Like Floss,* p. 97; June, 2000, Piper L. Nyman, review of *Little Puppy, Little Calf,* and *Little Lamb,* p. 118; June, 2001, Rachel Fox, review of *Little Baa,* p. 124.
Times Educational Supplement, March 29, 1991, p. 23.

*   *   *

MacDONALD, Amy 1951-
(Del Tremens)

Personal

Born June 14, 1951, in Beverly, MA; daughter of Alexander S. (a doctor) and Mary (a psychotherapist; maiden name, Wright) MacDonald; married Thomas A. Urquhart (an environmental conservationist), June 26, 1976; children: Emily, Alexander, Jeremy. *Nationality:* American. *Education:* University of Pennsylvania, B.A., 1973; Centre de Formation des Journalistes, 1982-83, fellow. *Politics:* Democrat. *Religion:* Unitarian.

Addresses

Home—10 Winslow Rd., Falmouth, ME 04105. *E-mail*—amymac@maine.rr.com.

Career

Proposition Theatre, Cambridge, MA, publicity directory, 1975-76; *Harvard Post,* Harvard, MA, editor, 1976-82; *Highwire* magazine, Lowell, MA, senior editor, 1983-84; Cambridge University Press, Cambridge, En-

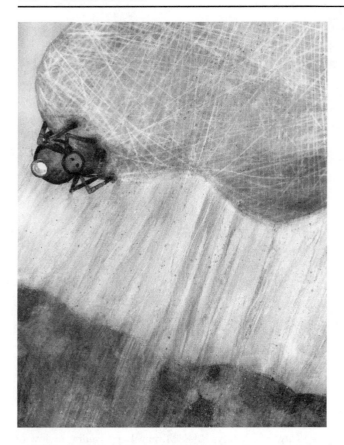

Nobb the spider weaves a net to make a home for her egg in Amy MacDonald's **The Spider Who Created the World.** *(Illustrated by G. Brian Karas.)*

gland, copy editor, 1984-88; full-time freelance journalist, editor, and children's book author, 1988—. Harvard University, summer writing instructor, 1988; Stonecoast Writers' Conference, instructor, 1991, 1992, 1993; University of Maine, Farmington, ME, instructor, 1995; Kennedy Center for the Performing Arts, workshop leader, 2003—. Board member, Figures of Speech Theater, 1990—, and Presumpscot River Watch.

Member

Society of Children's Book Writers and Illustrators, Maine Writers and Publishers Alliance (president, 1995-98), numerous environmental groups.

Awards, Honors

Columnist of the Year Award, New England Women's Press Association, 1980; Silver Stylus Award for best children's book, Collectieve Propaganda van her Nederlandse Boek (Dutch Book Association), 1990, for *Little Beaver and the Echo; Little Beaver and the Echo* was named one of the ten best children's books by *New York Times, Horn Book* and *Fanfare,* a Book-of-the-Month-Club selection, and shortlisted for the Newbery Medal and Children's Book Award, England; Oppenheim Platinum Award, 2003, for *Please, Malese!: A Trickster Tale from Haiti.*

Writings

(Compiler) *The Whale Show* (play), first produced at Proposition Theatre, Cambridge, MA, 1975, produced in New York, NY, 1977.

(Under pseudonym Del Tremens) *A Very Young Housewife* (parody of children's books), Harvard Common Press (Boston, MA), 1979.

Little Beaver and the Echo, illustrated by Sarah Fox-Davies, Putnam (New York, NY), 1990.

Rachel Fister's Blister, illustrated by Marjorie Priceman, Houghton (Boston, MA), 1990.

Let's Do It, illustrated by Maureen Roffey, Candlewick Press (Cambridge, MA), 1991.

Let's Make a Noise, illustrated by Maureen Roffey, Candlewick Press (Cambridge, MA), 1991.

Let's Play, illustrated by Maureen Roffey, Candlewick Press (Cambridge, MA), 1991.

Let's Try, illustrated by Maureen Roffey, Candlewick Press (Cambridge, MA), 1991.

Let's Pretend, illustrated by Maureen Roffey, Candlewick Press (Cambridge, MA), 1993.

Let's Go, illustrated by Maureen Roffey, Candlewick Press (Cambridge, MA), 1993.

The Spider Who Created the World, illustrated by G. Brian Karas, Orchard Books (New York, NY), 1994.

Cousin Ruth's Tooth, illustrated by Marjorie Priceman, Houghton (Boston, MA), 1996.

No More Nice, illustrated by Cat Bowman Smith, Orchard Books (New York, NY), 1996.

No More Nasty, illustrated by Cat Bowman Smith, Farrar, Straus (New York, NY), 2001.

Quentin Fenton Herter III, illustrated by Giselle Potter, Farrar, Straus (New York, NY), 2002.

Please, Malese!: A Trickster Tale from Haiti, illustrated by Emily Lisker, Farrar, Straus (New York, NY), 2002.

Little Beaver and the Echo has been published in twenty-five languages. Contributor to national and international magazines, including *Child, Parents, Parenting, Guardian, Times,* and *New Yorker.*

Sidelights

Amy MacDonald's first picture book, *Little Beaver and the Echo,* tells the story of a lonely little beaver who calls out his need for a friend and hears the exact same plea echoing from across the pond. He goes in search of this voice to befriend it and comes across a duck, an otter, and a turtle, also in need of friends. When the group reaches the other side of the pond, the mystery of the echo is explained by a wise old beaver. At the book's end, the pond echoes with the gleeful noises made by the four new friends. While one reviewer found this story somewhat predictable, many considered it a gentle and satisfying parable for young children. Carolyn Phelan, writing in *Booklist,* described *Little Beaver and the Echo* as "a simple, satisfying picture book.... There's a bit of Little Beaver in every kid."

MacDonald once related to *SATA* the genesis of *Little Beaver and the Echo:* "I have always loved children's books, but I never intended to write one. [*Little Beaver* and the Echo] came about entirely by accident. I was staying at a beautiful lake and playing with the echo there when my one-year-old son asked me what an echo was. Instead of answering, I wrote a story. The setting, of course, was the lake where I had spent so many happy summers as a child. And the main character was a beaver—like the ones who lived on the lake. The resulting book combines my love of a simple story with my love of the outdoors."

After completing her first book, MacDonald decided to continue to write for children. *Rachel Fister's Blister* is the humorous, rhyming story of Rachel, who has a blister on her toe, and all the people in her town, from the fireman to the priest and rabbi, who offer silly solutions to her problem. A reviewer for *Publishers Weekly* commented, "MacDonald's sparkling tale has the exceptional virtue of making her verse seem effortless," while Kathy Piehl remarked in *School Library Journal:* "This book's infectious rhythm and rhyme demand that it be read aloud."

The outrageous antics of the Fister clan make another appearance in *Cousin Ruth's Tooth,* "a great read-aloud story," according to *School Library Journal* critic Anne Parker, that "will also be enjoyed by beginning readers." After the youngster tells her aunt that she has lost her first tooth, Mrs. Fister sends the whole house into an uproar trying to locate it. Instead of treating this event as a normal part of growing up, the Fisters scramble about their home, searching for Ruth's missing tooth. As Cousin Keith suggests buying a new one at the department store, Uncle Drew insists that gluing in a new tooth would fix the problem. Chaos ensues as the family members struggle to find the missing part and eventually decide to ask the Queen for help in deciding what to do. As the Fisters anxiously await the Queen's solution, little Ruth makes a surprise announcement. A replacement tooth is growing where the old one was, a fact she knew about the whole time, but kept to herself, enjoying the panic she created. Reviewers praised MacDonald's text. For instance, a *Kirkus Reviews* contributor wrote that "a sophisticated vocabulary and carefully composed cadence make it a perfect piece to read aloud or perform." "It's a perfect romp," remarked a *Publishers Weekly* critic, "and readers can only hope for more collaborations between" MacDonald and illustrator Marjorie Priceman.

In another work, the author turned to an original creation story, *The Spider Who Created the World.* Explaining the development of the Earth, MacDonald devised a tale about a young spider called Nobb who is looking for a home to lay her first egg. Suffering rejections from Sun, Moon, and Cloud, Nobb decides to create a place of her own, stealing pieces from the three rude elements. Mixing these parts together, the spider designs a home of her own, the Earth. Here she lays her egg, and when it hatches all of the creatures of the world are released to inhabit the new world. *Booklist*'s Hazel Rochman observed that *The Spider Who Created the World* "has an easy rhythm for reading aloud, with satisfying reversals in the echoing text," while a *Publishers Weekly*

critic claimed that "MacDonald finds poetry in concise, repetitive language, and explores a metaphor that young naturalists will easily grasp." Speaking of the difficulty in creating original *pourquoi* tales, *Bulletin of the Center for Children's Books* reviewer Deborah Stevenson found the work "an elegant and well-structured one that spins its story thread with a gentle formality, careful progression, and pleasing rhythm."

Readers are introduced to eleven-year-old Simon and his eccentric Aunt Mattie and Uncle Philbert in *No More Nice,* a book about the young boy as he leaves for a week-long stay with the pair one spring vacation. Imagining that the two will be old, feeble, and impatient with young children, Simon dreads the trip. To his surprise, however, the two are exactly the opposite of what he expected, with his aunt telling him he needs to ask more questions and his uncle explaining to him the art of cussing creatively. Unlike his neat and orderly home life, the home of Simon's aunt and uncle is in disarray, with the boy finding out that he has to sleep with the couple's ornery cat. But Simon slowly begins to appreciate Mattie and Philbert's nonconformity, and by the end of the week, he heads off for home with his newfound knowledge and a greater appreciation for the role of manners in civilized society. According to *Booklist* critic Susan DeRonne, "This book ... tells a humorous story with a warm message."

Simon's zany relatives return in *No More Nasty,* described by *Horn Book* contributor Martha V. Parravano as "light but proficuous fare ... for elementary readers." After his fifth-grade teacher leaves the school in mid-year, Simon learns that his Aunt Mattie has been

The whole Fister family searches for a missing tooth in **Cousin Ruth's Tooth.** *(Illustrated by Marjorie Priceman.)*

hired to fill in for the absent teacher. Loving his aunt's unusual ways but at the same time embarrassed by her crazy antics, Simon keeps his relationship with the new teacher a secret from the other kids in the class. While initially dismissive of Aunt Mattie, who seems unfazed at all of the pranks the children attempt, the students eventually begin to enjoy her unorthodox teaching methods and become the highest-achieving class in the school. "The delightful black-and-white illustrations highlight moments of the humorous plot, which readers will enjoy as a read-aloud or read-alone," remarked *School Library Journal* critic Betsy Fraser.

MacDonald has also written the text for several board books in the "Let's Explore" series from Candlewick Press. The books combine simple ideas and bright, colorful drawings that together introduce the youngest children to activities and objects around them. Phelan remarked of the series in *Booklist,* "Simple, bright, and appealing, this set of board books offers a pleasant introduction to the world of reading."

Biographical and Critical Sources

PERIODICALS

Booklist, January 1, 1991, Carolyn Phelan, review of *Little Beaver and the Echo,* p. 938; March 15, 1992, Carolyn Phelan, review of *Let's Do It* and *Let's Make a Noise,* p. 1385; April 1, 1996, Carolyn Phelan, review of *Cousin Ruth's Tooth,* p. 1372; April 15, 1996, Hazel Rochman, review of *The Spider Who Created the World,* p. 1446; September 1, 1996, Susan DeRonne, review of *No More Nice,* p. 130; September 1, 2001, Chris Sherman, review of *No More Nasty,* p. 106.
Bulletin of the Center for Children's Books, May, 1996, Deborah Stevenson, review of *The Spider Who Created the World,* p. 307.
Horn Book, November-December, 1990, Ellen Fader, review of *Rachel Fister's Blister,* p. 731; July-August, 1992, p. 457; September-October, 1996, Ellen Fader, review of *The Spider Who Created the World,* p. 582; November-December, 2001, Martha V. Parravano, review of *No More Nasty,* p. 754.
Kirkus Reviews, February 1, 1996, review of *Cousin Ruth's Tooth,* p. 230; October 1, 1996, review of *No More Nice,* p. 1471.
Publishers Weekly, June 29, 1990, review of *Little Beaver and the Echo,* p. 100; August 31, 1990, review of *Rachel Fister's Blister,* p. 63; February 12, 1996, review of *The Spider Who Created the World,* p. 76; February 19, 1996, review of *Cousin Ruth's Tooth,* p. 215; August 27, 2001, review of *No More Nasty,* p. 86; January 14, 2002, review of *Quentin Fenton Herter III,* p. 58; May 27, 2002, review of *Please, Malese!: A Trickster Tale from Haiti,* p. 59.
School Library Journal, November, 1990, Kathy Piehl, review of *Rachel Fister's Blister,* p. 96; March, 1991, Margaret Bush, review of *Little Beaver and the Echo,* p. 175; June, 1992, Steven Engelfried, review of *Let's Do It* and *Let's Try,* p. 99; August, 1992, Gale W. Sherman, review of *Let's Make a Noise* and *Let's Play,* p. 143; May, 1994, Linda Wicher, review of *Let's Go,* p. 100; March, 1996, Patricia (Dooley) Lothrop Green, review of *The Spider Who Created the World,* p. 178; May, 1996, Anne Parker, review of *Cousin Ruth's Tooth,* p. 94; September, 1996, John Sigwald, review of *No More Nice,* p. 204; September, 2001, Betsy Fraser, review of *No More Nasty,* p. 230.

OTHER

Any MacDonald Web Site, http://www.amymacdonald.com (November 13, 2002).*

*   *   *

McKENNA, Colleen O'Shaughnessy 1948-

Personal

Born May 31, 1948, in Springfield, IL; daughter of Joseph F. (a civil engineer) and Ruth Short (an office manager) O'Shaughnessy; married J. Frank McKenna III (an attorney), March 25, 1972; children: Collette, Jeff, Laura, Steve. *Nationality:* American. *Education:* Slippery Rock University, B.S., 1970; post-graduate studies at Carnegie Mellon University and Pitt University. *Religion:* Roman Catholic.

Addresses

Home—101 Fox Ridge Farms, Pittsburgh, PA 15215.

Career

Third and fourth grade teacher in Bethel Park, PA, 1970-1973; writer. Member of St. Lucy's Auxiliary.

Member

Society of Children's Book Writers and Illustrators.

Awards, Honors

Award of Excellence, Slippery Rock University, 1992.

Writings

"MURPHY" SERIES

Too Many Murphys, Scholastic (New York, NY), 1988.
Fourth Grade Is a Jinx, Scholastic (New York, NY), 1989.
Fifth Grade: Here Comes Trouble, Scholastic (New York, NY), 1989.
Eenie, Meanie, Murphy, No, Scholastic (New York, NY), 1990.
Murphy's Island, Scholastic (New York, NY), 1991.
The Truth about Sixth Grade, Scholastic (New York, NY), 1991.
Mother Murphy, Scholastic (New York, NY), 1992.
Camp Murphy, Scholastic (New York, NY), 1993.

"GORDIE BARR" SERIES

Third Grade Stinks!, illustrated by Stephanie Roth, Holiday House (New York, NY), 2001.

Third Grade Ghouls!, illustrated by Stephanie Roth, Holiday House (New York, NY), 2001.

Doggone . . . Third Grade!, illustrated by Stephanie Roth, Holiday House (New York, NY), 2002.

FOR CHILDREN

Merry Christmas, Miss McConnell!, Scholastic (New York, NY), 1990.

Not Quite Sisters ("Cousins" series), Scholastic (New York, NY), 1993.

Stuck in the Middle ("Cousins" series), Scholastic (New York, NY), 1993.

Good Grief . . . Third Grade, Scholastic (New York, NY), 1993.

The Brightest Light (for young adults), Scholastic (New York, NY), 1993.

Live from the Fifth Grade (sequel to *Good Grief . . . Third Grade*) Scholastic (New York, NY), 1994.

New Friends (novelization of the television show *Dr. Quinn, Medicine Woman*), Scholastic (New York, NY), 1995.

Queen of May (novelization of the television show *Dr. Quinn, Medicine Woman*), Scholastic (New York, NY), 1996.

Valentine's Day Can Be Murder, Scholastic (New York, NY), 1997.

Sidelights

Colleen O'Shaughnessy McKenna's series chapter books and stand-alone titles contain compellingly humorous tales which chronicle the small distresses and goofy hi-jinks of pre-teens. The kids in her stories think and talk like kids and are people other children can identify with. Reviewers have called her books warm, funny, and insightful, and have noted the way her "Murphy" books capture the chaos, struggles, and joys of a loving, boisterous family. Since *Too Many Murphys* was first published in 1988, McKenna's books have become popular with children between the ages of eight and twelve. Added to the "Murphy" books is a further series featuring Gordie Barr and friends in a third-grade classroom, as well as the tales of the children at Sacred Heart Elementary School.

McKenna began serious attempts at writing while in the eighth grade. Because she loved the character of Little Joe from the television series *Bonanza,* she began to write her own scripts for the show. "I wanted him to notice me. The best way to do that was to make myself the main character," she once recalled to *SATA.* In all, McKenna wrote twenty-seven scripts, mailing the best three to *Bonanza.* "It was a good experience because I learned about the opening, middle, and end of a story."

After graduating from Slippery Rock University with a degree in elementary/special education, McKenna taught third and fourth grades in Bethel Park, Pennsylvania. While there, she began writing plays for her classes. Noting that her students enjoyed working on the plays,

Gordie makes plans to "stink out" the girl with whom he has to share a locker in Colleen O'Shaughnessy McKenna's **Third Grade Stinks!** *(Illustrated by Stephanie Roth.)*

McKenna did not hesitate to use them to gain control of her classroom. "I guess we can't have rehearsal today because someone is throwing spitballs," she would say. The kids disciplined each other in order to rehearse.

In 1972 she married J. Frank McKenna III, and when they started their family, she stopped teaching. Within six years their family had grown to include children Collette, Jeff, Laura, and Steve. When her husband, an attorney, announced that he would be away from home for about fourteen weeks trying a case, he encouraged McKenna to find something to do that she would really love. "You'll go crazy being alone with four children for more than three months," he told her. She began to think, "If I could do *anything,* what would it be?" The one thing she really missed was writing, so she signed up for a course in children's literature.

One important piece of advice McKenna gained from the class was "write about what you know." She realized that being a full-time mother, it would be natural to write about her own children. "One day, my oldest daughter, Collette, came up to me and said, 'None of my friends want to come to our crazy house. No offense, Mom, but you have too many babies. Sometimes I just wish I could be an only child.'" McKenna thought that sounded like a good story idea, and she began work on her first book, *Too Many Murphys.* The story became the first in a series of books depicting the often disastrously humorous antics of the Murphy family, based on the experiences of McKenna's own children and their friends.

Too Many Murphys focuses on Collette, a third-grader who is the oldest child in her family. She feels the weight of being the one who is always responsible, setting a good example for the other three children: Jeff, Laura, and Stevie. Collette describes herself as a "midget mother" and often wishes she had more time with her parents all to herself. In her review in *School Library Journal,* Carolyn Jenks stated that "the outstanding quality" of *Too Many Murphys* is realism. "The characters and the things that happen to them will be familiar to many young readers," she observed.

In the "Murphy" books, Collette deals with all the pains and joys of growing up. *Fourth Grade Is a Jinx, Fifth Grade: Here Comes Trouble,* and *The Truth about Sixth Grade* all focus on learning how to relate to parents, teachers, and classmates in school. Nancy P. Reeder, reviewing *The Truth about Sixth Grade* for *School*

Gordie tries to come up with the meanest, scariest costume for the school Halloween parade in* Third Grade Ghouls! *(Illustrated by Stephanie Roth.)

Library Journal, commented that "all of the characters may be found in any sixth grade classroom," where "students live in the moment . . . and every event is a crisis." Making friends in new situations such as camp and a new school are explored in *Eenie, Meanie, Murphy, No* and *Murphy's Island.* Collette also learns to adjust to big changes, such as her mother's pregnancy in *Mother Murphy.* Of her own writing, McKenna once commented: "In my 'Murphy' books I deliberately stretch out the awfulness, and I make Collette wade through it all, not just to get the laugh, but to force her to react. It is her reactions that draw readers to her, giving them a chance to identify with her because she really is a lot like them."

Another of McKenna's books for middle-grade readers is *Merry Christmas, Miss McConnell!,* in which fifth-grader Meg Stafford and her family discover that Christmas need not be filled with expensive decorations, dinners, and presents to be celebrated. McKenna balances the serious story of a family with financial difficulties with the humorous antics of Meg's friend, Raymond. In her *School Library Journal* assessment of *Merry Christmas, Miss McConnell!,* Susan Hepler declared that "McKenna has a good ear and eye for sketching fifth graders in a Catholic school."

With *Good Grief . . . Third Grade,* and its companion volume, *Live from the Fifth Grade,* McKenna presents the ongoing adventures of a group of kids at Sacred Heart Elementary School. In *Good Grief,* Marsha is determined at the beginning of third grade not to get in any more trouble. She even signs a declaration to that effect. The new student teacher, Miss Murtland, seems fun too, but all Marsha's good intentions come to nothing when her enemy, Roger, is assigned as her classroom partner. She goes through all sorts of schemes to get rid of Roger and finally tells an outright lie that gets him suspended from school. Now Marsha knows she has gone too far and must face up to the consequences; she has to make things right and take the blame. Elaine E. Knight, writing in *School Library Journal,* felt that McKenna "integrates humor and serious interpersonal issues well."

Roger and Marsha make another appearance in *Live from the Fifth Grade,* told from Roger's point of view. In this installment, Roger's love of a good practical joke not only alienates him from his old enemy, Marsha, but also gets him in hot water with Sister Mary Elizabeth. When he puts a snake in Marsha's locker, it is the last straw, and Roger finds himself serving detention by helping out the kindly Mr. Doyle, a custodian who is developmentally disabled. Roger does not mind this sort of detention at all, but then the school's laser printer disappears and the fault is laid at Doyle's feet. Roger and his friends—and even non-friend Marsha—develop an outlandish scheme to save Doyle, a plan "as harebrained as they come," according to *Booklist*'s Stephanie Zvirin.

Gordie Barr is the star of several tales set in a third-grade classroom. In *Third Grade Stinks!,* Gordie is upset when his teacher, Miss Tingle, tells him that he has to share a locker with Lucy, the class show-off, instead of with his best friend, Lamont Hayes. He and Lamont were going to cover the locker with baseball cards, but now these plans have to be put on hold. Gordie tries to think of how he can get rid of Lucy as a locker mate, and he eventually comes up with a scheme to find something smelly enough to make her want to change partners. The subsequent quest for the appropriately stinky object "propels the story along, resulting in a fast-paced easy chapter book," according to Teri Markson in *School Library Journal.* The stinky object in this case is a piece of Limburger cheese, but it turns out that Lucy loves Limburger and takes this as a gift, which leads to a reconciliation between the two. *Booklist*'s Lauren Peterson felt that "more sophisticated readers will groan at the unbelievable ending," but she still had praise for this "lightweight, lighthearted story."

Halloween is fast approaching in *Third Grade Ghouls,* and Gordie is worried about finding a great costume. Lamont, his friend, tries to help out, but his suggestion about wearing a toilet paper box does not work for Gordie. To make matters worse, Gordie brags to the school bully, Lumpy, that he is going to wear a scary costume, and to further complicate matters, he has also volunteered to accompany a timid first grader during the Halloween parade. This kid is so scared of costumes that he throws up at the sight of a scary one. But in the end, everything works out in this "universal, if predicable, story," according to a *Kirkus Reviews* contributor. Gordie comes up with a cat costume, and during the parade he helps the first grader overcome his fears when a dog runs loose on the school grounds. This canine helps Gordie solve his problem with the bully, as well, for Lumpy is terrified of dogs. Gillian Engberg, writing in *Booklist,* praised some of the "groan-worthy jokes" and details that "ring true" in this tale.

With *New Friend* and *Queen of May,* McKenna contributed two volumes to the novelization of *Dr. Quinn, Medicine Woman,* a television series. Set in a small Colorado town after the Civil War, the books and television show feature a female doctor, Dr. Quinn, who has adopted the three Cooper children and married a Native American named Sully. In *New Friends,* a girl named Laura comes to school and is in Colleen Cooper's class. When Laura begins telling lies about Colleen, trouble brews, and the tension only increases when it is announced there will be a spelling bee and only two students get to participate.

McKenna has also penned a young adult novel, *The Brightest Light.* The book follows the trials of Kitty Lee, a sixteen year old who grows as she confronts a number of new and confusing issues, including her best friend's mysterious romance and elopement with an older man. She also experiences new feelings for her old friend Cody, who asks her out on a date, and for the man whose children she babysits while his wife battles alcoholism. Although Carol A. Edwards, writing in *School Library Journal,* found *The Brightest Light* a fairly predictable teenage romance novel, she also lauded McKenna's

refusal to happily resolve all difficult issues: "To give McKenna credit, anything that couldn't be fixed in the last ten pages is realistically left hanging." A *Bulletin of the Center for Children's Books* reviewer praised the "subtle strength" of McKenna's heroine and suggested that *The Brightest Light* is "steadily told, entirely contemporary, and deeply romantic." Claire Rosser, reviewing the novel in *Kliatt,* similarly noted that Kitty Lee is "an admirable person, and readers will be happy in her happiness as she finds her true love at the end of the story."

McKenna enjoys making presentations about herself and her writing to young readers. She wants her love of reading and writing to help inspire children to succeed in these fields. "The first thing you have to do is entertain them," she told *SATA.* "I start by acting out scenes from *Bonanza* to show them what I was like in the eighth grade. Basically I show them I'm an ordinary person who chose writing as a career." She also explains to these groups how a story is written, using *The Three Little Pigs* to illustrate what makes a story work. She talks to the children about the importance of being a reader and gives them writing tips. "I want to represent a persistent kid who loved books so much I decided to write some of my own."

Biographical and Critical Sources

PERIODICALS

Booklist, September 15, 1992, Mary Romano Marks, review of *The Brightest Light,* pp. 138-139; March 15, 1993, Chris Sherman, review of *Camp Murphy,* p. 1319; September 1, 1993, Janice Del Negro, review of *Good Grief . . . Third Grade,* p. 61; November 15, 1994, Stephanie Zvirin, review of *Live from the Fifth Grade,* p. 602; December 15, 2001, Lauren Peterson, review of *Third Grade Stinks!,* pp. 731-732; January 1, 2002, Gillian Engberg, review of *Third Grade Ghouls,* p. 858; July, 2002, Hazel Rochman, review of *Dog-gone . . . Third Grade!,* p. 1848.

Book Report, March-April, 1993, Ann Gieseler Bryan, review of *The Brightest Light,* p. 42.

Bulletin of the Center for Children's Books, October, 1988, p. 47; February, 1989, p. 152; October, 1989, p. 39; October, 1990, p. 38, review of *The Brightest Light,* p. 183-84; February, 1992, p. 163.

Horn Book Guide, spring, 1995, Amy Quigley, review of *Live from the Fifth Grade,* p. 80.

Kirkus Reviews, September 1, 1988, p. 1325; February 1, 1989, p. 211; January 1, 1992, p. 54; December 1, 2001, review of *Third Grade Ghouls,* pp. 1687-1688; May 15, 2002, review of *Doggone . . . Third Grade!,* p. 736.

Kliatt, January, 1995, Claire Rosser, review of *The Brightest Light,* p. 10.

Publishers Weekly, August 26, 1988, p. 90; April 27, 1992, p. 272.

School Library Journal, December, 1988, Carolyn Jenks, review of *Too Many Murphys,* p. 109; March, 1989, p. 178; September, 1989, p. 254; March, 1990, p. 219; October, 1990, Susan Hepler, review of *Merry Christ-*

mas, Miss McConnell!, p. 38; December, 1990, p. 105; April, 1991, Nancy P. Reeder, review of *The Truth about Sixth Grade,* p. 121; February, 1992, p. 87; December, 1992, Carol A. Edwards, review of *The Brightest Light,* p. 133; April, 1993, Elizabeth Hanson, review of *Camp Murphy,* pp. 122-123; January, 1994, Elaine E. Knight, review of *Good Grief ... Third Grade,* p. 116; October, 1994, Jacqueline Rose, review of *Live from the Fifth Grade,* p. 126; November 2001, Teri Markson, review of *Third Grade Stinks!,* p. 129; February, 2002, Rosalyn Pierini, review of *Third Grade Ghouls,* p. 108; July, 2002, Marilyn Ackerman, review of *Doggone ... Third Grade!,* p. 95.

Wilson Library Bulletin, May, 1990, p. 4; January, 1991, p. 6.*

* * *

McMILLAN, Naomi
See GRIMES, Nikki

* * *

MEYER, June
See JORDAN, June (Meyer)

* * *

MONK, Isabell 1952-

Personal

Born October 4, 1952, in Washington, DC; daughter of Henry (a farmer and construction worker) and Jane (a beautician; maiden name, Barrett; later surname, Bradshaw) Monk. *Education:* Towson State University, B.F.A.; Yale University, M.F.A.

Addresses

Home—421 Upton Ave. S., Minneapolis, MN 55405.

Career

Professional actress. Tyrone Guthrie Theater, Minneapolis, MN, member of the company for nine seasons; storytelling resident at local public schools. Appeared in the films *Rosewood, Grumpy Old Men, Untamed Heart, Trauma, Family Business, Heartburn, Swing Shift, The World According to Garp, Here on Earth, Sugar and Spice,* and *Black Knight.* Television appearances include the solo show *We Ain't What We Was,* for the Public Broadcasting System, the special *Our Own Kind,* for ABC-TV, and the movies *Emma and I,* for CBS-TV, *Calamity Jane,* for NBC-TV, and *When She Says No,* for ABC-TV, and appearances in episodes of the series *The Equalizer, Benson,* and *Family Ties;* also appeared in *Things That Matter,* a local production of KTCA-TV, c. 1991. Appeared in numerous stage plays, including the role of Antigone in *The Gospel at Colonus,* c. 1985, and

Isabell Monk

a policewoman in *The Execution of Justice,* both Broadway productions; Dorine, *Tartuffe,* Arena Stage, Washington, DC, c. 1986; and Gloucester, *Lear,* New York Shakespeare Festival, c. 1990; appeared with other theater companies throughout the United States. Performed as a standup comic at Bud Friedman's Improvisation clubs in New York, NY, and Los Angeles, CA.

Member

Actors' Equity Association, Screen Actors Guild, American Federation of Television and Radio Artists.

Awards, Honors

National Award, Public Broadcasting Service, 1976, for writing and performing in *We Ain't What We Was;* Drama Desk Award, 1985, for *The Gospel at Colonus;* Helen Hayes Award nomination, 1986, for *Tartuffe;* Obie Award, *Village Voice,* 1990, for *Lear;* Midwest Emmy Award, 1991, for *Things That Matter;* McKnight fellow, 1998; fellow of Twentieth Century-Fox, 1998; Parents' Choice Honor Award, 2001, for *Family.*

Writings

We Ain't What We Was (solo special), broadcast by Public Broadcasting Service, c. 1976.
Hope, illustrated by Janice Lee Porter, Carolrhoda Books (Minneapolis, MN), 1999.

Family, illustrated by Janice Lee Porter, Carolrhoda Books (Minneapolis, MN), 2001.

The Story of Hope (play), produced in St. Paul, MN, at SteppingStone Children's Theater, 2001.

Work in Progress

Come to Me, for Carolrhoda Books (Minneapolis, MN), completion expected in 2004; research on *A Child's Retreat,* a center for recreational reading and conflict resolution.

Sidelights

Isabell Monk told *SATA:* "I am very interested in working with young people, specifically with helping them become more active recreational readers. I also feel that young people need to feel that they can go to a safe place within themselves to get away from the pressures of school, work, and home.

"My work in the Minneapolis Public Schools has been most rewarding for me. I'm not teacher material, but I do so enjoy helping to make a teacher's job more fun and less stressful by bringing in the crafts of acting, storytelling, and reading aloud to their students. For the students I feel that I become one more adult who loves

The kind words of her great-aunt make Hope proud of her biracial heritage. (From Hope, *written by Monk and illustrated by Janice Lee Porter.)*

Hope wonders if her unusual dessert will be accepted at the annual family potluck. (From Family, *illustrated by Janice Lee Porter.)*

them and takes the time to be with them. This is my small way of touching the future."*

*   *   *

MUNRO, Roxie 1945-

Personal

Born September 5, 1945, in Mineral Wells, TX; daughter of Robert Enoch (an automotive shop owner and boat builder) and Margaret (a librarian; maiden name, Bissey) Munro; married Bo Zaunders (an artist and photographer), May 17, 1986. *Nationality:* American. *Education:* Attended University of Maryland, 1963-65, Maryland Institute College of Art, 1965-66, and Ohio University, 1969-70; University of Hawaii, B.F.A., 1969, graduate work, 1970-71. *Hobbies and other interests:* Travel, reading.

Addresses

Home—20 Park Ave., New York, NY 10016. *Office*—43-01 Twenty-First St., Studio #340, Long Island City, NY 11101.

Roxie Munro

Career

Roxie (dress company), Washington, DC, dress designer and manufacturer, 1972-76; television courtroom artist in Washington, DC, 1976-81; freelance artist, 1981—. *Exhibitions*—Group shows: New York Public Library, New York, NY, 1986; Detroit Institute of Arts, Detroit, MI, 1987; High Museum, Atlanta, GA, 1987; Boston Atheneum, Boston, MA, 1987; Corcoran Gallery of Art, Washington, DC, 1988; Victoria and Albert Museum, London, England, 1988; Art Gallery of Ontario, Toronto, Canada, 1988; Fine Arts Museum of San Francisco, San Francisco, CA, 1988. Solo shows: Foundry Gallery, Washington, DC, 1977-79, 1983, 1986; Delaware Museum of Art, 1980; Gotham Book Mart, New York, NY, 1986; Marin-Price Gallery, Chevy Chase, MD, 1990-2002; Michael Ingbar Gallery of Architectural Art, New York, NY, 1991-2002. Works are included in many private and public collections.

Member

Artists' Equity, Society of Children's Book Writers and Illustrators.

Awards, Honors

Yaddo Painting Fellowship, 1980; Best Illustrated Children's Books citation, *New York Times,* and Best Children's Books citation, *Time,* both 1985, both for *The Inside-Outside Book of New York City;* Best Book selection, *School Library Journal,* 2001, for *Feathers, Flaps, and Flops.*

Writings

SELF-ILLUSTRATED

Color New York, Arbor House (New York, NY), 1985.
The Inside-Outside Book of New York City, Dodd (New York, NY), 1985.
The Inside-Outside Book of Washington D.C., Dutton (New York, NY), 1987.
Christmastime in New York City, Dodd (New York, NY), 1987.
Blimps, Dutton (New York, NY), 1989.
The Inside-Outside Book of London, Dutton (New York, NY), 1989.
The Inside-Outside Book of Paris, Dutton (New York, NY), 1992.
The Inside-Outside Book of Texas, SeaStar Books (New York, NY), 2001.
Mazescapes, SeaStar Books (New York, NY), 2001.
Doors, SeaStar Books (New York, NY), 2003.

ILLUSTRATOR

Kay D. Weeks, *The Great American Landmark Adventure,* National Park Service and American Architectural Foundation (Washington, DC), 1982.
Diane Maddex, *Architects Make Zigzags: Looking at Architecture from A to Z,* Preservation Press (Washington, DC), 1986.
Kay D. Weeks, *American Defenders of Land, Sea & Sky,* National Park Service (Washington, DC), 1996.
Julie Cummins, *The Inside-Outside Book of Libraries,* Dutton (New York, NY), 1996.
Bo Zaunders, *Crocodiles, Camels and Dugout Canoes: Eight Adventurous Episodes,* Dutton (New York, NY), 1998.
Bo Zaunders, *Feathers, Flaps, and Flops: Fabulous Early Fliers,* Dutton (New York, NY), 2001.
Raymond D. Keene, *Learn Chess Fast: The Fun Way to Start Smart and the Game,* Bright Sky Press (Albany, TX), 2001.
Joseph Siano, editor, *The New York Times What's Doing around the World,* Lebhar-Friedman (New York, NY), 2001.
Bo Zaunders, *Gargoyles, Girders, and Glass Houses: Magnificent Master Builders,* Dutton (New York, NY), 2003.

Cover artist for *New Yorker.* Contributor of illustrations to *Washington Post, U.S. News & World Report, Gourmet, Historic Preservation,* and *New Republic.*

Sidelights

Author and illustrator of the popular "Inside-Out" books, including titles on New York, Texas, Washington, D.C.,

London, and Paris, Roxie Munro is an inveterate city watcher. Born in Mineral Wells, Texas, in 1945, Munro once told *SATA*, "Unlike many children's book creators, I don't have a lot of specific memories of my childhood. I remember mainly sensuous impressions: water running across rocks in a ditch, the dried fall leaves, the splash of waves across a boat's bow." Growing up in a small, rural town, much of her spare time was spent "reading and daydreaming." Her parents encouraged the children to engage in independent, creative activities: drawing, making their own toys, and reading. The family also traveled a good deal together, taking annual vacations to the Northeast, South, and West, getting to know urban as well as rural America.

"My work is therefore, I think, an art developing from perception," Munro told *SATA*. "It is very visual, spatial. Ideas develop from a kind of active seeing. When I walk down a street, ride a bus, or go up an escalator, I FEEL the changing space. I see patterns, paintings everywhere. My mind organizes reality. I'll notice two gray cars, a red car, a black car, and two more red cars—aha!—a pattern."

Munro pursued this love of art from her early years on. As a first grader she won a county competition; in high school she was editor of the school yearbook and named most talented. Studying art at the University of Maryland, the Maryland Institute College of Art, the University of Hawaii, and Ohio University, she thereafter began her own business as a dress designer, manufacturing for small boutiques in Washington, D.C., and subsequently freelancing for several years as a courtroom artist for newspapers and television. Then, in 1981, Munro moved to New York and began selling her artwork to the *New Yorker* for their covers. She sold sixteen paintings to that magazine, known for its creative cover art.

Soon she approached various publishers, hoping to get more work designing book covers. One editor she met with thought her art could work well with children. Asked to come up with some ideas for children's books, Munro thought about it, and the title *The Inside-Out Book of New York City* suddenly came to her. Munro tells the story of the city visually, taking unique vantage points on well-known sites. For the Statue of Liberty, for instance, she looks not only at its exterior, but also from the inside out at the city. There are views of the inside of the stock exchange and of busy traffic. Other landmarks, viewed from both outside and inside, include St. Patrick's Cathedral and the cages at the Bronx Zoo. In her witty pictorial, Munro looks through windows, behind bars, and even across theater footlights to get an intimate view of the city. Winner of a *New York Times* Best Illustrated Children's Book Award in 1985, *The Inside-Out Book of New York City* inaugurated a series of such books for other cities.

From cities, Munro turns to libraries in *The Inside-Out Book of Libraries,* which contains renderings of libraries throughout the United States paired with text by Julie Cummins, a children's librarian. Each library is shown from both the outside and from the inside, on sequential spreads. Munro chooses locations from a small one-room library on a North Carolina island to one on an aircraft carrier, and she even includes the library in Folsom prison in California. *Booklist*'s Carolyn Phelan felt that the book "provides a lively, colorful introduction to libraries." And Elizabeth Bush, reviewing the same title in *Bulletin of the Center for Children's Books,* concluded, "This title reminds listeners that libraries, like the literature and information they house, come in many packages."

The Lone Star State is featured in the 2001 title, *The Inside-Out Book of Texas,* in pictures "ranging from the dramatic ... to the mundane," as a critic for *Publishers Weekly* wrote. Among the various sites and topics covered are a skyline of Dallas, ranch hands eating, the Texas Stadium (home of the Dallas Cowboys football team), the Lyndon B. Johnson Space Center in Houston, and various wildlife scenes. "Bright, cheerful colors invite the eye," noted *School Library Journal*'s Ruth Semrau. A reviewer for *Horn Book* also praised this addition to the series, noting that Munro not only introduces young readers to landmarks of the state, "but also cleverly stretches the definitional boundaries of inside and outside." This same reviewer felt the artist "uses her illustrations to paint a high-spirited picture" of the state. And reviewing *The Inside-Out Book of Texas* in *Booklist,* Gillian Engberg thought Munro "adds

Munro challenges readers to find their way through thirteen highly detailed mazes while searching for hidden letters and more in her self-illustrated **Mazescapes.**

another winner to the series" with this "lively, informative" book.

Extending her view of cities to the airborne, in *Mazescapes* Munro invites children to find their way through aerial mazes of cities and the countryside using any of six punch-out cars provided with the book. Each maze in *Mazescapes* connects with the one on the following page. Alison Kastner, writing in *School Library Journal,* thought that graduates of the "Where's Waldo" books who are looking for "something a little more challenging will find it in Munro's brightly colored and intricate paintings." The game here is to find the way to the zoo and then back home again through this series of maze-like renderings of towns, cities, and countryside. Peter D. Sieruta observed in a *Horn Book* review that *Mazescapes* contains "the kind of dizzyingly detailed artwork that sends adults running for the Dramamine yet almost always entrances kids."

Dirigibles also get the Munro treatment in *Blimps,* a book done with "accurate and complete detail," according to a reviewer in *New Advocate.* "The fun thing here was the research," Munro noted in *Children's Book Illustration and Design.* "I got a three-hour ride in a blimp over Manhattan, and in England visited the biggest blimp-making factory in the world."

As an illustrator, Munro has also worked with a variety of writers, including her husband, the Swedish photographer, artist, and writer, Bo Zaunders. Illustrating his *Crocodiles, Camels and Dugout Canoes: Eight Adventurous Episodes,* Munro's illustrations add "even more liveliness," according to Susan Dove Lempke in a *Booklist* review, "and will help attract young readers." A reviewer for *Publishers Weekly* also commended this gathering of travelers and explorers, noting that the enthusiasm of Zaunders and Munro "shine[s] through the pages of this absorbing picture book." A second husband-and-wife collaboration, *Feathers, Flaps, and Flops: Fabulous Early Fliers,* depicts the exploits of some early aviators in seven sketches. In *School Library Journal,* Louise L. Sherman praised Munro's "fine illustrations" in this volume, as did a *Horn Book* reviewer, who wrote that "[p]layful perspective is a Roxie Munro hallmark." Additionally, *School Library Journal* selected *Feathers, Flaps, and Flops* as a "Best Book of 2001."

Biographical and Critical Sources

BOOKS

Children's Book Illustration and Design, edited by Julie Cummins, Library of Applied Design (New York, NY), 1992.

Children's Books and Their Creators, edited by Anita Silvey, Houghton Mifflin (New York, NY), 1995.

PERIODICALS

Booklist, October 15, 1996, Carolyn Phelan, review of *The Inside-Out Book of Libraries,* p. 426; October 15, 1998, Susan Dove Lempke, review of *Crocodiles, Camels and Dugout Canoes: Eight Adventurous Episodes,* p. 420; April 1, 2001, Gillian Engberg, review of *The Inside-Out Book of Texas,* p. 1475.

Bulletin of the Center for Children's Books, October, 1996, Elizabeth Bush, review of *The Inside-Out Book of Libraries,* p. 53.

Childhood Education, October, 1987, p. 46.

Horn Book, March-April, 1986, p. 223; May-June, 1987, pp. 358-359; January-February, 1989, pp. 91-92; November-December, 1989, pp. 792-793; March-April, 1992, Ellen Fader, review of *The Inside-Out Book of Paris,* p. 221; September-October, 1996, Roger Sutton, review of *The Inside-Out Book of Libraries,* p. 611; January-February, 1999, review of *Crocodiles, Camels and Dugout Canoes,* p. 85; May-June, 2001, review of *The Inside-Out Book of Texas,* p. 350; July-August, 2001, review of *Feathers, Flaps, and Flops: Fabulous Early Fliers,* p. 480; September-October, 2001, Peter D. Sieruta, review of *Mazescapes,* p. 577.

Language Arts, October, 1987, p. 68.

New Advocate, winter, 1990, review of *Blimps,* p. 69.

Publishers Weekly, September 13, 1985, p. 132; August 22, 1986, p. 98; May 8, 1987, p. 68; October 30, 1987, p. 66; October 14, 1988, p. 76; September 29, 1989, p. 65; November 29, 1991, review of *The Inside-Out Book of Paris,* p. 50; August 19, 1996, review of *The Inside-Out Book of Libraries,* p. 65; August 31, 1998, review of *Crocodiles, Camels and Dugout Canoes,* p. 76; February 26, 2001, review of *The Inside-Outside Book of Texas,* p. 88; July 30, 2001, review of *Mazescapes,* p. 86.

School Library Journal, January, 1986, p. 59; May, 1987, p. 88; February, 1989, p. 79; December, 1989, pp. 95-96; February, 1992, p. 83; August, 1996, Nancy Menaldi-Scanlan, review of *The Inside-Out Book of Libraries,* p. 134; November, 1998, Patricia Manning, review of *Crocodiles, Camels and Dugout Canoes,* p. 144; June, 2001, Ruth Semrau, review of *The Inside-Out Book of Texas,* p. 140; July, 2001, Louise L. Sherman, review of *Feathers, Flaps, and Flops,* p. 101; August, 2001, Alison Kastner, review of *Mazescapes,* p. 171.

Time, December 23, 1985, Stefan Kanfer, review of *The Inside-Out Book of New York City,* p. 62.

O

OPPENHEIM, Joanne 1934-
(Jane Fleischer, Kate Jassem)

Personal

Born May 11, 1934, in Middletown, NY; daughter of Abe P. (an electrical engineer) and Helen (Jassem) Fleischer; married Stephen Oppenheim (a lawyer), June 27, 1954; children: James, Anthony, Stephanie. *Nationality:* American. *Education:* Attended University of Miami, FL, 1951-52; Sarah Lawrence College, B.A., 1960; Bank Street College of Education, M.S., 1980. *Hobbies and other interests:* Community theater.

Addresses

Home—55 East 9th St., New York, NY 10003. *Office*—Oppenheim Toy Portfolio, 40 East 9th St., #14M, New York, NY 10003. *E-mail*—joanne@toyportfolio.com.

Career

Elementary school teacher in Monticello, NY, 1960-80; Bank Street College of Education, New York, NY, member of Writer's Laboratory, 1962—, senior editor in publications department, 1980-92; *Oppenheim Toy Portfolio* (consumer organization), New York, NY, president and cofounder, 1989—. Monthly contributor to NBC's *Today Show,* 2000—. Member of board of directors, U.S.A. Toy Library, 1993—.

Awards, Honors

Outstanding Teachers of America Award, 1973; Children's Choice citation, International Reading Association, 1980, for *Mrs. Peloki's Snake,* and 1981, for *Mrs. Peloki's Class Play;* Ruth Schwartz Children's Book Award, Ontario Arts Council, 1987, Elizabeth Mrazik-Cleaver Award, 1987, and Outstanding Science Book citation, all for *Have You Seen Birds?;* Outstanding Science Book citation, 1994, for *Oceanarium;* various book club selections for books, including *James Will*

Joanne Oppenheim

Never Die, The Story Book Prince, and *Choosing Books for Kids.*

Writings

FOR CHILDREN

Have You Seen Trees?, illustrated by Irwin Rosenhouse, Young Scott Books (New York, NY), 1967, illustrated by Jean and Mou-sien Tseng, Scholastic (New York, NY), 1995.

Have You Seen Birds?, illustrated by Julio de Diego, Young Scott Books (New York, NY), 1968, illustrated by Barbara Reid, Scholastic (New York, NY), 1986.

179

Have You Seen Roads?, illustrated by G. Nook, Young Scott Books (New York, NY), 1969.

Have You Seen Boats?, Young Scott Books (New York, NY), 1971.

On the Other Side of the River, illustrated by Aliki, F. Watts (New York, NY), 1972.

Have You Seen Houses?, Young Scott Books (New York, NY), 1973.

Sequoyah, Cherokee Hero, illustrated by Bert Dodson, Troll (Mahwah, NJ), 1979.

Osceola, Seminole Warrior, illustrated by Bill Ternay, Troll (Mahwah, NJ), 1979.

Black Hawk, Frontier Warrior, illustrated by Hal Frenck, Troll (Mahwah, NJ), 1979.

(Under pseudonym Jane Fleischer) *Tecumseh, Shawnee War Chief,* illustrated by Hal Frenck, Troll (Mahwah, NJ), 1979.

(Under pseudonym Jane Fleischer) *Sitting Bull, Warrior of the Sioux,* illustrated by Bert Dodson, Troll (Mahwah, NJ), 1979.

(Under pseudonym Jane Fleischer) *Pontiac, Chief of the Ottawas,* illustrated by Robert Baxter, Troll (Mahwah, NJ), 1979.

(Under pseudonym Kate Jassem) *Chief Joseph, Leader of Destiny,* illustrated by Robert Baxter, Troll (Mahwah, NJ), 1979.

(Under pseudonym Kate Jassem) *Pocahontas, Girl of Jamestown,* illustrated by Allan Eitzen, Troll (Mahwah, NJ), 1979.

Oppenheim describes in verse the looks, behavior, and benefits of a number of insects in **Have You Seen Bugs?** *(Illustrated by Ron Broda.)*

(Under pseudonym Kate Jassem) *Sacajawea, Wilderness Guide,* illustrated by Jan Palmer, Troll (Mahwah, NJ), 1979.

(Under pseudonym Kate Jassem) *Squanto, the Pilgrim Adventure,* illustrated by Robert Baxter, Troll (Mahwah, NJ), 1979.

Mrs. Peloki's Snake, illustrated by Joyce Audy dos Santos, Dodd (New York, NY), 1980.

James Will Never Die, illustrated by True Kelly, Dodd (New York, NY), 1982.

Mrs. Peloki's Class Play, illustrated by Joyce Audy dos Santos, Dodd (New York, NY), 1984.

Barron's Bunny Activity Books, Barron's (Hauppauge, NY), 1985.

You Can't Catch Me!, illustrated by Andrew Shachat, Houghton (Boston, MA), 1986.

(With Betty Boegehold and William H. Hooks) *Read-a-Rebus: Tales and Rhymes in Words and Pictures,* illustrated by Lynn Munsinger, Random House (New York, NY), 1986.

The Story Book Prince, illustrated by Rosanne Litzinger, Harcourt (San Diego, CA), 1987.

Mrs. Peloki's Substitute, illustrated by Joyce Audy Zarins, Dodd (New York, NY), 1987.

Left and Right, illustrated by Rosanne Litzinger, Harcourt (San Diego, CA), 1989.

"Not Now!" Said the Cow, illustrated by Chris Demarest, Bantam (New York, NY), 1989.

Could It Be?, illustrated by S. D. Schindler, Bantam (New York, NY), 1990.

Wake Up, Baby!, illustrated by Lynn Sweat, Bantam (New York, NY), 1990.

Follow That Fish, illustrated by Devis Grebu, Bantam (New York, NY), 1990.

Eency Weency Spider, illustrated by S. D. Schindler, Bantam (New York, NY), 1991.

The Donkey's Tale, illustrated by Chris Demarest, Bantam (New York, NY), 1991.

Rooter Remembers: A Bank Street Book about Values, illustrated by Lynn Munsinger, Viking (New York, NY), 1991.

(With Barbara Brenner and William H. Hooks) *No Way, Slippery Slick!: A Child's First Book about Drugs,* illustrated by Joan Auclair, HarperCollins (New York, NY), 1991.

Show-and-Tell Frog, illustrated by Kate Duke, Bantam (New York, NY), 1992.

(With William H. Hooks and Barbara Brenner) *How Do You Make a Bubble?,* illustrated by Doug Cushman, Bantam (New York, NY), 1992.

(Adaptor) *One Gift Deserves Another* (based on the story by the Brothers Grimm), illustrated by Bo Zaunders, Dutton (New York, NY), 1992.

Row, Row, Row Your Boat, illustrated by Kevin O'Malley, Bantam (New York, NY), 1993.

Do You Like Cats?, illustrated by Carol Newsom, Bantam (New York, NY), 1993.

(Reteller) *The Christmas Witch: An Italian Legend,* illustrated by Annie Mitra, Bantam (New York, NY), 1993.

"Uh-Oh!" Said the Crow, illustrated by Chris Demarest, Bantam (New York, NY), 1993.

Oceanarium, illustrated by Alan Gutierrez, Bantam (New York, NY), 1994.

Floratorium, illustrated by S. D. Schindler, Bantam (New York, NY), 1994.

Money, Atheneum (New York, NY), 1995.

Have You Seen Bugs?, illustrated by Ron Broda, North Winds Press (Richmond Hill, Canada), 1996, Scholastic (New York, NY), 1997.

Painting with Air, illustrated by Stephanie Carr, Little Simon (New York, NY), 1999.

Big Bug Fun: A Book of Facts and Riddles, illustrated by Jerry Zimmerman, Scholastic (New York, NY), 2000.

Have You Seen Dogs?, illustrated by Susan Gardos, North Winds Press (Markham, Canada), 2001.

Also author of six activity books for children on maps, time, money, communications, and safety. Contributor to "Bank Street Readers" basal series, Macmillan (New York, NY), 1965.

FOR ADULTS

Kids and Play, Ballantine (New York, NY), 1984.

(With Betty D. Boegehold and Barbara Brenner) *Raising a Confident Child: The Bank Street Year-by-Year Guide,* Pantheon (New York, NY), 1984.

(With Betty D. Boegehold and Barbara Brenner) *Growing Up Friendly: The Bank Street Guide to Raising a Sociable Child,* Pantheon (New York, NY), 1985.

KidSpeak about Computers, Ballantine (New York, NY), 1985.

(With Betty D. Boegehold and Barbara Brenner) *Choosing Books for Kids: Choosing the Right Book for the Right Child at the Right Time,* Ballantine (New York, NY), 1986.

Buy Me! Buy Me! The Bank Street Guide to Choosing Toys for Children, Pantheon (New York, NY), 1987.

The Elementary School Handbook: Making the Most of Your Child's Education, Pantheon (New York, NY), 1989.

(With daughter, Stephanie Oppenheim) *The Best Toys, Books and Videos for Kids: The 1994 Guide to 1000+ Kid-Tested, Classic and New Products for Ages 0-10,* HarperCollins (New York, NY), 1993.

(With daughter, Stephanie Oppenheim) *Oppenheim Toy Portfolio Baby & Toddler Play Book,* illustrated by Joan Auclair, Oppenheim Toy Portfolio (New York, NY), 1999.

Oppenheim Toy Portfolio, Oppenheim Toy Portfolio (New York, NY), 2000.

Contributor to *Pleasure of Their Company,* Chilton (Radnor, PA), 1980. Contributor of articles to magazines, including *Family Circle, Parent and Child,* and *Working Mother.*

Work in Progress

La Noche Buena, for Barefoot Books, due fall of 2003.

Sidelights

Twenty years as an elementary school teacher and another twelve as a senior editor of the Bank Street College of Education's publication department supply the experience behind Joanne Oppenheim's entertaining and educational books for children. From her first books, which provide new looks at everyday things, to her retellings of traditional tales, Oppenheim is known for works that appeal to children with their pleasing rhymes and sense of humor. Her realistic stories have also been praised for creating characters and situations with which young readers will identify.

Oppenheim's first books in the "Have You Seen?" series combine fanciful verse with illustrations that use unusual perspectives to give children new looks at ordinary items such as roads, trees, birds, boats, and houses. In *Have You Seen Trees?,* Oppenheim's "pleasant, read-aloud rhythms" and "touch of humor" distinguish it from other science books, according to *New York Times Book Review* writer Alice Fleming. Similarly, George A. Woods noted in *New York Times Book Review* that "the rhythm of Joanne Oppenheim's descriptive verse text" in *Have You Seen Roads?* will "transport" the reader, while a *Kirkus Reviews* critic wrote that the rhymes in *Have You Seen Boats?* "titillate, educate, [and] play with the mind's ear." Although the series does not provide information directly, as a *Junior Bookshelf* reviewer observed, the aim "seems mainly to put their subjects in an environmental context and this is well done in an easy unforced style." "Oppenheim's poetry is magical," stated Susan Perren in a *Quill & Quire* review of the 1986 edition of *Have You Seen Birds?,* and she praised the author's "use of alliteration and repetition. Her poetry swoops and rolls, pecks and hoots, bringing the birds alive on the page."

Developing the series for a span of over thirty years, Oppenheim continues to add new titles to the "Have You Seen?" books. The author turns to the insect world in *Have You Seen Bugs?,* a picture book illustrated by Ron Broda that features three-dimensional paper artwork to accompany Oppenheim's text. Told in rhyming verse, *Have You Seen Bugs?* shares with young readers different characteristics of a wide range of small creatures, including spiders, caterpillars, and dragonflies. How bugs grow, what they eat, and how they move are covered, as are functions that specific creatures fulfill in the environment. Calling the work "a sensational book in praise of insects," a *Publishers Weekly* critic claimed that Oppenheim and Broda "cover a lot of ground and . . . pack in a surprising amount of information." Writing in *School Library Journal,* Patricia Manning also noted the wealth of information *Have You Seen Bugs?* offers, remarking that "it's perfect for any youngster."

Canines receive the "Have You Seen?" treatment in Oppenheim's *Have You Seen Dogs?* Here the author details the wide variety of shapes, sizes, and colors in which dogs appear. While not offering information on specific breeds, the author does explain to young readers how dogs differ in their looks and barks. Told in verse, *Have You Seen Dogs?* also shares the many different responsibilities some canines have, including helping handicapped people, protecting livestock, and entertaining crowds. Described as a "must for dog lovers," the book is "a good read-aloud . . . and useful resource when researching certain aspects about dogs," according to *Resource Links* contributor Judy Cottrell.

Oppenheim brings her classroom experiences to life in her stories about elementary teacher Mrs. Peloki. In *Mrs. Peloki's Snake,* the discovery of a reptile in the boys' bathroom prompts a classroom uproar. This "sprightly tale of reptilian high jinks [is] nicely tuned to the first-grade funny bone," Kristi L. Thomas commented in *School Library Journal.* The trials of staging a production of "Cinderella" is the topic for *Mrs. Peloki's Class Play,* which *School Library Journal* contributor Catherine Wood called "true to life," with "class members' personalities and humor [that] emerge on almost every page." Ilene Cooper likewise praised Oppenheim in *Booklist* for her "real grasp of second graders and their habits." Another true-to-life episode of classroom escapades is found in *Mrs. Peloki's Substitute,* according to a *Kirkus Reviews* writer, who said the book "has enough humor and verisimilitude to entertain children." In this story, after their cherished teacher leaves class sick, the students try to misdirect her unfortunate replacement to avoid a spelling test. While some critics faulted the book for potentially inspiring misbehavior, *Bulletin of the Center for Children's Books* writer Zena Sutherland found the story "nicely appropriate" in length and vocabulary, adding that most young readers "will enjoy a story about a familiar situation."

Another situation familiar to many children—sibling rivalry—is portrayed in *James Will Never Die.* In this tale, young Tony can never beat his older brother in their imaginary games, for James always manages to turn everything Tony thinks of into a victory. Tony's efforts to finally best his brother make for a "zippy story of sibling rivalry and affection," a *Publishers Weekly* critic noted. Barbara McGinn likewise found the brothers' adventures "refreshingly imaginative," even though they all involve someone dying, adding in *School Library Journal* that despite this negative aspect the book is "otherwise fast-moving [and] well-written." Another book about troublesome brothers is *Left and Right,* in which two cobbler brothers learn that they make better teammates than rivals. "Invitingly told in a rhythmic rhyme," according to *Booklist* reviewer Beth Herbert, the book explains concepts of left and right as well as cooperation and "entices with its amusing insights on siblings."

A catchy refrain distinguishes *You Can't Catch Me!,* in which an annoying insect bothers every animal on the farm without fear: "'No matter how hard you try try try you can't catch me!' called the pesky black fly." Oppenheim's rhymes "are deft and simple," remarked a *Kirkus Reviews* writer, who added that the story "has the rolling accumulative power of an old tale like *The Gingerbread Boy.*" Betsy Hearne similarly observed in *Bulletin of the Center for Children's Books:* "It's rare to find contemporary verse with a true nursery rhyme ring, but this has it." Another rhyming story with an old-time air is *The Story Book Prince,* which tells of the efforts of a royal household to get the Prince to sleep. "The couplets frolic along," Susan Powers commented in

School Library Journal, making this "a book for those [who] really enjoy clever word romps."

Oppenheim has also turned to familiar songs and fairy tales for material, updating them for today's children. Based on a story by the Brothers Grimm, for example, *One Gift Deserves Another* relates how two brothers are rewarded by their king for their gifts. The poor brother, who unselfishly gives the king the giant turnip from his garden, is given wealth, while his greedy rich brother, in exchange for a calculated gift of money and jewels, is given the king's most treasured possession—the turnip. Karen K. Radtke praised Oppenheim's retelling, noting in *School Library Journal* that by eliminating several adult elements from the original Grimm Brothers tale, the author "has distilled the remaining premise into an enjoyable story for children." "Oppenheim's lively retelling . . . captures its delicious ironies while lining out its tasty moral," a *Publishers Weekly* critic likewise stated. And Kathryn Jennings also had warm words for Oppenheim's "upbeat version," concluding in the *Bulletin of the Center for Children's Books* that "this has the humor of a 'Fractured Fairytales' episode and could become a storyhour favorite."

The above-ground world of flora and undersea world of the oceans are featured in two works by Oppenheim, *Floratorium* and *Oceanarium,* both using a make-believe museum to structure the information. In the first work, the author creates a floor plan for her museum that looks like a flower, with each petal branching off to a individual chapter explaining different types of plants, including deciduous, saltwater, and desert ones. At the end of the tour, readers are encouraged to visit the museum store, which, instead of selling souvenirs, offers information about important scientists in the field of botany, as well as the beneficial role plants play in the environment. *Oceanarium* takes readers on a different type of journey, this time exploring changes in sea life as one travels farther to the bottom of the ocean. Oppenheim covers topics such as life in a coral reef, a shark tank, and in the tidal waters, with each chapter providing material about the types of creatures found in their respective environments. Finishing *Oceanarium* with an explanation about the importance of keeping the ocean free from pollutants, the author also shares with readers the dangers of exhausting limited fish supplies from the ocean as that may disrupt the delicate balance of the ocean's ecosystem.

Writing in *Science Activities,* reviewer Albert C. Jensen found the two books "ingenious and intriguing in design," going on to claim that they "represent an impressive melding of accurate text and interesting artwork that actually illustrates what it is intended to illustrate." Also commenting on both volumes, *School Library Journal* writer Carolyn Angus believed that "these appealing books offer good introductions to their topics," while *Booklist* critic Janice Del Negro found "the two titles . . . accessible and enjoyable introductions to a wide variety of ecosystems."

Biographical and Critical Sources

PERIODICALS

Booklist, September 1, 1984, Ilene Cooper, review of *Mrs. Peloki's Class Play,* p. 70; November 1, 1989, Beth Herbert, review of *Left and Right,* p. 556; January 1, 1994, Janice Del Negro, review of *Floratorium* and *Oceanarium,* p. 823; January 15, 1995, Julie Corsaro, review of *Have You Seen Trees?,* p. 993; April, 1998, Carolyn Phelan, review of *Have You Seen Bugs?,* p. 1326.

Bulletin of the Center for Children's Books, July, 1973, p. 174; November, 1984; September, 1986, Betsy Hearne, review of *You Can't Catch Me!,* p. 15; June, 1987, Zena Sutherland, review of *Mrs. Peloki's Substitute,* p. 193; September, 1992, Kathryn Jennings, review of *One Gift Deserves Another,* p. 11.

Christian Science Monitor, May 1, 1987, p. B7.

Junior Bookshelf, December, 1977, review of *Have You Seen Roads?* and *Have You Seen Houses?,* p. 339.

Kirkus Reviews, August 1, 1971, review of *Have You Seen Boats?,* p. 804; September 1, 1980, p. 1159; July 15, 1986, review of *You Can't Catch Me!,* p. 1121; December 15, 1986, p. 1858; January 15, 1987, review of *Mrs. Peloki's Substitute,* p. 136.

New York Times Book Review, May 7, 1967, Alice Fleming, "First Steps in Science," p. 49; October 5, 1969, George A. Woods, review of *Have You Seen Roads?,* p. 34.

Publishers Weekly, October 22, 1982, review of *James Will Never Die,* p. 56; August 24, 1984, p. 79; October 5, 1992, review of *One Gift Deserves Another,* p. 69; April 10, 1995, review of *Have You Seen Trees?,* p. 61; May 4, 1998, review of *Have You Seen Bugs?,* p. 213.

Quill & Quire, December, 1986, Susan Perren, "Picture-Book Plums for Christmas Gift-Giving," p. 16.

Resource Links, June, 2001, Judy Cottrell, review of *Have You Seen Dogs?,* p. 20.

School Library Journal, August, 1980, pp. 63-64; October, 1980, Kristi L. Thomas, review of *Mrs. Peloki's Snake,* p. 138; February, 1983, Barbara McGinn, review of *James Will Never Die,* p. 70; October, 1984, Catherine Wood, review of *Mrs. Peloki's Class Play,* p. 150; April, 1987, Susan Powers, review of *The Story Book Prince,* pp. 87-88; June-July, 1987, p. 88; August, 1987, p. 72; December, 1989, p. 87; June, 1991, p. 87; February, 1993, Karen K. Radtke, review of *One Gift Deserves Another,* p. 83; April, 1994, Carolyn Angus, review of *Floratorium* and *Oceanarium,* p. 142; April, 1995, Wendy Lukehart, review of *Have You Seen Trees?,* pp. 126, 128; September, 1998, Patricia Manning, review of *Have You Seen Bugs?,* p. 196.

Science Activities, spring, 1995, Albert C. Jensen, review of *Oceanarium* and *Floratorium,* p. 44.

P

POULTON, Kimberly 1957(?)-

Personal

Born c. 1957, in NH; married John Poulton; children: Rachel, Laura. *Nationality:* American. *Education:* Attended college in Vermont.

Addresses

Home—Westport, MA. *Agent*—c/o Author Mail, Moon Mountain Publishing, 80 Peachtree Rd., North Kingstown, RI 02852. *E-mail*—Kim@hellowillow.com.

Career

Writer. *Rhode Island Medical Journal,* managing editor; Blue Cross/Blue Shield of Rhode Island, writer of physician communications; primary school teacher in New Hampshire and Maine.

Awards, Honors

Honorable mention, *Providence Journal*'s Holiday Short Story Contest, for "Christmas for Joel."

Writings

Hello Willow, illustrated by Jennifer O'Keefe, Moon Mountain Publishing (North Kingstown, RI), 2000.

Also the author of poems and short stories, including "Christmas for Joel," some of which have been published in *Osprey* (a literary magazine of the Westport Point United Methodist Church, Westport, MA).

Sidelights

Kimberly Poulton is the author of one picture book, as well as numerous short stories. *Hello Willow,* the story of a little girl's imaginative adventures in and under a backyard willow tree, was published in the year 2000. Illustrated by Jennifer O'Keefe, the picture book was the

A little girl imagines she is a butterfly, explorer, and monkey as she plays under a willow tree in Kimberly Poulton's **Hello Willow.** *(Illustrated by Jennifer O'Keefe.)*

debut not only of its author/illustrator team, but also of Moon Mountain, its publishing house.

Born in New Hampshire, Poulton grew up in Connecticut and has spent her entire life in New England. However, Poulton has "traveled to many wonderful places since early childhood through the power of words," as she noted on her Web site. Reading was an early and favorite activity of Poulton: she devoured children's books, novels, short stories, newspapers, and magazines alike. After attending college in Vermont, Poulton taught kindergarten through second grade in schools in New Hampshire and Maine.

Writing was a long-time desire for Poulton, and after several years in education she decided to switch careers. Working as an editor of a medical journal for a time, Poulton also wrote newsletters for physicians, but the birth of her second child convinced Poulton to work out of her home. She began to focus more and more on children's books, taking part in a local writers' group and attending conferences of the Society of Children's Book Writers and Illustrators to familiarize herself with all aspects of children's publishing. "I have always been very perceptive in my observations of people and surroundings, so it was a natural step to channel that into writing," Poulton commented on her publisher's Web site.

Employing her own childhood memories as well as the experiences of her two daughters, Poulton creates a playful world of the imagination in her debut picture book, *Hello Willow.* "I have a willow tree in my yard," Poulton writes in the book. "It greets me with a wave at my window each morning." The narrator, a little girl of four or five, loves to play under the tree's branches, which "fall to the ground like feathers." This plucky and creative child pretends she is by turns a monkey, a butterfly, an explorer, and a tea-party hostess, as she climbs and swings in the tree and dances, naps, and snacks under its sheltering boughs. At the end of the day, she returns to the snug security of her home in time for bed, but once in bed, the little girl wonders if her beloved willow tree is sleeping too.

Critical response to this first book was generally positive. A contributor for the online *Children's Bookwatch/Midwest Review* praised Poulton's "superbly written, whimsical story," and Alan Caruba, writing in *Bookviews,* thought that *Hello Willow* was a "good debut," which offers "life-affirming values." Remo Picchietti, writing in *BookReview,* called Poulton's title a "delightful" and "whimsical, but believable" children's book that will "entertain and delight every child who reads it or has it read to them."

Poulton continues to work on new story lines, spending as much time as she can both writing and visiting the children's sections of bookstores to educate herself about current children's book favorites.

Biographical and Critical Sources

BOOKS

Poulton, Kimberly, *Hello Willow,* illustrated by Jennifer O'Keefe, Moon Mountain Publishing (North Kingstown, RI), 2000.

PERIODICALS

Children's Book Review Service, December, 2000, review of *Hello Willow,* p. 52.

OTHER

BookReview, http://www.bookreview.com/ (February 27, 2002), Remo Picchietti, review of *Hello Willow.*
Bookviews, http://www.bookviews.com/ (February 27, 2002), Alan Caruba, review of *Hello Willow.*
Children's Bookwatch/Midwest Review, http://www.execpc.com/~mbr/bookwatch/ (February 27, 2002), review of *Hello Willow.*
Kimberly Poulton Web Site, http://www.hellowillow.com/ (February 27, 2002).
Moon Mountain Publishers, http://www.moonmountainpub.com/ (February 22, 2002).
Word Ravelings, http://wordweaving.com/ (February 27, 2002).*

* * *

POWELL, Patricia Hruby

Personal

Born in Arlington Heights, IL; married Morgan Powell (a composer and jazz trombonist). *Nationality:* American. *Education:* London School of Contemporary Dance; University of Illinois, B.F.A. (dance); Temple University, M.F.A. (dance); University of Illinois, M.S.

Patricia Hruby Powell

Powell retells fourteen international folktales about flowers in Blossom Tales. *(Illustrated by Sarah Dillard.)*

(library science). *Hobbies and other interests:* Organic gardening, Yoga, T'ai Chi, trapeze work, social dancing.

Addresses

Home—675N, C.R. 1375E, Tuscola, IL 61953. *Agent*—Moon Mountain Publishing, 80 Peachtree Rd., North Kingstown, RI 02852. *E-mail*—phpowell@tales-forallages.com.

Career

Dancer, choreographer, storyteller, writer, illustrator, dance teacher, mime, librarian. Artist-in-residence in schools and organizations, sponsored by the Illinois and Indiana arts councils, the Detroit Art Institute, and the Kennedy Center; taught and performed throughout Central and South America with sponsorship of U.S. Information Agency. One Plus One dance company, founder, choreographer, and dancer in London, England, Winnipeg, Canada, and New York, NY; writer in residence seven times, Ragdale Foundation, Lake Forest, IL. Conducts workshops in dance, drama, storytelling, and writing.

Awards, Honors

Recipient of National Endowment for the Arts and Illinois Arts Council fellowships; runner-up, Storyteller

of the Year, 1996, for "Gramma Lilac" from *Mothers, Daughters, Sisters, Grandmothers.*

Writings

Blossom Tales: Flower Stories of Many Folk, illustrated by Sarah Dillard, Moon Mountain (North Kingstown, RI), 2002.

Powell's essays and stories have appeared in *Cricket, Spider, Calliope, Storytelling, New Stone Circle, Prairie Wind, Riverwind, Storytelling World, Canadian Gardening, Green Prints,* and *Adventures in Storytelling.* Also the author/performer/reteller of two storytelling recordings, *Hans and Gret: The Rap and Other Stories from Around the World* and *Mothers, Daughters, Sisters, Grandmothers,* both from One Plus One.

Work in Progress

Zinnia, a bilingual English/Navajo picture book, for Salina Bookshelf, due in 2003; a young adult novel, tentatively titled *Waiting for Rain,* about a teenager who finds an entryway into the Amazonian rainforest in his attic.

Sidelights

"I used to talk in my dances, now I dance in my stories," commented Patricia Hruby Powell on her Web site. This Illinois community artist has blended dance, music, and words for over twenty-five years in performances that offer a unique storytelling experience. With her debut picture book, *Blossom Tales: Flower Stories of Many Folk,* Powell moved such multimedia experiences to the printed page, combining her love of story with her passion for gardening in a bouquet of stories written with "beautiful simplicity," according to Joanne S. Carpender in *National Gardener.*

Born and raised in Arlington Heights, Illinois, Powell and her brother and sister "played in barns and the construction sites of hundreds of new neighborhood houses" as children, the author noted on her Web site. "They piled dirt up from the new foundations and they waited so long that for years we had prairie-covered hills and tadpole-filled creeks and a bicycle route to the park over those hills." Powell wrote about these experiences in her first, and still unpublished, novel, *Maddy.* A dancer from an early age, Powell studied dance in London, at the University of Illinois, and at Temple University in Philadelphia, Pennsylvania, ultimately earning a M.F.A. in dance. Following the maxim of never quitting one's day job in the world of art and performance, Powell also earned a master's degree in library science and works as a substitute librarian.

Performing solo and with her dance company, One Plus One, Powell performs in England, Canada, Central and South America, the Caribbean, and around the United States, from New York City to her native Illinois. Powell's performances blend storytelling and movement in a dramatic form that reaches audiences of all ages.

Slowly, Powell moved from performances of dance with some story to storytelling performances illustrated with some dance and movement. From performing storyteller to writer was the next obvious step, one that she accomplished with the publication of stories and essays in such magazines as *Cricket* and *Calliope.*

Powell also wrote book-length manuscripts, both for novels and for picture books. She illustrated one such attempt, the unpublished *Frog Plus Frog.* Then, in 2002 her first picture book, *Blossom Tales,* appeared. In this title, Powell collects fourteen flower-themed folktales from around the world and retells them for a contemporary audience "with beautiful simplicity," as *National Gardener* reviewer Joanne S. Carpender described it. In the Sicilian tale, a crocus grows because of a poor boy's kindness, and in the Arabian tale, the prophet Mohammed's linen shirt transforms a common plant into the vibrant and aromatic geranium. In the English tale of the lily of the valley, that beautiful flower is the result of a battle between a brave dragon fighter and the dragon Sin. The fighter ultimately conquers the dragon, but where the man's blood was spilled, the flower sprang up. A Russian woodcutter who shares his bread with a dwarf is rewarded when the dwarf squeezes oil from snapdragon seeds to put onto the peasant's bread, and thereafter the woodcutter prospers by making snapdragon oil. Fairies turn tulips from drab brown to bright colors in another English folktale, and an Ojibwa myth tells of the dandelion coming from a beautiful golden-haired maid who stood waiting so long for her lover to come back to her that her hair turned white and blew away. The book also has an appeal for gardeners: as Powell explains in its pages, she has grown each of the flowers mentioned in her own garden.

Critical reception was positive for this debut title. Writing for the Web site *Ravelings,* Cindy Penn noted how Powell brings "her love of drama and storytelling to the written page in this collection." Lynne Schwartz-Barker, writing in the *Sunday Gazette-Mail,* felt it would be a "nice spring present for a beginning reader." And, writing in *Fearless Reviews,* Cindy Appel called *Blossom Tales* a "fascinating glimpse into a myriad of cultures."

Powell's second picture book, *Zinnia,* follows this flower theme in a bilingual text in English and Navajo and is expected to appear in 2003. The author has also compiled her stories on audiocassette. *Hans and Gret: The Rap and Other Stories from Around the World* and *Mothers, Daughters, Sisters, Grandmothers* are both award-winning recordings featuring Powell's storytelling technique, something that can also be experienced firsthand in her workshops and in her performances such as "An Evening with Jane Austen, Emily Brontë, and Emily Dickinson." Combining storytelling with movement, Powell reads from Austen's *Emma* and *Pride and Prejudice,* shares memories of her dead brother with sisters Charlotte and Anne as Brontë, and writes poetry in Amherst as Dickinson.

Powell lives in the countryside of central Illinois with her husband, a yellow lab named Jazzabelle, and a cat named Billie, and is at work on a young adult novel about a boy who finds he can travel to the Amazonian rainforest through a portal in his attic. "It started as a dream," Powell noted on her Web site, "as many of my projects do. I visited the rainforest while in South America with my dance company. And I did research on a collection of folklore and mythology from Amazonian peoples plus additional general research about the rainforest. The novel is set in New Bedford, Massachusetts, so I visited there to do research. New Bedford has a shipping and whaling history that is perfect for the plot of my novel."

"On days I don't tell stories," Powell concluded on her Web site, "I walk along the nearby river with Jazzabelle and tell her my new stories (she's not critical at all, so I don't feel intimidated by her hearing the stories that I'm just learning). Or better yet are the days I get to think. Usually I think about what I'm going to write that day. Then I write."

Biographical and Critical Sources

PERIODICALS

Sunday Gazette-Mail (Charleston, SC), March 17, 2002, Lynne Schwartz-Barker, "Garden Potpourri."

OTHER

Fearless Reviews, http://www.fearlessbooks.com/ (May, 2002), Cindy Appel, review of *Blossom Tales.*
Moon Mountain Publishing, http://www.moonmountainpub. com/ (July 6, 2002), "Patricia Hruby Powell, Author of *Blossom Tales.*"
National Gardener, http://www.gardenclub.org/book_ reviews/ (July 6, 2002), Joanne S. Carpender, review of *Blossom Tales.*
Patricia Hruby Powell Web Site, http://www.talesforallages. com/ (July 7, 2002).
Ravelings, http://www.wordweaving.com/ (July 6, 2002), Cindy Penn, review of *Blossom Tales.*

*   *   *

PRAGER, Ellen J. 1962-

Personal

Born April 30, 1962, in Bethpage, NY; daughter of Lawrence and Phyllis Prager. *Nationality:* American. *Education:* Wesleyan University, B.A., 1984; University of Miami, M.S., 1987; Louisiana State University, Ph.D., 1992. *Hobbies and other interests:* Scuba diving, swimming, cycling, reading, nature.

Addresses

Home—201 Crandon Blvd. #1036, Key Biscayne, FL 33149. *Office*—c/o Rosenstiel School of Marine and Atmospheric Science, University of Miami, 4600 Rickenbacker, Miami, FL 33149. *E-mail*—elprager@ aol.com.

Career

Marine scientist, researcher, and educator; freelance writer and consultant. Sea Education Association, Woods Hole, MA, faculty scientist, 1993-95; Caribbean Marine Research Center, Lee Stocking Island, Bahamas, associate director, 1995-96; U.S. Geological Survey, St. Petersburg, FL, marine geologist, 1997-99; Rosenstiel School, University of Miami, Miami, FL, assistant dean, 2000—. National Ocean Conference, co-chair of the subcommittee on research, education, and exploration, 1998; Florida Ocean Alliance Board, 2000. Often appears as a expert guest on NBC, ABC, and CNN; frequent public speaker at regional and national events.

Member

American Geophysical Union, International Society on Reef Studies, Oceanographic Society.

Awards, Honors

Parents Choice Award, 2001, for *Sand.*

Writings

FOR CHILDREN

Sand, illustrated by Nancy Woodman, National Geographic Society (Washington, DC), 2000.
Volcano!, illustrated by Nancy Woodman, National Geographic Society (Washington, DC), 2001.
Earthquakes, illustrated by Susan Greenstein, National Geographic Society (Washington, DC), 2002.

FOR ADULTS

(With Sylvia A. Earle) *The Oceans,* McGraw-Hill (New York, NY), 2000.
Furious Earth: The Science and Nature of Earthquakes, Volcanoes, and Tsunamis, McGraw-Hill (New York, NY), 2000.

Also the author of *EcoWatch,* a bi-weekly column for WTVJ-TV; contributor of articles to popular journals and magazines, including *Scientific American* and *Sea Frontiers;* author of numerous technical publications for scientific journals.

Work in Progress

Ocean Waves, for National Geographic, publication expected in 2003, and *Living under Water.*

Sidelights

A specialist in marine geology and assistant dean of the University of Miami's prestigious Rosenstiel School of Marine and Atmospheric Science, Ellen J. Prager is also a freelance writer with several children's and adult titles to her credit. Her book *The Oceans* has been called a must-have title for those interested in the sea by famous ocean explorer Jean-Michel Cousteau, while her series of children's science books for National Geographic,

Sand, Earthquakes, and *Volcano!,* have been praised by critics as being both kid-friendly and informative.

As Prager told *SATA,* she has been "literally immersed in marine science research for the last two decades." She began her career in marine science as a safety diver and research assistant at an underwater habitat in St. Croix, United States Virgin Islands in 1983, and since that time has participated in research expeditions to the Galapagos Islands, Papua New Guinea, and the deep waters of the Florida reef, among others. Prager also worked at the noted Sea Education Association (SEA) for several years. "I have spent many days on ships out at sea, on remote islands surrounded by aqua blue waters, and even living in an underwater research laboratory," Prager told *SATA.* "The ocean and surrounding environments continue to fascinate me and inspire me to learn more, explore, and share my enthusiasm and knowledge with others. I believe that we have not done an adequate job of educating the public and our politicians about the oceans and their importance to humans and the planet."

In 1999, Prager left her research and teaching job at the U.S. Geological Survey to concentrate on bringing earth and ocean science to a broader audience through writing. *Sand,* one of her children's titles, presents information on the composition and creation of sand that "is all accurate, interesting, brief, and presented in short blocks of text," Martha Scholl wrote in *Science Books and Films. Booklist's* Shelley Townsend-Hudson also had praise for *Sand,* noting that "Prager's part science, part fun-and-games approach gives this book lots of appeal." The "sand sleuth," a magnifying glass-toting cartoon sandpiper dressed like fictional detective Sherlock Holmes, displays magnified images of sand for the reader and also inserts some humor. Such kid-friendly devices prompted a contributor for *Publishers Weekly* to comment that the "informal approach should broaden this volume's audience." Reviewing *Sand* in *School Library Journal,* Ellen Heath concluded that the book was a "striking success" and an "outstanding choice" with a "fascinating, lively presentation." Further children's books by Prager for National Geographic include *Volcano!* and *Earthquakes,* both with similar informal approaches.

For older readers, Prager authored *The Oceans* and *Furious Earth: The Science and Nature of Earthquakes, Volcanoes, and Tsunamis,* the former title being coauthored with Sylvia A. Earle. These books received equally positive response from reviewers. Gilbert Taylor, reviewing *The Oceans* in *Booklist,* noted that Prager and Earle, both scientists and divers, "are well licensed to condense oceanographic knowledge" and to explain "the integrality of the ocean to geological history." Proceeding from the Paleozoic age to today's oceans, the authors discuss how the ocean got its present chemical make-up, how its currents can affect weather, and how important the ocean is to the life of this planet. Referring to the same work, a *Publishers Weekly* reviewer concluded that this "elegant study is an excellent resource for scientists, teachers and all lovers of the ocean."

Prager again lived underwater for a length of time in 2000, this time for the Jason Project, and during her two weeks underwater, she was broadcast live on ABC and CNN. In that same year she accepted an academic post once again, as assistant dean at the Rosenstiel School in Miami, Florida. She continues to write and to give frequent talks and presentations in which she shares her love for the oceans with others.

"I consider myself extremely fortunate," Prager concluded to *SATA*. "I am passionate about what I do for a living, and it has brought me joy and adventure, as well as wonderful friends and colleagues. I left the traditional track of a marine scientist in teaching and research to focus my efforts on bringing ocean science to the public and helping to bring attention to and support for continued research and education in marine science.... Unfortunately, we live in a society where the majority of students and adults are nearly scientifically illiterate. Yet science plays such an important role in society, ranging from technologies that provide for everyday needs to the understanding of policies that protect our environment. It is my hope that one day, science will share an equal spotlight with celebrity gossip and legal battles in the media, thus giving it the public visibility deserved and needed."

Biographical and Critical Sources

PERIODICALS

Booklist, March 1, 2000, Shelley Townsend-Hudson, review of *Sand,* p. 1246; May 1, 2000, Gilbert Taylor, review of *The Oceans,* p. 1634; December 1, 2001, Donna Seaman, review of *The Oceans,* p. 617; June 1, 2002, Carolyn Phelan, review of *Earthquakes,* p. 1727.

Choice, June, 2000, E. R. Swanson, review of *Furious Earth: The Science and Nature of Earthquakes, Volcanoes, and Tsunamis,* p. 1845.

Geotimes, August, 2000, Robert L. Kovach, review of *Furious Earth,* pp. 32-33.

Publishers Weekly, March 13, 2000, review of *Sand,* p. 83; April 24, 2000, review of *The Oceans,* p. 78.

School Library Journal, April, 2000, Ellen Heath, review of *Sand,* p. 124.

Science Books and Films, March-April, 2002, Martha Scholl, review of *Sand,* p. 77.*

S–T

SANCHEZ, Sonia 1934-

Personal

Original name Wilsonia Benita Driver; born September 9, 1934, in Birmingham, AL; daughter of Wilson L. and Lena (Jones) Driver; married Albert Sanchez (divorced); children: Anita, Morani Neusi, Mungu Neusi. *Education:* Hunter College (now Hunter College of the City University of New York), B.A., 1955; New York University, post graduate study; Wilberforce University, Ph.D., 1972. *Politics:* "Peace, freedom, and justice."

Addresses

Home—407 W. Chelten Ave., Philadelphia, PA 19144. *Office*—Department of English/Women's Studies, Temple University, 10th Floor Anderson Hall, 1114 W. Berks St., Philadelphia, PA 19122.

Career

Staff member, Downtown Community School, San Francisco, CA, 1965-67, and Mission Rebels in Action, 1968-69; San Francisco State College (now University), San Francisco, CA, instructor, 1966-68; University of Pittsburgh, Pittsburgh, PA, assistant professor, 1969-70; Rutgers University, New Brunswick, NJ, assistant professor, 1970-71; Manhattan Community College of the City University of New York, New York, NY, assistant professor of literature and creative writing, 1971-73; City College of the City University of New York, teacher of creative writing, 1972; Amherst College, Amherst, MA, associate professor, 1972-75; University of Pennsylvania, Philadelphia, PA, 1976-77; Temple University, Philadelphia, PA, associate professor, 1977, professor, 1979—, faculty fellow in provost's office, 1986-87, presidential fellow, 1987-88. Distinguished Minority Fellow, University of Delaware; Distinguished Poet-in-Residence, Spelman College; and Zale Writer-in-Residence at Sophie Newcomb College, Tulane University.

Sonia Sanchez

Member

Literature Panel of the Pennsylvania Council on the Arts.

Awards, Honors

PEN writing award, 1969; National Institute of Arts and Letters grant, 1970; National Endowment for the Arts award, 1978-79; Honorary Citizen of Atlanta, 1982; Tribute to Black Women Award, Black Students of Smith College, 1982; Lucretia Mott Award, 1984;

American Book Award, Before Columbus Foundation, 1985, for *homegirls & handgrenades;* Pennsylvania Governor's Award in the humanities, 1989, for bringing great distinction to herself and her discipline through remarkable accomplishment; Welcome Award, Museum of Afro-American History (Boston, MA), 1990; Oni Award, International Black Women's Congress, 1992; Women Pioneers Hall of Fame Citation, Young Women's Christian Association, 1992; Roots Award, Pan-African Studies Community Program, 1993; PEN fellowship in the arts, 1993-94; Legacy Award, Jomandi Productions, 1995.

Writings

FOR CHILDREN

It's a New Day: Poems for Young Brothas and Sistuhs, Broadside Press (Detroit, MI), 1971.

The Adventures of Fat Head, Small Head, and Square Head, illustrated by Taiwo DuVall, Third Press (New York, NY), 1973.

A Sound Investment and Other Stories, Third World Press, 1979.

FOR ADULTS

Homecoming (poetry), Broadside Press (Detroit, MI), 1969.

We a BaddDDD People (poetry), with foreword by Dudley Randall, Broadside Press (Detroit, MI), 1970.

(Editor) *Three Hundred and Sixty Degrees of Blackness Comin' at You* (poetry), 5X Publishing Co., 1971.

Ima Talken Bout the Nation of Islam, TruthDel, 1972.

Love Poems, Third Press (New York, NY), 1973.

A Blues Book for Blue Black Magical Women (poetry), Broadside Press (Detroit, MI), 1973.

(Editor and contributor) *We Be Word Sorcerers: 25 Stories by Black Americans,* Bantam (New York, NY), 1973.

I've Been a Woman: New and Selected Poems, Black Scholar Press (Sausalito, CA), 1978.

Crisis in Culture—Two Speeches by Sonia Sanchez, Black Liberation Press, 1983.

homegirls and handgrenades (poetry), Thunder's Mouth Press (New York, NY), 1984.

(Contributor) Mari Evans, editor, *Black Women Writers (1950-1980): A Critical Evaluation,* introduced by Stephen Henderson, Doubleday-Anchor (Garden City, NY), 1984.

Under a Soprano Sky, Africa World (Trenton, NJ), 1987.

(Compiler and author of introduction) Allison Funk, *Living at the Epicenter: The 1995 Morse Poetry Prize,* Northeastern University Press (Boston, MA), 1995.

Wounded in the House of a Friend (poems), Beacon Press (Boston, MA), 1995.

Does Your House Have Lions? (poems), Beacon Press (Boston, MA), 1997.

Like the Singing Coming off the Drums: Love Poems, Beacon Press (Boston, MA), 1998.

Shake Loose My Skin: New and Selected Poems, Beacon Press (Boston, MA), 1999.

PLAYS

The Bronx Is Next, first produced in New York, NY, at Theatre Black, October 3, 1970 (included in *Caval-cade: Negro American Writing from 1760 to the*

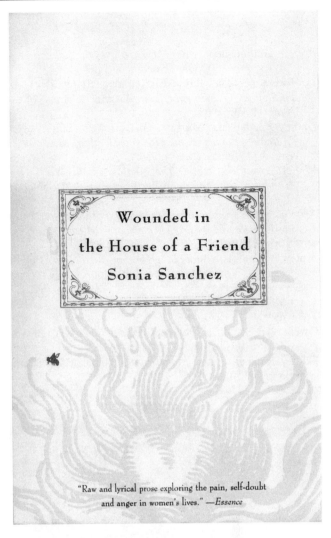

Sanchez's poetic tribute to women explores the tragedy and anger in their lives, yet the work also offers hope.

Present, edited by Arthur Davis and Saunders Redding, Houghton [Boston, MA], 1971).

Sister Son/ji, first produced with *Cop and Blow* and *Players Inn* by Neil Harris and *Gettin' It Together* by Richard Wesley as *Black Visions,* Off-Broadway at New York Shakespeare Festival Public Theatre, 1972 (included in *New Plays from the Black Theatre,* edited by Ed Bullins, Bantam [New York, NY], 1969).

Uh Huh; But How Do It Free Us?, first produced in Chicago, IL, at Northwestern University Theater, 1975 (included in *The New Lafayette Theatre Presents: Plays With Aesthetic Comments by Six Black Playwrights, Ed Bullins, J. E. Gaines, Clay Gross, Oyamo, Sonia Sanchez, Richard Wesley,* edited by Bullins, Anchor Press [Garden City, NY], 1974).

Malcolm Man/Don't Live Here No More, first produced in Philadelphia, PA, at ASCOM Community Center, 1979.

I'm Black When I'm Singing, I'm Blue When I Ain't, first produced in Atlanta, GA, at OIC Theatre, April 23, 1982.

Also author of *Dirty Hearts,* 1972.

CONTRIBUTOR TO ANTHOLOGIES

Robert Giammanco, editor, *Poetro Negro* (title means "Black Power"), Giu, Laterza & Figli, 1968.

Le Roi Jones and Ray Neal, editors, *Black Fire: An Anthology of Afro-American Writing,* Morrow (New York, NY), 1968.

Dudley Randall and Margaret G. Burroughs, editors, *For Malcolm: Poems on the Life and Death of Malcolm X,* Broadside Press (Detroit, MI), 1968.

Walter Lowenfels, editor, *The Writing on the Wall: One Hundred Eight American Poems of Protest,* Doubleday (Garden City, NY), 1969.

Arnold Adoff, editor, *Black Out Loud: An Anthology of Modern Poems by Black Americans,* Macmillan (New York, NY), 1970.

Walter Lowenfels, editor, *In a Time of Revolution: Poems from Our Third World,* Random House (New York, NY), 1970.

June M. Jordan, editor, *Soulscript,* Doubleday (Garden City, NY), 1970.

Gwendolyn Brooks, editor, *A Broadside Treasury,* Broadside Press (Detroit, MI), 1971.

Dudley Randall, editor, *Black Poets,* Bantam (New York, NY), 1971.

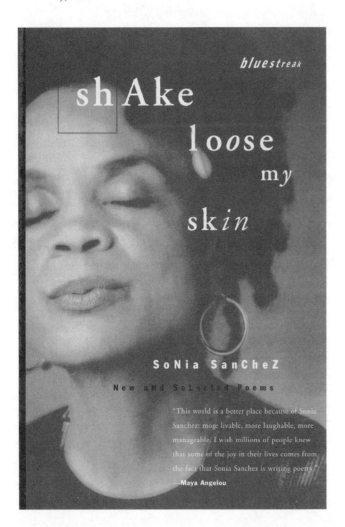

This retrospective covers more than thirty years of Sanchez's work. *(Cover photo by Sigrid Estrada.)*

Orde Coombs, editor, *We Speak as Liberators: Young Black Poets,* Dodd (New York, NY), 1971.

Bernard W. Bell, editor, *Modern and Contemporary Afro-American Poetry,* Allyn & Bacon (Boston, MA), 1972.

Arnold Adoff, editor, *The Poetry of Black America: An Anthology of the 20th Century,* Harper (New York, NY), 1973.

JoAn and William M. Chace, *Making It New,* Canfield Press (San Francisco, CA), 1973.

Donald B. Gibson, editor, *Modern Black Poets,* Prentice-Hall (Englewood Cliffs, NJ), 1973.

Stephen Henderson, editor, *Understanding the New Black Poetry: Black Speech and Black Music as Poetic References,* Morrow (New York, NY), 1973.

J. Paul Hunter, editor, *Norton Introduction to Literature: Poetry,* Norton (New York, NY), 1973.

James Schevill, editor, *Breakout: In Search of New Theatrical Environments,* Swallow Press, 1973.

Lucille Iverson and Kathryn Ruby, editors, *We Become New: Poems by Contemporary Women,* Bantam (New York, NY), 1975.

Quincy Troupe and Rainer Schulte, editors, *Giant Talk: An Anthology of Third World Writings,* Random House (New York, NY), 1975.

Henry B. Chapin, editor, *Sports in Literature,* McKay (New York, NY), 1976.

Cleanth Brooks and Robert Penn Warren, editors, *Understanding Poetry,* Holt (New York, NY), 1976.

Ann Reit, editor, *Alone Amid All the Noise,* Four Winds/Scholastic (New York, NY), 1976.

Erlene Stetson, editor, *Black Sister: Poetry by Black American Women, 1746-1980,* Indiana University Press (Bloomington, IN), 1981.

Amiri Baraka and Amina Baraka, editors, *Confirmation: An Anthology of African-American Women,* Morrow (New York, NY), 1983.

Burney Hollis, editor, *Swords upon This Hill,* Morgan State University Press (Baltimore, MD), 1984.

Jerome Rothenberg, editor, *Technicians of the Sacred: A Range of Poetries from Africa, America, Asia, Europe and Oceania,* University of California Press (Berkeley, CA), 1985.

Marge Piercy, editor, *Early Ripening: American Women's Poetry Now,* Pandora (New York, NY), 1987.

Poems also included in *Night Comes Softly, Black Arts, To Gwen With Love, New Black Voices, Blackspirits, The New Black Poetry, A Rock against the Wind, America: A Prophecy, Nommo, Black Culture,* and *Natural Process.*

OTHER

Author of column for *American Poetry Review,* 1977-78, and for *Philadelphia Daily News,* 1982-83. Contributor of poems to *Minnesota Review, Black World,* and other periodicals. Contributor of plays to *Scripts, Black Theatre, Drama Review,* and other theater journals. Contributor of articles to several journals, including *Journal of African Civilizations.*

Sidelights

In addition to being an important activist, poet, playwright, professor, and a leader of the black studies movement, Sonia Sanchez has also written books for children. She introduced young people to the poetry of black English in her 1971 work *It's a New Day: Poems for Young Brothas and Sistuhs*, created a moral fable for younger children in 1973's *The Adventures of Fat Head, Small Head, and Square Head*, and produced a collection of short tales for children in 1979's *A Sound Investment and Other Stories*. As William Pitt Root noted in *Poetry* magazine: "One concern [Sanchez] always comes back to is the real education of Black children."

Sanchez was born Wilsonia Benita Driver on September 9, 1934, in Birmingham, Alabama. Her mother died when she was very young, and she was raised by her grandmother until she too died when the author was six years old. Her father was a schoolteacher, and as a result she and her siblings spoke standard English instead of a southern or black dialect. It was not until she and her brother rejoined her father in Harlem, New York, when she was nine years old, that Sanchez learned the speech of the streets that would become so important to her poetry. Sanchez also stuttered as a child; this led her to writing, which she has done since she was very young.

Sanchez also learned about racism at a very young age. She recalled in an interview with Claudia Tate for Tate's *Black Women Writers at Work:* "I also remember an aunt who spat in a bus driver's face—that was the subject of one of my first poems—because he wanted her to get off as the bus was filling up with white people.... Well, my aunt would not get off the bus, so she spat, and was arrested. That was the first visual instance I can remember of encountering racism." She did not leave racism behind when her family moved north, however. She told Tate that "coming north to Harlem for 'freedom' when I was nine presented me with a whole new racial landscape." Sanchez continued, "Here was the realization of the corner store, where I watched white men pinch black women on their behinds. And I made a vow that nobody would ever do that to me unless I wanted him to. I continued to live in the neighborhood, went to that store as a nine-year-old child, and continued to go there as a student at Hunter College. When I was sixteen to eighteen they attempted to pinch my behind. I turned around and said, 'Oh no you don't.' They knew I was serious." She has been fighting racism and sexism ever since.

After graduating from Hunter College in 1955, Sanchez did postgraduate study at New York University. During the early 1960s she was an integrationist, supporting the ideas of the Congress of Racial Equality. But after listening to the ideas of Black Muslim leader Malcolm X, who believed blacks would never be truly accepted by whites in the United States, she focused more on her black heritage as something separate from white Americans. She began teaching in the San Francisco area in 1965, first on the staff of the Downtown Community School and later at San Francisco State College (now University). There she was a pioneer in developing black studies courses, including a class in black English.

In 1969, Sanchez published her first book of poetry for adults, *Homecoming*. She followed that up with 1970's *We a BaddDDD People*, which especially focused on black dialect as a poetic medium. At about the same time her first plays, *Sister Son/ji* and *The Bronx Is Next*, were being produced or published. In 1971, she published her first work for children, *It's A New Day: Poems for Young Brothas and Sistuhs*. Shortly afterwards, she joined the Nation of Islam, also referred to as the Black Muslims. Sanchez enjoyed the spirituality and discipline of the religion, but she always had problems with its repression of women. She explained to Tate: "It was not easy being in the Nation. I was/am a writer. I was also speaking on campuses. In the Nation at that time women were supposed to be in the background. My contribution to the Nation has been that I refused to let them tell me where my place was. I would be reading my poetry some place, and men would get up to leave, and I'd say, 'Look, my words are equally important.' So I got into trouble." Sanchez stated: "One dude said to me once that the solution for Sonia Sanchez was for her to have some babies.... I already had two children.... I fought against the stereotype of me as a black woman in the movement relegated to three steps behind. It especially was important for the women in the Nation to see that. I told them that in order to pull this 'mother' out from what it's under we gonna need men, women, children, but most important, we need minds." She added: "I had to fight. I had to fight a lot of people in and outside of the Nation due to so-called sexism. I spoke up. I think it was important that there were women there to do that. I left the Nation during the 1975-76 academic year."

While she was a Black Muslim, however, Sanchez produced her second children's book, *The Adventures of Fathead, Smallhead, and Squarehead*. A moral fable about a pilgrimage to Mecca, the tale began as a story for her own children. In an interview with *African American Review* contributor Susan Kelly, Sanchez remembered, "my children had asked me to make up a story one night in New York City before we moved to Amherst. They would always say, 'Read, read, read!' So I would read to them. And one night, they said, 'Don't read; make up a story.'" The resulting tale became *The Adventures of Fathead, Smallhead, and Squarehead.*

Another Sanchez book of interest to a teenaged audience is *Shake Loose My Skin: New and Selected Poems.* Featuring verse from her older publications, as well as four new entries, *Shake Loose My Skin* offers a sampling of Sanchez's work spanning over thirty years. In her poems, she tackles topics ranging from bigotry to poverty to drug abuse. "This collection should draw wide attention to the consistency of Sanchez's achievement," believed a *Publishers Weekly* contributor. *Library Journal* critic Ann K. van Buren found that this book "leaves one in awe of the stretches of language Sanchez has helped to legitimize."

Because of the political nature of most of her writings and her involvement in black power causes, Sanchez feels that her academic career has suffered from persecution by government authorities. She told Tate: "While I helped to organize the black studies program at San Francisco State, the FBI came to my landlord and said put her out. She's one of those radicals." Sanchez continued: "Then I taught at Manhattan Community College in New York City, and I stayed there until my record was picked up. You know how you have your record on file, and you can go down and look at it. Well, I went down to look at it, because we had had a strike there, and I had been arrested with my students. I went to the dean to ask for my record, and he told me that I could not have my record because it was sent downtown." Sanchez said: "That's when I began to realize just how much the government was involved with teachers in the university. I then tried to get another job in New York City—no job. I had been white-balled. The word was out, I was too political.... That's how I ended up at Amherst College, because I couldn't get a job in my home state. That's what they do to you. If they can't control what you write, they make alternatives for you and send you to places where you have no constituency."

After leaving Amherst, Sanchez eventually became a professor at Temple University in Philadelphia, Pennsylvania, where she has since taught for many years. She has also edited several books, and contributed poetry and articles on black culture to anthologies and periodicals. Summing up the importance of Sanchez's work, Kalamu ya Salaam concluded in *Dictionary of Literary Biography:* "Sanchez is one of the few creative artists who have significantly influenced the course of black American literature and culture."

In her interview with Kelly, Sanchez concluded, "It is that love of language that has propelled me, that love of language that came from listening to my grandmother speak black English.... It is that love of language that says, simply, to the ancestors who have done this before you, 'I am keeping the love of life alive, the love of language alive. I am keeping words that are spinning on my tongue and getting them transferred on paper. I'm keeping this great tradition of American poetry alive.'"

Biographical and Critical Sources

BOOKS

Children's Literature Review, Volume 18, Gale (Detroit, MI), 1989.

Dictionary of Literary Biography, Volume 41: *Afro-American Poets since 1955,* Gale (Detroit, MI), 1985, pp. 295-306.

Dictionary of Literary Biography, Documentary Series, Volume 8, Gale (Detroit, MI), 1991.

Tate, Claudia, editor, *Black Women Writers at Work,* Continuum, 1983, pp. 132-148.

PERIODICALS

African American Review, spring, 2000, Yoshinobu Hakutani, review of *Like the Singing Coming Off the Drums,*
p. 180; winter, 2000, Susan Kelly, "Discipline and Craft: An Interview with Sonia Sanchez," p. 679.

American Visions, October, 1999, Denolyn Carroll, review of *Shake Loose My Skin: New and Selected Poems,* p. 35.

Booklist, February 15, 1999, Donna Seaman, review of *Shake Loose My Skin,* p. 1028.

Library Journal, February 1, 1999, Ann K. van Buren, review of *Shake Loose My Skin,* p. 93.

Poetry, October, 1973, William Pitt Root, pp. 44-48.

Publishers Weekly, December 21, 1998, review of *Shake Loose My Skin,* p. 63.

OTHER

Sonia Sanchez—The Academy of American Poets, http://www.poets.org/ (December 15, 2001).*

*   *   *

SCHWEITZER, Byrd Baylor
See BAYLOR, Byrd

*   *   *

STINE, G(eorge) Harry 1928-1997
(Lee Correy)

OBITUARY NOTICE—See index for *SATA* sketch: Born March 26, 1928, in Philadelphia, PA; died of an apparent stroke, on November 2, 1997, in Phoenix, AZ. Writer and model rocket design specialist. Stine attended the University of Colorado (1946-50), and received his B.A. degree in 1952 from Colorado College. He began his career as editor of his college newspaper, *The Window* (1948-49). His first nonfiction book was *Rocket Power and Space Flight* (1957). He penned over thirty books during his career, and contributed to many others, most in the nonfiction space and rocketry field, and many in the science fiction genre. His first science fiction book was *Starship Through Space* (1954), a sequel to his best-known short story, "... And a Star to Steer Her By." Most of his science fiction titles were written, at least initially, under the pseudonym of Lee Correy. His science fiction stories are represented in many of the more popular anthologies, including *Science Fiction '58: The Year's Greatest Science Fiction and Fantasy, The Sixth Annual of the Year's Best Science Fiction* (both edited by Judith Merril), and *Analog Six* (edited by John W. Campbell, Jr.). He was a contributor to *Collier's Encyclopedia,* and the author of the columns "Conquest of Space" for *Mechanix Illustrated* (1956-57), and "The Alternate View" for *Analog* (beginning in 1980). He contributed over two hundred science fiction stories and nonfiction articles on science and rocketry to the major magazines and periodicals in the field, including *Omni, Science Digest, Saturday Evening Post, Astounding,* and *Magazine of Fantasy and Science Fiction.* He was founder and editor of *Missile Away!* (1953-57), *Model Rocketeer* (1958-64), and *Flow Factor* (1973-76), and he was senior editor of *Aviation/Space* (beginning in 1982). He was a member of the American

Institute of Aeronautics and Astronautics (associate fellow), the Instrument Society of America, the Academy of Model Aeronautics, the National Aeronautic Association of Rocketry (founder; president, 1957-67; honorary trustee), the American Society of Aerospace Education, Science Fiction Writers of America, the L-5 Society, the National Fire Protection Association, the British Interplanetary Society (fellow) the New York Academy of Sciences, Theta Xi, and the Explorers Club (New York City; fellow). He was co-founder of the Citizens Advisory Council on National Space Policy in 1980. He received a special award from the American Rocket Society for founding and editing *Missile Away!* (1957), Bendix Trophies from the National Association of Rocketry (1964; 1965; 1967; 1968), a Silver Medal, American Space Pioneer, from the U.S. Army Association (1965), a Silver Medal, payload category, from the First International Model Rocket Competition, Dubnica, Czechoslovakia (1966), a special award from the National Association of Rocketry (1967), and was the first recipient of the annual award in Model Rocketry Division, from the Hobby Industry Association of America (1969). Stine is the acknowledged "father of model rocketry," and as the author of its definitive texts and rules, he helped establish it as a safe and enduringly popular hobby—and an inspiration to future scientists, engineers, and astronauts.

OBITUARIES AND OTHER SOURCES:

PERIODICALS

Locus, December, 1997, p. 78.

*   *   *

STOEKE, Janet Morgan 1957-

Personal

Born April 30, 1957, in Pittsfield, MA; daughter of Julius Paul (a mechanical engineer) and Carolyn S. (an artist) Stoeke; married Barrett L. Brooks (a marine botanist), July 21, 1990; children: Harrison and Colin (twins), Elliott, Hailey. *Nationality:* American. *Education:* Colgate University, B.A., 1979; George Washington University, M.F.A., 1987.

Addresses

E-mail—janet@minervalouise.com.

Career

Author and illustrator. Worked variously as a gymnastics instructor, waitress, baby photographer, museum docent, bookstore clerk, and advertisement designer.

Member

Washington Children's Book Guild.

Janet Morgan Stoeke

Awards, Honors

Dutton Picture Book Competition Award, 1988, for *Minerva Louise;* Parents' Choice Silver Award and American Library Association Notable Book citation, both 1994, both for *A Hat for Minerva Louise.*

Writings

FOR CHILDREN; SELF-ILLUSTRATED

Minerva Louise, Dutton (New York, NY), 1988.
Lawrence, Dutton (New York, NY), 1990.
A Hat for Minerva Louise, Dutton (New York, NY), 1994.
Minerva Louise at School, Dutton (New York, NY), 1996.
A Friend for Minerva Louise, Dutton (New York, NY), 1997.
Five Little Kitty Cats, Dutton (New York, NY), 1998.
One Little Puppy Dog, Dutton (New York, NY), 1998.
Hide and Seek, Dutton (New York, NY), 1999.
Minerva Louise at the Fair, Dutton (New York, NY), 2000.
Minerva Louise and the Red Truck, Dutton (New York, NY), 2002.

FOR CHILDREN; ILLUSTRATOR

Katie Evans, *Hunky Dory Ate It,* Dutton (New York, NY), 1991.
Katie Evans, *Hunky Dory Found It,* Dutton (New York, NY), 1994.

Sidelights

Janet Morgan Stoeke has received high praise for her brightly colored, simple picture books featuring Minerva Louise, a hen whose cheerful optimism and inquiring spirit is never daunted by her many mistakes. "At the merest stroke of her pen," stated a *Publishers Weekly* reviewer, "Stoeke invests her poultry protagonist with an abundance of character." In addition to writing her own stories, Stoeke has also illustrated the books of other authors in artwork critics have describes as cheerful and silly. Her drawings feature endearing characters in appealing scenarios, and her work has been singled out for the visual humor it has added to the tales of other authors.

Stoeke did not plan to become a writer and illustrator. "I have had a number of other careers which came to me after some serious effort," she once explained. "But happily for me, this children's bookmaking one came along unforeseen, nearly out of the blue. I have been a gymnastics instructor, bookstore clerk, waitress, museum docent, and advertising designer. Throughout all of these jobs I painted and felt that being a painter was the most important part of me. I still feel the need to paint, and sometimes call myself a painter, but the children's book creator title suits me best of all those I've so far tried out.

"In the middle of completing my master's thesis, and while working full time at my most serious job (ad designer), a small article about a contest came across my desk. A contest for a picture book. I thought about all of the time I'd spent in that bookstore, working primarily with children's books. I had developed a lot of uppity opinions during that time. Most of them revolved around how I might have better accomplished what others had tried to do. The contest was closing in two weeks. I decided to try it.

"My main objectives were to avoid the pitfalls that glared out at me from books at the store. Don't write down to children, be didactic, gimmicky, trite, or the least bit imitative of a previously successful illustrator/ author. All this, and be funny and original." Although Stoeke soon realized that her goal was a difficult one, she was successful, and her submission won first prize in the 1988 contest. It also became her first book, *Minerva Louise,* as well as what Stoeke admitted was "the start of a new, ever-surprising, and probably endless education, and a very happy change of direction for me."

Minerva Louise is a gentle story about a somewhat discombobulated hen who succumbs to temptation and ventures into a house with red curtains. Once inside, she turns everything topsy turvy, making a nest in the fireplace logs and befriending a rubber duck and a tabby cat she mistakes for a cow. A *Publishers Weekly* writer dubbed Stoeke's debut picture book "a lighthearted story that will tickle the funny bone of the youngest child,"

Chilly chicken Minerva Louise mistakes a pair of mittens for hats to warm both head and tail in Stoeke's self-illustrated A Hat for Minerva Louise.

and praised the brightly colored, simple drawings that accompany Stoeke's story.

Stoeke has continued the adventures of her feathered protagonist in an ongoing series of picture and board books for the very young. In her second award-winning effort, *A Hat for Minerva Louise,* Stoeke's hen wants to play outside on a cold winter day and goes in search of clothes to keep her warm. "*A Hat for Minerva Louise* took a long time to come to me," Stoeke recalled. "I tried and tried to make Minerva Louise come to life again. Somehow she'd change or repeat herself too much when I worked at it. Then, when I looked the other way, and concentrated on something else—it fell into place, like a gift." Other books in the series include *A Friend for Minerva Louise,* which is about Minerva's excitement when her neighbors' activities signal that they have a new bunny—which turns out to be a human infant—and *Minerva Louise at the Fair,* in which the plucky hen becomes waylaid and ultimately rescued while exploring a local fair in her characteristically confused fashion.

Critics noted that much of the humor in Stoeke's "Minerva Louise" books is found in the author/illustrator's depiction of what a *Kirkus Reviews* critic called Minerva's "comically bland certitude," a characteristic exhibited when she mistakes a hose for a scarf and ends up proudly wearing a mitten for a hat in *A Hat for Minerva Louise,* or mistakes a baby's play pen for an outdoor rabbit hutch in *A Friend for Minerva Louise.* "Stoeke's second book about that intrepid screwball, Minerva Louise, is a rare find: a picture book exactly on target for preschoolers that sacrifices none of the essential elements of plot, character, and humor," asserted *Horn Book* contributor Martha V. Parravano. Maintaining that Minerva "deserves a blue ribbon," *School Library Journal* reviewer Marlene Gawron said of *Minerva Louise at the Fair:* "Anyone who has ever made an error in perception will appreciate [the hen's] ... logic as she figures everything out entirely wrong."

In addition to her "Minerva Louise" books, Stoeke has branched off into other realms of the animal kingdom. *Lawrence* is the story of a shy hedgehog who longs for a nibble of coconut cream pie but fears leaving his snug home and going out in the world to track some down. "Shy children who share Lawrence's fears will find a friend" in her "endearing" protagonist, according to a *Publishers Weekly* reviewer, adding that Stoeke's "upbeat" story is complemented by her "delightfully unaffected" drawings. In her board books *One Little Puppy Dog* and *Five Little Kitty Cats,* she illustrates basic counting concepts by having playful puppies illustrate going up the number scale and kittens going back down from five to one. Stoeke's "sweet, full-color" illustrations provide "enough detail to complement [her] ... simple texts," noted Marsha McGrath in her review for *School Library Journal. Booklist* critic Carolyn Phelan noted that the author/illustrator's simple approach "makes this pair of board books appealing and accessible even to very young children."

Stoeke has also garnered praise for the uncluttered, brightly colored illustrations she has created for two books by Katie Evans. Critics found her depiction of an eager young puppy who eats everything in sight and who sneaks off with "lost" socks and other items in *Hunky Dory Ate It* to be both endearing and amusing. A *Publishers Weekly* reviewer, for example, commented that the "suitably bare-bones, large-scale pictures convey the spunkiness of the eponymous pooch." "People enjoy hearing that I used my family and friends as models throughout," Stoeke once told *SATA.* "I didn't have a dog; sketches for Hunky Dory were already started when my husband and I got a puppy. He grew up to look a lot like Hunky Dory and was a terrific model!"

Biographical and Critical Sources

PERIODICALS

Booklist, February 1, 1992, Karen Hutt, review of *Hunky Dory Ate It,* p. 1039; January 15, 1994, Ellen Mandel, review of *Hunky Dory Found It,* pp. 935-936; October 15, 1994, Lauren Peterson, review of *A Hat for Minerva Louise,* p. 440; July, 1997, Lauren Peterson, review of *A Friend for Minerva Louise,* p. 1822; December 1, 1998, Carolyn Phelan, review of *One Little Puppy Dog* and *Five Little Kitty Cats,* p. 673; September 1, 2000, Connie Fletcher, review of *Minerva Louise at the Fair,* p. 125.
Bulletin of the Center for Children's Books, September, 1996, pp. 32-33; January, 1998, Elizabeth Bush, review of *A Friend for Minerva Louise,* p. 179.
Horn Book, January, 1995, Martha V. Parravano, review of *A Hat for Minerva Louise,* pp. 55-56.
Kirkus Reviews, September 15, 1994, review of *A Hat for Minerva Louise,* p. 1283.
New York Times Book Review, May 22, 1988, p. 30.
Publishers Weekly, February 12, 1988, review of *Minerva Louise,* p. 82; April 27, 1990, review of *Lawrence,* p. 59; November 22, 1991, review of *Hunky Dory Ate It,* p. 55; August 1, 1994, review of *A Hat for Minerva Louise,* p. 77; June 28, 1999, review of *Hide and Seek,* p. 81; September 13, 1999, review of *Minerva Louise at School,* p. 86.
School Library Journal, March, 1988, David Gale, review of *Minerva Louise,* p. 177; April, 1990, Luann Toth, review of *Lawrence,* p. 98; March, 1992, p. 214; February, 1994, p. 83; October, 1994, Karen James, review of *A Hat for Minerva Louise,* p. 103; August, 1996, Beth Tegart, review of *Minerva Louise at School,* pp. 130-131; November, 1997, Susan Garland, review of *A Friend for Minerva Louise,* p. 101; December, 1998, Marsha McGrath, review of *One Little Puppy Dog* and *Five Little Kitty Cats,* p. 92; July, 1999, Shelley Woods, review of *Hide and Seek* and *Rainy Day,* p. 81; August, 2000, Marlene Gawron, review of *Minerva Louise at the Fair,* p. 165.

OTHER

Janet Morgan Stoeke Web Site, http://www.minervalouise. com (October 15, 2002).

TANAKA, Shelley

Personal

Children: two daughters. *Nationality:* Canadian.

Addresses

Home—Kingston, Ontario, Canada. *Office*—Ground-wood Books, 720 Bathurst St., Ste. 500, Toronto, Ontario M55 2R4, Canada.

Career

Groundwood Books, Toronto, Canada, editor of fiction, 1984—; author and editor of books for children.

Awards, Honors

Mr. Christie's Book Award, 1997, for *Discovering the Iceman: What Was It Like to Find a 5,300-Year-Old Mummy?;* Silver Birch Information Award, Ontario Library Association, 1997, for *On Board the "Titanic": What It Was Like When the Great Liner Sank,* and 1998, for *The Buried City of Pompeii: What It Was Like When Vesuvius Exploded;* Science in Society Award; Red Cedar Award for Nonfiction nomination, British Columbia Library Association, 2000-01, for *Graveyards of the Dinosaurs: What It's Like to Discover Prehistoric Creatures,* and 2002-03, for *In the Time of Knights: The Real-Life Story of History's Greatest Knights.*

Writings

Michi's New Year, illustrated by Ron Berg, PMA Books (Toronto, Canada), 1980.

(With Ernie Coombs) *Mr. Dressup's Birthday Book: Painless Parties for Young Children and Their Parents,* illustrated by William Kimber, Douglas & McIntyre (Toronto, Canada), 1988.

(Editor) *The Anne of Green Gables Diary,* illustrated by Wes Lowe, Madison Press (Toronto, Canada), 1990.

The Heat Is On: Facing Our Energy Problem, illustrated by Steven Beinicke, Douglas & McIntyre (Toronto, Canada), 1991.

A Great Round Wonder: My Book of the World, illustrated by Debi Perna, Groundwood (Toronto, Canada), 1993.

The Disaster of the "Hindenburg": The Last Flight of the Greatest Airship Ever Built, illustrated by Jack McMaster and others, Scholastic (New York, NY), 1993.

The Illustrated Father Goose, illustrated by Laurie McGaw, Little, Brown (Boston, MA), 1996.

(With William Kaplan) *One More Border: The True Story of One Family's Escape from War-Torn Europe,* illustrated by Stephen Taylor, Groundwood Books (Toronto, Canada), 1998.

(Adaptor) L. M. Montgomery, *Anne of Green Gables,* Delacorte-Seal (New York, NY), 1998.

Attack on Pearl Harbor: The True Story of the Day America Entered World War II, illustrated by David Craig, Hyperion (New York, NY), 2001.

In **Attack on Pearl Harbor,** *Shelley Tanaka recreates the "date which will live in infamy" through the memories of people who were there. (Illustrated by David Craig.)*

(With Frank Augustyn) *Footnotes: Dancing the World's Best-Loved Ballets* (based on a television series), Key Porter Books (Toronto, Canada), 2001.

(With Tenzing Norbu Lama) *Himalaya,* Groundwood Books (Toronto, Canada), 2002.

(Translator) Heinz Janisch, *The Fire: An Ethiopian Folk Tale,* illustrated by Fabricio Vandenbroeck, Ground-wood Books (Toronto, Canada), 2002.

New Dinos! The Latest Finds! The Coolest Dinosaur Discoveries, illustrated by Alan Barnard, Atheneum (New York, NY), 2003.

"I WAS THERE" SERIES; FOR CHILDREN

On Board the "Titanic": What It Was Like When the Great Liner Sank, illustrated by Ken Marschall, Hyperion (New York, NY), 1996.

Discovering the Iceman: What Was It Like to Find a 5,300-Year-Old Mummy?, illustrated by Laurie McGaw, Hyperion (New York, NY), 1996.

The Buried City of Pompeii: What It Was Like When Vesuvius Exploded, illustrated by Greg Ruhl, photographs by Peter Christopher, Hyperion (New York, NY), 1997.

Graveyards of the Dinosaurs: What It's Like to Discover Prehistoric Creatures, illustrated by Alan Barnard, Hyperion (New York, NY), 1998.

The Lost Temple of the Aztecs: What It Was Like When the Spaniards Invaded Mexico, illustrated by Greg Ruhl, Hyperion (New York, NY), 1998.

In the Time of Knights: The Real-Life Story of History's Greatest Knights, illustrated by Greg Ruhl, Hyperion (New York, NY), 2001.

Sidelights

Canadian author Shelley Tanaka is best known for her nonfiction books for children and has won attention from critics for her engaging "I Was There" series, which draws readers into some of the more interesting events from history. Featuring such intriguing titles as *Discovering the Iceman: What Was It Like to Find a 5,300-Year-Old Mummy?,* the series mixes fact and fiction in a way that engages even the most history-averse reader. In addition to her nonfiction efforts, Tanaka has shared her affection for the classic coming-of-age story *Anne of Green Gables* by early-twentieth-century Canadian author L. M. Montgomery by adapting the book for younger readers and editing the *Anne of Green Gables Diary.* She has also worked with William Kaplan to tell the story of Kaplan's father and his family's efforts to flee Nazi Germany during the Holocaust in *One More Border: The True Story of One Family's Escape from War-Torn Europe.* Beginning in Lithuania in 1939, the book follows the Kaplan family as they are aided by the heroic Japanese envoy Sugihara in crossing Russia and then Japan, before making the final trip by sea that would bring them to their new home in the Canadian prairie. *Booklist* contributor Hazel Rochman called *One More Border* a "stirring picture book" that also pays homage to Sugihara, "who defied his government and personally issued transit visas for hundreds of [Lithuanian] Jews."

While Tanaka had authored a picture book earlier in her career, her first work of juvenile nonfiction, *The Heat Is On: Facing Our Energy Problem,* was published in 1991. The book explains what energy is, why it is important, where it can be found, and how to lower consumption of it. She followed *The Heat Is On* with several more standalone nonfiction titles, among them *The Illustrated Father Goose,* a biography of Canadian artist and environmentalist Bill Lishman, and *A Great Round Wonder: My Book of the World,* which focuses on our planet's environment, particularly on air, land, and water pollution and their possible remedies. Reviewing *A Great Round Wonder* for *Quill and Quire,* Martin Dowdling noted that Tanaka presents an "effective warning about what we have done to our environment."

Tanaka's most popular books are her "I Was There" series, which includes *The Lost Temple of the Aztecs: What It Was Like When the Spaniards Invaded Mexico, Graveyards of the Dinosaurs: What It's Like to Discover Prehistoric Creatures,* and *In the Time of Knights.* Beginning the series in 1996 with *On Board the "Titanic": What It Was Like When the Great Liner Sank,* Tanaka frames each event from history within a fictional narrative, then provides a factual backdrop, photographs, and other illustrations to ground her story. In *The Buried City of Pompeii: What It Was Like When Vesuvius Exploded,* for example, Tanaka spins a story taking place two thousand years in the past involving Eros, the steward to an elderly man of great wealth whose opulent dwelling in Pompeii is filled with belongings that readers know are destined to be buried beneath the volcano's ash. Reviewing the book for *Quill*

and Quire, critic John Wilson commented that the series "stakes out a definite niche" for Tanaka in the field of juvenile nonfiction.

Discovering the Iceman draws readers into the fascinating stories surrounding the discovery of mummies around the world, from the bog men of Denmark to discoveries from the Inca civilization of South America. Praising Tanaka for setting her central story of the Iceman in a "worldwide historic context," *Magpies* contributor Joan Zahnleiter added that the author introduces readers to a "fascinating topic . . . explored in quite some detail." Equally imbedded in the past, Tanaka's *Graveyards of the Dinosaurs* was dubbed a "sure hit with dinosaur fans" by *School Library Journal* reviewer Cathryn A. Camper. Camper particularly praised the author's inclusion of "new discoveries, energetic sidebars, and 'you are there' fictionalized accounts of dinosaur life [that] keep the book jumping."

Long-dead civilizations continue to mystify young students, and none is more mystifying than that of the Aztecs, which was destroyed following its clash with European conquistadores. In the "I Was There" series installment *Lost Temple of the Aztecs,* Tanaka spins what *Bulletin of the Center for Children's Books* contributor Elizabeth Bush called "a riveting account" of the sixteenth-century invasion of the Aztec empire, which is

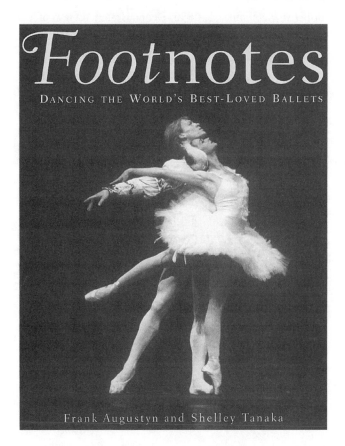

Dancer Frank Augustyn and Tanaka write a behind-the-scenes look at seven classic ballets from the dancer's point of view. (Cover photo by Jack Vartoogian.)

"told exclusively from the point of view of the van-quished and based largely on their own accounts." The clash of cultures is epitomized by the portraits of Aztec leader Montezuma and the Spaniard Hernán Cortéz, with the story of the conquest interspersed with information regarding the archaeological exploration of Mexico City's Great Temple after it was unearthed in a 1978 subway construction project. Praising *Lost Temple of the Aztecs* in *Canadian Children's Literature*, Martha J. Nandorfy called the book "a rich testimony of cultural memory ... combining direct testimony, thoughtful interpretation, paintings, and artifacts that will bring alive the Aztec heritage for young readers."

The Disaster of the "Hindenburg": The Last Flight of the Greatest Airship Ever Built examines the cause of the horrific explosion that occurred on the German-built, seventy-two-passenger zeppelin as it motored over New Jersey in May of 1937. Tanaka relates the event through the viewpoint of two teens, one a passenger and the other a cabin boy, on the ill-fated ship. *School Library Journal* contributor Valerie Childress praised the work, noting that "if the *Hindenburg* was the greatest airship ever built, then Tanaka's book is perhaps the best one ever written about the giant zeppelin."

Biographical and Critical Sources

PERIODICALS

Booklist, September 1, 1996, Denia Hester, review of *On Board the "Titanic": What It Was Like When the Great Liner Sank,* p. 132; April 15, 1997, Ilene Cooper, review of *Discovering the Iceman: What Was It Like to Find a 5,300-Year-Old Mummy?,* p. 1428; December 1, 1997, Ilene Cooper, review of *The Buried City of Pompeii: What It Was Like When Vesuvius Exploded,* p. 635; September 1, 1998, Ilene Cooper, review of *Graveyards of the Dinosaurs: What It's Like to Discover Prehistoric Creatures,* p. 118, and Hazel Rochman, review of *One More Border: The True Story of One Family's Escape from War-Torn Europe,* p. 115; April 15, 2001, Carolyn Phelan, review of *Footnotes: Dancing the World's Best-Loved Ballets,* p. 1548; August, 2001, Chris Sherman, review of *Attack on Pearl Harbor: The True Story of the Day America Entered World War II,* p. 2118.

Bulletin of the Center for Children's Books, May, 1997; January, 1999, Elizabeth Bush, review of *The Lost Temple of the Aztecs: What It Was Like When the Spaniards Invaded Mexico,* p. 184; February, 2001, Elizabeth Bush, review of *In the Time of Knights: The Real-Life Story of History's Greatest Knights,* p. 238.

Canadian Children's Literature, winter, 1999, Martha J. Nandorfy, review of *The Lost Temple of the Aztecs,* p. 103.

Magpies, March, 1998, Joan Zahnleiter, review of *Discovering the Iceman,* pp. 43-44.

Publishers Weekly, May 27, 2002, "For the Love of the Dance," p. 61.

Quill & Quire, February, 1981; September, 1993; October, 1993, Martin Dowdling, review of *A Great Round Wonder: My Book of the World,* p. 42; February, 1996; April, 1996; November, 1996; February, 1997; September, 1997, John Wilson, review of *The Buried City of Pompeii: What It Was Like When Vesuvius Exploded,* p. 72; March, 1998, Susanne Baillie, review of *Anne of Green Gables,* p. 74; September, 1998; February, 1999, review of *The Lost Temple of the Aztecs,* p. 43.

School Library Journal, May, 1981, Lorraine Douglas, review of *Michi's New Year,* p. 54; September, 1993, Valerie Childress, review of *The Disaster of the "Hindenburg,"* p. 246; October, 1996, Steven Engelfried, review of *On Board the "Titanic,"* p. 126; December, 1996, Elizabeth Talbot, review of *Anastasia's Album,* p. 149; June, 1997, Pam Gosner, review of *Discovering the Iceman,* p. 148; March, 1998, Jeanette Larson, review of *The Buried City of Pompeii,* p. 243; July, 1998, Cathryn A. Camper, review of *Graveyards of the Dinosaurs,* p. 111; December, 1998, Cheri Estes, review of *One More Border,* p. 106; February, 1999, Patricia Manning, review of *Lost Temple of the Aztecs,* p. 128; March, 2001, Betsy Barnett, review of *In the Time of Knights,* p. 279; June, 2001, Amy Kellman, review of *Footnotes: Dancing the World's Best-loved Ballets,* p. 160; November, 2001, Eldon Younce, review of *Attack on Pearl Harbor,* p. 187.

OTHER

Red Cedar Awards, http://redcedar.swifty.com/ (November 15, 2002), biography of Shelley Tanaka.

* * *

TREMENS, Del
See MacDONALD, AMY

W

WALLACE, Barbara Brooks 1922-

Personal

Born December 3, 1922, in Soochow, China; daughter of Otis Frank (a businessman) and Nicia E. Brooks; married James Wallace, Jr., February 27, 1954; children: James. *Education:* Attended schools in Hankow, Tientsin, and Shanghai, China; in Baguio, Philippines; and in Claremont, CA. Attended Pomona College, 1940-41; University of California—Los Angeles, B.A., 1945. *Religion:* Episcopalian.

Addresses

Home—2708 George Mason Pl., Alexandria, VA 22305.

Career

Children's book author. Foote, Cone & Belding, Hollywood, CA, script secretary, 1946-49; Wright MacMahon Secretarial School, Beverly Hills, CA, teacher, 1949-50; American Red Cross, Commerce and Industry Division, San Francisco, CA, head of fund drive, 1950-52.

Member

Children's Book Guild of Washington, DC; Alpha Phi.

Awards, Honors

National League of American PEN Women Juvenile Book Award, 1970, for *Claudia,* and 1974, for *The Secret Summer of L.E.B.;* International Youth Library Choice Book, 1975, for *Julia and the Third Bad Thing;* International Youth Library's Best of the Best, 1975, for *Claudia;* William Allan White Children's Book Award, 1983, for *Peppermints in the Parlor; Booklist* Editors' Choice Book, 1993, and Edgar Award, Mystery Writers of America, 1994, both for *The Twin in the Tavern;* Edgar Award, Mystery Writers of America, 1998, for *Sparrows in the Scullery.*

Recently orphaned Amelia is the target of a fiendish plot to cheat her out of her fortune in Barbara Brooks Wallace's Victorian melodrama. (Cover illustration by Richard Williams.)

Writings

Claudia, Follett (Chicago, IL), 1969.
Andrew the Big Deal, Follett (Chicago, IL), 1971.

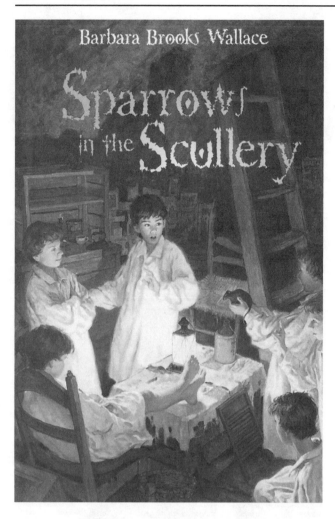

Kidnapped and abandoned in a miserable boys' home, eleven-year-old Colley finds friendship and learns to survive until his unexpected rescue. (Cover illustration by Richard Williams.)

The Trouble with Miss Switch, Abingdon (Nashville, TN), 1971.

Victoria, Follett (Chicago, IL), 1972.

Can Do, Missy Charlie, Follett (Chicago, IL), 1974.

The Secret Summer of L.E.B., Follett (Chicago, IL), 1974.

Julia and the Third Bad Thing, Follett (Chicago, IL), 1975.

Palmer Patch, Follett (Chicago, IL), 1976.

Hawkins, Abingdon (Nashville, TN), 1977.

Peppermints in the Parlor, Atheneum (New York, NY), 1980.

The Contest Kid Strikes Again, Abingdon (Nashville, TN), 1980.

Hawkins and the Soccer Solution, Abingdon (Nashville, TN), 1981.

Miss Switch to the Rescue, Abingdon (Nashville, TN), 1981.

Hello, Claudia!, Modern Curriculum Press (Parsippany, NJ), 1982.

Claudia and Duffy, Modern Curriculum Press (Parsippany, NJ), 1982.

The Barrel in the Basement, Atheneum (New York, NY), 1985.

Argyle, Abingdon (Nashville, TN), 1987.

The Interesting Thing That Happened at Perfect Acres, Inc., Atheneum (New York, NY), 1988.

The Twin in the Tavern, Atheneum (New York, NY), 1993.

Cousins in the Castle, Atheneum (New York, NY), 1996.

Sparrows in the Scullery, Atheneum (New York, NY), 1997.

Ghosts in the Gallery, Atheneum (New York, NY), 2000.

Secret in St. Something, Atheneum (New York, NY), 2001.

Miss Switch Online, Atheneum (New York, NY), 2002.

Peppermints in the Palace, Atheneum (New York, NY), 2003.

Sidelights

"Nothing in my childhood that I can think of pointed toward an interest in writing," Barbara Brooks Wallace once commented. "Though I treasured books (the newest *Oz* book from Grandmother in America or the latest *Tiger Tim Annual* from England—both books that were joyfully discovered under the Christmas tree each year), I didn't read avidly, at least not hundreds of books. Nor did I start writing at eight, or some other wonderfully early age. I envy all writers who have done both of these things, as so many have.

"It was my sister, Connie," Wallace continued, "who finally persuaded me to start writing, something I had been told I should do when in college. Connie apparently managed to do what a college professor had not succeeded in doing."

Both sisters were born and spent their childhood years in China, where their father was a businessman. They attended schools in several cities in China and the Philippines before moving back to the United States. Wallace went to college in California, but it was not until some fifteen years later that Wallace—by then married and with a young son—began writing. She worked on adult short stories until she discovered her love of writing for children.

Wallace's first children's book, *Claudia,* was named to the International Youth Library's Best of the Best list of 1975, some six years after it was published. *Claudia* tells of the often hilarious adventures of an eleven-year-old girl and her relationships with friends and family. Claudia reappears in *Hello, Claudia!* and *Claudia and Duffy. Hello, Claudia!,* which takes place before the events of the first Claudia book, begins as Claudia's best friend moves away. Eight-year-old Claudia is reluctant to become friends with the new boy next door, a precocious six-year-old named Duffy. The friendship, of course, blooms and carries on through all three books. "All of the [Claudia] books have a good balance of interests (home, friends, school) as well as warm familial relationships; all are discerning in their characterizations and have good dialogue," commented a reviewer in the *Bulletin of the Center for Children's Books.* A review of *Claudia and Duffy* in the same issue of the periodical called the three books "brisk, bouncy, warm in family relationships and often very funny."

Wallace's 1972 book *Victoria* tells the story of an eleven-year-old girl who dominates her three roommates at a boarding school by convincing them of the powers of a little book she owns. Trouble follows Victoria's adventures, and she makes increasing demands on her roommates. Only after the three reject Victoria do they learn of her unhappy background and her need for attention and importance. In reviewing *Victoria,* a *Bulletin of the Center for Children's Books* critic called it "a perceptive story, adroitly written; perhaps not since *Harriet (the Spy)* has there been a young heroine so self-centered, so complex, and so touching." A *Publishers Weekly* contributor praised the work as "an unusual and entertaining novel."

Wallace followed *Victoria* with *Can Do, Missy Charlie*—a book inspired by her childhood in China—*The Secret Summer of L.E.B., Julia and the Third Bad Thing*—an International Youth Library Choice Book of 1975—and *Palmer Patch,* an animal fantasy about which a critic wrote in the *Bulletin of the Center for Children's Books:* "For children who love animal stories, this has a sure appeal." These books were followed by the first in a series of lively, humorous books about a young American boy, Harvey, who inadvertently wins the services of a British gentleman's gentleman—*Hawkins, The Contest Kid Strikes Again,* and *Hawkins and the Soccer Solution.* Three other purely humorous books by Wallace, *The Trouble with Miss Switch, Miss Switch to the Rescue,* and *Miss Switch Online,* are fantasies, all featuring the popular teacher-witch Miss Switch.

Courage is the primary theme in *The Barrel in the Basement,* a *Borrowers*-like story of Pudding and Muddle, two elves—called Furkens—looking for a new basement dwelling. They meet Old Toaster, a Furken who lives in a barrel provided by Noah, an elderly human scholar of all things elfin, and they become friends. When Noah embarks on a trip and mysteriously does not return, Pudding discovers that he has been placed in a nursing home. Afraid for Noah, the elf gathers up his courage and sets out to rescue his friend. "These endearing creatures are fully developed," said reviewer Charlotte W. Draper in *Horn Book,* expressing a hope for "further exploits of these newest denizens of Faerie."

Argyle, published in 1987, is a humorous, nonsensical, fable-like story about the comfort of sameness and the fickleness of fame. A sheep named Argyle is happiest when he blends in with the rest of the flock, but when he finds a patch of strange little colored flowers and eats them, his wool coat turns multicolored—thus leading to the invention of argyle socks and a lucrative business for his owners. But fame is sometimes painful and passes quickly. Without the enchanted flowers, Argyle loses his colors and happily returns to the security of the fold. Calling the book "delightful nonsense," a *Bulletin of the Center for Children's Books* reviewer described Wallace's writing as "honed to simplicity and ... given humor by the union of fantastic development and bland style."

Following *Argyle* was *The Interesting Thing That Happened at Perfect Acres, Inc.,* the story of ten-year-

old Perfecta Deportmenta, the only child living in a sterile housing development owned by the evil Mr. Snoot, who hates animals and children. One lovely old house in the neighborhood is not controlled by Mr. Snoot, and it is there, as Perfecta and her new friend Puck discover, that Mr. Snoot is imprisoning story book characters, zoo animals, and other creatures in an attempt to make children's literature boring. A lively adventure follows, complete with magically appearing helpers, cloaks of invisibility, and wallpaper animals coming to life. The adventure has an important meaning, leading Perfecta to a surprising—and welcome—discovery. "The book's intriguing beginning will capture readers' imaginations," asserted a reviewer in *Booklist.*

Peppermints in the Parlor, which won the William Allan White Children's Book Award in 1983, is a Gothic mystery set in San Francisco in the 1890s. Wallace's eleven-year-old heroine, Emily, has been orphaned and sent to Sugar Hill Hall, the mansion of her wealthy aunt and uncle. She is horrified to find that her uncle is missing and her aunt is practically enslaved by two evil women who have turned the mansion into a home for the elderly. Emily, too, is forced into near-slavery, but she

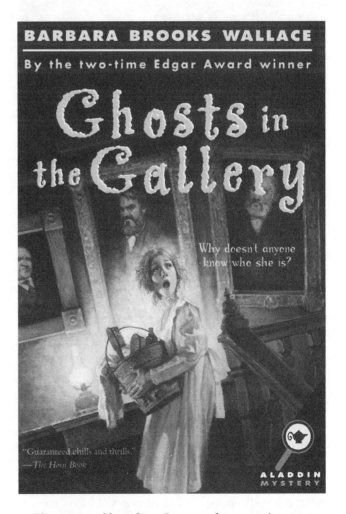

Eleven-year-old orphan Jenny endures service as a scullery maid in her grandfather's house when no one recognizes that she is part of their family. (Cover illustration by Richard Williams.)

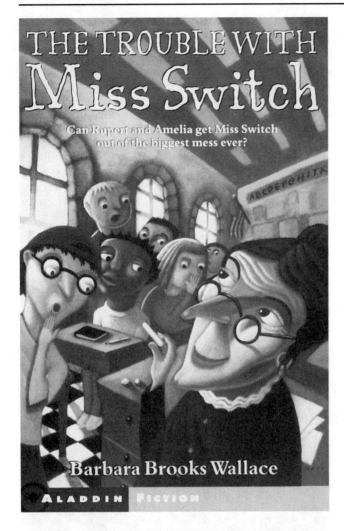

Scientist Rupert and his friend Amelia must confront the computowitch machine and the Witches' Council to save their favorite teacher. (Cover illustration by Russell Gordon.)

sets out to help the old people, who are locked in a dungeon-like cell called the Remembrance Room if they take a peppermint from a tantalizing dish kept in the parlor. Horror builds upon horror in the shadowy mansion as Emily tries to solve the mystery of her uncle's disappearance and thus obtain the key that will unlock all the other mysteries haunting Sugar Hill Hall. Ann A. Flowers, reviewing the book for *Horn Book,* likened *Peppermints in the Parlor* to Frances Hodgson Burnett's *A Little Princess* and Joan Aiken's *The Wolves of Willoughby Chase,* and described it as "an amusing Gothic romp with a shadowy, gaslit atmosphere, moving briskly and sweeping the reader along with it."

Wallace's Edgar Award-winning novel *The Twin in the Tavern* is another Victorian mystery. A young boy, Taddy, is twice orphaned, first by the death of his parents, and then by the sudden death of his aunt and uncle. He ends up the captive of two villainous thieves and is taken to live as an unpaid servant at the Dog's Tail, a grim tavern owned by one of the crooks on the Alexandria, Virginia, waterfront. Taddy has been warned by his dying uncle that he must find his twin to

know who he is—and thereby hangs the tale and the mystery. Writing in *School Library Journal,* Sally Margolis called *The Twin in the Tavern* "a worthy successor to" *Peppermints in the Parlor* and praised Wallace's "fine hand for Gothic embroidery" and the book's "nifty surprise conclusion."

"I have a clear recollection of how I felt as a child about many things," Wallace once said in explanation of her ability to relate to her young audience. "Christmas, the terror of waking alone at night, having a friend, and an understanding, I believe, of why I felt as I did. And I love children, especially the ages of seven to twelve. They are eager, enthusiastic, and so tremendously responsive." Another inspiration has been her son Jimmy. "My husband and I have only one child, Jimmy, who has been my main source of material for almost all my book children, three-year-old girls, twelve-year-old boys, all of them. (Even my witches, dragons, and talking mushrooms tend to sound like Jimmy.)" Wallace also once commented that children are her most valuable critics. "One little girl brought back a manuscript she was trial-reading for me and said, 'I never got past chapter one because I didn't know what you were talking about.' Just like that!

"The book I had most fun writing was *Peppermints in the Parlor,*" Wallace continued. "I didn't know what the ending was going to be until the ending arrived. I often didn't know what was going to happen from page to page and would sit up late at night writing because I couldn't wait until the next morning to find out. I guess my readers must have felt the same way in reading it as I did in writing it, or so I'm told. *The Twin in the Tavern* wasn't fun to write, the first half anyway, but the end result has been wonderful. I hope I'll be lucky enough to create another Victorian mystery, another book that's pure humor, or another fantasy—all my favorites to write. But whatever I do write, I know it will always be for children and will always have a happy ending. And that's the wonderful thing about being a writer—*I* get to choose!"

Wallace followed through on her desire to write more Victorian mysteries with *Cousins in the Castle, Sparrows in the Scullery, Ghosts in the Gallery,* and *Secret in St. Something,* all of which transport readers back to the nineteenth century, both in England and America. "The plot twists and turns at an alarming rate in this story of dastardly crimes and firm friendships," *Booklist*'s Ilene Cooper wrote of *Cousins in the Castle.* Orphaned Amelia must leave her London home to take up residence with distant cousins in America, and her adventures only just begin when she meets Primrose aboard the ship. This girl, however, turns out to be a boy in disguise who becomes fast friends with Amelia, saving her more than once.

Wallace continues her Victorian intrigues with *Sparrows in the Scullery,* in which the wealthy, sickly, and recently orphaned Colley is suddenly kidnapped and left at a home for orphans. Although the living conditions are severe, Colley becomes close to the other boys and learns hard lessons about friendship and survival.

"Wallace is deliberately Dickensian in her portrait of the home and the boys," noted a critic for *Kirkus Reviews,* "yet the tale is full of hope." More Victorian orphans in hot water are served up in *Ghosts in the Gallery,* "a gothic orphan story that introduces a soupçon of the exotic with references to China," according to *Horn Book*'s Mary M. Burns. Jenny Graymark, born in the East, is newly orphaned and must travel alone to the United States to a new home with relatives there. However, instead of being welcomed with open arms, Jenny is accused of being an impostor once she arrives. Thus starts a chain of events that keeps the reader guessing and turning pages. "Guaranteed thrills and chills," Burns further commented. Writing in *School Library Journal,* Jeanette Larson felt that Wallace "spins a delightful tale of Dickensian treachery, betrayal, and triumph."

Another alliterative title and nineteenth-century mystery are presented in Wallace's 2001 novel *Secret in St. Something.* Chris Sherman, writing in *Booklist,* felt that the book "has all the elements [readers have] come to expect from the Edgar [Award]-winning author," including a "plucky" heroine who braves dangerous situations, a page-turning plot, and a well-developed historical setting. Robin takes his baby brother Danny with him when he runs away from his cruel stepfather, Hawker. Robin is saved by unlikely new friends: four street toughs who take him in and teach him how to survive on the streets. Then Hawker catches up with him, and the suspense mounts. "Give this to both historical fiction and mystery fans, who will enjoy the unique blend of genres," wrote Kristen Oravec in a *School Library Journal* review.

Wallace once remarked, "Years ago, I wrote a book entirely different from anything I'd ever done before, a Victorian mystery melodrama titled *Peppermints in the Parlor.* My then publisher apparently loved it and accepted it at once. Shortly thereafter, they returned it and informed me they couldn't publish it after all. It was only later I learned that the company was on its way out. But they left me thinking the fault lay with me and the book. It was a crushing blow, especially since I knew I had a book on my hands that would be tough, if not impossible, to sell. And I was right.

"But several editors who returned the book for one reason or another, seemed to like it well enough to offer valuable criticism. Still no sale, however. A former editor and good friend from the above-mentioned publisher had told me I should try the legendary Jean Karl at Atheneum, but I didn't have the courage to send her the book. At last, discouraged, I thought I'd try it with an agent in London, but with the book virtually wrapped and ready to go, I suddenly changed my mind. I rewrote the cover letter, and sent the book off to Jean Karl. She took the book, and remained my wonderful editor until the end.

"If the other publisher had in fact taken it, my sense is they would have left the book pretty much as it was, despite some serious flaws. I believe it would have probably had a very short life, and died with the company. As it was, I rewrote much of it several times in accordance with some of the critiques I'd received, and then was lucky enough to have Jean guide it the rest of the way to a successful end. *Peppermints in the Parlor* is still in print now after twenty years, and I have to say, the book changed my life. I love to tell this story, especially to a young person who has suffered a big disappointment, because if it isn't a story of how one of the worst things that has happened in your life can in the end be one of the best, I don't know what is."

Biographical and Critical Sources

BOOKS

Holtze, Sally Holmes, editor, *Sixth Book of Junior Authors and Illustrators,* H. W. Wilson (New York, NY), 1989.

PERIODICALS

Booklist, July, 1980, review of *The Contest Kid Strikes Again;* December, 1980, review of *Peppermints in the Parlor;* May, 1981, review of *Hawkins and the Soccer Solution;* December, 1981, review of *Miss Switch to the Rescue;* February, 1983, reviews of *Hello, Claudia!* and *Claudia and Duffy;* April, 1985, review of *The Barrel in the Basement;* March 15, 1988, review of *The Interesting Thing That Happened at Perfect Acres, Inc.,* p. 1269; November 1, 1993, Ilene Cooper, review of *The Twin in the Tavern,* p. 524; April 1, 1996, Ilene Cooper, review of *Cousins in the Castle,* p. 1363; September 15, 1997, Ilene Cooper, review of *Sparrows in the Scullery,* p. 236; April 1, 2000, Hazel Rochman, review of *Ghosts in the Gallery,* p. 1475; May 15, 2001, Chris Sherman, review of *Secret in St. Something,* p. 1754.

Bulletin of the Center for Children's Books, April, 1970, review of *Claudia;* March, 1973, review of *Victoria,* p. 114; March, 1977, review of *Palmer Patch,* p. 116; February, 1983, reviews of *Claudia and Duffy* and *Hello, Claudia!,* p. 119; April, 1985, review of *The Barrel in the Basement;* September, 1987, review of *Argyle,* p. 19; April, 1996, Elizabeth Bush, review of *Cousins in the Castle,* p. 280.

Horn Book, October, 1980, Ann A. Flowers, review of *Peppermints in the Parlor,* p. 522; September-October, 1985, Charlotte W. Draper, review of *The Barrel in the Basement,* p. 561; July-August, 2000, Mary M. Burns, review of *Ghosts in the Gallery,* p. 469.

Kirkus Reviews, May, 1969, review of *Claudia;* October, 1971, review of *Andrew the Big Deal;* October 15, 1997, review of *Sparrows in the Scullery,* p. 1590; May, 2001, review of *Secret in St. Something.*

New Yorker, December 1, 1980, Faith McNulty, review of *Peppermints in the Parlor,* p. 220.

Publishers Weekly, January 22, 1973, review of *Victoria,* p. 71; December, 18, 1981, review of *Miss Switch to the Rescue,* p. 71; July 24, 1987, review of *Argyle,* p. 185; May 13, 2002, "In the Next Episode," p. 72.

School Library Journal, April, 1977, review of *Palmer Patch;* September, 1980, Liza Bliss, review of *The Contest Kid Strikes Again,* p. 78; October, 1980, Holly Sanhuber, review of *Peppermints in the Parlor,* p. 152; May, 1981, Chris Hatten, review of *Hawkins and the Soccer Solution,* p. 87; March, 1982, review of *Miss Switch to the Rescue,* p. 152; April, 1983, reviews of *Claudia and Duffy* and *Hello, Claudia!,* p. 119; September, 1985, Christina Olson, review of *The Barrel in the Basement,* p. 140; November, 1987, Julie Corsaro, review of *Argyle,* p. 97; April, 1988, David Gale, review of *The Interesting Thing That Happened at Perfect Acres, Inc.,* p. 105; October, 1993, Sally Margolis, review of *The Twin in the Tavern,* p. 134; November, 1997, Mary M. Hopf, review of *Sparrows in the Scullery,* p. 124; July, 2000, Jeanette Larson, review of *Ghosts in the Gallery,* p. 112; July, 2001, Kristen Oravec, review of *Secret in St. Something,* p. 116; June, 2002, Linda Bindner, review of *Miss Switch Online,* p. 148.*

*   *   *

WATT, Mélanie 1975-

Personal

Born August 20, 1975, in Trois-Rivières, Québec, Canada; daughter of John (a senior manager at Petro-Canada) and Francine (an administrative assistant; maiden name Leblanc) Watt. *Nationality:* Canadian. *Education:* C.E.G.E.P. Marie-Victorin (Québec, Canada), diploma in graphic design, 1997; University of Québec—Montreal, B.A. (graphic design), 2000. *Hobbies and other interests:* Music, art, design.

Addresses

Home—90 Robert Cauchon, St. Stanislas de Kostka, Québec J0S 1W0, Canada. *E-mail*—melanie_watt@hotmail.com.

Career

Author and illustrator.

Awards, Honors

Leon the Chameleon received the Honor Book award, Society of School Librarians, 2001; Our Choice List, CCBC, 2002; Magazine Book of the Year award, finalist, 2002; Children's Choices for 2002, Children's Book Council and the International Reading Association, 2002.

Writings

(Self-illustrated) *Leon the Chameleon,* Kids Can Press (Toronto, Canada), 2001.

(Illustrator) *Where Does a Tiger Heron Spend the Night?,* Kids Can Press (Toronto, Canada), 2002.

(Self-illustrated) *Learning with Animals* (gift package of five concept books), Kids Can Press (Toronto, Canada), in press.

Sidelights

Canadian author and illustrator Mélanie Watt began her first picture book for children, *Leon the Chameleon,* in 1999 her final year as a student at the University of Quebec in Montreal. Praised by *Quill and Quire*

Leon the chameleon turns red, purple, or orange rather than the normal green, yellow, or blue, but he discovers that his difference is an advantage. (From Leon the Chameleon, *written and illustrated by Mélanie Watt.*)

contributor Jessica Higgs as "not only a lesson on the interaction of colour but a celebration of being different," *Leon the Chameleon* focuses on a little chameleon who doesn't blend into the background like his other chameleon friends. Instead he turns the *opposite* color of his environment. It is hard to hide a problem like this—when hiding behind something yellow, Leon turns bright purple—and soon everyone is aware that young Leon is somehow different. In addition to praise for her sensitive storyline, Watt received kudos for her use of "vibrant, eye-popping primary and complementary colors" in illustrations that make *Leon the Chameleon* a "visually effective choice for children just learning colors," according to *Booklist* contributor Shelle Rosenfeld.

Born in Québec, Canada, in 1975, Watt had a passion for drawing at an early age. "Classmates often asked me to sketch little cartoon characters on pieces of paper or on the back of their hands," she explained. "I later developed my art by drawing portraits in pencil."

In college, Watt "decided to follow safe advice." She enrolled in a business administration program for two years before realizing that she needed a change. Entering a graphic design program, she eventually enrolled in the bachelor's program at the University of Québec. It was there, as part of an illustration class assignment, that Watt got the idea for *Leon the Chameleon.* "We had to make a book about colour," she recalled. "It was up to us to decide what the content would be. Having always been interested in children's books, I decided to make one that would teach complementary colours in a fun and simple way. I had a great time thinking up a story for little Leon, in fact, I think I spent more time on the storyline than working on the actual illustrations."

With the encouragement of her teacher, Michéle Lemieux, Watt translated her story into English and submitted it to Kids Can Press, where it was quickly accepted. One of the aspects of the book that intrigued the publisher was Watt's inclusion of an appendix providing an introduction to color theory via a color wheel. "This is certainly a fine way to extend the book," maintained Kathryn McNaughton in her review of the "absolutely delightful" *Leon the Chameleon* for *Resource Links,* "and children will enjoy experimenting with paints or gels which can help them see how colours are mixed."

Watt's advice to budding picture book creators is to "have a good message to tell. Then find a way to tell it by choosing the best possible character and setting to explore it. Think like a kid again and have fun creating."

Leon the Chameleon caused a great change in Watt's life, not only because it was her first published book. "I was planning on making a career in publicity," the author/illustrator explained. "I never knew that I could write a story before this opportunity was presented to me. But now, I'm certain this is something I want to continue to explore."

Biographical and Critical Sources

PERIODICALS

Booklist, April 1, 2001, Shelle Rosenfeld, review of *Leon the Chameleon,* p. 1480.
Childhood Education, winter, 2001, review of *Leon the Chameleon,* p. 112.
Kirkus Reviews, February 1, 2001, review of *Leon the Chameleon,* p. 191.
Quill and Quire, May, 2001, Jessica Higgs, review of *Leon the Chameleon,* p. 32.
Resource Links, June, 2001, Kathryn McNaughton, review of *Leon the Chameleon,* p. 7.
School Library Journal, April, 2001, Maura Bresnahan, review of *Leon the Chameleon,* p. 126; May, 2002, Lynn Dye, review of *Where Does a Tiger Heron Spend the Night,* p. 134.

*   *   *

WHEELER, Jill C. 1964-

Personal

Born March 12, 1964, in Sibley, IA; daughter of Norman J. (a farmer) and Carol L. (a homemaker; maiden name, Bensch) Wheeler; married Paul D. Libra (an auditor), September 5, 1987; children: Anna G. *Nationality:* American. *Education:* South Dakota State University, B.A., 1986. *Politics:* Independent. *Religion:* United Methodist. *Hobbies and other interests:* Motorcycle riding, cooking, Jungian psychology.

Addresses

Home and office—13025 Court Pl., Burnsville, MN 55337.

Career

Owner of Wheeler & Grace (marketing communications consulting firm), 1995—.

Member

International Association of Business Communicators (board of directors, Minnesota Chapter, 1992-94).

Writings

NONFICTION

Lost in London, Abdo Publishing (Edina, MN), 1988.
Bound for Boston, Abdo Publishing (Edina, MN), 1989.
The Story of Crazy Horse, Abdo Publishing (Edina, MN), 1989.
The Story of Geronimo, Abdo Publishing (Edina, MN), 1989.
The Story of Hiawatha, Abdo Publishing (Edina, MN), 1989.
The Story of Pontiac, Abdo Publishing (Edina, MN), 1989.

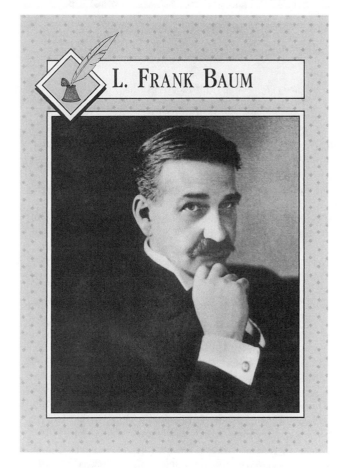

Jill C. Wheeler writes a brief biography of the author of the classic **The Wizard of Oz.** *(Cover photo from Bettmann Film Archive/Wide World Photos.)*

Wheeler describes the events of the terrorist attack of September 11, 2001.

The Story of Sequoyah, Abdo Publishing (Edina, MN), 1989.

The Story of Sitting Bull, Abdo Publishing (Edina, MN), 1989.

Corazon Aquino, Abdo Publishing (Edina, MN), 1991.

Earth Day Every Day, Abdo Publishing (Edina, MN), 1991.

Earth Moves: Get There with Energy to Spare, Abdo Publishing (Edina, MN), 1991.

The Food We Eat, Abdo Publishing (Edina, MN), 1991.

Healthy Earth, Healthy Bodies, Abdo Publishing (Edina, MN), 1991.

Nancy R. Reagan, Abdo Publishing (Edina, MN), 1991.

The People We Live With, Abdo Publishing (Edina, MN), 1991.

The Throw-Away Generation, Abdo Publishing (Edina, MN), 1991.

A. A. Milne: Creator of Winnie the Pooh, Abdo Publishing (Edina, MN), 1992.

Coretta Scott King, Abdo Publishing (Edina, MN), 1992.

Dr. Seuss, Abdo Publishing (Edina, MN), 1992.

Laura Ingalls Wilder, Abdo Publishing (Edina, MN), 1992.

Michael Landon, Abdo Publishing (Edina, MN), 1992.

Mother Teresa, Abdo Publishing (Edina, MN), 1992.

Princess Caroline, Abdo Publishing (Edina, MN), 1992.

Raisa Gorbachev, Abdo Publishing (Edina, MN), 1992.

Beastly Neighbors, Abdo Publishing (Edina, MN), 1993.

Branch Out: A Book about Land, Abdo Publishing (Edina, MN), 1993.

Earth Kids, Abdo Publishing (Edina, MN), 1993.

Every Drop Counts: A Book about Water, Abdo Publishing (Edina, MN), 1993.

For the Birds: A Book about Air, Abdo Publishing (Edina, MN), 1993.

The Midwest and the Heartland, Abdo Publishing (Edina, MN), 1994.

The Northeast, Abdo Publishing (Edina, MN), 1994.

The Pacific West, Abdo Publishing (Edina, MN), 1994.

The Southeast and Gulf States, Abdo Publishing (Edina, MN), 1994.

The West, Abdo Publishing (Edina, MN), 1994.

L. Frank Baum, Abdo Publishing (Edina, MN), 1997.

Judith Viorst, Abdo Publishing (Edina, MN), 1997.

Gwendolyn Brooks, Abdo Publishing (Edina, MN), 1997.

Peggy Parish, Abdo Publishing (Edina, MN), 1997.

Virginia Hamilton, Abdo Publishing (Edina, MN), 1997.

Lloyd Alexander, Abdo Publishing (Edina, MN), 1997.

Tara Lipinski, Abdo Publishing (Edina, MN), 1998.

Brett Favre, Abdo Publishing (Edina, MN), 1998.

Princess Diana, Abdo Publishing (Edina, MN), 2000.

Julia Roberts, Abdo Publishing (Edina, MN), 2001.

Shania Twain, Abdo Publishing (Edina, MN), 2001.

Michael J. Fox, Abdo Publishing (Edina, MN), 2001.

Tom Cruise, Abdo Publishing (Edina, MN), 2001.

Tom Hanks, Abdo Publishing (Edina, MN), 2001.

Jim Carrey, Abdo Publishing (Edina, MN), 2001.

Madeleine Albright, Abdo Publishing (Edina, MN), 2002.

Madonna, Abdo Publishing (Edina, MN), 2002.

Jennifer Lopez, Abdo Publishing (Edina, MN), 2002.

Amelia Earhart, Abdo Publishing (Edina, MN), 2002.

America's Leaders, Abdo Publishing (Edina, MN), 2002.

Oprah Winfrey, Abdo Publishing (Edina, MN), 2002.

Nelson Mandela, Abdo Publishing (Edina, MN), 2002.

Hillary Rodham Clinton, Abdo Publishing (Edina, MN), 2002.

Clara Barton, Abdo Publishing (Edina, MN), 2002.

Colin Powell, Abdo Publishing (Edina, MN), 2002.

Denzel Washington, Abdo Publishing (Edina, MN), 2002.

Martin Luther King, Jr., Abdo Publishing (Edina, MN), 2002.

Mel Gibson, Abdo Publishing (Edina, MN), 2002.

Laura Bush, Abdo Publishing (Edina, MN), 2002.

Rosa Parks, Abdo Publishing (Edina, MN), 2002.

Faith Hill, Abdo Publishing (Edina, MN), 2002.

George W. Bush, Abdo Publishing (Edina, MN), 2002.

Brad Pitt, Abdo Publishing (Edina, MN), 2002.

September 11, 2001: The Day that Changed America, Abdo Publishing (Edina, MN), 2002.

The Red Cross, Abdo Publishing (Edina, MN), 2002.

Pope John Paul II, Abdo Publishing (Edina, MN), 2002.

Firefighters, Abdo Publishing (Edina, MN), 2002.

Gandhi, Abdo Publishing (Edina, MN), 2002.

Cesar Chavez, Abdo Publishing (Edina, MN), 2003.

E. R. Doctors, Abdo Publishing (Edina, MN), 2003.

Enrique Iglesias, Abdo Publishing (Edina, MN), 2003.

George Washington Carver, Abdo Publishing (Edina, MN), 2003.

Harriet Tubman, Abdo Publishing (Edina, MN), 2003.

Jackie Robinson, Abdo Publishing (Edina, MN), 2003.

Kelly Clarkson, Abdo Publishing (Edina, MN), 2003.

Susan B. Anthony, Abdo Publishing (Edina, MN), 2003.

Thurgood Marshall, Abdo Publishing (Edina, MN), 2003.

Sidelights

Jill C. Wheeler is a very prolific author of nonfiction biographies, regional descriptions, and ecology books for children. In addition to her writing, she owns her own marketing communications consulting firm. Wheeler's biographies for children range from those of historically well-known Native Americans such as Geronimo, Chief Crazy Horse, Hiawatha, and Chief Sitting Bull to black American leader Coretta Scott King, politician Corazon Aquino of the Philippines, author Laura Ingalls Wilder, humanitarian Mother Teresa, and media stars like Princess Caroline of Monaco. Some crucial subjects Wheeler has written about in her ecology books include air quality, global warming, pesticides, renewable energy issues, land conservation, and refuse recycling.

When asked to describe how she is able to write about so many different subjects, Wheeler once told *SATA*, "I approach writing with the belief that there's something of interest in everything and everyone on the planet. It's the writer's job to find out what that is and share the excitement with readers. I also believe books remain the widest and most easily opened doors to a better understanding of the world around us. Life is too short to see and experience all the world has to offer, yet books allow us to cheat and catch a glimpse of that wonder."

Wheeler suggested that "Everyone should write something—even if it's never published. The words you commit to paper will be a gift to yourself, regardless of whatever else happens."

Biographical and Critical Sources

PERIODICALS

Booklist, May 1, 2002, Carolyn Phelan, review of *September 11, 2001: The Day That Changed America,* p. 1524.
Horn Book Guide, spring, 1998, review of *L. Frank Baum,* p. 171.
School Library Journal, June, 2002, John Peters, review of *September 11, 2001: The Day That Changed America,* p. 122.*

*   *   *

WYNNE-JONES, Tim(othy) 1948-

Personal

Born August 12, 1948, in Bromborough, Cheshire, England; son of Sydney Thomas (an engineer and lieutenant colonel in British Army) and Sheila Beryl (a homemaker; maiden name, Hodgson) Wynne-Jones; married Amanda West Lewis (a writer, calligrapher, director, and teacher), September 12, 1980; children: Alexander, Magdalene, Lewis. *Education:* University of Waterloo, B.F.A., 1974; York University, M.F.A., 1979. *Avocational interests:* Cooking, crosswords, cross-country skiing.

Addresses

Home and Office—Rural Route No. 4, Perth, Ontario K7H 3C6, Canada. *Agent*—Leona Trainer, Transatlantic Literary Agency, 72 Glengowan Rd., Toronto, Ontario M4N 1G4, Canada. *E-mail*—twj@perth.igs.net.

Career

Writer. PMA Books, Toronto, Ontario, designer, 1974-76; University of Waterloo, Waterloo, Ontario, instructor in visual arts, 1976-78; Solomon & Wynne-Jones, Toronto, graphic designer, 1976-79; York University, Downsview, Ontario, instructor in visual arts, 1978-80.

Member

International PEN, Writers Union of Canada, Association of Canadian Television and Radio Artists, Society of Composers, Authors, Music Publishers of Canada, and Canadian Society of Children's Authors, Illustrators, and Performers.

Awards, Honors

Seal First Novel Award, Bantam/Seal Books, 1980, for *Odd's End;* I.O.D.E. Award, 1983, and Ruth Schwartz Children's Award, 1984, both for *Zoom at Sea;* ACTRA Award, best radio drama, 1987, for *St. Anthony's Man;* Governor-General's Award for Children's Literature, 1993, Canadian Library Association Children's Book of the Year award, 1993, and *Boston Globe-Horn Book* Award for Fiction, 1995, all for *Some of the Kinder Planets;* Notable Books for Children citation, American Library Association, and Mister Christie Award shortlist, 1994, both for *The Book of Changes;* Governor-General's Award for Children's Literature, 1995, Young Adult Book of the Year, Canadian Library Association, Mister Christie Award shortlist, and Books for the Teen Age citation, New York Public Library, 1997, all for *The Maestro;* Vicky Metcalf Award, Canadian Authors Association, 1997, for body of work; Children's Book of the Year, Canadian Literary Association, 1998, for *Stephen Fair;* Books for the Teen Age citation, New York Public Library, 1999, for *Lord of the Fries;* Arthur Ellis Award of the Crime Writers of Canada, and Edgar Allen Poe Award short list, 2002, both for *Boy in the Burning House.*

Writings

FOR CHILDREN

Madeline and Ermadello, illustrated by Lindsey Hallam, Before We Are Six (Hawkesville, Ontario, Canada), 1977.
Zoom at Sea, illustrated by Ken Nutt, Douglas & McIntyre (Toronto, Ontario, Canada), 1983, illustrated by Eric Beddows, HarperCollins (New York, NY), 1993.
Zoom Away, illustrated by Ken Nutt, Douglas & McIntyre (Toronto, Ontario, Canada), 1985, illustrated by Eric Beddows, HarperCollins (New York, NY), 1993.
I'll Make You Small, illustrated by Maryann Kovalski, Douglas & McIntyre (Toronto, Ontario, Canada), 1986.

Mischief City (verse), illustrated by Victor Gad, Groundwood (Toronto, Ontario, Canada), 1986.

Architect of the Moon, illustrated by Ian Wallace, Groundwood (Toronto, Ontario, Canada), 1988, published as *Builder of the Moon,* McElderry (New York, NY), 1988.

The Hour of the Frog, illustrated by Catharine O'Neill, Little, Brown (Boston, MA), 1989.

Zoom Upstream, illustrated by Eric Beddows, Groundwood (Toronto, Ontario, Canada), 1992, HarperCollins (New York, NY), 1994.

Mouse in the Manger, illustrated by Elaine Blier, Viking (New York, NY), 1993.

The Last Piece of Sky, illustrated by Marie-Louise Gay, Groundwood (Toronto, Ontario, Canada), 1993.

Some of the Kinder Planets (short stories), Groundwood (Toronto, Ontario, Canada), 1993, Orchard (New York, NY), 1995.

(With Amanda Lewis) *Rosie Backstage,* illustrated by Bill Slavin, Kids Can Press (Toronto, Ontario, Canada), 1994.

The Book of Changes (short stories), Groundwood (Toronto, Ontario, Canada), 1994, Orchard (New York, NY), 1995.

The Maestro, Groundwood (Toronto, Ontario, Canada), 1995, Orchard (New York, NY), 1996.

(Reteller) *The Hunchback of Notre Dame,* illustrated by Bill Slavin, Key Porter Books (Toronto, Ontario), 1996, Orchard (New York, NY), 1997.

(Reteller) Bram Stoker, *Dracula,* illustrated by Laszlo Gal, Key Porter Books (Toronto, Ontario, Canada), 1997.

Stephen Fair, DK Ink (New York, NY), 1998.

On Tumbledown Hill, Red Deer College Press (Alberta, Ontario, Canada), 1998.

Lord of the Fries and Other Stories, DK Ink (New York, NY), 1999.

The Boy in the Burning House, Douglas & McIntyre (Toronto, Ontario, Canada), 2000.

(Editor) *Boy's Own,* Penguin (New York, NY), 2001.

Also author of a children's opera titled *A Midwinter Night's Dream* and a musical version of *Mischief City.* Author of regular column of children's book reviews for the Toronto *Globe and Mail,* 1985-88.

NOVELS; FOR ADULTS

Odd's End, Little, Brown (New York, NY), 1980.

The Knot, McClelland & Stewart (Toronto, Ontario, Canada), 1982.

Fastyngange, Lester & Orpen Dennys (Toronto, Ontario, Canada), 1988, published as *Voices,* Hodder & Stoughton (London, England), 1990.

RADIO PLAYS; BROADCAST BY CANADIAN BROADCASTING CORPORATION

The Thinking Room, 1981.

The Road Ends at the Sea, 1982.

The Strange Odyssey of Lennis Freed, 1983.

The Testing of Stanley Teagarden, 1985.

The Enormous Radio (from the story by John Cheever), 1986.

St. Anthony's Man (from his own story), 1987.

Mr. Gendelman Crashes a Party, 1987.

Dust Is the Only Secret, 1988.

We Now Return You to Your Regularly Scheduled Universe, 1992.

Work in Progress

At John O'Dogs, adult fiction; *The Outrageous Tiny Rathbone,* young adult.

Sidelights

Tim Wynne-Jones is a British-born Canadian writer whose works range from award-winning adult and young-adult fiction to such popular children's picture books as the "Zoom" series of tales about an adventurous cat. One of Canada's most popular authors among pre-schoolers and primary graders, Wynne-Jones is recognized as the creator of works that capture the mystery, fantasy, and wonder of childhood while addressing such realistic concerns as the conquering of personal fears and the relationship of children with their parents. He is known and appreciated for his rich language, zany plots, and a sophistication of theme that does not proclaim itself didactically, but that "reverberates beneath the simple surface of image and dialogue," as Gwyneth Evans noted in *Twentieth-Century Children's Writers.* A scriptwriter and composer, Wynne-Jones is also known for his work as lyricist for the television program *Fraggle Rock.*

The son of an engineer, Wynne-Jones was born in Cheshire, England, in 1948, but grew up in Ottawa, Canada. Attending the University of Waterloo, he began to study children's literature as part of a research project. A group of sociology students secured a grant to study racism and sexism in books for young readers, and Wynne-Jones, studying visual arts at the time, was included in the grant proposal as someone on the creative side of things. In an interview with Dave Jenkinson in *Emergency Librarian,* Wynne-Jones explained that having examined a plethora of children's books and finding fault with many of them, "the group decided that, because they knew what was wrong with children's books, they could then write good ones. It was a great lesson in how you do *not* write a children's book." While the publishing venture created by the grant was short-lived, it did produce Wynne-Jones's first creative effort, *Madeline and Ermadello,* a "quietly charming story about a young girl's fantasies," according to Linda Smith in *In Review: Canadian Books for Children.* Ermadello is Madeline's friend, the third in a trio that includes her carpenter father, Ernie, and her next door neighbor, Barnell. But Ermadello is special: he is imaginary, and Madeline can make him be anything she wants him to be. The quiet climax to this picture book comes when Madeline introduces Ermadello to her real-life friends at a tea party. A *Children's Book News* reviewer concluded that this "is a charming story of friendship that younger readers are certain to enjoy."

Wynne-Jones's first book highlighted the elements of fantasy and wonder common to the author's subsequent efforts for children. It was several years, however, before Wynne-Jones published a second picture book. During this time he worked as a designer at a publishing company, as a visual arts instructor at Waterloo University and York University, and as a graphic designer in his own company. He earned an M.F.A. in visual arts and was married. He also wrote and published his first adult novel, a psychological thriller, *Odd's End,* which won him Canada's prestigious Seal First Novel Award and a cash prize of $50,000. Understandably, Wynne-Jones stuck with adult fiction for his next title, *The Knot,* but he returned to children's books in 1983.

"I didn't start writing children's books because I had children," Wynne-Jones told Jenkinson in his *Emergency Librarian* interview. "I'd always had ideas for children's stories." Although a visual artist himself, Wynne-Jones does not illustrate his own books. Rather, he visualizes stories with the illustrations of other artists he respects. One such case was Ken Nutt (Eric Beddows), an acquaintance of his whose artwork Wynne-Jones wanted to see in book form. The direct inspiration for his first successful children's book was the family cat, Montezuma, or Zuma for short. Writing early one morning, Wynne-Jones observed the cat sitting on the kitchen counter batting at water from a dripping faucet. The idea for an adventure-loving and water-loving cat came to the author quickly. "The story, *Zoom at Sea,* was written in 20 minutes," Wynne-Jones told Jenkinson. "I don't quite know how those things happen." In the story, Zoom the cat goes to the home of the mysterious Maria, who helps him realize a lifelong dream of going to sea. Maria coaxes the cat as the foam gathers around him, "Go on. It's all yours." Linda Granfield, writing in *Quill and Quire,* noted that these words are "an irresistible, exciting invitation to the cat and the reader alike." Granfield added that the book was a "perfect balance of text and illustration" and served as a reminder to children and adults alike to "live our dreams."

Wynne-Jones initially had no intention of creating a sequel to this first popular "Zoom" title. However, a letter from his mother-in-law suggested further possibilities for Maria's magical powers, and *Zoom Away* was launched. In this story, a trip upstairs to Maria's attic becomes the magical metaphor for a trip to the North Pole. Zoom goes in search of the nautical tomcat, Uncle Roy, who set sail for the North Pole and has not been heard from since. Again, Nutt employed simple black and white illustrations to "complement ... perfectly" Wynne-Jones's text, according to Bernie Goedhart in *Quill and Quire.* Goedhart concluded that the two "seem destined to carve themselves a permanent niche in the world of Canadian picture-books." Though some reviewers, including Jon C. Stott in *Canadian Literature,* felt that the simple text lacked "depth," others found deeper resonances. Sarah Ellis, writing in *Horn Book,* commented that "*Zoom Away* is one of those rare picture books that combines absolute simplicity with mythic resonance.... The story is bigger that its plot." Drawing comparisons to such elemental Canadian myths as the search for the Northwest Passage and the romance involved in such adventure, Ellis concluded that the "satisfaction we feel at the book's safe ending goes beyond the satisfaction of putting a tired child to bed." Reviewing both "Zoom" books in *Canadian Children's*

Literature, Ulrike Walker reminded the reader of Wynne-Jones's theory of thresholds, developmental steps that everyone must take or risk to reach maturity, and placed the books in the context of mythic test or quest tales. "The Zoom books," Walker noted, "are composed of wonderful, multi-layered mixtures of images and text that masterfully combine a comforting sense of security with an equally compelling evocation of less innocent sensual gratification." The critic concluded: "These remarkable works ... bear eloquent witness to the complex levels of realization which all of us must undergo before we reach that stage we label 'adult.' "

If Zoom traveled to the Arctic via Maria's attic, the next obvious question—and one posed by a student to Wynne-Jones—was what would a trip to the basement hold in store for Zoom? The answer came in a third "Zoom" book, *Zoom Upstream,* "a book of reunion and probably a book about death, but I don't think any child will read that into it," Wynne-Jones explained to Jenkinson in *Emergency Librarian.* Set in ancient, cat-revering Egypt, *Zoom Upstream* has Zoom following a mysterious trail through a bookshelf to Egypt where he joins Maria in a further search for Uncle Roy. It is Maria who shows Zoom five silver buttons from a sailor's coat, the clues that ultimately lead the two to Uncle Roy and safety. The book's ending is, as noted by Janet McNaughton in *Quill and Quire,* "more like a beginning," with the trio sailing away in search of the source of the Nile. "A very special book," concluded McNaughton.

With *I'll Make You Small,* Wynne-Jones moves away from the voyaging world of cats to the more prosaic but no less dangerous world of the neighborhood. Young Roland's next door neighbor is crotchety old Mr. Swanskin, who threatens to make Roland small if he catches him trespassing on his property. But when Swanskin is not seen for several days, Roland is sent by his mother to investigate, only to find the eccentric old man repairing toys he broke during his own childhood. The gift of a pie saves Roland from Swanskin's threats, and he learns the man's secret—of how he was made to feel small as a child. "A child who likes scary stories, but is too young for Poe or Hitchcock, should enjoy this book," commented Bernie Goedhart in *Quill and Quire.* Appearing the same year as *I'll Make You Small* was Wynne-Jones's *Mischief City,* twenty-five poems that humorously explore subjects from a young child's frustration with adults to sibling rivalry. Joan McGrath, reviewing the book in *Quill and Quire,* felt that it was, with the illustrations of Victor Gad, "big, bold, and bright."

Another popular picture book from Wynne-Jones, and one that *Five Owls* contributor Anne Lundin compared to Sendak's *Where the Wild Things Are,* is *Architect of the Moon* (published in the United States as *Builder of the Moon*). Young David Finebloom receives an urgent message one night via a moonbeam and flies away, building blocks in hand, to repair the moon. Lundin went on in her review to note that "Wynne-Jones's text is spare, simple, poetic," while Catherine Osborne, writing in *Books for Young People*, commented that Wynne-Jones and illustrator Ian Wallace "make a strong contending team in the moon-book category." Walker, writing in *Canadian Children's Literature*, remarked that *Architect of the Moon* "is a subtle work" and one that "does not enclose but encourages the child to take a decisive step toward change." Also writing in *Canadian Children's Literature*, Michael Steig noted that *Architect of the Moon* is a true "visual text," in which pictures and text are finely integrated and one that "achieves a highly gratifying level of literary and artistic complexity and interest."

Wynne-Jones has written several other picture books for young readers, including *The Hour of the Frog, Mouse in the Manger,* and *The Last Piece of Sky,* all of them well received, but the "Zoom" books remain his most popular achievement in that genre. He has also written juvenile and young adult fiction, including two short story collections and a young adult novel. The award-winning *Some of the Kinder Planets* consists of nine stories which tell of children making encounters with other worlds, both metaphorically and realistically. Deborah Stevenson commented in *Bulletin of the Center for Children's Books* that the writing "is thoughtful, inventive, and often humorous," while a *Publishers Weekly* reviewer noted that "ordinary moments take on a fresh veneer in this finely tuned short-story collection." More short stories are offered up in *The Book of Changes,* a "fine collection" according to a *Kirkus Reviews* critic and "a delight" in the estimation of Annette Goldsmith, writing in *Quill and Quire.* Goldsmith added that Wynne-Jones attempted to "conjure up a sense of wonder" in these stories and that the "wonderful moments in this book ... will stay with readers." Writing in *Horn Book,* Nancy Vasilakis concluded that "Wynne-Jones tells his readers in these perceptive short stories that we all have the power to create the music of our own lives."

With *The Maestro,* Wynne-Jones again broke new ground for himself. The story of fourteen-year-old Burl and his struggle for survival, *The Maestro* was Wynne-Jones's first young adult novel. Fleeing his brutal father, Burl seeks shelter in a remote cabin by a Canadian lake. The cabin is inhabited by Nathaniel Gow, a musical genius, himself in flight from the mechanized world. Gow, patterned after the real-life Canadian musician Glen Gould, takes Burl in for a time. He also allows Burl to stay at his cabin when he returns to Toronto, and when Burl learns of Gow's subsequent death, he tries to claim the cabin for his, then goes on a mission to save Gow's final composition, confronting his father along the way. Roderick McGillis, writing in *Canadian Children's Literature,* noted that the book is "redolently Canadian," but that it also offers much more. "Its prose is dense and its themes move into challenging areas for young readers," McGillis remarked. Stevenson concluded in a *Bulletin of the Center for Children's Books* review that "Wynne-Jones has displayed a knack for the unusual made credible in his short story collections" and that it was "nice to see that skill expanded into a well-crafted and accessible novel." Writing in *Quill and Quire,* Maureen Garvie commented that *The Maestro* is

"tightly and dramatically scripted" and that this first young adult novel is a "peach."

In 1994 Wynne-Jones published a second collection of short stories, *The Book of Changes.* Told from the point of view of their male narrators, the seven stories "hold wonder and fascination for inquisitive readers," according to *School Library Journal* reviewer John Sigwald. "Wynne-Jones deals in moments, and these are carefully chosen and freshly realized," Sarah Ellis remarked in *Horn Book.* In "The Clark Beans Man," for instance, a boy uses a Donald Duck impersonation to fend off a schoolyard bully; in "Dawn," a teenager on a bus trip develops a brief friendship with a tough-looking older girl. Wynne-Jones published another collection, titled *Lord of the Fries and Other Stories,* in 1999. A reviewer in *Bulletin of the Center for Children's Books* observed that the author's "creative plotting and faith in the power of imagination ... keeps events sparking along in absorbing and unpredictable ways."

Wynne-Jones turned to psychological suspense with *Stephen Fair,* a 1998 novel about a fifteen year old plagued by nightmares. With the support of his friend Virginia, Stephen begins to question his troubled family life, including his mother's erratic behavior and the disappearances of his father and older brother. Stephen Fair received strong praise. "Wynne-Jones is an impressive stylist," remarked a critic in *Bulletin of the Center for Children's Books,* "and his depiction of Stephen's family, friends, and thoughts are unforcedly deft." A critic in *Kirkus Reviews* noted that the author reveals his characters' feelings "through quick, telling details and comments, or heavily symbolic background events," and a *Publishers Weekly* reviewer declared that Wynne-Jones "maintains the suspense while Stephen slowly unveils family secrets."

Wynne-Jones has proved himself a versatile and perceptive writer on many levels. Whether writing children's picture books, young adult titles, or adult fiction and plays, his message of the power of fantasy and fiction comes through loud and clear. As he once commented, "I like to tell stories—to entertain and instruct—about ordinary people in extraordinary circumstances or extraordinary people in very ordinary circumstances." Regarding his efforts for children, Wynne-Jones commented: "I write for children out of the child I was and am. I cannot write for an audience—where children's books are concerned, I am the Selfish Giant, shooing my audience away in order to reclaim the garden for myself!"

Wynne-Jones told *MAICYA:* "It is the spring of 2002 and I am writing a book tentatively titled *The Outrageous Tiny Rathbone.* In this novel a boy in a small Ontario town finds the ruby slippers worn by Judy Garland in the 1939 Warner Brothers movie *The Wizard of Oz.* The idea grew from a little article in the newspaper about an auction in New York in which the ruby slippers were sold for a million dollars. The article also mentioned, however, that there were seven pairs of slippers made for the movie. The whereabouts of several of the pairs is unknown. Where are they now?

"While my new book is only nominally a mystery story, in the genre sense of the word, there is a mystery at its heart. The book isn't about the ruby slippers, it's about the people who come in contact with this mystery. I think this is true of every story I write.

"Alfred Hitchcock talks about the 'McGuffin' in his films, meaning the thing that everybody is after, the drugs, the fabled necklace, or what have you. If I understand him correctly, he intimates that it isn't really important what the McGuffin actually is only that it gets the ball rolling and keeps the characters on their toes. It is the hub around which the events of the story swirl. Let me update. To me this plot device is more like a 'snitch' as in the Harry Potter books. You never know quite when the snitch might whiz by your head—that's suspense. Suspense intrigues me—but Hey! That's what it is supposed to do.

"Someone once said that Jane Austen is suspenseful and I know what he meant. Suspense is that essential fictional ingredient that keeps the reader turning pages to get to the bottom of the mystery. I do not, however, write straight 'Suspense Thrillers' anymore than I write straight 'Mysteries.' This must be annoying for those who wish to categorize authors. I'm just interested in the human condition to reduce a story to a basic 'and then' kind of state with the required cliff-hanger finish to every chapter.

"Which is why I don't write plot outlines. Can't do it. Hate it! I write the same way I read (though not as fast, unfortunately). I never quite know what's going to happen on the next page. I want to surprise myself and by so doing, hopefully, surprise my reader. Sooner or later, I get an idea where the story is going. That's what happens when I read, too. But even when I know where I want to take a story, I keep my options open. You never know when one of your characters will come up with a better idea than you!

"My new novel deals with the idea that amazing things show up even in your own small neck of the woods. This is an article of faith to me. I am firmly convinced that there is nowhere that is 'ordinary' nor is there such a thing as an 'ordinary' kid. A treasure is nothing more nor less than an article imbued with some intrinsic value. And an extraordinary person is pretty well anyone you send enough time getting to know.

"In my story, the ruby slippers are not important so much for their monetary value, but for the magic they contain, a magic that comes from a connection, however slight, with history and legend. They are a source of wonder to tiny Rathbone. I am heavily into Wonder.

"Mystery, Suspense, Wonder. That about sums it up."

Biographical and Critical Sources

BOOKS

Children's Literature Review, Volume 21, Gale (Detroit, MI), 1990, pp. 226-231.
Twentieth-Century Children's Writers, 4th edition, St. James Press (Detroit, MI), 1995, pp. 1049-1051.
Wynne-Jones, Tim, *Zoom at Sea,* HarperCollins (New York, NY) (New York, NY), 1993.

PERIODICALS

Booklist, April 15, 1993, p. 1524; January 1, 1994; June 1, 1994, p. 1846; March 1, 1995, p. 1241; October 1, 1995; December 15, 1996, p. 724.
Books for Young Readers, October, 1988, Catherine Osborne, review of *Architect of the Moon,* p. 10.
Bulletin of the Center for Children's Books, May, 1995, Deborah Stevenson, review of *One of the Kinder Planets,* p. 328; October, 1996, Deborah Stevenson, review of *The Maestro,* p. 81; March, 1999, review of *Lord of the Fries and Other Stories,* p. 260.
Canadian Children's Literature, number 60, 1990, Ulrike Walker, "A Matter of Thresholds," pp. 108-116; number 70, 1993, Michael Steig, "The Importance of the Visual Text in *Architect of the Moon:* Mothers, Teapots, et al.," pp. 22-33; number 81, 1996, Roderick McGillis, review of *The Maestro,* pp. 58-59.
Canadian Literature, spring, 1987, Jon C. Stott, review of *Zoom Away,* p. 160.
Canadian Materials, January-February, 1994, Joyce Mac-Phee, "Profile: Tim Wynne-Jones," p. 4.
Children's Book News, June, 1979, review of *Madeline and Ermadello,* p. 2.
Emergency Librarian, January-February, 1988, Dave Jenkinson, "Tim Wynne-Jones," pp. 56-62.
Five Owls, May-June, 1989, Anne Lundin, review of *Builder of the Moon,*
Horn Book, May-June, 1987, Sarah Ellis, review of *Zoom Away,* pp. 378-381; May, 1990, p. 332; January, 1995, p. 99; January-February, 1995, Sarah Ellis, review of *Some of the Kinder Planets* and *The Book of Changes;* May, 1995, p. 334; February, 1996, Nancy Vasilakis, review of *The Book of Changes,* pp. 76-77.
In Review: Canadian Books for Children, winter, 1978, Linda Smith, review of *Madeline and Ermadello,* p. 70.
Kirkus Reviews, July 15, 1995, review of *The Book of Changes,* p. 1032; April 1, 1998, review of *Stephen Fair,* pp. 503-504.
Publishers Weekly, April 12, 1993, p. 61; May 1, 1995, review of *One of the Kinder Planets,* p. 59; October 30, 1995, p. 62; October 14, 1996, p. 84; March 16, 1998, review of *Stephen Fair,* p. 65.
Quill and Quire, March, 1984, Linda Granfield, review of *Zoom at Sea,* p. 72; August, 1985, Bernie Goedhart, review of *Zoom Away,* p. 38; October, 1986, Bernie Goedhart, review of *I'll Make You Small,* p. 16; December, 1986, Joan McGrath, "Poems for Kids Conjure up a Cockeyed World," p. 15; December, 1989, p. 22; October, 1993, p. 38; November, 1992, Janet McNaughton, review of *Zoom Upstream,* p. 33; November, 1993, p. 38; October, 1994, Annette Goldsmith, review of *The Book of Changes,* p. 38; Decem-

ber, 1995, Maureen Garvie, review of *The Maestro*, pp. 36-37.

Reading Time, August, 1997, p. 35.

School Library Journal, August, 1990, p. 136 March, 1984, Linda Granfield, review of *Zoom at Sea*, p. 72;

February, 1994, p. 92; August, 1994, p. 148; April, 1995, p. 138; October, 1995, John Sigwald, review of *The Book of Changes*, pp. 141-142.

*   *   *

Autobiography Feature

Tim Wynne-Jones

When I was three, I ran away from home with a tea cosy on my head. That was in England. A few months later I ended up in Canada. I like to pretend that these two events were connected; that somehow this intrepid three-year-old made it all the way to northern British Columbia in his gray flannel shorts, red tie, and open-toed sandals. The thing is, I don't know what my destination was that spring day, let alone what my motive for leaving might have been. It is not really my memory but a piece of family lore.

We were staying with my mother's parents at the time. They lived in a grand house called "Ravensheugh." It stood on the Spital Road in the town of Bromborough, Cheshire. Many years later, reading a book about Cheshire, I would learn that the Spital Road was named for an eleventh-century leper's hospital (ho'spital) to which it led. I don't think that was where I was heading.

Probably I was angry. We were staying with my grandparents because we were about to leave for Canada. A few days before my flight in the tea cosy, I was sitting in the upstairs window of our own house, "Just Home," a few miles from Bromborough in the village of Little Sutton, when my next-door neighbor, Nicky, came over to play. I opened the window and called down to him.

"I can't come out today," I said. "We're moving to Canada."

I remember Nicky nodding in an "Oh, I see" kind of way and then heading home. It was as if I had said, "Sorry, today we're moving to Canada but I'll see you tomorrow." A few days later at Ravensheugh maybe the penny dropped. We were never going back to Just Home; I would never see Nicky again. That would be a pretty good reason for running away. Saying goodbye to Nicky is my only real memory of England.

We came to Canada on a Cunnard ocean liner, the *Ascania,* my four sisters, my mother and I. My father had gone on ahead. He was always going on ahead. He was an engineer. Whatever it was he was building always had to get built right away and so Mum was left with the task of packing and closing up house.

My one memory of the Atlantic crossing is tomato soup. My family was seasick and bedridden. I remember going to the dining hall all on my own. The place was almost deserted and I was asked to join the captain at his table. It was like something from an Edward Ardizzone picture book. I was Brave Tim!

I had tomato soup. It was sweet and rich and creamy and perfectly satisfying. Everything tastes better at the captain's table. In my picture book *Zoom Away,* Zoom the cat and Maria stop in a snow covered sitting room on their way to the Arctic and have cups full of piping hot tomato soup. It had stayed warm all those years in the thermos of my memory.

Kitimat was a little boy's dream come true. It stands at the head of the Douglas Channel, southeast of Prince Rupert and less than a hundred miles south of the southernmost tip of Alaska. The town, such as it was, was named after the Kitamaat Indians, the "people of the snow," as the Hudson's Bay Company traders had dubbed them a hundred years earlier. The Kitamaat were still there. My father and I went hunting with them. Well, Dad hunted and I plucked feathers.

I remember one hunting trip. We had stopped in an abandoned, roofless log cabin. It was raining. It's always raining on the northwest coast. We strung up a tarp and waited for a break in the weather. I played soldiers with shotgun shells while the men chatted and smoked their pipes. Mum had sent along egg, onion, and tomato sandwiches. Her thinly sliced homemade bread was soggy from the tomatoes, but then everything else was soggy, too. The sandwiches were just like the day.

What few houses there were in Kitimat had been shipped by barge all the way from Vancouver. We bought our supplies at the Hudson's Bay Company. There was a place called the "town site" that became what is present-day Kitimat. So, here we were, living on the edge of a place that didn't yet really exist. We had come from a place where the houses had names to a place where there were so few people nobody even bothered with numbers. We had come to a pioneer town from a city founded by King Alfred's daughter, Aethelfred, in 912. Maybe Bromborough seemed like Kitimat to Aethelfred. There were probably tall trees in England back then and bears, too. But no Mounties.

My older sisters tell me what they expected to find in the new world: giant green trees, big black bears, and tall red-suited Mounties. Miraculously, that's exactly what we did find. I once got paid for painting the rocks around the Mounties' headquarters. I painted the rocks white.

Bears would wander down into the settlement now and then. I remember one scratching his back against the side of our house. The house rocked! I also met a bear once with my mother. (Actually, the bear wasn't with my mother, I was.) We were walking on a path through the woods. The mama bear had a cub with her. That usually means trouble, but I think the two mothers came to some kind of unspoken agreement. It was kind of like *Blueberries for Sal* without the blueberries.

As for trees, you couldn't see the forest for them. A few years ago I wrote a radio piece for the Canadian Broadcasting Corporation about my memories of that time. I talked fondly about the twig huts we built in the steep woods, huts that looked exactly like Ernest H. Shepard's ink drawings of the house at Pooh Corner. My sister Wendy wrote to me after hearing the radio piece. She and her friends had built those twig houses, she explained, not me. She must have been right. After all, she was nine and I was five. Which brings up an important point: memory is untrustworthy; it is like a not-so-real estate magnet confiscating the territories it desires.

I spent a lot of time with a tugboat operator and his wife. The Douglas was a deep channel, deep enough for ocean-going freighters. There was a gigantic aluminum smelter at Kitimat. It was the tugboat captain's job to bring those freighters into harbor. And it was my job to help in all the many ways a five-year-old can. I remember eating fresh apple pie cooked right on board. But an even better memory than the pie was an American destroyer.

I didn't question why an American destroyer was parked in the Douglas Channel. When you're five the world is just one miracle after another. I remember boarding the warship from the tug and a sailor showing me around. He sat me in the seat of a turret gun. I remember swiveling the gun so that it pointed towards our house. What a surprise for Mummy!

The firing mechanism, as I recall, was made of red rubber and was roughly the shape of the squeezer at the end of a turkey baster. I remember firing off a few imaginary rounds, the sailor laughing as I blew up Kitimat. Kitimat kind of looked bombed out, anyway, a series of prefab houses on a bulldozed scarp. I realize now that the destroyer must have been over from the war in Korea. Maybe the sailors needed a little down time building twig houses.

I started school in Kitimat but I don't remember going very much. I distinctly remember playing hooky one day and discovering an enormous shark washed up on the beach. It was already rotting and fabulously stinky. Sharks seldom washed up on the shore of my classroom. Only Ritz crackers and apple juice. But it was in that classroom that I first performed in a dramatic role. I was cast as a stalk of celery. I still remember my line.

"Celery from a seed. That is what you need."

Presumably, my teacher had discovered, like the RCMP officers before her, my gift for the arts.

We were only in Kitimat three years but it holds enormous sway over my life. Though I am a city guy in

Tim Wynne-Jones, 2001

many ways, Kitimat created in me a love of nature that many years of urban life never rooted out. It would be thirty-four years before I would escape to the country where I now live but the yearning was in me from those days onward.

I might have grown up more of the outdoors type if my father hadn't started to suffer from gout, a painful affliction he endured on and off for the rest of his life. He sold his hunting rifles and shotguns. We fished from time to time but didn't get out into the wilderness together much after Kitimat.

Children who have read my novel *The Maestro* often ask if I was an abused child. I wasn't at all. But, having said that, I did model Burl's father on my own dad to some degree. I just exaggerated a lot. It's what fiction writers do. My father was large—stout—and gruff at times. He had been a major in the British Army and was used to giving commands. He could be the life of the party, wickedly funny, and a singer of bawdy songs. But when he was angry, he was pretty scary, although he never hit me. I gave Cal Crow some of these characteristics. Fictional characters seem more lively when they are modeled on real flesh-and-blood people and my father was a man of considerable flesh and blood.

But I also gave Burl some of my good memories of my father. The soggy hunting trip mentioned above, for instance. Burl talks about a time "when he could still get close to the man." Though my father was around all the years of my growing up, he was moody and consumed by his work. It couldn't have been easy keeping a big bunch of children clothed and fed.

The Greek Titan, Prometheus, stole his father's fire. I stole my father's Welsh moodiness and his love of awful puns. But the best thing I got from him was words. He was not university educated but he spoke wonderfully well, and he sang and told stories.

I did not set out to be a writer. From the age of eleven I was bound and determined to become an architect when I grew up. I leaned towards the visual arts, in any case. I drew all the time. I drew on the cardboard sheets the dry cleaner put inside my father's starched white shirts. I pestered my mother: "What should I draw now?" I would ask.

"Your last breath," she would reply, exasperated. My mother is pretty handy with language herself.

No, I did not set out to be a writer, but you use what building material you have. And so the buildings I was destined to design were made, not of mortar and steel, but of language. I wrote a picture book called *Architect of the Moon* (retitled *Builder of the Moon* in the U.S.A.). The moon was the kind of thing I turned out to be okay at building. In my first novel, the adult thriller, *Odd's End,* the house is one of the main characters. And in my young adult novel, *Stephen Fair,* the Fair family live in a wonderful ark in the middle of the woods. It is not just a house, of course, but a metaphor of Stephen's journey into his own disturbing past. Metaphors are the nails that hold up my buildings.

My home was always littered with books and vibrant with conversation and song and jokes. Diana would sing duets from Gilbert and Sullivan with my father. Jennifer would do her very regal impersonation of Queen Elizabeth. She once stood on the table to do it! If things really got out of hand, my father would say, "Kindly contain your hilarity with a modicum of restraint." And we would all roar with laughter and pay no attention.

Storytelling was expected in my family. Indeed, we younger children were not allowed to sit at the dinner table until we were "suitably interesting enough." I remember the supper-hour banishment to the TV room with my younger sister and brother, where we sat, gloomily, at little tray tables watching television and eating dinner, wanting only to join the grown-ups chatting and laughing in the dining room. Is that why my favorite memories are so often connected with food?

Our family grew to fullness in Kitimat. Giles Philip was born there. There were now six children: Jen, who was nine years my senior; Di, who was two years younger than Jen; Wendy, who was two years younger than Di; then me; and then Bryony, three years my junior, and finally G.P., as we called him. This was the troop my mother hauled off to Vancouver in 1955. My father was already there. There was a bridge to build.

By the time I graduated from high school I had lived in twelve different houses and never in any one of them longer than three years. I don't know how my mother coped. But I know how I did. I learned to make friends quickly and not to expect to keep them. I am envious of people who still know childhood friends. Perhaps that is why many of my stories feature sturdy friendships: Fletcher and Shlomo in "Tashkent," Carrie and Sam in *Lord of the Fries.* But equally present in my writing are difficult friendships: Burl and NOG in *The Maestro* or Jim and Ruth Rose in *The Boy in the Burning House,* for example.

The golden dream of childhood continued for about another year. We moved into a wonderful old house, 2212 Bellevue Avenue in West Vancouver. It seemed a mansion to me but anything would have seemed palatial after living in a prefab. There was an upstairs. I played in a little nook underneath the first floor landing.

I fell down the stairs once. I remember it vividly. My mother holding me while I bawled, then my father arriving and saying how sad he was to have missed my fall and would I consider doing it again. He made me laugh and I hated him for it.

The house was right on the sea. There was an overgrown path, sharp with blackberry bramble and alive with garter snakes, that led from our back garden down to a rocky beach. All the children who lived along Bellevue owned parts of that otherwise inhospitable shoreline. We each claimed a boulder that was our very own pirate flagship. When the tide came in you could get stranded on your boulder. It was like being at sea without the fuss of going anywhere. It was a brilliant time. I had good chums, a huge and verdant garden, the Pacific Ocean. Life was grand.

The author's parents, Syd and Sheila Wynne-Jones, in London, 1951, six months before the family moved to Canada

Kitimat, in northern British Columbia, 1951, where the Wynne-Jones family lived for three years

Then my father had a fall and it wasn't down the stairs. He was working on the construction site of the Oak Street Bridge and a girder crushed his leg. He was put out of commission for a year. He had no insurance; there was no workman's compensation. We had to leave Bellevue Avenue. When I returned there some twenty years later, the house was gone and in its place stood a pink apartment building with semicircular windows. They had taken away the raging ocean of my pirate-youth, as well, and replaced it with some tame inland sea.

"As one door shuts another one closes." One of my father's favorite expressions.

The year of my father's injury we lived in a basement. My mother divided up the space into rooms with sheets on clothes lines. One day, baby G.P. ate a pound of butter left on the back step by the milkman. I remember my mother crying in her curtained room like a patient in a hospital. My mother's greatest gift to this day is patience.

When my father recovered and got back to work, we moved to a little house on Haywood Avenue just a few blocks away. It was half the size of Bellevue but luxurious after living in a cotton-walled labyrinth. Several important things happened there. I entered grade three at Irwin Park School and met Miss Schultz, the world's best grade-three teacher. She let me and another boy named Graham stay in at recess and draw. She gave us tons of paper. We drew nothing but war scenes, mostly Indians and cavalry. Graham was good at horses. I specialized at dramatic

deaths: soldiers shot through with arrows. The painter of rocks had graduated to gore.

It was while we were at Haywood that I got my first bicycle. It was a green Raleigh three speed and I burst into tears when I saw it.

But the gift that outshines all the rest was the day my father brought home the collected children's writing of A. A. Milne. Four books in a boxed set: *Winnie-the-Pooh, The House at Pooh Corner, When We Were Very Young,* and *Now We Are Six.* It wasn't for any event I can recall. It must have been my father's way of trying to make up for the hardships of the previous year. In any case, to this day, *The House at Pooh Corner* ranks among my favorite books, right up there with *The Hitchhiker's Guide to the Galaxy* and *The Golden Compass.*

Were I to list all the books I have read that have moved me and all the sad songs I have ever loved, it would make a pretty good autobiography all by itself. I'm sure that when science finally has good enough equipment they will find that the universe is really made out of music.

If Miss Schultz was the epitome of a kind and inspired primary teacher, the following year at Pauline Johnson School I met the archetypal bully of a principal. His name was Mr. Egbert. We called him Eggbeater. I remember Eggbeater hanging over me while I scrambled the alphabet and simultaneously peed my pants. The boy who sat next to me was the only one other than the principal who saw the steaming puddle at my feet. That boy spent an eternity of

The author's father, Syd Wynne-Jones

recesses tormenting me, threatening to expose me. Bullying begets bullying.

I recall another incident where a Vancouver classmate beat me up because I said "garage" in the English way, as if it rhymed with "carriage" instead of with "barrage." Which only goes to show that the inspired bully always finds a reason to pound you out without even resorting to things like race, creed, or color.

As a subspecies, bullies figure prominently in many of my stories. I delight in thinking up imaginative ways of dealing with them. I'm not into Stephen King-like revenge, but it is nevertheless true that writing is a great way of getting back at someone!

The ultimate bully of my childhood was Howie in grade six. I got him back but good in "The Clark Beans Man" (in *The Book of Changes.*) While Howie's fictional stand-in straddled poor weak Dwight, the hero of my story, drooling spit on his face, Dwight suddenly let loose. He started quoting Wordsworth's poem, "The World Is Too Much with Us," in the voice of Donald Duck. What defense would a bully have for that?

When did I begin to write? The answer varies. My first published book came out in 1977. The oldest manuscript I have in my possession is from 1970, *The Fable of the Lady on the Hill,* a painfully sentimental little love story. I was twenty-two when I wrote and illustrated it. I had just failed out of architecture school. I had no idea what I was doing or where I was going. It was a scary time. I know I started several novels around then and never got farther than fifty

pages. There is a quotation from Peter London's *No More Second Hand Art* that my wife calligraphed and put up on her studio wall. "Reflect upon that quality of yourself without which you would no longer be the person you take yourself to be." I suppose, in a way, that was what I was doing in the early seventies. I sang in a band. I drew a lot. I started writing stories. Writing and drawing and singing—that's who I am.

I began to write song lyrics at that time, both for the band and for a "folkie" friend with whom I ended up forming a singing duo. The duo, Raffi and Tim, played cafés and college pubs around Toronto. Raffi went on to a fabulously successful career as a children's performer. I ended up back at school. Art school. I still didn't take my writing seriously.

But writing lyrics was a good start. Since we were going to perform the songs live I remember thinking that the words really *mattered,* which is a pretty important step in becoming any kind of a writer. Mark Twain puts it this way: "The difference between the right word and the nearly right word is the same as that between lightning and a lightning bug."

The difficulty in saying exactly when I began to write is that there are various component parts to the process that have to come together. I was always imaginative. But if imagination provides the impulse for artistic creation, there still has to be an opportunity for that impulse to kick in, to pick up momentum. There has to be a condition in which the germs of ideas begin to shape themselves into stories. And those story-making conditions began for me a long, long time before I actually put pen to paper. This condition, which marks the beginning of my life as an author came the summer my family moved from Vancouver to Ottawa, Ontario. It was 1958. I was ten. I knew no one.

I was bored out of my mind.

The nation's capital. Big deal! What good are parliament buildings when you haven't got a friend to parley with?

We lived in a particularly peaceful neighborhood called the Glebe (an Old English word referring to land granted to the church). We lived on Clemow Avenue, a wide, tree-lined street of brick houses. In Brian Doyle's wonderful novel *Easy Avenue,* I'm pretty sure the title refers to Clemow. I had my green Raleigh, so off I rode to explore the dappled avenues of the Glebe, busy Bank Street, the Rideau Canal which winds through the heart of Ottawa, and Landsdowne Park where the stock cars used to race on Wednesdays. You could get into the races for six bottle caps if your dad took you. My favorite car was "Duff's Taxi." It was yellow.

There were ponds in the Glebe where you could catch tadpoles and then leave them frying in the sun, we had a dog to run, a milkman you could ride with in his horse-drawn cart, and there was always a ball to bounce against a wall. It was the most boring time in my life!

Boredom, however, has its up side.

I am not by nature a solitary person. But solitude, finally, is the necessary state for creative writing. (I mean, if you've got a life, why bother making one up?) Anyway, acute, sluggish, what-do-I-do-now boredom is like a kind of bargain-basement solitude. And I had a lot of it that summer of '58. I have tried to recapture something of the feel of that time in my story "Hard Sell" (in *The Book of*

Changes). That's where the story-making began. Observing the games you are not a part of, eavesdropping on other people's fun, manufacturing events out of borrowed experience and a story out of a shapeless summer day.

Mercifully, there was the library. I was a reader. In fact, when we unpacked after the move east, I found a library book from West Van. It was an adventure story set in the Yukon with dogs in it. I lived in real terror that the Library Hit Squad would track me down. Now I wish I still had that purloined book. My daughter lives in Vancouver; I could get her to take it back for me. It would be so cool. I can see Maddy approaching the librarian with her perfect ballerina poise. "My dad asked me to bring this back," she would say. And then pulling out her purse, she might add, "How much will the fine be?"

My greatest joys were the various adventure series written by Enid Blyton, and the Freddy the Pig stories of Walter R. Brooks. They weren't good literature. But whenever I get uppity about bad children's books, when my critic's hat gets too tight and cuts off my circulation, I try to recall the sheer comfort and exhilaration of *Freddy and the Baseball Team from Mars* or *The Mountain of Adventure*.

One Sunday morning, wandering about the Glebe with nothing to do, I ran into a school mate who was on his way to Saint Matthews Anglican Church where he sang in the choir. They got paid! So I went, too. I ended up singing in that choir for four years. I didn't get rich, but under the guidance of Gerald Wheeler, Saint Matthews became the best boys' choir in Ottawa and I eventually became the head boy. I won at the Kiwanis Music Festival three years in a row as a treble soloist.

Success can make you giddy. Too much of it is intoxicating. I have won some awards as a writer and that has been very gratifying. But you have to write what you want to write, not what you think people expect you to write. My worst writing comes when I try to write like Tim Wynne-Jones.

But when I was eleven, how great it was to win at something. What a confidence booster. Later, when I was plagued by adolescent insecurity, there was always buried inside me the idea that it was possible to do better. That it was possible to come out on top.

I am terribly competitive. I realized just how bad this affliction was when my eldest son, Xan (Alexander) was playing a lot of soccer. I coached his teams for a number of years and the nastiness of my winning-is-everything attitude shocked me. At its worst, my rabid competitiveness seems a needy kind of thing. I think it might stem from always being the new boy. One reaction is to make yourself invisible. Not me. My approach was to stand up and shout, "Hey, look at me. Quick! I won't be here long."

The Wynne-Jones family, c. 1954. Left to right: Diana, Tim, Syd, Wendy, Sheila, Bryony, Jennifer, and "Captain Rafferty"

There were other, better lessons I learned singing in the choir: the way a lyric rides a melody line, the hard work it takes to excel at anything, how to entertain yourself through a mind-numbing sermon, and this important safety message: when you have just carried a tall candle in a procession around the church, don't let a tall boy blow it out!

But perhaps best of all, at Saint Matthews I experienced the thrill of singing in harmony. Neurologists have done tests and apparently your brain lights up all over the place when you sing in harmony. I believe it.

And choir was fun. The hockey broadcast scene described in my story "Fallen Angel" (in *Lord of the Fries*) really happened.

Choir also added a note of continuity to my life. In the four years I was at Saint Matthews my family lived in three different houses in three different suburbs of Ottawa and I went to four different schools.

My favorite school year ever was grade eight at Connaught Elementary in the west end of Ottawa. I made a best friend, Danny Sigler; became a champion receiver at schoolyard peewee football; got the role of the romantic lead, Frederick, in *The Pirates of Penzance*; and fell in love with Mabel, the other romantic lead. I even got pretty good grades.

We started going to Ocean Park, Maine, for summer holidays. All eight of us and a dog in one car. Those sixties' cars were big.

I loved Ocean Park. We would rent a cottage for two weeks. One cottage had a piano. I remember coming home from the beach, one day, and hearing someone playing the piano. Really well. My mother had come up earlier to fix dinner and, to my great surprise, it turned out to be her. Who knew she played? When she realized I was there, she blushed and immediately retired to the kitchen. Apparently, she had done her grade-ten musical exams back in England. But nothing more was said about the matter. My mother kept her ego in close harness. My father's ego took up a lot of room. And when, as a teenager, my own ego started to emerge, all gawky and full of itself, I remember thinking how little space there was—how little *air* there seemed to be around our house.

I read my last Hardy Boys book in Ocean Park, Maine. For a couple of years, I was a big fan of Bayport's famous detectives, gobbling up the stories as fast as I could lay hands on them. There was a little lending library in Ocean Park. I remember arriving at our cottage one summer, changing into my beach clothes, and racing to the library. *The Missing Chum.* Perfect.

But it was not perfect. I didn't get past page two. A profound lack of interest swept over me like a wave and just as devastating in its own way. Suddenly, I didn't care if anyone ever found Chet. I didn't care if the Hardy Boys crashed their new coupe and burned to death. It was over between us. Sadly, I returned the book and perused the shelves for something to fill the void. *Travels with Charley,*

The author (left) with sister Bryony and brother Giles Philip in the garden at the house on Bellevue Avenue, Vancouver, c. 1956

by John Steinbeck looked okay. I had never heard of Steinbeck but the story had a dog in it. And so I spent the summer of 1966 reading nothing but John Steinbeck. As far as I know Chet is still lost at sea.

That summer I stayed on in Ocean Park working in the kitchen at the Bassett Guest House. It was the first time I had ever lived away from home. Now, I thought, I'll get to do what the cool teens do: party on the beach, hang out 'til all hours of the night. Mostly what I did was spend a *lot* of time reading Steinbeck.

When I got to high school, I had one ambition: I wanted to be in with the *in* crowd. It seems pretty fatuous, but I have tried to forgive myself. It wasn't really me, I tell myself. An alien took over my skinny body. I was transmogrified into a joiner of clubs, a desperate *poseur,* and where girls were concerned, a heat-seeking missile. In the picture of the six lads in semi-drag, I'm the Great Pumpkin on the extreme left. But my politics weren't leftist—not then. I had no beliefs beyond girls, parties, and button-down, madras shirts.

The assembly of beauties known as the Ridgemont Rubies were a commando cheerleading squad prone to raiding assemblies and cheerleading competitions. Put that way, it sounds like we were anarchists. We weren't. We were just having fun.

I think I was having fun. I'm not sure. I know I spent a fair amount of time watching myself from the sidelines. I think a lot of teens feel that way.

For a long time I have been contemptuous of my teen years, how superficial and supercilious I was. It wasn't me, I protest. I was the pimply host of some alien whose greatest care in the world was whether his jeans were as tight as the Beach Boys' jeans.

Why the denial? Was I really so absurd? Why this betrayal? Why is my adult self, now almost as stout as his father, trying to distance himself from that skinny boy? Meanwhile, the boy in me feels like a kid alone in a room with a broken tea cup. "I didn't do it," he shouts. "Honest."

There were good times at Ridgemont High. There were parties and girls and madras shirts. The Beatles came along and we all became mods. For the first time ever, I actually got to stay at the same school right to the bitter end. True, my parents moved to the States, but I stayed on. I had lots of friends. At least, it seemed that way. Strangely, when I returned from university for commencement, I didn't go to any parties. Maybe my old friends didn't recognize me behind the beard I had grown that summer. Or, maybe the guy behind that beard failed to recognize them?

In my last year of high school, 1966-67, my family split in two. My parents didn't separate, but my father's business collapsed and, when the dust had settled, he and mum and Bryony and G.P. were living in Radnor, Pennsylvania, while the rest of us were still in Ottawa.

The Vietnam War was on and I would have been eligible for the draft had I moved. My father tended to tell funny and exciting stories about World War II but he kept a lot of bad stuff to himself. I learned much later that he had been among the first troops to arrive at the Bergen-Belsen Death Camp. As a Royal Engineer, it was his job to clean up the place. How those experiences must have haunted him. In any case, as poorly as he and I were getting along at the time, he was in no hurry to see me going off to fight in somebody else's war.

Tim Wynne-Jones, c. 1972

Wendy had been the first of my sisters to marry. I moved in with her and her new husband. The arrangement lasted less than three months. Who could blame them? One of the least favorite wedding presents you can give a young couple is a teenage brother. So I moved in with Jen and Di in their apartment downtown for the rest of the year. They were single and fun. If I cramped their style, they were kind enough not to mention it. I, myself, had no style to cramp. But I sure was working on it.

One last important footnote about high school. I failed English. I got 46 percent on my final exam. Ironically, my science marks were high enough that the school bumped me up to a pass so I could go to architecture school.

But what is more ironic is that I loved everything we read in English. It took me years to understand what my problem was. I just can't stay on the outside of a story.

One day in Mr. Partridge's senior English class, a crow flew into the room. How keenly I tried to convince the teacher that this was an event of real importance, that it was apt, somehow, considering we were discussing Hamlet.

"Don't you get it, sir?" I wish I had been able to say. "Elsinore is in Denmark, right? And in Norse mythology, two crows—well, ravens, actually—sit on either shoulder of Odin, the God of war and culture. One of those crows is Hugin, which means *thought*; the other is Munin, which means *memory*. Maybe *this* crow knows something we don't?"

Of course, I didn't know anything like that. What I knew but could not articulate was that when I am reading, the story is happening to me, just like the crow. Or the air, for that matter.

Later, in my twenties, I read all of the works of the British novelist, Graham Greene. He refers to his first memoir as "a sort of a life" partially because he has, as he says, "spent almost as much time with imaginary characters as with real men and women." I know the feeling, both as a reader and a writer. When I am in the middle of writing a novel, my characters are with me all the time. I am always listening for what they are going to say next. When I see something, I wonder what Burl or Stephen or Jim or Tiny might make of it. They don't see things from the same point of view as me. How could they? Not with the mess they've got themselves into! In writing, finally, I am allowed to live inside the story without flunking!

An autobiography can be many things. This one is almost three quarters done and I have barely gotten out of my childhood. But since I have made childhood my profession, so to speak, for the last twenty odd years, maybe that is as it should be. When I say profession, I don't simply mean my livelihood; I mean that I *profess* to this renewable resource called childhood. I affirm my faith in it, my allegiance to it. I guess in some ways I'm still trying to get it right. Maybe it's my way of hanging out indefinitely at all those schools I merely visited while passing through my childhood.

Entering the University of Waterloo in 1967 I was still ten years away from publishing a book and thirteen years from writing anything half good. How did I get there? How did the painter of rocks, the celery boy, the angelic chorister, the flunking English Lit senior, the would-be Master Builder end up pushing a pen for a living?

The author (bottom center, wearing leather and plywood glasses) and his wife, Amanda (far left, in leotard), with the cast of the musical Rumours of Our Death.

The last stage of the journey began, I guess, with a grumpy, quite troubled, but brilliant English professor.

You have to study all kinds of things to be an architect: design, systematic layout planning, structural physics, math, psychology, sociology, and, mercifully for me, cultural history. I had two fine instructors in that wide-ranging subject, but I credit the first of them, Murray MacQuarrie, with getting me to think. My classmates and I were a bit of an experiment, the first year of architecture students at the University of Waterloo. The faculty weren't quite sure what to do with us. Professor MacQuarrie wanted to ring our necks. He was astounded at how stupid we were. So, he gave us a monumentally long reading list. The Bible, for beginners, and then Ovid's *Metamorphosis,* Dante's *Divine Comedy,* Machiavelli's *The Prince,* and so on and so on, ending up some twenty books later with *The Lord of the Rings* trilogy. All to be read in one term.

He made us watch movies, too. With subtitles. Eisenstein's *The Battleship Potemkin,* Renoir's *The Rules of the Game,* Fellini's *8 1/2.* I fell in love with the films of Ingmar Bergman. My friends and I would go around pretending to speak Swedish.

To use a phrase coined around that time, MacQuarrie blew my mind. Structural physics didn't stand a chance. The writing, as they say, was on the wall.

Though I managed to stave off getting kicked out of architecture for a couple more years, I eventually left Waterloo and went to Toronto where I sang for a time in a band called Boogie Dick. We were hippies, outrageous, irreverent. We burned things on stage, I painted my face paisley, played electric baseball bat. Don't ask. For a while, we had a regular gig at a club called the Paramount on Spadina Avenue, until an enterprising journalist wrote a piece about us in the *Globe & Mail,* revealing what we thought of the club's management. The article got us fired and we took our mad act on the road.

Writing kept me sane, which, in Boogie Dick, was no mean trick. We were all crazy, some more than others. One of the band ended up a few years later in a hospital for the criminally insane.

I left Boogie Dick one cool summer morning, after a gig in Pembroke on the Ottawa River. It was a long way from Toronto, my new home, but only a couple of hours from my old home, Ottawa. I stole away without saying goodbye. I hitched to Ottawa, to my sister Diana's place. Her baby daughter was frightened of me with my afro and my bushy beard. I think I was a little frightened of me, too. I hurried back to the safety of Waterloo. The following fall, I enrolled in visual art.

Back in Waterloo, I moved with my buddy Doug Jamieson, another ex-architecture student, now a composer, into a house full of nutty musicians. Nutty isn't the same as crazy. Nutty is fun.

The house was called the Toadstool. One morning I counted sixteen guitars in that house. Sometimes there were that many people. We were all in bands or between bands. We were all in school or between schools. We all read Herman Hesse and Richard Brautigan. We listened to everything from Bach to the Beatles. We listening to Frank Zappa's "Hot Rats" and Antonin Dvorak's "New World Symphony." We pretended the latter was the score to a movie and made up the story to go along with it. The story changed with every listening.

I got a new band, Alabaster: a good band, a sane band. We didn't burn things on stage. We enjoyed each other's company. We played all over southwestern Ontario and I earned enough from that, plus working in the university library, to pay my way through school. Our drummer, Klaus Gruber, is to this day a great friend. I dedicated *Some of the Kinder Planets* to him and his wife, Margie, "two of the kinder people you could ever hope to meet." When you are licking your wounds it's nice to find a nice safe, friendly place to do it.

I kept writing. My lyrics were pretty pretentious. My biggest problem was in trying too hard to be clever. Growing up on Gilbert and Sullivan operettas, I was attuned to patter songs and so I piled way too many words into my lyrics.

Meanwhile, a new professor arrived in the Fine Arts Department. He was from Chicago. Virgil Burnett was a graphic artist who worked primarily in pen and ink. So did I (my architecture "rapidograph pens"—I had to use them for something!). Virgil was something of a surrealist. Me too. He wrote stories as well. It hadn't occurred to me you could get away with doing both!

I suppose Virgil became something of a father figure for me. I seldom saw my parents after they moved to the States. They kept moving: to Dover, Delaware; Dallas, Texas; Ridgewood, New Jersey. Virgil and his wife Ann were worldly and sophisticated. Ann taught at the University of Chicago and "commuted" to Stratford, Ontario. They had a place in France as well, in Flavigny-sur-Ozerain, where the movie *Chocolat* would later be filmed.

It was while they were in France, in the summer of 1974, that I stayed in their beautiful home in Stratford to look after the dog and cat. Virgil also had a horse which he kept at a stable out of town. He asked if I would mind sharing his Volkswagen bug with a girl who was going to groom and ride his horse. How could I refuse? The girl, as it turned out, was an acting student at York University, working backstage at the Stratford Shakespearean Festival that summer while also working in her grandmother's beautiful bookstore and, of course, riding Virgil's mare. She thought I was a friend of Virgil's from Chicago, which made me seem a lot more exotic than I really was. Her name was Amanda Lewis. It still is. We've been together ever since.

I think introducing you to your future wife goes well beyond the duties of a first-rate mentor, but that was what Virgil did and was. He gave me a glimpse into a world I had only imagined existed. People who wrote and drew and acted for a living.

I moved with Amanda to Toronto that fall where I found work in a small publishing company as a book designer. I didn't know anything about book design but PMA Books was a very small company. We were all kind of making it up as we went along. Besides, as luck would have it, Amanda's mother was a very good book designer for the University of Toronto Press. So my introduction to the book world was from the other side of the table, so to speak. I worked on manuscripts for several years before I sent one off with the hope of getting it published. I knew a little bit about what drives editors crazy. That's useful information.

I left PMA after a year and a half, the longest day job I ever held. Amanda and I traveled to Europe and upon

Tim Wynne-Jones and his wife, Amanda, with their children (left to right) Xan, Maddy, and Lewis, 1990

returning I set up a graphic design company with a friend from Waterloo, Michael Solomon. He is now one of the truly great children's book designers in Canada.

Amanda finished theatre school in 1978 and I decided it was time to go back, myself. I went to York to do a master's in visual arts. I didn't much enjoy it but there were several good teachers there, especially Toby McLennan, a performance artist. She asked me to be in several of her pieces. It was great—even better than being a stalk of celery. It was art and music and theatre all rolled into one.

Nobody at York much liked my drawing. So I started writing my own performance pieces. My performances tended to be weird little fanciful narratives with scores and furniture. I think that is when the final puzzle piece fell into place. A performance piece, you see, doesn't have any particular structure. It can be anything you want it to be. So, if there are words involved, they just have to be the words you need. I realized, for the first time, that this was exactly what all writing should be: whatever is needed, no more, no less. It seems a simple enough idea. It had taken me a long time to get it.

Upon graduating from York, I gave myself the summer off. That's a big gift when you have no money. I had been offered a part-time teaching post at York the next fall, so I got a bank loan to tide me over, rented a little Smith Corona electric typewriter and wrote a novel. Amanda was away. She was driving across America to visit relatives in California. I was all alone. I had no responsibilities, no deadlines, no one to have to be nice to or to feed. I wrote a mystery thriller called *Odd's End.* It only took six weeks to write the first draft. I loved every moment of writing it, climbed right inside the story—lived it. I scared myself silly, but it was good scary.

I entered *Odd's End* in the Seal First Novel Competition run by Bantam Books and McClelland & Stewart. And it won.

The prize was fifty thousand dollars and a three-publisher book contract which saw *Odd's End* come out in Canada, the United States, and England. It later came out in Germany as well, and was made into a movie in France many years later. The movie is called *The House That Mary Built.* Don't go out of your way trying to find it. Maybe it's better in French than it is in English.

Nowhere in that original book contract did it say anything about having a baby. But that's what we did. Amanda and I call Xan the Seal First Baby Award. He just seemed to come right along with the prize. If we had hoped to have a family before then, we knew it wouldn't be for some time. Amanda was acting and directing; I was teaching art. Who could afford children? The Seal Award changed all that, although it must be said that fifty thousand doesn't last long when you start buying things like a house and a car and, most important of all, a washing machine.

Xan turned out to be such a good idea that we had Maddy and then Lewis. Since Amanda was an only child and I had come from a family of six, we split the difference. Mind you, we didn't plan it that way.

One morning, when Amanda was already pregnant with Xan but only guessed that she might be and hadn't bothered to tell me about it, I sat at my kitchen table in our first floor flat on Sackville Street in Cabbagetown, Toronto, and wrote *Zoom at Sea.* I was watching our cat Montezuma playing in the sink with the drops of water that fell from the tap, batting them back up the spout. Zoom, as we called him, loved water. And that's how I began my story about a cat who goes to sea in a miraculous house. When it was done, I showed it to an artist I had met who worked at the art gallery in Stratford. He had never illustrated a book but I had a feeling he would be good. His name was Ken Nutt, although he later changed it to Eric Beddows. We did three Zooms together over the years.

In retrospect, *Zoom at Sea* made a bigger splash in my life even than *Odd's End.* It was my first children's book, and while I went on to write two more adult novels, I became, over the years, a dedicated writer of children's books. Picture books at first and then, increasingly, short stories and novels. People wonder if I wrote for my children, but that isn't really true. I wrote because of them. I wrote because they reminded me of my own youth.

The titles of all those books appear in the bibliography. But such a list represents only the barest facts of a working life. This story, so far, has been about the part of my life that launched me into a writing career. I like to think of it like that, as a launch. The first part of one's life is the rocket, the huge energy-packed vehicle that strains against the tug of gravity to get you up there, then falls away, used up in having released its tiny payload. But that makes it sound almost as if life after writing one's first book is some kind of effortless floating orbit. Not so. In truth, every book is a new launch. Gravity is always around.

There have been many professional highlights. In Canada I have won the Governor General's Award twice: for *Some of the Kinder Planets* in 1993, and for *The Maestro,* in 1995. I have also won the Canadian Library Association's Children's Book of the Year Award three times and the CLA Young Adult Book of the Year Award once. In 1997, I was given the Vicky Metcalf Award from the Canadian Author's Association for my body of work. In the United States, I am most proud of having won the *Boston Globe-Horn Book* Award, for *Some of the Kinder Planets*; and in 2002, the Edgar Award presented by the Mystery Writers of America, for best young adult crime fiction, for *The Boy in the Burning House.* My books have been published in all kinds of languages all over the world.

My love of music has resulted in writing the book and libretto for an opera called *A Midwinter Night's Dream,* the score for which was written by the preeminent Canadian composer, Harry Somers. With my good friend, John Roby, I wrote the book and lyrics for a musical based on my book of poems, *Mischief City. Mischief City* is the only thing I have written directly about my own children and family life in general. It isn't all true, mind you. Family life is far too complicated a business to be represented by something as formal and proper as the truth! The truth is about what happens. Fiction gives what merely happens some kind of shape. That's what I like about fiction. Life, after all, can be a pretty messy business.

I was fortunate to cowrite sixteen songs for the Jim Henson show *Fraggle Rock.* I worked with composer Phil Balsam, filling in for the wonderfully zany poet Dennis Lee when he got fraggled out for a bit.

Amanda and I lived in Toronto for fourteen years. She did theatre and I wrote books and a dozen or so radio plays for the Canadian Broadcasting Corporation. I love radio drama. Like books, so much of it is up to the listener to imagine.

Now and then Amanda and I worked together. She directed a play of mine called *Death of a Mouth* in the Rhubarb, Rhubarb Theatre Festival. I performed in the George F. Walker/John Roby musical, *Rumors of Our Death.* Amanda was the assistant director. I got to play a punk terrorist. In those days, terrorism was something you could poke fun at, something that happened somewhere else.

We lived, by then, on Winona Drive in a tiny house in a lovely neighborhood with good friends and a good school, but the city was beginning to get me down. I found, increasingly, that I was noticing the bad side of it rather than the good side: the desperate street people, the lost people, the angry people.

Kitimat loomed large in my memory. I had no particular desire to move back to northern B.C., but I wanted my children to experience the country so that when they grew up they would know there were choices a person could make. In 1988 a job offer came along, to be the writer-in-residence for ten months at a library in the little town of Perth, Ontario. I accepted, we rented out our home in Toronto and moved. We never left.

It is not dramatic countryside around here. No mountains, no ocean. No destroyers or sharks. We live on the southern edge of the pre-Cambrian Shield, the oldest mountain range in the world. Those mountains are pretty well worn right down.

We live fifteen minutes from Perth in Brooke Valley on seventy-six acres of mostly scrubby, swampy bush land, of cedar and ironwood, tall white pines, and, in the meadow, juniper and prickly ash. There are deer and coyotes, and pesky porcupines. Lately, a black bear has been knocking over our composter. We think it's a sow. I should get my mother to have a talk with her.

But if the countryside isn't dramatic, the change it has brought to our lives certainly is. Amanda left behind professional theatre but has gone on to create a wonderful children's theatre camp here. Lately her theatre work has taken her to Ottawa, as well, both to teach and direct. But she has over the years concentrated more on her visual art and also her writing. She has written five books, mostly on calligraphy and crafts. We wrote a book together, *Rosie Backstage,* an exploration for children of the theatre and how it works in the form of a story. The book is set at the Stratford Festival, where we met. We are currently working together on turning two of my short stories into one-act plays.

The last book I wrote in Toronto was the dark and gloomy adult novel *Fastyngange.* The first book I wrote in Brooke Valley was *Some of the Kinder Planets.* No two of my books could be more different. Ironically, the advance copies of *Fastyngange* arrived by courier at my door on Winona Drive just as my friend Doug Barnes was helping me pack up the van for the three-hour trip to Brooke Valley. Amanda and the kids had gone ahead. (A reversal of the way my dad did things!) Though the book received some critical success and went on to be published in England and Spain, it was not a high point in my life. Typically, by the time I finish writing a book I am glad to be done with it. In the case of *Fastyngange,* I could hardly believe I had written it! "Who is this guy?" I would ask myself later, flipping through the pages. "What's his problem?" Well, whatever the problem was, writing the book got me over it. Writing is a great form of therapy.

And ridding myself of all that darkness evidently cleared the way for *Some of the Kinder Planets,* my happiest writing experience ever. It was in writing *Planets* that I became my favorite writer. That might sound conceited; let me explain. I came to realize when I was working on *Planets* that I would never be anyone else. That's an important thing to figure out. I was able to happily concede that I would never be John Le Carré or Graham Greene or Jane Austen or Timothy Findley or any other of my literary heroes. It is important to emulate writers you respect; they are like trainer wheels on your bike. But at some time the trainer wheels have to come off. I felt, when I was writing *Planets,* that I was riding on my own at last.

I owe a lot of that feeling to Brooke Valley. It is a very special place. I felt an overwhelming sense of peace as soon as we moved here. Driving into the valley in the rental truck that very first time, we came to a low swampy area and a blue heron flew across our path. It was like a sign. I'm not sure of what, but an elegant one.

Our lives centered around little Brooke Valley School for several years. It is a cooperative one-room schoolhouse built in the woods with a student enrollment that varies but never gets much above sixteen. All the parents were involved—the whole community was involved. That was the best thing about Brooke Valley. Community was

something I had yearned for in all the restless years of my youth without even knowing it.

Roots. A sense of belonging.

I still play rock 'n' roll from time to time with my favorite band ever, The Usual Suspects, sometimes known as Louis the Dreamer. With Franc van Oort and Jack Hurd and Cam Gray, I've written forty songs or so. I still pack too many words into my songs. Sometimes there are so many, I end up writing a story instead.

I like to cross-country ski. There are old logging roads through our property and that's where Amanda and I go, out to the high meadow and the swamp land. Sometimes there are coyote tracks in the snow.

The winters are long here. We heat with wood; there's lots of it. I like to cook and do crossword puzzles or read in front of the fire. It is so quiet you can hear yourself think. I like that best of all. That and the full moon. You can see the shadow of chimney smoke on the snow.

Sometimes it doesn't seem quite far enough away. So we have bought a cabin on the Lake of Many Narrows, a couple of hours north of Sudbury, Ontario, where the only human sound you are likely to hear is the train to White River or the occasional float plane. Our good friends the Mason family introduced us to the lake. We have spent quite a few summers there now with them. There are no roads. You have to fly in or take the "Budd Car" and ask the conductor to stop at the trail head. Then it's a half-hour hike. The trail is ten thousand years old. I kind of feel that old myself after carrying in a heavy pack!

I designed the house we live in here in Brooke Valley, so my three years of architectural training were not a waste of time. But nothing you do in putting a life together is truly a waste of time. That would suggest there was some designated path you were supposed to be traveling and if you had stuck to it you would have arrived at your destination more quickly. There is no such path. There is no destination. This is where I am now and happy to be so. It would be a very good life indeed if one could say the same every step along the way. But if that were the case, how would you know when you had arrived somewhere just right?

Maybe you will understand why I am a person who doesn't really like to travel. But I wonder if you could explain to me why I often wish that I were somewhere else? I guess I just never learned how to unpack properly. As a writer I have traveled all over North America. I've done readings as far south as Miami and as far north as Norman Wells on the Mackenzie River in the Northwest Territories. I've been to Bologna, Italy, for the Children's Book Fair; to Melbourne, Australia, for their International Writer's Festival; and to Cambridge University in England to deliver a talk. I could imagine living in any of those places. In your imagination you can travel light and you don't need a passport.

Where next? There's only Lewis at home, these days. He's in grade ten as I write this, with dreams of becoming an actor. Amanda sometimes daydreams about us moving to Manhattan where she was born. I talk about England, a little cottage on the coast somewhere. We both kind of like Toronto all over again. Who knows? As glad as I am to have landed somewhere, there's still a part of me that wants to run away. I keep a tea cosy near at hand, just in case.

Oh, yes, and I *did* see Nicky again. On television. And then, many years later, for lunch when I happened to be in London. It was good to be able to explain to him, after forty-seven years, that moving to Canada had taken longer than I expected. He understood. He had been pretty busy himself becoming a successful actor.

And on another trip to England with Amanda and the children in the spring of 1997, I visited Little Sutton one afternoon and found Just Home. No one was home. But there was a lady next door tending her roses. She had lived in the same house all of her eighty plus years. Just as I was about to explain who I was and why I was there, she got a startled look in her eyes all of a sudden. "Why, you're Sid Jones's boy," she said.

What a shock. Was it my gray flannel shorts, red tie, and open-toed sandals? Hardly. But I was just about the age my father must have been when they left for the new world. She graciously thought to invite me into her house where she led me to the landing of the stairs. There was a large window there looking down on the backyard of Just Home.

"You'll want to see your garden," she said, smiling. It was as if she knew something about me I didn't know myself. I wonder . . .